THE BEST IN
THEOLOGY

VOLUME ONE

GENERAL EDITOR
J. I. Packer

EDITOR
Paul Fromer

AREA EDITORS

Old Testament: Bruce Waltke
New Testament: D. A. Carson
Church History: Nathan Hatch
Systematic Theology: David F. Wells
Ethics/Spiritual Life: Klaus Bockmuehl
Pastoral Psychology and Counseling: David G. Benner
Missions: Miriam Adeney
Homiletics: Haddon W. Robinson
Christian Education: Kenneth O. Gangel

Carol Stream, Illinois

THE BEST IN THEOLOGY

Published by Christianity Today, Inc. Distributed by Word, Inc.

Administrative Editor: Marty L. White
Cover Design: Dwight Walles

Library of Congress Cataloging-in-Publication Data

The Best in theology.

1. Theology. 2. Evangelicalism. I. Packer, J. I.
(James Innell) II. Fromer, Paul.
BR50.B444 1987 230 86-31777
ISBN 0-917463-14-5 (pbk.: v. 1)
Printed in the United States of America

EDITOR'S PREFACE

PAUL W. FROMER
Associate Professor of English, Wheaton College
Deputy Editor, *Christianity Today*

"A theology annual? How can you get the best scholarly articles in nine fields inside the covers of one book? Laid on the lap, it would cut off circulation to the feet."

Such a wry comment from a theology professor sums up a problem with selecting articles for this book. Back in the halcyon days of yore, when many of the writers printed here were getting their Ph.D.'s, wags were asking a similar question, "How do you get six elephants into a Volkswagon bug?" Three in front and three in back.

The volume you hold in your hands (without strain, one hopes, to the circulatory system) is our best answer to squeezing our article-elephants in a relatively small space. A single volume setting out all the best articles may not be possible. But it is less impossible than the alternative of no volume at all. Picture the thoughtful pastor or lay Christian trudging up and down the seeming miles of aisles of racks displaying scholarly theological journals in a top-notch library. He or she hopes to be led to those articles that really should be read if one is to keep track of the leading edge of theology today. The exercise is good for the circulation, but a strain on the eyes, not to mention the conscience.

To illustrate: one Old Testament scholar, when told of Patrick Miller's superb survey of recent thinking on interpreting the Psalter, said, "*Word and World?* I don't think I know that journal. Is it in our library?" (It isn't, yet that library buys over 800 journals of various types, primarily theological.) And a librarian, hearing of Richard Peace's article on how families can handle TV, said, "*The Journal of the Academy for Evangelism in Theological Education?* Never heard of it. Probably we should get it. What's its address?" This journal only just began publication, but a scholar working with *The Best in Theology* was on top of his field.

This hints at what we feel is the solution to the problem of selecting the best theological articles of the past year. The key is selecting a group of editors each of whom is on top of the literature of his area. He (or she, in the case of missions) can interact with the journals on one hand, and the editor on the other, to select the articles most likely to help the pastor or lay reader.

How were the area editors selected? First, no two were from the same school. Second, they range geographically from Gordon-Conwell to Fuller, and Dallas to Regent. Further, they range denominationally from Southern

Baptist to Anglican. They also range in schools that granted their doctor-
ates—Harvard (Waltke), Cambridge (Carson), Manchester (Wells), Basle
(Bockmuehl), York (Benner), Illinois (Robinson), and so on. (Biographical
sketches of area editors follow their Introductions.)

But the proof of the pudding is in the eating, and here we faced the
problem of space. At the outset, we envisioned 200 pages, covering articles
from five areas (OT, NT, Church History, Systematics, and Practical Theology). At forty pages each, this would allow eight pages for five articles in each
area. But Practical Theology is a cluster of disciplines—Pastoral Psychology,
Missions, Homiletics, Christian Education. Eight pages to each of these
seemed skimpy so we assigned eighty pages and increased the size of the
book slightly. We also separated Ethics/Spiritual Life from Systematics, thereby creating an additional area.

Then one area editor submitted 169 pages of copy for his forty-page
section. Solomon proposed dividing in half a child of disputed parentage,
and we considered asking him to join our staff. Solomonic or not, our best
judgment was to double the size of the original book to 400 pages—and
hope circulation to the feet was not seriously impaired for the weak-kneed
among us.

How were the articles chosen? Bruce Waltke, area editor for Old Testament, asked editors of about 150 journals to nominate the best OT article
they had carried in the past year. Kenneth Gangel secured the help of three
colleagues to filter through the Christian Education journals. Various procedures, such as conversation between the area editor and me, narrowed the
list to a half dozen; then we here made final choices in light of space, the
willingness of some writers to condense their material, and the larger question of balance. Church History is represented by only two articles (science
and religion; reasons for growth of pentecostalism), but those by David
Bosch (emergence of apartheid), Robert Linder (U.S. civil religion from the
Puritans to the present), René Padilla (twenty years of discussion on evange-
lism/social responsibility), and Bruce Shelley (three American parachurch
groups), are also historical treatments, though formally located in other
categories.

Since this is the first of what will become an annual event—if you find
that the project performs a necessary service—we have felt free to reach
behind the past twelve months for some of the selections. The plan is,
however, to search the literature appearing from September to September,
and publish around the beginning of the following year.

The authors of the resulting articles (thirty-four from four continents)
are as diverse as Pretoria and Buenos Aires in the south to Vancouver in the
north, and from London in the Far East to Pasadena in the West. Author
sketches appear at the end of this volume under the title "About the
Authors." References occur in thirteen languages (regularly translated),
including classical (Latin, Greek, Hebrew), Near Eastern (Akkadian, Sumeri-

an, Egyptian), and modern. One Britisher thinks we should separate English and American, or we would have twelve, not thirteen languages.

Incidentally, in keeping with the worldwide nature of the sources, we have generally maintained the spelling, documentation, and linguistic distinctives of the original article, unless it caused significant confusion. Thus a person wishing to pursue the documentation of an article will find it helpful to consult the appropriate issue of that journal for lists of abbreviations it uses in its footnotes for other scholarly journals. The world of scholarship has not entirely rid itself of the effects of the Tower of Babel.

Selecting articles poses the special issue of balance. When one walks into the average living room he sees magazines that almost unanimously reflect the view of the person living there. That has the value of reinforcing and cultivating cherished positions. But walk into the living room of a person whose mind is alert, and who is interested in the alternatives, and who finds differences not threatening but invigorating, and you will be looking at a range of magazines that print a decided spectrum of opinions.

In *The Best in Theology* you will find articles that develop positions you already hold. But as you continue to read, you will find others that seem to take a different tack. Both sets of authors may place their confidence in Scripture (though not always); but the emphases, or perhaps the basic viewpoints on a subject, may contrast sharply. To be specific: Peter Wagner's concern centers on evangelism, while René Padilla focuses on the added factor of social involvement. Are they in full agreement? Also one gets the impression that Richard Peace's suggestions on learning from TV's short, active segments might not appeal so much to the Puritan instincts of J. I. Packer. And does Norman Geisler's confidence in our ability to discover natural law as the basis for civil law mesh with David Bosch's suggestion that we are all to a surprising extent captive to the historical forces that characterize our own subculture or age?

This volume makes little attempt to uncomplicate these complexities. Such is the nature of a volume that presents the best in print over the short span of a year. In fact, some positions in dispute in society generally are treated by one article with no answering article elsewhere in this volume. No article disputes Robert Linder's view on the place of God in American politics, though some readers would no doubt be eager to try.

And Norman Gottwald's focus on the clash of social forces that helped form the canon leaves little place for "the mighty acts of God" as He breaks into our social system. What exactly is the relation between divine initiative and secondary causes as they are seen from a behavioral science viewpoint? No particular answer is found in this volume.

We may at this time lack the wherewithal to disagree intelligently with an article that raises our questions or our dander. No doubt this can be troublesome—even frustrating. I suggest we view these articles as friends—ones that stimulate our grey cells into red-blooded activity. In time they may pry loose some thoughts we did not know we could generate, and help us reach depths of profundity we did not know we could plumb.

The selection of articles also is designed to present materials of ranging complexity. Some will be just right for a fairly quick reading. A glance at the "Contents" page may help locate them. Others may remind us of the little girl who asked the librarian for a book on penguins. Not wanting to pass up the chance to encourage such a burst of scholarly interest, she brought forth a thick book of commendable thoroughness. A day later the girl returned the book, saying, "This book tells me more about penguins than I really want to know."

Some articles in this volume may appear that way on first reading. They are ones to return to later, after that first reading. They require time, and a growing maturity that may have to struggle to emerge. But these articles can become the most memorable. No article in this book is beyond the comprehension of the reader who is ready to roll up his (or her) sleeves, shift into the reflective mode, and *think*.

To help the reader see the setting of *The Best in Theology*, an introduction by J. I. Packer sets it in the context of what is currently going on generally in the world of theology. Reading his thoughts should prove specially helpful.

Any book has its models—the volumes it looks to for stimulation and general guidance. We turned repeatedly to *Journal of Biblical Literature, Catholic Biblical Quarterly,* and *Quarterly Review* (published by the United Methodists for pastors). There we found ideas on content, style, and appearance. These journals have our special thanks. Ronald Youngblood of the *Journal of the Evangelical Theological Society* also gave invaluable advice during the formative days of the project.

The concept of *The Best in Theology* emerged in some discussions of the senior editors of *Christianity Today*. The idea was specially championed by CTi president, Harold Myra, and J. I. Packer, the latter expressing concern at the pile of scholarly journals growing by his bedside, which he could not find time to sift through. Terry Muck, executive editor of *Christianity Today*, then wrote a prospectus that proposed some of the controlling factors of such a volume (at that time going by the working title of *Theology Annual*). And as I expanded this basic paper, I had the continual help of these men. Also consulted were the scholars and fellows of the Christianity Today Institute, who generally greeted the project with enthusiasm.

In addition, Harold Smith, managing editor of *Christianity Today*, contributed valuable ideas and took special interest in the visual appearance of Volume 1. He also correlated the work of the several departments of Christianity Today, Inc. that cooperated to produce the final work. I wish to give special recognition to Marty White, editorial coordinator for *Christianity Today*. She oversaw the typing of the copy, and kept a weather eye out for deadlines and slip-ups in the editorial process, and imposed a degree of organization on the flow of material that I could not have achieved. The computerized typesetting was handled by Karla Anderson, and production was overseen by Carolyn Barry, vice president of production for Christianity Today, Inc. Cindy Cronk made possible the use of Greek in the text by solving innumerable problems connected with adding a new language to the existing system's capability to handle English. Adapting an English keyboard to user-hostile software proved a feat.

Looking back on the project, which took six months, we have a special sense of gratitude to the area editors who accepted our invitation with alacrity, worked conscientiously, and proved gracious in all our dealings. A new project is filled with the need for innumerable changes, and their flexibility was a delight to see.

Finally I wish to note the pleasure the editing of this volume has brought me personally. It has stimulated my devotional life, enlivened my brain cells, given me a new respect for the careful thought that constitutes scholarly endeavor, thrust me into thoughts about continents beyond my own, and centuries before my own. The project has refined my judgment and produced a high sense of satisfaction in playing a part in a venture with such potential for the Kingdom of God.

The studies of Scripture and theology have brought repeatedly to mind the words of John Donne with which James Houston's article in the section on Ethics/Spiritual Life begins:

> Wilt thou love God as He thee! then digest,
> My soul, this wholesome meditation,
> How God the Spirit by angels waited on
> In heaven, doth make His Temple in thy heart.
>   John Donne, *Holy Sonnet* 15

About the Editor

Paul W. Fromer (B.S., in Chemistry, Syracuse University; graduate work in the Ph.D. program, California Institute of Technology; M.Div., Fuller Theological Seminary, M.A., Wheaton College) is associate professor of English, Wheaton College. He has been Deputy Editor of *Christianity Today* since 1979. He was staff member (1954-57) and area director (1957-60) for Inter-Varsity Christian Fellowship in Southern California. He was editor of *His* magazine from 1960 to 1971. His books, co-authored with Margaret Fromer, include one on Colossians, *Putting Christ First* (1986); and *A Woman's Workshop on Philippians* (1982).

CONTENTS

10

Section 6: PRACTICAL THEOLOGY/PASTORAL PSYCHOLOGY AND COUNSELING

Section 7: PRACTICAL THEOLOGY/MISSIONS

Section 8: PRACTICAL THEOLOGY/HOMILETICS

12

Section 9: PRACTICAL THEOLOGY/CHRISTIAN EDUCATION

INTRODUCTION

J. I. PACKER
General Editor, *The Best in Theology*
Professor of Historical and Systematic Theology
Regent College

Pity the pastor! and the parachurch worker! and the lay leader! Why? Not because they want our pity (if they are good specimens of their kind, they don't), but because of the vast demands that we make on them, and that as good specimens of their kind they make on themselves. Nowadays, when I hear the phrase "great expectations," I think not of Charles Dickens's young man who thought he was to go up in the world, but of the starry-eyed way modern Christians look to their leaders always to be on top of everything. One great expectation of this sort is that leaders will invariably be well-informed and up to date in every matter pertaining to their own field, namely the establishing and applying of biblical truth. In this age of the knowledge explosion, when one segment of one discipline, in theology as in the physical sciences, is all that a single person can hope to master, and several hundred theological journals in English roll off the press each quarter to supplement the far larger number of books on Christian themes published every year, such an expectation is a tall order indeed. Just here, however, it is hoped that Christianity Today's *The Best in Theology* may prove to be of help.

What is the purpose of this volume? It has been brought into being so that front-line leaders who lack time and opportunity to scan scholarly journals may year by year have access to some of the best articles that have appeared in print during the twelve months prior to each September's selection. The articles will regularly come from the areas of mainstream theological education all over the world: biblical studies (Old and New Testaments); church history; systematic theology (dogmatics and ethics, including spiritual life); and practical theology (subdivided into pastoral psychology, mission studies, homiletics, and Christian education). Each member of the team of specialist selectors is a working scholar in the field in which he or she makes the choices, and this will guarantee quality. Thus, if all goes well, the reader of *The Best in Theology* will be presented year by year with the cream of what the journals have carried—or some of it, at least; for if this first year's experience is anything to go by, there will always be enough good material to produce a volume twice the present size.

Books are shaped and packaged with particular readers in mind, and *The Best in Theology* is no exception. Its intended reader, as has been indicated already, will be a nonspecialist (the specialists will already have looked through the journals from which the selections come), and one who is ready to be sympathetic to evangelical viewpoints. It should be said at once that, just as no confessional test was applied in selecting the articles (the sole criterion was, what would most help the evangelical front-line worker), so it is hoped that many pastors and church officers who might not call themselves evangelical will find as much help here as self-identified evangelicals will. It is true that most of the material does in fact come from evangelical pens (nowadays, I suppose, one should rather say, computers), but no one should be surprised at that, for it is a fact that something like a tenth of the material in academic theological journals these days is written by avowedly evangelical authors, and it is also a fact, explain it how you will, that evangelical readers regularly get most help from the work of other evangelicals. The appropriate response to this latter fact must surely be to hope and expect that others will get help from it too.

The special significance of journal material is not always appreciated. It is true that, since the law of the Medes and Persians in modern universities and graduate schools is *Publish, or you miss promotion,* academic journals regularly contain a good deal of writing that the world could very well manage without. But it is also true that significant ideas get tried out first in the journals, and that key papers from conferences also appear in them. Only by keeping up with the journals can any scholar stay abreast of the progress of his own discipline, so as to remain professionally on the cutting edge. The quantity of chaff mixed in with the wheat in the journals can be a headache for full-time academics, and would be a bigger headache for amateur readers not involved in the technicalities of the field. If I am any judge, however, what has been creamed off for the present volume will both interest and instruct anyone who has had a seminary education, and much of it will ring bells with Christian leaders who have not.

What positive benefits, then, will *The Best in Theology* bring? In the first place, it will *inform,* both about the state of particular disciplines and the terms of particular problems. (Did you have any idea, for instance, about the ethnic elements in North America as these are displayed in Peter Wagner's article?) Then, second, it will *stimulate,* evoking fresh thought: critical, deep-level analysis and argument always does that, and such we have here. I believe that the area editors have done a fine job in making their choices, and I feel very confident about the value of this volume which their labor has produced.

Overview of Today's Theology

A bird's-eye view of some things currently happening in the world of theology could helpfully set the stage for the reading of this material; therefore I shall attempt one. Probably I am foolish to do so, for just as it is true that scholars generally are nowadays hard put to it to keep track of what goes on across the board in their own disciplines, so it is much more true that no one person can grasp all that goes on across the board in all the many distinct disciplines of theological study. So I am bound to fall down on the job one way or another, if not indeed every way. Specialists in each field will see at once just how short I have come, so I had better apologize to all of them for my inadequacies in each area before I start. Jerome K. Jerome wrote a book titled *Idle Thoughts of an Idle Fellow*: learned men may think this a suitable heading for the paragraphs that follow. I can only ask the learned ones to bear in mind that my purpose is to help nonspecialist readers, and never to forget those famous Wild Western words: "Don't shoot the pianist; he's doing his best."

Sociology

First, then, note the sociology of modern theological study. It is concentrated in universities and denominational or cross-denominational seminaries (called theological colleges in the British Commonwealth), where good library facilities exist and scholars are employed as professional academics to educate students by their teaching and to advance knowledge in their own discipline by researching. As in other fields of learning, so here, there are professional societies to which scholars worth their salt are expected to belong and journals that they are expected to read and publish in. In the West most universities are post- and sometimes anti-Christian in spirit. Persons employed to teach Christian studies there (often in departments of world religion rather than faculties of Christian theology) easily become low-profile figures whose confidence in confessing the faith and concern for the church's spiritual life constantly ebbs away, while a concessive attitude to secular skepticism becomes more and more deeply ingrained in them. Seminaries, by contrast, are to some extent cut off from the wider world of university life, and so may house teachers who are loud and clear confessionally but cannot tune in sensitively to secular thought. Steering between the Scylla of secular drift and the Charybdis of self-contained confessionalism is no easy task. *The Best in Theology,* for its part, aims to offer material that will help its readers to combine firmness on biblical beliefs with an openness that takes seriously the questions of nonevangelical and non-Christian participants in the dialogue about those beliefs; for that, so we believe, is the temper that the watching world most urgently needs to see in Christian leaders and spokesmen at all levels of expression and instruction.

Pluralism

Second, note the pluralism of modern theological thought. By pluralism I mean not only the existence of competing alternative theologies, which different thinkers develop in different ways to explicate and undergird Christian faith and life (that aspect of pluralism, like the poor, is always with us). I mean also the acceptance of this state of affairs as normal and healthy. This acceptance, now general in the mainstream Western churches, including the Roman Catholic communion (not the Orthodox, though), is a twentieth-century novelty to which, understandably enough, many find it hard to adjust. The assumption that the more theologies there are together, the healthier and livelier we shall all be, is a startling departure from the traditional conviction that, because truth is one, unanimity of thought about it, and unanimous expression of it, is the only proper goal for the church to seek. But it seems clear that, whether it be wisdom or folly (my readers will make up their own mind about that), this novel assumption has come to stay, and will hardly be uprooted in our lifetime.

Whence did it derive? The following factors, at least, contributed to spawning it.

(1) *The heavy emphasis among liberal Protestants on the impossibility of treating biblical teaching as revealed and therefore normative truth.* This has led to a non-normative, phenomenological conception of theology in the church as a discipline of describing what Christians do think rather than of directing them to what they should think. The fact that Christians think differently from each other on vital matters now gets treated as something inevitable, to be accepted with a cheerful shrug of the shoulders, rather than as something tragic, to be overcome by rational biblical argument.

(2) *The heavy emphasis among neo-orthodox Protestants on the notion that new truth, never before seen, might at any time break forth from new selective combinations of biblical strands of thought.* Whether or not they acknowledged that they were working with what has been called "a canon within the canon," that is, a selection of texts and passages detached from the rest of Scripture to a greater or lesser degree, the pundits of neo-ortho-doxy all in fact did work this way, from Barth on the right wing past Brunner and the Niebuhrs in the middle to Bultmann and Tillich on the left. And each offered individual interpretations of God's revelation that were not in full accord either with historic Christianity in any of its standard forms or with each other. This has led to a lively but bewildering resurgence of theological endeavor in which the proposing of new formulations suggested by recogni-tion of the thrust of some texts, along with energies of reaction against proposals based by others on recognition of the thrust of other texts, keeps the pluralist pot boiling merrily. The older demand that churchly theology be constructed under the control of the analogy of Scripture, so as to be a total presentation of the total teaching of the Bible from the totally consistent evangelical and doxological standpoint that all Scripture exhibits, is thus honored in the breach rather than the observance. Everyone pays lip-service to it, but no child of the neo-orthodox movement seems ever to have accepted the discipline of being rigorously bound by it.

(3) *The heavy emphasis among Roman Catholics on the distinction, canonized by John XXIII and Vatican II, between the unchanging substance of*

the faith and changing ways of expressing it. This has produced a relativistic type of theology among Catholics that is methodologically close to Protestant liberalism, and for which neo-modernism would be a fitting name. Its goal is to restate God-given truth in terms of the changed culture that is now current, which of course is something that all who want to exhibit God-given truth as truth for today must try to do. But uncertainty about what was content and what was only a form of expression in earlier declarations and definitions of that truth has resulted in there being great grey areas. Here, as conservative Roman Catholics along with conservative Protestants see it, liberal Catholics are in fact absolutizing the relativities of current culture and relativizing in relation to them not just older formulations of divine absolutes, but those absolutes themselves. This accusation may be true or false in particular cases (as, for instance, in the well-publicized papal slapping down of Küng, Schillebeeckx, Boff, and Curran, gestures on the propriety of which Roman Catholics continue to be sharply divided). But, nevertheless, the very fact of Roman Catholic commitment to the task of presenting ancient truth in modern dress contributes much to present-day pluralism in theology, and must of necessity continue to do so for the foreseeable future.

(4) *The heavy emphasis in ecumenical theological dialogue on the defensive provincialism of historic confessional traditions.* Attempts to recognize this and, as is said, to "get beyond" it, involve the diagnosing of what is essential substance as distinct from contingent form in all the traditional heritages, in the same way that the domestic Roman Catholic debate does. Individual efforts at this task produce a plurality of analyses and restatements that appear to their critics to be idiosyncratic and concessive to a fault. This criticism then prompts further efforts of the same sort, and so *ad infinitum*, with each theologian's representative and unitive purpose treated as excusing and indeed justifying the series of misshapen concepts that from time to time he comes up with.

The net result of all these impulses to pluralism is that except among evangelical Protestants, right-wing Catholics, and the Eastern Orthodox, there are just about as many theologies as there are theologians to devise them; the concept of heresy has almost lost its meaning; and loyalty to the institutional church has for the most part taken the place of loyalty to the faith once for all delivered to the saints, for no one is quite sure any more what the essence of that faith really is.

This does not mean, however, that there is no light or wisdom to be found amid the extraordinary Confused Noise (to borrow a phrase from A. A. Milne's Eeyore) that today's professional theological discussions create. What it means, rather, is that wisdom and insights are fragmented and scattered among many different writers and writings, and that he who would garner these riches must range widely in his hunt for them. Samuel Hopkins wrote of Jonathan Edwards: "He read all the books, especially books of divinity, that he could procure, from which he might hope to derive any aid in

his pursuit of knowledge. . . . Thus he was all his days like the busy bee,
collecting from every opening flower, and storing up a stock of knowledge
which was indeed sweet to him. . . ." We, too, need to be like the busy bee if
we are to build up a worthwhile stock of wisdom in an age of theological
pluralism; and I think we may hope to find that the selections offered each
year in *The Best in Theology* will give us useful leads to some of the more
heavy-laden flowers from which to seek precious theological nectar. Certainly, ongoing guidance in the areas where the Confused Noise is being
raised is something for which every thoughtful Christian must surely be
grateful.

Disciplines
Then, third, note the disciplines of modern theological thought. Look at
them directionally; see where they are trying to go, and how *The Best in
Theology*'s material can help you travel with them. As in life, so in scholarship (which, after all, is one department of life), nothing stands still. The
church's quest (mankind's quest, really) for more truth, deeper understanding, and greater wisdom is unending, and I hope it is your quest too, just as I
should be ashamed of myself if it were not mine. Theology—talk about
God—should therefore be seen, not as a pastime for Christian mandarins,
but as a quest for truth, understanding, and wisdom. A directional analysis of
its constituent elements will help us to catch this vision of what its true
purpose is.
     Theology is an organism of thought, a complex of disciplines each of
which feeds and is fed by the others. It used to be analyzed as a quadrilateral:
biblical theology (exegesis and synthesis—with "higher," "lower," and historical criticism as a means to more skillful performance in these two departments); systematic theology (including ethics); church history (including
historical theology); and practical theology, which covered spirituality, pastoral care, liturgy, and any mission studies that might be done. It has sometimes been exhibited as a circle, or better, a spiral, round all of which you
must go before you can reach any adequate understanding of the point from
which you started. William Perkins, the Puritan, defined theology as *the
science of living blessedly for ever*, thereby sweetly uniting the thoughts that
theology is a form of cognition, that it is concerned with eternal realities, and
that as a study it has a practical, disciple-making, nurturing thrust. But for
our purposes it is best to display theology as a sequence of distinct disciplines, with a certain logical progression from one to the other, thus:
     (1) *Exegesis* is the foundational discipline. It seeks to answer the ques-
tion: what was this biblical text, or passage, or book, written to convey?
What were its envisaged first readers meant to gather from it? What was the
human writer consciously telling them? What awareness of God was he
sharing with them? Only when exegesis has shown us what the passage
meant as communication from the writer to his intended readers can we

move on to draw out of it the universal truths about God and man that it is crystallizing or applying, re-apply them to ourselves in our own situation, and so see what it *means* as a word from God to us. *Interpretation* is the process of getting to the meaning of Scripture as God's word to present-day readers, and of this process exegesis is part one and application part two.

The Best in Theology contains two major pieces of exegesis: Douglas Moo's thorough demonstration of the sense in which Jesus affirmed the continuing validity of the Mosaic law in the kingdom of God, and Robert Gundry's necessary correction of E. P. Sanders's account of what Paul thought and taught concerning law, works, grace, and faith. Both are matters about which it is vitally important for us to apply Scripture rightly to ourselves, and without right exegesis of the relevant texts right application is not possible. Patrick Miller's review of current work on the Psalms yields a mind-expanding framework of questions to ask in exegeting them. Norman Gottwald's stimulating launch of a dialogue between social-scientific and canonical criticism that might ultimately broaden both, yields a comparable framework for all biblical exegesis—though the evangelical reader will need to do a little refocusing at some points, where Gottwald's thoughts about the nature of Scripture will seem to him inadequate.

Do these selections illustrate any significant trends in present-day exegesis? In a broad sense, yes: for they bear witness to the deep contemporary awareness, far deeper than ever marked the pre-critical era, that a great deal of the historical understanding of a text is missed if you do not fully appreciate the historical and cultural situation out of which it came and into which it was spoken. Sanders setting Paul against his Jewish background, and Miller reviewing the background of the Psalms, and Gottwald laboring to fill in the sociological background of each Old Testament passage, all illustrate this quest for more of the background as a means to grasping more of the expressed sense. And though particular scholars pursuing this quest may on occasion take the wrong turning, the quest itself is obviously right, and should be applauded.

(2) *Biblical theology* is the discipline that synthesizes and organizes the fruits of exegesis, both topically and historically. It seeks to answer such questions as: What is the total message of each biblical writer about this? and that? and God? and godliness? What is the total message of the Bible as a whole about these matters? By what stages was this teaching revealed? How much of the total revelation is presupposed by each writer in saying the particular things that he does say? All questions of the interrelation of the message of one part of Scripture with the message of another come under the scrutiny of biblical theology. It is a unifying, integrating discipline.

The procedures of biblical theology necessarily assume a view about the proper extent and limits of the biblical canon, and with that at least a provisional opinion about the date and provenance of the various books of which the canon is made up. One criterion of good biblical theology is that it works from views on these matters that are sober and not wild.

Another such criterion, in my view, is avoidance of the foolish fashion, so prevalent today, of forcing one Bible writer's theology to contradict another's, and representing different strands of tradition in the Scriptures as if they were at loggerheads. To anyone who believes that all Scripture is ultimately the product of a single divine mind, who remembers that it is possible to give the same thoughts different verbal clothing without them thereby ceasing to be the same, and who (I venture to say) looks dispassionately at the evidence, this fashion appears painful and perverse, groundless and gratuitous, unnecessary and unjustified. It is much to be hoped that professional biblical theologians, who have pursued internal theological contradictions in Scripture indefatigably for several decades, might soon tire of this particular game.

The particular virtues of disciplined biblical theology will be found displayed in R. T. France's "Liberation in the New Testament," which is by any standards a model of impeccable method and good judgment.

(3) *Historical theology* is the discipline that explores how Christians in the past have understood this or that element in the biblical faith, and how they have grasped that faith as a whole. What questions did they ask about it? What answers did they offer? What were their certainties, and what were their problems? What challenges were they seeking to meet, and what influences, both conscious and unrecognized, were they under as they did their thinking? The essays by Grant Wacker on early Pentecostalism, and by David Lindberg and Ronald Numbers on the post-Reformation interface between Christian belief and science, are illuminating ventures in historical theology on themes that cannot but be of deep interest to lively and alert Christian hearts.

(4) *Systematic theology* is a watershed discipline. Gathering to itself the results of exegesis, biblical theology, and historical theology, it seeks to tell us how we should state the whole faith today, topic by topic and as a whole, in the light of current interests, assumptions, questions, and challenges, both outside and inside the church. In idea, at least, systematic theology controls the confession of faith that both individual believers and Christian churches make before the world. It shows us how much needs to be said if the fullness of the faith is to be transmitted, and how it all needs to be angled if it is to make its proper impact on contemporary minds. It states and then reflects on the contents of Scripture from the standpoint of their application today. Thus it is, when properly managed, a discipline of biblical interpretation, fitly called *systematic* because it does not treat biblical themes in isolation, but thinks them all together in the way that Scripture itself does, and then sets each one forth as part of a whole. Thus it delineates particular truths as elements in that one ordered truth for which the Puritan name was *the body of divinity*. And it appeals to the comprehensive biblical understanding of the backbone structure of that body, namely the great good news that our

Maker has become our Redeemer, in all its discussions of any aspect of Christian belief. And it never allows itself to be drawn away from that gospel message.

This, at least, is what evangelical systematic theology does, and that is the only sort that concerns me here. True systematic theology should, and will, commend itself as demonstrably a testimony to the God of the gospel, the triune Creator-Redeemer, and as a transcript of the divine mind that is disclosed to us in the inspired Scriptures. Speculative religious schemes have sometimes called themselves systematic theology (that of Paul Tillich, for instance), but though philologically correct—since any talk about God, however he is conceived, constitutes theology—the description is in such cases mischievously misleading. The Christian idea of theology has always been that theology declares the apostolic gospel, and those whose theologies do not even attempt to do this would serve us well if they dropped the word and classified their works as systematic philosophies of religion instead.

To generalize about current trends in systematic theology is not easy. To be honest, I think we are somewhat in the doldrums. The towering figures of this century (Barth, Brunner, Bultmann, Rahner, Lonergan) have all gone, and we are still in process of digesting their legacy. Trinitarianism has made quite a spectacular comeback after a century during which crypto-unitarian thought-forms prevailed, and the attenuated Christologies that went with subchristian accounts of God are falling out of favor. Perhaps a conservative renewal in theology is beginning, and perhaps not: it is really too soon to say.

The systematic theology articles in *The Best in Theology* focus on concrete perplexities that arise when Christianity and culture interact: when, that is, Christian convictions seek to find expression in the mindset and socio-political structures of specific communities, while other influences and motivations from within the selfsame communities operate to deflect, disorient, and derail these endeavours. The material has great existential significance and is *angst*-laden in a very obvious way, for aggressive secularism, Afrikaner apartheid, and the New Religious Right are potent realities of our time, the future of each of which is fraught in different ways with vast possibilities of what can only be called disaster. These are, as the area editor points out, case studies in the problematical field of how Christians should deal with the world around them; they are also traumatic analyses, informed by full-orbed theological vision, of current forces and tensions that no Western Christian dare ignore, and thus have something of a prophetic quality as words of insight for our time.

(5) *Apologetics* is a discipline that squares up to the question: how should we commend and defend the Christian faith, as systematic theology formulates it for us, when we find ourselves confronted by modern unbelief, misbelief, and sheer puzzlement? What arguments are available to us, and what principles of procedure should direct us? Apologetics is almost a

department of systematic theology (indeed, it is often taught as such), and we have not allotted it separate space in *The Best in Theology* this year.

(6) *Ethics* is also a department of systematic theology. It asks: What are the ideals and standards of Christian behavior, both for individuals and for communities? How may we justify them as authentically wise, and beneficial, and fruitful, when we are confronted with criticisms of them based on a non-Christian view of human nature and destiny? How should we bring them to bear in particular cases? Ethics draws its material ultimately from Scripture, but mediately from the accounts of God and man that systematic theology provides. The selection by Norman Geisler on law and government illustrates this, for it resolves a question of social ethics by reference to one aspect of the doctrine of God's kingdom.

Spirituality (Christian life, lived in communion with God) is a sister field of study to ethics, and has often been subsumed under ethics, though the tendency today is against doing that; it too draws material from the digested theological doctrines of God and man, as well as from biblical passages that deal directly with the realities of fellowshiping with God, opening one's life to him, receiving both good and evil (in Job's sense) from him, and being nurtured in grace by him. The study of spirituality—ascetic theology, as it was once called—has blossomed in our time, and much of its range, fascination, and allure (I do not apologize for that word; all true Christians know the allure of fellowship with God) is brought out for us in James Houston's treatment of devotional reading.

(7) *Practical theology* is an umbrella term covering a wide range of applicatory studies. The general question to which it addresses itself is: how should we do God's work and glorify his name in our particular serving roles and situation, ministerial, evangelistic, pastoral, ecclesiastical, or whatever? Missiology, the study of how we are to understand and fulfill those of our ministering tasks that exhibit and extend God's kingdom in this world, may be seen as a department of practical theology, along with homiletics (preaching), Christian education, and pastoral psychology. All these are interface disciplines, in which biblical truth about God and man, and secular data about the modern world and people in it, come together, sometimes with great poignancy and urgency. I think you will agree with me that *The Best in Theology*'s material from each of these fields demonstrates this in a series of very striking ways.

Conclusion

Such, then, are the disciplines of theology at the present time, and such is the first annual Christianity Today volume of *The Best in Theology*. Whether it will become an annual in the true sense—that is, a perennial—will depend largely on the reception that this first one receives. It is, I believe, reasonably priced for what it is, and should certainly enrich and enliven any pastor who reads it. I could wish that all churches that want their pastors' minds to stay awake and in touch would see fit to give them copies! Any suggestions for making *The Best in Theology* even more helpful in future years will be gratefully received by the publishers. And now it is over to you. Good reading!

About the General Editor

J. I. Packer (B.A., M.A., D.Phil., Oxford University) is professor of historical and systematic theology, Regent College (Vancouver, B.C., Canada). He was ordained by the Church of England, and now attends St. John's (Anglican) Church, Shaughnessy, B.C. Many will have read several of his earlier books: *"Fundamentalism" and the Word of God* (1958); *Evangelism and the Sovereignty of God* (1961); and *Knowing God* (1973). A few of his recent books include *Your Father Loves You* (1986); (with Thomas Howard) *Christianity, the True Humanism* (1985); and *Keep in Step with the Spirit* (1984).

OLD TESTAMENT

Bruce Waltke, area editor

OLD TESTAMENT

BRUCE WALTKE
Professor of Old Testament
Westminster Theological Seminary

Introduction

Biblical studies are based on the belief that God *in some way* speaks to mankind in Scripture. Scholars within the discipline differ, however, in their understanding of the manner and the extent to which he speaks in them. For example, to state the matter cartoonishly, Protestant fundamentalists stand *under* Scripture in what appears to liberals as mindless assent and a tendency to absolutize their subjective interpretations; Catholics consciously, and confessionally-oriented Protestants unconsciously, stand *alongside* Scriptures with their traditions; and classic liberals stand *above* them with an arrogance that through the historical critical method they can find the truth in them. These differences have historically distinguished the journals and their contributors.

The present state of the study, according to Albert C. Outler,[1] is distinguished by the postliberal posture: to stand *before* the Scriptures and "to reposition Holy Scripture as a unique linguistic medium of God's self-communication to the human family." "Standing before the Scripture" entails putting a new priority on biblical studies, and "repositioning" them entails putting an emphasis on what the text and the canon say, instead of on what happened behind the text. In sum, rhetorical and canonical criticisms have replaced form and historical criticisms.

This editor welcomes these new emphases that revitalize biblical theology and biblical studies, but cautions that in postliberalism the discernment of the more than historical and/or literary values in the Bible—that is, its transcendent authoritative doctrine and normativeness—remain subjective and fluctuating. In addition, the foundations for faith in historical events remain as shaky as in classic liberalism. With the focus on text and canon for their own value, and not on the event behind the text, modern scholars tend subtly to reduce the text to fiction.

Several excellent articles on biblical theology, that is, the attempt to hear the canon as a whole, appeared this past year. Walter Brueggemann made the most significant contribution[2]; he suggests that it take the shape of a dialectic between "common theology" that denies pain by maintaining "there are orders, limits, and boundaries within which humanness is possible and beyond which there can only be trouble" (p. 40), and a theology of pain, which is a protest against the common theology. In an independent study H. H. Schmid[3] argues that Israel modified the notion of order because of its historical experience, and first expressed a theology of disorientation in pre-exilic prophecy, followed by other reflexes. S. Talmon[4] distinguishes a Jewish approach to revelation from a Christian one. Samuel Terrien[5] maps the contour of biblical theology in an objective and comprehensive overview of the vast literature on the subject published during the past fifteen years, along with linkage to preceding surveys.

In an attempt to hear the diverse portions of biblical literature many superb studies appeared this last year. C. S. Rodd, editor of *Expository Times*, along with John Ziesler is presenting a judicious series, "Which is the best commentary?" "Genesis" appeared in March 1986,[6] and "Job" in September.

Four essays by B. P. Kyle McCarter, D. L. Petersen, J. L. Mays, and J. M. Bassler[7] brilliantly profile David. Petersen[8] creatively exegetes the texts by comparing the biblical portrait of David with the symbols found in the portrait of David by the late Marc Chagall. Mays implies that the David of the Bible has a social reality similar to that of Scarlett O'Hara, a reality more significant than the names of women in the Atlanta telephone directory.

Outstanding studies on biblical books include: Daniel J. O'Connor, "Reverence and Irreverence in Job"[9]; and Carole Fontaine, "Proverb Performance in the Hebrew Bible,"[10] which illustrates the recent impact of other disciplines upon biblical studies, in this case the influence of paroemiology. To represent this genre of Old Testament studies the writer selected Patrick D. Miller, Jr., "Current Issues in Psalms Studies,"[11] the lead article in an issue devoted entirely to the Psalms.

As a result of the replacement of form criticism with rhetorical criticism, and the ascendancy of canonical criticism over against historical criticism, "courses in biblical introduction are in the throes of revision, but as yet without consensus," as Outler notes (285). The main challenge against this priority to assess the final form of biblical books and canon comes from those who stress the process of canonization over against the product of the canonization, and correlatively from social scientific criticism. For publication the writer selected Norman K. Gottwald, "Social Matrix and Canonical Shape,"[12] because, although Gottwald wants to leave the impression that his social scientific criticism correlates with canonical criticism, in fact he joins in sharp battle against it regarding the authority of the canon. A serendipity of his criticism is its exposé of how shallow is the canon's foundation when grounded on the faith of an arbitrarily chosen community, as argued by Brevard Childs, followed by R. Rendtorff (in *The Old Testament: an Introduction*, tr. by John Bowden [1985]), rather than on the solid rock of inspiration by the Holy Spirit.

In spite of the new emphases many studies still address themselves to the question of historicity. The best representative of this genre is Sara Japhet, "The Historical Reliability of Chronicles."[13] It should be read together with Tamara C. Eskenazi, "The Chronicler and the Composition of 1 Esdras."[14]

Archaeological and historical studies continue to sharpen the church's memory of the Bible's stories and its historical background. Erica Reiner's presidential address to the American Oriental Society, "The Uses of Astrology,"[15] and Stephanie Dalley, "Foreign Chariotry and Cavalry in the Armies of Tiglath-Pileser III and Sargon II,"[16] are outstanding and of interest to serious lay students. William H. Shea, "Some New Factors Bearing Upon the Date of the Exodus,"[17] collects new evidence supporting John Bimson's theory that Middle Bronze II should be lowered into the fifteenth century. To represent this genre the writer selected James L. Crenshaw, "Education in Ancient Israel,"[18] because it is a model of scholarly writing: erudite, cogent, lucid, and relevant.

Though no article has been selected for the field of textual criticism, the writer calls attention to Robert Bascom, "The Targums: Ancient Reader's Helps?"[19] because Bascom replaces the common misunderstanding that the Targums are "free" or "paraphrastic" translations with the theory that they added to the Hebrew text "coded" words or phrases that represented a condensed form of Jewish oral tradition.

Finally, note that *Sword of the Lord* published twenty-five sermons on the Old Testament by such outstanding preachers as R. G. Lee, G. W. Truett, H. Appelman, etc.

For a relatively full bibliography of literature relating to the Old Testament, see *Old Testament Abstracts*, Vols. 8 (1985) and 9 (1986) published by the Catholic Biblical Association. The writer wishes to thank publicly the scores of editors who recommended to him the articles they thought most appropriately fit *The Best in Theology*'s criteria. The editor regrets that he could not mention many more outstanding suggestions. What is needed is more scholarly articles that stand *with* Scripture pointing sinners to Jesus Christ.

Notes

[1] "Towards a Postliberal Hermeneutics," *TT*, 42/3 (Oct. 1985): 281-91.

[2] "Shape for Old Testament Theology." Parts I and II, *CBQ*, 47 (1985): 28-46; 395-415.

[3] "The notion of history in the Old Testament and in the ancient Near East," *OTE*, 4 (1986): 14-27.

[4] "Revelation in Biblical Times," *HS*, 26 (1985): 53-70.

[5] "Biblical Theology: The Old Testament (1970-1984) A Decade and a Half of Spectacular Growth," *BTB*, 15/4 (Oct. 1985): 127-35.

[6] *ET*, 97 (1986): 163.

[7] *Interpretation*, 40/2 (April, 1986).

[8] Originally published in *The Iliff Review* (Fall, 1985): 2-21.

[9] *ITQ*, 51/2 (1985): 85-104.
[10] *JSOT*, 32 (1985): 87-103.
[11] *Word and World*, 5 (1985): 132-43.
[12] *TT*, 42/3 (Oct. 1985): 307-31.
[13] *JSOT*, 33 (1985): 83-107.
[14] *CBQ*, 48 (1986): 39-61.
[15] *JAOS*, 105 (1985): 589-95.
[16] *Iraq*, 47 (1985): 31-48.
[17] *Catastrophism and Ancient History* (May, 1986): 29-35.
[18] *JBL*, 104/4 (Dec. 1985): 601-15.
[19] *BT*, 36/3 (July 1985): 301-16.

About the Area Editor

Bruce Waltke (Th.M., Dallas Theological Seminary; Th.D., Dallas Theological Seminary; Ph.D., Harvard University) is professor of Old Testament at Westminster Theological Seminary. He is affiliated with the Orthodox Presbyterian Church. Until 1985 he was assistant editor of the Expositor's Bible Commentary. He currently serves on the Committee for Bible Translation of the *New International Version of the Holy Bible*. His books include *Micah* in the Tyndale Old Testament Commentary series (Leicester: InterVarsity Press, forthcoming); *Intermediate Hebrew Grammar* (Winona Lake: Eisenbrauns, forthcoming); and *Theological Word Book of the Old Testament* (1980).

CURRENT ISSUES IN PSALMS STUDIES

PATRICK D. MILLER, JR.
Professor of Old Testament Theology
Princeton Theological Seminary

Article from *Word & World*

The scholarly investigation of the Psalms is now as always a matter of lively discussion on a variety of issues. In these pages no effort is made to cover that discussion exhaustively. The focus is on those issues that seem to this writer to be at the forefront and of potential importance for persons whose primary task is the interpretation of the Psalms in the context of the community of faith.

I. The Function of the Psalms in Ancient Israel

Form critical study has dominated, if not controlled, the way the Psalms have been handled during this century—a fact as evident in popular treatments of the Psalms and commentaries as in scholarly literature. Attention to the type and character of the Psalms with an effort to understand how they functioned in the life and worship of individual and community can offer either direct clues or heuristic suggestions for their continuing role in personal piety and public worship. However, the very character of the Psalms as relatively brief individual units, for the most part now loosed from any context but the literary one, means that many questions about type, and especially about the setting in life of the various types, are uncertain of answer or open to various answers.

The basic schema set forth by Gunkel and Begrich in their *Einleitung in die Psalmen*[1] remains the foundation on which others continue to build. The most important comprehensive treatment since that time is found in the work of Claus Westermann.[2] He has made a very strong case for seeing praise and lament as the two poles of human address to God and by far the dominant categories of the Psalms. With regard to the first pole, praise, the primary issue raised by Westermann and debated by others is whether there is any separate category of thanksgiving to God that can be distinguished from praise of God—either in Hebrew thought generally or in the types of psalms—as Gunkel so indicated in separating the song of thanksgiving from the hymn of praise. Westermann argues that both categories in the Psalter are distinct from expressions of thanks in the human sphere, in that they are totally directed toward God in exaltation by persons who in spontaneous joy think not of themselves but only of God.

In this writer's judgment, Westermann's description to some extent caricatures thanksgiving in the process of virtually eliminating it from the Psalter and Hebrew thought. Expressions of blessing toward human beings and toward God, as well as the more explicit declarations of praise, express gratitude as well as exalting God and bearing testimony to the Lord's grace and power. Westermann is correct, however, in identifying *praise* as the primary category, and in fact he essentially preserves Gunkel's distinction in differentiating *tᵉhillāh* (Gunkel = hymn; Westermann = descriptive praise) and *tôdāh* (Gunkel = song of thanksgiving; Westermann = declarative praise). The latter category does explicitly represent psalms that praise God by making joyful response to God's deliverance of persons from distress, in distinction from those that praise God more generally for majesty and creative power. The discussion is not unimportant for thinking theologically about the nature of praise and its relationship to thanksgiving and confession or proclamation, all of which are terms that have to do with what goes on in the *tôdāh*.[3]

The lament or complaint psalms in the Psalter and elsewhere in the Old Testament have been the subject of even more attention than the psalms of praise. Various proposals have been put forth to try to explain the situation and purpose of the laments of individuals. These represent efforts to understand who the *speaker* in the individual laments (the "I") is, who the *enemies* are, and what is the human need. Related to such questions is the matter of the cultic character of these psalms. References in various psalms to the sanctuary, sacrifice, help in the morning, and purification suggest a cultic connection. But is that universally the case, and does the ritual activity that may be associated with the laments take place in public cult or worship, or does it happen privately, perhaps in the context of the family? Some interpreters have noted and emphasized those places in the psalms that seem to identify the speaker as someone who has been accused of something. Noting places in the Old Testament where legal cases could be handled at the sanctuary (e.g., Exod 22:8-9; Deut 17:8-13; 19:16ff.; 21:1-9; 1 Kings 8:31-32), H. Schmidt suggested that a number of individual laments arise out of the language and activity of a sacral judicial procedure. One who claimed to be falsely accused prayed to God against his or her enemies (accusers) and received from the priests the verdict of God, which if favorable then elicited a further prayer of thanksgiving. (Examples: Pss 3, 4, 5, 7, 17, 26, 27, 54, 55, 69, etc.)[4] Walter Beyerlin more recently has proposed a modification of this view, seeing in a number of psalms (3, 4, 5, 7, 11, 17, 23, 26, 27, 57, and 63) a plea for divine judgment that is not understood as threatening or tied to a regularized sacral procedure in which the accused is brought to the priests for judgment, but is a protection; and the sanctuary provided asylum.[5] More sweepingly L. Delekat has proposed that these psalms along with many

others are prayers of persons who, seeking asylum in the sanctuary, wrote a   (2)
short prayer for help on the temple wall, probably in the evening upon
arrival. After the certainty of a hearing had been received, a short note to that
effect was added. In time, according to Delekat, the prayers became longer
and more artful. They could be engraved on a stele, perhaps by one who had
not composed the prayer.[6]

Neither Schmidt nor Beyerlin would ascribe all of the laments to an
occasion of judicial procedure or protection from false accusers in the
sanctuary. They both have acknowledged that a number of the laments seem
to cry out not for divine justice, but for deliverance from sickness and misery
(e.g., Pss 6, 13, 22, 28, 38, and 102). This view, accentuated earlier by
Mowinckel and affirmed by Gunkel as probably the origin of some of the
psalms before they were loosed from any cultic setting, has more recently
been elaborated by Klaus Seybold, who summarizes as follows:

> According to these texts, the psalm of the individual sick person was vari-
> ously anchored in the lament phase and was a prayer for preservation and
> healing. In keeping with this context, it was often simultaneously a confes-
> sion of guilt and a request for mercy, spoken within the private sickroom,   (3)
> probably with the aid of a priest. It was very likely not performed by the sick
> person himself during a pilgrimage to a holy place, since anyone seriously
> sick was generally not up to the rigors of such a trip. Or the psalm belonged
> in the thanksgiving phase as a laudatory prayer and personal (sacrificial)
> contribution within the framework of a community meal, celebrated at the
> sanctuary after successful recovery and as part of the reconciliation and
> rehabilitation of the recovered person. This could happen . . . "twice, three
> times" during the course of life. The actual, individual, and liturgically
> formed psalms of sickness originated in this way.[7]

The most impressive proposal in recent years for understanding the
form and function of the individual laments is that of Erhard Gerstenberger.
His analysis is shaped by three contributing factors that have not played so
large a role in other interpretations: (a) sociological analysis of the relation
of the individual to the group and the function of the group in society, as well
as of the relation between word and act in ritual matters; (b) the everyday
scheme of prayer as uncovered in the *narrative* texts of the Old Testament;
and (c) Mesopotamian ritual texts.[8] The result of his investigation is to place
the individual laments outside the official cult and the Temple. These
laments belong rather to healing ceremonies within the circle of the family.   (4)
A person who may be threatened by any of a wide range of troubles goes
to a ritual expert (trained in the ritual but not a priest) within the family or
clan, participates in a healing rite involving both words and actions, and gets
rid of the threat or trouble. The final goal and consequence of such activity
is the rehabilitation of the individual as a member of the primary social
sphere (clan or family) and thus the restoration of clan harmony.

If all this sounds more like family or group therapy than prayer and

worship in the church, that is neither surprising nor accidental. In his concluding remarks, Gerstenberger, noting the increasing isolation of individuals in a modern technological society, compares the rehabilitation of the
sufferer in the Old Testament with contemporary group therapy movements
that seek to reintegrate a distressed person into the primary group in a
process of words and actions under a group leader who is an expert in the
process or "ritual."[9] In this same connection Gerstenberger sees in Old
Testament scholarship's inability to think about these matters except in
terms of individual prayer and piety, or the official and corporate worship of
the people, a reflection of the Protestant tendency to understand prayer as
either an individual matter or a part of public worship. The lament psalms
are an indication of the fact that individuals live their lives "above all in the
small world of the primary group" (translation mine) rather than in the
larger—albeit secondary when viewed sociologically—sphere of community
or people. It is in the small group that meaning is found and religion
experienced.[10]

Gerstenberger's analysis, which has impressed many, will continue to be
tested and modified. His work is at least a challenge to others to assess
theologically the sociological reality of the significance for human existence
of small groups (e.g., families, circles of friends, groups with common interests or needs) as the context for meaningful existence. Both with regard to
Gerstenberger's work on the lament psalms as well as the contemporary
experience of church and synagogue, the relation of these smaller groups to
the larger spheres (e.g., church, community, nation) that give identity and
evoke loyalty remains to be developed.[11]

It would not do to characterize major approaches to the understanding
of the laments without recognizing another fact. Birkeland,[12] the later
Mowinckel,[13] and others believe that the "I" of the laments is the king acting
in behalf of or as representative of the people in crying out for help against
national enemies. This has been taken up afresh and impressively by J. H.
Eaton, who sees some fifty-odd psalms of the individual as being in fact royal
psalms.[14] Such a construal of the texts is plausible and undergirded by the
centrality of the king in ancient Israel and possibly in the official cult, as well
as by the ascription of so many psalms to David. The connection of the
psalms to the Messiah and the christological use of them by the early church
would be even more direct should such an interpretation be on the right
track.

The search for a readily identifiable situation as the context for understanding the laments may, however, be illusory or unnecessary. The language of these psalms with its stereotypical, generalizing, and figurative
style is so open-ended that later readers on the one hand are stopped from
peering behind them to one or more clearly definable set of circumstances or
settings in life, and on the other hand are intentionally set free to adapt them
to varying circumstances and settings. Indeed one can relate some of the

laments to persons and events in the Old Testament even though the psalms did not *originally* belong to such persons' experience in the sense of being composed by them or for them.[15] Gunkel, Westermann, and others have helped us see the distinction between original purpose and later use even when we may not be absolutely certain about either one.[16] Indeed in the work of Westermann the laments are not at all seen in the context of cultic and ritual activity but as one of the primary modes of prayer (the other being praise) that characterize human address to God.[17]

Theological concerns come very much to the fore in Westermann's analysis of the laments when compared with other treatments. Two issues that have theological implications stand out in the current discussion. One of these is what seems to be the simple question of how to label the genre under discussion. Should these psalms be called *laments* or *complaints (Klage/ Anklage)*, as is the standard approach, or should one designate them *petitions* or *supplications (Bitte)*? Westermann is a good example of the former, Gerstenberger of the latter, though each uses the other terminology also. While this may seem to be simply another case of form critics unable to agree on standard terminology, it is really more than that. Does such prayer function primarily to lay out complaint against God and others, articulating the human need, and giving form to the anguish and despair of one in trouble?[18] Or do these prayers place before God specific petitions for help in the hope and expectation that God will intervene in the situation to deliver one from trouble? Clearly both dimensions are present in the lament psalms, but the accent one places (or discerns) may affect one's theology. The emphasis may tend to create an understanding of prayer as an expression of human distress and a struggle with God that is in itself healing and restorative and a notion of God as present and involved in suffering more than delivering persons out of it. Or one's sense of these prayers as petitions for help may focus one's theology on prayer as effective in bringing about the power of God who is able to deliver and does so. It is of course possible also that the theology of prayer held by the interpreter of these Psalms may shape the way the genres are understood. If the "passion" of Jesus, i.e., God's incarnational com-passion with a suffering humanity (see below) and God's resurrection of the crucified Jesus are any clue, we would seem to be compelled to try to hold complaint and petition together.[19]

A second theological issue that may be identified in the ongoing study of the lament psalms is the question of how they identify the fundamental human need. Traditionally these psalms have been seen as reflecting the human condition of sinfulness before God, a condition that is directly attested in the so-called penitential psalms (Pss 6, 32, 38, 51, 102, 130, and 143) and inferred from the association between sickness and sin and judgment that may be discerned in various Old Testament contexts. In contemporary interpretation of the psalms that view is being regarded as much too simple if not misleading. Most of the psalms either do not identify the plight of the lamenter with sin, or at least are ambiguous on that score. Westermann again is the one who has addressed some of the theological implications of this fact by suggesting that Pauline theology has shifted the lament of the suffering one to the confession of the sinner. As he suggests, this shift has had large ramifications for Christian understanding of the work of Christ. The focus has been upon the forgiveness of sins rather than ending human suffering, even though the Gospels offer the Old Testament lament, especially Psalm 22, as a reference for understanding the Passion of Jesus, i.e., his identification with the suffering of those who cry out in the laments.

More recently Samuel Balentine has demonstrated that while the motif of the hiding of the face of God and related themes such as God's rejecting, forgetting, and being silent, and the like, are frequently understood as manifestations of divine judgment for sin when appearing in prophetic texts, that is not the case in the Psalms. There such expressions reflect more a sense of doubt, despair, and alienation from God, a condition that is frequently quite inexplicable, as is evidenced by the occasional protestations of innocence, protestations that are hardly very congruent with a Pauline anthropology.[20] Most Christian readers have as much difficulty with these claims of innocence as they do with the imprecations against enemies—in both cases because they cut against the grain of what is heard from the New Testament. It might seem that the communal laments of the people (Pss 44, 60, 74, 79, 80, 83, and 89) would be primarily cries for forgiveness of sin rather than pleas for help, but that assumption also may be a reflection of a prophetic-Christian reading of the texts. In a dissertation in progress,[21] Murray Haar demonstrates that these psalms subordinate the issue of sin to the claim on the covenantal relationship with God, which means that God's fate is bound up with that of Israel and the enemies of Israel are the enemies of God. Confession of sin is not a prominent feature of the communal laments.

Before leaving the issue of the form and function of the Psalms, one should note the stimulating hermeneutical efforts in this area by Walter Brueggemann. In a study published a decade ago he laid out the lament-deliverance relationship as a basic structure of Israel's faith that is prominent not only in the Psalms but runs throughout the Old Testament.[22] Subsequently Brueggemann placed the lament psalms over against the analysis by Elizabeth Kübler-Ross of the death-grief process that she discovered in her work with terminally ill patients. Brueggemann thus highlighted the significance of form and structure for persons handling loss, grief, and death, while underscoring some of the distinctiveness of the process in the community that is formed by faith.[23] The most extensive general treatment of the form and function of the Psalms by Brueggemann is a very heuristic proposal, growing out of the work of Paul Ricoeur, that the Psalms speak to or from situations of *orientation* (especially hymns), *disorientation* or *dislocation* (laments), and *reorientation* (especially songs of thanksgiving or declarative praise).[24] In all of this Brueggemann draws together psychological, philosophical, and hermeneutical strands in ways that suggest points of reference for a contemporary reading of the Psalms.

II. Re-Interpretation of the Psalms

While the term "re-interpretation" is not fully adequate, it does point to an aspect of Psalms study that focuses more on the final form of a psalm than on its original genre and character. A number of psalms are in some fashion composite or the result of earlier psalms or parts of psalms being re-interpreted in a new time. The result is often very different from the original form and function, but the dynamic present in the Psalms' capacity to speak in and for different situations is well illustrated in the very growth of the Psalter itself. Many psalms are seen as the result of the scribal activity in Exilic and post-Exilic times, impacted more by concerns of wisdom and torah and the search for true piety than by the influence of the cult. Some of these psalms have been described as "anthologies" (e.g., Pss 25, 33, 34, 103, 111, 112, 119, and 145)[25] because they are created by drawing upon pieces, expressions, verses, and language of other psalms—as well as other Old Testament traditions—which were not only composed earlier but possibly for quite specific cultic occasions. Here expressions for "seeking the Lord," "fearing God," God as "refuge" as well as references to "the afflicted," "the poor" and the like, which may have identified activities of persons in poverty or oppressed by others, have been spiritualized to describe the state of the pious Israelite before God.[26]

Such literary creations expressive of a torah piety are clearly present in the Psalter. Indeed one can identify obvious use of certain psalms in the composition of other psalms, e.g. in the relationships between Psalms 18 and 144 or Psalms 115 and 135 (the latter drawing on a number of psalm texts as well as other Old Testament material), the identity of Psalm 70 with Psalm 40:14-18, and the composition of Psalm 108 out of Psalms 57:8-12 and 60:7-14 as well as I Chronicles 16 out of Psalms 105:1-15, 96:1-13, and 106:1, 47-48. The issue that remains the subject of debate, however, is how far one can go in assigning psalms to this process of composition growing out of the concerns identified above. The language is so stereotyped that one may claim an early lament as a later spiritualized creation when that may not be the case at all. Nevertheless, enough clear examples exist that one may see the foundations laid for an ongoing process of re-interpreting the Psalms.

Another aspect of this new (or re-) interpretation that went on in the formation of the Psalter is the transformation of individual psalms possibly from the pre-Exilic era into psalms of the community in the Exilic and post-Exilic periods. The "I" of these individual psalms became Israel when the psalms were edited and rewritten at a later period. That process was not merely a mechanical, nonsubstantive one. On the contrary the psalms were given a new meaning in a new time. Joachim Becker, a primary advocate of such an understanding of the Psalms, sees a significant number of them as examples of reworking to give a new interpretation in a new time (Pss 9-10, 22, 40, 45, 54, 56, 59, 66, 68, 69, 85, 93, 102, 107, 108, and 118).[27] For Becker the most noticeable form of the new interpretation is the transformation of original cultic songs of lament or thanksgiving into eschatological songs reflecting the Exilic or post-Exilic situation of Israel in conflict with its neighbors.[28] He sees four central ideas in the eschatological salvation word of these psalms: Yahweh, whose power is revealed in creation and deliverance from exile, enters into rule and appears on Zion; deliverance from exile, return, and renewal as a people occupy a central place; the nations recognize the saving act of Yahweh, assemble to worship on Zion, and are punished and destroyed; Israel's posterity shall possess the land and inherit the blessing.[29]

A further mode of new interpretation that has been recognized for a long time but is also the subject of current interest is the *historicizing* of psalms, a feature primarily of titles added to psalms, associating them primarily with David and his life and experiences.[30] Such ascriptions served not only to identify a presumed author but to provide some hermeneutical clue to understanding the psalms thus titled.[31] Such historicizing, however, was not confined to the process of adding titles, according to Becker. For example, an individual song of thanksgiving in Psalm 18:2-31 became a royal song of David with the addition of vv. 32-51 and the title. The whole was then placed into the David story (II Sam 22). One can cite other examples of psalms that have been historicized by being ascribed to figures in the biblical story, e.g. I Samuel 2:1-10 (Hannah), Isaiah 38:10-20 (Hezekiah), and Jonah 2:3-10 (Jonah).[32]

III. The Psalter As a Collection

The interest in the way in which various Psalms may have been edited and given a new interpretation in the Exilic and post-Exilic age has contributed to a growing appreciation of the Psalter as a collection or book of psalms. Both the process of formation and the significance of the final shape of the Psalter have been matters of debate or discussion. Investigations of smaller collections and interrelationships among the Psalms have suggested a more conscious composition of the whole than has been sometimes recognized. Klaus Seybold has done a very careful study of the psalms of ascents (Pss 120-134) to show that they are interrelated not only by a common title "Song of Ascents" but by linguistic expressions, content, theology, and redactional activity. He sees them arising out of a lay context but collected together as a kind of handbook of songs and prayers for the pilgrim to Zion. They reflect a communal orientation that affirms the close relation to God and rejoices in

Zion as God's chosen abode.[33] Pierre Auffret has tried to demonstrate the interrelationships of Psalms 120-134 by analysis of literary structure and has also suggested that Psalms 135-138 are a consciously constructed group that have clear relation to Psalms 120-134, and more daringly, that Psalms 15-24 are a group arranged chiastically around Psalm 19 as a center.[34]

Westermann has identified several features of the present shape of the Psalter, including the fact that to some extent the Psalms are grouped according to distinctions that have been recognized form-critically.[35] There are groupings of psalms that are primarily individual (e.g., the David psalms) and some that are largely psalms of the community (in the Korah and Asaph psalms as well as the Songs of Ascents). The lament psalms occur more in the first half of the Psalter and hymns of praise more in the latter—a literary movement from dominant strains of lament to dominant shouts of praise that reflects a basic theological structure as well as the movement encountered in individual laments. Westermann has also suggested that the original Psalter may have been Psalms 1-119, to which the Songs of Ascents and others were added.[36] Whether or not that can be proven, it is clear from the beginning and ending of the Psalter that some guides have been given for understanding the whole. Psalms 1 and 2 form an introduction which suggests first that one finds here a true torah piety that will show the way for those who love the Lord and the law, and secondly that these psalms also show the way of God's rule over the larger human communities. The conclusion to the Psalms, i.e., Psalm 150, and the title of the Psalter (*tehillîm* = hymns) give the Psalter to the community as a book of praise to God.

The appearance of a number of Psalms manuscripts at Qumran, including the large Psalms scroll from Cave 11 with a decidedly different order and arrangement of the Psalms that are on it, has raised the issue of whether or not there may have been another "authoritative" or "canonical" Psalter than the one that presently exists in the Hebrew Bible—one that could have been a genuine rival or alternative to the form preserved in the Masoretic Text.[37] While the matter is hardly settled, the evidence tends toward the conclusion that the Qumran manuscripts are dependent on the received canonical Psalter of the Hebrew Bible. The Cave 11 Psalms scroll containing only the latter third of the Psalter is where the most variation occurs, both in reordering and in the inclusion of non-canonical psalms. But over two-thirds of the Psalms manuscripts or fragments show only canonical materials extant and in the expected sequence.[38] The grouping of Psalms 105, 95, and 106 in I Chronicles 16 shows us both that Book IV of the Psalter already existed as a unit (because the conclusion to that Book which follows the end of Ps 106 is included in I Chron 16:36), and that psalms from the canonical text could be regrouped for liturgical purposes. It may be that the unusual contents and ordering of the Cave 11 scroll reflect liturgical concerns as well as the desire to create "a library edition of the putative works of David."[39] Patrick Skehan was probably correct in his judgment that we cannot learn anything from the Qumran texts about "the formative period of the building up of the standard collection of 150 Psalms."[40]

IV. Literary Study of the Psalter

Finally, attention should be called to the fact that the growing interest in the literary study of the Bible has had its impact also on the study of the Psalms, and in two ways. One of these is the renewed and intense interest in trying to define the nature and character of Hebrew poetry, with particular attention to the poetic line and its function in building larger blocks. The question whether or not meter exists in Hebrew poetry, or can be described if it does exist, remains much debated.[41] The phenomenon of parallelism has been the subject of major treatments in recent years. Stephen Geller has proposed a system for analysis of aspects of parallelism that sets up some basic categories and applies the concept of grammatical paradigm to produce a reconstructed sentence out of poetic couplets.[42] In a somewhat different direction, James Kugel claims that parallelism is not a poetic device that breaks down into many types but is essentially a way of heightening, reinforcing, or—to use his term—"seconding" a point or statement made in the first colon of a poetic line.[43] The most complex recent proposal about the nature of Hebrew poetry is that of Michael O'Connor, who combines analysis of lines on a syntactical basis with the examination of various tropes or figures as the way to approach small numbers of lines, i.e., bicola and tricola.[44] These studies raise the question whether parallelism in Hebrew poetry is one thing (Kugel) or many (Geller and O'Connor). They effectively rule out the usual handbook approach that suggests all lines can be seen in terms of three types of parallelism (synonymous, antithetic, and synthetic). While this writer has found Kugel's approach particularly helpful in analyzing poetry, it is also the case that both Geller and O'Connor provide categories that, when applied to lines of poetry, give us handles for grasping both logical and aesthetic dimensions of Hebrew poetry.

Beyond the focus of parallelism and the nature of Hebrew poetry, which of course encompasses much more than simply the Psalms, literary study of the Psalter has sought to apply stylistic and rhetorical analysis. Here issues of formation and function are less to the fore, and the particular mode of expression of each psalm takes precedence over its place as a typical example of a genre. The concern is for the medium as well as the message, and the claim is that form and content cannot be separated. One is led to appreciate any psalm as a unique literary expression that unfolds its word in various traditional poetic devices and features. Interpreters who have moved in this direction have given particular attention to formal features of structure and the figures of speech that create that structure, such as repetition, chiasmus, inclusion, alliteration and word play, ambiguity, and the like.[45]

Such stylistic analysis belongs to the study and indeed the understanding of any poetic text. It is consistent with larger trends in contemporary biblical study toward a primary focus on the final form of a text. It remains to be seen how well those whose sensitivity is to formal and poetic features will be able to place their work in the service of hermeneutics. To date stylistic analysis often stands by itself without engaging other issues of interpretation.[46] But it is also the case that interpreters of the Psalms whose attention is particularly given over to form critical exegesis or to theological, liturgical, and pastoral dimensions of interpretation, have tended on the whole to ignore stylistic aspects as features of the text's expression. No modern commentary in English reflects any serious concentration on matters of style.[47] The full hearing of the Psalms will be greatly enhanced when the familiar tendency to abstract content from form or to empty form of its content is overcome. To know the Psalms are poetic is not to forget that they are Scripture. To read and hear them as Scripture requires that one receive them also as poetry. From either direction, *understanding* is all.

Notes

[1] Herman Gunkel and Joachim Begrich, *Einleitung in die Psalmen* (Göttingen: Vandenhoeck und Ruprecht, 1933).

[2] Claus Westermann, *Praise and Lament in the Psalms* (Atlanta: John Knox, 1981).

[3] On the praise of God in the Psalms see the January, 1985 issue of *Interpretation.*

[4] Hans Schmidt, *Das Gebet des Angeklagten im Alten Testament* (BZAW, 49; Giessen, 1928).

[5] Walter Beyerlin, *Die Rettung der Bedrängten in den Feindpsalmen der Einzelnen auf institutionelle Zusammenhänge untersucht* (FRLANT, 99; Göttingen: Vanderhoeck und Ruprecht, 1970).

[6] L. Delekat, *Asylie und Schutzorakel am Zionheiligtum* (Leiden: E. J. Brill, 1967).

[7] Klaus Seybold and Ulrich B. Mueller, *Sickness and Healing* (Biblical Encounter Series; Abingdon: Nashville, 1981) 44. Seybold's more elaborated development of this view appears in *Das Gebet des Kranken im Alten Testament* (BWANT, 19; Stuttgart: W. Kohlhammer, 1973).

[8] Erhard Gerstenberger, *Der bittende Mensch* (WMANT, 51; Neukirchen Vluyn: Neukirchener, 1980).

[9] Ibid., 167-69.

[10] Ibid.

[11] A similar point of view has been set forth in two works by Westermann's student, Ranier Albertz: *Weltschöpfung und Menschenschöpfung* (CTMA 3; Stuttgart: Calwer, 1974) and *Persönliche Frömmigkeit und offizielle Religion* (CTMA 9; Stuttgart: Calwer, 1978). In distinction from the laments of the people, which are rooted in the history of salvation and thus associated with the official theology of the nation, the individual laments are rooted in the history of the individual and that person's relationship with God. They belong therefore to the personal religion that has its locus in the sphere of the small group and the family. The lament is an appeal to one's personal God to be present and protect and is intended to rehabilitate and restore the person to the small group. In a long conclusion to the second work Albertz suggests some implications of this perspective for the focus of ministry, seeing it involved more in the family and its life and worship, helping to give family members a better understanding of themselves and their situation as well as to actualize and strengthen in each new phase or turning-point in

life their personal relationship of trust in God (*Persönliche Frömmigkeit*, 208). In his treatment of the biblical material Albertz gives some attention to the integration of the personal religion of the individual in the small group into the official religion and worship of the larger community.

[12] H. Birkeland, *The Evildoers in the Book of Psalms* (Oslo: J. Dybwasd, 1955).

[13] Sigmund Mowinckel, *The Psalms in Israel's Worship* (Oxford: Basil Blackwell, 1962), chapters III, VII, and VIII.

[14] John H. Eaton, *Kingship and the Psalms* (SBT, 32; London: SCM, 1976).

[15] Cf. Patrick D. Miller, Jr., "Trouble and Woe: Interpreting the Biblical Laments," *Interpretation* 37 (1983) 32-45.

[16] With regard to the prevalence of interpretations that focus upon sickness and false accusation as the primary conditions of the lamenters, Joachim Becker's summary words are appropriate: "It is no accident that sickness and accusation dominate in the prayer speech of the individual lament songs. These have to do with the two fundamental human needs. Sickness is the threatening of physical existence by lessening life. The sick person in the Old Testament believes himself or herself to be near the entrance to the realm of the dead. Accusation is the threatening of moral existence in the community and no less dangerous." J. Becker, *Wege der Psalmenexegese* (SBS, 78; Stuttgart: Katholisches Bibelwerk, 1975), 33; translation mine.

[17] Westermann, *Praise and Lament*, 15-35.

[18] Cf. Samuel Balentine, *The Hidden God: The Hiding of the Face of God in the Old Testament* (OTM; Oxford: Oxford, 1983).

[19] Both the modern consciousness vis-à-vis the intervention of God in the nexus of events and the loosing of the lament psalms from a possibly highly specific cultic event to a more spiritual setting in the ongoing experience of worship and piety have probably contributed to an emphasis upon the complaint character of these psalms more than the petition for help.

[20] See note 8.

[21] At Union Theological Seminary in Virginia.

[22] "From Hurt to Joy, From Death to Life," *Interpretation* 28 (1974) 3-19.

[23] "The Formfulness of Grief," *Interpretation* 31 (1977) 263-75.

[24] "Psalms and the Life of Faith: A Suggested Typology of Function," *JSOT* 17 (June, 1980) 3-32. See now W. Brueggemann, *The Message of the Psalms: A Theological Commentary* (Minneapolis: Augsburg, 1984).

[25] Becker, *Wege*, 75.

[26] See the summary discussion of Becker, *Wege*, Ch. IX and the works by Deissler, Gelin and Robert referred to there.

[27] In addition to his *Wege der Psalmenexegese*, one should consult his more extended study, *Israel deutet seine Psalmen: Urform und Neuinterpretation in den Psalmen* (SBS 18; Stuttgart: Katholisches Bibelwerk, 1975).

[28] Cf. B. S. Childs, *Introduction to the Old Testament as Scripture* (Philadelphia: Fortress, 1979) 517-18.

[29] Becker, *Wege*, 93ff.

[30] Cf. Becker, *Wege*, Ch. XIII; Childs, *Introduction*, 520-22.

[31] Childs sees this interpretative move as follows: " . . . the incidents chosen as evoking the Psalms were not royal occasions or representative of the kingly office. Rather David is pictured simply as a man, indeed chosen by God for the sake of all Israel, but who displays all the strengths and weaknesses of all human beings. He emerges as a person who experiences the full range of human emotions, from fear and despair to courage and love, from complaint and plea to praise and thanksgiving. . . . The effect of this new context has wide hermeneutical implications. The psalms are transmitted as the sacred psalms of David, but they testify to all the common troubles and joys of ordinary human life in which all persons participate." *Introduction*, 521. Cf. M. Fishbane, "Torah and Tradition," in *Tradition and Theology in the Old Testament*, ed. D. A. Knight (Philadelphia: Fortress, 1977) 287; and P. D. Miller, "Trouble and Woe."

[32] Becker, *Israel*, 33.

[33] K. Seybold, *Die Wallfahrtspsalmen* (Biblisch-Theologische Studien, 3; Neukirchen-Vluyn: Neukirchener Verlag, 1978).

[34] Auffret, *La sagesse a bati sa maison: études de structures littéraires dans lÁncien Testament et spécialement dans les Psaumes* (OBO 49; Fribourg, Suisse: Editions Universitaires, 1982) 407-549.

[35] C. Westermann, *Praise and Lament*, 250-58.

[36] Ibid.

[37] J. A. Sanders, "Cave 11 Surprises and the Question of Canon," *McCormick Quarterly* 21 (1968) 1-15. Cf. Sanders, *The Dead Sea Psalms Scroll* (Ithaca: Cornell, 1967) 14.

[38] P. W. Skehan, "Qumran and Old Testament Criticism," *Qumran: Sa Piété, sa théologie et son milieu*, ed. M. Delcor (BETL 46; Leuven, University Press, 1978) 167.

[39] Ibid., 169.

[40] Ibid., 164.

[41] See, for example, James Barr's review of Kugel's *The Idea of Biblical Poetry* in *The Times Literary Supplement*, December 25, 1981, 1506. See n. 43 below.

[42] S. A. Geller, *Parallelism in Early Biblical Poetry* (HSM 20; Missoula: Scholars Press, 1979).

[43] J. Kugel, *The Idea of Biblical Poetry* (New Haven: Yale, 1981).

[44] M. O'Connor, *Hebrew Verse Structure* (Winona Lake: Eisenbrauns, 1980).

[45] Some representative examples of rhetorical or stylistic analysis of the Psalms are N. H. Ridderbos, *Die Psalmen—Stilistischen Verfahren und Aufbau* (BZAW 117; Berlin: W. de Gruyter, 1972); M. Weiss, "Wege der Neuen Dichtungswissenschaft in ihrer Anwendung auf die Psalmen-forschung," *Biblica* 42 (1961) 255-302; L. Alonso-Schökel, *Trienta Salmos: Poesia y Oracion* (Estudios de Antiguo Testamento 2; Madrid: Ediciones Christiandad, 1981); J. Trublet and J.-N. Aletti, *Approche poétique et théologique des psaumes* (Paris: Cerf, 1983); and P. Auffret, *La sagesse.*

[46] Some of the works cited above are refreshing exceptions in this regard.

[47] It is worth noting that the great form critic Herman Gunkel gave major attention to the aesthetic features of the Psalms in his commentary on them.

EDUCATION IN ANCIENT ISRAEL

JAMES L. CRENSHAW
Professor of Old Testament
Vanderbilt University Divinity School

Article from *Journal of Biblical Literature*

Present knowledge about education in ancient Israel is astonishingly incomplete. This deficiency of hard evidence exists despite many attempts to recover the actual learning situation prior to the first explicit reference to a school, Ben Sira's invitation to acquire an education at his house of study *bêt hammidrāš*, 51:23).[1] The flurry of recent activity in researching the problem has failed to alter the state of knowledge appreciably, although it has introduced fresh evidence from Palestinian inscriptions[2] and from the Hellenistic world.[3] The resulting extravagant claims about an elaborate system of schools throughout Palestine prior to the monarchy and after its disappearance require cautious assessment.[4] That is the modest task envisioned in this brief paper.

The disputed issue concerns the context within which education occurred: did parents assume primary responsibility for educating their children, or did they entrust boys (and girls)[5] to professional educators? In short, were there schools during the formative period of the monarchy or, more generally, before Ben Sira? Since differences of opinion arise from considering the same evidence, the problem could be partly semantic. After all, the term "school" is used in scholarly discussion with reference to a dominant intellectual perspective, as in the Uppsala school, and to a kind of discipleship, as in the Isaianic school. Neither sense is intended here; rather, by school is meant professional education, which involved both reading and writing, at a specific location to which young people came and for which fees were paid to a teacher. This is the sense in which recent interpreters seem to use the word, although they do not formulate the matter so explicitly. The disagreement, therefore, concerns the interpretation of the three kinds of evidence pertaining to the existence of schools in Israel. It comes as no surprise that these three possible sources of clarification are (1) the Hebrew Bible, (2) Palestinian inscriptions, and (3) ancient Near Eastern parallels. We shall examine the evidence from each of these sources in the light of recent scholarship.

I. Education in the Hebrew Bible

Evidence from the Hebrew Bible is largely circumstantial, and some texts say more about literacy in general than about how that ability to read and write was acquired. In August Klostermann's pioneer study of education in Israel, only three texts are taken as conclusive evidence for schools: Isa 28:9-13; 50:4-9; Prov 22:17-21.[6] The first is complicated by its reference to children who have just been weaned. Is it likely that the teaching of reading and writing began at such a tender age? Friedemann Golka answers this question with an emphatic "No" and understands the text as a mockery of infant's babble.[7] Although he thinks of a family setting, such a reading of the passage is not absolutely required; as a matter of fact, Golka must assume that parents instructed their own children in reading and writing. Now it is certainly clear that fathers and mothers taught their offspring moral precepts and instructed them in the art of coping, but all of this may easily have been achieved through oral instruction. What is not so clear is the context in which children learned to read and write, and that is the matter at issue in Isa 28:9-13.[8]

The second passage from the Isaianic corpus uses an expression for a trained tongue[9] and specifically refers to those who are taught. The decisive issue here is whether the prophet's appeal to an authoritative training is adequately explained by parental instruction or whether a greater source of authority is implied. Still, that enhanced authority could be a reference to prophetic discipleship and to the oral instruction involved in such a relationship with a prophetic master. The third text, Prov 22:17-21, is so closely related to the Egyptian Instruction of Amen-em-opet that it loses much of its evidentiary value.[10] It is conceivable that this foreign material was assimilated into the Israelite ethos[11] at the popular level, although a more probable explanation for the borrowing is that Israelite teachers needed a text for instructing scribes, and this one was precisely the kind of classic instruction for which they were searching. In light of such ambiguous evidence within the Hebrew Bible, modern critics must decide whether the virtual silence about schools is because none existed[12] or because they were so common that no one ever thought it necessary to mention what was obvious to all.

Evidence of a different sort from the Hebrew Bible has often been mustered in defense of professional schools, although it addresses the broader issue of literacy in Israel.[13] The evidence includes, among other things: (1) the existence of a city named Qiriath-Sepher (City of the Book, or City of the Scribe);[14] (2) the story in Judg 8:13-17 about Gideon's enlisting the aid of a local youth to write down the names of the city officials;[15] (3) Isaiah's determination to bind up the testimony and seal the teaching among his disciples (8:16);[16] (4) Job's desire to have the charges against him written on a document so that he could display them and demonstrate his innocence (31:35-37);[17] (5) Habakkuk's reference to a vision that could be read while one ran

through the streets (2:2);[18] (6) allusions to buying knowledge, which is
understood as tuition (Prov 4:5; 17:16);[19] (7) presumed scribes and courtiers
in the royal court, particularly in the time of David, Solomon, and Hezekiah;[20]
(8) references to parental instruction in Proverbs (especially 4:1-9; 8:32-36);
(9) scattered references to writing (e.g., Isa 10:19; 29:11-12; Prov 3:3; 7:3
[the tablet of the heart]; Jer 8:8 [the false pen of scribes]; Deut 24:1, 3
[a bill of divorce]; Jer 32:12 [deed of purchase]; Josh 18:9; 2 Sam 18:17); (10)
vocabulary for teaching and knowledge in Proverbs (cf. also the Oak of
Moreh in Gen 12:6; Deut 11:30).

The evidence clearly points to the existence of literate persons at an
early period in Israel. What remains unclear, however, is the place where that
literacy was acquired. Was the teaching of reading and writing exclusively a
parental responsibility, or did professional teachers supplement the learning that occurred at home? Unfortunately, the evidence presented above
does not permit a definitive answer to this question.

II. Palestinian Inscriptions

André Lemaire has recently gathered together the cumulative evidence from
Palestinian inscriptions. His analysis of the inscriptional data makes free use
of qualifying adverbs such as "perhaps" and "probably," which signals the
provisional nature of his conclusions. However, the use to which he puts this
understanding of the evidence is considerably less cautious, and the results
are necessarily problematic.[21] Lemaire isolates the following kinds of evidence that require, in his judgment, the presence of schools throughout
Palestine from premonarchic times: (1) abecedaries (Lachish, Kadesh-Barnea, Kuntilat-Ajrud, perhaps Aroer); (2) isolated letters of the alphabet or
groups of letters (perhaps Arad); (3) letters of the alphabet grouped by
similarities in appearance (perhaps Lachish); (4) words written several
times (Arad, Kadesh-Barnea, perhaps Kuntilat-Ajrud); (5) personal names
(perhaps Arad and Aroer); (6) formulary beginnings of letters (Kuntilat-
Ajrud); (7) lists of months (Gezer); (8) symbols (Kadesh-Barnea); (9) sequence of signs (Kadesh-Barnea); (10) drawings (Kuntilat-Ajrud, probably
Lachish); (11) exercises in reading a foreign language, that is, Phoenician
(Kuntilat-Ajrud).

The nature of the evidence encourages considerable speculation, both
with regard to actual content and intention. Lemaire thinks that many features arose from students' efforts to master the Hebrew script and alphabet,
to memorize correct epistolary form and essential information about the
agricultural year, to acquire refined techniques in drawing, and to familiarize
themselves with proper names. Poor drawings and very large characters are
attributed to learners, as are mistakes such as transposed letters. Similarly,
the juxtaposition of characters of the alphabet that resemble one another is

taken as proof that students are expressing their powers of discrimination.[22]

The evidence to which Lemaire appeals is in some respects impressive: the existence of a clear Phoenician hand, which may indicate a trained scribe; two abecedaries, one of which is in a superior hand; and the juxtaposition of similar letters of the alphabet. One might add to these data the paleographic consistency throughout ancient Israel, which seems to imply authoritative instruction in the art of writing. Alternative explanations for some of the evidence to which Lemaire appeals readily come to mind. The size of script may indicate poor eyesight, and the disparity in the quality of drawings may mean nothing more than that some persons draw better than others. Nevertheless, the cumulative inscriptional evidence seems to suggest that some people were practicing writing at a few locations. If that is a proper assessment of the evidence, it still leaves unanswered the issue of where children received their instruction.[23] When one takes into account the possibility that the pithoi were brought to the sites from somewhere else, conclusions about where the writing on them occurred are extremely hazardous.

One other bit of evidence has often been brought forward as proof that a school existed in ancient Shechem. W. F. Albright claimed that an Akkadian letter was written by a school teacher to request payment for services rendered.[24] This interpretation of the letter has been challenged,[25] and alternative explanations carry greater conviction, particularly since they do not require textual emendation of the crucial verb.[26] Nevertheless, the letter seems to mention writing, which is being taught, even if to domestics. Perhaps the so-called Gezer Calendar belongs to the discussion at this point, if it actually represents a school boy's practice lesson.

Bernhard Lang has introduced yet another kind of corroborative evidence, the virtual absence of scribal errors in ostraca from Palestine.[27] Here he relies on Lemaire's observation that only four ostraca in about 250 contain errors. It may be that such expertise says more about the simplicity of the Hebrew language than it does about the locus of education. Albright's oft-quoted remarks about the relative simplicity of Hebrew are very much to the point here,[28] especially in the light of such complex languages as Akkadian, Egyptian, and, to a lesser degree, Ugaritic. It follows that the evidence from Palestinian inscriptions, although impressive, is less persuasive than Lemaire admits, and the elaborate system of schools among the Israelite and major neighboring cities that he envisions may never have existed.

III. Education in Egypt, Mesopotamia, and Ugarit

A third kind of evidence is often cited as decisive proof that schools existed in Israel: the irrefutable fact that schools played a vital role in major cultures of the time, specifically in Egypt, Mesopotamia, and Ugarit. The argument usually assumes two forms: first, that many features from these schools appear in biblical texts; and, second, that administrative necessity would have required a presence of schools in Israel's royal courts. For example, use of "my son" as a technical expression for student and "father" for teacher is often taken as decisive proof of Egyptian influence, particularly when combined with common practices such as a free use of corporal punishment. In addition, it is often said that Israel's kings could not have carried out their official business without the assistance of trained officials who understood foreign languages and had mastered various literary skills. For these accomplishments, so it is argued, schools were indispensable.[29]

Now the importance of schools in the ancient world need not be debated. In Egypt from about 1900 B.C.E. a royal school existed for the express purpose of training courtiers, and a specific body of literature bears the identifying title "instructions" (seboyet). In these government schools training was provided for potential courtiers, who learned the art of persuasive speech, proper conduct in public, moral values, human psychology, and much more. Most important, they acquired an ability to read and write hieroglyphics. Given the difficulty of this task, it occasions little surprise that numerous errors in the school copies have survived, which suggests that learning did not always accompany copying, inasmuch as students seem often not to have understood the text. A premium fell on handwriting, not understanding; gaps in texts were left without any attempt to fill them in with familiar material, which implies that students did not exercise much original thinking.

One thing is certain: scribes thought highly of their profession. In one text, The Satire of the Trades, the scribal profession is exalted above all other occupations (biblical scholars have long known a similar text in Ben Sira 38:24-39:11). Perhaps the excessive cruelty in Egyptian pedagogy could be endured because of the high status bestowed on graduates. In any event, we possess various scribal controversies that testify to the harsh context within which training took place.

These observations apply to secular schools; the existence of temple schools is generally assumed, but conclusive evidence is lacking until comparatively late,[30] when education became remarkably democratic and concentrated on middle-class values.

Sumerian schools are well documented;[31] the school possessed a name, the edubba ("tablet house"), and its occupants spoke a special guild language. Members of the tablet house designated themselves "sons" to outsiders, "brothers" to colleagues. The master teacher was "father," and "older brothers" were the preceptors. According to S. N. Kramer, five texts have survived: (1) a schooldays essay; (2) an account by an unhappy father because his son did not choose to be a scribe; (3) a courteous disputation between a supervisor and a scribe; (4) a vituperative debate between two seniors nearing graduation; and (5) a quarrel between two young schoolboys that was resolved by a supervisor. In time the tablet house disappeared, and scribal education fell under the control of families. In Egypt, on the other hand, it appears that education in the family context gave way to governmental instruction.

Certain types of scribal activity had a purely practical aim, for example, the writing of economic contracts. But what about the nonpractical texts? For whom did Sumerian scribes compose their *literary* works? Surely not for the general populace, since most people were illiterate. This included priests, judges, and kings. Only three Mesopotamian kings boasted literacy (Ashurbanipal, Shulgi, and Lipit Ishtar), and their boasts seem empty. Then did scribes write such texts exclusively for themselves and thereby compile a literary canonical tradition? Thus it would seem, and art for art's sake characterized the scribal profession. In a real sense, scribes were caught in a bind. On the one hand, they wanted to guard the prerogatives of their profession and thus to preserve their ranks as "poor aristocrats," whereas on the other hand, they wished to be more responsive to the people and thus to incorporate folklore into their own esoteric teachings. In addition to the complexity of the language, which certainly safeguarded their profession, there was frequent use of technical jargon and secret language (and outright pedantry on occasion). Nevertheless, these Sumerian scribes found a place for popular songs, riddles, and jokes that arose outside their ranks. It seems that rhetoric played a minor role in Mesopotamian education, whereas original thinking was not altogether scorned. We do not know the precise nature of exams, but one such text has survived, as has encouragement to a student who was fast becoming too old. Those who persevered most probably found employment within the government, with rare exceptions.

Scant information on the Hittites suggests that scribal schools existed,[32] despite the concentration on the royal family in these sources, according to H. G. Güterbock. Nevertheless, a stone at a gate has been discovered with hieroglyphs of a personal name together with the logogram for scribe. Güterbock thinks that this discovery indicates that trained scribes sat at the city gate and transacted business there. A similar paucity of information exists where Ugarit is concerned, although Anson Rainey has endeavored to piece together the evidence.[33] He thinks that scribes played an important role in ancient Ugarit, a deduction that seems reasonable in light of the literary remains from Ras Shamra.

In short, there were undoubtedly schools in Egypt and Mesopotamia, and their existence in Ugarit is also probable. The emergence of Israel on the historical scene came centuries later than the heyday of schools in either Egypt or Mesopotamia. Is it conceivable that Israel's kings would have imitated her successful neighbors, particularly during Solomon's era? What then do we make of this evidence from Egypt and Mesopotamia? Once again conclusive proof is lacking that these two regions have shaped the form education took in Israel.

The matter is more complicated than is commonly acknowledged. Israel and Egypt were at quite different stages of development in the tenth century.[34] By that time Egypt was an advanced culture, having achieved political sophistication over the course of two millennia, whereas Israel was just beginning her political existence. If comparison is to be made one must set Israel over against a comparable stage in Egypt's development. This correct intuition led Golka to conclude that since early Egyptian education was in the hands of parents, the same was true during the initial stages of Israel's monarchy. The fallacy of the argument lies in the fact that nations do not develop at the same rate, especially when one country can benefit from another's long experience.[35] Besides, differences in complexity of a government affect the picture. The relatively simple Israelite culture made rapid strides, so it will not do to insist that Egypt and Israel developed at the same rate of speed. It follows that Golka's dismissal of the Egyptian and Mesopotamian parallels is less conclusive than he thinks.

Those parallels are impressive, but do they require a theory of dependence and an equation of settings? Close examination of the extent of similarities[36] must include, among other things, (1) technical language for students and teachers, (2) the use of harsh punishment to reinforce learning, (3) Egyptian loanwords for scribal kit and ink,[37] (4) instructions within the book of Proverbs that closely resemble their Egyptian counterpart,[38] and (5) formal similarities between Job and Qoheleth, on the one hand, and Mesopotamian texts, on the other hand. Besides the striking affinities between Prov 22:17-24:33 and the *Instruction of Amen-em-opet*, several images occur in Egyptian wisdom and in Israelite (for example, righteousness as the foundation of the throne,[39] a little child [*Ma^cat*] playing before the Lord and a goddess who has life in one hand and wisdom in another,[40] weighing the heart in just scales, the reference to heaping coals of fire on an enemy's head [presumably a ritc of expiation], a garland around the neck, and a tree of life). Some of these are easily explained on the premise of polygenesis, that is, on the assumption that certain responses naturally accompany the asking of existential questions. Moreover, even if the items in question were actually borrowed by Israelite sages, that fact alone would not necessarily prove that schools existed there. The family setting is equally appropriate for the use of these images and literary genres.

The case for Israelite schools has been reinforced by appeals to the character of wisdom literature. Both Hans-Jürgen Hermisson and Bernhard Lang have argued that the book of Proverbs is didactic in form and therefore functioned as a textbook for students in school.[41] The claim is that conscious rhetoric renders Proverbs an instructional text rather than the product of popular wisdom. Furthermore, didactic units and the portrait of Dame Wisdom are comprehensible, in Lang's view, only if one acknowledges the central position of a school.[42] Gerhard von Rad stated the matter quite simply—one must say, too simply. For him two kinds of deductive arguments were decisive: (1) one from the circumstances in neighboring cultures, and (2) another from the quality of Israel's literary achievement. He concluded: "In Israel, too, writing was known. But writing has to be taught. Handwriting, however, was never taught without accompanying material. It follows from this that there must have been schools of different types in Israel."[43] Von Rad distinguishes several kinds of schools: priestly, royal, levitical, and scribal training required for Ezra's chancellery.

Some of the specifics of von Rad's argument lack cogency. This judgment applies especially to his supposed examination questions and to so-called noun lists (onomastica). The former are common phenomena in popular wisdom, which seems fascinated with such impossible questions.[44] As for the latter, nothing suggests that the authors of Job and Sirach are actually working with noun lists. Rather, they are merely enumerating natural phenomena in a manner that would readily occur to people anywhere.

Yet another line of reasoning has led Tryggve Mettinger to the belief that Israel had schools during Solomon's era.[45] That evidence consists of the list of state officials, which Mettinger thinks indicates strong Egyptian influence. That claim can scarcely be denied, but it hardly adds up to the existence of schools. As a matter of fact, the silence in these texts about an official in charge of education is hard to imagine if alongside all the other royal officials there actually stood a head of schools.[46]

In sum, schools played a vital role in Egyptian and Mesopotamian life, and their influence has certainly reached Israel's learned centers. But precisely what those centers of education in Israel consisted of remains unclear, so much so that R. N. Whybray has even denied the existence of a professional class of sages.[47] In the long run, however, he simply substituted another concept, intellectual tradition, for what others call wisdom and located that mental activity in upper-class landowners.

IV. Conclusions: Assessing the Evidence

What then can one say about education in ancient Israel when the three lines of evidence fail to provide a clear picture? In what follows an attempt will be made to work backwards and to describe the situation as nearly as possible. In doing so, a minimalist perspective seems appropriate. In all probability Israelite education was far richer than the resulting account, but erring on the side of caution is preferable to extravagant claims that exceed the evidence.

According to one tradition the high priest Joshua ben Gamla decreed in 63 C.E. that every town and village would have a school and that all children would attend from the age of six or seven.[48] Regardless of the credence one gives to this tradition, a school certainly existed some 250 years earlier, although its proprietor, Ben Sira, restricted his teaching to those who could afford to pay for it. His professional pride is well known,[49] even if he did also respect other vocations in a way that is entirely absent from the Egyptian *Satire of the Trades*. We cannot be sure just what made up the curriculum in Ben Sira's school, but a combination of scripture and sapiential tradition seems to have occupied his thought.[50] In this respect the curriculum was quite different from the Alexandrian one reflected in Wisdom of Solomon 7:17-22, which includes, among other things, philosophy, physics, history, astronomy, zoology, religion, botany, and medicine.[51]

In the late third century an unknown admirer of Qoheleth described his mentor as one who taught the people ($h\bar{a}^c\bar{a}m$).[52] This looks like a claim that a democratization of knowledge occasioned Qoheleth's appearance on the scene. Perhaps that turning to the people dictated his special interest in aesthetics, integrity, and context.[53] Moreover, this description of Qoheleth's activity mentions the proverbial form in which he couched his teaching ($m^e\check{s}\bar{a}l\hat{i}m$).[54] From the rest of the book attributed to Qoheleth we can guess that these proverbs and lessons drawn from them were characterized by utter realism and a healthy skepticism.[55] The contrast with Ben Sira's piety can scarcely be greater and may have arisen in part from the two distinct patrons—the people in Qoheleth's case, and elite young men in the case of Ben Sira. It follows that Qoheleth's educational setting can hardly have developed into that over which Ben Sira presided. James F. Ross has proposed an intermediate stage of learning that could link both types of instruction.[56] In trying to understand the decisive shift in perspective within Psalm 73, he envisions a school adjacent to the divine sanctuary. In his view, scholars discussed the perennial problems that threaten faith, such as theodicy, in the immediate environs of the sanctuary. Unfortunately, such an understanding of Ps 73:17 is entirely conjectural.

Education of a different kind is reported in 2 Chr 17:7-9, where King Jehoshaphat is said to have sent five princes, nine Levites, and two priests throughout Judah to teach the book of the law to the people. Of course, this text reveals more about the special interests of its author than about actual history.[57] Nevertheless, it suggests that in the late fifth century a premium was placed on religious education in certain quarters. The earlier task resting on the shoulders of parents, according to the idealized picture in Deut 6:7, is here entrusted to a small band of teachers who enjoy royal favor. For this concept of royal patronage, we can also appeal to the superscription in Prov 25:1, which refers to scribal activity by certain "men of Hezekiah." This brief allusion to copying earlier manuscripts is tantalizingly obscure, but it opens the door to speculation about scribal training under the king's sponsorship. Since Hezekiah consciously imitated Solomon in many ways, it is at least arguable that he did so in this matter as well. After all, the Hebrew text of the Queen of Sheba's praise of Solomon includes the words, "Happy are your men" (1 Kgs 10:8), even if the Greek and Syriac texts have "Happy are your wives."[58] In other words, there is some textual warrant for the presence of a group called "the men of Solomon," at least in the mind of the author responsible for 1 Kgs 10:8.

However, the Deuteronomistic language in the Solomonic legends suffices to give one pause, and the presence of courtiers under David hardly requires the existence of royal schools at this time.[59] The decisive argument would seem to concern the nature of the proverbial sayings transcribed by the men of Hezekiah, for royal interests are conspicuously missing from the collection, and the few references to the king may reflect no more than the usual fascination with persons in authority.[60] In the case of the proverbs attributed to Solomon, the picture is even more astonishing, for the peculiar concerns of the court have made little impact on the authors.

Now if a royal school cannot be documented, where did education take place? An answer to this question can certainly be given: Parents instructed their children in their own homes. No one contests this fact, for the evidence is compelling indeed. The primary sense of father and son within Proverbs must surely reflect a family setting, and the occasional reference to mother cannot rightly be attributed to the demands of parallelism.[61] As a matter of fact, every single use of father and son within Proverbs can be understood as precisely that, a father instructing his son, rather than technical language for teacher and student. But exclusive residence in Whybray's camp may be costly, for it necessitates giving up the sages as a professional group within ancient Israel. Therefore, it seems unwise to insist that all education occurred in the home, despite the paucity of evidence for royal schools.

It follows that the bulk of education may very well have taken place in the family setting, where practical instruction in daily life was provided for boys and girls according to the opportunities open to them. Guilds of various kinds probably broadened the clientele beyond the immediate family while narrowing the scope of learning.[62] For a chosen few, special scribal training may have been provided in Hezekiah's court, and that elite training continued with Ben Sira and eventually fell into priestly hands. Still another kind of education, represented by Qoheleth, sought to reach the adult population in general, and this effort had its religious counterpart (2 Chr 17:7-9). In short, considerable diversity characterized education in ancient Israel, and scholarly preoccupation with the existence or nonexistence of a school threatens to obscure this significant fact.[63]

Notes

[1] André Lemaire lists the various studies dealing with schools in ancient Israel (*Les écoles et la formation de la Bible dans l'ancien Israël* [OBO 39; Fribourg: Editions Universitaires; Göttingen: Vandenhoeck & Ruprecht, 1981] 93 n. 70). These entries cover the period from 1908 through 1979.

[2] Lemaire gives the most complete analysis of inscriptional evidence to date insofar as their relevance to the existence or nonexistence of schools is concerned (*Les écoles et la formation de la Bible dans l'ancien Israël*, 7-33, 86-92).

³ Bernard Lang, *Frau Weisheit* (Düsseldorf: Patmos, 1975).

⁴ Lemaire concludes that Canaanite capitals had schools (Aphek, Gezer, Megiddo, Shechem, Lachish, Jerusalem), as did Israelite centers (Shiloh, Shechem, Gilgal, Bethel, Hebron, Beersheba). He believes that local schools (Arad, Kadesh-Barnea, Kuntilat-Ajrud) gave elementary education and that regional schools (Lachish) were more advanced. Royal schools at Jerusalem and Samaria taught international relations. Alongside these schools were priestly and prophetic ones, and learning took place at the gates, in the temple, and at the royal palace. From the age of five, boys (and a few girls from elite families) studied, taking advantage of an elaborate curriculum, which Lemaire describes in considerable detail. Naturally, such schools had to develop adequate textbooks. Lemaire traces the formation of the canon as the composing of appropriate texts for classroom use. He thinks such a hypothesis explains the original setting of the Bible, its transmission, and the formation of a canon. Although more modest, Hans-Jürgen Hermisson's claim that "die israelitische Weisheit hat ihr Zentrum, ihre Ursprungs- und Pflegestätte in der israelitischen Schule" says far more than the data warrant (*Studien zur israelitischen Spruchweisheit* [WMANT 28; Neukirchen-Vluyn: Neukirchener, 1968] 192).

⁵ Roland de Vaux (*Ancient Israel: Its Life and Institutions* [New York, Toronto, London: McGraw-Hill, 1961] 48-50) is clearly indebted to Lorenz Dürr, *Das Erziehungswesen im Alten Testament und im antiken Orient* (Leipzig: J. C. Hinrichs, 1932). That debt is especially noticeable in de Vaux's remark about education for girls. He writes: "Girls remained under the control of their mothers, who taught them what they needed to know for their duty as wives and housekeepers" (p. 50), but one has the impression that Dürr's views are less subject to the charge of patriarchalism (see p. 113, where he emphasizes the breadth of learning acquired by daughters, particularly in Torah).

⁶ "Schulwesen im alten Israel," in *Theologische Studien Th. Zahn* (Leipzig: A. Deichert [Georg Böhme], 1908) 193-232.

⁷ "Haben denn gerade Entwöhnte, also höchstens Dreijährige, einen *Lehrer?* Natürlich nicht! Es sind die *Eltern*, in Israel wie bei uns, die sich bei Kindern dieses Alters der Kindersprache zur Unterweisung bedienen" ("Die israelitische Weisheitsschule oder 'des Kaisers neue Kleider,' " *VT* 33 [1983] 260).

⁸ A. van Selms understands the text in the light of Akkadian ("Isaiah 28:9-13: An Attempt to Give a New Interpretation," *ZAW* 85 [1973] 332-39). He translates, "Go out! Let him go out! Go out! Let him go out! Wait! Let him wait! Wait! Let him wait! Servant, listen! Servant, listen!"

⁹ The Hebrew word is *limmûdîm*. The further emphasis on hearing in this verse is appropriate to the educative process in the ancient world. The conclusion to the Instruction of Ptahhotep even has an extended pun on the word for hearing. In Egypt "a hearing heart" was essential to learning (cf. the similar expression in Solomon's request to the Lord, 1 Kgs 3:9).

¹⁰ This is also the case if Irene Grumach's theory of a common source for the biblical text and Amen-em-opet should prove true (*Untersuchungen zur Lebenslehre des Amenope* [Munich: Münchner Ägyptologische Studien 23, 1972]).

¹¹ Glendon Bryce has discussed the process of adaptation, assimilation, and integration (*A Legacy of Wisdom* [Lewisburg, PA: Bucknell University Press, 1979]).

¹² "Dass Keine Schulen erwähnt werden, erklärt sich immer noch am besten daraus, dass es keine gab" (Golka, "Die israelitische Weisheitsschule oder 'des Kaisers neue Kleider,' " 265).

¹³ Some critics emend the text of 2 Sam 12:25 to read that David committed Solomon to Nathan's care, and they understand the reference in 2 Kgs 10:1, 5 to guardians of Ahab's sons as scribal education (cf. 1 Chr 27:32, which states that Jehiel attended David's sons). Others interpret the phrase in 1 Kgs 12:8 ("who had grown up with him," that is, Rehoboam) in a pregnant sense of "attended school with him" (Hermisson, *Studien zur israelitischen Spruchweisheit*, 117-18).

¹⁴ The meaning of this expression remains hidden. Even if it alludes to a book, it may identify the city as a depository for a document that required periodic public reading. Alternatively, a reference to scribes may suggest that a guild of scribes existed in the city.

¹⁵ Ephraim A. Speiser's remarks about this story have no basis in the text. He describes the youth as an "urchin on the street" and observes that the text almost suggests "that he was a

juvenile delinquent" (*City Invincible: A Symposium on Urbanization and Cultural Development in the Ancient Near East* [ed. Carl H. Kraeling and Robert M. Adams; Chicago: University of Chicago Press, 1960] 119).

[16] Scholars have long recognized the existence of a professional group of prophets who gathered around a prophetic leader such as Elijah or Elisha. The close bond between disciples and teacher seems particularly clear in the Isaianic corpus. This fact has often helped to illuminate the so-called Servant Songs and the additions to First Isaiah in general.

[17] Antony R. Ceresko stresses an influence on this text other than the usual Egyptian oath of innocence (*Job 29-31 in the Light of Northwest Semitic* [BeO 36; Rome: Biblical Institute Press, 1980]).

[18] There is some question about who the reader is — the prophet who announces the vision or the people.

[19] The language may be symbolic. In that case it would have nothing to say about tuition, but would rather refer to the difficulty one endures in acquiring knowledge.

[20] R. N. Whybray, *The Succession Narrative* (SBT 2d Series 9; London: SCM, 1968). E. W. Heaton writes: [The book of Proverbs] "affords the most direct evidence we possess for the school or schools which Solomon must have established in order to train candidates for his new bureaucracy" (*Solomon's New Men* [New York: Pica, 1974] 123).

[21] For specifics, see the author's review in *JBL* 103 (1984) 630-32. Incidentally, Ahiqar instructs his adopted son in the home, although Nadin is destined for the role of a royal courtier. This is strange if James Lindenberger is right that the Ahiqar tradition was compiled "under royal auspices for the purposes of instructing young people who were to be attached to the court" (*The Aramaic Proverbs of Ahiqar* [Baltimore and London: Johns Hopkins University Press, 1983] 21).

[22] Lemaire gives a convenient summary of his findings (*Les écoles et la formation de la Bible dans l'ancien Israël,* 32). He discusses the inscriptions on pp. 7-33 and provides fourteen figures for clarification.

[23] Golka writes, "In keinem Fall kann er jedoch den Beweis erbringen, dass diese Funde einer Schule, und nicht dem Privatunterricht nach dem Famulussystem entstammen" ("Die israelitische Weisheitsschule oder 'des Kaisers neue Kleider,' " 263 n. 19). Golka thinks the situation would be entirely different if all the evidence had been found in a single place, especially in Jerusalem.

[24] "A Teacher to a Man of Shechem about 1400 B.C.," *BASOR* 86 (1942) 28-31. Albright could not make up his mind whether the author was a woman who taught music and dance or a man who headed a school for future cuneiform scribes.

[25] F.M.T. de Liagre-Böhl, "Der Keilschriftbrief aus Sichem," *Baghdader Mitteilungen* 7 (1974) 21-30. In line 10 ṣuḫārū is understood as servants, and lapātu in line 11 is taken in the sense of "to write." The result is a letter requesting immediate economic relief. The setting is a domestic one and has nothing to do with a school ("Zwar bleibt er ein Bittbrief, jedoch in der Sphäre des Handels- und Geschäftslebens, was das Verständnis erleichtert," p. 28).

[26] Apalu ("to pay") for abalu.

[27] "Schule und Unterricht im alten Israel," *La Sagesse de l'Ancien Testament* (ed. M. Gilbert; BETL 51; Gembloux: Duculot, 1979) 191.

[28] "Since the forms of the letters are very simple, the 22-letter alphabet could be learned in a day or two by a bright student and in a week or two by the dullest; hence it could spread with great rapidity" (*City Invincible,* 123). Lang is considerably less optimistic about the learning skills of youngsters; he therefore suggests a year or even two years for mastering the Hebrew alphabet ("Schule und Unterricht im alten Israel," 190-91).

[29] Tryggve N. D. Mettinger, *Solomonic State Officials* (ConBOT 5; Lund: Gleerup, 1971). Hermisson offers the most complete argument and reviews the copious secondary literature (*Studien zur israelitischen Spruchweisheit,* 113-36; cf. also Heaton, *Solomon's New Men*).

[30] For an extensive bibliography on Egyptian schools, see Lemaire, *Les écoles et la formation de la Bible dans l'ancien Israël,* 94 n. 73. The following works are particularly important: Hellmut

Brunner, *Altägyptische Erziehung* (Wiesbaden: Harrassowitz, 1957); Eberhard Otto, "Bildung und Ausbildung im Alten Ägypten," *Zeitschrift für ägyptische Sprache und Altertumskunde* 81 (1956) 41-48; R. J. Williams, "Scribal Training in Ancient Egypt," *JAOS* 92 (1972) 214-21; idem, " 'A People Come Out of Egypt': An Egyptologist Looks at the Old Testament," *Congress Volume: Edinburgh, 1974* (VTSup 28; Leiden: Brill, 1975) 238-52.

[31] Kraeling and Adams, *City Invincible*, 94-123; Lemaire, *Les écoles et la formation de la Bible dans l'ancien Israël,* 94 n. 74; S. N. Kramer, *The Sumerians* (Chicago and London: University of Chicago Press, 1963) 229-48.

[32] Kraeling and Adams, *City Invincible*, 121-22.

[33] "The Scribe at Ugarit, His Position and Influence," *Proceedings of the Israel Academy of Sciences and Humanities* 3, no. 4 (1969) 126-47; Lemaire gives a good bibliography of relevant works (*Les écoles et la formation de la Bible dans l'ancien Israël*, 94-95 n. 75).

[34] Golka, "Die israelitische Weisheitsschule oder 'des Kaisers neue Kleider,' " 264-65.

[35] Gerhard von Rad acknowledged the cultural difference between Israel and Egypt, but this admission did not prevent him from concluding that Israel had a school at the royal court (*Wisdom in Israel* [Nashville and New York: Abingdon, 1972] 17).

[36] See my *Old Testament Wisdom* (Atlanta: John Knox, 1981) 212-28.

[37] Williams, " 'A People Come Out of Egypt': An Egyptologist Looks at the Old Testament," 238-39. He understands Hebrew *qeset* (scribal kit) as a borrowing from Egyptian *gsti* , and he reads the Hebrew term *d^{e}yô* in Jer 36:18 as a copyist's error for *reyo* , which "might also be an Egyptian loanword" (239).

[38] William McKane, *Proverbs* (OTL; Philadelphia: Westminster, 1970) 51-150.

[39] Hellmut Brunner, "Gerechtigkeit als Fundament des Thrones," *VT* 8 (1958) 426-28.

[40] Christa Kayatz, *Studien zu Proverbien 1-9* (WMANT 22; Neukirchen-Vluyn: Neukirchener, 1966).

[41] Hermisson, *Studien zur israelitischen Spruchweisheit,* 122-25; Lang, "Schule und Unterricht im alten Israel," 192-201; idem, *Die Weisheitliche Lehrrede* (SBS 54; Stuttgart: Katholisches Bibelwerk, 1972). Margaret B. Crook thinks that the description of the virtuous woman in Proverbs 31 is a sort of academic catalogue for a school that trained wealthy young women in home economics, which includes household administration and instruction in the arts and crafts ("The Marriageable Maiden of Prov. 31:10-31," *JNES* 13 [1954] 137-40).

[42] Frau Weisheit, 23-53.

[43] *Wisdom in Israel*, 17. The ideal Israelite education, for von Rad, is reflected in 1 Sam 16:18 and consisted of music, warfare, eloquence (and physical attractiveness); see *Old Testament Theology* (Edinburgh and London: Oliver & Boyd, 1962) 1. 430.

[44] See my "Questions, dictons et épreuves impossibles," in *La Sagesse de l'Ancien Testament*, 96-111.

[45] *Solomonic State Officials*, 143-57.

[46] Mettinger describes the following royal titles: secretary, herald, friend of the king, "house minister," chief of district prefects, and superintendent of the forced levy (*Solomonic State Officials*, 25-139). It would simplify matters greatly if we knew exactly what the responsibility of certain Israelite officials was, for example *mazkîr* and *sōpēr* .

[47] *The Intellectual Tradition in the Old Testament* (BZAW 135; Berlin and New York: Walter de Gruyter, 1974).

[48] De Vaux, *Ancient Israel*, 50. Some scholars think such education began during the time of John Hyrcanus about 130 B.C.E. (Dürr, *Das Erziehungswesen im alten Testament*, 112 n. 1). R. A. Culpepper acknowledges competing traditions in the Babylonian and Palestinian Talmuds (*Ketub*. 8.8 and *B. Bat.* 21a) with regard to the beginnings of elementary education ("Education," in *The International Standard Bible Encyclopedia* [Grand Rapids: Eerdmans, 1982] 2. 25).

[49] See my *Old Testament Wisdom*, 28-65, for discussion of the sages as a professional class. Whybray argues quite differently (*The Intellectual Tradition in the Old Testament,* 15-54).

[50] The scriptures made a strong impression on Ben Sira (discussed in my *Old Testament Wisdom*, 149-73, particularly 149-54).

[51] David Winston describes the global nature of the Greek curriculum alluded to here (*The Wisdom of Solomon* [AB 43; Garden City, NY: Doubleday, 1979] 172-77).

[52] On this text, see G. T. Sheppard, "The Epilogue to Qoheleth as Theological Commentary," *CBQ* 39 (1977) 182-89.

[53] Aarrhe Lauhe correctly recognizes an aesthetic dimension alongside the ethical one (*Kohelet* [BKAT 19; Neukirchen-Vluyn: Neukirchener, 1978] 217-20).

[54] Timothy Polk, "Paradigms, Parables, and Mᵉšālîm : On reading the Māšāl in Scripture," *CBQ* 45 (1983) 564-83 is the latest in many important studies of Māšāl . Two others deserve special notice, George M. Landes, "Jonah: A Māšāl ?" in *Israelite Wisdom* (ed. J. G. Gammie et al.; Missoula, MT: Scholars Press, 1978) 137-58 and William McKane, *Proverbs,* 22-33.

[55] See my essay "The Birth of Skepticism in Ancient Israel," in *The Divine Helmsman* (ed. James L. Crenshaw and Samuel Sandmel; New York: Ktav, 1980) 1-19.

[56] "Psalm 73," in *Israelite Wisdom*, 169. For my understanding of this psalm, see *A Whirlpool of Torment* (Overtures to Biblical Theology, 12; Philadelphia: Fortress, 1984) 93-109.

[57] On this text, see Jacob M. Meyers, *II Chronicles* (AB 13; Garden City, NY: Doubleday, 1965).

[58] *BHS* favors the reading in the LXX and Syriac, but leaves the matter open.

[59] W. Lee Humphreys discusses the minor role of the court in the book of Proverbs ("The Motif of the Wise Courtier in the Book of Proverbs," in *Israelite Wisdom*, 177-90).

[60] Udo Skladny described Prov 16:1-22:16 as instruction to officials and diplomats and Proverbs 28-29 as an instruction to a prince (*Die ältesten Spruchsammlungen in Israel* [Göttingen: Vandenhoeck & Ruprecht, 1962] 46, 66).

[61] The appeal to stylistic demands as a poetic allusion to the teacher's function *in loco parentis* occurs in Lang, "Schule und Unterricht im alten Israel," 193-95. The Hebrew poet could have invented appropriate expressions to serve in parallelism with father (e.g., the one who begot you); this possibility reduces the cogency of Lang's argument. If father and mother were a "fixed pair," the introduction of the second word may have been almost automatic. However, the variety in Prov 23:22-25, as well as in 31:2, makes that highly unlikely.

[62] Various guilds come to mind: priests, prophets, pottery makers, metal workers, dancers, musicians and so forth.

[63] The article by André Lemaire ("Sagesse et Écoles," *VT* 34 [1984] 270-81) appeared too late for me to benefit from its contents. Among other things, Lemaire urges scholars to distinguish between oral and written proverbial material, recognizes the inappropriateness of Golka's sociological argument about Egypt and Israel, interprets archaeology's "silence" about schools, and reemphasizes inscriptional evidence for widespread schools in preexilic Israel.

SOCIAL MATRIX AND CANONICAL SHAPE

NORMAN K. GOTTWALD
Professor of Biblical Studies
New York Theological Seminary, New York

Article from *Theology Today*

The catch phrases "social matrix" and "canonical shape" suggest the relationship between social scientific criticism and canonical criticism in Old Testament studies. In particular, I want to stake out the intrinsic compatibility of their respective concerns, and even the necessity of their collaboration, in order properly to fulfill what each approach hopes to achieve. In the process, I will offer a critique of certain inadequacies and dangers in the formulations of both types of critics.

I.

Social scientific criticism, also known as sociological criticism or biblical sociology, starts from the premise that biblical writings are social products.[1] They were written by people shaped by and interacting within institutional structures and symbolic codes operative in the primary sectors of communal life, such as economy, family, government, law, war, ritual, and religious belief. These Israelite-Jewish social networks, always in flux and full of tension and contradiction, supply an indispensable context for grounding other insights of biblical studies, including the results of historical critical methods and the newer literary methods, as well as canonical criticism itself. The guiding question for social science approaches to the Bible might be framed in this way: What social structures, processes, and codes are explicit or implicit in the biblical literature, in the scattered social data it contains, in the overtly political history it recounts or touches on, and in the religious beliefs and practices it attests?

Social scientific criticism is many-faceted, proceeding along several fronts or axes of inquiry and employing a variety of methods and theories. For example, it works along a continuum from limited inquiries into particular offices, roles, and institutions toward more inclusive analyses and reconstructions of the larger social system. At times, it operates with synchronic analysis of social realities at a particular historical juncture or in a posited representative moment that gives a cross section of social life. At other times, it operates with a diachronic analysis of how the social phenomena, of whatever scale, developed over time. Typically, it organizes the inquiry and the results into the rubrics supplied by the social sciences, but it may also bring a social scientific perspective into exegesis that follows the discursive form of the biblical texts.

Social scientific criticism, in addition to drawing on archaeology, cautiously employs comparative method for studying social formations cross-culturally in order to theorize about the social history of Israel, since it is well known that the biblical texts are frequently too restrictively religious, too fragmentary, or too anachronistic to be able by themselves to give us a balanced picture of Israelite society. All in all, in contrast to past erratic or undisciplined efforts, there is currently good reason for confidence in proposing controlled hypotheses about Israelite society. Granted that important social data are lacking for ancient Israel, we can nonetheless formulate testable models for conceiving the society, models that are necessary for interpreting the knowledge we do have and suggestive of additional research needed to refine and revise our tentative mappings of biblical societies.

Insofar as the whole of biblical societies is the object of study, global social theorists such as Karl Marx, Emile Durkheim, and Max Weber are key influences and guides. The use of Marxian, Durkheimian, and Weberian tools of analysis and synthesis is often highly eclectic. What is especially important in the work of these theorists is that they held broad and coherent perspectives which, in varying ways, viewed the components of society as multi-dimensional and interactive, giving rise to contradictions in society that fuel social change. Furthermore, after a long era of reaction against crude social evolutionary schemes of the nineteenth century, neo-evolutionary social theory is being cogently applied to ancient Israel, allowing as it does for different rates of social change from society to society, for leaps in stages or retrograde developments, and for calculations of trends or tendencies in terms of probabilities instead of heavy-handed determinisms.

I do not hesitate to claim that social scientific criticism completes the task of historical criticism by providing more or less detailed social referential readings of the biblical texts. Admittedly, these texts differ greatly in their accessibility to social analysis. One might generalize that laws and prophetic texts have been somewhat more amenable to social scientific exegesis than have imaginative narratives, such as sagas and legends, and wisdom genres. Yet it is fair to state that some headway is being made in the social interpretation of texts composed of all the major genres of biblical literature.

A word should be said about where I see my own study of premonarchic Israel falling within this description of social scientific criticism. In *The Tribes of Yahweh* and subsequent studies,[2] I propose in considerable detail that the body of literature identifiable as probably premonarchic is most satisfactorily explained as the creation of a social revolutionary movement, largely of a peasant populace, carving out its own material and cultural liv-

ing space in the highlands of Canaan in a trans-tribal, village-based revitalization process that consciously broke with centralized government in the
Canaanite form of city-state hierarchy.

The religion of these Israelite folk arose co-terminously with their social
and political struggle and was both the ideological propulsion for and the
most distinctive cultural expression of their movement. This social organization, along with its religious ideology, continued as an active force
throughout the changing conditions of later Israelite and Jewish social history. In my recent overview of the Hebrew Bible, I attempt to trace the social
organizational and conflictual threads that run unbroken throughout biblical history and literature.[3]

My hypothesis is comprehensive and many-stranded and it is comparative. It also includes major efforts at sociological exegesis of texts, especially
in Joshua and Judges. The hypothesis stands or falls on the sum total of
evidence it appeals to in biblical and extrabiblical texts, material culture,
and comparative studies. Of course, this "evidence" is not piled up and
counted, so to speak, for it has to be interconnected, weighed, and prioritized, which necessarily leaves considerable room for differences of interpretation, even among those who share my broad perspective. It is also to be
expected that the hypothesis will have to be modified, enlarged, and cor-
rected over time. Also, while this whole approach raises critical questions
about our own religious faith, the truthfulness of my hypothesis is not deter-
minable by whether it suits piety, church tradition, theology, or politics.

II.

Canonical criticism has set for itself the task of showing how the biblical text
was shaped and interpreted as Scripture and what that means for properly
understanding it in its own setting and in properly appropriating it in our
settings. While social scientific criticism draws upon a body of methods and
theories developed in the social sciences, canonical criticism has a less
sharply demarcated set of analytic tools.

Canonical criticism draws mainly on aspects of literary theory and hermeneutics in order to push beyond redaction criticism's interest in single
books and series of books to an examination of the final form of the text as a
totality, as well as the process leading to it, and to raise issues of theological
authority and hermeneutics in a manner that grows organically out of the
historical literary description of the canonizing of Scripture. But precisely
where the emphasis falls in canonical study and how the elements at work
interact is heatedly discussed among canonical critics. For instance, does
the emphasis fall on the final shape of canon or on the shaping process that
culminates in canon?

The most prolifically published representative of canonical criticism,

Brevard S. Childs, focuses heavily on "the canonical shape" of the final form of the text conceived as determinative for historical and theological interpretation.[4] The actual role of historical criticism in the canonical task posited by Childs has been the subject of much controversy. I conclude that, in practice, Childs builds regularly on historical critical insight, but that in his theoretical formations he often appears to denigrate historical criticism per se, which is either outright self-contradictory or, more likely, a miscommunication on his part, since he may be meaning to say that historical criticism is necessary but not sufficient to canonical criticism. More problematic and crucial to his enterprise is exactly how the final shape of the canon is normative for interpretation.

In the main, Childs' canonical shape seems to be the final redactional stroke that disposes the contents in certain ways and thereby accents or interconnects motifs and perspectives that control the overarching reading of the text. Examples of this canon-controlled structuring are intricate arrangements of judgment and salvation patterns, and oscillating movements between past, present, and future in the operative hermeneutic of the final hand (redactor/canonizer?). I credit Childs with an acute intuitive eye for seeing redactional constructs, especially in the prophetic literature. For me, the most original and perceptive aspect of his work is redaction critical, in which he advances toward a phenomenology of canonical form.

In his recent canonical analysis of the New Testament, Childs tends to replace the earlier term "canonical shape" with "canonical form," and he offers a section on "Methodology of Canonical Exegesis."[5] Canonical exegesis seeks for "traces either of how the author intended the material to be understood, or of the effect which a particular rendering has on the literature."[6]

Among the signs of canonical shaping are the following features: (1) the overall structure of the book; (2) prescripts, conclusions, and superscriptions; (3) assignments of historical setting for the book; (4) the relation between the author's stated vantage point and the probable audience of the document; (5) the function of the addressee; (6) the function of indirect authorship or pseudonymity; (7) the effect of putting certain books side by side so that material is dropped, added, or separated. I should also add that, with this new book, Childs removes all doubt about his emphatic rejection of literalistic, univocal, fundamentalist readings of the canon.

James A. Sanders, in distinction from Childs, does not give excessive or privileged stress to the final form of the canon. What interests him is the canonical process operative through all the stages of Israel's literary history.[7] The canonical process was a trend toward repeating communal values and resignifying them in textual form. Furthermore, the various ways in which biblical writers repeated and resignified these values along the trajectory toward the final canon provides us appropriate canonical hermeneutics for our own reading of the Bible. Scripture is seen as "adaptable for life" throughout its entire course from initial composition and collection down to its present appropriation.

Gerald T. Sheppard attempts to nuance and refine Childs' approach, which he prefers to call "canon contextual criticism." He does so by trying to include all the compositional and redactional moments in the development of Scripture within the paradigm of the "final" canonical perspective.[8] For Sheppard, canon contextual reading sees the final text dimensionally, and includes a careful delineation of numerous ways that Scripture comments on Scripture. Sheppard seeks to overcome a narrow theory of intentionality (Childs' inclination), but also to contest the assumption that theological exegesis simply imitates the technical hermeneutics of biblical writers (Sanders' inclination). For example, Sheppard describes three forms of inner-biblical exegesis that represent different expressions of canon consciousness: (1) midrash, in the sense of reemploying set phrases in an anthological manner; (2) "canon conscious redaction," which relates one canonical book or part of a book to some other canonical book or collection; (3) thematization of historically disunified traditions under the canonical rubrics of Law, Prophets, and Wisdom.[9] It may be added that Joseph Blenkinsopp's work on prophecy and canon argues a particular case of canon-conscious redaction in the sense that the Law and Prophets have been accommodated to one another, notably in the inter-textual formulation of the conclusions to Deuteronomy and Malachi.[10]

III.

Suppose we now undertake a conversation between the two forms of criticism, chiefly but not exclusively with Childs as the voice for canonical criticism. It is acknowledged that I speak primarily as a practitioner of social scientific criticism, but I do so as one who takes canonical criticism's concerns seriously and who respects what it aims to accomplish even when dissenting on the presuppositions and conclusions of certain of its advocates. Immediately, we can recognize a systemic drive and a comprehensive impulse in canonical criticism that is analogous to the systemic drive and comprehensive impulse in social scientific criticism. Each can be conceived as total in its aims and formulations. Each attempts to resolve the multiplicity of the texts into common denominators, whether the common denominator of social matrix, which birthed the texts and is more or less reflected in them, or the common denominator of canonizing consensus in the religious community, which put its stamp of approval on the present scope and form of the texts and which urges us to locate particular texts within a body of texts viewed as an authoritative theological complex.

So the question arises: Are these two "totalisms," these comprehensive canonical and social scientific methods, irreconcilable and exclusive of one another? Is either of them mistaken from the outset? Or are they schemata which can each get at something important, leaving us with the problem of how to relate them in a historical understanding of ancient Israel and in a contemporary appropriation of the literature?

It seems to me that, while they are totalistic in methodological thrust, the two methods are not intrinsically "totalitarian," by which I mean that I cannot see anything in the essential enterprise of either form of criticism that excludes the other on principle. Nevertheless, to carry through a methodology properly, all the way to its limits so that it gives maximal yield, means that a single-mindedness must be applied. This does not mean that the advocate of the method, much less the whole community of scholars and interested people at large, necessarily accepts that this method alone yields truthful and valid results. It means only that the results achieved by this method are significant and must be addressed. The overall significance of such a comprehensive method, and especially its precise relation to other valid methods, is hardly assessable prior to the results of detailed inquiry and certainly not by fiat of single scholars, including those most committed to the new method and those opposed to it.

One way of exploring the contact points between social scientific criticism and canonical criticism is to examine what happens when the essence of the claims of each is carried into the territory of the other.

To begin with, what has canonical criticism to say to social scientific criticism? When assertions about canonical process and shape are brought into play, what is their legitimacy and pertinence for social scientific criticism? Through the categories of sociology of literature, ideology, and symbolic interaction, it is at once obvious that canonical criticism poses a set of issues altogether proper to social scientific criticism.

Consider canonical process for a start. The Pentateuchal themes, by way of example, are selective and highly arbitrary in their accents. Narratives, poems, and laws are brought into an ordered design around key nuclear themes or motifs. At the earliest stage of Israelite traditioning, there was a stylizing and patterning impulse at work that condensed, expanded, juxtaposed, interwove, and prioritized elements in the tradition without any strict regard for actual spatio-temporal relationships. This tendency systematically centralized the experiences of diverse groups in early Israel as if they had happened to a united Israel. The centralizing manipulation of the traditions gives them, at an early stage, the character of "canonical traditions."[11]

Consequently, we can say with confidence, and precisely as an aspect of the sociology of Israel's literature, that from Israel's beginnings as a tribal confederation in Canaan an ordering transmutation of historical events and social processes was decisively at work, doubtless because this revolutionary people relentlessly asked for its own *mythos,* its own foundation charter, its own objectified validation for being what it was and what it was struggling to become in a sociopolitically alien environment. Thus something like a "canonical process" was indeed operative as a basic communal activity at an early date, and this very tendency or process had a social matrix.

It is more difficult to form a judgment about canonical shape, if only because its various literary and theological dimensions have yet to be sorted out and the status of canonical shape seems to mean somewhat different things to different canonical critics. Immediately, however, it must be acknowledged by social scientific critics that late biblical society produced a canon of set books, and that the adoption of this canon was highly significant of and for the direction that early Judaism took. A social reconstruction of post-exilic Israel that ignored the emergence of "the religion of the book" would be truncated and inadequate social description and social analysis.

Both canonical process and canonical shape are ways of underscoring the ideological component of Israelite society and religion. The scripturalizing tendency in Israel brings its symbolic world front and center as part of the agenda of social scientific criticism. In a recent article on Old Testament theology,[12] Walter Brueggemann points out that the radical social equality of Israel and its embrace of the pain of the oppressed and the deprived has its counterpart in a radical deity who affirms the oppressed and embraces their pain. He goes so far as to say that the struggle between a severe contract theology and a theology of pain and oppression is internal to God as "a question of God seeking to present and represent himself as taking all of these data into account."[13] For the social study of religion as ideology, it is certainly a datum of importance that the picture of God in ancient Israel has this characterization of a deity who struggles to overcome conceptions of gods as endorsers of social inequality and despisers of the underclasses of society. Israel's characterization of God contends with exactly the points of a just and humane public order that Israel contends with.

For the sake of a social understanding of Israel, it is appropriate and necessary that biblical theology should examine carefully what is said about the thoughts, feelings, and actions of this Yahweh. There is, for instance, solid ground for social symbolic reflection in the discovery of Raymund Schwager that, while there are no less than 600 Old Testament passages about instances of violence that are condemned by Yahweh, there are a full 1000 cases that display Yahweh's own violence.[14] I contend that this is a social datum because it correlates both with the forms of violence that Israel suffered and that Israel practiced, as it also correlates with Israel's ambivalent assessments of and copings with violence. I would, therefore, argue that theological *and* social inquiries into biblical violence are greatly limited when they are separated, and that correspondingly they gain depth and explanatory reinforcement when associated.[15]

What now does social scientific criticism have to say to canonical criticism? When the assertion that all religious expressions have a social context and a social counterpart is brought into play, how does this impact our discernment of the canon?

To begin with, there is the question of the positions of various social groups with respect to their preferences for and their interests in this or that canonical shaping of the literature. It is not sufficient to speak of an undifferentiated "communal mind or will" as the stimulus to canonical process and the arbiter of canonical closure. Literature, especially canonical literature, is not disinterested. Every text has its social matrix and represents one or more social interests, whether we can easily identify them or not. And the final act or series of acts that fix a canonical boundary and content have a social matrix and interest as well.

Childs refers to social factors in the shaping of the canon, but in little more than a formal way, with little specificity, and never—as far as I can see even in his most recent work—in such a way as to grant that the very act of canonization, conceived as the ultimate religious act in a literary mode, is itself a thoroughly social act conditioned by a social locus in which this particular canon won out over other possible canons or over against resistance to canonization itself.

As Sanders concedes, and Sheppard and Blenkinsopp more explicitly recognize, social scientific criticism helps us to grasp the tensions and conflicts expressed in the inclusion and exclusion of texts and in their articulation in relation to one another. Without this sensitivity and method, canonical criticism may lapse into harmonization that simply accepts a communal decision to validate a collection and arrangement of literature as somehow overcoming, flattening out, and resolving all the prior and continuing socio-religious struggle in the community. In the absence of social scientific criticism, canonical criticism may obscure the reality that the mere assertion of what has been affirmed as canon does not tell us precisely enough what the force and thrust of the canonical decision actually was for the canonizing community, and thus derivatively or analogously what its force and thrust might be for us.

Blenkinsopp has put this social ingredient of canonical studies very well indeed:

> The biblical canon cannot be taken as an absolute, in the sense of providing in a straightforward way a comprehensive legitimation or normative *regula fidei*. For the canon itself arose out of the need to resolve conflicting claims to authority in the religious sphere, and the resolution did not come in the form of a final verdict. These claims, moreover, can be traced back to the prophets whose language about the nature and activity of God simply rules out the idea of a canon as it is generally understood. . . . [I]n the last analysis we cannot dissociate religious authority from personal experience.[16]
>
> The idea of a canon, in particular, would call for examination as an aspect of social history, implying as it does claims to authority and comprehensive attempts at legitimation on the part of different groups and individuals. For the most part this work still remains to be done, and it is no wise derogatory to the religious claims being made to insist that it needs to be done.[17]

At this point, a word of caution to both parties in this dialogue of criticisms is advisable. All comprehensive methods and forms of criticism, including theology I should add, can go awry by turning into dogmatism and positivism, and dead-ending in a sort of methodological fundmentalism. The same can happen with social scientific criticism and canonical criticism, and it is most likely to happen when critics of one persuasion talk only or mainly among themselves.

Social scientific fundamentalism results when one lapses into thinking that a social matrix can be conjured out of thin air, or that knowledge of a social matrix directly accounts for a text in all its features, or that everything in a text that is not immediately traceable to a social rootage is inconsequential.

Canonical fundamentalism results when one lapses into thinking that the religious community's authority-affirming fiat floats trascendently above history and society, or that the canonical decision gives us an indisputable clue to meaning that can shortcut the inquiry into the entire history of the text and its changing shapes, or that from the canonical form of the text we can directly read off prescriptions for our situation in the absence of information and sensitivities about what is at stake in their and our social contexts.

Both forms of methodological fundamentalism can produce flat or monolithic readings of texts that ignore individualities in the growth and functioning of texts in the communities where they were at home, and in particular may miss the special complexity of language in its relation to social and intellectual history, both in biblical times and in our own socioreligious situations.

Semiotics or sociolinguistics will be increasingly vital both to a proper social criticism and a proper canonical criticism. How do the special interests of groups get articulated and how are they given compelling currency in particular genres and aggregations of texts? What is the social status of texts that seek to give large-scale interpretations of the origins, meanings, and obligations of communities? Why do some texts make more direct allusions to social data, and others more indirect allusions, and some no allusions at all, at least in any denotative sense? What are the different kinds of socially perceived texts signifying, *really* signifying: that one should do or not do certain things, think or not think certain thoughts, obey or not obey certain leadership claims, side with or oppose this or that interest group, social tendency, or governmental act or regime?

If we make a distinction between penultimate canonical process and a culminating canonical shaping, what in fact happens when the meanings of texts are re-signified along the way and in the final closure, sometimes *sharply* re-signified? Certainly, the way we should understand canon will be affected by what we understand the function of these canonical texts to be as signifiers of particular meanings to the canonizing community. For example, are the significations from earlier stages of canonical process carried over into the "canonical intentionality" so-called? Or are the earlier significations abolished or altered so that a higher order intentionality cancels out, heightens, spiritualizes, historicizes, or subordinates the preceding significations of texts as they functioned in prior contexts? Childs seems to be arguing some form of the latter, but his results to date, while suggestive and at times even brilliant, are impressionistic and appear far from definitive. A "final shape" that is suppposed to be determinative of our interpretation ought to be demonstrable according to widely agreed criteria.

At issue is not only how significations may change through stages of literary development, but also the question of the status of language offered as authoritative language. What did the canonizing community think it was commending when it singled out this particular literature? This may seem a relatively easy question to answer when the language is directly prescriptive of particular ritual or social behavior. Even in that case, however, we observe prescribed behavior that may no longer have been able to be done, or may not have been of much relevance to the canonizing community's preferred repertory of behavior. When it comes to language of celebration, admonition or warning, or history-like narratives, the authority claimed is especially problematic. The intended and actual results of conferring authority on these texts may have been manifold: to secure particular kinds of ritual or social behavior, to strengthen internal unity or consensus in the community, to insure obedience to authorities whose entitlements to be obeyed or whose interpretations, instructions, and policies were in dispute, or simply to preserve cherished stories.

Much the same questions about what authority of the canon specified apply equally wherever later generations have affirmed this canon as their own. New social factors and new comprehensions of language continuously reshape the range and quality of authority which the ongoing communities assign to the canon. In our own time, how do changing notions of the relation between the oral and the written, between factuality and interpretation, between literal and symbolic meanings, and of the very import of language as metaphor—how do all these intellectual and sociocultural developments give different colorations to what is signified by accepting a canon? Then and now, *how closely* and *over what range* were and are behaviors and meanings in the community expected to be regulated by this normative literature? What sanctions, if any, have been applied for violating the canon? An astute canonical criticism, informed by social critical awareness, should be able to help us with such questions.

IV.

To sharpen the dialogue, I conclude with a focus on the canonical closure of the Law to bring out the agreements and differences in the ways that Childs and I approach the issues. The shared ground between Childs and myself can perhaps best be seen by noting our criticisms of the biblical theology movement. Walter Brueggemann has made a most interesting, if fleeting, association between my attitude toward biblical theology and Childs' attitude toward the same subject.

> Gottwald has found a way (even if he is not interested in it) of giving substance and credibility to the now discredited "mighty deeds of God" construct. As is well known, Childs saw the problem: "Mighty deeds of God" is a way of speaking that seems to float in the air without historical basis. The approach of Wright and von Rad had not solved the problem of "actual" history and "sacred" history. The recital of sacred history appeared to have no rootage in historicality. Gottwald has found a way for those who will speak in terms of "mighty acts." But now it must be faced that the recital is an ideological articulation of a radical social movement. Obviously the implications for doing Old Testament theology are acute.[18]

What Brueggemann correctly notes is that Childs and I are looking for a way to anchor biblical theology in something broader and deeper than a series of confessional statements abstracted from biblical texts and communities. Childs' manner of doing this has been to lodge biblical theology in the broad contours of the scriptural collections as designed and affirmed by a canonizing community which serves as our authoritative ancestor in the faith. For Childs, the canon itself as a total content becomes an enlarged confession of faith whose accents and proportions are to be determined by a continuous reading of the whole.

On the other hand, I choose to locate biblical theology in its metaphorical range of reference to Israelite socioeconomic, political, and cultural life by showing how the basic assertions of that theology correspond to socioeconomic, political, and cultural interests and desiderata in ancient Israel. I claim that anything experienced or claimed with respect to God has a counterpart experience or claim with respect to human life in the concrete Israelite community.

So what is at stake between these two views of biblical theology? The difficulty I find with Childs' way of anchoring biblical theology, broader gauged though it is by far than the acts of God theology, is that it rests in the end on the narrow base of the canonizing community. It overlooks the special pleading of that community and misses the tremendous social systemic tensions and conflicts integral to the final outcome of the community's canonical decisions, of the sort initially explored in the work of Burke O. Long and Paul D. Hanson.[19] Moreover, the canonical appeal tends not only to negate, or at least slide over, the social problematic of the canonizing community, but also to obscure the social problematic of the interpreting communities in which we are discerning the ancient canon's applicability to us. That Sanders to a degree, and Sheppard and Blenkinsopp more explicitly, are open to the social placement of the canon, implies that canonical criticism *need* not be, and I would say *should* not be, as "a-social," even "anti-social," as Childs makes it out to be.

Let me now illustrate these issues with respect to the canonical closure of the Law. I begin with the widely held view that the thrust of the community in canonizing the Law was to achieve order, stability, and fidelity to established priestly leadership and interpretations, assuming for the moment that P-like tendencies were principally at work in the scripturalizing of the Law. If that was the social matrix of the canonizers of the Law, does that not already orient us, the interpreters, toward an ordering and stabilizing purpose in our use of Scripture? What then are we to do with the challenge and threat to order and stability in our own social and ecclesial milieus and in many parts of the biblical canon itself? (Likewise, is not the sharpness of radical prophecy toned down by engulfing it in the moderating and comforting wrappings of the redacted collection of the prophets?) Does it not seem likely that a canonical criticism uncorrected by social scientific criticism, and not greatly concerned with historical criticism, will "stack the deck" toward a kind of biblical theology that is ecclesially circumscribed and committed in advance to preserving and reinforcing the current churchly and academic privileges and outlooks of contemporary official interpreters?

It is true that at a number of points Childs attempts to guard against this kind of circular exegesis and theology. But by accenting the surface structure of the finished text and by underplaying history and society, much the same kind of hypostatizing or reifying of the canon can result as occurred with the elevation of confessions of the acts of God to normative rank. I detect just such a dangerous leaning in some of Childs' remarks, especially where he excludes from consideration social factors that were not in the conscious minds of the canonizers or which they deliberately expunged from the text. For example, Childs says:

> It is clear from the sketch of the [canonical] process that particular editors, religious groups, and even political parties were involved. . . . But basic to the canonical process is that those responsible for the actual editing of the text did their best to obscure their own identity. . . . Increasingly the original sociological and historical differences within the nation of Israel were lost, and a religious community emerged which found its identity in terms of sacred scripture. Israel defined itself in terms of a book! The canon formed the decisive Sitz im Leben for the Jewish community life, thus blurring the sociological evidence most sought after by the modern historian. When critical exegesis is made to rest on the recovery of these very sociological distinctions which have been obscured, it runs directly in the face of the canon's intention.[20]

A little later, Childs speaks of " 'a canonical intentionality' which is coextensive with the meaning of the biblical text."[21]

To the contrary, it seems to me that only through recovery of "sociological distinctions which have been obscured" by collectors, redactors, and canonizers can we get a true sense of the pluriformity of the canon, and thus give a full hearing to its various voices in relation to all the factors at work in our own situations as interpreters.

By way of recovering these lost dimensions of canonical politics, we can identify two sets of vested interests at work in the canonizing of the Law, one from outside the restored Jewish community and one from within it.

(1) The Demotic Chronicle from Egypt discloses the Persian initiative in commanding the priests of Egypt to codify the ancient laws of the land which then became Persian provincial law. Precisely the same Persian intervention makes sense as the governmental instrument by which the reforming Jews from exile were able to make the Torah both the distinctively Jewish religious and civil charter and the Persian provincial or district law honored in Judah.[22]

(2) Secondly, the curious combination of P Torah in Genesis through Numbers with D Torah in Deuteronomy probably signifies that the priestly establishment favoring P had to make concessions to other groups who favored D, such as Levites and prophets, in order to effect a broad enough coalition of forces to make the new law persuasive and enforceable. Thus, the first stage of canonization can be seen to have produced a "new consensus Torah."[23]

If we grant social conflictual origins to the canon, Childs is not very convincing or self-consistent when he says:

> The canonical interpreter stands within the received tradition, and, fully conscious of his own time-conditionality as well as that of the scriptures, strives critically to discern from its kerygmatic witness a way to God which overcomes the historical moorings of both text and reader.[24]

In my judgment, neither the sociohistoric process of canonization nor the requisites of theology itself give warrant for using the Bible "to discern . . . a way to God which overcomes the historical moorings of both text and reader." As far as I can see, *the canon* is very historically and socially moored, and *I as interpreter* am very historically and socially moored, and *the God shown in Scripture* is very historically and socially moored. Childs may here be confusing the capacity of widely separated historical contexts to address and inform one another with a severance from historical moorings altogether.

V.

As I view the future of canonical criticism, which I take to be a bright and promising one, it will not lie along the route of collapsing the meaning of the biblical text into what the final canonizers made of it. It will have to embrace all the varied fought-over meanings and their social settings, from the beginning, and not excluding the canonizers. To capitulate to the obscuring process of the canonizers in effacing the identities and conflictual stances of editors, religious groups, and political factions, would be to default both as historians and as theologians.

Theology does have truth at stake, including the truth of how theologies have arisen in our past.[25] A moment's reflection tells us that one of the prime reasons for obscuring the identity of those who advocate authoritative decisions and interpretations is to make their judgments look unquestioned and ancient, even timeless, and certainly descended from divine authority. To overlook this psychosocial reality of ideology and mystification in religious assertions, canonical assertions included, is to deliver theology into an uncritical subjection to the unexamined self-interests of canonizers and contemporary interpreters. This, in turn, leaves us vulnerable to unconscious captivity within our own horizons, at a loss for a critical perspective by which the Bible could tell us anything we did not already know or by which it could come to bear tellingly on thought and practice today.

I conclude with the confidence that canonical criticism is not inconsistent with social scientific criticism, provided that each sees the element of the other that is intrinsic and necessary to its own enterprise. As Sheppard concisely formulates it, the two criticisms belong together:

> Better theological exegesis requires a recognition that all the words of scripture are human words, historically conditioned, and contextually relativized in service to a larger theological claim upon a later believing community.[26]

A social hermeneutic open to the social locus of original texts and canon and to the social locus of interpreters will have both a linguistic canonical sensibility and a sociological bent toward uncovering the self interests, past and present, through which the divine interests are asserted. In plain truth, in biblical traditions, every assertion of divine interest is also someone's human interest. The collaboration of canonical criticism and social scientific criticism will improve our chances of discerning, focusing, and critiquing the admixture of divine-human interests which form the content of biblical revelation.

Notes

[1] On social scientific methodology, see the essays by Bruce J. Malina, Norman K. Gottwald, and Gerd Theissen in N. K. Gottwald (ed.), *The Bible and Liberation: Political and Social Hermeneutics* (Maryknoll: Orbis, rev. ed., 1983), pp. 11-58. For bibliography, see N. K. Gottwald, "Bibliography on the Sociological Study of the Old Testament," *American Baptist Quarterly*, 2 (1983), pp. 168-184.

[2] Norman K. Gottwald, *The Tribes of Yahweh: A Sociology of the Religion of Liberated Israel, 1250-1050 B.C.E.* (Maryknoll: Orbis, 1979); *idem*, "John Bright's New Revision of *A History of Israel*," *Biblical Archaeology Review*, 8 (1982), pp. 56-61; *idem*, "Two Models of the Origins of Ancient Israel: Social Revolution or Frontier Development," in *The Quest for the Kingdom of God: Studies in Honor of George E. Mendenhall*, ed. H. B. Huffmon *et al.* (Winona Lake: Eisenbrauns, 1983), pp. 5-24; *idem*, "The Israelite Settlement as a Social Revolutionary Movement," in *The Proceedings of the International Congress of Biblical Archaeology Marking the 70th Anniversary of the Israel Exploration Society* (forthcoming).

[3] Norman K. Gottwald, *The Hebrew Bible: A Socio-Literary Introduction* (Philadelphia: Fortress, 1985).

[4] Brevard S. Childs, "The Old Testament as Scripture of the Church," *Concordia Theological Monthly*, 43 (1972), pp. 709-722; *idem*, "The Exegetical Significance of Canon for the Study of the Old Testament," *Vetus Testamentum Supplements*, 28 (1977), pp. 66-80; *idem, Introduction to the Old Testament as Scripture* (Philadelphia: Fortress, 1979); *idem, The New Testament as Canon: An Introduction* (Philadelphia: Fortress, 1985).

[5] Childs, *New Testament as Canon*, pp. 48-53.

[6] *Ibid.*, p. 49.

[7] James A. Sanders, *Torah and Canon* (Philadelphia: Fortress, 1972); *idem*, "Adaptable for Life: the Nature and Function of Canon," in *Magnalia Dei—The Mighty Acts of God: Essays on the Bible and Archaeology in Memory of G. Ernest Wright,* ed. F. M. Cross *et al.* (Garden City: Doubleday, 1976), pp. 531-560; *idem*, "Canonical Context and Canonical Criticism," *Horizons in Biblical Theology*, 2 (1980), pp. 173-197; *idem. Canon and Community. A Guide to Canonical Criticism* (Philadelphia: Fortress, 1984).

[8] Gerald T. Sheppard, "Canon Criticism: The Proposal of Brevard Childs and an Assessment for Evangelical Hermeneutics," *Studia Biblica et Theologica*, 4 (1974), pp. 3-17; *idem, Wisdom as a Hermeneutical Construct: A Study in the Sapientializing of the Old Testament* (New York/Berlin: Walter de Gruyter, 1980); *idem*, "Canonization: Hearing the Voice of the Same God through Historically Dissimilar Traditions," *Interpretation*, 37 (1982), pp. 21-33; see also, note 26 below.

[9] Sheppard, "Canonization."

[10] Joseph Blenkinsopp, *Prophecy and Canon. A Contribution to the Study of Jewish Origins* (Notre Dame/London: University of Notre Dame Press, 1977).

[11] Gottwald, *Tribes*, pp. 35, 40, 63, 92, 111-183 *passim.*

[12] Walter Brueggemann, "A Shape for Old Testament Theology, I: Structure Legitimation," *Catholic Biblical Quarterly*, 47 (1985), pp. 28-46.

[13] *Ibid.,* p. 43.

[14] Summarized in Robert North, "Violence and the Bible: The Girard Connection," *Catholic Biblical Quarterly*, 47 (1985), pp. 14-15.

[15] For fuller elaboration, see Norman K. Gottwald, "Sociological Method in Biblical Research and Contemporary Peace Studies," *American Baptist Quarterly*, 2 (1983), pp. 142-156.

[16] Blenkinsopp, *Prophecy and Canon*, pp. 142-143.

[17] *Ibid.*, p. 148.

[18] Walter Brueggemann, *"The Tribes of Yahweh:* An Essay Review," *Journal of the American Academy of Religion*, 48, (1980), p. 445; *The Bible and Liberation*, pp. 175-176.

[19] Burke O. Long, "Social Dimensions of Prophetic Conflict," *Semeia*, 21 (1982), pp. 31-53, with response by Norman K. Gottwald, pp. 107-109; Paul D. Hanson, *The Dawn of Apocalyptic. The Historical and Sociological Roots of Jewish Apocalyptic Eschatology* (Philadelphia: Fortress, 1975).

[20] Childs, *Introduction to the Old Testament as Scripture*, p. 78.

[21] *Ibid.*, p. 79.

[22] S. Dean McBride, Jr., has so far offered the fullest account of this Persian intervention in Jewish canonization (lecture on the Pentateuch and the Law of the Temple in Ezek. 40-48, Yale Divinity School, February 1977; to my knowledge McBride has not published on the subject); see also George Widengren in *Israelite and Judaean History*, ed. J. H. Hayes and J. M. Miller (Philadelphia: Westminster, 1976), p. 515, indebted to Egyptologists W. Spiegelberg and F. K. Kienitz.

[23] Sheppard's term in "Canonization," p. 25; see also Robert R. Wilson, *Prophecy and Society in Ancient Israel* (Philadelphia: Fortress, 1980), pp. 305-306. Gottwald, *The Hebrew Bible*, pp. 103, 106, 436-437, 459-469 elaborates on the impact of the conjunction of Persian intervention and Judahite political compromise on canonization and social history.

[24] Childs, *New Testament as Canon*, pp. 51-52.

[25] Norman K. Gottwald, "The Theological Task After *The Tribes of Yahweh*," in *The Bible and Liberation*, pp. 190-200.

[26] Gerald T. Sheppard, "The Use of Scripture Within the Christian Ethical Debate Concerning Same-Sex Oriented Persons," *Union Seminary Quarterly Review*, 40 (1985), p. 31.

NEW TESTAMENT

D. A. Carson, area editor

NEW TESTAMENT

D. A. CARSON
Professor of New Testament, Trinity Evangelical Divinity School
Acting Warden, Tyndale House Library for Biblical Research,
Cambridge, England

Introduction

To be asked to choose five or six articles representative of the best of New Testament scholarship during the past year is to be given a task demanding the wisdom of Solomon. To be assigned no more than fifty pages for these articles renders the task impossible: most of the truly ground-breaking articles are thirty or forty pages long.

And so I have compromised. I selected two which together ran to 87 pages, and asked their authors to reduce them. This they have cheerfully done, largely by eliminating footnotes and some of the more technical arguments. Experts will have already read the original, uncut versions; perhaps these simplified versions will encourage others to do so.

The article by Dr. Gundry is important because it engages tellingly with the work of E. P. Sanders—work that has set the agenda for studies in Paul and in the Jewish background of the New Testament. In brief, Sanders holds that the principal issue that divided Paul from his Jewish opponents was not justification by works of the law versus justification by grace, but Christology. Both Jews and Christians understood themselves to be God's people on the grounds of God's grace; but in both groups, adherents were then expected to persevere by obedience. One enters the covenant by grace, and remains in it by works. Sanders labels this stance "covenantal nomism"; and since in his view it accurately describes both Jews and Christians, we are compelled to look elsewhere for what divides them. The brief answer is that Christians believed Jesus to be the Messiah, and Jews did not.

Sanders's work is based on detailed discussion of both Jewish and Christian sources. Only rarely does a scholar set the agenda of discussion, and this is what Sanders has achieved. Implicitly, of course, his work calls in question the dominant Protestant exegesis of much in the Pauline epistles, and even of the validity of Protestantism itself, considered historically. Dr. Gundry's thoughtful evaluation and critique of Sanders is an excellent example of the growing literature that insists Sanders's work be circumscribed by major qualifications.

Especially since the discovery (1947) and progressive publication of the Dead Sea Scrolls, more and more attention has been devoted to the way the New Testament uses the Old. Such study can devote specialist monographs to the text form of citations, to different kinds of appropriation techniques, to parallels in various strata of Jewish literature, and so on. Once again, however, the issues transcend the specialist. At stake, finally, is the way the canon fits together. If you envisage that the pieces fit together in one way, you are a dispensationalist; if in another, you are a covenant theologian; if in another, you uphold a Barthian view of *Heilsgeschichte* ("salvation history"). Of course, the categories are not neat: there is a spectrum, not quantum definitions. Yet the fact remains that the way we relate, say, the law of Moses and the gospel of Jesus Christ, is intimately related to our entire theological system. That is why the essay by Dr. Moo is so important. It canvasses part of the ground that must be studied, the synoptic Gospels, with careful exegesis and restrained conclusions.

Like many other students of the Old Testament, I try to scan between eighty and a hundred journal fascicles a quarter. The range of topics is enormous. Among the articles that caught my eye, but which could not be admitted here for want of space, were several of no less merit than the two I have just mentioned. As an excellent example of the primary staple of New Testament scholarship, viz., careful, painstaking exegesis that illuminates the text, Linda Belleville's treatment of Galatians 3:21-4:11 in *Journal for the Study of New Testament* 26 (1986) 53-78, stands out. At a time when there is renewed interest in worship, but when most treatments are an awkward mixture of the insightful and the trivial, it is a pleasure to commend the most recent reflections of D. G. Peterson in *Reformed Theological Review* 44 (1985) 34-41.

Other topics that command continued attention are the synoptic problem, the reconstruction of New Testament history, the relation between the New Testament documents and other first century streams of thought, the exact place of Gnosticism, and assorted streams of biblical theology. Recently two more topics have been added: the new literary criticism that goes beyond structuralism in analyzing ancient documents as they stand; and the impact of the social sciences on the analysis of social groupings in the New Testament. As might be expected, one can find in these outpourings examples of careful work (e.g., the essays of Prof. E. A. Judge), and the rawest forms of uncontrolled speculation. But if *The Best in Theology* flourishes, I shall try to provide the best samples in all these areas in later years.

About the Area Editor

D. A. Carson (B. Sc., McGill; M. Div., Central Baptist Seminary, Toronto; Ph.D., Cambridge University) is professor of New Testament, Trinity Evangelical Divinity School, and Acting Warden, Tyndale House Library for Biblical Research, Cambridge, England. He was ordained in 1972 by the Fellowship of Evangelical Baptist Churches in Canada. With John D. Woodbridge he edited *Hermeneutics, Authority, and Canon* (1986). Other recent publications include *Matthew*, in the Expositor's Bible Commentary (1984); *From Sabbath to Lord's Day* (1982); and *Divine Sovereignty and Human Responsibility* (1981).

the prob. here: wrong formulations (artificial) of the prob. forcing of data into either-or categories. failure to allow for vaguer, more complex interaction of the various strands in Paul. (Räisänen)

GRACE, WORKS, AND STAYING SAVED IN PAUL

R. H. GUNDRY
Professor of New Testament and Greek
Westmont College

Article slightly condensed by the author from *Biblica*

The publication of E. P. Sanders' *Paul and Palestinian Judaism* (from here on *PPJ*—Philadelphia: Fortress Press, 1977) stirred up the study of Paul's theology. In *PPJ*, however, Sanders gave far more space to Palestinian Judaism than to Paul. Now he has written another book, *Paul, the Law and the Jewish People* (from here on *PLJP*),[1] which redresses that imbalance and enables us to take fuller and fairer account of his thoughts. Their growing influence on Pauline studies calls for examination.

The present article is written to refute one of the most important of Sanders's thoughts, viz., that "on the point at which many have found the decisive contrast between Paul and Judaism—grace and works—Paul is in agreement with Palestinian Judaism... salvation is by grace but judgment is according to works; works are the condition of remaining 'in', but they do not earn salvation".[2] But if we treat the literatures (the Pauline and the Palestinian Jewish) *materially*—i.e., if we weigh their emphases—quite a different impression may be gained, an impression of Palestinian Judaism as centered on works-righteousness and of Paul's theology as centered on grace.

Weighing the materials of Palestinian Judaism shows a preponderance of emphasis on obedience to the law as the way of staying in. The covenant, based on God's elective grace, may be presupposed; but it has no prominence (as Sanders admits).[3] Rather, a body of interpretative or applicatory traditions starts piling up, also a body of oral legal traditions (written down finally in the Mishnah) which parallel the written law of the OT. These traditions draw the criticism in the NT outside Pauline literature that they smother the original intent of the law (see Mark 7,6-13; par. Matt 15,3-9 for the classic passage). The very raising of the issue establishes a Palestinian Jewish preoccupation with the law and with its careful observance, and indicates a basic disagreement between Palestinian Judaism and Christianity at this point. *Hellenistic*

Josephus' descriptions of the Jewish sects confirm this preoccupation (*Life* 38 § 191; *J.W.* 1.5.2. § 110; 2.8.6, 9, 12, 14 §§ 136, 147, 159, 162; *Ant.* 17.2.4 § 41; 18.1.3-4 §§ 12-18), as do the contents of the Mishnah and other early rabbinic literature. The punctiliousness of the sect at Qumran proves that we cannot legitimately use endtime fervor to dilute preoccupation with careful observance of the law. And whatever enjoyment Palestinian Jews derived from such observance is immaterial to the fact of this preoccupation. Sanders has succeeded in undermining the notion that in Palestinian Judaism the retention of salvation always depended on producing at least a bare majority of good deeds; but he has not succeeded in relating the law to elective grace in a way that materially scales down preoccupation with legal interpretation, extension, application, and observance.

Though obedience is integral and important to Paul's theology, along-side Palestinian Jewish absorption in legal questions his comments on obedience look proportionately slight. Furthermore, they usually take the form of exhortations, not of legal interpretation, extension, and application. Where amoral questions arise (as concerning meat offered to idols in 1 Cor 8-10; cf. Rom 14), Paul tends to freedom of conscience rather than to legal definition. The moral demands of the law he takes, not as distinctive of Judaism, but as matters of universal obligation (see esp. Rom 1,18-32); therefore it would not cross his mind that commanding Gentile as well as Jewish Christians to meet these demands might disagree with his insistence on freedom from the law. In the Judaizing debate, he is concerned with specially Jewish features of the law (circumcision, "days and months and seasons and years" [Gal 4,10], and dietary restrictions), the kind that capture most attention in Palestinian Judaism.

As noted, Sanders sees a principial agreement between Paul and Palestinian Judaism: a person gets in by God's elective grace and stays in by works of the law. But for Paul, of course, God's elective grace works through Christ. Sanders' view therefore requires us to think that after defining in an un-Jewish, Christological way the grace that gets a person in, Paul lapses back to his inherited Jewish, un-Christological way of thinking with regard to staying in: "Christians are judged according to how well they fulfill the law" and will be excluded if they do not fulfill it well enough.[4] This view of Paul's thought implies that the question of staying in was not a theological point of debate between him and the Judaizers; for otherwise we would have expected him to carry over his un-Jewish thinking from getting in to staying in so as to avoid a charge of inconsistency and keep the focus of his soteriology on faith in Christ.

In fact, however, the question of staying in *is* the issue, at least the primary one, in Galatians. There, contrary to Sanders' statement that "the subject of Galatians is... the condition on which Gentiles enter the people of God",[5] Paul does not deal with the question of whether believing Gentiles had *gotten* in; rather, he deals with the question of whether believing Gentiles could *stay* in without submitting to circumcision and keeping other parts of the law. "Having begun by the Spirit, are you now being perfected by the flesh?" (3,3). It is a question of "abiding", not of starting, according to Paul's quotation of Deut 27,26 (3,10). "You have been severed from Christ, you who are seeking to be justified by law; you have fallen from grace... You were running well; who hindered you from obeying the truth?" (5,4.7). Even in the less polemical Romans, staying in by faith in Christ seems to be as much on Paul's mind as getting in; for he devotes chaps. 6-8 to the ongoing life of believers as being not under law, but under grace; and the phrase "from faith to faith" in 1,17a means that from beginning to end, faith alone (which Paul expressly contrasts with works—see esp. 4,4-5) forms the overarching principle of soteriology, staying in as well as getting in. Similarly, we read in Rom 11,20, "You stand by faith."

Outside Galatians and Romans, too, Paul repeatedly identifies faith and rejects works as the principle of continuance in salvation; he repeatedly affirms the activity of God and denies human effort as the fundament of perseverance. Human effort is an effect, not a cause. "For you stand by faith" (2 Cor 1,24). "Not that we are adequate in ourselves so as to consider anything as [coming] from ourselves, but our adequacy is from God" (2 Cor 3,5). "Being confident of this very thing, that he who has begun a good work in you will perfect it until the day of Jesus Christ" (Phil 1,6). "Work out your salvation with fear and trembling, for it is God who effects in you both the willing and the doing for his good pleasure" (Phil 2,12b-13). "We... put no confidence in the flesh... I count [N.B. the present tense after the preceding perfect tense 'I counted'] all things to be loss... and I count [them] rubbish in order that I should be found in him, not having my righteousness from the law, but the [righteousness] through faith in Christ, the righteousness from God, [based] on faith" (Phil 3,3.8-9). Likewise in disputed epistles: "Striving according to his working which works in me with power" (Col 1,29); "being established by the [probably = 'your'] faith" (Col 2,7); "that Christ may dwell in your hearts through faith" (Eph 3,17). Cf. 2 Cor 4,7.10; 12,9; 13,4; Eph 2,10; 6,10.[6]

So then, Paul did not dispute with the Judaizers because he thought they taught that believing Gentiles had to be circumcised and start keeping the rest of the law as means of getting in. In *PPJ* Sanders himself showed that, strictly speaking, not even non-Christian Palestinian Judaism represented such a view. Instead, entering the covenant preceded taking the yoke of the commandments; thus, Gentile proselytes entered the covenant by indicating their acceptance of it and their intention to obey the commandments in it, and circumcision and similar acts that followed constituted evidence rather than means of entry.[7] We can hardly suppose, then, that the Judaizers in the church taught that believing Gentiles had to be circumcised and start keeping the rest of the law to get in; on the contrary, he battles against circumcision and keeping the rest of the law as necessary to stay in, i.e., against *falling* from grace, not against failure to enter it (Gal 5,4).

At the same time he demands good works. But his un-Jewish extension of faith and grace to staying in makes good works evidential of having received grace through faith, not instrumental in keeping grace through works.[8] This extension also means we cannot accept Sanders' view that Paul's attacks on

DIFF. TW° SOPHISTICATED UND. OF RABBIS
+ COMMON UND. OF MOST FOLKS.

84   The Best in Theology

the Judaizers' teaching are to be explained simply as a dogmatic denial: Judaism (and therefore the Judaizing element in the church) is wrong because it is not Christianity.[9] On the contrary, Paul attacks the Judaizers' teaching as a *corruption* of grace and faith (again see Gal 3,3.10; 5,4.7). For Paul, then, getting in and staying in are covered by the seamless robe of faith as opposed to works, with the result that works come in as evidential rather than instrumental.

Paul's insistence on faith rather than on law for staying in as well as getting in raises the question, Why did he regard law and faith as excluding each other? Sanders offers an answer limited to salvation-history: "God's will to save by Christ is changeless... the law was *never* intended by God to be a means of righteousness. It is not only *lately* that it has come to an end as such".[10] But an historical intention of God that salvation should *always* be by faith in Christ for all people, Gentiles as well as Jews, does not explain why Paul can speak of faith as "coming" late in history (Gal 3,23-29), why he can speak of the salvation of Gentiles as an only recent historical development (see esp. Rom 11,11-32), why he can assume that faith and the law were compatible in the OT, or why Paul can say that "the righteous ordinance of the law should be fulfilled in us, who walk not according to the flesh but according to the Spirit" (Rom 8,4). Apparently there is something about the law in human experience as illustrated in Palestinian Judaism that is incompatible with faith, whereas the law as originally given by God and as now immersed in the Spirit and revised in accordance with Christ's coming, the hardening of Israel, and the grafting in of Gentiles is not incompatible with faith.[11] Statements that speak of fulfilling the law imply the new work of the Spirit; statements such as "faith came" (Gal 3,23) and "you are not under the law, but under grace" (Rom 6,14.15) reflect failure of the law in past human experience.

Where in past human experience does the incompatibility of the law with faith lie? We are forced back to an answer Sanders rejects: for Paul, the incompatibility lies in the self-righteousness to which unbelievers who try to keep the law succumb. Sanders counters that we find Paul's main objection to Jewish self-righteousness, not in self-dependent pride of accomplishment, but in the Jews' dependence on their status as God's covenant people who possess the law and in their consequent missing of the better righteousness based solely on believing participation in Christ, not on having the law: "what is wrong with Judaism is not that Jews seek to save themselves and become self-righteous about it, but that their seeking is not directed toward the right goal... They do not know that, as far as salvation goes, Christ has put an end to the law and provides a different righteousness from that provided by Torah obedience (Rom. 10.2-4)".[12] Thus the difference between Jewish righteousness and God's righteousness in Christ "is not the distinction between merit and grace, but between two dispensations. There is a righteousness which comes by law, but is now worth nothing because of a different dispensation... It is this concrete fact of *Heilsgeschichte* which makes the other righteousness wrong...".[13]

To be sure, Paul sees a shift in dispensations. But he sees more than that. The key-passage Phil 3,2-11 starts with his boasting in the givens of Jewish status ("as to circumcision, an eight-dayer; from the stock of Israel; of the tribe of Benjamin"), but goes on to confidence in personal accomplishments ("a Hebrew of the Hebrews; as to the law, a Pharisee; as to zeal, persecuting the church; as to the righteousness in the law, having become blameless"). Sanders admits that in Phil 3,2-11 Paul makes personal accomplishments as well as the givens of Jewish status the objects of his former confidence in the flesh; but he argues that Paul does not charge himself with "the attitudinal sin of self-righteousness".[14] But a long list of items in Phil 3,2-11 points to the attitudinal sin of self-righteousness alongside the mistake of missing God's righteousness in Christ: (1) "boast"; (2) "have confidence"; (3) "*think* (δοκεῖ) to have confidence"; (4) "to me (μοι)" in connection with "gain"; (5) "I regard"; (6) Paul's setting out his past achievements as superior to the achievements of his opponents who boast in the flesh—as though there is a contest over who can boast the most; (7) his following denial that he now "considers" himself to have arrived (vv. 12-16); and (8) his exhortation to be similarly "minded (φρονῶμεν)" (v. 15).

That a dispensational shift does not by itself account for all Paul says is evident also in his parade example, Abraham; for he, according to Paul, was justified by faith long before Christ ushered in the new dispensation (Gal 3; Rom 4). David is just as troublesome to Sanders' purely salvation-historical explanation; for Paul has David, too, justified by faith (Rom 4,6-8)—yet David lived not only long before the new dispensation, but also right within the old dispensation of law.

Since Paul's own righteousness had included works accomplished as well as status granted, we must say that his opposing the works of the law to faith in Christ includes an attack on self-dependence as well as an indication of dispensational shift. What Paul says about Abraham in Rom 4,2.4 supports the point: "for if Abraham was justified by works, he has ground for boasting... to the one who works the reward is not reckoned according to grace, but according to debt" (contrast Pr Man 8; *Jub.* 23,10; m. *Kidd.* 4,14). Sanders tries to avoid the force of these statements by noting that in fact the reward was given to Abraham on the basis of faith and that Paul neither mentions nor criticizes an attempt by Abraham to be justified by works.[15] Nevertheless, Paul's statements imply that Abraham *could* have boasted if his justification *had* come by works.

Sanders recognizes that according to Paul "it was never... God's intention that one should accept the law in order to become one of the elect".[16] "It has always been by faith".[17] Well, then, so far as God's intention is concerned, salvation-history did not shift from righteousness which comes by law to God's righteousness in Christ (as Sanders self-contradictorily says in his attempt to load everything on Paul's notion of salvation-history),[18] but from promise to fulfillment (cf. Gal 3-4). The use of the law to establish one's own righteousness is what Paul finds wrong in Palestinian Judaism, including his past life.

Rom 9,30-10,13 comes into play here. Sanders admits that "at first blush" and taken alone 9,30-32 means that Israel failed to fulfill the law because they rested on works rather than on faith. But the rest of the passage, Sanders argues, identifies the reason for this failure, not with a wrong manner of trying to fulfill the law (works instead of faith), but with lack of faith in Christ, so that "their own righteousness" (10,3) means "that righteousness which the Jews alone are privileged to obtain" rather than "self-righteousness which consists in individuals' presenting their merits as a claim upon God".[19] We may agree that Paul blames Israel for lack of faith in Christ. But to make that lack displace rather than complement wrong dependence on one's own works fails to carry conviction. Sanders is reduced to saying that in 9,31 Paul uses νόμος a second time even though he means "the righteousness of God which comes by faith in Christ", that this use is "certainly curious", and that "Paul did not say precisely what he meant" but "the desire for a balanced antithesis [νόμος having just occurred for the Mosaic law] led Paul to an almost incomprehensible combination of words". Sanders then draws a parallel with 8,10.[20] But in 8,10 Paul achieves balance with pairs of antonyms: "body" vs. "Spirit", "dead" vs. "life", and "sin" vs. "righteousness"; whereas Sanders asks us to believe that in 9,31 the *same* word "law" refers in one breath to the Mosaic law, in the next breath to the righteousness of God which comes by faith in Christ.

Another view is preferable. Paul's speaking of faith in 9,32 looks like a contrast with νόμον in the sense of law; indeed the strongly adversative ἀλλ᾽ ὡς ἐξ ἔργων, "but as [if it were] by works", confirms this contrast and interprets νόμον in v. 31 as the law used for works-righteousness. Otherwise the question, "Why [did they not attain it]?" and its answer, "Because [they did] not [pursue it] by faith, but as [if it were] by works", makes doubtful sense; for if the second occurrence of νόμον in v.31 means the righteousness of God by faith, Paul has *already* (in the first phrase of v. 31) told why Israel did not attain it: they were pursuing the law. As it is, the contrast in pursuing but not attaining requires that the object be the same: thus νόμον has one referent, the law; and the second occurrence of νόμον has no qualifier attached because the qualifier attached to the first occurrence—viz., "of righteousness"—carries over. The verb ἔφθασεν means "attained", not "fulfilled", says Sanders.[21] But "attained" in the sense "achieved" comes out to much the same as "fulfilled". The verb κατέλαβεν means "took hold of" and, by virtue of synonymous parallelism, determines a similar meaning for ἔφθασεν. Therefore, we do best to understand Paul as saying that Israel pursued the law as a way of establishing self-righteousness but, because of sin (cf. esp. 2,1-3,23), failed to attain it.[22] In view of the statement that it is

Gentiles who have taken hold of righteousness (v. 30), Paul probably chooses ἔφθασεν to indicate not only that Israel did not arrive at all, but also that Israel did not arrive *first* (the basic meaning of φθάνω), i.e., ahead of the Gentiles.

At 10,3 the infinitive "to establish" in the phrase "seeking to establish their own [righteousness]" and the contrast with subjection to God's righteousness show that it is not pride of privilege so much as self-reliance Paul is objecting to. Yet again, in 10,5 it is performance rather than privilege which contrasts with faith: "for Moses writes that the one who *does* [ποιήσας] the righteousness which is from the law will live by it". And in 10,8 Paul's *dropping* "that you may do it" from his quotation of Deut 30,14 concerning "the word of faith" favors the view that here faith contrasts with the Jewish attempt to perform the law, not with Jewish privilege in having the law.

We conclude, then, that Paul is not criticizing the Jews' unbelief in Christ *instead of* their attempt to perform the law, but that he is criticizing their unbelief *as caused by* an attempt to perform the law. That attempt leads to self-righteousness, but not because of any fault in the law itself or in obedience as such. Rather, boasting corrupts Spirit-less obedience to the law. Such obedience ends in man-made religion (if it does not already arise out of man-made religion). The law itself, however, is Spiritual (Rom 7,14—πνευματικός, related to the Holy Spirit in Paul's usage and therefore capitalized here in English translation), so that Spiritual believers naturally fulfill the righteous ordinance of the law (Rom 8,4). The same Spirit that determines their conduct determined the precepts of the law. And no true believer is un-Spiritual (Rom 8,9; hence, prolonged carnality calls in question a profession of faith—see esp. Gal 5,19-24). In view of Sanders' discussion, it may be too much to say that in Palestinian Judaism good works were always thought to earn God's favor according to a bookish weighing of merits. But in view of the many passages in Palestinian Jewish literature that Sanders cites concerning atonement by good works,[23] it is not too much to say that in Paul's presentation of Palestinian Judaism good works constitute a righteousness necessary at least to activate God's grace for the forgiveness of sins.[24] Paul will have none of this synergism. For him, salvation is *wholly* by grace through faith (cf. Eph 2,8-10). Good works are an outgrowth of the new creation in Christ.

BUT...
IMBAL'D.?

Paul is not content to argue that trying to keep the law is incompatible with faith. He takes unbelieving Jews and Christian Judaizers on their own terms and argues also that trying to keep the law never turns out to be successful. This failure of the Jews is the point of Rom 2,1-3,23, which leads into the detailed explanation of justification by faith in 3,24-5,21.[25] In support of Sanders, N. T. Wright argues that "Paul's accusations are not against legalism, but against sin, the breaking of the law".[26]

They are against breaking the law, yes; but Paul levels his accusations to puncture Jewish boasting in the law. Such boasting arises from legalism.

Sanders, seconded by Wright, argues back that this boasting does not have to do with merits, but with a special relation to God,[27] as in Rom 2,17-20.23a. But Paul's contextual exposé of the Jews' disobedience to the law keeps him from saying they boast in their obedience. To avoid appearing to contradict himself, he says only that they boast in the law, in God, etc. It is simply assumed they boast in the law because they think they keep it well enough. As we have already noted, Rom 4,2 clearly shows that boasting includes works of obedience as well as pride of possession: "for if Abraham was justified by works, he has a ground of boasting" (cf. Phil 3,4.6). Sanders is correct to deny that for Paul obedience to the law is bad, but wrong in denying Paul's criticism that such obedience has led to the sin of pride.

According to Sanders, however, the inconsistency and unconvincingness of Paul's statements concerning universal sinfulness show that he posited justification by faith before thinking of universal sinfulness rather than that he reached justification by faith as a conclusion based on universal sinfulness.[28] Sanders seems to miss Paul's meaning in Rom 5,12-14 that death reigned prior to the law, not because all people between Adam and Moses sinned for themselves apart from the Mosaic commandments, but because they sinned in Adam's disobedience to the commandment not to eat from the tree of knowledge; i.e., Adam's original sin was imputed to them (see esp. 5,19a). In the end, however, it does not matter whether in Paul's mind universal sinfulness came before justification by faith or vice versa, or whether the two occurred to him simultaneously. The fact remains that he includes Jews with Gentiles as law-breakers in order to undermine legalistic dependence on the law and thereby support justification by faith.

Sanders also argues that in the early chapters of Romans Paul is not attacking legalism, but is trying to put Jews and Gentiles on an equal footing so as to establish faith as a universal way of salvation instead of the law as a peculiarly Jewish way.[29] But could there not have been equality *under the law* for Jews and Gentiles? Why should not Paul have seen equal footing for Gentiles if they, like proselytes to Judaism, submitted to circumcision and tried to keep the rest of the law on coming into the church? Sanders answers by pointing to Gal 2,14 as indicating that Paul did not think Gentiles were able to live by the law.[30] But Gal 2,14 says nothing of the sort. The question of ability does not come in. Paul makes only a factual statement that Cephas, a Jew, is living like the Gentiles rather than like the Jews; and he asks why Cephas is trying to force Gentiles to live like Jews.

Elsewhere the question of ability does arise, but with particular reference to *Jews*. Whether Paul or someone else, the "I" in Rom 7,7-25 is under the law and therefore must be Jewish. At least the "I" must *include* the Jew. This "I" despairs over inability to keep the law.[31] So Paul strengthens his attack on works-righteousness by calling attention to Jewish inability not to sin as well as to the actuality of Jewish sinning. Sanders attributes the passion of Rom 7,7-25 "partly" to Paul's desire to exonerate God from intending the law to bring sin and from having given a law that brought death.[32] But where did the rest of the passion come from? And the passion in the passage relates directly to human inability, not to God's honor: "Wretched man that I am! Who will rescue me from the body of this death?" (v. 24). At the end of his discussion, Sanders betrays the weakness of his position by saying, "We must back away from strict exegesis of Romans 7 to understand Paul's thought".

According to Paul, obedience would have to be total to be successful in establishing one's own righteousness before God. Apparently the fact that repentance and forgiveness have to take up the slack caused by disobedience shows the inadequacy of works-righteousness. Thus he will not allow the law to be divided, as though a person could work up sufficient righteousness by keeping part of the law but not the rest:"for as many as are of the works of the law are under a curse; for it is written, 'Cursed is everyone who does not abide by all things written in the book of the law, so as to do them' " (Gal 3,10, with a quotation of Deut 27,26). Sanders thinks Paul chose to quote Deut 27,26 because only here does the LXX connect "law" with "curse"; that therefore Paul's emphasis falls on those words, not on the word "all", which only happens to appear; and finally that the weight of Paul's argument rests in the quotations of Gen 15,16 and Hab 2,4 (Gal 3,8.11), since the further quotation of Lev 18,5 in v. 12 shows the law to be wrong because it does not rest on faith, not because it is impossible to fulfill the law completely. The quotation in Gal 3,10 is designed, then, as a sidelight "to discourage Gentiles from accepting circumcision",[33] for "failure to fulfill the law perfectly leads to damnation by the law; while true life *cannot in any case* come by obedience to the law, even if the obedience is faultless".[34]

But should we shunt aside Gal 3,10 as an "even if", a mere spur alongside the main track of Paul's argument? A whole train of considerations favors that we should not. Sanders lays down the principle that it is not the OT quotations that tell us what Paul means, but Paul's own words that tell us what he took the OT quotations to mean; then Sanders notes that in his own words Paul mentions only the curse that comes on those who accept the law.[35] For the sake of argument let us accept Sanders' principle and ask whether Paul's own words are in fact limited to the curse. The answer is no. Paul starts introducing the quotation with the words, "For as many as are of the *works* of the law". If he has in mind merely acceptance of the law, we would have expected a reference only to the law, not to the works of the law. "Works" shows that he has in mind performance, which relates to the bulk of the quotation, "everyone who does not continue in all things written in the book of the law, so as to do them".[36] The large amount of space he devotes in Rom 2,1-3,23 to Jewish failure to abide by everything in the law confirms this observation.

Furthermore, within the quotation of Deut 27,26 Paul takes from the LXX the verb ἐμμένει, "abides by", which requires legal perfection, rather than giving a more accurate translation of the Hebrew *yāqîm*, "confirms", which requires only a basic intention to keep the law. This point gains in strength from the fact that in several other respects he does *not* follow the LXX of Deut 27,26.

Yet again Paul returns to the question of performance in v. 12: "but the law is not of faith; rather, 'the one who does them [the things written in the law] will live [ζήσεται, which for Paul means to have eternal life] by them' [Lev 18,5]". Is Paul pitting Hab 2,4, which he quotes in the preceding verse for righteousness or eternal life by faith, against Lev 18,5 and disagreeing with the Mosaic statement? His defense of the law in Romans casts doubt on an affirmative answer. The interest in the question of performance evident in Gal 3,10 ("works of the law" and "abides by") substantiates the doubt. More probably, Paul quotes Hab 2,4 to show that in fact faith underlies righteousness or eternal life and quotes Lev 18,5 to show that eternal life might have come through complete obedience to the law.[37] Then in v. 13, he returns to the theme of the curse which comes because of a breakdown in obedience. Since according to v. 10 the curse falls on the one who fails to abide by everything in the law, Paul's statement "Christ redeemed us from the curse of the law" clearly implies that it is failure to abide by everything in the law that necessitates faith in Christ's redemptive work. Otherwise Paul has no reason to bring up the curse again. Thus non-performance lies on the main track, not on a spur, of his argument; and his argument is not that eternal life *could* not come *even though* a person perfectly obeyed the law, but that eternal life *does* not come *because* a person obeys the law only imperfectly.[38]

Final confirmation comes from Gal 5,3, which, Sanders admits, "shows that, although Paul quoted Deut. 27,26 for the connection of 'curse' and νόμος, he did not forget that it said 'all' "[39]: "But I testify again to every man who is circumcised [or 'gets himself circumcised'] that he is a debtor to do the whole law". We may note first that these are Paul's own words, which therefore show what he got from the quotation of Deut 27,26 in Gal 3,10. Secondly, the adverb "again" shows that he is indeed reflecting on the earlier passage. And the accusation in Gal 6,13, "For not even those who are getting circumcised keep the law themselves", shows that he is contrasting incomplete performance, such as mere submission to circumcision, with complete performance.

According to Sanders, however, Paul infers that accepting circumcision entails accepting the whole law, "not to argue that the law should not be accepted *because* all of it *cannot* be kept, but as a kind of threat: if you start it *must* all be kept". Sanders goes on:

> To make this support the view that Paul argues against the law because it is impossible to keep all of it quantitatively, one must make a long list of assumptions about Paul's and the Galatians' presuppositions about the law: one must keep it all; one cannot do so; there is no forgiveness of transgression; therefore accepting the law necessarily leads to being cursed. The

middle terms of this thought-sequence are never stated by Paul, and this sequence of views cannot be found in contemporary Jewish literature.[40]

Actually, these presuppositions need be only Paul's, not the Galatians' as well. The first, that one must keep all the law is not an assumption on our part, but Paul's outright statement in Gal 5,3. The second, that one cannot keep all the law is hardly missing. We have seen that Gal 3,13a compared with 10 clearly implies such failure, that Gal 6,13 states it outright, that Rom 2,1-3,23 details it, and that Rom 7,7-25 adds pathos to it. Moreover, Gal 5,17-21, which comes not very far after the verse presently in question, indicates that without the Spirit a person does not avoid the works of the flesh, which will prevent the inheriting of God's kingdom. The third presupposition, that there is no forgiveness of transgression, is put wrongly; rather, Paul adopts the earlier Christian view that Jesus' vicarious death (therefore not our obedience to the law) takes care of transgression; and he does not leave this presupposition unstated (see Gal 3,13; cf. Rom 3,23-25; 4,25; 5,6-10; 1 Cor 15,3; 2 Cor 5,21; Gal 1,4). Thus the "middle terms" *are* stated by Paul; and for *his* theology it makes no difference whether or not they can be found in contemporary Jewish literature. As Sanders does not deny, the fourth pre-supposition, that accepting the law necessarily leads to being cursed, appears in the text (Gal 3,10). It stands fast, then, that Gal 5,3 confirms the necessity and failure to keep the whole law as a main feature of Paul's argument for justification by faith alone.

Paul twists the screw harder by saying that the law actually increases sin (Gal 3,19.22; Rom 5,20; 6,15-16; 7,5-6.7-25, esp. 13; 11,32). Since Sanders does not dispute the point, but affirms it,[41] we have only to ask how he can deny that the unfulfillability of the law poses a major problem to Paul. Why does Paul attempt this tour de force of saying the law *increases* sin if not even inability to keep it perfectly troubles him? It appears that the twin pillars of human weakness and salvation-history, not just salvation-history, uphold justification by faith alone. To counter that Paul's thinking runs from the solution in Christ to the human plight, so that Paul's anthropology is only a reflex effect of his Christian soteriology,[42] makes the strength of his empha-sis on the lordship of sin using the law and the pathos in his description of life under that lordship hard to explain adequately. Sanders does not appre-ciate these problems enough, but emphasizes corresponding problems in seeing a development from plight to solution.[43] We should call in question that there was any development, in either direction. The problems suggest that Paul thought simultaneously rather than consecutively of plight and solution.

But as Paul's soteriology needs balancing by the lordship of sin in his thinking, so the lordship of sin needs balancing by the forensic meaning of justification and the concept of sin as guilt which that meaning implies. As is popular to do nowadays, Sanders stresses the power of sin more than the guilt of sin as the quintessence of Paul's hamartiology[44]; thus justification denotes transferral from sin's lordship to Christ's lordship more than an exchange of guilt and righteousness between the believer and Christ.[45] But in Galatians Paul introduces justification as the solution to the problem of transgressions, which cause the law to bring a curse. Only then does bondage come into his discussion; and even so, primarily bondage to false religion (4,1-10.21-5,1), only secondarily to sinning (3,22;5,17-21).[46] This pattern repeats itself in Romans: the problem of guilt comes first, reaching a climax in 3,19-23; forensic justification follows in 3,24-5,19; only later come the classic passages dealing with sin's lordship (5,20-8,17). See also 1 Cor 6,9-11; 2 Cor 5,21.

It is not satisfactory to pass off the earlier passages as merely traditional and undistinctive of Paul's thought. He spends too much papyrus on guilt and on its replacement with Christ's righteousness. Sanders rightly calls attention to the possibility of substituting "life" and "Spirit" for "righteousness" in Rom 6,16; Gal 3,3.6.21.[47] But this possibility in no way negates or scales down the forensic element. Since union with Christ makes possible the exchange of guilt and righteousness (see esp. Phil 3,7-11), Paul naturally mixes the forensic benefit of that union, "righteousness", with other benefits (cf. the mixture of forensic language, "one died for all", with participatory language, "therefore all died", in 2 Cor 5,14). Furthermore, since death is the penalty for sin (Rom 5,12-21; 6,15-23), it is only natural that Paul should associate life in the Spirit, who gives life, with the forensic negation of that penalty (Rom 8,1-2). The benefits of union with Christ are not equivalent to each other; they accompany each other and are distinguished from each other (cf. Rom 5,17-21; 8,1-11).

Sanders objects that even in Rom 1,18-3,23 Paul does not reach the conclusion "guilty"; rather, "under sin" (3,9).[48] But how can we read about the inexcusability of pagans in the latter half of chap. 1, about the inexcusability of Jews in chap. 2, about the accountability of Jews and pagans alike in 3,19, and about propitiation or expiation in Christ's blood and the passing over of sins committed beforetime (3,25) without taking "under sin" as referring to sin that brings guilt as well as (or perhaps at this point in Romans, more than) sin that brings bondage?

Certainly, illegitimate sexual unions contradict union with Christ (1 Cor 6,12-20; 10,1-22). But Paul warns against other sins which by their nature have nothing to do with union (e.g., thievery, covetousness, drunkenness, reviling, and rapaciousness in 1 Cor 6,10—the list could grow longer with additions from Gal 5,20-21 and other passages). And why should he be so concerned about the lordship of sin if not for the reason that sinning brings guilt? Otherwise not even certain sexual unions would contradict union with Christ. It is simply untrue to say Paul never presses his participatory language into the service of his juristic language as he sometimes presses his juristic language into the service of his participatory language (for the latter see Gal 3,21, where "righteousness" appears instead of the expected "life", and Rom 6,7, where "justified from sin" has the contextual meaning "set free from the domination of sin"). In Gal 5,16-24 participation in Christ and the Spirit serves the warning against the works of the flesh. The fact that Paul describes the contrasting fruit of the Spirit as that "against which there is no law" reveals a juristic frame of reference to which the language of walking by the Spirit and belonging to Christ is bent. Similarly, where union with Christ in Rom 6,1-11 would lead us to expect a recapitulation of that idea in v. 14, which supports the intervening exhortation (vv. 12-13), Paul is not content to stop with the statement, "For sin shall not lord it over you" (v. 14a), but locates the ultimate ground of his exhortation in a juristic theologoumenon: "for you are not under law, but under grace" (v. 14b). And instead of reading that in Christ there is liberation from the lordship of sin, as we would expect from Rom 7,7-25, we read in 8,1 the juristic statement that there is "no condemnation" to those who are in him.[49] Not till v. 2 does Paul write about liberation, but he immediately goes back to juristic language in the phrases "as a sin-offering", "condemned sin", "righteous ordinance of the law" (vv. 3-4). In short, the dynamics of union with Christ are pressed into the service of forensic justification as well as vice versa.[50]

But if juristic thinking marks Paul's theology deeply, why does he not write more about atonement, repentance, and forgiveness?[51] He may not write very much, and at least some of what he does write comes from early Christian tradition. But in addressing the already converted he can, in the main, assume that tradition. Atonement, repentance, and forgiveness need not be any the less foundational to his theology or important to his thinking for being traditional. (Sanders should be the first to grant the principle behind this statement, since in Palestinian Judaism the covenantal side of nomism admittedly gets little attention in the literature but, according to his interpretation, has fundamental importance).[52] In fact, when citing the tradition concerning Christ's death "for our sins" Paul describes the tradition "as of first importance" (1 Cor 15,3). Whether traditional or not, the statement concerning propitiation or expiation in Rom 3,25 comes at a crucial juncture in his argument, viz., at the point of transition from sin to justification. Paul hardly needs to cite a juristic tradition here if he is mainly concerned about the power, not the guilt, of sin. Furthermore, this juristic tradition, if tradition it is and not Paul's own words, agrees with his emphasis on the inexcusability of sin in 1,18-3,23[53]; with further statements in 4,7-8.25; 5,6-11; 8,3.32; 14,15 (most of which are obviously juristic and the rest of which are most naturally taken so); with his doctrines of the imputation of sin and, where there is faith, the imputation of righteousness in 5,12-19; and with his delaying a discussion of the lordship of sin till 5,21 and the following chapters. Even Sanders admits that the juristic statements in 2 Cor 5,11-21 belong to Paul.[54] When we add to these 1 Cor 5,7; 11,24-25; Gal 1,4; 2,20; 3,13; 1 Thess 5,10 (cf. Eph 2,13; Col 1,20), Paul's supposed lack of interest in the juristic value of Christ's death looks false. Two recent studies by H. Ridder-bos and J. D. G. Dunn strengthen this verdict.[55]

On the other hand, repentance and forgiveness, which are prominent in Palestinian Judaism, do not appear so often in Paul as atonement does (but see Rom 2,4-5; 4,6-8; 2 Cor 3,16; 7,9-10; 1 Thess 1,9-10). Why not? Sanders offers the reason: Paul was too interested in the problem of sin's lordship, for which repentance and forgiveness provide no solution but for which union with Christ and receiving his Spirit do provide a solution.[56] Here Sanders is partly right. Unlike faith, which has Christ as its object, repentance does not sound a Christological note. Nor does forgiveness in comparison with justifi-cation, which entails an exchange of guilt and righteousness between the believer and Christ. But Sanders misses the boat in thinking Paul favored the Christologically oriented terms and avoided the Judaistic terms purely for the dogmatic reason that Christianity is not Judaism. Rather, as we have seen, Paul so deeply felt the falling short of God's glory through sin that he did not think trying to keep the law, *let alone repenting to receive forgiveness for failure to keep it*, adequate. The more the law abets sin's lordship because of human weakness, the less adequate is repentance to take care of guilt; *for repentance implies a change of behavior.*

For this same reason Paul cannot ascribe atoning value to good works. Juristically, Christ's self-sacrifice makes them unnecessary and, by compari-son, inferior. Dynamically, sin's lordship, exercised through the law, frus-trates efforts to keep the law well enough to make atonement. Despite his very full discussions of atonement by good works in Palestinian Judaism,[57] Sanders neglects to emphasize how differently Paul thinks of atonement. This neglect grows out of a mistaken belief that Paul has little concern over the question of guilt. A greater appreciation of just such a concern enables us to understand his rejection of Judaism better.

Even Paul, however, says that in the end people will be judged according to their works. Sanders, citing Rom 2,12-16; 11,22; 14,10; 1 Cor 3,10-13; 4,2-5; 6,9-10; 10,21; 11,29-32; 2 Cor 5,8-10; Gal 5,21, uses such statements to argue that on the question of staying in Paul holds fast the Jewish mode of thinking, according to which avoiding evil works and doing good works are the condi-tion of staying in, but do not earn salvation.[58] "The point is that God *saves* by grace, but that *within* the framework established by grace he rewards good deeds and punishes transgression".[59]

But we cannot afford to let this apparent similarity between Paul and Palestinian Judaism go unscrutinized. Again it is necessary to recall that Paul's phrase "from faith to faith" (Rom 1,17) means that salvation continues as well as starts on the principle of faith alone, which, as Paul makes clear, excludes works (see Rom 4,4-5 for the most explicit statement; cf. 11,17-22). And we have already noted that his letter to the Galatians, which emphasizes faith instead of works, deals more with staying in than with getting in. So we have to ask whether in Paul's doctrine of judgment according to works synergism has watered down the doctrine of grace or whether the danger is false profession (so that loss of salvation is only apparent) rather than the negating of a salvation genuinely received. The evidence Sanders cites from Palestinian Jewish literature shows overwhelmingly that good works are a condition as well as a sign of staying in. It appears, however, that for Paul good works are only (but not unimportantly) a sign of staying in, faith being the necessary and sufficient condition of staying in as well as of getting in. He expresses his thought unambiguously in 2 Cor 13,5: "Test yourselves whether you are in the faith". "Test yourselves" points to evidence rather than means. Paul goes on to talk of doing good and not evil (v. 7). Thus good works are a way of proving the genuineness of salvation.

Contrastingly, the rabbis make varying and sometimes contradictory statements about merit and the weighing of fulfillments and transgressions at the last judgment.[60] Sanders takes these statements as unsystematically hortatory rather than as contrary to grace. Even so, the rabbis' mixing of merit-language and grace-language makes synergism an applicable designation and stands in sharp opposition to Paul's avoiding all talk of merit, indeed, denying merit outright.

Everyone recognizes that judgment according to works provides Paul a basis of exhortation, and that his affirmations of justification by faith, not by works, are theological, even polemically so. But his waxing polemical on the doctrine casts a shadow on Sanders' insistence that works-righteousness in Palestinian Judaism was only a hortatory device, not a soteriological principle as well. Paul had been a zealous proponent of Palestinian Judaism. His statements not only comment on others in Palestinian Judaism, but also reflect on the nature of his own participation in it (Gal 1,13-14). To be sure, he converted to Christianity; but conversion does not necessarily blind a person to past realities; so we are not at liberty to say Paul miscontrued his own experience of Judaism.[61]

It is hard to imagine Paul as engaging in the careful attempts to define the commandments exactly and, further, to "build a fence" around them by adding regulations in order to keep people from even coming close to breaking them.[62] Sanders interprets such attempts on the part of the rabbis as growing out of sincere desire to please God. Well and good. But Paul's failure to follow the rabbinic pattern reveals a world of difference between him and the rabbis: they show much more confidence in human nature than he does.[63] His dependence on the Holy Spirit relates to this malism and forestalls the need for scholastic definition and protection of the commandments.

Sanders tries to counteract a relatively sanguine estimate of human nature in Palestinian Judaism by stressing the language of unworthiness and dependence on God's grace that we find especially in Jewish prayers *to* God, as opposed to descriptions *of* God, where the language of justice, reward, and punishment prevails.[64] But Paul characteristically stresses God's grace in speaking *of* him. Furthermore, in the literature of Palestinian Judaism the people of God are typically called "the pious" and "the righteous"—terms that point to good conduct; but in Paul's letters, "the believers", "the called", and "the saints"—terms that reflect God's grace.[65] Despite some formal similarities, then, Paul and Palestinian Judaism look materially different at the point of grace and works.[66]

We may conclude that Paul rejected Judaism and Judaistic Christianity not only because of a conviction that God had revealed His Son Jesus in him (Gal 1,15-16)—after all, he could have preached Christ as the messianic establisher of the law—but also because of a conviction that works-righteousness lay at the heart of Judaism and Judaistic Christianity and that it would corrupt what he had come to believe concerning God's grace in Jesus Christ.[67]

Notes

[1] (Fortress Press, Philadelphia 1983).

[2] *PPJ*, 543.

[3] See, e.g., *PPJ*, 236.

[4] SANDERS, *PLJP, 112;* see again *PPJ*, 543, and almost identical statements on pp. 517, 518; also *PLJP*, 10. SANDERS' statement that Paul opposes obeying the law as the condition of remaining among the elect ("Paul's Attitude Toward the Jewish People", *USQR* 33 [1978] 184) seems to contradict these other, repeated statements.

[5] SANDERS, *PLJP*, 17-20. Sanders describes the point as "absolutely vital".

[6] Cf. K. T. COOPER, "Paul and Rabbinic Soteriology", *WTJ* 44 (1982) 137; and the comments on a different but related topic by E. SYNOFZIK, *Die Gerichts- und Vergeltungsaussagen bei Paulus* (Göttinger Theologische Arbeiten 8; Göttingen 1977) 59-61. Sanders does not believe, of course, that "faith stopped functioning after entry" (*PLJP*, 114). In a letter to me dated Dec. 3, 1981, he says, "I need to sharpen the formulation and clarify the point... I did not intend to imply that 'entry' is only momentary. There is nevertheless a distinction between an entry requirement (what is necessary in order to be considered a member *at all*) and behavioural requirements within the group. Circumcision, I think, is the former in the Galatians debate. When considered in the latter category, it is a matter of indifference (*Gal. 6.15;* I Cor. 7.19), as are 'days' and food (Rom. 14.1-6)". These words and longer statements in *PLJP*, 20, 52 (n. 20), 159, represent a basic shift rather than the sharpening and clarification of an original point. For it used to be in Sanders' view that getting in was solely by God's elective grace in both Paul and Palestinian Judaism. Now Sanders is saying that getting in requires circumcision in Palestinian Judaism and among Christian Judaizers; otherwise a person cannot be considered a member at all. It used to be in Sanders' view that for both Paul and Palestinian Judaism, keeping the law was only the means of staying in. Now Sanders is saying that at least one aspect of keeping the law— viz., submitting to circumcision—is a means of getting in for Palestinian Judaism and Christian Judaizers, whereas Paul goes in the opposite direction by making circumcision a matter of indifference. It seems that the fundamental and original thesis that Paul and Palestinian Judaism were at one on getting in by grace and staying in by obeying the law has broken down. In effect, Sanders now admits that Jews and Judaizers were synergists on the topic of getting in, and that at least on the question of circumcision Paul was not a synergist even with respect to staying in, let alone with respect to getting in.

[7] SANDERS, *PPJ*, 206-212; cf. 85-101.

[8] Cf. E. JÜNGEL, *Paulus and Jesus* (Tübingen [3]1967) 66-70. We may partly agree with Sanders that in Paul "good deeds are the *condition* of remaining 'in', but they do not *earn* salvation" (*PPJ*, 517; IDEM, *PLJP*, 114). On the other hand, the condition must be evidential rather than instrumental if it is to stand beside Paul's much stronger emphasis on staying in by faith, not by works.

[9] So SANDERS' understanding of Paul (*PPJ*, 550-552 *et passim*; IDEM, *PLJP*, 27, 47). He stresses Paul's "exclusivist soteriology" so one-sidedly that he thinks Paul's own, emphatic, and extended formulation "by faith and not by works... actually misstates the fundamental point of disagreement [with Judaism and Judaizing]" (*PPJ*, 551).

[10] SANDERS, *PLJP*, 85-86 (his italics); so also 47.

[11] Paul does not, however, carefully and consciously distinguish the revisions. See the well-balanced comments by SANDERS, *PLJP*, 97-105.

[12] SANDERS, *PPJ*, 550.

[13] SANDERS, *PLJP*, 140.

[14] SANDERS, *PLJP*, 44.

[15] SANDERS, *PLJP*, 33-34. Sanders notes the expressions "law of works" (3,27) and "the one who works" (4,4), but by-passes them in favor of expressions concerning status: "Jews" (3,29); "the circumcision" (3,30; 4,9.12); "those of the law" (4,14.16). Yet the textual data require a both-and rather than an either-or.

[16] SANDERS, *PLJP*, 46.

[17] SANDERS, *PLJP*, 33-34.

[18] SANDERS, *PPJ*, 550-551 ("He [Paul] simply saw the old dispensation as worthless in comparison with the new"); IDEM, *PLJP*, 140-141.

[19] SANDERS, *PLJP*, 36-38; cf. N. T. WRIGHT, "The Paul of History and the Apostle of Faith", *TynBul* 29 (1978) 82-83.

[20] SANDERS, *PLJP*, 42.

[21] SANDERS, *PLJP*, 42.

[22] SANDERS' strongest argument against this understanding—viz., the argument that Phil 3,6.9 shows righteousness by the law to be attainable (*PLJP*, 43-45)—rests on failure to recognize that Paul there speaks from the standpoint of a false human estimate: "If anyone else *thinks*... I more" (v. 4b). He is not implying that except for the better righteousness in Christ, God would have been satisfied with Paul's righteousness. Paul's rhetorical contest with the Judaizers determines his taking the standpoint of a false human estimate. Against Sanders, understanding "my righteousness" as "my individual righteousness" does not depend on a conflation with Rom 3,27; 4,2; for right within Philippians 3 the phrases "according to [the] law, a Pharisee; according to zeal, persecuting the church; according to the righteousness in [the] law, having become blameless" point to individual performance alongside Jewish status. Sanders admits as much in his statement, "Paul says that his former confidence in the flesh was partly in status... and partly in accomplishment..." (*PLJP*, 44).

[23] See the pages cited under "Atonement" in the subject-index of *PPJ*.

[24] See W. L. LANE, "Paul's Legacy from Pharisaism: Light from the Psalms of Solomon", *Concordia Journal* 8 (1982) 130-138.

[25] See U. WILCKENS, *Rechtfertigung als Freiheit* (Neukirchen-Vluyn 1974) 79-84.

[26] WRIGHT, "The Paul of History and the Apostle of Faith", 82.

[27] SANDERS, *PLJP*, 32-35; Wright, "The Paul of History and the Apostle of Faith", 82.

[28] SANDERS, *PLJP*, 35-36; cf. 123-135.

[29] SANDERS, *PPJ*, 490-491; cf. IDEM, *PLJP*, 29-30 *et passim*.

[30] SANDERS, *PPJ*, 496.

[31] For a full discussion, see R. H. GUNDRY, "The Moral Frustration of Paul Before His Conversion: Sexual Lust in Romans 7:7-25", *Pauline Studies* (Essays presented to Professor F. F. Bruce; ed. D. A. HAGNER and M. J. HARRIS; Grand Rapids 1980) 228-245. This discussion includes a consideration of Acts 22,3; Gal 1,13; and especially Phil 3,4-6, which implies only that it is possible to keep the law perfectly from the standpoint of outward observance, not that it is possible to be sinlessly perfect in obedience to the law (pp. 233-234).

[32] SANDERS, *PLJP*, 76-81, 124.

[33] SANDERS, *PPJ*, 483; cf. IDEM, *PLJP*, 17-27.

[34] SANDERS, "On the Question of Fulfilling the Law", 105-106; cf. IDEM, *PLJP*, 152.

[35] SANDERS, *PLJP*, 20-22.

[36] Cf. D. J. MOO, " 'Law,' 'Works of the Law,' and Legalism in Paul", *WTJ* 45 (1983) 90-99.

[37] See HÜBNER, *Das Gesetz bei Paulus* (FRLANT 119; Göttingen 1978) 39-42, though his explanation that "quantitative Erfüllung ist nicht möglich, weil die Torah Bestimmunger besitzt, die 'qualitativ erfüllt' werden müssen" does not carry conviction.

[38] See U. WILCKENS, "Zur Entwicklung des paulinischen Gesetzverständnisses", *NTS* 28 (1982) 166-169 et passim; IDEM, *Rechtfertigung als Freiheit*, 84-94; IDEM, *Der Brief an die Römer* (EKK 6/1; Köln/Neukirchen-Vluyn 1978) 93, 178-180, 201, 233-243. Despite the criticisms of G. KLEIN, "Sündenverständnis und theologia crucis bei Paulus", *Theologia Crucis—Signum Crucis* (FS E. Dinkler; ed. C. ANDRESEN and G. KLEIN; Tübingen 1979) 249-282, Wilckens is correct in seeing the importance of concrete transgressions in Paul's thought.

[39] SANDERS, *PLJP*, 27.

[40] SANDERS, *PLJP*, 27 (his italics).

[41] SANDERS, *PLJP*, 70-71. HÜBNER, *Das Gesetz bei Paulus*, 71-76, (cf. WILCKENS, "Zur Entwicklung...", 182-183), does dispute the point so far as Romans is concerned. His strongest argument—viz., that the singular of τό παράπτωμα, "the transgression", in Rom 5,20 points away from increased sinning on the part of individual human beings and toward an increase in the transsubjective rule of sin—comes to grief in chap. 6, where the transsubjective rule of sin works out in individual sinning (see, e.g., the exhortation in v. 12: "Therefore do not let sin reign in your mortal body with the result of obeying its lusts [plural!]").

[42] SANDERS, *PPJ*, 442-447, 474-511; IDEM, *PLJP*, 68, 125. RÄISÄNEN, "Legalism and Salvation", *Die paulinische Literatur und Theologie* (ed. S. Pedersen; Teologiske Studier 7; Aarhus/Göttingen 1980) 69, singles out Gal 2,21 as the strongest support for the view that Paul rejected the law for a Christological rather than an anthropological reason; but P. GARNET, "Qumran Light on Pauline Soteriology", *Pauline Studies*, 29-31, points to a slightly earlier statement in Gal 2,15 as indicating that the human problem precedes the Christological solution. For a modern example of psychological turmoil over failure to keep the law perfectly, see the autobiographical statement of the Jewish scholar E. RIVKIN in his book *A Hidden Revolution: The Pharisees' Search for the Kingdom Within* (Nashville 1978) 22.

[43] SANDERS, *PLJP*, 68-70, 81, 138, 149-154. It is hard to understand why Sanders thinks the universality of sin implies that Paul thought backwards, from solution to plight. Why could not Paul have thought that since all need salvation, Christ came to save all? According to Gal 2,15-16, SANDERS argues, Paul "knows full well that observant Jews are not in fact sinners by the biblical standard" (*PLJP*, 68, in reference to Paul's mentioning "Jews" who are "not sinners from [the] Gentiles"). But because of the contrast with "Jews", the term "Gentiles" rather than the phrase "not sinners" receives the emphasis, as is confirmed by the emphatic position of ἐξ ἐθνῶν before ἁμαρτωλοί, against normal word order. Paul's formal use of the Jewish epithet "sinners" for Gentiles does not imply that he did not regard Jews, too, as sinful (cf. Rom 2,1-3,24; 7,7-25). We may appreciate, even endorse, SANDERS' argument for rhetorical exaggeration in Rom 1,18-3,23; 7,7-25 (see *PLJP*, 123-135). But his deduction that such exaggeration is due to Paul's moving from solution to plight does not follow. We might equally well say that Paul uses rhetorical exaggeration because of his preoccupation with the human plight. In fact, such a view would make it easier to understand the rhetorical flights, which gain rather than lose pathos in the hyperbole Paul uses.

[44] Much modern psychology views guilt as an incapacitating complex. Though this view may have alerted us to sin as an incapacitating power in Paul's theology, it may also have dulled many of us to sin as objective guilt in his theology. Adding moral relativism to such a psychological view of sin insures a theological devaluation of objective guilt. This devaluation carries with itself, of course, a corresponding devaluation of the propitiatory or expiatory value of Jesus' death. To the extent psychology is a natural science it is merely descriptive and lacks the capacity to address moral questions.

⁴⁵ SANDERS, "Patterns of Religion", 470-474; IDEM, *PPJ*, 502-508.

⁴⁶ Against SANDERS, "Patterns of Religion in Paul and Rabbinic Judaism: A Holistic Method of Comparison," *HTR* 66 (1973) 478.

⁴⁷ SANDERS, "Patterns of Religion", 470-474.

⁴⁸ SANDERS, *PPJ*, 503.

⁴⁹ Rom 8,1 harks back to Rom 5,16.18, where κατάκριμα does not refer to the lordship of sin over conduct, but to the sentence of death and its execution because of the one sin of Adam. In 8,1, then, Paul is reminding his readers of the reversal for those who are in Christ Jesus of the condemnation they had in Adam. The argument that "condemned sin" in 8,3-4 means "broke the power of sin in human conduct", because the condemnation was something the law could not do whereas the law certainly could, and did, condemn sin in the sense of pronouncing judicial sentence against it—this argument overlooks the possibility that the inability of the law has its counterpart, not in God's condemning sin in the flesh, but in the ἵνα-clause concerning the fulfillment of the righteous ordinance of the law. God's condemning sin in the flesh would then lay the juristic foundation for the superstructure of freedom from sin's lordship.

The argument that the inferential ἄρα, "then", in v. 1 relates "condemnation" to the preceding discussion of sin's lordship rather than to guilt is overrated. We can see a tight connection drawn with the preceding context by ἄρα οὖν, "therefore then", in 7,25. But here in 8,1 Paul drops οὖν. As a result, ἄρα draws only a loose connection, probably with earlier discussions of forensic justification, especially the one in chap. 5, the only preceding passage in Romans where κατάκριμα has occurred. The γάρ-clause in v. 2 does indeed talk of deliverance from sin's lordship (described in 7,7-25). In so doing it does not define "condemnation" in v. 1; rather, it makes deliverance from sin's lordship a sign or evidence of the judicial pronouncement "no condemnation". The γάρ-clause in v. 3 starts with the same purpose, but returns in its second half to the judicial aspect, grounded in Jesus' sacrifice for sin.

God's sending his son in the likeness of sinful flesh and as a sin-offering defines God's condemning sin in the flesh much more easily (these expressions all occur in the same clause in relation to each other) than does the subsequent ἵνα-clause concerning the fulfillment of the righteous ordinance of the law. That fulfillment gives the purpose, not the definition, of God's condemning sin in the flesh and makes up for the inability of the law. Some commentators, admitting the well-known use of περὶ ἁμαρτίας for "sin-offering" in the LXX, shy away from it here with a generalizing interpretation which they fail to support with counter-evidence. The phrase is so frequent in the LXX for sin-offerings, however, that we need powerful reasons not to accept this meaning in Rom 8,3. The bond between "condemned sin in the flesh" and περὶ ἁμαρτίας gives us a positive reason to accept it (cf. 2 Cor 5,21); a general meaning "for sin" or "to deal with sin" would be superfluous in the context. Therefore, eliminating v. 1 (usually along with 7,25a) as an alien juristic gloss does not leave the way clear to see only a discussion of liberation from sin's power and to deny a reminder of liberation from the guilt of sin (against R. BULTMANN, *Exegetica* [Tübingen 1967] 279, and others in his wake; cf. H. HÜBNER'S complaint ["Pauli Theologiae Proprium", *NTS* 26 (1980) 468-469] that Sanders separates the juristic and the participatory too much).

⁵⁰ Therefore it is hard to accept Sanders' waving aside 1 Cor 6,9-11, which he recognizes to be non-participatory, as hortatory (*PPJ*, 498, 500). It would be truer to say that the levitical and juristic language of the passage provides the firm foundation of Paul's exhortation.

⁵¹ SANDERS, *PPJ*, 497-508.

⁵² See esp. the response to Neusner in SANDERS, "Puzzling Out Rabbinic Judaism", *Approaches to Ancient Judaism* (ed. W. S. Green; Brown Judaic Studies 9; Chico, CA 1980) 2, 72-73; also IDEM, *PPJ*, 234-237, 420-421.

⁵³ The point stands whether or not we accept Sanders' thesis that much of Rom 1,18-3,23 stems from Jewish homiletical tradition, for Paul would at least be using such tradition to stress the inexcusability of sin.

⁵⁴ SANDERS, *PPJ*, 502-503.

⁵⁵ H. RIDDERBOS, "The Earliest Confession of the Atonement in Paul", and J. D. G. DUNN, "Paul's Understanding of the Death of Jesus", both in *Reconciliation and Hope* (NT Essays on

Atonement and Eschatology presented to L. L. Morris; ed. R. BANKS; Grand Rapids 1974) 76-89, 125-141. See also R. H. GUNDRY, Sōma *in Biblical Theology* (SNTSMS 29; Cambridge 1976) 204-216; P. STUHLMACHER, "Achtzehn Thesen zur paulinischen Kreuzestheologie", *Rechtfertigung* (FS E. Käsemann; ed. J. FRIEDRICH *et al.*; Tübingen/Göttingen 1976) 512-514; IDEM, "Zur paulinische Christologie", *ZTK* 74 (1977) 455-460. S. KIM, *The Origin of Paul's Gospel* (WUNT 2/4; Tübingen 1981) 276-277, n. 3, criticizes Dunn for playing down the penal, substitutionary character of Jesus' death in Paul's theology after having presented good evidence for it.

[56] SANDERS, "Patterns of Religion", 468-469; IDEM, *PPJ*, 499-501, 507, 549-551.

[57] See "Atonement" in the subject-index of *PPJ*. With regard to Paul's view of staying in, SANDERS thinks 1 Cor 3,5-4,6; 5,1-5; 11,27-34; and 2 Cor 12,21 indicate a belief in atonement through repentance and the suffering of punishment by the Christian who has sinned (*PLJP*, 107-109). But Paul does not use the language of atonement in these passages, only that of discipline; the language of atonement he reserves for Christ's death alone.

[58] SANDERS, *PPJ*, 515-518; IDEM, *PLJP*, 113-114. See also *PLJP*, 123-135, esp. 125-126, for a retraction of Rom 2,12-16 from this point.

[59] SANDERS, *PPJ*, 543; cf. K. P. DONFRIED, "Justification and Last Judgment in Paul", *ZNW* 67 (1976) 92-103.

[60] SANDERS, *PPJ*, 125-147.

[61] For merit theology in Palestinian Judaism, see D. A. CARSON, *Divine Sovereignty and Human Responsibility* (Atlanta 1981) 49-53, 68-74, 78 (in part), 89-92, 104-121.

[62] Cf. SANDERS, *PLJP*, 95-96, 106-107. Saldarini, *JBL* 98 [1979] 300, notes that "halaka is not derived from covenant in any concrete way in Tannaitic literature; it is itself central and primary". As a result of the rabbis' preoccupation with legal minutiae, CAIRD wonders whether their religion "was not *in toto* at the third remove from principles which are central to Christian theology" (*JTS* ns 29 [1978] 539).

[63] See CARSON, *Divine Sovereignty*, 92-93.

[64] See, e.g., SANDERS, *PPJ*, 395.

[65] "The saints" emphasizes divine consecration rather than holy living, though, of course, holy living stems from such consecration. Presumably Paul might have used the Jewish terms, too, had they not in his view become overlaid with legalistic connotations. The QL forms a partial exception to typical Jewish usage (see G. L. CARR, "The Provenance of the Term 'Saints': A *religionsgeschichtliche* Study", *JETS* 24 [1981] 107-116).

[66] This judgment runs opposite that of M. D. HOOKER, "Paul and 'Covenantal Nomism' ", *Paul and Paulinism* (Essays in honour of C. K. Barrett; ed. M. D. HOOKER and S. G. WILSON; London 1982) 47-56. She agrees with Sanders that Paul and Palestinian Judaism look similar at the point of grace and works, and uses that agreement to argue against Sanders that the patterns of religion therefore look similar despite the intrusion of Paul's "participation theology".

[67] Of course, Paul did not think that by becoming a Christian he had departed from his ancestral religion as represented in the OT and in the remnant of grace (see esp. Rom 11). Nor did he think it wrong to practice Judaism apart from an attempt to establish one's standing before God (see esp. 1 Cor 9,20; Rom 14). But the great autobiographical reversal Paul details in Gal 1,13-14; Phil 3,4-9 and his battle against the Judaizers show it is appropriate to speak of his getting out of Judaism. For present purposes it has not seemed necessary to discuss the question whether or not justification by faith is the center of Paul's theology (see R. Y. K. FUNG, "The Status of Justification by Faith in Paul's Thought: A Brief Survey of a Modern Debate", *Themelios* 6 [3, 1981] 4-11).

My thanks to Sanders for graciously and voluntarily sending a manuscript of *PLJP* long before its publication.

JESUS AND THE AUTHORITY OF THE MOSAIC LAW

DOUGLAS J. MOO
Associate Professor of New Testament
Trinity Evangelical Divinity School

Article from *Journal for the Study of the New Testament*

The question of the relevance of the Mosaic law for Christian ethics, a perennial theological issue, has assumed new importance with the popularity of relativistic ethics, the 'new morality'. Proponents of this approach generally reject any appeal to moral 'rules', including especially those found in the OT. On the other hand, sometimes in response to this approach, others stress the eternal and absolute validity of at least the OT 'moral' law. The debate has focused attention on the teaching and example of Jesus, to which both sides appeal for support. And an initial glance at Jesus' teaching would seem to provide support for both alternatives. This article surveys some relevant aspects of Jesus' life and teaching in the hope of discovering his fundamental approach to the issue of the authority of the Mosaic law for his followers.

The breadth and complexity of the topic may make this project appear to be overly ambitious. While acknowledging the problem, the study is, I think, manageable, granted the following limitations. First, the discussion will be confined to the synoptic gospels. This should not be taken to imply an *a priori* rejection of the historical value of material within the fourth gospel, but is simply to recognize that study of the synoptic and Johannine traditions demands different methodologies. Second, while some necessary reference to the history of the traditions studied will be made, the focus of the study will be on the final, canonical shape of the Jesus tradition. The validity and importance of such a focus is being increasingly recognized. It is only by careful exegetical examination of the extant material in its context that the degree of coherence within the tradition, so important in making *traditionsgeschichtlich* decisions, can be assessed. This is not to deny the need to take into consideration the perspective each evangelist brings to bear on the material. Again, however, the study is not primarily devoted to a delineation of the evangelists' theologies. A final limitation relates to the focus of the discussion. 'Jesus and the law' is a many-faceted topic involving, potentially, Jesus' attitude toward the oral law and the various forms of Jewish piety. Our investigation will be confined to the single question: to what extent and in what manner did Jesus conceive the Mosaic law to be binding on people who had entered the Kingdom of God?

Before proceeding to an analysis of the relevant passages, it will be helpful to outline briefly some representative positions on the question of Jesus' relationship to the law. While a bewildering variety of views, with varying differences in detail, has been espoused, the following list adequately summarizes the main tendencies.

1. Jesus summarily abrogated the law. While requiring mention, this view is almost universally rejected by serious scholars.
2. Jesus' teaching is a new law, the Messianic law, which replaces the Mosaic law.[1]
3. Jesus is the last and greatest expositor of the law of God. He entirely upholds the moral law, showing complete obedience to its demands in his own life, and demonstrating in his teaching the original intent of the law's demands.[2]
4. Jesus 'radicalized' the law, intensifying the demands of the law beyond what they originally included. This 'Toraverscharfung', carried out on the basis of Jesus' immediate awareness of the will of God[3] and/or the paramount demand of love,[4] results in the abrogation of some commands.[5]
5. Jesus intensified the requirements of the law and brought new demands of his own, without, however, clearly abrogating any moral commands.[6]
6. Jesus' teaching *fulfills* the law, in the sense that the law pointed forward to his teaching. His demands move in a different sphere, above and apart from the law, whose continuing validity exists only in and through him.[7]

This general survey enables us to isolate several key questions which are crucial for our purposes. First, what does Jesus' own behavior imply about his view of the law? Second, did Jesus establish a critical principle(s) by which the validity and meaning of the Mosaic commands could be evaluated? Third, what was the place of the Old Testament in Jesus' ethical teaching? Fourth, did Jesus, in fact, implicitly or explicitly teach the abrogation of any commandment? Fifth, what did Jesus claim would be the effect on the law of his coming? These questions furnish the outline for the study.

Jesus' Personal Observance of the Law

Robert Banks, in the most important modern treatment of Jesus and the law, correctly stresses the need to distinguish among the written law, the oral law and customs in assessing Jesus' relationship to the Judaism of his day.[8] With respect to the written law, it cannot be demonstrated that Jesus personally violated any of its commands.[9] He is seen in attendance at the great festivals in Jerusalem, pays the half-shekel temple tax (Mt. 17.24-27), wears the pre-scribed tassel on his robe (Mt. 9.20; cf. Num. 15.38-41) and, whatever may be said about his teaching on the subject of commands relating to the Sabbath and ritual purity, he does not transgress them.[10]

While it has been argued that Jesus displays an equal fidelity to the oral law,[11] it seems, on the contrary, that a clearer distinction can be made. His association with various 'impure' elements of society and his nonemergency Sabbath healings are rather clear infringements of the accepted *halaka*.[12] However, the verdict that there is no evidence Jesus kept *any* of the oral law cannot be sustained[13]; his regular attendance at synagogue services and his habits at meals and in prayer suggest behavior in conformity with, if not in obedience to, the oral law.[14] With respect to both the oral law and the customs of his day, Jesus' behavior seems to have been dictated more by the needs of the ministry than by a sense of subservience.[15]

That the synoptic tradition portrays a Jesus fundamentally subservient in his behavior to the written law is clear, but it is impossible to infer from this that Jesus wished his followers to observe it equally faithfully.[16] Apart from an obvious problem inherent in this argument (there is no evidence that Jesus was less faithful to the stipulations of the 'ceremonial' law than to the 'moral'), it suffers from a basic failure to recognize the place of Jesus' minis-try in the history of revelation. While Jesus' coming undoubtedly inaugu-rated a decisively new era in the *Heilsgeschichte*, the period of time before the culminative redemptive events of the Cross and Resurrection remains one of transition in which elements of the previous dispensation persist. Jesus' adherence to the written law *could* simply reflect an aspect of the old age which was destined to pass away in the new age.[17] Thus, the evidence from Jesus' personal observance of the law is, *taken by itself*, of almost no value for our purposes and, again, the need to determine Jesus' view of the role of the law in the new age is indicated.

Critical Principles for the Evaluation of Commands

It is frequently asserted that Jesus established love for others, or humanitar-ian considerations, as a principle on the basis of which the meaning and applicability of OT commands could be evaluated. The passage which most clearly suggests such an interpretation is the 'Great Commandment' peric-ope (Mt. 22.34-40; Mk 12.28-34; cf. Lk. 10.25-28). In response to the question of an inquirer, 'Which is the greatest commandment in the law?', Jesus cites two texts from the Pentateuch, which respectively command love for God (Dt. 6.5) and love for one's neighbor (Lev. 19.18). The conjunction of the commands clearly suggests that, for Jesus, love for God and for others are inseparable and *together* constitute the 'greatest' commandment (note par-ticularly Matthew's 'the second is like it').[18]

What is involved in establishing the double love commandment as the 'greatest' is explicated more fully in Jesus' concluding assertion (according to Mt.): 'on these two commandments depend [κρέμαται] all the law and the prophets'. The phrase 'law and prophets' is found only rarely in Jewish literature as a denotation of the OT Scriptures but is used with this meaning in the NT.[19] However, Matthew's use of the term here and in 5.17 and 7.12, clearly gives a particular nuance to the phrase, so that the 'commanding' or ethical aspect of the Scriptures is highlighted.[20] Crucial for the understanding of the relationship between the 'law and the prophets' and the love commandment is the meaning of the word κρεμάννυμι. The term is often compared with the Heb. tālui , which is used by the rabbis in formulations similar to that in the gospels.[21] But the purpose of the rabbis is to isolate a command or principle from which the rest of the law could be derived,[22] and this essentially scholastic exercise is foreign to the context in the gospels.[23] A second alternative is to view the love command as constituting the fundamental hermeneutical principle, which can serve to discriminate among the different Old Testament laws.[24] This approach, typical of relativistic ethics but by no means confined to it, is supported by reference to occasions on which Jesus allegedly treated the OT in just this manner. Perhaps the most important of these comes in Jesus' defense of his disciples' plucking and eating corn on the Sabbath. In response to Pharisaic objections to this behavior, Jesus cites the example of David and his followers, who broke the law by eating consecrated bread when they were 'hungry and in need' (Mk 2.25-26; Mt. 12:3-4; Lk. 6:3-4; cf. 1 Sam. 21.1-6). Many argue that Jesus here indicates the priority of human need over the ceremonial law.[25] But Jesus' disciples have not technically violated the ceremonial law—only the oral law—and there is no hint that the disciples were in any great need. Others suggest that Jesus is attempting to revise the overly stringent interpretation of the Sabbath among his fellow Jews,[26] but it is better to view the argument as more Christological than this. Jesus is suggesting a comparison between David and his followers and himself, David's 'Son' and his disciples. He is directing the attention of his critics away from the Sabbath issue to the larger issue: 'The Son of Man is Lord of the Sabbath' (Mk 2.28).[27] In any case, there is no indication that Jesus holds up humanitarian concern as a basis for disobeying the law.

Other passages are also cited as support for this approach to the OT law—Mk 2.27, Mt. 9.13 and 12.7, Mt. 7.12, Mt. 23.23—but none are at all decisive. The second interpretation of the love command suffers decisively, then, from lack of support elsewhere in Jesus' teaching. A third alternative would then seem to be necessary, according to which the role of the love commandment as denoted by κρεμάννυμι has been compared to the hinges of a door or the nail from which objects are suspended.[28] According to this analogy, the love commandment is set apart from all others as the most basic demand of the law, but does not displace any other commandments.[29]

In no instance are love or humanitarian concerns shown to effect the abrogation of a commandment; with respect to the Sabbath, concern for the fellow man was recognized as an important factor in the original promulgation of the commandment itself. For Jesus, it is not a question of the 'priority of love over law'[30] but of the priority of love *within* the law. Love is the greatest commandment, but it is not the *only* one; and the validity and applicability of other commandments can not be decided by appeal to its paramount demand.

The Place of the Old Testament in Jesus' Ethical Demands

Of perhaps the most direct relevance for the topic under consideration is the way in which Jesus employed the OT in his own ethical teaching. The nature of his application of the OT, while not necessarily normative, is nevertheless of great significance. However, the investigator who hopes to draw determinative conclusions from a study of this material is doomed to disappointment, for perhaps the most significant aspect of this topic is the paucity of references to the OT. Before discussing the significance of this fact it is necessary to examine the relevant texts.

A number of examples have already been introduced in the previous section. The fundamental demand of love is expressed by means of two OT commands, although the significance of this is mitigated by the fact that the question which led to these quotations was framed in terms of the OT.[31] Jesus appealed on three occasions to the prophetic tradition in order to highlight the need for inner obedience in addition to outward conformity to the law's demands (Hos. 6.6 in Mt. 9.13 and 12.7; Mic. 6.8 in Mt. 23.23). However, in view of the polemical contexts, it cannot be certainly concluded that Jesus is doing anything more than pointing out that his Jewish detractors' behavior is inconsistent with their own principles.

In the discussion about divorce common to Mark and Matthew (Mk 10.2-12; Mt. 19.3-12), Jesus appeals to Genesis 1.27 and 2.24 in order to correct the commonly accepted interpretation of Deuteronomy 24.1-4. This procedure is sometimes compared with the rabbinic practice of seeking to construe harmoniously two apparently conflicting statements in the law.[32] Yet this view does not take sufficient cognizance of the emphases in the text. While little should be made of the fact that the Deuteronomy quotation is attributed to *Moses* and the Genesis statement to *God*,[33] it is important to note that Jesus characterizes the legislation in Deuteronomy as having been given because of 'hardness of heart'.[34] Rather than harmonizing the passages, Jesus rather clearly suggests that the need for the Mosaic legislation arose from a new factor—human sinfulness. Further, it has been claimed that Jesus utilizes the Genesis account not as OT revelation *per se*, but as an indication of God's original purposes.[35] However, this is a distinction which is illegitimate and it is necessary to see in this incident an appeal to the will of God revealed in the OT as indicative of what is forever appropriate in the marriage relationship.

An undoubted example of an appeal to a Mosaic commandment in ethical debate is encountered in the narrative of the conflict over ritual defilement (Mk 7.1-23; Mt. 15.1-20). Jesus, in responding to the criticism that his disciples 'eat with unwashed hands', broadens the issue by launching an attack on the 'tradition of the elders'. The implications of this attack for Jesus' view of both the oral and written law will be considered in due course, but our interest here is in the fact that the tradition is criticized primarily because it has the effect of 'making void the word of God'. The portion of God's word at issue, the fifth commandment, is clearly held up as a norm applicable to the Jews, who are criticized for their failure to take it into consideration in the development of their tradition. Once again, all that can be definitely proved from this is that Jesus expected the Jews of his day to observe the commandments under which they lived.

Another incident in which the commandments of the decalogue play a role is the encounter between Jesus and a rich enquirer, who asks about the means of attaining eternal life (Mt. 19.16-22; Mk 10.17-22; Lk. 18.18-23). Jesus responds by quoting five of the ten commandments (Mark adds 'do not defraud', Matthew, 'you shall love your neighbor as yourself'). When the young man asserts that he has observed these, Jesus goes on to demand that he also sell all that he has and follow him. Although it is argued that these further demands are simply attempts to bring out the real meaning of the commandments in the case of this particular individual,[36] this interpretation must be rejected: while the command to 'sell all' might conceivably be construed as implied in the commandments, it is impossible to interpret the demand of discipleship ('follow me') in the same way. Clearly this climactic demand is something that goes well beyond any requirement of the OT.[37] Moreover, it may be that Jesus' citation of the commandments was simply a 'set-up,' intended to expose the man's shallowness in terms of his own religious framework and to pave the way for the enunciation of the really applicable demands.[38] This understanding of the citation is possible, but it is not certain that it should be accepted: it is perhaps better to view the decalogue commands as genuine, though incomplete, demands of discipleship.[39]

These references exhaust the evidence for Jesus' direct use of the OT in his ethical teaching (the 'antitheses' of Mt. 5 will be considered below). It is clear that they provide little support for the view that Jesus simply took over and applied the moral demands of the OT for the new age. Not only are Jesus' demands made, for the most part, independently of the OT, but those occasions on which the law is cited are exclusively polemical in character. However, it is illegitimate to conclude from this that Jesus saw no place for the OT in the ethics of the Kingdom, for it could be argued that Jesus simply *assumes* the relevance and acceptance of the OT demands in the Jewish context of his ministry. The independent authority on the basis of which Jesus formulated his ethical demand *is* obvious, however, and the next stage of our inquiry will illuminate that further.

Abrogation of Old Testament Commands?

In attempting to assess the applicability of OT commandments to Christian believers, it is important to determine whether Jesus abrogated any commandments. By 'abrogation' is meant the declaring invalid of the natural meaning of a commandment for the Christian dispensation. Put in this way, virtually all Christians at all times have accepted the abrogation of *some* OT commandments—those relating to the sacrifical system, for example. A more crucial question is whether the abrogation of commandments with a distinctly ethical thrust occurs.

Two matters in the dispute over ritual defilement require comment. We have seen that Jesus came to the defense of his disciples' transgression of the *halaka* concerning the washing of hands by criticizing the oral law as a whole for its effectual negation of Scriptural commands. As an example of this, Jesus cites the prevalent scribal interpretation according to which something declared *Corban*, dedicated to God, could not be used by anyone but its possessor. By insisting on the inviolability of the vow, the scribes were creating a situation in which parents could be legally denied the use of their children's possessions, a state of affairs Jesus viewed as a transgression of the fifth commandment. The *Corban* example is not directly relevant to the original point of dispute, but this issue is taken up at the end of the narrative, when Jesus solemnly announces to the crowd: 'there is nothing outside a man which by going into him can defile him; but the things which come out of a man are what defile him' (Mk 7.15; Mt. 15.11 is briefer, but makes the same point). Immediately afterward, Jesus reiterates the point privately to his disciples, in the course of which Mark parenthetically notes 'thus he declared all foods clean' (7.19b). This remark interprets Jesus as having effectively annulled the Levitical food laws, and this interpretation appears to be a legitimate conclusion from the principle enunciated in v. 15: 'Was er aber hier sagt muss die alten Reinheitsgesetze sprengen' ('What he says here must transcend the old laws of purity' [my translation]).[40]

The different elements in the pericope we have just been considering raise an important question: how can Jesus first appeal to the written law to castigate the scribal tradition (Mk 7.7-13), and then, if only implicitly, overturn part of that written law (v.15)?[41] Many would respond by advocating the need to observe a distinction between the moral and the ceremonial law.[42] It is claimed that such a distinction was unknown in Judaism and that it is thereby illegitimate to introduce this principle into Jesus' teaching on the law.[43] While it is true that a theoretical distinction of this sort was not made, there emerges, for instance in Philo and at Qumran, a *practical* differentiation of this nature. Jesus' appropriation of the prophetic emphasis on the need for *inner* obedience, his comment about 'the weightier matters', the elevation of the love command and his transformation of the Passover meal all suggest that he may have operated with a similar distinction.[44] Thus, while the evidence does not allow us to assume that Jesus and his hearers presupposed a clear and conscious demarcation between the moral and cermonial law, it is not illegitimate to find the seeds of this kind of a distinction in passages such as Mark 7.1-23. Ultimately, the basis for the acceptance or abrogation of laws lies elsewhere. As Cranfield, commenting on Mark 7, says, 'the key is rather that Jesus spoke as the one who is, and knew himself to be τέλος νόμου (Rom. x.4)'.[45]

The synoptic evangelists recount four conflicts between Jesus and various Jewish authorities over the observance of the Sabbath. Jesus' attitude toward the Sabbath and his justification of his own and his disciples' conduct is frequently cited as constituting an abrogation of the Sabbath command.[46] Basic to the decalogue Sabbath commandment is the prohibition of work. What precisely is meant by 'work' is not clearly defined in the OT, although there are indications that all types of normal activity were included.[47] As the Sabbath became increasingly important in post-exilic Judaism, the need was felt to define more clearly the kinds of activity prohibited, and this led to the development of the oral Sabbath law.[48] It appears that it was only this scribal tradition, not the written law, which Jesus and the disciples violated.[49] The case for finding an abrogation of the written Sabbath law rests on the justifications given by Jesus for this activity. These justifications can be grouped into two types according to whether humanitarian or Christological concerns predominate.

The humanitarian arguments have already been dealt with in a previous section, but it must be asked whether Jesus' definition of what is allowed is somewhat broader than what the OT seems to indicate. Particularly significant is the fact that all the healings which Jesus performed on the Sabbath were nonemergency cases; indeed the duration of the illness is often stressed.[50] The synagogue ruler in Luke 13.14 objects to Jesus' performance of Sabbath healing. Jesus' reply is interesting in that he asserts that it was necessary (δεῖ) for the miracle to fall on the Sabbath (Lk. 13.16). This indicates that Jesus regarded the Sabbath as a particularly appropriate time for his ministry of healing and may represent a slight shift from the trend of the Old Testament Sabbath tradition. Nevertheless, Jesus' working of miracles stands in a unique category and too much can not be made of this.

In the second line of the argument Jesus highlights his own status as a means of justifying his disciples' Sabbath behavior. As we have argued, this is the point of the allusion to 1 Samuel 21.1-6 found in Mark 2.25-26 and parallels. A similar typological appeal to the OT is recorded by Matthew immediately after this (Mt. 12.5-6): if the priests who serve in the Temple on the Sabbath are innocent of wrong-doing (according to the rabbinic dictum that the 'Temple service takes precedence over the Sabbath'[51]), how much more innocent are the disciples, who are 'serving' Jesus, 'one greater than the Temple'?[52] Both of these allusions to the OT focus attention on the person of Christ, in whose service disobedience to the letter of the law can sometimes be justified. The third Christological argument is the climax of this approach: 'the Son of Man is Lord of the Sabbath' (Mt. 12.8; Mk 2.28; Lk. 6.5). It is impossible to understand this other than as an assertion of superiority over the Sabbath and, hence, of the authority to abrogate or transform the Sabbath law.[53] The significance of this claim must not be missed: as I. H. Marshall says, 'Jesus claims an authority tantamount to that of God with respect to the interpretation of the law'.[54] But while Jesus undoubtedly claimed this right, there is no evidence that he exercised it; the most that can be said is that his Sabbath healings 'stretch' the written Sabbath law. Whether the NT church acted on the authority inherent in Jesus' claim is a question that is not of legitimate concern here.[55]

The single most important passage in determining the relationship between Jesus and the law is undoubtedly Matthew 5.17-48. Inasmuch as Jesus' direct statements about the OT in vv. 17-19 are difficult to interpret and can be properly understood only in relation to vv. 21-48, it will be advantageous to consider the latter passage first.

Scholars are deeply divided over the nature of the relationship which is exhibited between the OT quotations and Jesus' demands.[56] It is proper that the antitheses be considered at this point in our discussion because most scholars hold that Jesus clearly abrogated commandments of the OT, but there is no agreement on which of the antitheses fall into this category. It will be necessary to examine each of them in turn, but first some comments should be made about the introductory formula all six have in common.

Although the introductory formulas are not identical, it is almost certain that they are all variations of a single basic formula, represented most fully in v. 21 and v. 33: ἠκούσατε ὅτι ἐρρέθη τοῖς ἀρχαίοις . . . ἐγὼ δὲ λέγω ὑ-μῖν. There has been some question about the meaning of the dative with ἀρχαίοις but it seems certain that it should be given a purely dative ('to the ancients') rather than an ablatival ('by the ancients') sense.[57] With this meaning, it is difficult to exclude some reference to the generation who received the law at Sinai,[58] although it should not be too quickly concluded that the *written* law only must thereby be involved; it was the Jewish belief that the *oral* law, too, was given at Sinai (cf. Abot 1.1-2).[59] Similarly, it is most natural to interpret 'you have heard' as a reference to the reading of the Scriptures in the synagogue,[60] but it should not be forgotten that the Scripture was usually read in interpreted ('targumized') form.[61] An important alternative to the view that the formula refers to the reading of the law in the synagogue is the possibility that Jesus is utilizing a standard rabbinic formula which was employed to contrast the teaching of one sage with another.[62] But this alternative must probably be discarded; the attestation for the formula is rather late, the Sermon presents anything but the academic milieu in which the rabbinic formula appears, and the Christological ἐγώ introduces a strongly distinctive element into the formula in Matthew 5.[63] Therefore it can be concluded that the formula used by Jesus suggests he is quoting the OT as it is usually heard by his audience. Whether that 'hearing' involved interpretative elements not properly a part of the text can be determined only by carefully studying the actual quotations and Jesus' response to them. One final point should be made: while it has become standard to label the six citations with Jesus' responses as 'antitheses', this term itself might represent an illegitmate assumption. The grammar allows at least three different nuances of translation: 'you have heard, but I (*in contrast to that*) say to you'; 'you have heard, and I (*In addition to that*) say to you'; 'you have heard, and I (*in agreement with that*) say to you'.[64]

It is generally agreed that no abrogation of the law occurs in the first two antitheses, but it is more difficult to determine whether Jesus is simply drawing out the actual meaning of the commands or whether he is *extending* their application. The numerous parallels to Jesus' teaching on anger and adultery in the OT and Jewish literature are frequently cited to prove that Jesus' demands would not be unfamiliar to his hearers.[65] But it is not clear that these sentiments were widely taught or accepted in Jesus' day,[66] nor do any of the parallels give evidence that such sentiments were derived from the sixth and seventh commandments. It is the *conjunction* of inner motive with the decalogue commandments that is distinctive to Jesus' demands.

But that Jesus understood this conjunction to be implied in the OT law, at least with respect to the sixth commandment, is shown, it is argued, by the clause quoted after the commandment. 'Whoever kills shall be liable to judgment' is often interpreted as a reference to a scribal tradition which prescribed punishment only for the outward deed and ignored the inner motive. Against this, Jesus associates anger with murder by prescribing the same punishment for each.[67] But this clause is more likely to be a representation of the OT laws pertaining to the punishment of the murderer.[68] The same point can be made if this is so, however: the error would then lie in the juxtaposing of the penalty for 'case law' with the general ethical principle, thereby suggesting an illegitimate restriction on the latter.[69]

Certainty on this question is almost impossible, but the apparent lack of evidence for the subsuming of anger and lust under the prohibitions of the decalogue might suggest that Jesus' interpretation does go beyond the legitimate intent of the law. Should we therefore speak, as do many, of the 'radicalization' or 'deepening' of the law in these first two antitheses? The difficulty with these descriptions is that they suppose Jesus is 'doing something to' the law, whereas this is not obvious. Rather it would appear that Jesus, with the emphatic 'but *I* say to you', enunciates principles neither derived from, nor intended to extend, the meaning of the laws quoted.[70]

In contrast to the first two antitheses, it is commonly asserted that in the third antithesis Jesus revokes the OT law concerning divorce.[71] In order to determine the validity of this assertion, it will be necessary to deal with several difficult questions and to take into consideration Jesus' teaching elsewhere on the question.

First, it is important to note that in none of the passages recording Jesus' teaching on divorce does he present the right of divorce as a Mosaic *command*. In Matthew 5.31, the quotation from Deuteronomy 24.1 presents the giving of the certificate of divorce as the command, and Mark 10.2-11 // Matthew 19.3-12 is in agreement with this.[72] Inasmuch as divorce is not *commanded* in Deuteronomy 24.1-4,[73] nor, indeed, anywhere in the OT, it is incorrect to speak of an abrogation of the divorce command.

Second, it is necessary to ask whether Jesus withdraws the *permission* of divorce granted by Moses. In Mark 10 and Luke 16.18, this would seem to be the case, for the prohibition of divorce appears to be absolute. According to Mark 10.5 (see also Mt. 19.8), Jesus views the Mosaic toleration of divorce as a concession to the people's stubborn insensibility to the divine will (= 'hardness of heart').[74] In contrast to this (δέ, v. 6) stands the original creation intention of God which, it would appear, Jesus seeks to restore and uphold (οὖν, v. 9).[75] This view can be defended in Mark, but it fails to explain the Matthean parallel. For the effect of the 'exception clause' (Mt. 19.9; cf. also Mt. 5.32) is to bring Jesus' teaching on the legitimacy of divorce into rather close agreement with that of the Deuteronomic legislation.[76] Indeed, this is often denied, it being argued on grammatical grounds that no exception exists in Matthew or that πορνεία, the basis for the exception, is significantly narrower in meaning than the equivalent concept in Deuteronomy 24.1. Lending weight to these arguments is the fact that Jesus' line of argument in Matthew, as in Mark, appears to point toward a teaching which is stricter than Moses' and in harmony with the creation will of God. Despite the plausibility of this approach, it does not appear that either the grammatical or the lexical argument cited above can be sustained.[77]. Of course, another alternative is to deny the authenticity of the exceptive clauses in Matthew, but real difficulties exist for this possibility also.[78] Thus it must be concluded that both the Matthean pericopae give teaching on divorce closely similar to the Mosaic provisions. This being the case, the 'hardness of heart' to which Jesus attributes the Mosaic teaching is not done away with in the new age of the Kingdom; indeed, the case of 'serious sexual sin' (πορνεία) which justifies divorce is a prominent example of just that. As under the Mosaic law, the fact of human sin is recognized and provision made for it.

To return to Matthew 5.31-32, it is now important to determine what effect Jesus' teaching has on the actual commandment quoted—viz., to give a bill of divorce. The pronouncement of Jesus juxtaposed with this quotation suggests that the root problem which Jesus attacks is a liberal divorce procedure based on the Deuteronomy passage. As such, the bill of divorce command is never really addressed, though it might be inferred that Jesus envisages a context in which such a provision would be inappropriate.[79]

Thus, it is not clear that Jesus abrogates any Mosaic commandments respecting divorce and remarriage. On the other hand, Jesus *does go beyond the OT* in forthrightly labelling remarriage after an improper divorce 'adultery.'[80] Once again, then, more than straightforward 'exposition' of the OT is involved in the third antithesis. Nor does Jesus 'deepen' or 'intensify' the commandment that is quoted, or any part of the Mosaic divorce legislation. Jesus' purpose is to emphasize in a new way the seriousness of initiating an illegitimate divorce ('causes her to commit adultery') and to place blame on the one who marries an improperly divorced person. His agreement with Deuteronomy 24.1-4 as far as the basis for a legitimate divorce is concerned is, as it were, incidental to his central intention.

The fourth 'thesis' cited by Jesus as a springboard for his own teaching is an accurate summary of a number of OT passages commanding the faithful performance of oaths and vows.[81] The rabbis accepted with reluctance the need for oaths, but they never prohibited them, although the Essenes may have.[82] Jesus' prohibition appears, however, to be absolute: 'do not swear at all'—in which case a clear difference with respect to the OT is found.[83] On the other hand, the examples cited in vv. 34-36 strongly suggest that Jesus had in mind the casuistic development regarding oaths in the scribal tradition.[84] This feature, combined with undoubted examples of hyperbole in the Sermon and the conclusion in v. 37a, may serve to indicate that Jesus' main point is the need for absolute truthfulness and that he intends to prohibit only those oaths whose purpose is to avoid that truthfulness.[85] In this case, Jesus' teaching would be almost indistinguishable from the OT position. Nevertheless, it is difficult to uphold any restriction on Jesus' prohibition: the final words of v. 37, 'anything more than this comes from the evil one', repeat the categorical abolition of oaths. Furthermore, James, who *may* preserve an independent witness to Jesus' words, also gives an absolute prohibition (5.12). However, the forbidding of all *voluntary* oaths cannot be legitimately styled an abrogation of an OT command because there is no OT text which *commands* oaths; the custom is presumed and regulations are given for its practice.[86] Again, Jesus does not exposit or deepen the commandment, but effectively cancels legislation that is no longer needed since the practice it regulated is prohibited in the coming Age.[87]

John P. Meier claims that Jesus' teaching with regard to the *lex talionis* is 'perhaps the clearest and least disputable case of annulment in the antitheses'.[88] While it is precarious to contest so strong a statement, it does not seem that this judgment can be sustained. The law requiring equivalent compensation, found at three places in the Pentateuch, had the purpose not to justify, but to restrain private retribution, by establishing a judicial procedure to which all could appeal.[89] Jesus does not question the legitimacy of this policy (nor does he uphold it), but prohibits his disciples from using the principle in personal relations. Inasmuch as application of the *lex* to private parties is not envisaged in the OT, it is likely that Jesus is opposing a misuse of the law among his contemporaries.[90] Thus, nothing is done to the OT law as such.[91]

The final statement quoted by Jesus in Matthew 5 is unique among the antitheses as including a clause that is not drawn from, nor representative of, the OT. This is sometimes contested, it being urged that the restriction of the love command in Leviticus 19.18 to the fellow-Israelite ($r\bar{e}a^c$) and the frequent expressions of hostility to Israel's enemies in the OT render 'you shall hate your enemy', 'die logische und praktische Konsequenz'.[92] But even within Leviticus 19, the command of love is widened to embrace the 'resident alien' (v. 34) and, when the entire thrust of the OT is considered, a command to hate can hardly be considered a fair extrapolation.[93] The source from which the sentiment is taken cannot be certainly identified, although perhaps most likely is the demand that the members of the Qumran sect hate the 'sons of darkness'.[94] In contrast to this, Jesus demands that his followers love even their enemies, which in the context particularly includes their persecutors. Once again, the demand of Jesus does not abrogate any OT commandment, but neither can it be regarded as a natural extrapolation from OT teaching.

Having examined each of the antitheses, it can be concluded that none of the usual characterizations of Jesus' handling of the OT is sufficient to embrace all of the evidence. 'Exposition' can in no manner account for the situation in the final four antitheses, although it cannot be ruled out as a description of the first two. Besides the inadequacy of the term to do justice to the evidence, it is highly questionable whether the antithetical formula would have been chosen had simple exegesis been Jesus' goal. Likewise, the process observed in the first two antitheses *might* be best described by the terms 'deepening' or 'radicalization', but the latter four cannot be understood in this way. What is the dominant note, hinted at in the emphatic 'I say to you', testified to by the crowds at the conclusion of the Sermon and observed in all the antitheses, is the independent, authoritative teaching of Jesus, which is neither derived from nor explicitly related to the OT.

As a summary of the evidence relating to Jesus' abrogation of the OT, it should be noted that only one commandment, that a bill of divorce be given, was seen to be implicitly revoked, and it is important to note that Jesus explicitly characterizes it as a less-than-adequate statement of God's perfect will. One practice (swearing) allowed in the Mosaic law was forbidden by Jesus to his disciples and in two other instances (Sabbath observance and food laws), Jesus enunciated principles that would allow for the abrogation of laws.

Direct Statements about the Old Testament

We have argued that, to determine the manner in which the Christian believer can use the OT as a guide for behavior, it is necessary to understand the impact of Jesus' coming on the older revelation. In this final section, it is our task to examine the text that most directly treats that question: Matthew 5.17-19 and the partial Lukan parallel, 16.16-17.

In Luke 16.16, Jesus clearly announces a fundamental shift in Salvation-history: 'The law and the prophets were until John; since then the good news of the Kingdom of God is preached, and every one enters it violently'. Especially in light of v. 17, it is impossible that Jesus intends to announce the *termination* of the relevance of the OT;[95] rather, the period during which men were related to God under its terms has ceased with John. Matthew's parallel (11.13a) presents some interesting differences: 'all the prophets and the law prophesied until John'. Unique and particularly striking is the notion of the law 'prophesying', but it is difficult to know what to make of it. Banks sees in it an indication of a Matthean theological theme which regards the law as well as the prophets as pointing forward to Christ.[96] This understanding will have to be pursued further in discussing Matthew 5.17, but the present verse need only indicate that the entire OT is being viewed as the first member in a 'prophecy-fulfillment' understanding of history.[97]

Study of Matthew 5.17-19 is complicated by the complex and debated tradition history of the verses. According to some, each of the three verses has to be assigned to a different stratum of the early community as they present differing views of the law.[98] The validity of the various suggestions concerning the history of these verses can be assessed only after their meaning has been determined. But as a working procedure, we will seek to determine the meaning of each verse within its present context, since it is certainly legitimate to suppose that the final redactor, at least, intended them to be understood in relation to one another.

The meaning given to the phrase 'the law and the prophets' has an important bearing on the exegesis of v. 17. We have already noted that the phrase appears to connote the OT Scriptures in the NT generally, but that Matthew gives the phrase a particular nuance, stressing the normative or imperatival aspect of the OT. The fact that νόμος is used alone in v. 18 and that v. 19 speaks of 'commandments' strongly suggests that this connotation is present in 5.17 as well.[99] But it is not legitimate to press this distinction to the extent that the phrase is taken to imply simply 'the will of God'[100]; reference to the written Scriptures cannot be eliminated.[101]

It is not to 'abolish' the demands of the OT Scriptures that Jesus has come but to *fulfill* them. The determination of the meaning of 'fulfill' in this context is a notorious *crux*, for while the sense of the term as applied to prophecies appears easy to establish, its significance with respect to commands is much less obvious. Any acceptable interpretation will have to do justice to the following factors:

1. When Septuagintal usage is considered, it is almost certain that πληρόω is more closely related to *mālē*² than to *qûm* .[102]
2. The term with which πληρόω is contrasted, καταλύω, means 'abolish', 'annul'.[103]
3. The focus in Matthew 5 is clearly on the relationship between the OT and Jesus' *teaching*, not his actions.

A number of suggested interpretations can be immediately eliminated when these factors are given sufficient consideration. The remaining possibilities posit a relationship between Jesus' teaching and the OT according to which the former (1) 'fills up' the law by expressing its full intended meaning[104]; (2) 'fills up', or 'completes' the law by extending its demands[105]; or (3) 'fulfills' the law by bringing that to which it pointed forward.[106] Two further considerations are crucial in deciding which of these positions is correct: the usage of πληρόω in Matthew and the implications of the use of the OT in the antitheses.

The most obvious and distinctive use of πληρόω in Matthew comes in the introductions to the so-called 'formula quotations', which declare the 'fulfillment' of an OT prophecy or historical event in the life of Jesus. It is this aspect of Matthew's employment of πληρόω that is stressed by Banks, who argues that 'precisely the same meaning should be given to the term πληρόω when it is used of the Law as that which it has when it is used of the prophets'.[107] The fact that the Law itself is said to 'prophesy' according to Matthew (11.13) demonstrates that the law as well as the prophets can be regarded as possessing a 'prophetic' function. Thus, it is suggested, as Jesus fulfilled the OT prophecies in his activity so he 'fulfilled' the OT law in his teaching.[108]

Against this view, however, it can be argued that the closest parallel to the use of πληρόω in Matthew 5.17 is found not in the formula quotations, which all have the passive form, but in Matthew 3.15, which, like 5.17, has the active infinitive. And 'to fulfill all righteousness' in 3.15, it is argued, must mean something like 'to obey (e.g., "complete") every righteous demand of God.'[109] Furthermore, Matthew uses πληρόω elsewhere, albeit in non-theological senses, to mean 'fill up' or 'complete' (13.48; 23.32).

It is difficult to determine which of these lines of evidence should be taken as most significant in determining the meaning of πληρόω in Matthew 5.17. On the one hand, the difference between the passive formulation in the formula citations and the active in Matthew 5.17 may preclude their association, but, on the other hand, the meaning of Matthew 3.15 is not clear and not much may be gained by comparing Matthew 5.17 with it. On the whole, there would appear to be a slight balance of evidence in favor of Banks's interpretation. The reference to the law 'prophesying' (11.13), taken in conjunction with the dominant use of πληρόω in the formula quotations, is very suggestive. Moreover, the idea of the fulfillment of the law is in accord with the broad scope of fulfillment in Matthew, including, as it does, historical events with no clearly predictive element (cf. 2.15).

More decisive support is given this interpretation of πληρόω if the understanding of the antitheses developed above is correct. Most scholars recognize the need to interpret the basic 'theory' enunciated in vv. 17-19 in light of the specific practical examples of vv. 21-48. Hence, those who regard 'fulfill' as connoting the bringing out of the true intention of the law find exposition of the OT in the antitheses; while 'deepening', 'radicalizing', or 'intensifying' the law is found by supporters of the view that 'fulfill' implies an extension of the law's demands. Yet if Jesus in the antitheses is doing neither, but is rather bringing new demands only indirectly related to the OT commands which are cited, then the law can perhaps be best viewed as an *anticipation* of Jesus' teaching. Jesus fulfills the law by proclaiming those demands to which it looked forward.

Can this interpretation be reconciled with vv. 18-19? At first sight, no stronger endorsement of the eternal validity of even the most insignificant item in the law could be found than appears in these verses. But such an interpretation poses insuperable problems for anyone who is concerned to discover a consistent position within Matthew. Many scholars simply deny that this is possible and find in vv. 18-19 a tradition stemming from the conservative Jewish community in the early church, a tradition which Matthew has for some reason inserted in its present context.[110] While it is possible that one could be forced to this view, it must be said that it seems a very difficult one; is it likely that the final redactor would have deliberately inserted sayings that appear, when compared with vv. 21ff., to present Jesus as 'the least in the Kingdom of Heaven'? Surely it is incumbent on us to seek out other alternatives before this position is accepted.

Attempts to avoid the conclusion that there is in these verses an absolute endorsement of every demand in the law focus on three things: the scope of the ἕως clauses in v. 18, the meaning of νόμος in v. 18 and the antecedent of τούτων in v. 19.

The first ἕως clause in v. 18, 'until heaven and earth pass away', must be compared with Luke 16.17: 'it is easier for heaven and earth to pass away, than for one dot of the law to become void'. It is probable that the Lukan verse must be understood as an assertion of the continuing validity of the law, in order to guard against the drawing of antinomian conclusions from v. 16.[111] Almost certainly, the Matthean ἕως clause must be given the same meaning: 'until heaven and earth pass away' is simply another way of saying, 'until the end of the present world order'.[112]

The second ἕως clause in v. 18 is less easy to interpret, since πάντα, 'all things', has no clear antecedent and the precise meaning of γένηται is uncertain.[113] One approach understands πάντα to refer to the demands of the law which are to be 'done' or 'obeyed'.[114] But, when Matthean usage is considered, γένηται must almost certainly be translated 'happen', 'come to pass', so this approach must be excluded.[115] A second interpretation takes πάντα as a reference to *events* which are to come to pass, and inasmuch as this interpretation gives a natural sense to both γένηται and πάντα, it should probably be accepted. The events denoted by πάντα have been variously identified: the death or resurrection of Christ;[116] those things prophesied of his first coming or of his entire career;[117] or the end of the Age.[118]

A consideration of Matthew 24.34-35, which presents several striking linguistic parallels to v. 18, can aid in making a decision. In that context, 'until all these things come to pass' is probably to be interpreted as a reference to the signs enumerated by Jesus earlier in the chapter.[119] πάντα ταῦτα, then, indicates *predicted events*. πάντα in 5.18, without the ταῦτα, leaving it unspecified, is likely to mean much the same thing: all predicted events, the 'whole divine purpose'.[120] While it is claimed that this interpretation makes the second ἕως clause tautologous to the first and hence superfluous, this is not really the case: the second introduces the idea, absent from the first, of God's redemptive purposes. If these interpretations of the ἕως clauses are correct, then they provide no help in delimiting the statements of vv. 18-19.

νόμος in v. 18 probably means, basically, the OT Scriptures,[121] although, it is probable also that the imperatival aspect of the Scriptures is still particularly in view. Another kind of delimitation is suggested by those who suppose that νόμος here is a reference to the *moral* law only.[122] But such a meaning is unlikely in view of the lack of attestation for any clear distinction in Judaism among moral, ceremonial and civil law and the stress on detailed parts of the Scriptures in 5.18.[123] A better suggestion is that the continuing validity of the law is to be understood in the light of its 'fulfillment' (v. 17).[124] In all its details, the Scripture remains authoritative, but the manner in which men are to relate to and understand its provisions is now determined by the one who has fulfilled it. While this view cannot be demonstrated exegetically, the position of v. 18 between v. 17 and the antitheses surely suggests that it can be understood only in conjunction with the new approach to the law. It is precisely the same with Luke 16.17, placed between v. 16 and the saying about divorce in v. 18.

This statement about the permanent validity of the law leads to the practical conclusion (οὖν) of v. 19: even 'the least of these commandments' must be practiced and taught; not to do so is to risk exclusion from the Kingdom. But what are *these* commandments? Attempts to restrict the reference to the decalogue, Jesus' commands, or the antitheses cannot be justified.[125] Most likely, the antecedent of τούτων is to be located in νόμος, the whole (v. 18) being broken down into its parts (v. 19). In the same way, then, as νόμος in v. 18 must be understood in light of its fulfillment, so 'these commandments' should be understood as referring to the commandments as fulfilled (and thereby, perhaps re-interpreted) in Jesus.[126]

The function of vv. 18-19 is rather clearly to guard against a possible antinomian interpretation of v. 17 and, perhaps, of the following antitheses. While it is generally held that it was Matthew's concern about antinomian tendencies in his church that led him to insert these Jewish-Christian sentiments here, it must be asked whether Jesus, too, would not have been concerned about the possibility of his listeners drawing such a conclusion. Could not he have appropriated a perhaps popular Jewish saying about the eternal validity and applicability of the law and applied it to the 'fulfilled law' in order to demonstrate his essential continuity with it? It would appear that such an evaluation is at least as probable as supposing that Matthew has done the same.[127]

Conclusion

In his direct statements about the law Jesus upholds the continuing validity of the entire OT Scriptures, but also asserts that this validity must be understood in light of its fulfillment. It can be readily seen that the evidence gleaned from other lines of investigation in the course of the study is compatible with this position. No sensation-causing revolutionary, Jesus adhered to the law in his own life, but used it remarkably little in his teaching about the righteousness expected of members of the Kingdom. Jesus evidenced in the antitheses and claimed in his statement about the Sabbath an authority over the law, such as only God possesses. On the basis of this authority, Jesus denied to his disciples at least one practice tolerated in the old dispensation (vows), and set forth a principle destined to abrogate large segments of Pentateuchal laws (cf. Mk 7.15). But none of this occurs as a deliberate attack on the law; rather the validity or abrogation of laws appears to be decided entirely by their relationship to Jesus' teaching and to the new situation which his coming inaugurates.[128]

This general perspective is found in all three synoptic gospels with differences in emphasis, but without significant contradictions. Each evangelist combines statements upholding the validity of the law with pronouncements of Jesus regarding his authority over the law. Little use of the law is made in any gospel in the formulation of kingdom ethics, and dietary regulations receive criticism in all three also. These conclusions depend for their cogency on the exegetical decisions reached in the course of the study; and particularly Matthew 5.18-19, and the general approach to the law in the first gospel, are likely to be raised as fundamental objections to this unified outlook. Yet for all Matthew's concern with Judaism and his apparent reluctance to sever relationships with the synagogue, he transmits some of Jesus' most far-reaching claims with respect to the law (5.17, 21-48; 12.8), and it seems preferable to understand more conservative statements within this 'fulfillment' motif rather than speak of contradictions in his material. The unanimity in outlook found in the synoptics on this matter, when contrasted with first-century Jewish beliefs and even some circles in the early church, suggests that we are in touch here with the authentic teaching of Jesus.

What may we then conclude from this about the authority of the Mosaic law in the new age of fulfillment? Any conclusions drawn from Jesus' teaching must, of course, be tentative and subject to the correction and expansion of the more explicit treatment of some of these questions in the epistles. The most that can be done here is to suggest some directions in which the evidence would seem to lead.

First, and most basically, every Mosaic law must be, as Ridderbos puts it, 'placed under the condition of its fulfillment'.[129] On the basis of Jesus' teaching, it does not seem that any Mosaic commandment can be assumed to be directly applicable to the believer. Jesus' authority as the law's fulfiller stands even over the decalogue, as his claim of lordship over the Sabbath shows; and most believers have utilized that authority in refusing to 'honor the *seventh* day'.[130] Nor do statements about the discontinuity/continuity of the law presume the tripartite division of the law, so popular in much of Christian history. The *whole* law came to culmination in Christ. As the sole ultimate authority of the Messianic community, he takes up the law into himself and enunciates what is enduring in its contents. In doing so, it may be inaccurate to speak of a 'new law',[131] but it cannot be denied that Jesus' commandments include both general principles and some detailed demands— much more than the bare requirement of love is involved. The change in redemptive 'eras' brings with it a change in the locus of authority for the people of God,[132] but it does not bring a liberation from authority as such.

Thus, secondly, the teaching of Jesus gives little support to those who would want to apply the criterion of love to discriminate among the applicability of Mosaic commandments. It was not on the basis of 'the demands of love', but on the basis of his unique intuitive knowledge of God's will that Jesus interpreted and applied the law.

Finally, Jesus by no means countenances the abandonment of the Mosaic law; indeed (if Mt. 5.18-19 be accepted as authentic), he explicitly commands that it be taught. However, this teaching must always be done with due attention to the fulfillment of the law (v. 17) and the way in which this fulfillment affects the meaning and applicability of its provisions.

Notes

[1] This position is usually identified in Matthew's Gospel. Cf. B. W. Bacon, 'Jesus and the Law: A Study of the First "Book" of Matthew (Mt. 3-7)', *JBL* 47 (1928), 203-31. Davies finds fewer Mosaic traits and is more cautious in speaking of a new law, but finds a 'Messianic torah' in Matthew (*The Setting of the Sermon on the Mount* [Cambridge: University Press, 1964], 94-107).

[2] This was the position held by most of the reformers (cf. Harvey K. McArthur, *Understanding the Sermon on the Mount* [London: Epworth, 1960], 36). Among modern scholars: Carl F. H. Henry, *Christian Personal Ethics* (Grand Rapids: Zondervan, 1957), 316; Greg L. Bahnsen, *Theonomy in Christian Ethics* (Nutley, N.J.: Craig, 1977) 141-83; Herman Ridderbos, *The Coming of the Kingdom* (Philadelphia: Presbyterian and Reformed, 1962), 314; Ned B. Stonehouse, *The Witness of the Synoptic Gospels to Christ* (combining *The Witness of Matthew and Mark to Christ* and *The Witness of Luke to Christ* (Grand Rapids: Baker, 1979 [= 1944], 197-211). Hans Windisch (*The Meaning of the Sermon on the Mount* [Philadelphia: Westminster, 1951], 132-50) argues that Jesus stayed essentially within the framework of Judaism in his attitude to the law.

[3] Cf. Werner Georg Kümmel, 'Jesus und der jüdische Traditionsgedanke', *ZNW* 33 (1934), 121-27.

[4] Cf. W. Gutbrod, 'νόμος', *TDNT*, IV, 1063.

[5] Late in the nineteenth and early in the twentieth centuries, scholars especially stressed the 'prophetic' character of Jesus' approach to the law (Adolph Harnack, 'Hat Jesus das alttestamentlich Gesetz abgeschafft?' *Aus Wissenschaft und Leben* [Giessen: Töpelmann, 1911], II, 230-34; Bennett Harvie Branscomb, *Jesus and the Law of Moses* [New York: Richard A. Smith, 1930], 262-66; C. G. Montefiore, *Some Elements of the Religious Teaching of Jesus according to the Synoptic Gospels* [New York: Arno, 1973], 44). More recently, Jesus' approach to the law has been compared with that of the Qumran sectarians (Herbert Braun, *Spätjüdische-häretischer und frühchristlicher Radikalismus: Jesus von Nazareth und die essenische Qumransekte* [2 vols.; 2nd edn; BHT, 24,2; Tübingen: Mohr, 1959]). Probably the majority of modern scholars hold something like this general view.

[6] This seems to have been the dominant view in the Patristic period (cf. McArthur, *Sermon*, 26-32). Cf. also Ernst Percy, *Die Botschaft Jesu: Eine traditionskritische und exegetische Untersuchung* (Lunds Universitets Arsskrift, n.s. 49; Lund: Gleerup, 1953), 122-23, and Pieter Godfried Verweijs, *Evangelium und neues Gesetz in der ältesten Christenheit bis auf Marcion* (Domplein/Utrecht: Kemink en Zoon, 1960), 350-51.

[7] Robert Banks argues for this position in his important monograph, *Jesus and the Law in the Synoptic Tradition* (SNTSMS 28; Cambridge: University Press, 1975). His basic position is accepted by John P. Meier (*Law and History in Matthew's Gospel* [An Bib, 71; Rome: Biblical Institute Press, 1976], 87-88).

[8] *Jesus and the Law*, 90-91. Branscomb (*Jesus and the Law*, 126-28) contests the validity of separating the oral from the written law, but against this it must be maintained that as long as a significant Jewish group (the Sadducees) rejected the validity of the oral law, such a distinction is not only possible but necessary.

[9] Gutbrod, 'νόμος' *TDNT*, IV, 1062.

[10] Jesus' contact with ritually unclean people in the course of his healing ministry cannot be viewed as a transgression of the law, since this kind of activity is hardly covered in the law (Banks, *Jesus and the Law*, 105).

[11] Branscomb, *Jesus and the Law*, 170-74. Gerhard Barth argues that, at least in Matthew, the oral law is not rejected as such ('Matthew's Understanding of the Law', *Tradition and Interpretation in Matthew*, by Günter Bornkamm, Gerhard Barth and Heinz Joachim Held [Philadelphia: Westminster, 1963], 86-89).

[12] The deliberateness and frequency with which Jesus performs miracles on the Sabbath suggests that more than 'isolated incidents' are involved (as argued by M. Hubaut, 'Jésus et la loi de Moïse', *RTL* 7 [1976], 406).

[13] Contra Banks, *Jesus and the Law*, 237-38.

[14] Branscomb, *Jesus and the Law*, 126-28. Banks argues that Jesus attended the synagogue solely to minister (regarding κατά τό εἰωθός in Lk. 4.16 as a reference to habits of ministering [cf. Acts 17.2]) (*Jesus and the Law*, 91). But it is more likely that such ministry grew out of regular attendance for worship (Robin Nixon, 'Fulfilling the law: The Gospels and Acts', *Law, Morality and the Bible*, ed. Bruce Kaye and Gordon Wenham [Downers Grove, Ill.: InterVarsity Press, 1978], 60).

[15] Banks, *Jesus and the Law*, 99, 237-38.

[16] *Pace,* Robert MacKintosh, *Christ and the Jewish Law* (London: Hodder & Stoughton, 1886), 59-62.

[17] Cf. the position adopted by W. D. Davies ('Matthew 5.17, 18', *Christian Origins and Judaism* [Philadelphia: Westminster, 1962], 50-58).

[18] Victor Paul Furnish, *The Love Command in the New Testament* (Nashville: Abingdon, 1972) 26-27; David Hill, *The Gospel of Matthew* (NCB; London: Oliphants, 1972), 307.

[19] 2 Macc. 15.9; 4 Macc. 18.10; Midr. Ps. 90 #4; Mt. 5.17; 7.12; Lk. 16.16; 24.44; Jn 1.45; Acts 13.15; 24.14; 23.23; Rom. 3.21. SB (I, 240) note that the phrase is rare in Jewish literature; it may be that it reflects a Christian emphasis on prophecy.

[20] Wolfgang Trilling, *Das wahre Israel: Studien zur Theologie des Matthäus-Evangeliums* (SANT, 10; Munich: Kösel, 1964), 173-74; Georg Strecker, *Der Weg der Gerechtigkeit: Untersuchungen zur Theologie des Matthäus* (FRLANT, 82; Göttingen: Vandenhoeck & Ruprecht, 1962), 144; A. Feuillet, 'Morale ancienne et morale chrétienne d'après Mt. V. 17-20; Comparison avec la doctrine de L'Épître aux Romains', *NTS* 17 (1970-71), 124.

[21] E.g., TB Ber. 63a; SB I, 907-908. Cf. also Berger, *Gesetzesauslegung,* 230; Rudolph Schnackenburg, *The Moral Teaching of the New Testament* (New York: Seabury, 1965), 93.

[22] SB I, 907-908.

[23] Furnish, *Love Command,* 32-34.

[24] Furnish, *Love Command,* 74; Branscomb, *Jesus and the Law,* 263. Barth ('Matthew's Understanding', 78-85) views love as the basis upon which Matthew re-interpreted and thereby retained the law. J. L. Houlden (*Ethics and the New Testament* [New York: Oxford University Press, 1973], 107) sees the love commandment as interpreting the law in Matthew, but in Mark and Luke, he claims, the law is 'rivaled and supplanted'.

[25] Verweijs, *Evangelium,* 23; Hugh Anderson, *The Gospel of Mark* (NCB; London: Oliphants, 1976), 110.

[26] C.E.B. Cranfield, *The Gospel According to Saint Mark* (CGTC; Cambridge: University Press, 1966), 115; William L. Lane, *The Gospel According to Mark* (NICNT; Grand Rapids: Eerdmans, 1974), 116-17.

[27] Rudolph Pesch, *Das Markusevangelium* (HTKNT; 2 vols.; Freiburg/Basel/Vienna: Herder, 1977), I, 181-82; Heinz Schürmann, *Das Lukasevangelium* (HTKNT; Freiburg/Basel/Vienna: Herder, 1969), I, 303-304; R. T. France, *Jesus and the Old Testament* (London: Tyndale, 1971), 46-47; cf. I. Howard Marshall, *The Gospel of Luke* (NIGTC; Grand Rapids: Eerdmans, 1978), 232; L. Goppelt, 'πεινάω', *TDNT,* VI, 19. Banks contests the typological interpretation, claiming that '. . . nowhere else in the gospels does Jesus portray himself as David's successor' (*Jesus and the Law,* 115). But against this, cf. especially Sherman E. Johnson, 'The Davidic-Royal Motif in the Gospels', *JBL* 87 (1968), 136-50.

[28] For the former, cf. Arndt, 451; and Ceslaus Spicq. *Agape in the New Testament,* Vol. 1: *Agape in the Synoptic Gospels* (St. Louis/London: B. Herder, 1963), 30; for the latter, Bertram, 'κρεμάννυμι', *TDNT,* III, 920.

[29] Banks, *Jesus and the Law,* 169.

[30] Charles Carlston, 'The Things that Defile (Mark VII.14) and the Law in Matthew and Mark', *NTS* 15 (1968-69), 87.

[31] Banks downplays the role of love in Jesus' ethics, claiming that the love command is a decisive demand only within the law (*Jesus and the Law,* 243-44). But passages such as Mt. 5.43ff. suggest that love plays a prominent part in the demands of the Kingdom also (Strecker, *Der Weg,* 136-37).

[32] J. Duncan M. Derrett, *Law in the New Testament* (London: Darton, Longman & Todd, 1970), 377; Davies, *Setting,* 104-105; Stonehouse, *Witness,* 204-205; Anderson, *Mark,* 241-42.

[33] Banks, *Jesus and the Law,* 149; contra, e.g., Wolfgang Trilling, *Israel,* 205-206; Victor Hasler, 'Die Herzstuck der Bergpredigt: zum Verständnis der Antitheser in Matth. 5,21-48', *TZ* 15 (1959), 96.

[34] Kenneth J. Thomas correctly notes the differences between the rabbinic technique and

Jesus' approach. As he says, '. . . one citation is used to interpret the other by placing it in a new context' ('Torah Citations in the Synoptics', *NTS* 24 [1977-78], 88; cf. also Banks, *Jesus and the Law*, 147-50).

[35] Trilling, *Israel,* 205-206.

[36] Henry, *Ethics,* 375; Ridderbos, *Kingdom,* 293; Cranfield, *Mark,* 330; Lane, *Mark,* 367; Thomas, 'Torah Citations', 89.

[37] C.F.D. Moule, 'Prolegomena: The New Testament and Moral Decision', *Exp T* 74 (1962-63), 370; Bacon, 'Jesus and the Law', 214; Banks, *Jesus and the Law,* 162-63; Meier, *Law and History,* 88.

[38] Banks, *Jesus and the Law,* 164.

[39] Gutbrod, 'νόμος', *TDNT,* IV, 1063.

[40] Verweijs, *Evangelium,* 22; Siegfried Schulz, *Die Stunde der Botschaft. Einführung in die Theologie der vier Evangelisten* [Hamburg: Furche, 1967], 174; Kümmel, 'Jüdische Traditionsgedanke', 124-25; Pesch, *Markusevangelium,* I, 384; Davies, 'Matthew 5.17, 18', 40-41. Contra Barth, 'Matthew's Understanding', 89-90.

[41] Cf. Quesnell, *Mark,* 93-94.

[42] Bahnsen, *Theonomy,* 214.

[43] Cf. Banks, *Jesus and the Law,* 242-43.

[44] Walter C. Kaiser, Jr., 'The Weightier and Lighter Matters of the Law: Moses, Jesus and Paul', *Current Issues in Biblical and Patristic Interpretation*, ed. Gerald F. Hawthorne (Grand Rapids: Eerdmans, 1975), 181-185; David Wenham, 'Jesus and the Law: An Exegesis of Matthew 5.17-20', *Themelios* 4 (April, 1979), 95.

[45] *Mark,* 244.

[46] Ernst Käsemann, 'The Problem of the Historical Jesus', *Essays on New Testament Themes* (SBT, 41; London: SCM, 1964), 40; Willy Rordorf, *Sunday: The History of the Day of Rest and Worship in the Earliest Centuries of the Christian Church* (Philadelphia: Westminster, 1968), 65-71; Kümmel, 'Jüdische Traditionsgedanke', 121-22.

[47] Activities specifically prohibited are: regular plowing and harvesting (Ex. 34.21); kindling a fire (Ex. 35.3); carrying burdens (Jer. 17.21-27); trade (Neh. 10.32); treading the winepress, loading beasts, and holding markets (Neh. 13.15-22); long journeys and the pursuing of business (Is. 56.2). Cf. Lohse, 'Σάββατον', *TDNT,* VII, 5.

[48] The Mishnah tractates 'Erubim and Shabbat are devoted to this task. Cf. SB, I, 616-18.

[49] D. A. Carson, 'Jesus and the Sabbath in the Four Gospels', *From Sabbath to Lord's Day: A Biblical, Historical and Theological Investigation,* ed. D. A. Carson (Grand Rapids: Zondervan, 1982), 61. Cf. also, for Matthew's narrative, Hill, *Matthew,* 211-12, and Davies, *Setting,* 103-104; and for Luke's, Jacob Jervell, 'The Law in Luke-Acts', *HTR* 64 (1971), 29.

[50] Rordorf, *Sunday,* 65-66. The rabbis allowed medical attention that was necessary to prevent death on the Sabbath (SB, I, 622-29).

[51] TB Shabb, 132b.

[52] The aptness of the parallel between the priests, innocent because they serve the Temple, and the disciples, innocent because they follow Jesus, is too clear to overlook (cf. Birger Gerhardsson, 'Sacrificial Service and Atonement in the Gospel of Matthew', *Reconciliation and Hope: New Testament Essays on Atonement and Eschatology presented to L. L. Morris on his 60th Birthday,* ed. Robert Banks [Grand Rapids: Eerdmans, 1974], 28).

[53] F. Godet, *A Commentary on the Gospel of St. Luke* (5th edn; 2 vols.; Edinburgh: T. & T. Clark, n.d.), I, 290; Roland de Vaux, *Ancient Israel* (2 vols.; New York/Toronto: McGraw-Hill, 1961), II, 483.

[54] *Luke,* 233.

[55] On this, cf. further especially Rordorf, *Sunday,* and *From Sabbath to Lord's Day*, ed. D. A. Carson.

[56] Exposition of the law (Henry, *Ethics,* 300-307; Ridderbos, *Kingdom,* 299; Bahnsen, *Theonomy,* 90; John Murray, *Principles of Conduct: Aspects of Biblical Ethics* [Grand Rapids: Eerdmans, 1957], 158); deepening, radicalizing or intensifying the law (Martin Dibelius, *The Sermon*

on the Mount [New York: Scribner's, 1940], 69-71; Jacques Dupont, Les Béatitudes, Vol. I: Le problème littéraire—Les deux versions du Sermon sur la Montagne et des Béatitudes (3rd edn; Bruges: Abbaye de Saint-André, 1958), 146-58; Davies, Setting, 101-102); the promulgation of a new law (Spicq, Agape, I, 5-6); the setting forth of a new teaching which does not abrogate the law (Percy, Botschaft, 163-64).

   57 BDF, #191; cf. also Patrick Fairburn, The Revelation of Law in Scripture (Grand Rapids: Zondervan, 1957 [= 1869]), 228-29; Percy, Botschaft, 123-24; contra Ridderbos, Kingdom, 297-98; William Hendriksen, New Testament Commentary: Exposition of the Gospel According to Matthew (Grand Rapids: Baker, 1973), 295-96.

   58 Cf. the rabbinic zôrôt hariᵓšônîm (Barth, 'Matthew's Understanding', 93; Verweijs, Evangelium, 18). Included also is probably the 'chain' of teachers who transmitted the law (SB, I, 253; Meier, Law and History, 132).

   59 Percy, Botschaft, 124.

   60 M.-J. Lagrange, Evangile selon Saint Matthieu (EBib; 5th edn; Paris: Gabalda, 1941), 97; Robert A. Guelich, The Sermon on the Mount: A Foundation for Understanding (Waco, TX: Word, 1982), 182. Since Matthew consistently uses the passive form of λέγω to introduce quotations of Scripture, it is likely that some reference to the OT is included when ἐρρέθη is found in the formula (G. Kittel,'λέγω', TDNT, IV, 111-12; Meier, Law and History, 131; contra SB, I, 253; Barth, 'Matthew's Understanding', 93).

   61 Cf. Gustaf Dalman, Jesus-Jeshua: Studies in the Gospels (New York: Macmillan, 1929), 58. ἠκούσατε may well suggest the fact of 'traditionally interpreted' quotation (SB, I, 253; Matthew Black, An Aramaic Approach to the Gospels and Acts [3rd edn; Oxford: Clarendon, 1967], 300; Trilling, Israel, 268-69; Percy, Botschaft, 124).

   62 See especially David Daube (The New Testament and Rabbinic Judaism [New York: Arno, 1973 (= 1956)], 55-60) who suggests the paraphrase 'you have understood the meaning of the law to have been' for the first, second and fourth antitheses, 'you have understood literally' for the others. Cf. also I. Abrahams, Studies in Pharisaism and the Gospels, first series (New York: KTAV, 1967 [= 1924]), 16; Edward Lohse, ' "Ich aber sage euch" ', Der Ruf Jesu, 193-96; Davies, Setting, 101; Hill, Matthew, 120. Morton Smith has suggested that τοῖς ἀρχαίοις is parallel to the rabbinic bāriᵓšônāh , which would yield a meaning for the antithetical formula something like 'at first they used to say . . . they came around to saying' (Tannaitic Parallels to the Gospels [JBLMS, 6; Philadelphia: SBL, 1951], 28).

   63 Meier, Law and History, 133; Guelich, Sermon, 182. Percy points out that the rabbinic formula is always used in the context of a refutation of one opinion by means of appeal to Scripture; a process completely unlike that in the antitheses (Botschaft, 124-25).

   64 Pierre Bonnard, L'Evangile selon Saint Matthieu (CNT; Neuchâtel: Delachaux & Niestlé, 1963), 64.

   65 Gerald Friedlander, The Jewish Sources of the Sermon on the Mount (New York: KTAV, 1969), 40-53; C. G. Montefiore, Rabbinic Literature and Gospel Teachings (New York: KTAV, 1970 [= 1930]), 38-56; SB, I, 276 82, 298-301.

   66 Windisch, Sermon, 132.

   67 Alfred Plummer, An Exegetical Commentary on the Gospel According to St. Matthew (London: Robert Scott, 1915), 78; M'Neile, Matthew, 61.

   68 Banks, Jesus and the Law, 188-89. Cf. especially Gen. 9.6; Ex. 21.12; Lev. 24.17. κρίσις probably connotes the punishment of God rather than a 'court of law' (Arndt, 454) and is probably chosen so as to provide a clear connection between the penalties for murder and for anger. The second and third descriptions of punishment in v. 22 are probably not intended to represent a gradation in punishment, but to expand and explain the first (G. Bertram, 'μωρός', TDNT, IV, 841-42; J. Jeremias, 'ῥακά', TDNT, VI, 975-76). For another explanation, see C.F.D. Moule, 'Uncomfortable Words: I. The Angry Word: Matthew 5.21f.', ExpT 81 (1969-70), 10-13.

   69 On the distinction between the decalogue as 'principal' law and the developed system as 'case' law, see Gordon Wenham, 'Law and the legal system in the Old Testament', Law, Morality, and the Bible, 28.

124   The Best in Theology

[70] Banks, *Jesus and the Law*, 189, 191; Guelich, *Sermon*, 238, 258.

[71] Although some would view vv. 31-32 as a continuation of the second antithesis (Günther Schmahl, 'Die Antitheses der Bergpredigt: Inhalt und Eigenart ihrer Forderungen', *TTZ*, 83 [1974], 290), it is probably a separate unit (Meier, *Law and History*, 129; Guelich, *Sermon*, 197).

[72] Cf. Mt. 19.7 and Mk 10.5, in which 'this commandment' probably refers not to *divorce*, but to the need to give the bill of divorce, *when* divorce occurs (contra Banks, *Jesus and the Law*, 149).

[73] It is probable that the apodosis of Dt. 24.1-4 does not come until v. 4 (cf. RSV), in which case the only *command* is that a divorced woman, whose second husband has died, cannot remarry her first spouse (C. F. Keil and F. Delitzsch, *Commentary on the Old Testament*, Vol. 1: *The Pentateuch* [Grand Rapids: Eerdmans, n.d.], 416-17).

[74] The term in question is σκληροκαρδία, used only in this context in the NT. In the LXX this word, and its adjectival form (σκληροκάρδιος) are found four times, in each case with the sense 'spiritual obduracy'. Important also is the verbal form σκληρύνω which J. Behm defines as '. . . the persistent unreceptivity of a man to the declaration of God's saving will . . .' (*TDNT*, III, 614).

[75] Thus, essentially, Lane, *Mark*, 355.

[76] ʿerwat dābār , the phrase which appears to establish legitimate grounds for divorce, refers to a serious sexual sin (S. R. Driver, *A Critical and Exegetical Commentary on Deuteronomy* [ICC; 3rd edn; Edinburgh: T. & T. Clark, 1895], 270-71). The school of Shammai advocated this translation, stressing the word ʿerwat . Jesus' position in Mt. 5.32 and 19.9 would seem to be rather close to Shammai's (and λόγος πορνείας *may* be a rough translation of the phrase from Dt., since the word order *dᵉbar* ʿerwāh *does* occur [M. Git. 9.10; cf. SB, I, 313]).

[77] The grammatical case rests on understanding εἰ μή in Mt. 19.9 and παρεκτός in 5.32 in a 'preteritive' sense, in which case πορνεία is simply excluded from consideration (cf. Banks, *Jesus and the Law*, 153-59). But, as Fitzmyer says, this and other less likely grammatical reinterpretations are 'subterfuges to avoid the obvious' ('The Matthean Divorce Texts and Some New Palestinian Evidence', *TS* 37 [1976], 207).

More popular, and more defensible, have been attempts to give πορνεία a meaning other than the usual: anything forbidden by OT law (Bruce Malina, 'Does *Porneia* mean Fornication?', *NovT* 14 [1972], 10-17); premarital sex (Abel Isaakson, *Marriage and Ministry in the New Temple* [Lund: Gleerup, 1965], 127-41); marriage within prohibited degrees of kinship (Joseph Bonsirven, *Le divorce dans le Nouveau Testament* [Paris: Desclée, 1948], 50-60; Fitzmyer, 'Divorce Texts', 213-23; Meier, *Law and History*, 148-50; and especially Heinrich Baltensweiler, *Die Ehe im Neuen Testament* [Zurich: Zwingli, 1967], 87-102; Guelich, *Sermon*, 204-210). It is clear that πορνεία can have such a restricted meaning (particularly in the latter sense) when the context so indicates, but there are insufficient contextual factors to justify such a restriction in the Matthean texts.

[78] As Hill points out, Jewish law required divorce in cases of adultery, and it is quite possible that Matthew simply makes this explicit (*Matthew*, 124-25, 280-81). Moreover, the tendency in Matthew is uniformly to make the demands of the law stricter, not to provide 'loopholes'.

[79] Ridderbos, *Kingdom*, 299.

[80] Branscomb, *Jesus and the Law*, 152.

[81] Cf. especially Lev. 19.12; Num. 30.3; Dt. 23.21; Ps. 56.14. It is improbable that a reference to the third commandment is included (J. Schneider, 'ὀμνύω', *TDNT*, V, 178; Banks, *Jesus and the Law*, 193-94).

[82] For the former, see SB, I, 321-28; Friedlander, *Jewish Sources*, 60-65; Montefiore, *Rabbinic Literature*, 48-50. Josephus claims that the Essenes forbade swearing (*BJ* 2.8.6) but also mentions a solemn entry oath (*BJ* 2.8.7). The evidence from the Scrolls is inconclusive, but it is probable that an entrance oath alone was allowed (Davies, *Setting*, 240-41).

[83] Ernst Kutsch, ' "Eure Rede aber sei ja ja, nein nein" ', *EvT* (1960), 208-209; Schneider 'ὀμνύω', *TDNT*, V, 178; Montefiore, *Synoptic Gospels*, II, 68; Friedlander, *Jewish Sources*, 60; Banks, *Jesus and the Law*, 194-95; Meier, *Law and History*, 153-55. To view the phrases introduced by μήτε . . . μήτε as a list of oaths prohibited by Jesus is incorrect; μήτε is equivalent to μηδέ here and introduces examples of the kind of thing Jesus is combatting (SB, I, 328). Neither

is it legitimate to view v. 37a as a new oath introduced by Jesus (Schneider, 'ὀμνύω', *TDNT*, V, 180-81).

[84] For examples, cf. SB, I, 328-36.

[85] Hasler, 'Herzstück', 98-99; Stonehouse, *Witness*, 206-207; Murray, *Principles*, 171.

[86] Meier (*Law and History*, 152) claims that oaths are commanded in the OT, but there is only one text of which this can be said (Ex.22.10-13), and this is limited to a specific situation in the courts. Dt. 6.13 and 10.20, which Meier cites, should be regarded not as commands that vows be made, but that any vows made by God's people should be made to the Lord.

It would not appear that Jesus' words have relevance to the taking of an oath in a law court; he prohibits *all* oaths *voluntarily undertaken*.

[87] Dupont, *Béatitudes*, I, 158.

[88] *Law and History*, 157; cf. also Barth, 'Matthew's Understanding', 94.

[89] Cf. Martin Noth, *Exodus: A Commentary* (Philadelphia: Westminster, 1962), 132.

[90] Hasler, 'Herzstück', 101-102; Stonehouse, *Witness*, 209; Murray, *Principles*, 174-75.

[91] A number of scholars find in this antithesis the introduction of a new demand: whereas the law had *restrained* vengeance, Jesus *prohibits* it (Gutbrod, 'νόμος', *TDNT*, IV, 1064; M'Neile, *Matthew*, 69; Dupont, *Béatitudes*, I, 158; Marshall, *Luke*, 116).

[92] Schultz, *Botschaft*, 186 (quoting Klostermann). Cf. also Banks, *Jesus and the Law*, 199. Spicq (*Agape*, I, 9-10) and O.J.F. Seitz ('Love your enemies', *NTS* [1969-70], 42-43) allow that 'hate your enemy' is a not unnatural extrapolation from the OT teaching.

[93] Olaf Linton, 'St. Matthew 5,43', *ST* 18 (1964), 66.

[94] 1QS 1.3, 9-10; 2.4-9. Cf. H. Bietenhard, 'Enemy', *The New International Dictionary of New Testament Theology*, I, 554; Furnish, *Love Command*, 42-47; Davies, *Setting*, 245 (possibly). Otherwise, it is possible that a popular maxim is involved (SB, I, 353; Seitz, 'Love', 51; O. Michel, 'μισέω', *TDNT*, IV, 690). Morton Smith suggests that the phrase may have been a gloss in a targum ('Mt. 5.43: "Hate thine Enemy" ', *HTR* 45 [1952], 71-72).

Montefiore, in a thorough survey of the rabbinic evidence, concludes that the sages did teach, in theory, a universal love; many teachings, in practice, failed to express it (*Rabbinic Literature*, 59-104).

[95] Robert Banks, 'Matthew's Understanding of the Law: Authenticity and Interpretation in Matthew 5.17-20', *JBL* 93 (1974), 235.

[96] *Jesus and the Law*, 210; Meier, *Law and History*, 71-73; Albert Descamps, *Les Justes et la justice dans les évangiles et le christianisme primitif hormis la doctrine proprement paulinienne* (Louvain: Univ. of Louvain/Gembloux: Duculot, 1950), 161-62.

[97] Walter Grundmann, *Das Evangelium nach Matthäus* (THKNT; Berlin: Evangelische Verlag, 1968), 310.

[98] Hamerton-Kelly, 'Attitudes', 19-32, provides a convenient discussion.

[99] Theodor Zahn, *Das Evangelium des Matthäus* (4th edn; Leipzig: Deichert, 1922), 209-10, 215; Trilling, *Israel*, 173-74; Strecker, *Der Weg*, 144. (The use of ἤ rather than καί in 5.17 is probably due to the negative form of the sentence [Bonnard, *Matthieu*, 61].)

[100] As do Klaus Berger, *Die Gesetzesauslegung Jesu: ihr historischer Hintergrund im Judentum und im Alten Testament* (WMANTm 40, 1; Neukirchen/Vluyn: Neukirchener, 1972), 224; Alexander Sand, *Das Gesetz und die Propheten: Untersuchungen zur Theologie des Evangeliums nach Matthäus* (Biblische Untersuchungen, 11; Regensburg: Pustet, 1974), 186.

[101] Bahnsen, *Theonomy*, 50-51.

[102] Brevard S. Childs, 'Prophecy and Fulfillment: A Study of Contemporary Hermeneutics', *Int* 12 (1958), 204; Banks, *Jesus and the Law*, 208-209. The LXX never uses πληρόω to translate *qûm* (on the LXX usage of πληρόω, cf. Descamps, *Justes*, 124-25) and the interchange of *mālēʾ* and *qûm* in the targums (Meier, *Law and History*, 74) is insufficient basis to overturn this factor.

[103] The closest parallel to Mt. 5.17 in the use of καταλύω is 2 Macc. 2.22, where it is used with reference to the law and must mean 'abolish' or 'annul' (Grundmann, *Matthäus*, 145; Banks, *Jesus and the Law*, 207; contra Henrik Ljungman, *Das Gesetz Erfüllen: Matth. 5,17ff. und 3,15 untersucht* [Lunds Universitets Arsskrift, n.s. 50; Lund: Gleerup, 1954], 60-61).

[104] R.C.H. Lenski, *The Interpretation of St. Matthew's Gospel* (Minneapolis: Augsburg, 1943), 206-207; Henry, *Ethics*, 318; Ridderbos, *Kingdom*, 294; Bahnsen, *Theonomy*, 61-72; Nixon, 'Fulfilling', 56-57.

[105] Although the following authors disagree on the exact nuance, they are united in giving πληρόω the sense 'give the complete or perfect meaning': Kümmel, 'Jüdische Traditionsgedanke', 128-29; Lagrange *Matthieu*, 93-94; Dupont, *Béatitudes*, I, 138-44; Lohmeyer-Schmauch, *Matthäus*, 107-108; Wilder, *Eschatology*, 130; Schnackenburg, *Moral Teaching*, 57-58; Davies, 'Matthew 5.17, 18', 33-45; Floyd V. Filson, *A Commentary on the Gospel According to St. Matthew* (BNTC; London: Black, 1960), 83; Feuillet, 'Morale', 124; Grundmann, *Matthäus*, 145-46; Schweizer, *Matthew*, 107; Schulz, *Botschaft*, 182; Trilling, *Israel*, 174-79; Christoph Burchard, 'The Theme of the Sermon on the Mount', *Essays on the Love Command*, 73.

[106] Banks, *Jesus and the Law*, 207-10; Meier, *Law and History*, 75-85. Meyer (*Aims of Jesus*, 153) says: 'His [Jesus'] crowning revelation "fulfilled" the Torah by bringing it to its appointed eschatological completion'.

[107] *Jesus and the Law*, 210.

[108] Banks, *Jesus and the Law*, 210. Guelich similarly stresses the redemptive-historical focus of v. 17 and views the verse as a pronouncement of Jesus' bringing in the eschatological 'Ziontorah' (*Sermon*, 137-38, 163). And see also Meyer, *Aims of Jesus*, 143-51.

[109] Cf. G. Schrenk, 'δικαιοσύνη', *TDNT*, II, 198.

[110] E.g., Kümmel, 'Jüdische Traditionsgedanke', 127; Hans-Theo Wrege, *Die Überlieferungsgeschichte der Bergpredigt* (WUNT, 9; Tübingen: Mohr, 1968), 40.

[111] Marshall, *Luke*, 630.

[112] Inasmuch as Jesus, in both Mt. (24.35) and Lk. (21.33) clearly predicts the 'passing away of heaven and earth', it is incorrect to view this saying as equivalent to saying 'never' (H. Traub, 'οὐρανός', *TDNT*, V, 515; Meier, *Law and History*, 61).

[113] It seems clear, however, that the ἕως clause is temporal (contra Eduard Schweizer ('Noch einmal Mt. 5,17-20', *Das Wort und die Wörter* [für Gerhard Friedrich], ed. Horst Balz and Siegfried Schulz [Stuttgart: Kohlhammer, 1973], 71), who wants to give the clause a *final* meaning and A. M. Honeyman ('Matthew V. 18 and the Validity of the Law', *NTS* 1 [1954-55], 141-42), who finds a Semitic construction which yields an inclusive and modal sense).

[114] Wrege, *Bergpredigt*, 39; Sand, *Gesetz*, 38; Grundmann, *Matthäus*, 148; Schulz, *Botschaft*, 183; Hill, *Matthew*, 118. Schweizer has argued that the love command in particular is the subject ('Matth. 5.17-20: Anmerkungen zum Gesetzesverständnis des Matthäus', *Neotestamentica: Deutsche und Englische Aufsätze 1951-1963* [Zurich/Stuttgart: Zwingli, 1963], 400-405).

[115] Cf. especially Meier, *Law and History*, 53-54, 61-62.

[116] Jesus' death: Davies, 'Matthew 5.17, 18', 44-63; the Resurrection: Hamerton-Kelly, 'Attitudes', 30.

[117] Meier (*Law and History*, 62-64; cf. Guelich, *Sermon*, 145-48) argues for the former; for the latter, cf. Lenski, *Matthew*, 204.

[118] M'Neile, *Matthew*, 59.

[119] Banks, *Jesus and the Law*, 216. And for more evidence for this view of this difficult logion, see especially Cranfield, *Mark*, 407-408.

[120] Plummer, *Matthew*, 76.

[121] Arndt, 545; contra Gutbrod ('νόμος', *TDNT*, IV, 1059), Banks (*Jesus and the Law*, 214-15) and Meier (*Law and History*, 52) who restrict the reference to the Pentateuch.

[122] Fairbairn, *Law*, 226-27; MacKintosh, *Christ and the Law*, 23.

[123] Bahnsen, *Theonomy*, 48.

[124] Lagrange, *Matthieu*, 94; Bonnard, *Matthieu*, 62; Trilling, *Israel*, 179; G. Schrenk, 'ἐντολή', *TDNT*, II, 548-49; Wenham, 'Jesus and the Law', 95.

[125] For the first, see Schrenk, 'ἐντολή', *TDNT*, II, 548; for the second, Banks, *Jesus and the Law*, 221-23; for the third, Carlston, 'Things that Defile', 79. Against the last-named view, it does not appear that Matthew ever uses οὗτος prospectively.

[126] A. T. Lincoln, 'From Sabbath to Lord's Day: A Biblical and Theological Perspective', *From Sabbath to Lord's Day*, 374. James D. G. Dunn (*Unity and Diversity in the New Testament: An Inquiry into the Character of Earliest Christianity* [Philadelphia: Westminster, 1977], 246) sees Matthew to be advocating 'continuing *loyalty* to the law, that is, for him, *the law as interpreted by Jesus*'. Guelich (*Sermon*, 153-55) finds v. 19 to be restricted by v. 20, which introduces the idea of the eschatological 'Zion-torah' (the term is Harmut Gese's).

[127] Banks (Matthew 5.17-20', 236-40) defends the substantial authenticity of vv. 17-20. Although his interpretation differs slightly from mine, his arguments are nonetheless relevant here.

[128] Cf. especially Banks, *Jesus and the Law*, 242-45; and also Verweijs, *Evangelium*, 351.

[129] *Kingdom*, 308.

[130] The letter of the fourth commandment clearly specifies the *seventh* day, not simply a 'one-in-seven' principle.

[131] Davies has suggested that the early Christians, taking up some inchoate indications in this direction in contemporary Judaism, may have come to view Jesus' teaching as a new *torah* (*Torah in the Messianic Age and/or the Age to Come* [JBLMS, 7; Philadelphia: SBL, 1952]; *Setting*, 122-88). But this is contested by Peter Schäfer, 'Die Torah der messianischen Zeit', *ZNW* 65 (1974) 27-42; and Robert Banks, 'The Eschatological Role of Law in Pre- and Post-Christian Jewish Thought', *Reconciliation and Hope*, 175-85.

[132] Bahnsen's treatment (*Theonomy*) is flawed by a consistent failure to give adequate attention to such salvation-historical considerations. Similarly, approaches which emphasize the difference in *interpretation* of the law evidenced by Jesus and the Pharisees (cf. Stephen Westerholm, *Jesus and Scribal Authority* [CB, NT, 10; Lund: Gleerup, 1978]) often fail to come to grips with the radical shift in perspective brought by the coming of the Kingdom.

CHURCH HISTORY

Nathan Hatch, area editor

CHURCH HISTORY

NATHAN HATCH
Associate Dean, College of Arts and Letters
University of Notre Dame

Introduction

Professors David Lindberg and Ronald Numbers share the conviction that the interaction of science and Christianity has been of profound importance in the shaping of Western civilization. Both are distinguished historians of science whose scholarly work has often addressed questions having to do with the interface of science and religion. In April 1981, at the University of Wisconsin, they convened an international conference on the historical relations of Christianity and science. The final fruits of that effort are now contained in the book *God and Nature: Historical Essays on the Encounter between Christianity and Science* (University of California Press, 1986). The book includes eighteen original essays based on the best available scholarship and written in nontechnical language. The essay here, "Beyond War and Peace: A Reappraisal of the Encounter between Christianity and Science," (from *Church History*) is similar to their introduction to *God and Nature*. It represents a superb primer to the historical literature on the subject, particularly the effort of historians in recent years to move beyond depicting the encounter between science and religion as one of sustained warfare.

Modern Pentecostalism has been called *the* religious movement of the twentieth century, with several million adherents in North America and possibly sixty million worldwide. In "The Functions of Faith in Primitive Pentecostalism," a recent article in the *Harvard Theological Review*, Professor Grant Wacker explains the growth of this movement as a distinctly American creation, the confluence of several traditions within evangelical Protestantism in the late nineteenth century. He asks why so many ordinary men and women chose to stay with the movement despite persecution from outsiders and derision from former friends. In answering this question, Wacker sensitively explores the ways in which Pentecostal forms of Christianity functioned effectively at a personal level. Wacker suggests that the movement prospered because it offered certitude about the reality of the supernatural and afforded a deep sense of community. The movement, which Wacker finds to be surprisingly doctrinal in orientation, prospered not in spite of being out of step with the times, but precisely because it *was* out of step with them.

About the Area Editor

Nathan Hatch (M.A. and Ph.D., Washington University, St. Louis, Mo.) is associate dean, College of Arts and Letters, University of Notre Dame. He is affiliated with the Christian Reformed Church. Books include *The Sacred Cause of Liberty* (1977) and, co-authored with Mark Noll, *The Bible in America* (1981).

BEYOND WAR AND PEACE:
A REAPPRAISAL OF THE ENCOUNTER
BETWEEN CHRISTIANITY AND SCIENCE

DAVID C. LINDBERG and RONALD L. NUMBERS
Mr. Lindberg is Professor of the History of Science
Mr. Numbers is Professor of the History of Medicine
and the History of Science
University of Wisconsin, Madison

Article from *Church History*

On a December evening in 1869, with memories of civil war still fresh in their minds, a large audience gathered in the great hall of Cooper Union in New York City to hear about another conflict, still taking its toll—"with battles fiercer, with sieges more persistent, with strategy more vigorous than in any of the comparatively petty warfares of Alexander, or Caesar, or Napoleon." Although waged with pens rather than swords, and for minds rather than empires, this war, too, had destroyed lives and reputations. The combatants? Science and Religion.[1]

The bearer of this unwelcome news was Andrew Dickson White, a 37-year-old, Episcopal-bred historian who had taught at the University of Michigan and served in the New York State Senate before becoming the first president of Cornell University at the age of thirty-three. His refusal as president to impose any religious tests on students and faculty, and his declared intention of creating in Ithaca "an asylum for *Science*—where truth shall be sought for truth's sake, not stretched or cut exactly to fit Revealed Religion," had aroused the enmity of pious New Yorkers, who accused the young president and his school of religious indifference and infidelity. When "sweet reasonableness" failed to placate his critics, White fired his Cooper Union broadside, accusing them of possessing the same kind of narrow minds and mean spirits that had led to the persecution of Vesalius, Kepler, and Galileo.[2]

History showed, White declared, that "interference with Science in the supposed interest of religion—no matter how conscientious such interference may have been—has resulted in the direst evils both to Religion and Science, and *invariably*." To document this thesis, he surveyed "some of the hardest-fought battlefields of this great war," illustrating how rigid biblical literalists and dogmatic theologians had stunted the growth of science and prostituted religion—only to lose in the end.[3]

Some of the bloodiest battles, White believed, had been fought during the sixteenth and seventeenth centuries, the period of the so-called Scientific Revolution, when powerful church leaders repeatedly tried to silence the pioneers of modern science. Nicolaus Copernicus, who dared to locate the sun at the center of the planetary system, risked his very life to publish his heretical views and escaped "persecution only by death." Many of his disciples met a less happy fate: Bruno was "burned alive as a monster of impiety: Galileo tortured and humiliated as the worst of unbelievers; Kepler hunted alike by Protestants and Catholics." Andreas Vesalius, the sixteenth-century physician who laid the foundations of modern anatomy by insisting on careful first-hand dissection of the human body, paid for his temerity by being "hunted to death." The latest victim in this protracted war on science, said White in an obvious reference to his own experience, was a certain American university, denounced from pulpit and press as "godless" merely because it defended scientific freedom and resisted sectarian control. White no doubt felt that its president, too, deserved to be ranked among the martyrs of science for the persecution that he had endured.[4]

White's Cooper Union lecture appeared the next day as "The Battle-Fields of Science" in the *New-York Daily Tribune*. In the years following, White fleshed out his history of the conflict between science and religion with new illustrations, some drawn from contemporary hostilities between creationists and evolutionists. Along the way he also narrowed the focus of his attack: from "religion" in 1869, to "ecclesiasticism" in 1876, when he published a little book entitled *The Warfare of Science*, and finally to "dogmatic theology" in 1896, when he brought out his fully documented, two-volume *History of the Warfare of Science with Theology in Christendom*. In this last version of his thesis he distinguished sharply between theology, which made unprovable statements about the world and took the Bible as a scientific text, and religion, which consisted of recognizing "a Power in the universe" and living by the Golden Rule. Religion, so defined, fostered science; theology smothered it.[5]

No work—not even John William Draper's best-selling *History of the Conflict between Religion and Science* (1874)—has done more than White's to instill in the public mind a sense of the adversarial relationship between science and religion. His *Warfare* remains in print to the present day, having appeared also in German, French, Italian, Swedish, and Japanese translations. His military rhetoric has captured the imagination of generations of readers, and his copious references, still impressive, have given his work the appearance of sound scholarship, bedazzling even twentieth-century historians who should know better. In recent decades, for example, the intellectual historian Bruce Mazlish certified White's thesis to have been established "beyond reasonable doubt," and the late George Sarton, a distinguished historian of science at Harvard, found White's argument so compelling that he urged its extension to non-Christian cultures.[6]

Such judgments, however appealing they may be to foes of "scientific creationism" and other contemporary threats to established science, fly in the face of mounting evidence that White read the past through battle-scarred glasses, and that he and his imitators have distorted history to serve ideological ends of their own. Although it is not difficult to find instances of conflict and controversy in the annals of Christianity and science, recent scholarship has shown the warfare metaphor to be neither useful nor tenable in describing the relationship between science and religion.[7] In the remainder of this paper, we wish to support this conclusion with a series of examples drawn from recent scholarly studies—thereby giving White's thesis a more systematic critique than it has heretofore received.

I.

White viewed the early centuries of the Christian era as an unmitigated disaster for science. By his account, the church fathers regarded all scientific effort as futile and required any crumbs of scientific knowledge acquired through patient observation and reasoning to yield to puerile opinions extracted by dogmatic church leaders from sacred writings. Such "theological views of science," he wrote, have "without exception . . . forced mankind away from the truth, and have caused Christendom to stumble for centuries into abysses of "error and sorrow."[8] The coming of Christianity thus "arrested the normal development of the physical sciences for over fifteen hundred years," imposing a tyranny of ignorance and superstition that perverted and crushed true science.[9]

It is true, of course, that few church fathers placed high value on science and that some spurned it altogether. Augustine expressed reservations about the value of natural science: "When it is asked what we ought to believe in matters of religion, the answer is not to be sought in the exploration of the nature of things, after the manner of those whom the Greeks called 'physicists'. . . . For the Christian, it is enough to believe that the cause of all things, whether in heaven or on earth, whether visible or invisible, is nothing other than the goodness of the Creator."[10]

One must not conclude from such remarks, however, that the church fathers totally repudiated scientific knowledge or demanded that it always conform to dictates of scripture. The opening clause of the passage just quoted is often overlooked. Augustine is arguing only that *in matters of religion* there is little or nothing to be learned from the Greek physicists. In another context he argues that insofar as scientific knowledge is required, it must be taken from the pagan authors who possess it:

> It frequently happens that there is some question about the earth, or the sky, or the other elements of this world, the movement, revolutions, or even the size and distance of the stars, the regular eclipses of the sun and the moon, the course of the years and seasons; the nature of the animals, vegetables and minerals, and other things of the same kind, respecting which one who

is not a Christian has knowledge derived from the most certain reasoning or observation. And it is highly deplorable and mischievous and a thing especially to be guarded against that he should hear a Christian speaking of such matters in accordance with Christian writings and uttering such nonsense that, knowing him to be as wide of the mark as . . . east is from west, the unbeliever can scarcely restrain himself from laughing.[11]

White and other writers on science and religion have suggested that science would have progressed more rapidly in the early centuries of the Christian era if Christianity had not inhibited its growth. Counterfactual speculations about what might have occurred had circumstances been otherwise are of questionable value. But it is worth pointing out that the study of nature held a very precarious position in ancient society; with the exception of medicine and a little astronomy, it served no practical function and generally failed to win recognition as a socially useful activity. As a result, it received little patronage from either pagans or Christians, but depended for its existence on independent means and individual initiative. When the economic and political fortunes of the Roman Empire declined in late antiquity, people of wealth decreased in number, and the elites directed their initiative elsewhere. Moreover, changing educational and philosophical values were diverting attention from the world of nature. Inevitably the pursuit of science suffered.

Christianity did little or nothing to alter the situation. It contained more or less the same spectrum of attitudes toward natural science as did paganism. If there were differences, Christianity was perhaps a little less otherworldly than the major competing ideologies (Gnosticism, Neoplatonism, and the mystery religions) and afforded slightly greater incentive for the study of nature. The church fathers used Greek scientific knowledge in their defense of the faith against heresy and in the elucidation of scripture, thereby preserving and transmitting it during the social and political turmoil of the first millennium of the Christian era. Science was thus the handmaiden of theology—a far cry from its modern status, characterized by autonomy and intellectual hegemony, but also far from the victim of Christian intolerance that White portrayed. Christianity was not the enemy, but a valued (if not entirely reliable) servant.[12]

In addition to serving theology, Greek scientific knowledge occupied a prominent place in Christian world views, from the time of Basil of Caesarea and Augustine through the end of the Middle Ages and beyond. The notion that any serious Christian thinker would even have attempted to formulate a world view from the Bible alone is ludicrous. For example, contrary to popular belief (which White's *Warfare* has helped to shape), the church did not insist on a flat earth; there was scarcely a Christian scholar of the Middle Ages who did not acknowledge its sphericity and even know its approximate circumference. By the beginning of the thirteenth century, virtually all of the works of Aristotle had become available in Europe, and from this point onward we see a persistent effort to integrate Aristotelian natural philosophy, or science, with Christian theology. In the end, Christianity took its basic categories of thought, its physical principles, and much of its metaphysics and cosmology from Aristotle. By means of its power to organize and interpret human experience, Aristotelianism conquered Christendom.

But Christian theology impinged on science in return and altered its character. Certain aspects of Aristotelian natural philosophy, such as its determinism (everything that will occur must occur) and its denial of a creation, were diametrically opposed to central Christian doctrines. The ensuing struggles (which were not between Christianity and science, but rather, one must note, among Christians holding different views of the proper relationship between Christianity and science) led ultimately to a theological condemnation of these and other philosophical propositions in 1270 and 1277. The complexity of the encounter between Christianity and science is illustrated nicely by the aftermath of these condemnations.[13] The condemnations did place a lid on certain lines of scientific speculation; henceforth, philosophers or scientists were forbidden to uphold certain Aristotelian positions and forced to tread lightly whenever they approached theological territory. But while losing certain freedoms, they gained others. Theological condemnation of a considerable body of Aristotelian propositions weakened the heavy hand of Aristotelian authority and freed scientists to speculate in non-Aristotelian and anti-Aristotelian directions. Thus we see in the fourteenth century a steady stream of attacks on various Aristotelian doctrines and a veritable orgy of speculation about non-Aristotelian possibilities, including such notions as the rotation of the earth on its axis.

The condemnations affected the scientific enterprise in another way. One of the central themes of the condemnations was the proclamation of God's absolute sovereignty and omnipotence. From this doctrine follows the absolute contingency of nature—that the course of nature can be anything God chooses it to be and, therefore, that humankind's acquired knowledge of natural causes can be overturned simply by God's decision to do things otherwise. The condemnations thus generated a certain skepticism about the ability of the human mind to penetrate with certainty to the underlying causes of observed events; this attitude encouraged the view that science should restrict its attention to empirical fact and ignore the search for underlying causes, thus influencing the development of scientific methodology. Four hundred years later, the idea of God's absolute sovereignty and its corollary, the total passivity of matter, became central features of Isaac Newton's mechanistic world view."[14]

II.

In 1543 Nicolaus Copernicus (1473-1543), a Catholic church administrator from northern Poland, announced a heliocentric astronomy that removed the earth from the center of the universe and led, ultimately, to the overturn-

ing of the medieval world view. White's interpretation of these events is
almost as wide of the mark as his understanding of the Middle Ages. White
reports that Copernicus feared to publish his discoveries in Rome or Wittenberg—the centers, respectively, of Catholicism and Protestantism. Instead,
the astronomer turned to Nuremberg, where his work was published with a
"grovelling preface," written by the Lutheran clergyman Andreas Osiander
(1498-1552), which contained the "apologetic lie that Copernicus has pro-
pounded the doctrine of the earth's movement not as a fact, but as a hypothesis." "The greatest and most ennobling, perhaps, of scientific truths" was
"forced, in coming before the world, to sneak and crawl."[15] Copernicus died
within a few hours of receiving his first copy of the book and thus, in White's
words, placed himself "beyond the reach of the conscientious men who
would have blotted his reputation and perhaps destroyed his life."[16]

White's picture of unremitting religious hostility to heliocentrism is no
longer defensible—if, indeed, it ever was. If Copernicus had any genuine fear
of publication, it was the reaction of scientists, not clerics, that worried him.
Other churchmen before him had freely discussed the possible motion of the
earth—Nicole Oresme (a bishop) in the fourteenth century and Nicholas of
Cusa (a cardinal) in the fifteenth—and there was no reason to suppose that
the reappearance of this idea in the sixteenth century would cause a religious
stir.[17] Indeed, various churchmen, including a bishop and a cardinal, urged
Copernicus to publish his book, which appeared with a dedication to Pope
Paul III. Had Copernicus lived beyond its publication in 1543, it is highly
improbable that he would have felt any hostility or suffered any persecution.
The church simply had more important things to worry about than a new
astronomical or cosmological system. Although a few critics noticed and
opposed the Copernican system, organized Catholic opposition did not
appear until the seventeenth century.[18]

Concerning the Protestant response to the ideas of Copernicus, White
claims that "all branches of the Protestant Church . . . vied with each other in
denouncing the Copernican doctrine as contrary to Scripture."[19] He also
maintains (and his account has been repeated endlessly) that the theologians Martin Luther, Philipp Melanchthon, and John Calvin all bitterly
attacked the new theory. In fact, from Luther we have only a single off-the-
cuff remark, made during a "table talk" in 1539 (four years *before* publication
of Copernicus's book), in which he refers to "that fool who wants to overturn
the whole art of astronomy." Melanchthon expressed early disapproval of
heliocentrism as a description of reality, but later softened his position.
Calvin spoke out against heliocentrism in a sermon on 1 Corinthians 10 and
11 (dating from 1556), denouncing the propagators of such vain novelties for
their contentious spirit, which undermines the quest for truth; but his interest in such matters was not deep, and cosmological issues never entered
systematically into his theology.[20]

Significantly, the first sustained response to Copernicus came from a group of young Lutheran mathematical astronomers who worked under Melanchthon's general patronage.[21] One of them, Georg Joachim Rheticus (1514-1574), spent two years with Copernicus shortly before the latter's death and persuaded the elderly astronomer to publish his book. Rheticus saw it through the press, with Osiander's help. Osiander's prefatory letter, maintaining that astronomy makes mathematical predictions but does not necessarily describe physical reality, was no "grovelling" apology, but an expression of deeply held convictions, shared by many astronomers—a sincere attempt to save Copernicus from unnecessary criticism. Rheticus himself accepted the physical reality of heliocentrism and, contrary to White's claim, proclaimed his position openly. However, many of Rheticus's colleagues adopted Copernicanism simply as a mathematical reform, offering a better way of predicting planetary positions, while overlooking or rejecting the radical thesis that the earth really moves. Their reasons for opposing the motion of the earth were both scientific and theological: heliocentrism violated the principles of Aristotelian physics and conflicted with the literal interpretation of certain biblical passages that seemed to teach the fixity of the earth. To the latter objection, heliocentrists replied that such passages were written in the language of everyday speech and should not be taken as statements of scientific truth. By the end of the century, then, Protestants held a variety of cosmological views, the merits of which they freely debated.

The seventeenth century, according to White, produced a "new champion" of heliocentrism, the young Galileo, equipped with a new scientific instrument, the telescope. "Against him," White writes, "the war was long and bitter. . . . Semi-scientific professors, endeavoring to curry favour with the Church, attacked him with sham science; earnest preachers attacked him with perverted Scripture; theologians, inquisitors, congregations of cardinals, and at last popes dealt with him, and, as was supposed, silenced his impious doctrine forever."[22] This dramatic tale has come, for many, to symbolize the theological assault on science.

White experienced little difficulty identifying good and evil, truth and error, heroes and villains. Modern scholarship, however, offers a picture more subtle in its shadings. In order to grasp the events and understand why Galileo's fate differed from that of Copernicus, we must keep in mind the Counter-Reformation of the second half of the sixteenth century. Responding to the challenge of the Protestant Reformation, Catholicism grew more conservative and authoritarian; power became centralized, and ideological vigilance increased. One of the most sensitive issues was biblical interpretation, for Protestant rejection of the Catholic position that the church alone has the authority to interpret the Bible set the two sides in direct opposition. The Catholic church assumed a firm stance on this issue at the Council of Trent (1545-1563), forbidding the interpretation of scripture on any matter of faith or practice "contrary to the sense determined by the Holy Mother

Church."[23] The hermeneutic flexibility of the Middle Ages had become a thing of the past.

When Galileo burst on the scene in 1610, he came equipped not only with telescopic observations that could be used to support the heliocentric theory, but also with liberal arguments about how to interpret biblical passages that seemed to teach the fixity of the earth. Galileo argued that God spoke through both scripture and the "book of nature," that the two could not truly conflict, and that in physical matters authority should rest with reason and sense. Challenged by demonstrative scientific proof, any scriptural passage to the contrary would have to be reinterpreted. Galileo was flirting with danger, not only by entering the domain of the theologians, but also by defending hermeneutic principles clearly at odds with the spirit of the Council of Trent. Moreover, Galileo lacked the convincing physical proof of the mobility of the earth that his own position demanded. Every one of his telescopic observations was compatible with the modified geocentric system of Tycho Brahe, and Galileo's argument from the tides (that they represent a sloshing about of the oceans on a moving earth) convinced few. The trouble in which Galileo eventually found himself, and which led ultimately to his condemnation, then, resulted not from clear scientific evidence running afoul of biblical claims to the contrary (as White tells the story), but from ambiguous scientific evidence provoking an intramural dispute within Catholicism over the proper principles of scriptural interpretation—a dispute won by the conservatives at Galileo's expense.[24] Galileo never questioned the authority of scripture, merely the principles by which it was to be interpreted.

The details of Galileo's condemnation need not detain us long.[25] Galileo's campaign on behalf of Copernicanism was halted abruptly in 1616, when the Holy Office declared the heliocentric doctrine heretical—though at the time Galileo faced no physical threat. Eight years later Galileo received permission from the new pope, the scholarly Urban VIII, to write about the Copernican system as long as he treated it as mere hypothesis. After many delays, Galileo's *Dialogue Concerning the Two Chief World Systems* appeared in 1623. In it, Galileo not only unambiguously defended the heliocentric system as physically true, but also made the tactical mistake of placing the pope's admonition about its hypothetical character in the mouth of the slow-witted Aristotelian, Simplicio. Although the official *imprimatur* of the church had been secured, Galileo's enemies, including the now angry Urban VIII, determined to bring him to trial. The inquisition ultimately condemned Galileo and forced him to recant. Although sentenced to house arrest for the rest of his life, he lived comfortably in a villa outside Florence. He was neither tortured nor imprisoned—simply silenced.

The Galileo affair was a multifaceted event. Certainly it raised serious questions about the relationship between reason and revelation, and the proper means of reconciling the teachings of nature with those of scripture.

Nonetheless, it was not a matter of Christianity waging war on science. All of the participants called themselves Christians, and all acknowledged biblical authority. This was a struggle between opposing theories of biblical interpretation: a conservative theory issuing from the Council of Trent versus Galileo's more liberal alternative. Both were well precedented in the history of the church. Personal and political factors also played a role, as Galileo demonstrated his flair for cultivating enemies in high places.[26]

III.

Throughout the nineteenth century, but especially after the publication in 1859 of Charles Darwin's *Origin of Species*, the hottest battles in White's warfare were fought over the biblical account of creation. These conflicts allegedly pitted the "great body of theologians" against a coalition of scientists drawn from the fields of astronomy, geology, biology, and anthropology who sought to substitute a dynamic, natural history of the world for the static, supernatural account found in Genesis. Each encounter, says White, followed a predictable pattern: theologians first marshaled biblical texts against the offending scientific doctrine, then sued for peace, after the development of a scientific consensus, by offering "far-fetched reconciliations of textual statements with ascertained fact."[27]

As an example of this process, White cites the reception given to the nebular hypothesis of Pierre Simon Laplace, who in 1796 proposed that the solar system had developed naturally from a contracting, rotating nebula. "Throughout the theological world," White writes, "there was an outcry at once against 'atheism,' and war raged fiercely." Later, after various discoveries had made the hypothesis scientifically respectable, the faithful decided that Laplace's conjecture was not atheistic at all, but corresponded marvelously with the biblical declaration that "in the beginning . . . the earth was without form, and void" (Gen. 1:1-2).[28]

In his zeal to describe the battle, White neglects to inform his readers that clergy were among the first to embrace and popularize the hypothesis —and that the most successful and influential of the "far-fetched" efforts to harmonize the Mosaic and Laplacian cosmogonies came not from over-imaginative biblical scholars but from two of America's most distinguished scientists, Arnold Guyot of Princeton and James Dwight Dana of Yale. Instead of illustrating the eagerness of theologians to wage war on science, the history of the nebular hypothesis shows the extent to which orthodox Christians went to avoid conflict with science.[29]

The religious response to developments in historical geology provides another example of the fallacy of the science-versus-theology formula. As Charles C. Gillispie pointed out years ago, the problem in geology during the early nineteenth century was "one of religion (in a crude sense) *in* science rather than one of religion versus science." To illustrate the absurdity of pitting men of science against men of the cloth, we need only point out that the leading English geologists of the early nineteenth century—William Buckland, William Daniel Conybeare, and Adam Sedgwick—were all clergymen, as was the American geologist Edward Hitchcock. And for every theologian who labored to produce "more or less absurd" schemes for reconciling geology and Genesis, there were scientists—for example, the geologists Benjamin Silliman and John William Dawson—who did the same thing.[30]

Geologists who argued for the antiquity of the earth, the existence of pre-Adamic life, and a limited Noachian flood inevitably generated heated debate. But when conflict erupted, it did not find geologists facing theologians. Rather, as James R. Moore recently has argued, professional geologists, who subscribed to Charles Lyell's admonition to study geology "as if the Scriptures were not in existence," joined with professional biblical scholars, who adopted Benjamin Jowett's advice to "interpret the Scriptures like any other book," in an alliance against amateur geologists and exegetes who refused to accept these maxims.[31]

The appearance of Darwin's controversial theory of organic evolution, which made humans animals and left God virtually unemployed, understandably stirred passionate debate. But White's polemical analysis confuses rather than clarifies the issues. According to White, Samuel Wilberforce, the Bishop of Oxford, launched the theological offensive against Darwin—and set the tone of the debate—by writing an essay for *The Quarterly Review* in which he condemned Darwinism for contradicting the Bible. Later, on 30 June 1860, in an address at Oxford before the British Association for the Advancement of Science, Wilberforce repeated his objections, this time congratulating himself "that he was not descended from a monkey." Upon hearing this remark, Darwin's friend the zoologist Thomas Huxley shot back: "If I had to choose, I would prefer to be a descendant of a humble monkey rather than of a man who employs his knowledge and eloquence in misrepresenting those who are wearing out their lives in the search for the truth"—a shot, says White, that "reverberated through England" and indeed the world.[32]

To White's credit, he refrained from passing on an even more sensational (and apocryphal) version of the story, according to which the bishop impertinently asked Huxley whether it was "on your grandfather's or grandmother's side that you claim descent from the apes." Replied the irreverent zoologist: "I would rather be descended from an ape than a bishop." This is a dramatic and memorable story, but one, as J. R. Lucas and others have shown, that perpetuates many errors and places Wilberforce in a grossly unfair light.[33]

In his essay for *The Quarterly Review*, which provided the basis for his comments at Oxford, Wilberforce expressed concern about the theological implications of Darwinism, but he dwelt on the scientific, not the religious, objections to Darwin's theory. In fact, he professed a willingness to embrace the theory if it should be demonstrated to be correct:

> If Mr. Darwin can with the same correctness of reasoning [as Newton] demonstrate to us our fungular descent, we shall dismiss our pride, and avow, with the characteristic humility of philosophy, our unsuspected cousinship with the mushrooms . . . only we shall ask leave to scrutinise carefully every step of the argument which has such an ending, and demur if at any point of it we are invited to substitute unlimited hypothesis for patient observation. . . . We have no sympathy with those who object to any fact or alleged facts in nature, or to any inference logically deduced from them, because they believe them to contradict what it appears is taught by Revelation.

These are hardly the ravings of an intransigent fundamentalist, as even Darwin recognized. Writing to a friend, Darwin called the Bishop's review "uncommonly clever" and noted that his clerical critic "picks out with skill all the most conjectural parts [of the *Origin*], and brings forward well all the difficulties."[34]

The Huxley-Wilberforce exchange, far from setting the tone of the Darwinian debate, went virtually unnoticed at the time. The botanist Joseph Hooker, who later endorsed the legend, reported to Darwin shortly after the meeting that he, not Huxley, had responded most effectively to the bishop. And a writer covering the meetings for *The Athenaeum* neglected even to mention Huxley's alleged riposte. Wilberforce and Huxley did, without doubt, exchange words, but the words became memorable only with the passage of time, as victorious Darwinians began reconstructing the history of their struggle for recognition. In their memories Huxley won the day at Oxford, but contemporary records indicate otherwise: Wilberforce's supporters included not only the majority of clerics and laypeople in attendance, but "the most eminent naturalists" as well.[35]

In recent decades, the encounter between William Jennings Bryan and Clarence Darrow at the Scopes trial in 1925 has achieved similar legendary status as a major turning point in the war between science and religion. According to common opinion, the evolutionists, though defeated on legal grounds, scored a stunning public-relations victory, halted the anti-evolution crusade, and exposed the bumbling Bryan as an ignoramus. A more careful look suggests that they did nothing of the sort. Even liberal contemporaries, Paul M. Waggoner has shown, tended at first to view the trial as a disturbing fundamentalist victory, and the anti-evolution campaign continued to prosper for several years after the trial. By present standards, Bryan displayed remarkable openmindedness for a creationist. Publicly, he not only accepted the testimony of geologists regarding the antiquity of the earth, but conceded that the "days" of Genesis represented long periods of time. Privately, he allowed to friends that he had no quarrel with "evolution before man."[36]

144 The Best in Theology

White's seeming compulsion to reduce every episode in the history of science and Christianity to a simple warlike confrontation blinded him to the possibility that Darwin's critics might have been motivated by honest scientific objections or that his supporters might have been attracted for theological reasons. Thus he tells us that Harvard's venerable Louis Agassiz rejected evolution because he could not escape "the atmosphere of the little Swiss parsonage in which he was born" and that the Canadian geologist Sir William Dawson opposed Darwinism for theological reasons—ignoring in both cases their scientific complaints. Likewise, White overlooked the affinity between Darwinism and Calvinism that apparently encouraged such orthodox Christians as the botanist Asa Gray and the geologist-clergyman George Frederick Wright to accept natural selection.[37]

We are not suggesting that all was harmony—that serious conflict did not exist—only that it was not the simple bipolar warfare described by White. Recent scholarship suggests that Darwinism produced conflict in at least three different ways. According to James R. Moore, the Darwinian debates created conflict, not between scientists and theologians, but within individual minds experiencing a "crisis of faith" as they struggled to come to terms with new historical and scientific discoveries. It was, he writes, a "conflict of minds steeped in Christian tradition with the ideas and implications of Darwinism."[38]

Neal C. Gillespie has argued that the conflict involved competing systems of science or "epistemes," the older of which rested on theological assumptions while the newer one, associated with Darwin, rejected religion as a means of knowing the world and insisted on an interpretation of nature that involved only natural, secondary causes. "Because the new episteme for science differed from the old in having within it no place for theology," he explains, "serious questions were thereby raised that made the conflict, sometimes dismissed as an illusion or a mistake, very real indeed." Such conflict, arising from transformations *within* science, had little to do with warring scientists and clerics.[39]

Frank M. Turner has offered still a third way of viewing the Darwinian controversies. The "victorian conflict between religious and scientific spokesmen," he claims, resulted not from hostility between progressive science and retrogressive theology, as White would claim, but from a "shift of authority and prestige . . . from one part of the intellectual nation to another," as professionalizing scientists sought to banish the clergy from the scientific enterprise and end their control of education. According to Turner, the positivist episteme described by Gillespie

constituted both a cause and a weapon. The "young guard" agreed among themselves that science should be pursued without regard for religious dogma, natural theology, or the opinions of religious authorities. . . . The drive to organize a more professionally oriented scientific community and to define science in a more critical fashion brought the crusading scientists into conflict with two groups of people. The first were supporters of organized religion who wished to maintain a large measure of control over education and to retain religion as the source of moral and social values. The second group was the religiously minded sector of the preprofessional scientific community, which included both clergymen and laymen.

In Turner's view, then, the conflict had a social as well as an intellectual dimension.[40]

IV.

This brief excursion to some of White's old battlefields has demonstrated that the historical relationship between science and Christianity—or, more properly, scientists and theologians—cannot be reduced simply to conflict or warfare. Additional examples would only strengthen this conclusion.[41] However, discrediting the warfare thesis represents only the beginning of the historical task confronting us. We also must construct a satisfactory alternative, for until we do, it is likely that the military metaphor will continue to dominate historical analysis. We require a fresh history of science and religion, free (or as free as we can make it) of the distortion of malice and self-interest. Reinterpreting something as complex as the encounter between Christianity and science is a delicate and arduous task that can hardly be accomplished within the scope of one paper. Nevertheless, we wish to offer a few caveats and suggestions that may help to define a suitable program.

First, to insure that we will not be misunderstood, we wish to assert plainly that our displeasure with White's warfare thesis is matched by our aversion to its converse. That is, in denying that unremitting hostility and conflict have characterized the relationship between Christianity and science, we do not in any way mean to suggest that Christianity and science have been perennial allies. Such an interpretation, though widely held in some circles, particularly among Christian apologists, fails to pass historical muster.[42]

Second, one of the great attractions of White's view is its simplicity; few qualifications and nuances detract from the clarity of his picture. The memorable imagery found in his writings helps to explain their remarkable longevity. Unfortunately, we will never find a satisfactory alternative of equal simplicity. Any interpretation that begins to do justice to the complexity of the interaction between Christianity and science must be heavily qualified and subtly nuanced—clearly a disadvantage in the quest for public recognition, but a necessity nonetheless.

Third, we are convinced that traditional categories—enemies versus allies, conflict versus consensus—are misleading, even pernicious, because they direct us toward the wrong questions. For more than a century historians of Christianity and science like White have wasted their time and dissipated their energies attempting to identify villains and victims, often with polemical or apologetic intent, and always within a framework heavily laden with values. They tacitly have assumed that science has been, and continues to be, one of Western civilization's most valuable cultural artifacts—so valuable, indeed, that nothing should be allowed to interfere with it. Then they have proceeded to inquire why the most perfect expression of scientific activity (namely, modern science) was so long in coming into existence, as if its creation were a simple and inevitable matter; they have leapt quickly to the conclusion that science has suffered various indignities at the hand of assorted enemies, of which Christianity was chief. Such scientism must not pass unchallenged.

In offering these criticisms, we do not mean to question the significance or value of the scientific enterprise. We mean only to suggest that to start with scientific assumptions is no way to understand the nature and genesis of science. If we only celebrate the rise of science, we are not apt to understand it. Besides, partisan historians of religion can play a similar game: by supposing religion to be the premier cultural property, to which everything else (including science) must be subordinate, they discover that science frequently has interfered with the progress of religion. Both games, though seductive for their apologetic function, are of little merit to the historian, because the outcome is, in very large measure, predetermined by the value-laden rules of the game being played. Sound scholarship requires a more neutral starting point.[43]

Historical investigation to date has revealed a rich and varied interaction between science and Christianity. People of assorted scientific and theological persuasions and varieties of knowledge and commitment have, with varying degrees of skill and integrity, gone about the business of understanding themselves and their world, building institutions, creating careers, and pursuing sundry satisfactions. In the process, Christianity and science—as intellectual systems, as institutions, and as objects of personal commitment—have rubbed against each other, sometimes comfortably, sometimes with destructive force.[44] In the future we must not ask "Who was the aggressor?" but "How were Christianity and science affected by their encounter?" We are confident that research will show that the encounter has been multiform, the range of effects enormous. We will discover shifting alignments and dual memberships. We will uncover as much struggle and competition within the Christian and scientific communities as between them. Most important, we will see that influence has flowed in both directions, that Christianity and science alike have been profoundly shaped by their relations with each other. If, however, we fail to escape the trap of assigning credit and blame, we will never properly appreciate the roles of science and Christianity in the shaping of Western culture; and that will deeply impoverish our understanding.

Notes

[1] "First of the Course of Scientific Lectures—Prof. White on 'The Battlefields of Science,' " *New York Daily Tribune*, 18 Dec. 1869, p. 4.

[2] Bruce Mazlish, Preface to *A History of the Warfare of Science with Theology in Christendom*, by Andrew Dickson White (abridged ed., New York, 1965), p. 13; Andrew Dickson White, *A History of the Warfare of Science with Theology in Christendom*, 2 vols. (New York, 1896), 1: viii. On White, see Glenn C. Altschuler, *Andrew D. White—Educator, Historian, Diplomat* (Ithaca, 1979).

[3] "First of the Course of Scientific Lectures," p. 4.

[4] Ibid.

[5] Ibid.; Andrew Dickson White, *The Warfare of Science* (New York, 1876), p. 145; White, *A History of the Warfare*, 1: ix, xii. Although hints of White's distinction between religion and theology appear in his earlier works, the focus on dogmatic theology in his 1896 volumes seems to have been more of an afterthought—a misleading effort to distance himself from William Draper—than an essential premise. See Draper, *History of the Conflict between Religion and Science* (New York, 1874). Henry Guerlac corroborates this judgment in an unpublished memoire, "Sartoniana and Forward," where he notes that White had intended to entitle the 1896 book *A History of the Warfare of Science and Religion*, but was talked out of it by his collaborator, George Lincoln Burr.

[6] Mazlish, Preface, p. 18; George Sarton, "Introductory Essay," in *Science, Religion and Reality*, ed. Joseph Needham (New York, 1955), p. 14.

[7] For a brilliant critique of the warfare metaphor, see James R. Moore, *The Post-Darwinian Controversies: A Study of the Protestant Struggle to Come to Terms with Darwin in Great Britain and America, 1870-1900* (Cambridge, 1979), pp. 19-122. See also David C. Lindberg and Ronald L. Numbers, eds. *God and Nature: Historical Essays on the Encounter between Christianity and Science* (Berkeley, 1986), passim; and Ronald L. Numbers, "Science and Religion," in *Historical Writing on American Science*, ed. Sally Gregory Kohlstedt and Margaret W. Rossiter, *Osiris* 1, 2d ser. (1985): 59-80.

[8] White, *A History of the Warfare*, 1:325. For a fuller account of science and the early church, see David C. Lindberg, "Science and the Early Church," in *God and Nature*, pp. 19-58.

[9] White, *A History of the Warfare*, 1:375.

[10] Augustine, *Enchiridion* 3.9, trans. Albert C. Outler, Library of Christian Classics 7 (Philadelphia, 1955), pp. 341-42.

[11] Augustine, *De genesi ad litteram* 1.19; trans. Meyrick H. Carre, *Realists and Nominalists* (London, 1946), p. 19. For another translation, see Augustine, *The Literal Meaning of Genesis*, trans. John Hammond Taylor, S.J., 2 vols., Ancient Christian Writers 41-42 (New York, 1982), 1:42-43.

[12] The themes of this and the preceding paragraph are more fully developed in Lindberg, "Science and the Early Church," pp. 29-33.

[13] For a good account of the effects of the condemnations, see Edward Grant, "The Condemnation of 1277, God's Absolute Power, and Physical Thought in the Late Middle Ages," *Viator* 10 (1979): 211-44; reprinted in Edward Grant's *Studies in Medieval Science and Natural Philosophy* (London, 1981), article 13.

[14] See Gary Deason, "Reformation Theology and the Mechanistic Conception of Nature," in *God and Nature*, pp. 181-85.

[15] White, *A History of the Warfare,* 1:123.

[16] Ibid., 1:123-124.

[17] Oresme's discussion is translated and analyzed in Marshall Clagett, *The Science of Mechanics in the Middle Ages* (Madison, 1959), pp. 600-609.

[18] On the sixteenth-century Catholic response to Copernicanism, see Robert S. Westman, "Copernicanism and the Churches," pp. 81-85, 86-95.

[19] White, *A History of the Warfare*, 1:26. On the Protestant response to Copernicanism, see Westman, "Copernicanism and the Churches," pp. 81-85, 89-98.

[20] On Luther and Melanchthon see B. A. Gerrish, "The Reformation and the Rise of Modern Science," in *The Impact of the Church Upon Its Culture: Reappraisals of the History of Christianity*, ed. Jerald C. Brauer (Chicago, 1968), pp. 231-65. For the latest word in the long debate over Calvin's position, see R. Stauffer, "Calvin et Copernic," *Revue de l'histoire des religions* 179 (1971): 31-40; Robert White, "Calvin and Copernicus: The Problem Reconsidered. *Calvin Theological Journal* 15 (1980): 233-43.

[21] Robert S. Westman, "The Melanchthon Circle, Rheticus, and the Wittenberg Interpretation of the Copernican Theory," *Isis* 66 (1976): 164-93.

[22] White, *A History of the Warfare*, 1:130-31.

[23] The text of the decree is given in Olaf Pedersen, "Galileo and the Council of Trent: The Galileo Affair Revisited," *Journal for the History of Astronomy* 14 (1983): 28-29, n. 46.

[24] On the issues between Galileo and his critics within the church, see ibid; also William R. Shea, "Galileo and the Church," in *God and Nature*, pp. 118-33.

[25] On the course of events, see (in addition to the works by Petersen and Shea) Jerome J. Langford, *Galileo, Science, and the Church* (New York, 1966).

[26] The struggle over heliocentrism was not the only battle during the period of the scientific revolution identified by White. For his discussion of the biomedical sciences, see *A History of the Warfare*, 1:49-63. For contrasting views, see Ronald L. Numbers and Ronald C. Sawyer, "Medicine and Christianity in the Modern World," in *Health/Medicine and the Faith Traditions*, ed. Martin E. Marty and Kenneth L. Vaux (Philadelphia, 1982), pp. 134-36; and James J. Walsh, *The Popes and Science* (New York, 1908).

[27] White, *A History of the Warfare*, 1:22, 218.

[28] Ibid., 1:17-18.

[29] Ronald L. Numbers, *Creation by Natural Law: Laplace's Nebular Hypothesis in American Thought* (Seattle, 1977).

[30] Charles Coulston Gillispie, *Genesis and Geology: A Study in the Relations of Scientific Thought, Natural Theology, and Social Opinion in Great Britain, 1790-1850* (Cambridge, Mass., 1951); White, *A History of the Warfare*, 1:234. See also Nicolas A. Rupke, *The Great Chain of History: William Buckland and the English School of Geology, 1814-1849* (Oxford, 1983).

[31] James R. Moore, "Geologists and Interpreters of Genesis in the Nineteenth Century," in *God and Nature*, pp. 322-50. See also Martin J. S. Rudwick, "The Shape and Meaning of Earth-History," ibid., pp. 296-321.

[32] White, *A History of the Warfare*, 1:70-71.

[33] J. R. Lucas, "Wilberforce and Huxley: A Legendary Encounter," *The Historical Journal* 22 (1979): 313-30. See also Sheridan Gilley, "The Huxley-Wilberforce Debate: A Reconsideration," in *Religion and Humanism*, ed. Keith Robbins, Studies in Church History 17 (Oxford, 1981), pp. 325-40.

[34] Quoted in Lucas, "Wilberforce and Huxley," pp. 317-20.

[35] Ibid., pp. 313-30.

[36] Paul M. Waggoner, "The Historiography of the Scopes Trial: A Critical Re-evaluation," *Trinity Journal,* n.s. 5 (1984): 155-74; Ronald L. Numbers, "Creationism in 20th-Century America," *Science* 218 (1982): 538-44. See also Edward J. Larson, *Trial and Error: The American Controversy over Creation and Evolution* (New York, 1985).

[37] White, *A History of the Warfare*, 1:68, 82. On the relationship between Darwinism and Calvinism, see Moore, *Post-Darwinian Controversies*, pp. 280-98, 334-40. White's interpretation of the Darwinian debates is rejected also by A. Hunter Dupree, "Christianity and the Scientific Community in the Age of Darwin," in *God and Nature*, pp. 351-68.

[38] Moore, *Post-Darwinian Controversies*, pp. 102-103.

[39] Neal C. Gillespie, *Charles Darwin and the Problem of Creation* (Chicago, 1979), pp. 12-13, 18, 53. See also Alvar Ellegard, *Darwin and the General Reader: The Reception of Darwin's Theory of Evolution in the British Periodical Press, 1859-1872:* (Göteborg, Sweden, 1958), p. 337.

[40] Frank M. Turner, "The Victorian Conflict between Science and Religion: A Professional Dimension," *Isis* 69 (1979): 356-76. Owen Chadwick has argued that the conflict between science and religion "was hypostatized, necessarily, out of a number of conflicts"; *The Secularization of the European Mind in the Nineteenth Century* (Cambridge, 1975), pp. 163-64.

[41] See, for example, Edward E. Daub, "Demythologizing White's Warfare of Science with Theology," *American Biology Teacher* 40 (1978): 553-56.

[42] See, for example, R [eijer] Hooykaas, *Religion and the Rise of Modern Science* (Grand Rapids, Mich., 1972); and Stanley L. Jaki, *The Road of Science and the Ways to God* (Chicago, 1978).

[43] On the need for a neutral stance, see Martin Rudwick, "Senses of the Natural World and Senses of God: Another Look at the Historical Relation of Science and Religion," in *The Sciences and Theology in the Twentieth Century*, ed. A. R. Peacocke (Notre Dame, 1981), pp. 241-61.

[44] Although we are aware of the danger that some readers might interpret our use of the terms "science" and "Christianity" as an unwarranted reification of these entities, we have retained this terminology as a convenient way of designating the various manifestations of Christianity and science.

THE FUNCTIONS OF FAITH
IN PRIMITIVE PENTECOSTALISM

GRANT WACKER
Associate Professor of Religious Studies
University of North Carolina at Chapel Hill

Article from *Harvard Theological Review*

I.

On a foggy evening in the spring of 1906, nine days before the San Francisco earthquake, several black saints gathered in a small house in Los Angeles to seek the baptism in the Holy Spirit. Before the night was over, a frightened child ran from the house to tell a neighbor that the people inside were singing and shouting in strange languages. Several days later the group moved to an abandoned warehouse on Azusa Street in a run-down section of the city. Soon they were discovered by a Los Angeles *Times* reporter. The "night is made hideous . . . by the howlings of the worshippers," he wrote. "The devotees of the weird doctrine practice the most fanatical rites, preach the wildest theories and work themselves into a state of mad excitement."[1]

The Azusa Street revival is commonly considered the cradle of modern pentecostalism, the beginning of what Peter Williams has aptly called "*the popular religious movement*" of the twentieth century. Although no one knows how big the movement really is, scholars estimate that there are several million adherents in North America and possibly sixty million worldwide. In the United States alone there are more than three hundred pentecostal denominations. Most are quite small, yet the two largest, the Assemblies of God and the Church of God in Christ, each claim more than two million American followers and additional millions in other parts of the world. Nor has the respectability lagged far behind. The *Christian Century* recently judged Oral Roberts one of the ten most influential religious leaders in America, and pentecostal statesman David J. DuPlessis clearly has become a star in international ecumenical circles.[2]

There is considerable disagreement about the origin of the movement, but the broad outline of the story seems clear enough. Like Mormonism and Seventh Day Adventism, pentecostalism is a distinctively American creation which grew from the confluence of several traditions within evangelical Protestantism in the middle and later years of the nineteenth century. The immediate result of this confluence was a widespread conviction that the

151

conversion experience should be followed by another life-transforming experience known as baptism in the Holy Spirit. The latter was regarded as the prerequisite for the restoration of the gifts of the Spirit described in 1 Corinthians 12 and 14. By the end of the century these notions had combined with growing reports of miraculous healing experiences to fuel an urgent expectation that the Lord's return was at hand. In this context of mounting religious fervor, many men and women began to look for an indisputable sign, a proof, that they had truly received the baptism in the Holy Spirit. Thus in 1901 one Charles Fox Parham, an itinerant faith healer living in Topeka, Kansas, came to the conclusion that speaking in "unknown tongues" (technically called glossolalia) was in fact the biblical evidence of baptism in the Holy Spirit. Eventually a black holiness preacher named William J. Seymour carried this notion to Los Angeles, where his preaching ignited the Azusa Street revival described above.[3]

All of the major pentecostal denominations were formed in the next two decades. Between 1907 and 1911 several already thriving Wesleyan sects in the Southeast were drawn into the movement through the influence of persons who had visited the Azusa Mission. These included the predominantly black Church of God in Christ, centered in Mississippi and western Tennessee, the Church of God, based in the southern Appalachians, and the Pentecostal Holiness Church, concentrated in the Carolinas and Georgia. After a slow start the pentecostal message also caught fire among non-Wesleyan evangelicals in the lower Midwest and California. The Assemblies of God, organized in 1914, grew most luxuriantly in Missouri, Oklahoma, and Texas. A doctrinal dispute in the Assemblies of God over the nature of the Trinity soon led to the formation of numerous unitarian or "Oneness" groups. The two largest of these are now known as the United Pentecostal Church, International, and the Pentecostal Assemblies of the World, both centered in the Midwest. In the 1920s Aimee Semple McPherson also broke from the Assemblies of God to establish her own denomination in Los Angeles, the International Church of the Four-square Gospel.[4]

If there is a measure of consensus about the sequence of events that led to the formation of modern pentecostalism, there is little consensus about the underlying causes. Some pentecostal historians have argued that the revival came *Suddenly from Heaven*, as one standard history of the movement is titled. Other historians have traced pentecostalism's origins to the social and cultural changes of the 1880s and 1890s, and still others have sought to place it in the long context of ecstatic and millenarian movements throughout history.[5]

Understanding the causes of pentecostalism is an important task; nonetheless, in this essay I want to sidestep the problem of initial causes and ask a somewhat different question: Once the movement had started, why did it survive? While the great majority of evangelical Protestants clung to the old allegiances, why did a small but steady stream of believers year after year forsake the old commitments in favor of new ones? More significantly, why did thousands of ordinary men and women choose to stay with the movement, knowing that it meant persecution from outsiders and remorseless derision from former friends? Why, in short, did this new mix of old ingredients prove so durable?

I suggest that two factors were especially crucial. First, pentecostalism functioned effectively at the personal level. It offered certitude about the reality of the supernatural and, in the face of loneliness and death, it met enduring needs of the human spirit. Second, the movement's message was a preeminently traditional message, richly textured with mythic images of an undefiled and unchanging realm outside mundane history. Together, these factors insulated pentecostalism from the encroachments of the modern world. Scholars and skeptics could say what they wanted; the ideas and sensibilities of the movement unfolded—and rather luxuriantly at that—within a set of premises untouched and for many years impervious to the governing assumptions of twentieth-century culture.

II.

Pentecostalism prospered first of all, then, because it offered certitude about the truthfulness of inherited theological claims about the reality of the supernatural. "In an age filled with discordant and capricious theological sounds," one pentecostal historian has perceptively written, the movement provided a "retreat from the turbulence of doubt and denial." Certitude was, in short, the inner strength of the revival, the backbone that sustained it year in and year out. Yet in order to understand how certitude functioned, it is necessary to see how it grew from the interplay between the worldview and the religious experiences of the movement's adherents.[6]

Primitive pentecostals considered themselves orthodox heirs of the Protestant Reformation, yet their conceptual universe was thickly populated with supernatural beings. God the Father was barely one of them. He existed of course on paper, in a handful of theological books, and in printed Sunday School lessons. But in practice, in the daily devotional life of ordinary folk, God was eclipsed by Jesus. One historian's assertion that early pentecostalism was essentially a "Jesus-cult" may be too strong, yet no child of the movement could forget the lyrics of the countless songs about Jesus, sung over and over in Sunday evening meetings.

> All that thrills my soul is Jesus;
> He is more than life to me;
> And the fairest of ten thousand,
> In my blessed Lord I see.

Pentecostal songbooks were heavily oriented toward Jesus. "Roll your Burdens on Jesus," "He Was Nailed to the Cross for Me," "Jesus Is Calling," "Jesus Saves," "'Tis So Sweet to Trust in Jesus," and "We Shall See the King" were among the well-worn favorites.[7]

Nor did the Holy Spirit, formally conceived as the Third Person of the Trinity, receive much attention. Despite strenuous insistence by pentecostal writers that the Holy Spirit is a person and not an impersonal power, in the daily devotional life of the people the Spirit often emerged as just that: impersonal power. Once again, the songs tell the story: "Old-time Power," "Pentecostal Power," "Send the Fire," "When the Power Fell on Me," "Bring Your Vessels Not a Few (He will fill your heart to overflowing, With the Holy Ghost and power)." Autobiographical accounts of the baptism experience repeatedly used physical—and especially electrical—metaphors. Aimee Semple McPherson's recollection is typical: When "I began to speak in other tongues," she wrote, "ripples, waves, billows, oceans, cloudbursts of blessing flooded my being. . . . I shook as though I were holding the positive and negative handles of the electric battery in the school laboratory." A respected theologian similarly described the Holy Spirit as a "felt power" emanating from the Bible "like invisible rays eddying in irresistible arcs." The Spirit, he continued, flows from the Bible like a "rose plot that emits delicious perfume."[8]

Demons and angels were palpably real and always present. One historian has argued that the pentecostal worldview was thoroughly animistic. Participants would have found this characterization repugnant, but it is undeniable that their literature was filled with stories about Satan's direct interference in earthly affairs. Prominent political figures or groups were often identified as the Antichrist, and demonic spirits were held responsible for many sicknesses. In most instances, consequently, faith healing was conceived as exorcism of the afflicting demon. Belief in outright demon possession (independent of illness), requiring exorcism by persons specially gifted for this task, was universal. Fortunately, though, angels were equally real, often materializing as guardians in moments of grave physical danger. The "sky hung low" over the Early Church, Shirley Jackson Case once remarked, and he might well have added that in the first blush of the pentecostal revival a sky that had grown distant moved perceptibly closer.[9]

This thoroughly supernaturalistic conceptual horizon is the framework in which the hallmark of primitive pentecostalism, speaking in tongues, should be analyzed. Two autobiographical accounts from the earliest years illustrate the forcefulness of the experience. The author of the first was Nickels John Holmes, who attended the University of Edinburgh and the University of North Carolina at Chapel Hill (eventually earning a master's degree), and was probably the best educated of the original leaders. The second was written by Thomas Ball Barratt, who carried the message from New York to Norway in 1906 and was soon known as the father of European pentecostalism.

I fasted for three days without eating or drinking anything. . . . At times everything was dark, so dark that everything in my experience seemed to go away. . . . One night as my heart was going up for the Holy Ghost, it seemed that the whole room was filling with a mist of heaven, and my whole body was being permeated by it. And a great roll of mist above my head as waterfall. . . . I felt my tongue slightly moving up and down, the motion growing stronger and stronger. I was conscious that it was not I, that did it, and I was sure that it was the Holy Ghost, and immediately my teeth began to chatter without my effort or control. . . . I recognized the presence and power of the Holy Ghost in all this, and as soon as I discovered the control of my mouth I testified and praised God for Pentecost.

***

I constantly felt the need of a *still greater blessing* . . . thirsting for a full baptism of the Holy Ghost—*the experience itself*, and not only the intense longing for it. . . . [While] they were praying [for me] the doctor's wife saw a *crown of fire* over my head and *a cloven tongue as of fire* in front of the crown. . . . Others say *this supernatural highly red light.—The very same moment, my being was filled with light and an indescribable power, and I began to speak in a foreign language* as loudly as I could. For a time I was lying upon my back on the floor, speaking . . . "divers kinds of tongues." . . . There was an aching in my vocal chords. I am sure that I spoke seven or eight different languages.[10]

Ecstatic experiences of this sort fueled certitude in various ways. One of the most important was by satisfying a yearning for direct contact with the divine. The recollection of Agnes Ozman, who is often said to have been the first to receive the baptism with the evidence of tongues, was typical: "At times I longed for the Holy Spirit to come in more than for my necessary food and at night a desire was felt more than for sleep and I knew it was the Lord." A. J. Tomlinson, principal founder of the Church of God, said much the same: "I was so hungry for the Holy Ghost that I scarcely cared for food, friendship, or anything else." Another patriarch remembered that he had felt an "insatiable hunger for this experience" after someone told him that it had "everything in the religious world backed clean off the map." For others, ecstasy was proof of their salvation and sanctification. "After being saved I still felt blue and doubted," one convert explained. "I couldn't really tell when I was sanctified, but I must have been, for . . . I spoke in tongues." For many it was a badge of spiritual status. Pentecostals are "the heavenly people," one editor proclaimed, "the elite of the Universe." Another writer insisted that it was "a fact that the most pious and deeply spiritual people of the land . . . have been the first to receive their Pentecost." For some converts, however, baptism in the Holy Spirit was the beginning of genuine repentance. A Methodist minister in Kansas, who had groused that the problem with pentecostals was that they failed to keep "the niggers in their place," converted to the movement in a predominantly black revival. "I had to wade through a whole camp meeting of them when I got the Baptism," he wrote. "God surely broke me over the wheel of my prejudice."[11]

The important point here is that the certitude that early pentecostals manifested was not simply a rationalization of intense religious experiences, but the product of a dialectic between supernaturalism and ecstasy. This becomes evident, I think, when we recognize that the "signs and wonders" of the pentecostal revival cannot be readily equated with the involuntary motor phenomena of the Second Great Awakening, nor even with the turbulent holiness revivals of the late nineteenth century. Although pentecostalism certainly had its share of trance, dancing, prostration, screaming, laughing, weeping, and violent jerking, involuntary behavior of this sort was never the central focus. What made pentecostalism unique, rather, was its preoccupation with events that seemed starkly supernatural. "The common heartbeat of every service," as David Harrell has said of a somewhat later period, "was the miracle—the hypnotic moment when the Spirit moved to heal the sick and raise the dead."[12]

If speaking in tongues was the working heart of primitive pentecostalism, healing was its soul. Every conceivable form of healing, including the replacement of lost organs and resurrections from the dead, were reported endlessly, page after page, sometimes in the jargon of the camp meeting, sometimes in the seemingly straightforward prose of a daily newspaper. One reminiscence from 1903, drawn virtually at random, suggests something of the throbbing energy of a pentecostal meeting.

> People singing, shouting, praying and speaking languages that I couldn't understand; while all about the tent were empty cots and wheel-chairs, and numerous discarded canes and crutches were hung round about the tent, while those who had been delivered from using same leaped and shouted and rejoiced.

The healing testimonials are so astounding, and recur with such frequency, in so many contexts, one can hardly fail to be awed.[13]

Still more intriguing is, however, the movement's enduring fascination with xenoglossolalia, the ability to speak a foreign language one has never learned. Initially, pentecostals believed that all glossolalia is in fact xenoglossic. This idea soon faded to the more defensible claim that most glossolalic utterances are understood only by God. Even so, pentecostals have always insisted that some utterances are real languages. Early autobiographical accounts often claim the gift of one or more specific foreign tongues: a gift, they almost always add, corroborated by natural speakers of the language. The sources are rich with variations upon this theme: glossolalic singing in unison by congregations; glossolalic messages, which, when interpreted, contained information the speaker could not have acquired naturally; glossolalic messages by lifelong deaf mutes; glossolalic singing by disembodied voices; and so forth. In the first six years at least a score of missionaries left for foreign lands, not knowing the native language, but certain they would be divinely enabled to preach in it when they arrived.

Whether anyone ever had sustained use of a xenoglossic language is unclear, but to this day many pentecostals insist that they have heard it with their own ears, and denominational magazines continue to carry stories of these occurrences, usually among missionaries.[14]

First and foremost, then, pentecostalism offered invincible certitude that the supernatural claims of the gospel were really true, not the old-fashioned gospel of the nineteenth century, but the awesome wonder working gospel of the first century. As one enthusiastic convert put it, baptism in the Spirit had given him a "know-so salvation, not a reckon so, hope so, think so, guess so, may be so, nor anything of the kind."[15]

Another way that pentecostalism functioned effectively at the personal level was its ability to meet enduring needs of the human spirit. Simply stated, the movement provided a means for confronting the oldest of human foes: loneliness and the fear of death. The revival was, in Josef Barton's lovely phrase, a "language of aspiration," an effort to find warmth and security in a world increasingly alien to traditional values. The movement never had much of a social vision, but from first to last it was profoundly communal. Again, the choruses of the songs tell the story.

> It is joy unspeakable and full of glory
> Full of glory, full of glory;
> Oh, the half has never yet been told.

***

> It is truly wonderful, What the Lord has done!
> It is truly wonderful, It is truly wonderful!
> Glory to His name.

***

> This is like heaven to me
> I've crossed over Jordan to Canaan's fair land
> And this is like heaven to me.[16]

In the planned spontaneity of the pentecostal meeting, twenty or thirty minutes were ordinarily given to personal testimonies, an unselfconscious ritual that helped dispel doubt and reinforce commitment. The countless testimonials published in the movement's magazines are traces of what was said in those meetings. When the weekly *Pentecostal Holiness Advocate* was founded in 1917, eighteen-year-old Walter Brack wrote in to announce proudly that after "enjoying salvation" for three full years, he still had the "old time Holy Ghost religion" and expected to "stand true till Jesus comes." David Faulkner lamented that for nearly all of his ninety-nine years he had been a Baptist, but when the Lord saved him he "felt about like a boy sixteen

years old." J. W. Noble reported that he was "still alive and on fire for God."
Already there were memories of better days. Brother Pittman loved to "think
back to the good old camp meeting times of ten years ago . . . when there
were hungry souls praying through to God." Nor was it all roses. "The devil is
going to kill me," Reanie Hancock feared. Lilah Peppers grimly acknowledged that she had nearly succumbed to "temptations, doubts, fears, and
trials." Yet the central, fundamental mood of the revival was timelessly
captured by one A. D. Bayer: "The love is still burning in my heart. . . . How
good the Lord has been to me."[17]

Leafing through the thousands of testimonials, it is difficult to doubt that
what these persons wanted from life was pretty much what men and women
have always wanted: meaning for this world and salvation for the next. And in
this respect pentecostalism was eminently successful, for it made these
treasures available to everyone, however ignoble. "No instrument that God
can use is rejected on account of color or dress or lack of education," one
pioneer insisted. "That is why God has so built up the work." It is quite true
that early pentecostalism was afflicted with charlatans and autocrats, and it
is equally true that it soon succumbed to the race and gender prejudices of
its cultural environment. Yet that should not obscure the fact that in many
churches and in countless ways the old stratifications were razed and a new
order erected. A large part of the movement's secret, Roger Robins has
written, is that "the poor, the sick, the elderly, the ignorant and the
oppressed could take their rightful turn as priests at the altar." For having
been "touched by the fire of the Spirit, they found themselves made 'kings
and priests unto God.' "[18]

III.

The second major factor that helped guarantee the survival and eventual
prosperity of the pentecostal movement is that its formal belief system, the
doctrines articulated in the theology books, formed an island of traditional-
ism in a sea of modernity. More specifically, the distinctive theological ideas
pentecostals lived for and fought about invariably presupposed one of the
central features of folk religion: ahistoricism. Differently stated, pentecostal
ideology was built upon a foundation that was, they thought, untouched by
the limitations and corruptions of ordinary existence.

Here it is important to be precise. Early pentecostalism's principal doctrinal affirmations were squarely rooted in the theological traditions of the
Church. In this sense the movement was, like all evangelical sects, fundamentally continuous with historic Protestantism. But in three more restricted
respects pentecostal beliefs were not historical. First, pentecostals displayed little interest in the general history of the Church, and virtually no
interest in the period stretching from the Day of Pentecost to the Reforma-

tion. Second, they were, at best, only dimly aware of the pervasive modern assumption that human nature is plastic and that every human creation is conditioned by its historical setting. Third, much of the time they were preoccupied with apocalyptic eschatology, the "history" of the future. In practice all of this meant that pentecostal thought tended to be exempt from, respectively, adverse judgments drawn from the history of Christianity, rational refutations based upon relativistic cultural assumptions, and empirical disconfirmation by a future that did not yet exist.

The first form of pentecostal ahistoricism, disregard for the general history of the Church, was also characteristic of Latter-Day Saints, Stoneite Christians, Republican Methodists, Landmark Baptists, and a score of smaller restorationist groups that emerged in the United States during the nineteenth century. Like all of these groups, pentecostals were certain they had recaptured the essential feature of the Apostolic Church and, more importantly, that they had eluded the "men made creeds and traditions" of the intervening years. This longing to recover the "pure fountain," as one pentecostal leader put it, was fueled by the conviction that virtually everything that had happened since the Day of Pentecost was irrelevant. Although a few writers made desultory attempts to find precedents for tongues in the history of the church, one summed up the prevailing attitude when he proclaimed that precedent really did not matter. "To tell the truth, all of us are indifferent about it. . . . The Pentecostal Movement has no such history; it leaps the intervening years crying, 'BACK TO PENTECOST!' "[19]

As the years passed the restorationist impulse gradually faded, but in the beginning it brightly illumined the pentecostal horizon, drawing first-generation leaders into a complex "Latter Rain" theory to account for their place in God's "Plan for the Ages." The foundation of the theory was the word of the prophet Joel: "It shall come to pass afterward that I will pour out my spirit upon all flesh." Pentecostals assumed the prophet's proclamation was proleptic, simultaneously describing both the Day of Pentecost and the Last Days of history. Given this premise, it was easy to conclude that the contemporary outpouring of charismatic gifts was in fact the Latter Rain foretold by Joel. For centuries, said A. J. Tomlinson, the truth "has been buried beneath the debris of custom, tradition, and unbelief."

> Creeds, articles of faith, systems, doctrines, false Churches are even now quivering, ready to fall. The True Church of God is going to rise soon above the great host of modern churchianity, and shine out in her glory and beauty with conquering tread.

It was an intoxicating vision. What it really meant, said Tomlinson, is that the Church should "expect nothing less in glory and power in the evening light than that which broke out over the eastern hills in the early morning of the gospel age."[20]

Another manifestation of the pentecostal distaste for history was a trait that might be called conceptual ahistoricism. Like their fundamentalist cousins and, for that matter, most orthodox believers, pentecostals instinctively resisted the relativistic assumptions of modern culture in general and modern biblical scholars in particular. In the mind of the typical convert, one historian has aptly said, Scripture "dropped from heaven as a sacred meteor." The immediate result of this ahistorical outlook was an incorrigible belief that the Bible is without error. "I believe in the plenary inspiration of the Scriptures," said one leader at the turn of the century. "I detest and despise . . . this higher criticism, rationalism, and this seeking on the part of ungodly professors to do away with objectionable parts of the Word of God, and as fire-baptized people we stand on the whole Book, hallelujah!" Even so, while the Bible's inerrancy was an always-present presupposition, the really operative principle of interpretation was the conviction that exegesis is best when it is as rigidly literal as credibility can stand. A vivid but not atypical example was the assertion by an esteemed pentecostal theologian in 1930 that according to Gen 6:2 intercourse between angels and human women was the source of giants on the earth—and, he concluded, it "still happens today." The practice of handling poisonous snakes, which persisted for many years in and out of the Church of God in the southern Appalachians, was based on an unflinchingly literal reading of Mark 16:18. This and other isolated passages, taken literally, became the basis for drinking lethal doses of poison, handling live coals of fire, and refusing to use prescribed medicines even when it led to certain death for oneself or one's children.[21]

The conviction that tongues invariably accompanies baptism in the Holy Spirit, which soon became the litmus test of pentecostal orthodoxy, similarly grew from a literal reading of Acts 2:4, 10:44-46, and 19:1-7, in which the presence of the Holy Spirit and speaking in tongues are associated. As early as 1907 the movement's leading theologian admonished pentecostals not to get "hung up" (as he put it) on the fact that stalwarts such as "Charles G. Finney, Jonathan Edwards, and Hudson Taylor" had never professed to speak in tongues. They were "great and good men," he allowed, "but unless they had the Bible evidence of Pentecost, we cannot Scripturally say that they had the Baptism of the Holy Ghost." Winning the battle of proof texts, as they were certain they had done, was equivalent to winning the war, for historical and experiential evidence had nothing to do with the question.[22]

Conceptual ahistoricism led, then, to wooden principles of biblical interpretation; it also fostered a hair-trigger disposition to fight and separate rather than compromise on any point of doctrine. Pentecostals, no less than fundamentalists, were certain that the definition and defense of correct belief was a matter of eternal importance. This point should be stressed, for no stereotype is more pervasive than the idea that primitive pentecostalism represented a gentle flowering of the spirit, long on religious affection and short on creedal conviction. Actually, the opposite was true. Before William Seymour's Azusa Mission was five months old it issued a creedal statement and shortly afterward warned: "We recognize every man that honors the blood of Jesus Christ to be our brother. . . . *But* we are not willing to accept any errors, it matters not how charming and sweet they may seem to be." A year later, Seymour reiterated the point. He denounced those who would say " 'Let us all come together; if we are not one in doctrine, we can be one in spirit' " by pointing out that "impure doctrine" is the same as "spiritual fornication." The first book-length exposition of pentecostal theology, published in 1907, similarly admonished readers to remember that baptism in the Holy Spirit hinged upon a person's willingness to "lay aside any errone-ous theory" relating to the "primary doctrines of the Bible."[23]

It is true that early pentecostals did not forge extensive creeds or cate-chisms, but that does not mean that they were careless about doctrinal regularity. For one thing, the restorationist impulse disposed them to avoid association with the historic creeds of Christendom. "We have the bible for everything," A. J. Tomlinson boasted, "and we have no creeds, rituals or articles of faith." But that hardly meant that Tomlinson or any other pente-costal was willing to tolerate diversity of doctrine. "The standard of truth is fixed and any deviation from that standard is error," he solemnly warned. "Stick to your own crowd."[24]

There was, however, a more important reason for the brevity of their creeds: unblinking conformity was simply presupposed. This becomes evi-dent when we look at the way pentecostal authorities handled deviance. It is undeniable that the first ten or fifteen years were rocked by a succession of antinomian excesses, yet irregularities of this sort were crushed without a second thought. Moreover, pentecostal factions wrangled about questions most evangelicals have usually considered open for discussion. The proper form of church government, the exact purpose of each of the gifts of the Spirit, the timing of sanctification, the morality of seeking a physician, and other issues of this sort, triggered lock-outs, personal denunciations, and a general determination always to speak one's own convictions, regardless of the human cost.[25]

Examples are endless; fights between Wesleyan and non-Wesleyan pen-tecostals about the necessity of a distinct sanctification experience prior to baptism in the Holy Spirit illustrate the point. In 1912 William J. Seymour, who upheld the Wesleyan view, literally bolted the door of the Azusa Mission to his old friend, William H. Durham, pastor of Chicago's North Avenue Mission, because of the latter's public opposition to the Wesleyan position. Durham, in turn, was described even by his friends as a "sledgehammer" in the defense of truth. Charles Parham, who also disagreed with Durham about the nature of sanctification, publicly urged God to smite dead whoever was wrong. Florence Crawford, founder of Oregon's The Apostolic Faith, simi-larly hoped that "Hell will . . . increase its flames to swallow those who dare to preach Durham's damnable heresy." A difference of opinion on this matter prompted J. H. King, the Wesleyan patriarch of the pentecostal Holiness

Church, to order (non-Wesleyan) Aimee Semple McPherson off the platform of a church in Virginia. After a decade as General Superintendent of the denomination, King lamented that the "strife, contentions, divisions, judicial trials, and confusions" within the body had left him "exhausted and at the point of almost complete helplessness."[26]

So it went, year after year. Occasionally gentler spirits would call for more charity and less zealotry, but their pleas only underscore the fact that the movement was born and bred in a welter of doctrinal brawls. The large number of schisms between 1915 and 1935—most of which began as disputes over seemingly minor points of belief—indicates that the major pentecostal groups had no interest in compromise and little tolerance for diversity.[27]

To this point we have noted that pentecostals were ahistorical, first, in their lack of interest in the history of the Church, and second in their conceptualization of the relation between Scripture and the cultural context in which it arose. There was, however, still another form of ahistoricism which helped sustain and insulate pentecostals from outside criticism. They were ardent millenarians.

Robert Anderson, the foremost historian of American pentecostalism, has argued that the movement was, in the final analysis, essentially a millenarian eruption. His conclusion is debatable, but whatever the final verdict, it is indisputable that pentecostals were strongly influenced by an apocalyptic eschatology drawn indirectly from Adventist and directly from Plymouth Brethren traditions. They looked for the imminent rapture of the saints, followed by the return of the Lord and the events described in Daniel, Ezekiel, and Revelation. The early creeds, without exception, declared the nearness of the end. Scores of hymns and (we are told) virtually every vernacular interpretation of a message in tongues proclaimed it. The *Pentecostal Holiness Advocate* called the Second Coming the "greatest subject" in the whole of Christian theology. The first General Council of the Assemblies of God declared that the message "predominant in all this great outpouring . . . is 'Jesus is coming soon.' " The masthead of Aimee Semple McPherson's magazine, *The Bridal Call,* was typical.

> Believing as we do that Jesus Christ . . . is soon to come back to this earth for His waiting people . . . we endeavor to set forth . . . the plain message of Salvation, the Baptism of the Holy Ghost, Divine Healing and the Soon Coming of Jesus.

Word and Work, weekly magazine of an Apostolic Faith band based in Massachusetts, similarly averred that its main purpose was the "spread of the Good News of the Soon Coming of our Lord Jesus Christ and the need of a preparation to meet him in peace." The Azusa Mission's *Apostolic Faith* spoke for countless believers, in short, when it proclaimed that the pentecostal revival was the beginning of a "world-wide revival—to bring on Jesus."[28]

For pentecostals millenarian expectation was heightened by mixing dispensational premillennialism with the restorationist notion of a Latter Rain that would repristinate the early rain of the Day of Pentecost. There were several versions of dispensationalism, but Presbyterian, Congregationalist, and Baptist dispensationalists ordinarily contended that tongues and other gifts of the Spirit had ceased when the Apostolic Age ended and the Church Age began. Pentecostals reversed the argument, contending that the eruption of tongues on the Day of Pentecost signaled the beginning of the Church Age, and the twentieth-century Latter Rain revival signaled its end. The proof was glossolalia. "Why do I know this is the Latter Rain?" asked Susan Duncan, a founder of the Rochester Bible and Missionary Training Institute. Because, she answered, speaking in tongues is the only sign unique to the Day of Pentecost, and thus its reappearance in the twentieth century necessarily signifies the coming of the second and final Latter Rain.[29]

This intense millenarianism helps explain some of the behavior patterns outsiders found problematic. The movement's consistently conservative, if not reactionary, attitude toward secular society is a case in point. With the exception of pacifism, orphanage work, and a few soup lines, pentecostals showed little interest in social reform—individual, structural, or otherwise.[30] Yet to say that pentecostals had a barren social ethic is to tell only part of the story. The other and probably more important part is that they were simply uninterested in questions of public policy. This is illustrated by the war-years issues of the *Pentecostal Holiness Advocate* and Sister Aimee's *Bridal Call*. In the former, from the beginning of 1917 to the end of 1918, the Great War was rarely mentioned except in the context of eschatological discussions. In the latter the Armistice went unnoticed, although the war did remind Sister Aimee that there is always a "Red Cross Hospital atop Calvary's Hill." The one significant exception to this lack of interest in the workaday world was the abiding interest pentecostals showed in the fate of Jews. Spurred by the belief, common among dispensational premillenialists, that the restoration of Israel was proof of the imminence of the Second Coming, pentecostals consistently supported Zionism abroad and generally opposed anti-Semitism at home. Other than this, however, millenarian expectation seems to have deflected any measurable interest in the affairs of secular society.[31]

Personal asceticism is another behavior pattern illumined by fervent millenarianism. Pentecostals, like most evangelicals, routinely banned tobacco, alcoholic drinks, and worldly amusements such as gambling and dancing. Rules of this sort are sociologically (if not scripturally) explicable because they impose symbolic fences between the group and the world and thereby remind members that they do not belong to the world. Yet the traditional marks of evangelical identity, plus the stigma of attending a "Holy Roller" church and shouting in unknown languages, would seem to have been more than adequate to establish a separate culture. The problem here is that pentecostals often went much further. At different times and places they tried to ban common indulgences such as chewing gum or eating pork, catfish, candy, or ice cream; drinking coffee, tea, or soda pop; wearing neckties or wedding rings; playing sports or watching parades; reading novels or newspapers; visiting relatives or riding in cars on Sundays. They commonly warned against "excess in the marital relation" and occasionally proscribed marital sex entirely. This severity suggests that something else was involved. A letter left at home by a delegate to the 1917 General Council of the Assemblies of God, which specified "what should be done" if she were "caught up [in the Rapture] while away on her present trip," may offer the key. When people expect the Lord's return at any moment, frivolousness is not merely imprudent. It is immoral.[32]

The tendency to blur the distinction between frivolous and immoral behavior is seen in the promotional literature of the Holiness School in Falcon, North Carolina. In the entire town, the ads boasted, one could not buy tobacco, or "dope drinks" like Coca Cola, or find "Theaters, Circuses, Moving Picture Shows, Base Ball Games, Social Parties and Dances"—all "agencies of evil" sending young people to their "eternal destruction." The same blurring is evident in a Church of God admonition that "tobacco users, whiskey drinkers, dope gulpers, labor unioners, socialists, lodgers, adulterers, fornicators, politicians . . . murderers and all liars" are equally exposed to the "awful wrath" to come. Convinced that they were approaching the edge of history, the ability of pentecostals to make reasonable moral discriminations became blunted—and for good reason. One who constantly looked for the Lord's return could hardly afford to guzzle a dope drink, or squander a day in a union hall, when the Son of Man might at any moment burst through the clouds of glory.[33]

This leads to another behavior pattern sharpened by millenarian expectation: a determination to evangelize the world. The divine purpose in the revival, Charles Parham urged, is to "fit men and women to go to the ends of the earth to preach . . . before the end of the age." Within six months of its founding, thirty-eight missionaries fanned out from the Azusa Mission to Africa, India, and China. Many went overseas fully expecting never to return, to be raptured or martyred on the mission field. Pentecostal magazines were filled with reports from missionaries and endless pleas for more money and greater sacrifices to save the lost before it was forever too late.[34]

It was the same at home. "I sold my horse, rig, and everything I had and bought a ticket to Houston," one pioneer remembered of his call to the ministry in 1905. "We soon found an old abandoned saloon building. . . . When the building was cleaned and ready for use, *we set out to get a crowd.*"

Another patriarch lamented that a revival meeting in Alabama had to be postponed (not canceled) because the speaker's "boy got sick and his cow died." "Well do I remember," said another, "walking 75 miles to hold a meeting . . . where poor people were begging for me to go." To outsiders it looked like mindless zealotry, but as one of the earliest issues of the *Evening Light* made clear, "the end is near and we have no time to parley or reason with the devil."[35]

Anticipation of the Second Coming partly accounts for still another feature of pentecostal behavior, the militaristic imagery of their daily rhetoric. Again, the testimonials are revealing: "We are still on the firing line for God." "This [letter] leaves us still in the battle at Seymour." "All the artillery of hell was turned on us." "[We] rented the opera house and opened fire on the enemy." To some extent this siege mentality was a reflection of the age, a time when the memory of Shiloh and Gettysburg was still fresh enough that Teddy Roosevelt could use "Onward Christian Soldiers" as a campaign theme song. And to some extent it reflected the fact that early pentecostals were constantly harassed with peltings, beatings, arson, ridicule in the press, and merciless excoriation by their evangelical rivals. One holiness leader's observation that the movement was the "last vomit of Satan" was more graphic than most, but in substance not unusual.[36]

Even so, this militarism would have existed under any circumstances. In the approaching darkness of the Last Judgment, ordinary differences of opinion easily became ultimate differences, shadowed with eternal consequences. Opposition was not merely ill-considered, but blasphemous. To fail to seek baptism in the Holy Spirit was not merely to neglect, but to defy, God's commandments and to guarantee abandonment in the Great Rapture. To say (as many evangelicals did) that tongues is the work of the devil was not merely to fall into doctrinal error, but to commit the Unpardonable Sin, punished by everlasting damnation. Satanic powers struggled for the souls of men and women as the nations stumbled toward Armageddon. As one preacher phrased it, "A terrific battle is being fought between two great powers, the Hosts of the Almighty, and Satan and the hosts of evil." When pentecostals learned to read the *Book of Revelation* like a daily newspaper, it is not surprising that they also learned to express themselves in the rhetoric of the Apocalypse.[37]

I am not suggesting that any of these behavior patterns—diffidence toward worldly affairs, personal asceticism, missionary zeal, or militaristic rhetoric—is wholly explained by millenarianism. To some extent each was the product of other traditions pentecostals had inherited, and the atmosphere they breathed. The point, rather, is that millenarianism sharpened the edges, stoked the fires, intensified the colors of their world. If it is difficult for outsiders to imagine why anyone would willingly choose the stigma of "Holy Roller" religion, the exhilaration of living in the final watch of history may have had something to do with it.

IV.

In summary, what I have proposed in this essay is that the internal culture of pentecostalism, the texture of its faith, was the secret of its survival. To be sure, there were other factors, some wholly external and structural. From the earlier holiness movement, for example, pentecostals inherited an elaborate network of publications, conferences, and training institutes which helped them stabilize a molten revival. And while it is true that some evangelicals fought pentecostalism at every turn in the road, neither the established denominations nor the civil courts of law did much to impede its growth.[38] Historians have discerned other facilitating factors.[39] All things considered, however, it is evident that the principal causes of pentecostalism's survival and eventual prosperity were rooted deep within the religious culture of the movement itself.

For the most part this is a forgotten world, shrouded by the cloak of acculturation. But when the movement was young, and still effervescent with the original religious vision, it offered certitude about the reality of the supernatural and afforded coherence and meaning for ordinary lives fragmented, perhaps, by more than the ordinary share of human troubles. Beyond this it offered a worldview that was exempt from adverse judgments drawn from the history of the Church, insulated from rational refutation based on relativistic cultural premises, and protected from empirical disconfirmation by a future that did not yet exist. By defining the world in the traditional terms of a folk religion, pentecostals shielded their lives from the ambiguities of historical existence. They lived in the "ancient order of things," in that mythic realm where the Divine and the Satanic are locked in a terrible struggle and the frivolous pleasures of modern civilization are seen for what they really are. The movement flourished, in short, not in spite of the fact that it was out of step with the times, but precisely because it *was* out of step.

Still, there was more to pentecostalism than solutions for needs of the spirit or freedom from the ambiguities of history. The forces that animated primitive pentecostalism were also profoundly disruptive. In its defiance of social conventions, in its bellicosity and zealotry, in its ecstatic excess and deliberate scrambling of the glory of human language, the movement embodied a primordial urge toward disorder. And this too was part of its secret. For the chaos that stands outside the constraints and ordering principles of the social system, one anthropologist has written, is undeniably the source of the "noxious and the destructive," but it also is the "fount of most of our becomings."[40]

Of course primitive pentecostals would have put it differently. They would have said that the movement flourished because it afforded an exhilarating vision that life on earth could be a foretaste of heaven. And a warning of the wrath to come.

Notes

1 Los Angeles *Times* (10 April 1906) 1 and (18 April 1906) section 2, p. 1. The most detailed account of the Azusa revival is Douglas J. Nelson, "For Such a Time as This: The Story of Bishop William J. Seymour and the Azusa Street Revival: A Search for Pentecostal/Charismatic Roots" (Ph.D. diss., University of Birmingham, 1981) 189-96. The best general study of early pentecostalism in the United States is Robert Mapes Anderson, *Vision of the Disinherited: The Making of American Pentecostalism* (New York: Oxford University Press, 1979). For pentecostalism worldwide see Walter J. Hollenweger, *The Pentecostals* (trans. R. A. Wilson; Minneapolis: Augsburg, 1972; German original, 1961). For a comprehensive bibliography of primary and secondary materials pertaining to American and, to some extent, world pentecostalism, see Charles Edwin Jones, *A Guide to the Study of the Pentecostal Movement* (2 vols.; Metuchen, NJ: Scarecrow, 1983).

2 Peter W. Williams, *Popular Religion in America* (Englewood Cliffs, NJ: Prentice-Hall, 1980) 144. *Christian Century* (18 January 1978) 35. For DuPlessis see, e.g., Richard Quebedeaux, *The New Charismatics* (New York: Harper & Row, 1976) 92-95. For indications of the magnitude of contemporary pentecostalism, see Kenneth S. Kantzer, "The Charismatics among Us," *Christianity Today* (22 February 1980) 25-29, and David B. Barrett, *World Christian Encyclopedia* (New York: Oxford University Press, 1982) 838.

3 The historiographic debate about the beginnings of American pentecostalism is discussed in my "Taking Another Look at the *Vision of the Disinherited,*" *Religious Studies Review* 8 (1982) 15-22; Timothy L. Smith, "The Disinheritance of the Saints," ibid., 22-28; Donald Wilber Dayton, "Theological Roots of Pentecostalism" (Ph.D. diss., University of Chicago, 1983) chap. 1.

4 All of the denominations mentioned and many of the smaller pentecostal groups have authorized histories. The handiest guide to this literature is David W. Faupel, *The American Pentecostal Movement* (Wilmore, KY: Asbury Theological Seminary, 1972).

5 Carl Brumback, *Suddenly . . . from Heaven* (Springfield, MO: Gospel Publishing House, 1961).

6 Charles W. Conn, *Like a Mighty Army: A History of the Church of God* (rev. ed.; Cleveland, TN: Pathway, 1977) xxvii.

7 For "Jesus-cult" see Nils Bloch-Hoell, *The Pentecostal Movement* (London: Allen & Unwin, 1964; Norwegian original, 1956) 109. The theological ramifications of the preoccupation with Jesus are explored in Allen L. Clayton, "The Significance of William H. Durham for Pentecostal Historiography," *Pneuma: Journal of the Society of Pentecostal Studies* 1 (Fall 1979) 27-42, esp. 39-40. The songs can be found in *Assembly Songs* (Springfield, MO: Gospel Publishing House, n.d.).

8 Aimee Semple McPherson, *The Story of My Life* (ed. Raymond L. Cox; Waco: Word, 1973) 30. "Perfume" is from Harold Horton, *The Gifts of the Spirit* (Springfield, MO: Gospel Publishing House, 1975; original, 1934) 193-94.

9 For references to the Antichrist, Satan, demons, demon-caused illness, and angels see virtually any issue of early pentecostal periodicals such as *Apostolic Evangel* (Falcon, NC), *Apostolic Faith* (Baxter Springs, KS), *Apostolic Faith* (Los Angeles), *Bridal Call* (Framingham, MA), *Bridegroom's Messenger* (Atlanta), *Evening Light and Church of God Evangel* (Cleveland, TN), *Latter Rain Evangel* (Chicago), *Pentecost* (Indianapolis), *Pentecostal Evangel* (Springfield, MO), *Pentecostal Holiness Advocate* (Franklin Springs, GA), *Trust* (Rochester, NY), *Upper Room* (Los Angeles), *Word and Witness* (Malvern, AR), and *Word and Work* (Framingham, MA).

10 Nickels John Holmes, *Life Sketches and Sermons* (Royston, GA: Pentecostal Holiness Church, n.d. [ca. 1909]) 139-40; 143-44. Barratt, *When the Fire Fell* (1927), is excerpted in Frederick Dale Bruner, *A Theology of the Holy Spirit* (Grand Rapids: Eerdman's, 1970) 121, 124. Similar accounts are anthologized in Wayne Warner, ed., *Touched by the Fire: Patriarchs of Pentecost* (Plainfield, NJ: Logos, 1978). Sometimes the baptism experience was barely discernible. See the case of Joseph H. King, *Yet Speaketh: A Memoir* (Franklin Springs, GA: Pentecostal Holiness Church, 1949) 116-20.

[11] Agnes N. [Ozman] LaBerge, "History of the Pentecostal Movement from Jan. 1, 1901" (typescript in the Assemblies of God Archives, Springfield, MO). Tomlinson, *Answering the Call of God* (n.d.) 9, quoted in Conn, *Mighty Army*, 84. "Map" is from Frank J. Ewart, *The Phenomenon of Pentecost* (St. Louis: Pentecostal Publishing House, 1947) 5-6. "In tongues" is from an unnamed interviewee in William W. Wood, *Culture and Personality Aspects of the Pentecostal Holiness Religion* (The Hague: Mouton, 1965) 26. The elitism remarks are in *Upper Room* (July 1910) 8, and George Floyd Taylor, *The Spirit and the Bride* (Falcon, NC: privately printed, 1907) 43. I owe the latter reference to James R. Goff, "Millenarian Thought among Early Pentecostals, 1898-1908," (doctoral seminar paper, University of Arkansas, 1983). "Prejudice" is from *Pentecostal Evangel* (22 March 1924) 6-7, quoted in Anderson, *Vision*, 123.

[12] David Edwin Harrell, Jr., *All Things Are Possible: The Healing and Charismatic Revivals in Modern America* (Bloomington: Indiana University Press, 1975) 6.

[13] A. W. Webber, "Revival of 1903 in Galena, Kansas," *Apostolic Faith* (May 1944) 11. Again, see any issue—indeed, virtually any page of any issue—of the early periodicals listed in n. 9 above.

[14] Xenoglossolalia claims are almost as common in the early literature as healing claims. Some of these accounts have been reprinted in Warner, ed., *Touched*, and Ralph W. Harris, *Spoken by the Spirit* (Springfield, MO: Gospel Publishing House, 1973).

[15] A. C. Knight, *Pentecostal Holiness Advocate* (28 February 1918) 5.

[16] Josef J. Barton, "Pentecostalism and Rural Society in the Southern Highlands, 1890-1950," (paper presented to the American Academy of Religion, Dallas, November 1980); *Assembly Songs*, 27, 116, 39.

[17] All testimonials are from the 1918 *Pentecostal Holiness Advocate:* Brack: (10 January) 3; Faulkner: (11 April) 10; Noble: (11 April) 13; Pittman: (18 April) 13; Hancock (10 January) 9; Peppers: (10 January) 3; Bayer: (21 February) 9.

[18] The "pioneer" is quoted without attribution in Stanley H. Frodsham, *With Signs Following: The Story of the Pentecostal Revival in the Twentieth Century* (rev. ed.; Springfield, MO: Gospel Publishing House, 1946) 34. Roger G. Robins, "Worship and Structure in Early Pentecostalism" (senior seminar paper, Harvard Divinity School, 1984). The Frodsham reference and the main point of the paragraph are drawn from Robins's exceptionally perceptive study.

[19] "Men made" is from A. J. Tomlinson (?), "Brief History of . . . Church of God," prefixed to L. Howard Juillerat, compiler, *Book of Minutes . . . of the General Assemblies of the Church of God* (Cleveland, TN: Church of God Publishing House, n.d. [abridgment of 1922 original ed.]) 8. "Pure fountain" is from Donald Gee, *The Ministry Gifts of Christ* (Springfield, MO: Gospel Publishing House, 1930) 13. "To tell" is from B. F. Lawrence, *The Apostolic Faith Restored* (St. Louis: Gospel Publishing House, 1916) 12. The title of a booklet by P. C. Nelson said it best: *The Jerusalem Council: The First General Council of the Assemblies of God* (Enid, OK: Southwestern, n.d. [ca. 1930]).

[20] A. J. Tomlinson, *Evening Light and Church of God Evangel* (1 July 1910) 1 and (1 March 1910) 1.

[21] "Sacred meteor" is from Russell P. Spittler, "Scripture and the Theological Enterprise," in Robert K. Johnston, ed., *The Use of the Bible in Theology: Evangelical Options* (Atlanta: John Knox, forthcoming). "I believe" is from B. H. Irwin, *Live Coals of Fire* (13 October 1899) 2, quoted in James R. Goff, Jr., "Pentecostal Millenarianism: The Development of Premillennial Orthodoxy, 1909-1943," *Ozark Historical Review* 12 (1983) 19. "Still happens" is from D. M. Panton, *Verheissung Der Vaters* (June 1930) 13-16, quoted in Hollenweger, *Pentecostals*, 295. For snake-handling and related practices see Anderson, *Vision*, 92-96.

[22] Taylor, *Spirit*, 42.

[23] For the Azusa creed and Seymour's remarks see the *Apostolic Faith* (September 1906) 2; (December 1906) 1; and (October 1907-January 1908) 3. "Lay aside" is from Taylor, *Spirit*, 132.

[24] A. J. Tomlinson, *Evening Light and Church of God Evangel* (1 October 1910) 1; *Church of God Evangel* (2 May 1914) 3; *Evening Light and Church of God Evangel* (15 August 1910) 1.

[25] Anderson, *Vision,* 154-57.

[26] For Seymour versus Durham see Frank Bartleman, *How Pentecost Came to Los Angeles* (2d ed.; Los Angeles: privately printed, 1925) 139, 146-52, and Clayton, "Durham," esp. 31-32. "Sledgehammer" is from Ewart, *Phenomenon,* 73. For Parham and Crawford versus Durham see Edith L. Waldvogel, "The 'Overcoming Life': A Study in the Reformed Evangelical Origins of Pentecostalism" (Ph.D. diss., Harvard University, 1977) 187-88, and Edith [Waldvogel] Blumhofer, "The Finished Work of Calvary: William H. Durham and a Doctrinal Controversy," *Assemblies of God Heritage* 3 (Fall 1983) 9-10. For King versus McPherson, see Vinson Synan, *The Old-Time Power: A History of the Pentecostal Holiness Church* (Franklin Springs, GA: Advocate Press, 1973) 139. King's remark is from *Yet Speaketh,* 333.

[27] The growth of internal dissension and the stories of the numerous groups that resulted from this dissension are compactly surveyed in John Thomas Nichol, *Pentecostalism* (New York: Harper & Row, 1966) chaps. 7-9.

[28] Anderson, *Vision,* 80. Historians who support Anderson's thesis include Goff, "Pentecostal Millenarianism," and D. William Faupel, "The Function of 'Models' in the Interpretation of Pentecostal Thought," *Pneuma: Journal of the Society for Pentecostal Studies* 2 (Spring 1980) 51-71, esp. 64-69. The primary references are from the *Pentecostal Holiness Advocate* (21 February 1918) 8; Assemblies of God *Minutes* (1914) 1; *Bridal Call* (October 1918) inside front cover; *Word and Work,* as advertised in *Bridal Call,* ibid.; *Apostolic Faith* (September 1906) 4.

[29] Susan A. Duncan, *Word and Work* (August 1910) 239, quoted in Faupel, "Models," 68.

[30] Admittedly, early pentecostal pacifism was a significant exception to the general pattern of noninterest in humanitarian reforms. Roger Robins, "A Chronology of Peace: Attitudes Toward War and Peace in the Assemblies of God: 1914-1918," *Pneuma: Journal of the Society for Pentecostal studies* 6 (Spring 1984) 3-25. Jay Beaman, "Pentecostal Pacifism: The Origin, Development, and Rejection of Pacific Belief among Pentecostals" (M.Div. thesis, North American Baptist Seminary, Sioux Falls, 1982).

[31] Sister Aimee's remark is from *Bridal Call* (May 1919) 16. Pentecostalism's perennial fascination with the fate of the Jews is a recurring theme in Dwight Wilson, *Armageddon Now!: The Premillenarian Response to Russia and Israel since 1917* (Grand Rapids: Baker, 1977).

[32] "Present trial" is from Assemblies of God *Minutes* (1917) 20. The extreme restrictiveness of pentecostal mores is discussed in Synan, *Old-Time Power,* 261; idem, *The Holiness-Pentecostal Movement in the United States* (Grand Rapids: Eerdmans, 1971) 67, 180. See also Dillard L. Wood and William H. Preskitt, Jr., *Baptized with Fire: A History of the Pentecostal Fire-Baptized Holiness Church* (Franklin Springs, GA: Advocate, 1983) 16-17, 25, 33.

[33] "Eternal destruction" is from A. C. Holland, *Apostolic Evangel* (23 August 1916) 4. "Awful wrath" is from *Church of God Evangel* (11 April 1914) 3. The final sentence of the paragraph is a paraphrase from Timothy P. Weber, *Living in the Shadow of the Second Coming* (New York: Oxford University Press, 1979) 62.

[34] Sarah T. Parham, ed., *The Life of Charles F. Parham* (Baxter Springs, KS: Apostolic Faith Bible College, 1977; original, 1930) 51. Missions data are taken from Anderson, *Vision,* 71-72, and Nelson, "Seymour," 72-74.

[35] "Soon found" is from Howard A. Goss, in Ethel A. Goss, *The Winds of God* (1958) 41, quoted in Nichol, *Pentecostalism,* 58, emphasis added. "Boy sick" is from M. M. Pinson, to J. R. Flower, 19 December 1950 (Springfield, MO: Assemblies of God Archives). "Walking" is from F. M. Britton, *Pentecostal Truth* (Royston, GA: Pentecostal Holiness Church, 1919) 225. A. J. Tomlinson, *Evening Light and Church of God Evangel* (15 March 1910) 2.

[36] "Firing line" is from G. F. Patton, *Apostolic Faith* (April 1925) 17. "At Seymour" is from J. H. Bennett, *Christian Evangel* (9 May 1914) 8. "Artillery" is from Maria B. Woodworth-Etter, *Acts of the Holy Ghost* (Dallas: John F. Worley Printing, 1912) 171. "Opened fire" is from H. A. Goss, excerpted in Lawrence, *Apostolic Faith,* 63. Morgan quoted in Anderson, *Vision,* 142 (based upon Ewart, *Phenomenon,* 85).

[37] "Terrific battle" is from Seeley D. Kinne, *Evening Light and Church of God Evangel* (15

March 1910) 4. For a typical illustration of the pentecostal tendency to interpret routine doctrinal disagreements in ultimate terms see R. B. Kirkland, *"Speaking with Tongues": Evidence and Gift* (New York: privately printed, 1925) 52.

[38] Anderson, *Vision,* 150.

[39] See, e.g., Nichol, *Pentecostalism*, chap. 5, and Anderson, *Vision*, chap. 12.

[40] Kenelm Burridge, *Someone, No One: An Essay on Individuality* (Princeton: Princeton University Press, 1979) ix-x.

SYSTEMATIC THEOLOGY

David F. Wells, area editor

SYSTEMATIC THEOLOGY

DAVID F. WELLS
Andrew Mutch Professor of Historical and Systematic Theology
Gordon-Conwell Theological Seminary

Introduction

The four articles selected for inclusion comprise a unit, for all are looking at the same issue: Christ and culture. They are not, of course, looking at the whole issue. Many more than four essays would be required for that. Nevertheless, these are each important contributions.

The first essay by Klaus Bockmuehl gives an analysis of and provides a perspective on secularism, concluding with the salient elements of what he believes should be a Christian response to it. The three essays that follow constitute an examination of only one part of the process Bockmuehl describes. It is that part in which there is cross-pollination between political realities and religious convictions, specifically as these come to focus in the call for liberation.

There are at least three prevalent misconceptions about liberation theology. First, there is no such thing as liberation theology; there are, however, many liberation theologies. They differ from continent to continent—African, Asian, South American—and within these continents there are many variations on the theme. Second, liberation theology is nowhere a people's movement; liberation theology is everywhere an academic theology. It is the product of intellectual reflection upon painful and largely unchangeable sociological reality. As intellectual theorizing, it is far better known and far more talked about in Western academic circles than it is in many of the countries of South America. Nevertheless, it will be the dominant ecumenical theology for the foreseeable future, and will be the force behind many World Council of Churches initiatives and pronouncements.

Third, liberation theology is no novelty, though it periodically makes headlines in our secular newspapers. In some ways, it is simply a rekindling of older liberal Protestant ideas, but, in other ways, it also shares common interests with a wider range of theology. At its center is the question which is also at the center of many other theologies: how do we properly relate Christ and culture? More precisely, how does Christian salvation work itself out in social structures, and what is the effect of eschatology on our power structures? The answers liberation theologians have given to these questions are sometimes distinctive, but the questions they are addressing are shared with most other theologies.

The Best in Theology

These questions, in fact, are not at all foreign to evangelicals, for in the last three decades in particular, renewed attention has been given to questions of social responsibility and to how a Christian social ethic should function in the contemporary world. The questions raised by liberation theologians are therefore questions that must also be answered by evangelicals, different as their answers may be.

These questions cannot be addressed foundationally by recourse to ideological, political, or sociological theory; for evangelicals, the perspective upon issues of liberation and the means of adducing answers to them must come from sacred Scripture. For this reason, R. T. France's careful analysis of the New Testament is placed first. It is important to notice his insistence, which I believe is entirely proper, that the New Testament is unambiguously clear that liberation is primarily freedom from the penalty and bondage of sin; it is, of course, expected that social consequences will emerge from this, but precisely how these consequences are to be worked out is not given to us in blueprint fashion.

The essays by Robert Linder and David Bosch are fascinating and painful counterpoints to France's thematic study. Both are studies in the way civil religion has functioned, in the one case in the United States and in the other in South Africa. In both countries, civil religion is a loose profession of religious values that has guided the formation of national policy and structured national understanding. Civil religion, in both countries, found its genesis in Christian faith, but in order to be civil (national in scope and inoffensive in function), it has had to shed much of its Christian particularism. In South Africa, it is more obviously Christian than in the United States, but there it is also less eschatological. Indeed, the underlying eschatological force in American civil religion is also what invites comparisons with the various liberation theologies. This is why some authors have paired Jerry Falwell, who has a liberation theology for the ideological right wing, with Gutierrez or Segundo who have liberation theologies for the ideological left wing, but all are, oddly enough, exponents of a postmillennialism.

Whether this analysis is correct may be debated. What is clear, however, is that an uncritical alliance between evangelical faith and any ideology—of the left or the right—is an invitation to disaster. These provocative essays may not make welcome reading, and may, in fact, be most discomforting. The issues they raise, however, cannot be disregarded.

About the Area Editor

David Wells (B.D., London University, England; M.Th., Trinity Evangelical Divinity School; Ph.D., University of Manchester, England) is Andrew Mutch professor of historical and systematic theology at Gordon-Conwell Theological Seminary. Born in what is now Zimbabwe, he studied initially at University of Cape Town, where he became a Christian. He is a member of the Lausanne Committee for World Evangelization, and also serves on its theology working group.

He was general editor and part author of *Eerdmans Handbook to Christianity in America* (1983) and *Reformed Theology in America: A History of Its Modern Development* (1985). His recent books include *God the Evangelist: The Role of the Holy Spirit in Bringing Men and Women to Faith* (1987); *The Person of Christ: A Biblical and Historical Analysis of the Incarnation* (1984).

SECULARISATION AND SECULARISM: SOME CHRISTIAN CONSIDERATIONS

KLAUS BOCKMUEHL
Professor of Theology and Ethics, Regent College

Article condensed by the author from *Evangelical Review of Theology*

Two sections have been deleted from the original article. In the first, Dr. Bockmuehl establishes the topic of secularisation and secularism as one of primary importance for a church whose membership and influence are shrinking under the impact of secularism. He first looks at the past history of the concept, and the attitude that is signified by it. He arrives at the basic distinction between a secularisation that carries the gospel into the secular marketplace (illustrated, for example, by the Protestant Reformation), and a secularisation that implements the program of secularism, in which one lives 'without God in the world' (Eph. 2:12). Now, the author looks at the prospects of secularism and secularisation on the levels of mass psychology and social structures.—Editor

Two Phases of the Secular Mindset

The progress of the secular mind seems always to begin with a mood of euphoria. We have the testimony of exhilaration in the heyday of the Enlightenment at the beginning of the second half of the 18th century. The same mood seems to have pervaded Western culture around the end of the 19th century and into the beginning of the 20th century, when the educated elite consciously linked up with the Enlightenment and its optimistic view of human nature. Owen Chadwick quotes an advertisement for the *Encyclopaedia Britannica* of 1898 that exalts 'the wonderful story . . . of modern progress in the arts, sciences and industries', and promises to 'tell how the light was spread'. Spirits are waking everywhere: how glorious to be alive! Humanity is seen to be potentially almighty. However, these sentiments did not last. The atrocities of the French Revolution and its tyrannical pursuit of virtue had a sobering effect. It is surprising to see how, later, the mood of French historiography changes from the optimism of Michelet to the dejection of Hippolyte Taine, and how the public reception of Darwinism turns sour.[1]

The First World War had similar effects. The evangelists of materialism around the turn of the century made way for culture critics who brooded

177

over the relativism and meaninglessness of the technological age. Karl Heim observed the sobering of mood in the leading scientists.[2] At the time, many people already felt that the 'Roaring Twenties' resembled dancing on a volcano ready to erupt, and as Thornton Wilder characterized the mood, they tried to 'eat their ice cream while it is on their plate'. One theologian captured the cultural climate in a startling manner: 'Fear of God has died. But a new fear replaces it, fear of everything ['Weltangst']. . . . Adoration of culture turns into disdain. The dark gate, to which all secularisation leads, is pessimism'.[3] Man, having abolished God, now clamours about being a 'cosmic orphan'.

Peter Berger, the eminently readable sociologist, who has a wakeful eye on intellectuals, observes at one point that they 'are notoriously haunted by boredom'. For whatever reason, Berger feels that on the other side of secularism, 'there is no telling what outlandish religiosity, even one dripping with savage supernaturalism, may yet arise in these groups. . . .'[4] Ultramoderns develop a new belief in fate, turn to superstition in search for 'meaning', and make enlightenment perfect in a new obscurantism.[5]

The most remarkable instance of such a change in mood is the recent collapse of secular optimism in Western Europe. The sixties, with their booming economy, sported an exuberant mindset of confidence in limitless progress and human ability. But then the picture changed as the public faced the first oil crisis, some seemingly intractable ecological problems, a period of economic decline, and the renewed perception of the threat of nuclear war. Today visitors to Western Europe marvel at the weariness and melancholy, the doom and gloom that rule supreme. Problems may be far greater in India or in Latin America, but it is 'Euro-pessimism', 'the disappearance of hope', that characterizes the old countries.[6] People speak of themselves as the 'no-future generation'. All creativity is gone. Man has lost his moorings—he discarded faith in God, and he is now also through with the belief he was to have in himself. Sartre's prophecy of 'Huis clos' and 'La nausèe' is fulfilled. One wonders what happened to the 'principle of hope' and the 'theology of hope' that were hailed in the sixties—could they have become old hat in less than twenty years?

Disorientation and despondency again give rise to new eccentric faiths. David Martin observes: 'Amsterdam . . . one of the most secularised areas in Holland . . . at the same time is besieged by minor cults'.[7] People begin to dabble again in witchcraft and necromancy. Astrology is 'a burgeoning industry in the most "advanced" countries of the west'.[8] Where God and man have been abandoned, humanity discovers that the cult of Satan is next: it begins to dominate whole sectors of cultural expression, as, for example, in the rock music scene. Secular society quickly becomes a victim of fear and superstition as people have lost their anchorage in a ground that does not shift with the moods of the day. These perspectives make mandatory the question: 'After secularism, what?'

'Anomie', or: The Prospects for the Social Structures

The same question is well worth asking also in view of the social-structural consequences of a secularity that denies any allegiance to God. Secularism proves a terrifying solvent of social bonds. Secular sociologists today are the foremost witnesses to the quality of religion as providing both identity and bonding, as well as to the effects of the loss thereof in a largely secularized milieu. Dr. Martin comments: 'That religion has been a carrier of identity is axiomatic'; it also stipulates organic solidarity and looks after the 'coherent relation' of one's social and personal identity 'to a whole'.[9] Sociologists are aware of religious ethics as the running endorsement of the ancient teaching, 'God said to them: "Beware of all iniquity" and commended to everyone his neighbour' (Eccl. 17:12).

It is even more remarkable that modern sociology, beginning with Emile Durkheim, should have chosen a term—anomie—for the secular dissolution of social bonds that figures prominently in the eschatology of the gospel: 'Because *anomia* (lawlessness) will abound, the love of many will grow cold' (Mt. 24:12). Sociologists, philosophers, and historians see this disintegration of the social network in the progress of secularisation. This is evident, for example, in the field of economics, where emancipation from the traditional directives of religious ethics and the renunciation of the proprietor's responsibility before God have resulted in the theory and practice of an utter individualism. Consequently, misery has come to millions of people as society has fragmented, and overt acts of unmitigated class warfare have been committed.[10] Others observe the ominous rise of nationalism concurrently with the maturing of secularity, another fragmentation for which the world has already had to pay dearly in two world wars.[11] And the desacralization of religion can quickly turn into a sacralization of politics.

In more recent times we face a mounting disintegration of the family, the social unit that sociologists fifteen or twenty years ago still thought was highly resistant to the acids of secularisation. Here, too, social disorganization is under way.

The overall result is 'anomie', an atomism of social life that we only now recognize as the content of the prophecy found in the arts, music, painting, and literature of the first half of the 20th century. (Can we still speak of any sizeable creation of art in the second half of this century, except in reproduction?) This *anomie* expresses itself in the abolition of moral consensus, at first perceived as the opening up of individual freedom. Liberals like John Stuart Mill postulate that the individual must and can be trusted to be himself responsible for his morality. But what if others, like Friedrich Nietzsche, come and proclaim that not only religion, but also morality, is the 'opiate for the people', designed only to stifle genius?[12] How shall we then live together? Where there are no absolute values, all behaviour is arbitrary, and Adolf Eichmann and Mother Teresa represent only different individual predilections.

Nietzsche knew that secularism and anarchy go together, in the same way as faith in God and belief in structure: 'I fear we won't get rid of God, as [because] we still believe in grammar. . . .'[13] Only the dissolution of all structure, social or otherwise, seems to be able to give man the total autonomy that will supposedly facilitate the ultimate self-realization and gratification that he feels entitled to.

Enlightenment took individuality, a prominent boon from the inheritance of Christianity, and severed it from its organic links; it turned into individualism, an uncontrolled cancerous growth; in the same way brotherhood is being blown up into collectivism. A paradigm of the whole development can be seen in the evolution of types in the philosophical school of the 'Young Hegelians' after their rejection of Hegel's synthesis of Christianity and culture. Each position, as it were, coagulates in the stance of an individual person, the whole presenting an instructive genealogical tree: D. F. Strauss combines the apex of Bible criticism with the veneration of humanity; L. Feuerbach combines the overall criticism of religion with the worship of the I-Thou relationship. Next the Bauer brothers are atheists and anarchists, and the end product is Julius Stirner's philosophy of 'solipsism', neatly expressed in the title of his book *The Only One and His Property*. The road that began with the Enlightenment must be completed with Stirner; in its beginnings, the life of Rousseau granted already some glimpses of the end. The historian James Hitchcock shrewdly observes: Insofar as 'the ultimate demand of the secularised individual . . . is absolute personal moral autonomy', 'the most fundamental disease of the modern psyche is solipsism, the need for an empty universe to be filled by an infinitely expanding self.'[14] Stirner's *The Only One and His Property* can also be seen as the secret of Adam Smith's Political Economy divulged. Since we cannot afford to depopulate the globe for the benefit of the Only One, the logical conclusion must be civil war, be it a cold one. We can already understand Marx's desperate scramble to evade the consequences through the proclamation of socialism.

However, the logic is not one of theory alone. We are beginning to feel the palpable burden of the rising spiritual and material costs of social disintegration, of the international order as well as of the family, in terms of social expenditure the taxpayer has to answer for. There comes the moment when people are no longer willing to bleed. Attempts at setting up new goals on the basis of this worldly human responsibility fail. The consensus concerning mechanics and the 'How to' of science cannot be repeated either regarding morals or the question many ask about goals: 'What For?'[15] Pluralism comes to sense that no social system can exist without a basic commonality of norms. This impasse can, of course, be countered by growing institutionalism. More blatant than this, and sometimes replacing it, can be the emergence of an insurmountable public desire for a new ideological reintegration—if necessary, by force. Robespierre may serve as a classical example for the reversal of secularisation into sacralization.[16] Re-integration comes with the suggestion of a 'salutary' dictatorship, one that will make for us the decisions of renunciation and frugality we can no longer bring ourselves to make. It is the type of the beneficient dictator who steps in when, facing the confusion of goals and values, a majority begins to feel: 'It cannot go on like this'. The imminent change of mood is sometimes recognized in the shifting place of the concept of freedom. Most prominent as a slogan at the outset, it becomes obsolete, almost a pudendum, before the advent of the benevolent dictatorship, just as confidence in the potential of man will be replaced by the induction of fear and a feeling of powerlessness vis-à-vis pressing social problems, serving the same ultimate purposes of the impending dictatorship.

Sociologists are only too aware of these historical consequences of 'anomie'. At the end of his study of 'Religion in Secular Society', Bryan Wilson, the Oxford sociologist, himself reveals a remarkable change of mood. All through his book he sounded as though slightly sneering at the demise of religion, and fending off any sign of its meddling in public affairs again—as if to say, 'The secular world can do very well without it'. Towards the end he becomes quite thoughtful. He observes that Christianity has brought 'the extension of kin-group and neighbourhood affectivity into generalized and impersonal goodwill'. Also, it has been responsible for 'a strong internalized sense of impersonal individual honesty', as well as 'disinterested devotion to one's calling'—all qualities that render much social control dispensable and may well have been decisive in making our present culture possible.

Now when the liturgy, the theology, or the social life of the Church deteriorate, then only the Church is concerned. However, with ethics, things are different. Those moral qualities now appear 'as a type of moral capital debt which is no longer being serviced'. Therefore, 'whether indeed our own type of society will effectively maintain public order, without institutional coercion, once the still persisting influence of past religion wanes even further, remains to be seen.' What can be seen already and must be further expected, is the increase of crime and public disorder.[17]

Wilson's Oxford colleague David Martin comments on the disorientation in the wake of European secularism: '. . . the extension of pluralism can create the conditions under which either the older forms of integration will try and re-establish themselves in control, or the pluralistic tendency will be pushed dangerously close to anarchy and atomism, or the monism of the Eastern European system will come to seem attractive by virtue of the ideological vacua and disintegrations which have been created. . . . Anarchy in any context is frequently a prelude to totalitarian re-integration.'[18]

The state must then take over the enforcement of morals, and replace God as the guarantor of the morality of social life; that is, the state must become <u>totalitarian</u>. It must try to inspire awe and reverence, and must establish a secret police that if possible would know everything and could read the thoughts of the heart, just as God did, becoming the replacement of conscience as the representation of the objective moral law within the individual subject.

One can already determine what ideology would be favored by such a state. It must be socialism, nationalism, or preferably a mix of the two. Any of these approaches would be an attempt to recover social cohesion and to legitimise outward enforcement of the commonality of life. The German re-integration of 1933 gives all necessary instruction.

It is thus the secular sociologists who today seem to be most aware of the threatening corollaries of secularisation: <u>less religion must logically mean more coercion</u>. They substantiate William Penn's dictum: <u>Nations must be governed by God, or they will be ruled by tyrants</u>. If that is the truth we can glean from the pages of recent history, then secularism is the enemy not only of religion, but of humanity.

The problem that surfaces everywhere in these explorations is the old question of whether there can be legality without morality, and whether there can be morality without religion. Concerning the first half of the question, the secularists of a hundred years ago were convinced that one could not (as John Stuart Mill proposed) leave the basic moral decisions in the hands of the individual on a large scale. They therefore demanded that morality be taught in schools. Then, of course, they ran into the problem of motivation. Their materialist worldview and a natural history of accidents would not support the quality of mercy. It could not rule out Auschwitz. Nietzsche derided D. F. Strauss in his later attempt to combine a naturalist worldview of causality and contingency with the exhortation to humanism and brotherhood. Marxism still labours with this dilemma. Voltaire had quietly endorsed the necessity of faith as the foundation of morality when he refused to 'talk atheism in front of the maids'. Kant examined, as it were, the problem under laboratory conditions, and decided that morality must always lead to religion and rely on religion.[19] One French intellectual, F. Brunetière, as Chadwick relates, went through this argument existentially in the course of his life, beginning as an atheist, but returning to the Church under the conviction that 'society cannot dispense with religion in its acceptance of moral axioms'.[20] It cannot dispense with it because responsibility, the backbone of morality, is a theological concept, and the group or the state cannot serve as its point of reference.[21]

Cycles of Apostasy and Conversion

In our historical survey we have met with several examples of the different stages of development: the optimism of the Enlightenment, and then its recapture as the 19th century turned into the 20th, and again its recapture in the decade of the 1960s. We have witnessed repeated periods of social disorientation and decay. Karl Heim thought that the mindset of secularism was an age-old problem, only compounded in Christian culture.[22] Indeed, already the Psalmist was faced with a milieu ignoring God: 'Help, Lord; for there is no longer any that is godly; for the faithful have vanished from among the sons of men.' (Ps. 12:2)

What we observe is perhaps the 'natural' process of moral corrosion in a fallen world, a tendency to corrupt (Eph. 4:22b) that would finally tear down humanity if it were not for measures of divine preservation, disinfection, expurgation, and renewal. These are measures that may be well perceived as visible historical counterparts to the renewal of creation praised in Psalm 104:30: 'You send forth your Spirit . . . and you renew the face of the earth'.

These measures are of different kinds. Not only the dispersion of mankind, Genesis 11, but also the calling of Abraham in Genesis 12 must be seen as God's response to man's rebellious undertaking exemplified in the Tower of Babel. As we look into recent history, sometimes the secularist exultations ended in wars of an ever-increasingly terrible scale. Perhaps there is the other possibility of a culture, a nation, a creative minority, returning to the mercy of the Eternal God. Christ's parables of the Tenants (Luke 20:9ff.) and of the Prodigal Son (Luke 15:11ff.) seem to indicate this double outcome of secularisation. We would then be faced with a cycle of apostasy and conversion as already experienced by the people of Israel at the time of the early judges.

In light of this, the most advanced group of people would then be those Russian intellectuals who, having gone through the empty promises of rationalism, through nihilism, through the Marxist re-integration of society, and finally through the utter disillusionment and mortification of an ageing Marxist society, are now in growing numbers turning to the orthodox Christian faith. Of them we have recently been given a first glimpse in Tatiana Goricheva's disturbing and fascinating book *Dangerous to Speak of God*.[23] Through their witness, western society is once more given the grace of an opportunity to choose between the Road of Light and the Road of Darkness.

In a section omitted here, Dr. Bochmuehl looks at some 'available responses' to secularism and secularisation. He touches on several attempts at accommodation of Christianity to secularism, as proposed by Schleiermacher, Bultmann, and Gogarten, which necessitated the abandonment of certain 'unpopular' doctrines. He also looks at the recent change of mind (in the direction of Schleiermacher) of noted sociologist Peter Berger, a contemporary authority on the theme. In conclusion, the author meditates on some desirable Christian responses to today's mindset of secularism. These reflections follow.—Editor

Desirable Responses

1. It seems to be necessary to expose the mechanism of secularisation and secularism so as to reveal their inherent pitfalls. The recognition of a diffuse and hidden peril is of immense value. It needs to be said that secularism is the adversary of the gospel, that it will never engender love of God and love of neighbour, but only love of self, and that there is no future for faith in its appeasement. Such an analysis of secularism and its working can act as a necessary disinfectant.

2. However, we propose at the same time that a 'response' should not merely be shaped by the analysis of the opponent, be it in terms of accommodation or rejection. The 'response' should in no way be a reaction. It should be determined not by the milieu but by the Word of God. Taking an example from Barth's *Theological Existence Today* in the political crisis situation of Germany in 1933: Christian proclamation must in the last analysis go on 'as if nothing had happened'. Accommodation must be strictly in form of speech; but the content of the gospel cannot be contained by any secular epistemology. The church, furthermore, must not withdraw from the world, but, according to its marching orders in the New Testament, aim for holy living even in unholy places (Eph. 4:17ff.; Tit. 2:12ff.).

3. On this basis, three transactions are necessary to sustain Christian identity and outreach: prayer, sustenance of the fellowship, and proclamation.

(a) The first task is to strengthen the centre of Christian identity, that is, a person's relationship with God. This is done through prayer. Prayer is the expression of respect for, and love of God, clearly the extreme antithesis to secularism. In prayer, the Christian presents to God humanity and the course it is taking.

Prayer engenders steadfastness and independence, and yields the necessary orientation. The German author Ernst Jünger noted in the days of the turbulent dissolution of the National Socialist Empire: 'What could one recommend to help people, especially simple people, to avoid conformism with, and standardization by the system? Nothing but prayer. This is the point of leverage, even for the humblest. . . . It yields uncommon gain and tremendous sovereignty. This is also true apart from all theology. In situations where the most clever ones fail and the most courageous look in vain for ways out, you sometimes see a man quietly counsel the right and do what is good. You can trust that that is a person who prays.'[24] Prayer helps to recover perspective, and teaches us what Os Guinness has called 'a basic requirement of contemporary discipleship': to be 'ready to "think globally but act locally" '.[25] Perspective comes as a fruit of perceptive prayer and is, as such, the prerequisite of ministry to fellow believers and to the world.

Moreover, prayer needs to be followed up (2 Tim. 2:19!) by a life of sanctification, by the willingness to 'live soberly, righteously, and godly in this world' (Tit. 2:12), that is, to live differently from the rest, to stick to God's absolute moral standards and not yield to general permissiveness, to live conscientiously and yet not turn one's back on humanity, to withdraw from evil although not from people. There can be no Christian life without the struggle against secularism: a struggle against the will to autonomy and the forgetfulness of the things of God, which characterize the spirit of these times. The struggle also involves the daily battle to awaken to Him and to the hallowing of His name.

(b) *Diligite dominum. . . . Veriliter agite, et confortetur cor vestrum*, 'love God, act bravely, and He shall strengthen your hearts', is how the Vulgate translates Psalm 31:24f. The whole psalm speaks confidently of the possibility of courageous action in an alien environment, and reminds one of Paul's words of encouragement for his brethren in 1 Corinthians 15:58: 'Therefore, my beloved brethren, be steadfast, immovable, always abounding in the work of the Lord, inasmuch as you know that your labour is not in vain in the Lord.' The second task, combining the interests of identity and outreach, concerns the 'strengthening of the brethren' (Luke 22:32; Acts 14:22, etc.). It endeavours to 'fan the flame where you find it,' to support any discernible movement in the direction of faith, and to strengthen Christian commitment.

This will find expression in the conscious cultivation of cell groups, small circles that support those purposes. Bryan Wilson felt that any good that might still come from religion would come from 'the religion of the sects', by which he seems to have meant the unpolluted Christianity of small groups of committed people not associated with the churches. He may have underestimated the network of such groups *within* today's churches and denominations, successors of the *ecclesiola in ecclesia* of early Pietism and of Wesley's 'bands', which successfully countered institutional torpor and the dissolution of social bonding. David Martin seems to have been fascinated with the wide-reaching effects of Haugeanism, the corresponding movement within the Norwegian church.[26] Faith here proves once more not only the guarantor, but the source of salutary human relationships.

(c) Finally, proclamation. This concerns Christian outreach. In the first place, it is the calm re-announcement of the reality of God, both of his righteousness and mercy, to a secularity forgetful of these facts. In a secular environment religion may perhaps still be allowed as a topic, but the question of God (like death) has almost become a pudendum. It is of utmost importance that individuals, as well as society as such, be faced in a matter-of-fact way with the question of its relationship to God. It is the task of the Church to announce God again to 'a crooked and perverse generation' (Phil. 2:15). The Church is to remind the world that God 'has appointed a day on

which He will judge the world in righteousness by the Man whom He has
ordained' (Acts 17:31), and that this Man, Jesus Christ of Nazareth, at the
same time is the one ground of our salvation.

In the pursuit of these tasks the Church will be the light of the house (Mt.
5:15), which she shares with the rest of humanity. The Church will act like
leaven in the dough, and resemble the mustard in its surprisingly abundant
growth, making it the nesting-place for many. In the pursuit of these tasks, as
well as in the work of their callings under the creation mandate, Christians
will not only 'help to build the temple of the Lord' (Zech. 6:15), but, in the
meantime, will also unwittingly participate in God's own work of sustaining
His creation.

Notes

[1] O. Chadwick, *The Secularization of the European Mind in the Nineteenth Century,* Cambridge: University Press 1975, 153, 210.

[2] Karl Heim, 'Der Kampf gegen den Säkularismus', in: H. H. Schrey, Hrsg., *Säkularisierung,* Darmstadt: Wiss. Buchgesellschaft 1981, 123.

[3] H. Schreiner, as cited in Hermann Lübbe, *Säkularisierung. Geschichte eines ideenpolitischen Begriffs,* Freiburg u. München: Alber ²1975, 89.

[4] Peter L. Berger. *A Rumor of Angels. Modern Society and the Rediscovery of the Supernatural,* Garden City, N.Y.: Doubleday Anchor Books 1970, 24.

[5] Manès Sperber, *Die vergebliche Warnung. All das Vergangene . . . ,* Wien: Europaverlag 1975, 207.

[6] Cp. L. Newbigin, *The Other Side of 1984. Questions for the Churches,* Geneva: WCC 1983, 1.

[7] D. Martin, *A General Theory of Secularization.* New York, etc.: Harper Colophon Books 1978, 197.

[8] L. Newbigin, *op. cit.,* 18.

[9] D. Martin, *op. cit.,* 77, 83, 88, 108, 205.

[10] L. Newbigin, *op. cit.,* 11, 22.

[11] H. Lübbe, *op. cit.,* 77, 131.

[12] O. Chadwick, *op. cit.,* 28ff., 232.

[13] Friedrich Nietzsche, *Werke,* K. Schlechta, Hrsg., vol. 2, Darmstadt: Wiss. Buchgesellschaft 1966, 960.

[14] James Hitchcock, 'Self, Jesus, and God: The Roots of Religious Secularization', in: P. Williamson and K. Perrotta, eds., *Summons to Faith and Renewal: Christian Renewal in a Post-Christian World,* Ann Arbor, Mich.: Servant Books 1983, 29, 35.

[15] H. Lübbe, *op. cit.,* 70.

[16] O. H. von der Gablentz, as cited in H. Lübbe, *op. cit.,* 123f.

[17] Bryan Wilson, *Religion in Secular Society: A Sociological Comment* (1966), Harmondsworth (U.K.): Penguin 1969, 254, 261ff.—It is very doubtful whether the 'influx of Eastern religions' will continue to provide social bonding through 'impersonal goodwill', a sense of civil vocation, and the concern for the public square with which Christianity originally endowed Western civilization.

[18] D. Martin, *op. cit.,* 164, 89, cp. 46, 90, 188.

[19] Frederick Copleston, S.J., *A History of Philosophy,* vol. 6: *Modern Philosophy,* pt. II: Kant, Garden City, N.Y.: Doubleday Image Books 1964, 135.

[20] O. Chadwick, *op. cit.,* 243.

[21] Cp. H. H. Schrey, *op. cit.,* 130.

[22] K. Heim, *op. cit.*, 110, 112, 123. However, Heim felt in 1930 that Christians were approaching a final battle of the spirits, *op. cit.*, 127.

[23] Tatjana Goritschewa, *Von Gott zu reden ist gefährlich. Meine Erfahrungen im Osten und im Westen* (1984), Freiburg etc.: Herder ⁹1985.

[24] Ernst Jünger, *Strahlungen III*, München: dtv 1966, 14, cp. 27f.

[25] Os Guinness, *The Gravedigger File: Papers on the Subversion of the Church*, Downers Grove, Ill.: InterVarsity Press 1983, 233.

[26] D. Martin, *op. cit.*, 34, 69.

LIBERATION IN THE NEW TESTAMENT

R. T. FRANCE
Vice-Principal, London Bible College

Article from *The Evangelical Quarterly*

I. Jesus and the Kingdom of God

The *Pax Romana* was a good thing, but we should not let its virtues blind us to the fact that life in the provinces of the Roman empire was no utopia. In Palestine, where Christianity was born, political, economic and social grievances were sufficient to spark off a series of bloody revolts against the 'enlightened' government of Rome and, more important, its often less enlightened local representatives. The New Testament was written against the background of a society seething with discontent, and accustomed to brutality and injustice matched in few parts of the world today.[1]

It is against this background that the attitude of Jesus to the revolutionary movements of his day must be assessed. Strenuous efforts have been made to identify Jesus as the would-be leader of a violent revolution, a precursor of the Zealot leaders who a generation later plunged Palestine into the disastrous 'war of liberation' that culminated in the Roman destruction of Jerusalem.[2] Nowadays, however, it is generally agreed that such a position can be maintained only by both discarding most of the more direct evidence available (that of the Gospels) and also flying in the face of historical probability. Jesus, it would now be generally accepted, was no Zealot— indeed he took pains to dissociate himself publicly from the revolutionary option.[3]

In addition to the discussion of the standard texts, it is important that we set the question against the background of some of the more distinctive emphases of Jesus' life and teaching, which effectively put him at odds with violent revolution in general and with the Zealot position in particular. Without at this point going into any detail, we might suitably note the following themes, which are documented elsewhere:

(i). Jesus conceived of his role as Messiah in terms of the restoration of the relationship between man and God, not in terms of national aspirations or of political liberation; and he saw the appointed means as suffering and death, not conquest.[4]

(ii). His views on the place of the Jewish nation in the purposes of God, and his repeated warnings of God's judgment on it as a political institution, are in striking contrast with Zealot ideals.[5]

(iii). His constant stress on love, even of enemies, and on unlimited forgiveness contrasts sharply with the philosophy of hatred that underlies most revolutionary movements.[6]

This is well-trodden ground. My purpose in this article, however, is not to produce another critique of *Jesus and the Zealots*, but rather to consider on a broader front, and in more positive terms, what Jesus' mission was, rather than what it was not. In particular, we shall be considering how far the language of 'liberation' is appropriate to describe what Jesus came to achieve.

The term Jesus used most frequently to denote the new order he had come to bring, the purpose of his mission, is 'the kingdom of God'.[7] The English translation is unfortunate in that it suggests a political unit, whereas the Greek *basileia* refers to the act of reigning, the situation where God is in control, God's 'reign' or 'sovereignty'. Under this phrase Jesus speaks of many different aspects of his work, so that it becomes a very general designation of 'the state of affairs which God intends' and which it is Jesus' purpose to bring about. He speaks of the kingdom of God as something which is near (Mk. 1:15; Lk. 10:9, 11), which should be sought (Mt. 6:33) and which one may enter (Mk. 9:47; Mt. 5:20; 7:21; Jn. 3:5) or be near to (Mk. 12:34), but which can also be shut up (Mt. 23:13; cf. 16:19) or taken away (Mt. 21:43). It is preached (Mt. 24:14; Lk. 4:43; 9:60), it is forced (Mt. 11:12), it comes secretly (Lk. 17:20) and it will come in power (Mk. 9:1). It is to be looked forward to (Mt. 6:10; cf. Lk. 19:11) and yet it is already 'among you' (Lk. 17:21). It is only for the committed (Lk. 9:62), for children and those who are like children (Mk. 10:14f), for the poor in spirit and the persecuted (Mt. 5:3, 10); the poor disciple possesses it (Lk. 6:20), but the rich man can enter it only with difficulty (Mk. 10:23-25). It is above all a mystery (Mk. 4:11) that may take men unawares (Mt. 12:28).

But *what is it?* The list of characteristics above should be enough to show that a simple answer is not going to do justice to the teaching of Jesus. In fact it is seldom that anything approaching a definition or even description of the kingdom of God is given in the Gospels. It is apparently parallel to righteousness (Mt. 6:33), and to the accomplishment of God's will (Mt. 6:10). Sometimes, however, it seems to refer to the future state of those who please God (Mt. 8:11; 13:43). It is characteristically described in parables: 'the kingdom of God is like . . .'. But these parables sometimes refer to the preaching and penetration of the gospel (Mk. 4:26ff, 30ff; Mt. 13:33), sometimes to the present experience of the convert (Mt. 13:44-46) or his obligations (Mt. 18:23ff), sometimes to men's ultimate fate (Mt. 13:24ff, 47-50; 20:1ff; 22:2ff; 25:1ff).

All this points to the truth of Norman Perrin's argument that 'kingdom of God' is not a concept or idea with a single dictionary definition, but a 'tensive symbol', by which he means a phrase that may have a wide range of meanings or points of reference, and whose function is rather to evoke a certain complex of ideas related to the overall purpose of God than to refer to any specific concept, or event, or state of affairs.[8] If this is so, we must beware of simplistic assertions that the kingdom of God is 'all about' heaven, or 'all about' a conversion experience, or 'all about' a future cataclysmic event, or 'all about' social justice for the poor. It is a general expression for the purposes of God as they are focused in the ministry of Jesus, and any drawing of ethical or theological principles from this expression is only valid if it can be justified from the NT account of Jesus' ministry and teaching, not on the basis of a presumed 'meaning' of 'kingdom of God'.

In this context, then, it is not legitimate to claim, as is often done, that Jesus' use of the expression 'kingdom of God' demonstrates his concern with political liberation, or with the restructuring of society, or with an other-worldly life-style or with any other specific ethical ideal. More specific evidence is needed of what his aims were.

It should be noted also that the kingdom of God is almost always spoken of as an active subject—it 'comes', etc.—or as something already existing, with which men may identify themselves by 'entering into' it. We may seek and pray for its consummation, but it is not something that is brought about by human effort, even by obedience to the will of God. The old liberal idea, sometimes echoed in modern discussion, of men bringing the kingdom of God on earth has no basis in the gospels.[9]

'Kingdom of God' is not, then, a promising approach to the social and political implication of Jesus' ministry. We must look more widely at the emphases displayed in his life and teaching.

Helmut Gollwitzer[10] argues that Jesus, despite his dissociation from Zealot ideals, was revolutionary in the sense that he overturned existing values, thus precipitating an ultimate transformation of power structures, property relations, social conventions, etc. Whether or not this lighting of the fuse for explosions that might occur centuries later is what most of us would call 'revolution', the point is important; Jesus did preach and practise values in relation to society, race, and wealth, and indeed on the basic ethical issues of law-keeping and the will of God, which were uncomfortably radical,[11] and of which we are still only beginning to explore the practical implications. The time-bombs that he planted have been exploding in Christian-inspired social and political reform and in life-styles which have challenged society ever since, and they continue to do so in an exhilarating way today as Christians re-examine some of their inherited traditions of discipleship.

But how far does this '*bouleversement* [overturning] of the value scale'[12] add up to an endorsement of modern liberation theology? How did Jesus envisage his 'revolution' of values coming about? Has this anything to do with the struggle for political freedom today?

A disciple who takes the practice and teaching of Jesus as a practical guide for living will always be, simply by what he is, conspicuous and a challenge to the accepted values of society. A disciple group that consciously sets itself to live by Jesus' values will inevitably develop a 'counter-culture'. Did Jesus then aim to set up such a visible alternative as a means to overturn the existing system?

Luke records his stated programme as

> 'to preach good news to the poor.
> . . . to proclaim release to the captives
> and recovering of sight to the blind,
> to set at liberty those who are oppressed,
> to proclaim the acceptable year of the Lord.'
> (Lk. 4:18f; from Is. 61:1f)

While traditional Christian exegesis has interpreted these words in terms of spiritual release, some recent interpreters take them more literally, and specifically regard the 'acceptable year' as the OT jubilee, which Jesus campaigned to have literally observed, resulting in a redistribution of wealth and a new socio-economic deal for the poor.[13] The literal jubilee has not convinced many students of the Gospels, but the view that Jesus not only preached new values but also set out a specific programme for socio-economic reform has been welcomed by some. I have attempted to examine this suggestion in some detail with reference to Jesus' teaching on wealth,[14] and have concluded that for all the undeniably radical implications of the values Jesus inculcated, the Gospels do not support the view that he advocated or even countenanced any specific programme to change the existing socio-economic system. In other words, he was radical without being revolutionary (as I understand the term, to refer to the forcible overthrow of the *status quo*). His followers were and are at liberty to draw practical conclusions from the values he lived and taught, but they cannot claim his direct sanction for their chosen course of action, and may legitimately differ quite fundamentally over what programme is the most adequate way to implement his values.

What is true of Jesus' attitude to socio-economic reform seems equally true of his political attitude. His refusal to endorse the Zealot option is balanced by an attitude of detachment from, sometimes hostility toward, the Jewish establishment and, by implication, the political system to which they owed their status. He was conspicuously 'non-aligned', a fact that should be seriously pondered by those who claim his sanction for whole-hearted support of one side, whether right or left, in a political conflict. Jesus had the ideal situation in which to engage, or to urge his disciples to engage, in militant revolt or in authoritarian suppression of a discontented population, but he is as far from the one as from the other. This was not what he had come to do.

And yet he had talked about 'good news to the poor', 'release', 'liberty'. If he was not preaching political liberation, what *did* he mean? At the risk of sounding hopelessly traditional, I can say only that the liberation he proclaimed was from something far more deep-rooted than the political oppression of the Roman empire. He did not expect, and certainly did not advocate, a re-establishment of Jewish national freedom; indeed, he went out of his way to pour cold water on any such hopes.[15] His concern was with men's attitudes and relationships towards one another and towards God. In the latter respect he looked for liberation from sin, from hypocrisy, from alienation from God; in the former respect he attacked pride, greed, injustice, and the barriers of class, race, wealth, and respectability which divide man from man. These are all matters of attitudes and values, of a man's spiritual and social orientation, and it is here that Jesus' programme of liberation centred.

The disciple-group that grew out of Jesus' ministry was, therefore, a group of people who *were* different, rather than a group with a different philosophy or political system. They had experienced 'liberation' at the most fundamental level. It was inevitable that their community should become by its very nature a challenge to the existing structures, and we may fairly assume that Jesus expected and intended it to be so. But the Christian challenge was the positive one of demonstrating an alternative way of life, rather than the negative one of a programme to destroy and replace the existing order. It was radical but not revolutionary.

This is not to say that Jesus did not expect political change. He certainly did, as his predictions of the destruction of Jerusalem show. But it was not the change a Jewish 'liberationist' would have desired. And the kingdom of God to whose coming he taught his disciples to look foward was not to be a national triumph, but a new order that God would bring in his own time and way (Mk. 4:26-29), and that he did not suggest could be hastened by human effort, though it could and should be eagerly sought and prayed for.

Meanwhile, the kingdom of God was already available for those who were prepared to enter it, not by joining a political movement but by a personal reorientation of values resulting in a life focused on the love of God and of one's fellow-men. This was the liberation Jesus offered.

II. 'Liberation' Language in the New Testament

'Liberation' is not a direct equivalent of any one word in the Greek NT, but a study of a number of near-equivalents is valuable to highlight the NT perspective.

Aphienai and *aphesis* are used in the LXX particularly in reference to the release of captives and slaves and the remission of debts. *Aphesis* is thus a strong candidate for a 'liberationist' interpretation in the NT. It is striking, however, that of the 17 uses of *aphesis* in the NT all but two refer to the forgiveness of *sins*, and those two (both in Lk. 4:18) are in the course of a quotation from the LXX.[16] There is thus a remarkable change in the use of this term, from a socially oriented 'liberation' to a spiritual 'liberation'.[17]

Eleutheroun and its derivatives are little used in the LXX, predominantly of the freeing of slaves (though interestingly not of the Exodus, which is seen as a divine 'redemption', *lutrōsis*, rather than a human 'liberation'). In the NT they are used little outside Paul's letters, where they are used almost exclusively in a metaphorical reference to the Christian experience of freedom from the law, from moral bondage, or, in the case of the verb, from sin; such uses have no discernible socio-political application. One literal use is in the famous statement that in Christ 'there is neither slave nor free' (Gal. 3:28; cf. 1 Cor. 12:13; Col. 3:11), a statement whose eventual social implications are enormous, but these implications are not spelled out and the context does not suggest that they were in Paul's conscious intention at the time of writing. The one discussion of literal 'liberation' in the LXX sense (1 Cor. 7:20-24) is with reference to the Christian slave's personal decision whether he should seek freedom, but no programme of seeking freedom for others is mentioned. The eventual 'liberation' of the created order (Rom. 8:21) is something to be awaited with longing, but it will come apparently by the sovereign action of God. *Eleutheroun,* like *aphienai,* therefore moves from the sphere of human liberation in the LXX to a new spiritual dimension in the NT.

Luein has a wide variety of uses, but with reference to the release of *people* it is used in a clearly relevant way only in Rev. 1:5 of release from sins, and in Lk. 13:12, 16, of release from deformity, regarded (only here in the NT[18]) as a satanic bondage. The verb is used in Eph. 2:14 of the 'destruction' of the racial barrier, a theme of some importance to our subject, though not linguisitically relevant to the use of *luein* for the 'freeing' of people(s); this racial harmony is the result of Christ's reconciling work, and so is reported as a *fait accompli,* rather than as a goal to be achieved.

But if *luein* is only marginally relevant to our subject, its derivative *lutrousthai,* with the noun *lutron,* has more to offer. Basic to the usage of this group in the LXX is the idea of an equivalent payment as the means of freedom. It is used characteristically of the 'redemption' of the firstborn, and can have either people or things as its object. From its use for 'buying freedom for' slaves comes its characteristic use in Deuteronomy for God's 'redemption' of his people from slavery in Egypt. In this usage, where political liberation is of course clearly intended, the subject is always God; man may be responsible for the redeeming of an individual slave, but the redeeming of a people is only God's business, and Isaiah so uses it frequently of God's action on behalf of his people Israel. In the Psalms it develops further to be a fairly general term for rescuing the Psalmist from whatever danger threatens, but again the subject is, and must be, God.

In the NT *lutrousthai* seldom occurs, though it is interesting to see it reappearing in a nationalistic sense in the (inadequate) hope of the Emmaus disciples (Lk. 24:21; cf. *lutrōsis* for the pre-Christian hope in Lk. 1:68; 2:38). Elsewhere the root (usually with the prefix *apo-*, almost unknown in the LXX) occurs some 15 times in a clearly theological sense, related both to freedom from sin and to the ultimate salvation to which the Christian looks forward. In this usage it is charactertistically connected with the death or 'blood' of Jesus, and he is normally explicitly the agent of redemption. Thus a nationalistic (though God-centred) usage that still lingers in Luke's picture of pious Jewish hopes before Christ, gives way in the NT to a clearly soteriological meaning. The liberation that in the NT parallels the Exodus experience is a liberation from sin and its effects.

The most common NT verb to be considered here is _sōzein_. Its usage in both LXX and NT is of course very wide—as wide as the range of dangers and problems from which men need to be saved. In the Synoptic Gospels its most common use, beyond the literal sense of rescue from physical danger and death, is of healing from physical sickness, in which sense it is used almost as often as the more predictable _iāsthai_ and _therapeuein_. Liberation from sickness is a prominent aspect of Jesus' ministry. But 'to be saved' in an absolute sense is already in the Gospels beginning to take on its distinctive NT usage, where it stands parallel to 'entering the kingdom of God' (Mk. 10:23-26), and Jesus' mission is presented as one of saving the lost (Lk. 19:9-10), or more specifically, 'to save his people from their sins' (Mt. 1:21). This usage becomes almost invariable in the rest of the NT, where the nature of the 'saving' is rarely explicitly stated, but is clearly from the context a restoration of a broken relationship with God. Once, in a quotation from the LXX (Rom. 9:27) the verb is used of national salvation, but in a context which is explicitly opposed to an exclusive nationalism.[19] _Sōzein_ and its cognates are therefore in the NT concerned with men's physical and spiritual well-being, but not apparently with their social or political status.

This very sketchy study of possible 'liberation'-language in the NT therefore adds up to a remarkably unanimous concentration of men's liberation from sin and its effects (and in the case of _sōzein,_ from sickness), the emphasis falling all the time on a man's relationship with God and on the initiative of God in the saving process.[20] Frequently this involves a marked break with LXX usage, reflecting a new emphasis among the Christian writers.

No doubt there are many other ways in which 'liberation' ideals could be expressed, and the study of specific words is in any case at best only a partial guide to the underlying thought and concerns of the writer(s); a broader approach will be attempted in the next section. But for what they are worth, these word-studies provide some pointers to the essential interests of the NT that must not be ignored.

III. The New Testament Perspective on Liberation

'Liberation' is such an elastic word that we need to do some subdivision in order to set out what seem to be the main areas of NT concern. At the risk of some oversimplification, and of some inevitable overlap between the categories, I propose to work with three subheadings.

(a). Personal Liberation

By this term I mean the setting right of 'oppression' in terms of what a person is in himself, rather than in his surroundings. Here again an immediate subdivision is necessary, between physical oppression (illness) and spiritual oppression (sin and alienation from God).

We have seen the former as an important part of the usage of *sōzein* in the NT, and it was of course one of the most prominent parts of Jesus' active ministry. The 'release' of those held by sickness was his constant concern, and continued to be that of his followers as reported in Acts, though it is remarkable that in the epistles there is little sign of this healing activity beyond the lists of gifts in 1 Cor. 12 and a brief mention in James 5:14-16.

On one occasion a physical deformity was described by Jesus as a bondage inflicted by Satan, and the healing of the deformity as a 'liberation' (Lk. 13:16). The fact that Luke described the deformity as a 'spirit of infirmity' (verse 11) may suggest that this is one of those cases where an apparently physical complaint is described in terms of demonic possession (cf. Mk. 9:17-27, epilepsy?; Mt. 9:32f. dumbness; Mt. 12:12, blindness and dumbness). Generally illness and demon-possession are carefully distinguished in the Gospels, and the cure of the one described in different terms from the exorcism of the other. But whether due to a 'resident' demon or not, Lk. 13:16 suggests that Jesus regarded at least some forms of physical ill-health as a satanic oppression that demanded liberation, and in that liberation he and his earliest followers were actively engaged.

The mention of demon-possession brings us to the border-line between physical and spiritual liberation. But demon-possession is a special, and in the NT as a whole, a relatively less prominent form of spiritual bondage. In our survey of 'liberation' language we saw how the NT concentrates on personal liberation from sin and its effects, which include not only guilt and alienation from God, but also the false values of a godless world, such as legalism, greed, and all forms of selfishness and lack of love. Christian salvation (a more appropriate word than 'liberation' for the central concern of the NT, in that its modern usage is loaded towards spiritual rather than socio-political interests) is an all-round change affecting a man's total life and relationships, past, present and future, but it is focused in the restoration of a broken relationship with God, the cause to which NT thought traces our disorientation.

I hope this focus on personal liberation, especially in its spiritual aspect, is sufficiently obvious to any reader of the NT not to need extensive demonstration. We shall return to it later. The danger is that in according it its proper prominence in our approach to the NT we fall into the pietist trap of assuming that this is all the NT is interested in, as much evangelical thought has done until recent years. So having noted this as the primary concern of the earliest Christians, let us see whether their writings are interested also in other aspects of liberation.

(b). Socio-economic Liberation

I have argued above that Jesus did not set out a programme for achieving the redistribution of wealth or other socio-economic reforms. This was not what he had come to achieve, and his modern followers have a hard time when they try to reconstruct such an intention from his teaching in order to claim his sanction for their own reforming programmes. But that does not mean that he had nothing to say about social justice, or any interest in the economic facts of life. Far from it.

Jesus takes it for granted that it is right to give money to the poor (Mk. 10:21; 14:7; Lk. 19:8; cf. Jesus' own practice as reflected in Jn. 13:29). He goes further in recommending that they be invited to meals (Lk. 14:13). A special interest in the poor is shown in his praise of the widow's offering (Mk. 12:41-44), and there is an unmistakable note of indignation in his description of the poor man suffering at the rich man's gate (Lk. 16:19-21).

But a concern for the poor is not in itself a call for socio-economic change. What then was the 'good news to the poor' he claimed as part of his mission (Lk. 4:18; Mt. 11:5)? To call for charity is neither a new ideal nor an adequate solution to the economic problem. The Zealots and others went far beyond this in their call for social reform and the liberation of slaves;[21] did Jesus share these ideals?

'The poor' (in Hebrew, *ᶜanawîm*) was an honoured title in the OT and in later Jewish literature. It described not so much those who were materially deprived, but rather the pious, oppressed by the wicked but promised ultimate vindication by God. Their literal poverty was a result of their deliberate choice of the side of God against the godless order of society. They are also called 'the meek', a class distinguished by their attitude rather than by their material status alone.[22] It is against this background that we must read Jesus' remarkable pronouncement to his disciples, 'Happy are you poor, for yours is the kingdom of God' (Lk. 6:20). It was their deliberate choice of discipleship that had resulted in their literal poverty, and it was that chosen poverty rather than the state of destitution as such that Jesus congratulated. The word 'poor' here is not to be evaporated into a spiritual condition alone, under the influence of the very different beatitude of Mt. 5:3, but it speaks of the poverty of the disciple, who stands in continuity with the *ᶜanawîm* of the OT, not of material poverty as such.

Over against the poor disciple stands the rich man. It is hard for him to be saved (Mk. 10:23-25). The rival attraction of mammon (possessions as such, not just ill-gotten gains) militates against his relationship with God (Mt. 6:24; cf. Mk. 4:19). Greed is the great enemy of true discipleship (Lk. 12:15-21). The remedy is to give freely, even recklessly (Mk. 10:17-22; Mt. 5:40-42; Lk. 12:33f; Lk. 14:33).

Here is a radical enough call for the redistribution of wealth, but its focus is on the rich man's salvation rather than on the poor man's material needs. And this is typical of Jesus' approach. The 'good news' to the poor is not that they will become rich, or even equal, but that 'yours is the kingdom of heaven'. Poverty, in its OT sense, is a blessing, not a disaster to be escaped, because it frees a man to seek the kingdom where wealth would only get in the way. Hence the reversal of roles that is such a clear feature of Jesus' teaching about the poor (Mk. 12:41-44; Lk. 6:20-26; 16:19ff; etc.); it is not that the poor will become rich and the rich poor, but that the poor who seem in this world to be the losers will turn out in fact to be the winners, while the apparently well-off will turn out, for all their riches, to lack what really matters. Real wealth is in the kingdom of God, and in this sphere the poor man is at an advantage.

So Jesus *is* the liberator of the poor, as for instance James Cone so eloquently argues,[23] but this liberation consists not, directly at least, in the correction of economic injustice, but in opening to them a new sphere of life where the old values are transcended. It is like the 'liberation' of the tax-collectors and undesirables with whom Jesus mixed; they remained tax-collectors, but found with Jesus an acceptance and dignity that totally altered their condition.

Such an account of Jesus' message to the poor sounds dangerously like the 'opiate of the people'—a new spiritual wealth that makes material poverty more endurable, instead of doing anything about it. What prevents it from remaining at that level is the radical undercutting of the world's value system that is involved. If treasure on earth stands in antithesis to treasure in heaven, and if true discipleship involves sitting loose to and even disposing of material possessions, if materialism is the great enemy of godliness, then no man can be a follower of Jesus and live for material advantage. And if that is so the heart has gone out of the ruthless acquisitiveness that is the root of economic injustice. Christians, if they understand their Master's teaching, cannot climb over others to get rich. When you add also Jesus' teaching on love and compassion, not only have we no motive for exploitation, but we have a positive motive for seeking the material well-being of our fellow-men, and that must mean a concern for socio-economic justice. To be crudely simple, if all the world were Christian there would be no exploiters, but until that is the case love demands that the Christian be on the side of the exploited. For in Jesus' values people come before possessions, and in Jesus' ministry human need, physical as well as mental and spiritual, took precedence over the conventions of the contemporary social structure.

While, then, Jesus did not campaign for economic justice, nor did he set out for his disciples a programme for doing so, he nevertheless preached and lived such values and attitudes that those who take him seriously can neither exploit nor ignore the plight of the exploited. Socio-economic liberation, if it was not his direct aim, is the proper concern of those who accept his radical value-system.

The outworking of Jesus' values in the New Testament church is most clearly seen in the concern of the Christians for each other's material needs. The famous experiment with the sharing of property in the early Jerusalem church (Acts 2:44-47; 4:32-5:11), the daily distribution to widows (Acts 6:1-6), the famine relief of Acts 11:27-30, and Paul's later collection for the relief of the Jerusalem Christians, these all demonstrate a concern for the material well-being of others, but all operate apparently within the Christian group; they are not extended to socio-economic needs in the wider community, nor are they part of any general programme of reform. If they were intended as examples for imitation by non-Christian society, this intention is not explicit.

Similarly in the teaching of some of the Epistles on the removal of social barriers (James 2:1-9) or on giving to those in need (James 2:15f; 1 Jn. 3:17), the principles are shown as operating within the Christian fellowship. It is not often that one meets a more general principle of social action such as 1 Tim. 6:18f; James 1:27. Galatians 6:10 is particularly interesting in that it adds to the principle of doing good to all men, 'especially to those who are of the household of faith'.

It seems that the time had not yet come for Christians, as a minority group, to campaign for a restructuring of society at large, but within their own circles they could explore the practical implications of Jesus' radical values. In the process they no doubt made mistakes, of which the Jerusalem 'communism' is often thought to be an example. Values without specific prescriptions demand experiment, and mistakes can be made and learned from. As for society at large, their emphasis was clearly on winning people to Christ and to the new life he offered. It was thus that society could eventually be changed; for the time being they do not seem to have felt themselves in a position to try to change it.

Paul's attitude to slavery, for instance, is closely parallel to Jesus' approach to poverty. He envisages a situation where there will continue to be masters and slaves, and gives practical guidance on the proper Christian attitude in those states (Eph. 6:5-9; Col. 3:22-4:1; cf 1 Pet. 2:18ff); his advice to the Christian slave on seizing the chance of freedom is concerned only with the individual's choice, not with a disruption of the system (1 Cor. 7:21). But at the same time by his teaching that spiritual freedom makes men equal (1 Cor. 7:22; Gal. 3:28; Phm. 16) he undercuts the value-system of a slave-owning society and plants a time-bomb that was one day to explode in the abolition of slavery. The fact that he did not campaign for its abolition in his own time does not mean that he has nothing to say on the matter, only that what he says is in terms of attitudes, not of a programme for social reform.

Socio-economic reform, then, is an area for which the NT provides a lot of raw material, in the form of radical new values and attitudes, which began to find expression within the caring community of the faith. In relation to society at large, however, beyond the powerful examples of a new way of life among the followers of Jesus, these values had scarcely begun to be worked out in practice, so that the search for any specific programme for Christian social action in the NT is not a hopeful one.

(c). Political Liberation
The liberation of the nation Israel from political oppression was the grand objective of the Zealots and of several other groups of resistance fighters and activists of the NT period. In as far as we can find in the NT a parallel to the national liberation movements of today,[24] it will be in these Jewish liberation movements. The next chapter will show how far Jesus distanced himself from their revolutionary methods. But did he share their ideals? Did he and his early followers offer any support, however passive, to the cause of political liberation?

Jesus came as the fulfillment of the hopes of those who were 'looking for the consolation of Israel' (Lk. 2:25; cf. Lk. 1:54f, 68f; 2:38) and it is most unlikely that their hopes were purely spiritual. He was tried and convicted as a nationalist agitator, 'the king of the Jews', and after his death at least some of his followers looked back on a now shattered hope that he was to 'redeem Israel' (Lk. 24:21). Even after his resurrection his disciples still saw his mission in such terms (Acts 1:6). Such a view of his mission clearly accounts for much of the popular enthusiasm during his ministry (see especially Jn. 6:14f; Mk. 11:9f and parr.) and the subsequent disenchantment. Had Jesus wished to promote national liberation, he had a ready-made base from which to do it.

His rejection of a political role has been mentioned earlier. We have seen that the focus of his messianic mission was in a different area, summed up in the conversation with Pilate on the nature of his kingship (Jn. 18:33-38).

As for the hopes of Jewish nationalism, Jesus not only bypassed them, but went out of his way to repudiate them, warning his contemporaries of the divine judgment that was to fall on 'this generation' (Lk. 11:49-51; 13:34-5; 19:41-44; 23:28-31, etc.), and of the complete devastation of the temple that was the focus of their national life (Mk. 13:1ff, etc.). The one act of Jesus that seems to give credence to a revolutionary purpose (the Cleansing of the Temple) was directed not against the Romans but against the Jewish establishment. There is a good deal to suggest that he believed that the Jewish people as then constituted had forfeited their status as God's special people (Mk. 12:1-9; Mt. 21:43; 22:1-14; etc.); certainly he saw God's purpose as now embracing others, to the possible exclusion of Jews (Mt. 8:11-12). Even in the very context of his famous 'liberation'-manifesto at Nazareth (Lk. 4:16-21) Jesus went on to point out that God's concern could not be confined to nationalistic limits (4:24-27), a sentiment that did not please his compatriots (4:28f). His vision of the future of the nation as such is entirely of judgment, and his teaching gives no hint of a subsequent political restoration for Israel as a nation.[25]

In the specific context of first-century Palestine, therefore, Jesus not only avoided involvement in the movement for political liberation, but deliberately poured cold water on any such ideals. Neither his teaching nor his action gives any backing to an attempt to overturn the *status quo*. Indeed on one occasion he gratuitously introduced as an example of Christian nonresistance the recommendation that the unjust 'dragooning' methods of the occupying forces should be complied with even beyond what was inevitable (Mt. 5:41); the 'second mile' is powerful incidental proof of Jesus' acceptance of the political *status quo*.

In the rest of the NT the question of the Christian's attitude to the government (in all instances the 'imperialist' government of Rome, as exercised through its local representatives) arises from time to time. 1 Timothy 2:1-2 requires Christians to pray for those in political authority, with the understanding that through their efforts God will ensure 'a quiet and peaceable life.' 1 Peter has much to say on the Christian's conduct in the face of hostile authorities, and includes the specific injunction to be subject to political authorities (specifying both the emperor and his local representatives) 'for the Lord's sake', attributing the local governor's authority to God who 'sent' him (2:13-17). Most strongly of all, Romans 13:1-7 spells out the authority of the secular ruler as part of God's ordering of the world, and draws the conclusion that the Christian must 'be subject', not resist, and pay not only his taxes but also respect and honour.

A full discussion of Romans 13:1-7 is impossible here, but it must be insisted that if this passage is seen as an integral part of the discussion of the outworking of discipleship beginning in 12:1, it must be read as enshrining a general principle, theologically grounded, rather than as a pragmatic recommendation applicable only to the early days of Nero.[26] Civil government as such is a God-given institution; it is his way of running the world, and as such requires the Christian's submission. (This is the word Paul uses, rather than obedience.)[27]

Must the Christian then accept any government, however bad? Can political liberation never be right? In a useful exposition of Romans 13:1-7,[28] N. T. Wright suggests that when a government makes itself a god, it ceases to be 'government under God', and is therefore theologically on a par with anarchy; it then no longer falls under the principles expressed in Romans 13. The portrait of anti-God government in Revelation 13, which is often set in contrast with Romans 13, would be such an 'anarchy'.

This suggestion is worth exploring, but the apparently universal Christian conviction that at least *some* governments must be opposed (however much we may differ over which ones they are!) is surely better explained as a case of the 'lesser evil', where there is a conflict of principles, each in itself good and divinely sanctioned. To resist government is bad in itself, but the alternative may be worse. The famous decision of the apostles that 'we must obey God rather than men' (Acts 5:29) points in this direction. So while political disruption can certainly not be justified from Romans 13, and is in fact always a violation of the principle there set out, it may nonetheless sometimes be the Christian's duty, despite that principle, in a case where a greater principle of Scripture is at issue. The same 'conscience' that requires our submission to government (Rom. 13:5) may also cause us to defy a particular government's edicts to the point of advocating its overthrow.[29] Such decisions are always painful, and are seldom so clear as to command general Christian agreement. But the ethics of Christian discipleship in a fallen world will never be simple.

But in any case Romans 13 is not about changing governments and liberating nations, but about how a Christian should conduct himself in the *status quo*, and it is hazardous to look in this passage for teaching on liberation, for or against. That is not Paul's concern here. Indeed it is not his concern in any of his letters, and the same may be said of the other NT letter-writers. Paul was concerned rather with the practicalities of living within the existing order, and in that context he exemplified well the principle of Romans 13, respecting the legitimate authority of the High Priest in Israel (Acts 23:5), and of the authorities of Philippi, even though he took it upon himself to remind them of how their authority should properly be exercised (Acts 16:19-39), and expecting the Roman government to protect his legitimate rights as a citizen (Acts 22:25-29; 23:16ff; 25:10f; etc.).

But political liberation is a subject that simply did not come up. The NT writers, while they see the Christian as primarily a citizen of another type of kingdom (Phil. 3:20; Heb. 11:13-16; etc.), expect him to function as a responsible citizen of the earthly society in which he finds himself. They do not lay down how he should react to a government which makes this impossible for his Christian conscience, nor, apparently, do they expect this situation to occur.

HERM.

The NT, then, gives no direct approval to political liberation. We may, however, argue for Christian involvement in liberation movements as a necessary means to a good end, particularly as the means of achieving socio-economic justice for the subjects of an oppressive government. This, as we have seen, can be justified from NT thinking, even if it is far from being the main concern of the NT writers. Here we are in the grey area where principles must be weighed against one another, and good ends weighed against undesirable means. The NT gives us no firmer grounds. Not only does it refuse us direct sanction for political liberation in itself as a Christian ideal, but it makes it very clear that political insubordination is, for the Christian, wrong in itself. It is only as the lesser evil that it can be justified.

And let us not delude ourselves that this stance of the NT writers was due to the excellence of the political situation in which they lived. There was ample fuel for liberationist agitation in their situation. It was far harder for them to accept the *status quo* than it is for us in the modern West. But that is what they did, because their interest lay essentially elsewhere.

IV. Conclusions

The liberation that the NT offers is primarily liberation from sin and its consequences,[30] or, as we would more customarily put it, spiritual salvation. But among the consequences of sin is a twisted system of values, the self-centered materialism of unredeemed humanity; and liberation from these false values is an essential part of Christian salvation. This liberation makes distinctions of race, colour, class, sex, and wealth irrelevant to the Christian. Such liberation, rather than a direct attack on the structure of society, is the goal of Jesus and of the NT writers. Political liberation as such is not their concern.

Should Christians then ignore the cry of the oppressed for justice, and offer them only new values to make the injustice more palatable? Should they write off liberation theology as incurably worldly and at odds with the perspective of the NT?

Liberation theology calls our attention to areas where in practice the values of NT Christianity are flouted, where unredeemed humanity (and, too often, humanity that claims redemption but does not exhibit its fruits) has its way. Such situations are an affront to the values Jesus preached, and therefore a standing challenge to those who claim to follow him. The NT indicates plainly enough, and the Christian conscience shouts aloud, that these things ought not to be so.

But the NT does not tell us how to right these wrongs. It tells us the ends, but leaves the means for us to work out. It provides us with principles to guide us, but these principles can point in opposite directions, as when love demands a change in the system while the divine institution of government demands submission to the authorities. It is a very cavalier or a very simple Christian who can claim that his course is clearly laid down in Scripture.

But this is what liberation theology appears to do, when it elevates one approach to a quasi-canonical status. The ends it seeks, of social justice and freedom from oppression, are Christian ends, provided they are not allowed to usurp the saving mission of Christ as the essence of the Christian gospel. But the too frequent assumption that the political means favoured somehow also carries a divine stamp of approval is dangerous, especially when those means are so clearly at odds with Jesus' rejection of the revolutionary option.

Indeed it has been suggested that from the NT point of view the trouble with liberation theology is that it is not radical enough![31] It concentrates on the symptoms (social injustice, etc.) without prescribing a cure for the illness itself (the twisted values of selfish materialism). Jesus was radical without being revolutionary, but liberation theology is revolutionary without being radical.

That is, perhaps, an unfairly simplistic quip, but it may point to an underlying problem with much liberation theology. It has sometimes been noted how the biblical exegesis of many writers of this school is focused on the OT. It looks at the Exodus as the great paradigm of God's liberating work, seen in political terms.[32] But even in the OT itself, and overwhelmingly in the NT, the Exodus is interpreted as a pointer to God's redemption of his people from a more fundamental bondage, that of sin and alienation from God.[33] By concentrating on this OT aspect of God's saving work, has liberation theology forgotten the radical newness of the Christian gospel, which goes to the heart of those false values from which man's oppression and injustice stem? In its proper concern to eliminate the fruits of sin, has it prescribed a remedy that leaves the root intact?

For oppressing, exploiting, affluent man is in need of liberation too, at the deepest level. Clark Pinnock concludes a volume on *Evangelicals and Liberation*[34] with a brief, trenchant chapter entitled 'A Call for the Liberation of North American Christians'. He pleads for their 'liberation from bondage to Mammon'. It is a salutary warning; and it suggests the sobering thought that if *this* liberation had been achieved, as surely the NT demands, many of the crying needs that have called forth liberation theology might not have existed.

Notes

[1] So e.g. M. Hengel, *Victory over Violence* (English trans., London: SPCK, 1975) 71f, summarising the detailed account in previous chapters.

[2] Most notably, but by no means exclusively, by S. G. F. Brandon, *Jesus and the Zealots* (Manchester University Press, 1967).

[3] See especially the series of discussions by M. Hengel: in addition to *Victory over Violence* (note 1), see his *Was Jesus a Revolutionist?* (English trans., Philadelphia: Fortress, 1971); *Christ and Power* (English trans., Philadelphia: Fortress, 1977). Also A. Richardson, *The Political Christ* (London: SCM, 1973). More briefly, Myrtle Langley, 'Jesus and Revolution' in C. Brown (ed.) *New International Dictionary of New Testament Theology* (Exeter: Paternoster, 1978) vol. 3, 967-981; also my *The Man They Crucified* (Leicester, IVP, 1975) chapter 8. For extensive scholarly discussion of Brandon's thesis see the recent symposium *Jesus and the Politics of his Day,* ed. E. Bammel and C. F. D. Moule (Cambridge University Press, 1984).

[4] See my conclusion in *Jesus and the Old Testament* (London: Tyndale Press, 1971), 148-150.

[5] See below, 3 (c). *Political liberation.*

[6] See Hengel, *Victory over Violence,* 75-76, n. 103; Richardson, *op. cit.* 46-47.

[7] 'Kingdom of heaven' in Matthew is, of course, simply a stylistic variation. There is no difference in meaning or use.

[8] N. Perrin, *Jesus and the Language of the Kingdom* (Philadelphia: Fortress, 1976), especially 29-34.

[9] For a fuller discussion of the implications of the phrase 'the kingdom of God' and of the dangers involved in misappropriating it in modern usage, see my article 'The Church and the Kingdom of God' in D. A. Carson (ed.) *Hermeneutics and the Church* (Exeter: Paternoster, 1984).

[10] 'Liberation in History', *Interpretation* 28 (1974), 404-21, especially 410-11.

[11] For a brief survey of some of these values see my *The Man They Crucified* 80-106.

[12] Gollwitzer, *art. cit.* 411.

[13] So especially J. H. Yoder, *The Politics of Jesus* (Grand Rapids: Eerdmans, 1972), especially pp. 34-40, 64-77; following A. Trocmé, *Jesus Christ and the Non-Violent Revolution* (Geneva, 1961; English trans., Scottdale, Pa.: Herald Press, 1974).

[14] 'God and Mammon', *EQ* 51 (1979), 3-21; *cf.* a shorter version, 'Serving God or Mammon', *Third Way* 2/10 (1978), 3-8.

[15] See below, 3 (c). *Political liberation.*

[16] Note also that when the same passage is loosely quoted of the ministry of Jesus in Mt. 11:5, this clause is omitted, the emphasis falling on healing and preaching.

[17] See H. Vorländer in *NIDNTT* I, 698-701.

[18] Mk. 7:35 has been seen in a similar light, but the context requires no more than a picturesque metaphor; the agency of Satan is not mentioned.

[19] *Cf.* Jude 5 for another 'OT' use, in recalling the Exodus.

[20] Note, however, that *sōzein* is occasionally used with a human subject as the agent of reconciliation with God; Rom 11:14; 1 Cor. 7:16; 9:22.

[21] See M. Hengel, *Victory over Violence*, 59 and note 74.

[22] For this strand of thought in Judaism see e.g. E. Bammel in *TDNT* VI 888-99.

[23] *God of the Oppressed* (New York: Seabury Press, 1975), 72-81.

[24] See N. A. Dahl, 'Nations in the New Testament' in *New Testament Christianity for Africa and the World. Essays in Honour of Harry Sawyerr,* ed. M. E. Glasswell and E. W. Fasholé-Luke (London: SPCK, 1974), 54-68, for the inappropriateness of the term 'nation' for the various ethnic groups of the Roman Empire in NT times, as well as for the paucity of NT interest in 'nationalism'.

[25] On all this paragraph see the detailed argument of my article 'Old Testament Prophecy and the Future of Israel' in *Tyndale Bulletin* 26 (1975), 53-78. On alleged exceptions to the last observation in Lk. 21:24 and Mt. 23:39 see *ibid.,* 74-76, with note 41.

[26] For the latter view see e.g. B. N. Kaye in *Law, Morality and the Bible,* ed. B. N. Kaye and G. J. Wenham (Leicester: IVP, 1978) 104-108; *cf. idem TSF Bulletin* 63 (1972) 10-12; also, apparently, M. Hengel, *Victory over Violence* 88f. The implication that Paul would not have written this ten years later depends both on the assumption that no permanent principle is expressed and on the questionable belief that the early years of Nero's principate were years of 'good' government.

[27] On the importance of this distinction see C. E. B. Cranfield, *NTS* 6 (1959/60), 242-45, and his commentary *(ICC) ad loc.*

[28] *Third Way,* vol. 2, nos. 9-12 (May-June 1978).

[29] On the role on 'conscience' in this connection, see D. J. Bosch 'The Church and the Liberation of Peoples?', *Missionalia* 5/2 (1977), 25-26.

[30] *Cf.* H. Gollwitzer's stress on liberation from *judgement* as the heart of the gospel, *art. cit.,* 407-409.

[31] D. J. Bosch, *art. cit.* 37.

[32] See M. Hengel, *Victory over Violence*, 59, for a similar use of the Exodus theme by the Zealots.

[33] See R. E. Nixon, *The Exodus in the NT* (London: Tyndale Press, 1963); *cf.* D. F. Wells, *The Search for Salvation* (Leicester: IVP, 1978), 134-36.

[34] Ed. Carl E. Armerding (Nutley, NJ: Presbyterian and Reformed, 1977).

RELIGION AND THE AMERICAN DREAM:
A STUDY IN CONFUSION AND TENSION

ROBERT D. LINDER
Professor of History
Kansas State University

Article from *Mennonite Life*

"The American Dream" is an illusive concept.[1] Roughly speaking, it has something to do with freedom and equality of opportunity. As a matter of fact, in the political realm, it involves the shared dream of a free and equal society. The fact that the reality does not fit the dream is probably well known, for no society can be both free and equal at the same time. Even in a relatively open and mobile nation like America, there are still relatively few at the top of the heap, many more in the middle, and some at or near the bottom. Nevertheless, in the United States, even those who have the most reason to deny its reality still cling to its promise, if not for themselves, at least for their children. In any case, it can be said of the American Dream, in the words of sociologist W. Lloyd Warner, that ". . . though some of it is false, by virtue of our firm belief in it, we have made some of it true."[2] What is true in the case of the American Dream and society at large also seems to be true in the realm of religion and the Dream.[3]

Two views provide the background for understanding the historic tension between two aspects of the American Dream in religion. The first is expressed in Puritan John Winthrop's oft-cited and well-known 1630 metaphor of "A City upon a Hill." The second is found in sometime Baptist and Seeker Roger Williams' less known but equally hallowed vision of a country in which, as he observed in 1644, "God requireth not an uniformity of Religion to be inacted and inforced in any civil state. . . ." Over the years, the Puritan sense of cosmic mission as God's New Israel eventually became part of America's national identity and the Radical stand for religious freedom developed into the American ideal of religious and cultural pluralism. And so the two dreams of Americans for a religiously harmonious nation and a religiously free nation have existed side-by-side down to the present-day—sometimes in relative peace but often in considerable tension.[4]

The First American Dream and Religion: Puritan vs. Radical

The Puritans who gave the country its rich imagery of America as a City on a Hill and as a second Israel lived with a great deal of tension themselves. They

were, by self-definition, elect spirits, segregated from the mass of humankind by an experience of conversion, fired by the sense that God was using
them to revolutionize human history, and committed to the execution of his
will. As such, they constituted a crusading force of immense energy. However, in reality, it was an energy that was often incapable of united action
because the saints formed different conceptions of what the divine will
entailed for themselves, their churches, and the unregenerate world at large.
But, still, they were certain of their mission in the New World—to be an
example of how a covenanted community of heartfelt believers could function. Thus, in New England the relation of church and state was to be a
partnership in unison, for church and state alike were to be dominated by the
saints.[5]

This arrangement worked fairly well for the first American Puritans, but
in the second and third generations the tension began to mount between the
concept of a New Israel composed of elect saints on the one hand, and the
Puritan conviction that true Christians were those who had experienced a
genuine conversion to Christ on the other. Everything in the New Israel
depended on the saints. They were the church and they ruled the state. But
what if the second generation did not respond to the call for conversion and
the supply of saints ran out? The answer was eventually to create a device
usually called the halfway covenant, whereby those of the second generation
who did not experience conversion in the Puritan mold could be admitted
to church membership after making a profession of communal obedience,
and thereby have their children baptized in order to place them under the
covenant. The Puritans found how difficult it was to make certain that the
second and third generations were soundly converted and thus qualified to
keep the City on the Hill operating properly according to the ordinances of
God.

In any case, the Puritans maintained their sense of destiny and purpose
by means of this patchwork arrangement. However, the concept of New
England as God's New Israel was given new impetus during the First Great
Awakening in the first half of the seventeenth century. American theologian
and Congregationalist minister Jonathan Edwards, for one, saw the hand of
God at work in the awakening, in both a theological and social sense.
Edwards believed that there would be a golden age for the church on earth,
achieved through the faithful preaching of the gospel in the power of the Holy
Spirit. The world thus would be led by the American example into the
establishment of the millennium. In this, the New Englanders were surely
God's chosen people, his New Israel.[6]

As most people know, the millennium did not come in Edwards' day or
even immediately thereafter. Instead the First Great Awakening died out and
the original theistically-oriented chosen nation theme was metamorphosed
into a civil millennialism. This occurred in the period between the end of the
awakening in the 1740s and the outbreak of the American Revolution in 1775.

It was in this era that the transferral of the central concepts of seventeenth-century Puritan ideology to all America, including the New Israel motif, took place. Disappointed that the great revival did not result in the dawning of the millennium, many colonial preachers turned their apocalyptic expectations elsewhere. In short, when the First Awakening tailed off, its evangelical spokesmen had to reinterpret the millennial hope it had spawned. In the process, the clergy, in a subtle but profound shift in religious values, redefined the ultimate goal of apocalyptic hope. The old expectation of the conversion of all nations to Christianity became diluted with, and often subordinated to, the commitment to America as the new seat of liberty. First France and then England became the archenemies of liberty, both civil and religious. In his insightful study of this development, historian Nathan Hatch concludes:

> The civil millennialism of the Revolutionary era, expressed by the rationalists as well as pietists, grew out of the politicizing of Puritan millennial history in the two decades before the Stamp Act crisis. . . . Civil millennialism advanced freedom as the cause of God, defined the primary enemy as the antichrist of civil oppression rather than that of formal religion, traced the myths of its past through political developments rather than through the vital religion of the forefathers, and turned its vision toward the privileges of Britons rather than to heritage exclusive to New England.[7]

Thus the first Great Awakening was not only a significant religious event, but also a popular movement with wide-ranging political and ideological implications that laid the groundwork for an emotional and future-oriented American civil religion. The revolutionary generation began to build an American nation based upon religious foundations of evangelical revivalism. The latter-day New England Puritans were joined by many Anglicans, Presbyterians, and Dutch Reformed of equally evangelical persuasion in seeing themselves as jointly commissioned to awaken and guide the nation into the coming period of millennial fulfillment.

But in the process, where the churches moved out, the nation moved in. Gradually, the nation emerged in the thinking of most Americans as the primary agent of God's meaningful activity in history. They began to bestow on their new nation a catholicity of destiny similar to that which theology usually attributes to the universal church. Thus, the Declaration of Independence and the Constitution became the covenants that bound together the people of the nation and secured to them God's blessing, protection, and call to historic mission. Most important, the United States itself became the covenanted community and God's New Israel, destined to spread real freedom and true religion to the rest of the world.[8]

In the nineteenth century, this transmutation of the millennial ideal resulted in what became known as "Manifest Destiny," coined by journalist John L. Sullivan in 1845. Manifest Destiny came to mean for countless Americans that Almighty God had "destined" them to spread over the entire North American continent. And as they did, they would take with them their uplifting and ennobling political and religious institutions.[9]

But there was another religious dream abroad in the land, one that did not rest upon the model of a City on a Hill or God's New Israel. This was the belief in religious liberty that had grown out of the Protestant left, generally known as the Radical Reformation. This view originally stood alongside of and in many cases opposed to the idea that New England was God's New Israel. The classic spokesperson for this second concept was Roger Williams, founder of the Rhode Island colony—the first real haven for religious dissidents on American soil.

As already mentioned, Williams rejected the Puritan notion of a religiously covenanted community that could exercise political power. He valued religious liberty and religious individualism more than religious uniformity and religious communitarianism. In fact, he stoutly rejected the Puritan teaching that New England was God's New Israel and flatly stated that:

> The State of the Land of Israel, the Kings and people thereof in Peace and War, is proven figurative and ceremoniall, and no patterne nor president for any Kingdome or civill state in the world to follow.[10]

In sum, Williams boldly asserted his basic premises that civil magistrates are to rule only in civil and never in religious matters, and that persecution for religion had no sanction in the teachings of Jesus, thus undercutting the whole ideological foundation for the Puritan hope in creating a Christian state that would be a City on a Hill.

Quaker William Penn was also in this radical tradition. In both Baptist Rhode Island and Quaker Pennsylvania, religious liberty resulted in religious pluralism. This was all right with Williams and Penn, for both believed that this was the biblical way. But how could God's New Israel survive such a cacaphony of spiritual voices? How could the religious mosaic that soon emerged in the new nation be reconciled with the view that America was God's chosen nation? How could any semblance of religious unity be achieved if religious liberty prevailed? In short, how could this religious smorgasbord ever be regarded as a covenanted community?

The answer lay in the willingness of Enlightenment figures like Thomas Jefferson to reach out to the New Israel exponents on the right and the religious liberty champions on the left in order to create an American civil religion. Jefferson, the great champion of religious liberty and political individualism, also embraced the imagery of the United States as a second Israel. In his second inaugural address on March 4, 1805, Jefferson told the American people that during his second term as their national leader he would need:

... the favor of that Being in whose hands we are, who led our fathers, as Israel of old, from their native land and planted them in a country flowing with all the necessaries and comforts of life; who has covered our infancy with His providence and our riper years with His wisdom and power, and to whose goodness I ask you to join in supplications with me that He will so enlighten the minds of your servants, guide their councils, and prosper their measures that whatsoever they do shall result in your good, and shall secure to you the peace, friendship, and approbation of all nations.[11]

Thus Jefferson articulated the belief held by most Americans of that day that the United States and not just New England was a City on a Hill.

The American Amalgam: Civil Religion

Exactly what was the civil religion that was able to subsume, for a time at least, these two divergent strands of the American Dream? Briefly stated, civil religion (some call it public religion) is that use of consensus religious sentiments, concepts, and symbols by the state—either directly or indirectly —for its own purposes. Those purposes may be noble or debased, depending on the kind of civil religion (priestly or prophetic) and the historical context. Civil religion involves the mixing of traditional religion with national life until it is impossible to distinguish between the two, and usually leads to a blurring of religion and patriotism and of religious values with national values. In America, it became a rather elaborate matrix of beliefs and practices born of the nation's historic experience and constituting the only real religion of millions of its citizens.[12]

The first American civil religion was supported by both the nation's intellectuals—mostly children of the Enlightenment—and the country's Christians—mostly Bible-believing evangelicals. The intellectuals like Jefferson supported it because it was general enough to include the vast majority of Americans and because it provided the moral glue for the body politic created by the social contract. The evangelicals supported it because it appeared to be compatible (perhaps even identical) with biblical Christianity. In any case, from this confluence of the Enlightenment and biblical Christianity, American civil religion emerged to promote both the concept of religious liberty and the notion that America was God's New Israel![13]

Under the aegis of American civil religion, the idea of the City on a Hill and God's New Israel was advanced to that of the "redeemer nation" with a manifest destiny. In other words, gradually, the old Puritan notion was infused with secular as well as religious meaning, and joined with political as well as religious goals. This was accomplished in the course of American expansion and by means of political rhetoric and *McGuffey's Reader*.[14]

The result of these developments is perhaps best illustrated by the story of President William McKinley's decision to annex the Philippines following the Spanish-American War in 1898. In November of the following year, McKinley, himself a devout Methodist layman, revealed to a group of visiting clergymen just how he came to sign the bill of annexation, following a dreadful period of soul-searching and prayer.

> I walked the floor of the White House night after night until midnight; and I . . . went down on my knees and prayed to Almighty God for light and guidance. . . . And one night late it came to me this way—(1) That we should not give them back to Spain—that would be cowardly and dishonorable;
>
> (2) that we could not turn them over to France or Germany—our commercial rivals in the Orient—that would be bad business and discreditable;
>
> (3) that we could not leave them to themselves—they were unfit for self-government—and they would soon have anarchy and misrule worse than Spain's was; and (4) that there was nothing left for us to do but to take them all, and to educate the Filipinos, and uplift and civilize and Christianize them, and by God's grace do the very best we could by them. . . . And then I went to bed, and went to sleep and slept soundly. . . .[15]

In short, McKinley said that destiny and duty made it inevitable that the Americans should bring civilization and light—democratic civilization and biblical light—to the poor Filipinos! Manifest destiny had led God's New Israel down the primrose path of imperialism!

The concept that the United States is God's New Israel and a chosen nation is hardly dead. In his 1980 acceptance speech at the Republican National Convention in Kansas City, presidential nominee Ronald Reagan declared:

> Can we doubt that only a Divine Providence placed this land, this island of freedom, here as a refuge for all those people in the world who yearn to breathe free? Jews and Christians enduring persecution behind the Iron Curtain; the boat people of Southeast Asia, Cuba, and of Haiti; the victims of drought and famine in Africa, the freedom fighters in Afghanistan. . . . God Bless America![16]

In many ways, Reagan's words in that instance extended the concept from America as a City on a Hill to America as a Cosmic Hotel, from the nation as a Model of Merit to the nation as a Magnet to the Masses.

President Reagan has used the City on a Hill/Manifest Destiny motif with telling effect on many occasions since taking office in January 1981. For example, in September 1982, he received roaring approval from a large crowd at Kansas State University when he asserted: "But be proud of the red, white, and blue, and believe in her mission. . . . America remains mankind's best hope. The eyes of mankind are on us . . . remember that we are one Nation under God, believing in liberty and justice for all.[17] In March 1983, he brought cheering evangelicals to their feet in Orlando, Florida, when he

proclaimed to the annual convention of the National Association of Evangelicals: "America is great because America is good" and reiterated that this
nation was "the last best hope of man."[18] The idea that America is God's
chosen nation, in a religious as well as in a political sense, is alive and well
and living in Washington, D.C.!

While the former Puritan concept of a City on a Hill and God's New Israel
evolved over the years from an evangelical, communitarian application to a
religious, national one, there has been a parallel development from religious
liberty to cultural pluralism. Originally, religious liberty meant that the
various denominations were free to spread the gospel as they understood it,
without intrusion by either the government or a state church. In this context,
an evangelical Protestant consensus emerged that made the United States in
the nineteenth century into what historian William G. McLoughlin called "a
unified, pietistic-perfectionist nation" and "the most religious people in the
world."[19] However, that consensus began to crack near the end of the century as new immigrants from non-Protestant churches or no churches at all
flowed into the country and as the secularizing forces associated with Darwinism, urbanization, and industrialization made their presence felt in
American society. And as the country became more diverse, that diversity
was protected—some would even say encouraged—by the nation's commitment to religious liberty. Thus, slowly but surely, religious freedom was
translated into cultural pluralism.

However, by the post-World War II period, this cultural pluralism was
beginning to strain the very bonds of national unity. It was a time of increasing tension and confusion. Looking back on the period 1945-1960, the late
Paul Goodman lamented:

> Our case is astounding. For the first time in recorded history, the mention of
> country, community, place has lost its power to animate. Nobody but a
> scoundrel even tries it. Our rejection of false patriotism is, of course, itself a
> badge of honor. But the positive loss is tragic and I cannot resign myself to
> it. A man has only one life and if during it he has no great environment,
> no community, he has been irreparably robbed of a human right.[20]

Goodman's analysis was not only a modern jeremiad, however; it was also a
plea for the emergence of a modern unifying concept that would serve to
hold the republic together. The destruction of the old evangelical Protestant
consensus and with it the original American civil religion, and the emergence
of cultural pluralism based on the American doctrine of religious liberty—
and now reinforced by the melting pot myth—all spelled out the need for a
new civil religion based on the new facts of American life. Ironically enough,
during the very period when Goodman's observations most closely applied,
a rejuvenated civil faith was emerging. This new civil religion took shape
during the Eisenhower presidency and it was as amiable and ambiguous as
Ike. It was now a civil religion that had been enlarged to include not only the

three major faiths of the land—Protestant, Catholic, Jew—but virtually anyone who acknowledged a Supreme Being. The national mood of the 1950s
was congenial to an outpouring of religiousity, and examples of it abounded:
national days of prayer, the addition in 1954 of "under God" to the Pledge of
Allegiance to the flag, the authorization to place "in God we trust" on all
currency and coins, and the adoption of the same phrase as the national
motto in 1956, are a few examples.

Interestingly enough, hard on the heels of the new upsurge of civil
religion in the 1950s came a time of great political turmoil and widespread
religious renewal in the 1960s. It was in this context that the New Religious
Right emerged in the 1970s—galvanized by its hostility to theological and
political liberalism alike. In many ways, this New Religious Right resembled
the old Puritanism as it began to interact with the American civil religion. Its
first order of business was to purify the church and state, to restore old
values and old ideals, and, if possible, to put an end to the confusion and
tension of the age.

The American Civil Religion in the Hands of the New Religious Right: The Confusion and Tension Heightened

The leaders of the New Religious Right of the 1970s found a civil religion that
invested the civil officers of the country with a certain religious mystique;
one that linked the social order to a higher and truer realm; one that provided
religious motivation and sanction for civil virtue; one that, in short, served
the functions of an established religion—and they liked it! It was a public
religion that gave the majority of Americans an over-arching common spiritual heritage in which the entire nation supposedly shared. Because it did not
appear to contradict their understanding of the American past or their commitment to Bible Christianity, and because they did not have a profound
understanding of civil religion or American history, and, further, because
civil religion seemed suited to their goal of restoring America's spiritual and
political vigor, New Religious Right leaders embraced the American civil
religion as they found it. They did not seem to be aware of or understand one
perplexing feature of the American public faith, pointed out by historian
Sidney E. Mead and others—namely, that it included a central doctrine of
separation of church and state. This concept is, of course, a legacy of the
historic American emphasis on religious libery. As such, it greatly compli-
cates the operation of civil religion in America and provides the public faith
with a substantial element of self-contradiction. In any case, the New Religious Right hardly noticed this in the beginning and is often perplexed by
those who refuse to go along with such parts of its program as prayer in the
public schools—a perfectly logical civil religion activity—because of the
principle of religious liberty and its corollary, separation of church and
state.[21]

But this last point illustrates the fact that the appearance of the New Religious Right in the 1970s has exacerbated the old tensions associated with the two religious components of the American Dream. Most of the adherents of the New Religious Right come from traditions that accept the doctrine of religious liberty, but the movement has wholeheartedly embraced that part of American civil religion that emphasizes America's national mission as God's New Israel. How can a nation that is so culturally diverse speak in terms of a national mission? Unfortunately, the New Religious Right does not seem to acknowledge the reality of that cultural diversity, but prefers to think of America as it was throughout most of the nineteenth century—a religiously homogeneous nation.

Moreover, the New Religious Right's millennial vision for America seems inconsistent and confused. Belief in America as a City on a Hill and as God's New Israel requires a postmillennial eschatology—the view that the Kingdom of God is extended through Christian preaching and teaching as a result of which the world will be Christianized and will enjoy a long period of peace and righteousness called the millennium. During the nineteenth century, postmillennial views of the destiny of America played a vital role in justifying national expansion. Although there were other explanations for the nation's growth, the idea of a Christian republic marching toward a golden age appealed to many people. Millennial nationalism was attractive because it harmonized the republic with religious values. Thus America became the hope of the nations—destined to uphold Christian and democratic principles that would eventually bring spiritual and political freedom to the world.

This is exactly what the leaders of the New Religious Right, men like TV evangelist Jerry Falwell and best-selling author Tim LaHaye, believe. Falwell declares that the various activities of the Founding Fathers indicate that they "were putting together God's country, God's republic, and for that reason God has blessed her for two glorious centuries."[22] He has written approvingly: "Any diligent student of American history finds that our great nation was founded by godly men upon godly principles to be a Christian nation . . . Our Founding Fathers firmly believed that America had a special destiny in the world."[23] LaHaye proclaims: "America is the human hope of the world, and Jesus Christ is the hope of America."[24]

The only problem with all of this is that Falwell, LaHaye, and many other leaders of the New Religious Right are also premillennialists—adherents of that view of the future that claims that Jesus' return will be followed by a period of peace and righteousness before the last judgment, during which Christ will reign as king in person or through a select group of people. This kingdom will not be established by the conversion of individuals over a long period of time, but suddenly and by overwhelming power. Evil will be held in check during the millennial kingdom by Christ, who will rule with a rod of iron. Further, premillennialists believe that this kingdom will be preceded by a period of steady decline and by certain signs such as great tribulation, apostasy, wars, famines, earthquakes, and the appearance of the antichrist.

By way of contrast, nineteenth-century premillennialists, who then constituted only a minority of American Christians, did not believe that their nation was a recipient of God's special favor but was rather just another Gentile world power. In short, they did not support the view that the United States was God's New Israel. Moreover, premillennialists today still maintain a rather gloomy scenario of the future, including the concept of a time of great decline immediately preceding the second coming of Christ.[25]

There has always been inconsistency on the part of premillennialists with regard to the interpretation of world events and their desire to be patriotic Americans. This is particularly marked in the New Religious Right.[26] Individuals like Falwell and LaHaye have felt called to enter the social and political arena, but they do not have a consistent eschatological base for such activities. In essence, they want to support a certain type of postmillennial vision for America while maintaining a premillennial eschatology.

In fact, much of the New Religious Right's program seems to be contradictory and inconsistent. Perhaps this is because of its confused eschatology. A further problem with its millennialism is its encouragement of the new American civil religion, with its emphasis on the chosen theme, while ignoring the enormous cultural pluralism present in the United States today. There seems to be something bizarre about attempts to advocate any scheme to spread American political, cultural, and religious values to the world when nobody in this country seems certain what those values are anymore. Moreover, much that is proposed by the New Religious Right appears to contradict the historic American Dream of religious liberty—especially in terms of its drive to introduce state prayers into public schools, its advocacy of tax credits for these who send their children to parochial schools, and its insistence upon a large standing, professional army.[27]

Conclusions

There are many similarities between the adherents of the New Religious Right and the Puritans of the sixteenth and seventeenth centuries. Both seem to be movements composed of self-confessed godly people determined to change the moral and religious climate of their day. There also appear to be many of the same tensions in the two respective movements—especially the desire, on the one hand, for heartfelt religion to prevail, and the wish, on the other, to impose a certain level of morality on society in general. There is, if you will, a perplexing contradiction in the movement that makes it want to create some kind of national religion (or quasi state-church) of "true believers." As the Puritans discovered, it is impossible to combine the two elements in any meaningful way because true faith cannot be forced, especially in the context of religious freedom. It appears historically impos-

sible to achieve the Puritan goals of an elect society composed entirely of
genuine believers while at the same time allowing any sort of religious
freedom that, in turn, makes the conversion experience meaningful. That
was the Puritan dilemma and it may well be the dilemma of the New Religious
Right as well.

What happened to the Puritans when they tried to impose their values—
no matter how high-minded and uplifting to mankind they may have been—
on a larger society? They met first with frustration, then with disillusionment, and finally with the prospect of either acquiescing to a new regime or
going into exile. After three generations of attempting to bring godly government to England and after fighting and winning a civil war, Oxford don and
Puritan divine Dr. John Owen in 1652 could only survey the Cromwellian
regime and lament:

> Now, those that ponder these things, their spirits are grieved in the midst of
> their bodies;—the visions of their heads trouble them. They looked for
> other things from them that professed Christ; but the summer is ended, and
> the harvest is past, and we are not refreshed.[28]

In the end, what will happen to the New Religious Right if and when its
participation in politics comes to naught? What will come of its vision and
participation in the American Dream? If the concept of a New Israel and a
covenanted community could not be implemented and maintained in a
country like seventeenth-century England or a place like colonial New England with culturally and religiously homogeneous populations, how can
anyone expect such an idea to be successfully realized in an increasingly
pluralistic society like the United States in the 1980s?

The New Religious Right, like the Puritan movement of old, may have to
learn the hard way that the best that Christians can hope for in a largely
unconverted world is genuine religious freedom in which to practice the
Faith and preach the gospel. That part of the American Dream is still meaningful, precious, and possible. The live question of this generation is: can it
be preserved? Adherents of the New Religious Right are trying to save the
American Dream. But how ironic it would be if, in the process, they destroyed
it!

Notes

[1] This is a revision of a lecture originally presented at a Conference on the American Dream,
the Dwight D. Eisenhower Library, Abilene, Kan., April 21, 1983.

[2] W. Lloyd Warner, *Social Class in America* (New York: Harper and Row, 1960), pp. v-vi.

[3] Christopher F. Mooney, *Religion and the American Dream: The Search for Freedom Under
God* (Philadelphia: Westminster, 1977). This collection of essays focuses on the "power and
force of religion in civil affairs" and notes many of the contradictions and tensions in this aspect
of the American Dream.

[4] John Winthrop, *Papers*, A. B. Forbes, ed. (5 vols., Boston: The Massachusetts Historical Society, 1929-1947), 2:295; and Roger Williams, *The Bloudy Tenent of Persecution for Cause of Conscience* (London: n.p., 1644), Introduction. Also see Anson Phelps Stokes, *Church and State in the United States* (New York: Harper and Row, 1950); Leo Pfeffer, *Church, State, and Freedom* (Boston: Beacon Press, 1953); Loren Baritz, *City on a Hill: A History of Ideas and Myths in America* (New York: John Wiley, 1964); Ernest L. Tuveson, *Redemmer Nation: The Idea of America's Millennial Role* (Chicago: University of Chicago Press, 1968); Conrad Cherry, ed., *God's New Israel: Religious Interpretations of American Destiny* (Englewood Cliffs, NJ: Prentice-Hall, 1971); and John F. Wilson, *Public Religion in American Culture* (Philadelphia: Temple University Press, 1979).

[5] Alan Simpson, *Puritanism in Old and New England* (Chicago: University Press, 1955), pp. 19-38.

[6] Jonathan Edwards, *Apocalyptic Writings*, ed. Stephen J. Stein (New Haven: Yale University Press, 1977).

[7] Nathan O. Hatch, "The Origins of Civil Millennialism in America: New England Clergymen. War with France and the Revolution," *William and Mary Quarterly*, 31 (July 1974), 429. Also see Nathan O. Hatch, *The Sacred Cause of Liberty: Millennial Thought in Revolutionary New England* (New Haven: Yale University Press, 1977); and John F. Berens, *Providence and Patriotism in Early America, 1640-1815* (Charlottesville: University of Virginia Press, 1978), pp. 51-80.

[8] John E. Smylle, "National Ethos and the Church," *Theology Today*, 20 (Oct. 1963), 314; and Berens, *Providence and Patriotism in Early America*, pp. 81-111.

[9] Frederick Merk, *Manifest Destiny and Mission in American History* (New York: Knopf, 1963), pp. 31-32.

[10] Williams, *The Bloudy Tenet of Persecution*, Introduction.

[11] *Inaugural Addresses of the Presidents of the United States* (Washington, D.C.: United States Government Printing Office, 1974), p. 21.

[12] The basis for this definition of civil religion is found in the following: Robert N. Bellah, "Civil Religion in America," *Daedalus*, No. 96 (Winter 1967), 1-21; D. Elton Trueblood, *The Future of the Christian* (New York: Harper and Row, 1971), pp. 83-102; and Will Herberg, "American Civil Religion: What It Is and Whence It Comes," in *American Civil Religion*, ed. Russell E. Richey and Donald G. Jones (New York: Harper and Row, 1974), pp. 76-88. For an evaluation of civil religion from two different but complementary points of view, see Wilson, *Public Religion in American Culture*; and Robert D. Linder and Richard V. Pierard, *Twilight of the Saints: Biblical Christianity and Civil Religion in America* (Downers Grove, IL: InterVarsity Press, 1978).

[13] Jean-Jacques Rousseau, *The Social Contract and Discourses*, ed. G. D. H. Cole (New York: Dutton, 1950), p. 139; Jean-Jacques Rousseau, *Oeuvres Completes, Du Contrat Social*, ed. Bernard Gagnebin and Marcel Raymond (4 vols., Paris: Gallimard, 1964), 3: 368-375, 468; Ralph H. Gabriel, *The Course of American Democratic Thought*, 2nd ed. (New York: Ronald Press, 1956), pp. 14-25, 23-28. Sidney E. Mead, *The Nation With the Soul of a Church* (New York: Harper and Row, 1975), pp. 56-57; and Seymour M. Lipset, *The First New Nation* (New York: Basic Books, 1963), pp. 61-98.

[14] Robert W. Lynn, "Civil Catechetics in Mid-Victorian America: Some Notes About American Civil Religion, Past and Present," *Religious Education*, No. 48 (Jan.-Feb. 1973), 5-27.

[15] *The Christian Advocate*, Jan. 22, 1903. pp. 1-2. Also see Charles S. Olcott, *The Life of William McKinley* (2 vols., New York: Houghton Mifflin, 1916), 2: 109-111.

[16] Ronald W. Reagan, "Acceptance Address: Republican National Convention Presidential Nomination," *Vital Speeches of the Day*, 46, no. 21 (Aug. 15, 1980), 646.

[17] Ronald W. Reagan, "Believe in Her Mission," Landon Lecture at Kansas State University on Sept. 9, 1982, published in full in *The Manhattan Mercury*, Sept. 9, 1982. p. 82.

[18] "Text of the Remarks of President Ronald W. Reagan to the Forty-First Annual Convention of the National Association of Evangelicals." March 8, 1983, Sheraton Twin Towers Hotel, Orlando, Florida, released by the Office of the Press Secretary, The White House, p. 1. See the report of the speech in *The New York Times*, March 9, 1983, pp. 1-11.

[19] William G. McLoughlin, ed., *The American Evangelicals, 1800-1900* (New York: Harper and Row, 1968), p. 1.

[20] Paul Goodman, *Growing Up Absurd* (New York: Random House, 1960), p. 97.

[21] Mead, *The Nation With the Soul of a Church*, pp. 78-113: and Alfred Balitzer, "Some Thoughts about Civil Religion," *Journal of Church and State,* 16 (Winter 1974), 36-37.

[22] Jerry Falwell, *America Can Be Saved* (Murfreesboro, TN: Sword of the Lord Publishers, 1979), p. 23.

[23] Jerry Falwell, *Listen America!* (Garden City, NY: Doubleday, 1980), p. 29.

[24] Tim LaHaye, *The Bible's Influence on American History* (San Diego: Master Books, 1976), p. 59.

[25] For a discussion of this view, see Ernest R. Sandeen, *The Roots of Fundamentalism: British and American Millenialism, 1800-1930* (Chicago: University of Chicago Press, 1970); and Robert G. Clouse, ed., *The Meaning of the Millennium* (Downers Grove, IL: InterVarsity Press, 1977), pp. 17-40.

[26] For a first-rate examination of this particular problem, see Robert G. Clouse, "The New Christian Right. America, and the Kingdom of God," *Christian Scholar's Review*, 12, No. 1 (1983), 3-16.

[27] For a discussion of the tensions created by this last point, see Robert D. Linder, "Militarism in Nazi Thought and in the American New Religious Right," *Journal of Church and State*, 24 (Spring 1982), 263-279, esp. p. 276, n. 38.

[28] John Owen, "Christ's Kingdom and the Magistrate's Power," sermon published in *The Works of John Owen* (24 vols., Edinburgh: T. and T. Clark, 1850-1853), 8: 381. For the scriptural basis for Owen's allusion, see Jeremiah 8:20.

AFRIKANER CIVIL RELIGION
AND THE CURRENT SOUTH AFRICAN CRISIS

DAVID J. BOSCH
Professor of Missiology
University of South Africa

Article from *The Princeton Seminary Bulletin*
(based on a lecture given at Princeton in October, 1985)

The purpose of this paper is to illustrate how Afrikaner Civil religion developed and how religious and other forces, step by step, yet irrevocably,
prepared South Africa for the crisis it faces today. In tracing the course of
these forces my intention is neither to portray the Afrikaner as the villain of
the story nor to offer an apology for what he was and did. I merely wish to
illustrate how people—even those who believe themselves to be the makers
of history—easily and frequently fall victim to their own past and become
prisoners of their own history. In this respect Afrikaners are by no means
unique; but in their case, the forces of history were so overwhelming and
they themselves so puny in the face of those forces that the outcome of this
crucible could not but be more dramatic than it was elsewhere. In saying
this, I am not trying to absolve the Afrikaner from his personal responsibility;
I am suggesting only that all of us are at the same time shapers and victims of
history, and that, in a given context, the one element rather than the other
may predominate. In a classical Greek tragedy the actors are both subjects of
the events that take place and pawns on a chessboard. They are free to act,
and, yet again, not free to do so.

I shall return to the metaphor of tragedy. For the moment, however,
notice the outside world frequently has only one explanation for the Afrikaner's life, worldview, and his policy of racial discrimination: his Calvinism.
It is because they were Calvinists—so the argument goes—that Afrikaners,
ever since the founding of a Dutch colony at the Cape of Good Hope in 1652,
have regarded themselves as a race apart, a specially chosen people, a latter-
day Israel, sent by God to subdue Africa's original inhabitants and transform
the wilderness into a garden. They were, in fact, to quote the title of a well-
known popular book on the subject, *The Puritans in Africa*.[1] Dutch and
French Calvinists, so the theory has it, had emigrated to South Africa *before*
the major Calvinist tradition in Europe had relapsed into scholasticism or
had begun to adjust to the changing intellectual and social world of the
Enlightenment and the Industrial Revolution. The "primitive Calvinism" of
the early Dutch settlers at the Cape was transmitted essentially unchanged

to successive generations. Its most basic tenet was the Calvinist notion of predestination with its concomitant concept of the elect.[2]

The first person to have suggested that Calvinism was the key to understanding the Afrikaner was, significantly, not somebody from their own ranks but the famous missionary-traveller, David Livingstone.[3] From 1849 onwards he was putting forward, in ever clearer terms, the theory that it was the Afrikaners' Calvinism that had shaped their thinking and policies, particularly toward blacks. He attacked the Dutch Reformed Church as the ideological fountainhead of persistent injustice to blacks throughout the entire course of Afrikaner history.

Since Livingstone, this hypothesis became almost universally accepted as *the* explanation of the Afrikaner's mentality and actions, first in English liberal circles and subsequently by virtually all non-Afrikaner students of Afrikanerdom.

It is one of the ironies of history that, from the late nineteenth century onward, Afrikaners themselves began to propound the so-called "Calvinist paradigm" as the key to the understanding of their history. The Afrikaner version of the "Calvinist paradigm" included an important modification, however. Whereas English liberal scholars regarded Calvinism as the ogre responsible for the Afrikaners' idea of racial superiority and their policy of subduing black tribes and oppressing them, Afrikaner scholars of the late nineteenth and the twentieth centuries understood their ancestors as having regarded themselves as God's chosen people who had the duty to subdue the black tribes in order to civilize and uplift them. Thus both friend and foe agreed that it was Calvinism that shaped Afrikanerdom; the one, however, wished to prove how bad Calvinism was, the other how good it was.

A handful of modern scholars have, however, once again gone through the early records with a fine-toothed comb. The result of this research was an almost total rejection of the "Calvinist paradigm" as explanation of early Afrikaner history and thinking. Two points have to be identified in this respect.

First, it is becoming ever clearer that the parallel with the Puritans has little, if any, substance to it.[4] In New England no fewer than one hundred thirty university graduates, ninety-two of them ministers, were among the Puritans arriving before 1640. This factor together with others ensured vigorous theological and intellectual activities in seventeenth-century Massachusetts and Connecticut, something that was totally absent in the contemporary Cape Colony, which started as a refreshment post for ships bound for the East Indies. There, relatively little intellectual activity was in evidence, the rudimentary ministrations of the few early clergymen left no recognizable theological impact, and the farmers in the outlying districts lived largely in almost total isolation from the already limited intellectual and social activities at the Cape itself. Most of these early Afrikaners were unsophisticated and, in fact, barely literate. The Bible was often the only book they had and read, and they tended to interpret it literally, not only as the revealed Word of God but also as the final source of all knowledge. These characteristics they shared, of course, with virtually all religious communities of simple people; religious fundamentalism is, however, not the same as Calvinism. Neither did the fact that they all belonged to the Reformed Church automatically make them Calvinists. For more than a century and a half all their ministers came from Holland and even among those only very few could be regarded as classical Calvinists. Several of them had been influenced by the Dutch "Second Reformation," and by English and Scottish evangelicalism; toward the end of the eighteenth century the impact of Reformed pietism at the Cape was undoubtedly greater than that of original Calvinism, particularly because of the ministry of H. R. van Lier and M. C. Vos.

The contemporary records concur with this observation. Until approximately 1870, more than two centuries after the founding of the Dutch settlement at the Cape, there is no direct evidence of the Afrikaners themselves appealing to their Calvinist beliefs as explanation or justification for their peculiar way of life. Where a link is seen, this is done, without exception, by outside observers. They knew that all Afrikaners were members of the Dutch Reformed Church and had applied the Bible to their own situation by means of a literal interpretation. So these observers deduced that Afrikaner political and societal attitudes and acts were to be ascribed to Calvinism.

This leads me to a second observation: Livingstone's view that early Afrikaners regarded themselves as a chosen people with a manifest destiny, in fact, reveals more about Livingstone himself than about the Afrikaners. He and many other British colonial and missionary figures of this period were imbued with the belief that Britain had a divinely ordained civilizing mission in Africa and Asia. This kind of belief was simply in the air, as it were, among Western nations, most particularly Britain. Victorians, as Ronald Robinson and John Gallagher put it, were "suffused with a vivid sense of superiority and self-righteousness, if with every good intention."[5] Livingstone was no exception. He believed, however, that the Afrikaner settlers in the interior of southern Africa had no right to such divine claims and so, after first having imputed to them the general Western notion of manifest destiny, he immediately proceeded to reject the legitimacy and validity of such a notion among Afrikaners.

In summary, then, and in very broad outline, my argument so far has been that Afrikaners during the first two centuries of settlement in southern Africa were, on the whole, Calvinists only in name, had no sense of a manifest destiny, but were, by and large, unsophisticated folk who reacted to the challenges of their context in an ad hoc manner and by means of a very literalist interpretation of the Bible.

In the course of the nineteenth century, however, the situation would begin to change fundamentally. The forces that were operative here were many. I confine myself here to only four of these.

History

The first force or factor to take into consideration is the Afrikaners' peculiar history and the way it molded them and gave birth to the people we know today. I do not intend to recount Afrikaner history in capsule form. Rather, by comparing Afrikaner history with American history, I want to highlight some significant differences, and the influence of those on our two respective peoples.

In the year 1806, the budding Afrikaner nation was cut off from its mother country, Holland, not—as was the case with Americans—through a War of Independence which happened to be successful, but rather by means of exchanging a rather inefficient distant Dutch master for a much more efficient yet totally alien British one. This happened roughly in the same period that armed clashes with the Xhosa on the Eastern frontier became more and more common. Soon the Afrikaner settlers found themselves caught in a pincer movement between an alien and unsympathetic administration bent on Anglicizing them, on the one hand, and the advances of the numerically vastly superior black armies on the other.

Many Afrikaners chose to attempt escaping from the pincer by trekking north, crossing the Orange River, and establishing the three northern republics of Natal, the Orange Free State, and the Transvaal. Time and again, however, their efforts at political self-determination were thwarted, as the British annexed or conquered one newly acquired Afrikaner territory after the other: Natal (1842), Basutoland (1868), Griqualand West and the Kimberley diamond fields (1871), and the Transvaal (1877). In the First War of Independence (1880-81) the Transvaal was victorious, only to succumb, with the Orange Free State, during the Anglo-Boer War, twenty years later (1899-1902).

The Afrikaners' situation was, in fact, always tenuous—to put it mildly—not only with respect to the steady encroachments of Britain, but also because they were vastly outnumbered by blacks in their new republics.

Once again a reference to contemporary North America might be helpful to illustrate the differences. In 1830 President Andrew Jackson signed the Indian Removal Act, and eastern tribes were directed to the vast Central Plains area. In the course of the next seventy years scores of Indian tribes were relocated in the Central Plains; they came from Florida and Georgia; from New England, from Michigan and Wisconsin, from Idaho and Oregon, from Texas and New Mexico. The Central Plains were not, however, destined to be a permanent sanctuary for the Indians, since year after year thousands upon thousands of whites were still pouring across the Mississippi. By mid-century as many as fifty-five thousand westward trekkers a year were breaching the Indian frontier. Treaties signed, treaties broken, more treaties signed—these were the legal weapons used to appropriate Indian lands and confine tribes in shrinking areas. The creation of Oklahoma Territory in 1890 shrank Indian Territory by about fifty percent.[6] The white migrants and settlers never really doubted the outcome of the clash with the Indians: they were superior to them in numbers, in skills, in weapons, in sophisication, in resoluteness.

The contemporary scene in the interior of southern Africa was vastly different. At a time when fifty-five thousand whites per year were crossing the Mississippi, the total Afrikaner population of the two remaining republics—the Orange Free State and the Transvaal, then about twenty years of age—was still much less than fifty-five thousand, and they were vastly outnumbered by blacks within their borders and much more so beyond them. Once again Afrikaners were caught in a pincer movement: between the encroaching British in the South and the Zulu, the Ndebele, the Shangaan, the Pedi, and the Tswana to the East and to the North. In these circumstances the Afrikaners were to find their identity and security—in a literal *and* figurative sense—in the *laager*, where their ox-wagons, drawn into a circle, would protect them against the outside world.

The *laager* mentality was immensely strengthened in and by the Anglo-Boer War (1899-1902) in which the remaining Afrikaner republics lost their independence. F. Hertz is correct when he says ". . . more than anything else it is common grief that binds a nation together, more than triumphs."[7] For Britain the war was no more than a passing episode; for the Afrikaners, who lost eight times as many women and children in the concentration camps as soldiers on the battlefield, this was the most crucial event in their history, the matrix out of which a new people was born. Immediately after the war, Lord Milner embarked on a vigorous policy of Anglicization and forthwith banned the use of the Dutch language from all schools. This was regarded as a total onslaught in the extreme. After having lost their political freedom on the battlefield, Afrikaners were now to lose their identity as well, through the schools. In this, the Afrikaner's darkest hour, it was, above all, the Afrikaans churches that rallied to the people's aid. Church and people became virtually indistinguishable.

In the burgeoning civil religion of the postwar period the young Afrikaans language was utilized to foster Afrikaner sentiments. Poets, particularly Totius (J. D. du Toit), had an enormous influence. In one of his poems, *"Vergewe en vergeet"* ("Forgive and forget"), he compared the Afrikaner with a small thorn tree, which had been trampled down by a large ox-wagon, symbolizing Britain. The tree slowly stood up again, however, and healed its wounds with the ointment of its own resin. In another poem Totius selected a semi-desert weed, the hardy and resilient *besembos,* and made it a symbol of the Afrikaner people. The *besembos* flourishes where most other and stronger plants would die. Even if you burn it down, it just sprouts forth anew and flourishes as before. These and other poems became a lens through which Afrikaners were looking upon their past. They conveyed to generations of Afrikaners the notion that they are there to stay, that they are irrevocably part and parcel of the soil of Africa, of the veld and the mountains and the rivers, and that no earthly force would ever succeed in subduing them, let alone routing them.

Since the Anglo-Boer War, eighty years ago, this sentiment has, on the whole, grown in strength rather than weakened. For many decades the National Party and the Dutch Reformed Churches were seen as jointly responsible for keeping the *laager* intact, buttressing the weak spots, and keeping up the morale of the people. After the National Party came to power in 1948, the entire legislative machinery was harnessed with this one purpose in mind: to safeguard Afrikaner identity once and for all so that it would never again be exposed defenselessly to the onslaughts of the outside world.

This then, very briefly, is the historical matrix out of which the Afrikaner people was born. A small white tribe, in the extreme southern tip of a vast black continent, cut off from the mother country almost two centuries ago, threatened with extinction from two sides, the blacks and the British, they are determined to maintain and defend their identity. This historical reality in the course of time coalesced with the forces of the spirit to shape the contemporary Afrikaner. I want to draw attention, very briefly, to three.

Religious Forces

Reformed Evangelicalism. This is the first and oldest of these spiritual forces. During the latter part of the eighteenth century a few Dutch pastors who had been deeply influenced by the Dutch "Second Reformation" and the Evangelical Awakenings in the British Isles served at the Cape. The two best known ones were H. R. van Lier and M. C. Vos. Through their ministry an indelible stamp of evangelicalism was put on the Dutch Reformed Church there. In the course of the nineteenth century, this trait was immensely strengthened by the arrival at the Cape of Scottish Presbyterian ministers who, incidentally, at one stage outnumbered those of Dutch descent. The most famous person to come out of this group was Andrew Murray, Jr., whose pastoral career spanned an almost incredible sixty-nine years (1848-1917).

Toward the end of the nineteenth century the broad and rather amorphous evangelical tradition comprised, generally speaking, three groups:

1. A small, more peitistic and revivalistic group of people who were inclined to other-worldliness and eschewed politics.

2. A second and much larger group. During the period of the awakening of Afrikaner nationalism, particularly after the Anglo-Boer War, the idea of a *volkskerk* (church of the people; national or ethnic church) gradually took root among adherents of this group. The *volkskerk* idea took concrete shape, *inter alia,* in the church's concern for the plight of the Afrikaner after the war.

In this group the church's concern for people's social and political plight was, on the whole, limited to the Afrikaner.

3. A third group, smaller than the second, which kept alive the missionary spirit of the eighteenth century Awakening. They knew that it was impossible to concern oneself with the spiritual needs of blacks without at the same time getting involved in their very real bodily and social needs. The scores of Dutch Reformed Church missionaries who went to Malawi, Kenya, Nigeria, Zambia, and Zimbabwe as well as those who worked within the borders of South Africa, virtually all came out of this third group. In the course of time it is out of this group that the first voices of protest against Afrikaner politics would come.[8]

Kuyperian Calvinism. The second major religious force to have shaped Afrikaner civil religion was Kuyperian neo-Calvinism. When Abraham Kuyper and his supporters used the slogan, "In isolation lies our strength," their intention was to rally the small, scattered forces of authentic Calvinism in Holland, unite these, and spread their message throughout the Dutch nation. The slogan thus propagated isolation for the sake of mission; it aimed at winning the Dutch people back to original Calvinism. In fact, Kuyper was so imbued with missionary zeal for Calvinism that racial differences presented no problem to him. In his Stone Lectures, delivered at Princeton Seminary in 1898, he argued:

> . . . the commingling of blood [was] the physical basis of all higher human development . . . [G]roups which by commingling have crossed their traits with those of other tribes . . . have attained a higher perfection. It is noteworthy that the process of human development steadily proceeds with those groups whose historic characteristic is not isolation but the commingling of blood . . . [sometimes] of very different tribes . . . [T]he history of our race does not aim at the improvement of any single tribe, but at the development of [human-kind] taken as a whole, and therefore needs this commingling of blood in order to attain its end. Now in fact history shows that the nations among whom Calvinism flourished most widely exhibit in every way this same mingling of races.[9]

Kuyper's concern, therefore, was for a militant expansionist Calvinism. On South African soil, however, particularly after the Anglo-Boer War, Kuyper's ideals were adapted to local circumstances. As they blended with the existing socio-political realities they underwent some significant mutations. The very survival of Afrikanerdom was at stake during those years. Thus the slogan "In isolation lies our strength" was not understood, as it was in Holland, in terms of isolation-for-mission, but in terms of isolation-for-survival. For the first time in South African history one now encountered sustained theological (or ideological) arguments according to which Afrikaners should neither fraternize with foreigners nor break down the walls of racial separation instituted by God; like Israel, the Afrikaner's salvation lay in

racial purity and separate schools and churches. One of the first proposals
for a thoroughgoing political and social segregation was put forward by a
Kuyperian pastor, the Reverend W. J. Postma, in 1907. His suggestion was to
". . . give the black nations a piece of ground where they can establish their
own schools, churches, prisons, parliaments, universities. If we go there we
must not ask to own ground or vote. . . . If they come here to work they must
not play tennis. . . ."[10]

In this way Calvinism indeed became the basis of an ideology that was
used to keep Afrikaners apart from other people—not, however, the original
expression of Calvinism, and not, as often alleged, among seventeenth-,
eighteenth-, and early nineteenth-century Afrikaners, but Kuyperian neo-
Calvinism, and only at the dawn of the twentieth century. During the ensuing
decades it would grow steadily, both in strength and in sophistication. It
gradually began to overshadow the older evangelical tradition, which tended
to be much more pragmatic and less likely to justify its actions by an appeal
to unchanging biblical principles. "[I]t became increasingly difficult for any
Afrikaner theologian openly to oppose the Kuyperian system in its South
African version. Opposition to it could not only be misconstrued as treason
to the Afrikaner cause, but also as an indication of theological unreliability
and as a threat to the Reformed tradition as such."[11] Evangelicalism proved
to be too weak theologically to counter effectively the Kuyperian apartheid
theology.

Romantic Nationalism. The hope of any fundamental theological change
disappeared almost completely when, during the 1930s, Kuyperian neo-
Calvinism and the *volkskerk* current in Afrikaner evangelicalism blended
with a third religio-ideological force: romantic nationalism. Not that Afrikaners simply swallowed German National Socialism lock, stock, and barrel.
Rather, we had a repeat of what had happened a generation earlier: once
again Afrikaners would selectively adapt what they had received from Europe, in such a way that it would speak to their specific situation as an
embattled people struggling to define and protect their identity.

Romantic nationalist ideas were disseminated in South Africa by young
Afrikaners who had studied in Germany in the 1930s. Several of them rose to
prominence and dominated the political and cultural scene from the 1950s to
the 1970s. One of these was Dr. H. F. Verwoerd, who was to become the great
theorist of "separate development" and prime minister in the 1950s and
1960s. Another one was Dr. Piet Meyer, for many years chairman of the
Afrikaner Broederbond and head of the South African Broadcasting Corporation, and the man who shaped and molded that organization into what it is to
this day. A third person was Dr. N. J. Diederichs, who later served as cabinet
minister and also as state president. Yet another was Dr. Geoff Cronjé,
sociologist, who, in 1945, published his *'n Tuiste vir die nageslag* (A home
for posterity), which became the object of intense study and discussion in

Afrikaner circles. This book was dedicated to Cronjé's wife ". . . and all other Afrikaner mothers, because they are the protectors of the purity of blood of the Boer nation."

Let us look, briefly, at some of the contributions of two of these men, Meyer and Diederichs.

In December 1941 Meyer read a paper entitled *"Die vooraand van ons vrywording"* (The eve of our liberation) at an Afrikaner national youth congress. His definition of a Calvinist-Christian view of life (which he labelled "Krugerism") was clearly influenced by contemporary events in Germany. The organic national community is seen as a pyramidical structure with, at the top, the leaders who have acquired that position because of their charisma and drive. At the very top we have the "natural leader of the people, called by God and endowed with the necessary authority to rule the people according to God's will. . . ."[12] The leader called by God is apparently not elected by the people but only "confirmed" by them, since his authority is "organic."[13] Political groupings who oppose the implementation of the national calling cannot be allowed to operate.[14] The battle now (1941) raging in Europe was a battle for rejuvenation, between the emerging organic national idea and the liberal individualism of the previous century. The gist of the national idea is that the people is an organic community of soil, blood, language, culture, state, tradition, worldview, and destiny. This movement of the people *(volk)* has found its purest and most powerful manifestation first in Italian Fascism and then in German National Socialism.[15] Since the victory of the latter is imminent, the Afrikaners find themselves on "the eve of our liberation." Thus the title of the paper becomes transparent.[16]

In 1936 Nico Diederichs, then professor of philosophy in Bloemfontein, published his *Nasionalisme as Lewensbeskouing*. Only in the nation, as the most total comprehensive human community, can the individual find true fulfillment.[17] A nation is first and foremost a unity of love—of what is eternal and super-temporal.[18] It permeates everything and embraces the whole person. It is the most complete community imaginable. A person is first of all a member of the nation. Love for one's nation is the highest and most sublime love one can experience in the earthly realm, but only if it forms part of one's love to God. Service to one's nation is part of one's love to God.[19]

In an illuminating paragraph Deiderichs—and we should remember that this was written when Hitler was a dictator in Germany—redefines democracy.[20] The number of individual votes supporting a specific policy does not matter, he says. A democratic government is not one that enjoys numerically superior support, but one that is representative of the values, ideals, and principles of the nation—in other words, a government that mirrors the "totality of the nation." A national democratic government may consist of one person, or of several; he or they may be elected or self-appointed. The essential criterion is simply whether he or they truly represent the total essence of the nation as spiritual unity. The similarities between what Diederichs says here, and what Meyer was to say five years later, are striking indeed.

Some of these ideas were not further developed or were later abandoned by Diederichs. This general climate, however, became the springboard for the creation of the Ossewa-Brandwag and related movements (such as Oswald Pirow's Nuwe Orde and the anti-Semitic Gryshemde). In addition, Afrikaner nationalism was invigorated tremendously by the Simboliese Ossewatrek (Symbolic Oxwagon Trek) of 1938.

Less than a year after this, South Africa was involved in a war with Germany—a war in which the sympathy of the majority of Afrikaners was with Germany rather than with Britain. The secret semi-military Ossewa-Brandwag aimed at the establishment of a South Africa under exclusive Afrikaner rule. As early as 1934 the Broederbond made it clear in a circular to its members that the ultimate aim of the Afrikaner was to rule South Africa. As long ago as 1881, during the First War of Independence, Jorissen wrote: "Let it be from the Zambesi to Simons Bay: Africa for the Afrikaner!" These were also the words with which *Eene eeuw van onrecht* concluded, and the phrase was again taken up by P. J. Meyer in his 1941 paper.[21] The Osswea-Brandwag, which at one stage had a membership of over two hundred thousand, was prepared to work for this ideal with all means at its disposal. Only one nation could be recognized in a state, and the state had to be the vehicle of that nation's personality. In South Africa that nation was the Afrikaner, who claimed a birthright and with whom the English could not expect to be treated on an equal footing. The English had to relinquish their separate existence as a national group and be assimilated with the Afrikaner nation, or else emigrate.[22] Nobody even bothered to argue that the blacks had no stake in South Africa: this was simply taken for granted.

The excesses of the Ossewa-Brandwag brought it into confrontation with the National Party, under the strong leadership of Dr. D. F. Malan. A bitter struggle ensued until the Ossewa-Brandwag was suppressed in 1944. Despite wartime charges, neither Malan nor J. G. Strijdom was Nazi in belief, though both were staunch segregationists. Details of Malan's successful undercover fight against Nazism inside Afrikaner nationalism came to light only in the 1960s. Many Afrikaners, however, definitely cherished Nazi ideals and sentiments.

Quite apart from the complicated issue of overt or covert Nazi sympathies, however, it is beyond doubt that romantic nationalism made deep inroads into Afrikaner thinking. In the 1930s and 1940s the conviction grew that the ethnic purity of a nation had a metaphysical base. It was, therefore, divinely ordained and commanded. It is in this kind of thinking that the religious roots of the law prohibiting interracial marriage are to be found. A. P. Treurnicht proudly recalls that the petition presented to Parliament in 1939—pleading for segregation between white and black and for the prohibition of mixed marriages—was the one with the largest number of signatures ever—almost a quarter of a million. He adds: "And at the head of the petition-ers was a man of the church. Vader Kestell."[23] It was, once again, representa-tives of the Afrikaans Reformed churches who, in the 1940s, petitioned first the Smuts government and then the Malan government to introduce such a law. It was, in fact, one of the very first laws to be promulgated by the Nationalist government after it came to power in 1948.

The Current South African Crisis

The religious roots of Afrikaner nationalism, as it reached maturity in the 1940s and 1950s, are, then, to be traced back to the influences of Reformed evangelicalism, Kuyperian Calvinism, and romantic nationalism. It is, in-deed, a curious blend of all three of these, having gleaned from each what best suited the peculiar situation of the Afrikaner.

From the beginning of the 1960s, however, the monolith slowly began to crack and break up. To some extent this came because of the growing awareness of the domestic and international situation, as Afrikaners slowly became conscious of the reality of the winds of change blowing over Africa. Another reason for the breakup of the monolith was a theological awakening that began to manifest itself among a younger generation of Afrikaners. Most of these came from the Reformed evangelical wing of the Dutch Reformed Church, and many of them were working in and with the black church. The majority of them were, in addition, influenced by the theology of Karl Barth. Since the early 1960s Dr. Beyers Naudé (currently General Secretary of the South African Council of Churches), after having been banned for seven years, became the undisputed symbol of theological dissidence in the cir-cles of the Dutch Reformed Church. But there were many others besides Naudé who had been challenging the theological support for apartheid since the 1950s, and even earlier.[24]

These voices were, however, not heeded. During the 1960s, in particular, virtually every voice of protest, whether in church or in politics, in the ecclesiastical or secular press, was squashed. Those who nevertheless did speak out were ostracized. In the wake of the Cottesloe Consultations (De-cember 1960), the Dutch Reformed Church (Cape Province and Transvaal) terminated its membership in the World Council of Churches and increas-ingly isolated itself from other South African churches. Beyers Naudé founded the Christian Institute and became its first full-time director, a step that cost him his status as minister. When, soon after this, he was elected elder in the Parkhurst congregation, the Presbytery of Johannesburg declared the election null and void, arguing that Naudé, in accepting the directorship of the Christian Institute, had "disobeyed the guidance of the *Breë Moderatuur*" (Moderamen of the General Synod). The 1966 General Synod, with one dissenting voice, condemned the Christian Institute as representing false doctrine, and ordered all Dutch Reformed Church members and officials to resign from it. Henceforth only official National Party policy and official church views would be tolerated.

During the 1970s the climate began to change somewhat. It again became possible, though still only in a limited way, to propagate alternative political and ecclesiastical paradigms in Afrikaner circles. Meanwhile, however, frustration in the black community had reached breaking point. On June 16, 1976, Soweto erupted in violence, which soon spread across the whole country. Just over a year later (September 12, 1977) Steve Biko, the father of the Black Consciousness Movement, died in detention, after having been kept in police cells naked and manacled for weeks. When the Minister of Police was confronted with this in Parliament, his reaction was: "Steve Biko's death leaves me cold." A few weeks later (October 19, 1977) several organizations, including the Christian Institute, were banned, many people arrested, and others served with banning orders. Violence continued to erupt in the black townships, but was, on the whole, quelled reasonably effectively. White South Africa heaved a sigh of relief: it looked as though things were returning to "normal."

Since last year, however, the entire scene has changed fundamentally and permanently. Violence of both kinds—structural *and* revolutionary—is no longer sporadic; it has become endemic. In the black communities those who are regarded as collaborators with the system are no longer just ostracised; they are executed. The spiral of violence is rising.

The irony is that the year 1985 has seen more fundamental political reform in South Africa than the total preceding period: restoration of citizenship to blacks, scrapping of Influx Control and the passbook system, scrapping of the Mixed Marriage Act, assurances that blacks will be included in decision-making processes at the highest level, and so forth. These reforms, however, have not in the least changed the mood in the black community. Why not? For several reasons, I think. First, because these reforms are being introduced piecemeal, in small installments, and not as part of a comprehensive new strategy. Second, the reforms are clearly the result of black pressure; so they seem to suggest that pressure should be increased rather than decreased, in order to wring even more fundamental changes from the government, particularly to bring the government to the point where it might surrender altogether. A third reason is that none of the changes introduced, important as they are in themselves, really suggests that the white minority is willing to jeopardize even theoretically its position of power and privilege. Only two weeks ago [dated from October 1985] an opinion poll revealed that two-thirds of all white South Africans believe that South Africa will *never* have a (black) majority government.

The ruling National Party has indeed become more pragmatic in recent years. The pure and unadulterated expression of classical Afrikaner religio-political thinking is no longer embodied in the National Party. The two ultra right-wing parties (the Herstigte Nasionale Party, founded in 1969, and the Conservative Party, founded in 1982) can indeed claim to be the heirs to that legacy. Still, for all its growing pragmatism, the National Party finds it impossible to break out of the ideological straitjacket it itself donned generations ago. So we see the realities of present-day South Africa leading the main body of Afrikaners to a curious mixture of ideological motivations and pragmatic considerations. In the final analysis, however, the forces that molded the Afrikaner, and Afrikaner civil religion, continue to determine Afrikaner attitudes and prevent them from embracing a new paradigm. They are prepared to make concessions, but refuse to be pushed too far. While propagating changes and a modicum of compromise, they are developing a Masada complex. The resoluteness of the Afrikaner to fight literally to the bitter end should not be underestimated. Therefore, unless all parties can agree to meet around a table and thrash out a new political and societal blueprint, and do so very soon, the stage is set for a civil war that may last decades and leave the entire subcontinent in ruins. Whether we will have a negotiated settlement or a long drawn-out revolution is hard to tell. The portents are not too promising; in fact, the gap between white intransigence and black demands seems to be widening.

What we see unfolding, then, truly has the makings of a classical Greek tragedy. The stage for this tragedy is an area as large as Western Europe, and most of the millions of actors seem to be incapable of comprehending where they are heading. In George Steiner's words they "stride to their fierce disasters in the grip of truths more intense than knowledge,"[25] captives of their respective histories.

Tragedy, however—so Steiner reminds us—is by definition irreparable. We remain pawns, turned over to the capriciousness of a malevolent God, to blind fate, the solicitations of hell, or to the brute fury of our own animal blood, which is waiting for us in ambush at the crossroads, mocking us and destroying us.[26] But Steiner also points out that we encounter tragedy in Greek antiquity and in Shakespeare, not, however, in the Judaeo-Christian Scriptures and tradition.

But I stand in this latter tradition. This means that I am an anti-tragedy person. I am in the hope business. I know of judgment, which is not the same as tragedy. I also know of repentance and forgiveness, of reparation and restitution, of a new life beyond the grave, of a kingdom that is coming. And, of course, I am not alone in this. There are also the Desmond Tutus, the Beyers Naudés and tens of thousands of others; there is still a silver-haired Alan Paton who first aroused our consciences when he wrote *Cry, the Beloved Country*, forty years ago, and who, just a month ago, opened our National Initiative for Reconciliation with a reading from Psalm 130. The night is dark, indeed, but there have always been and there still are the watchmen crying out their messages of hope, reminding us that when the night is at its darkest, dawn has drawn near.

Notes

[1] W. A. de Klerk, *The Puritans in Africa* (London: 1975).

[2] Cf. also André du Toit, "No Chosen People: The Myth of the Calvinist Origins of Afrikaner Nationalism and Racial Ideology," *The American Historical Review* 88:4 (October 1983), pp. 920-28.

[3] For a summary of Livingstone's views on the Afrikaners, cf. Du Toit, op. cit., pp. 939-47.

[4] W. S. Hudson (ed.), *Nationalism and Religion in America* (New York: 1970), p. 3; quoted in André du Toit, *Puritans in Africa?* (Unpublished paper, n.d.), p.4.

[5] Robinson and Gallagher, *Africa and the Victorians: The Climax of Imperialism in the Dark Continent* (London: 1961), pp. 2-3; quoted in Du Toit. "No Chosen People," p. 939.

[6] Information gleaned from *Central Plains,* map no. 9 in the Making of American Series, supplement to the September 1985 issue of *National Geographic.*

[7] F. Hertz, *Nationality in History and Politics* (London: 1957), p. 12.

[8] Cf. J. J. F. Durand, "Afrikaner Piety and Dissent," in *Resistance and Hope: South African Essays in Honor of Beyers Naudé,* ed. Charles Villa-Vicencio and John W. de Gruchy (Cape Town/Grand Rapids: 1985), pp. 42-45.

[9] A. Kuyper, *Lectures on Calvinism* (Grand Rapids: 1961), pp. 35-36.

[10] Quoted by Irving Hexham, *The Irony of Apartheid* (1981), p. 180.

[11] Durand, op. cit., p. 41.

[12] P. J. Meyer, *Die Vooraand van ons vrywording* (Potchefstroom: 1941), p. 25 (my translation).

[13] Ibid., p. 25.

[14] Ibid., pp. 25-26.

[15] Ibid., pp. 30.

[16] A year later Meyer read a paper at the annual congress of the Afrikaanse Nasionale Studentebond in Pretoria, where he developed his ideas in more detail. Cf. "Die toekomstige ordening van die volksbeweging in Suid-Afrika," *Wapenskou* 3:3 (September 1942), pp. 28-37, 50-53.

[17] N. J. Diederichs, *Nasionalisme as lewensbeskouing* (Bleomfontein: Nasionale Pers, 1936), p. 18.

[18] Ibid., p. 37.

[19] Ibid., p. 63.

[20] Ibid., pp. 55-57.

[21] Cf. Meyer, op. cit., p. 37.

[22] References in H. Giliomee, "The development of the Afrikaner's self-concept," in *Looking at the Afrikaner Today,* ed. H. W. van der Merwe (Cape Town: Tafelberg, 1975), p. 25.

[23] A. P. Treurnicht, *Credo van 'n Afrikaner* (Cape Town: 1975), p. 78.

[24] The two first theologians who have, since the 1940s, been criticizing Nationalist paradigms were Professors B. B. Keet (Stellenbosch) and B. J. Marais (Pretoria).

[25] George Steiner, *The Death of Tragedy* (London: 1974), p. 7.

[26] Ibid., pp. 8-9.

ETHICS/SPIRITUAL LIFE

Klaus Bockmuehl, area editor

ETHICS/SPIRITUAL LIFE

KLAUS BOCKMUEHL
Professor of Theology and Ethics
Regent College

Introduction

Readers will join the present writer in appreciation of the editorial decision to combine the two topics of "Ethics" and "Spiritual Life" into one area in *The Best in Theology*. With this decision, we resume the ancient order of theological disciplines which linked "Ethics" and "Ascetics." More limited than the concept of "the Christian life," the word "ethics" has always meant merely dealing with the earthly behavior of persons, or with the second table of the Ten Commandments. So if we dealt only with "ethics" we might omit the actions of the "first table," concerning our relationship with God—among them prayer, the Great Commission, and the edification of the church.

This has become a fact in the history of much Protestant ethics. The damage it inflicts becomes especially evident today when Christian ethics yields to the pressures of secularism and reduces itself to the discussion of the morality of interhuman relationships. However, when severed from the study of communion with God, the ethics of human relations will be essentially altered and corrupted. A glance at Christ's double commandment of love reminds us that there are indeed two main fields of Christian action. The spiritual and the ethical together form the Christian life.

Overall, it would be desirable that this selection of essays touch on such subdivisions as spiritual life, fundamental ethics, personal ethics, and social ethics. It would do this both in terms of general foundations, and individual applications to problems (for instance, those in the field of professional ethics). However, as space is limited, we will have to pick and choose.

For the area of spiritual life, "A Guide to Devotional Reading" by James M. Houston, professor of spiritual theology at Regent College, Vancouver, B.C., seems particularly suitable because it provides a valuable introduction to the field as such. Since this is the first volume of *The Best in Theology*, it has been thought permissible to include an article of 1984. The area editor's second choice for this field is Leighton Ford's "The 'Finger of God' in Evangelism," from the journal *World Evangelization*.

For the field of social ethics, Norman L. Geisler's "A Premillennial View of Law and Government" has been chosen because it presents useful insights into today's decisive debates on the basic method of and approach to the questions of social ethics. The author, a professor at Dallas Theological Seminary, deals with the "theonomists" in particular, but his argument also covers other positions, such as the concept of "Christocracy" in the Barthian school, and the different theories of application of New Testament ethics (for instance, the Sermon on the Mount) to the realms of state and society. The area editor's second choice in this subdivision is C. René Padilla's summary of the recent discussions on social ethics among evangelicals, "Evangelism and Social Responsibility: From Wheaton '66 to Wheaton '83," in *Transformation*.

The coverage of other sub-divisions must wait for another year.

About the Area Editor

Klaus Bockmuehl (Th.D., University of Basle) is professor of theology and ethics at Regent College (Vancouver, B.C.). A citizen of the Federal Republic of Germany, he is an ordained minister in the Evangelical Church of the Rhineland. His most recent books are *Living by the Gospel* (1986), *The Challenge of Marxism: A Christian Response* (IVP, 1980; Helmers and Howard, 1986), and *Evangelicals and Social Ethics* (1979).

EVANGELISM AND SOCIAL RESPONSIBILITY
From Wheaton '66 to Wheaton '83

C. RENÉ PADILLA
Editor of *Misión*, and Co-ordinator of
Latin American Theological Fraternity

Article from *Transformation*

The relationship between evangelism and social responsibility has in the last few years been a matter of special concern to evangelicals in many parts of the world. Today, most evangelicals would hardly fit the stereotype of a person who is solely committed to 'saving souls' and who closes his or her eyes to bodily needs. However, the problem comes when an attempt is made to define what importance such needs should have in relation to missionary priorities.

A number of international and interdenomination conferences held between 1966 and 1983 reflect this debate. A gleaning of the documents that emerged from them, beginning with *The Wheaton Declaration* and concluding with the statement on *The Church in Response to Human Need*, shows that a more wholistic approach to mission has slowly gained ground in evangelical circles. The purpose of this study is to survey this development and to point to the role that Two-Thirds World theologians have played in it. The term Two-Thirds World is now widely preferred to refer to the majority of the world's population who live in conditions of poverty, powerlessness and oppression, mainly in Africa, Asia, and Latin America. This is also where the majority of Christians live.

From Wheaton '66 to Lausanne '74

The Congress on the Church's Worldwide Mission was held at Wheaton, Ill., April 9-16, 1966. It was sponsored jointly by the Evangelical Foreign Missions Association and the Interdenominational Foreign Mission Association: agencies that at that time represented 102 mission boards and 30,000 missionaries (almost one-half of the North American Protestant missionary force working overseas). Its declared purpose was to bring together evangelical leaders to study some of the problems confronting the Church 'both at home and overseas'. With an attendance of almost one thousand delegates from seventy-one countries, it was a significant effort to rethink the Church's mission on a world-wide scale.[1]

239

To be sure, *The Wheaton Declaration*, the 5,900-word document that came out of it with a unanimous endorsement by the participants, was regarded by some as 'a thoroughly conservative statement from a conservative source'.[2] It could hardly be expected that an evangelical conference dealing with subjects such as syncretism, neo-universalism, proselytism, and neo-Romanism would produce a document free from negative overtones. *The Wheaton Declaration* had, however, the great virtue of recognizing that 'we are guilty of an unscriptural isolation from the world that too often keeps us from honestly facing and coping with its concerns'. It confessed the failure 'to apply Scriptural principles to such problems as racism, war, population explosion, poverty, family disintegration, social revolution, and communism'. It articulated the desire of evangelicals to 'look to the Scriptures for guidance as to what they should do, and how far they should go in expressing [their] social concern, without minimizing the priority of preaching the Gospel of individual salvation'. It urged 'all evangelicals to stand openly and firmly for racial equality, human freedom, and all forms of social justice throughout the world'.[3]

Clearly, a new attitude with regard to Christian social responsibility was finding its way into evangelical circles at the time of the 1966 Wheaton Congress. The new concern for social problems shown in *The Wheaton Declaration*, however, was by no means unrelated to the presence of a good number of participants from the Two-Thirds World. These delegates from outside the United States read papers and delivered inspirational addresses. According to a conservative observer, 'their recommendations weighed heavily in determining the final shape of the Declaration'.[4] This fact goes a long way to explain how such a document could come out of a mission conference held in the United States at a time when, as Robert Booth Fowler has demonstrated, evangelicalism in that country was simply not interested in social change or social activism.[5] This was probably the first time that under the influence of people from the Two-Thirds World an important evangelical gathering produced a missiological statement that, despite its limitations, could be regarded by an ecumenical leader as important enough to be 'among the more widely welcomed and read missionary documents of this decade'.[6]

The next important meeting, the World Congress on Evangelism, was sponsored by *Christianity Today*, magazine in celebration of its tenth anniversary. It was held in Berlin, from October 25 to November 4, 1966, under the motto 'One Race, One Gospel, One Task'.[7] In his opening address evangelist Billy Graham, honorary chairman of the Congress, reaffirmed his often repeated conviction that 'if the Church went back to its main task of proclaiming the Gospel and people converted to Christ, it would have a far greater impact on the social, moral, and psychological needs of men than it could achieve through any other thing it could possibly do'.[8] He thus voiced a basic premise which was taken for granted by the organizers of the Congress.

This might have been the main reason why the question of the relationship of evangelism to social responsibility—a recurring theme in the discussion groups during the conference—was not given proper attention at the plenary sessions, despite the fact that 'many delegates felt there should have been more of an effort to crystallize thinking on it'.[9] As a result the conclusion could be drawn that 'Berlin did not establish the theological basis for social action, even though it stood firm on proclamation evangelism as *the* mission of the Church'.[10] Even so, the Closing Statement included the following important declaration related to the social implications of the Gospel: 'We reject the notion that men are unequal because of distinction of race or color. In the name of Scripture and of Jesus Christ we condemn racialism wherever it appears. We ask forgiveness for our past sins in refusing to recognize the clear command of God to love our fellowmen with a love that transcends every human barrier and prejudice. We seek by God's grace to eradicate from our lives and from our witness whatever is displeasing to him in our relations with one another. We extend our hands to each other in love, and those same hands reach out to men everywhere with the prayer that the Prince of Peace may soon unite our sorely divided world.'

The Berlin Congress was followed by several regional congresses on evangelism sponsored by the Billy Graham Evangelistic Association. At all of them, with surprising regularity, there were speakers who brought up the question of Christian social involvement as an issue intimately related to evangelism. At the Asia-South Pacific Congress on Evangelism (Singapore, November 5-13, 1968),[11] Benjamin E. Fernando of Columbo, Ceylon (now Sri Lanka), speaking on 'The Evangel and Social Upheaval', claimed that 'Part of the tragedy of our time is that evangelical Christians are avoiding the revolution that they themselves caused (by their earlier biblical social witness) and so others have stepped in'. He eloquently challenged his hearers to work for social change for 'there are no substitutes for social reformation'.[12] At the U.S. Congress on Evangelism (Minneapolis, September 8-13, 1969),[13] several speakers (notably Tom Skinner, Leighton Ford, Mark Hatfield and Ralph D. Abernathy) related evangelism to social responsibility so effectively that in the view of one reporter 'The consensus of the delegates was that any church or member thereof that whistles to the world a heavenly refrain, while not following Christ in alleviating oppression and human suffering, is a struck ship. At Minneapolis they watched the tide of God's Spirit float the church off its reef of social isolation and head it for the open sea of humanity'.[14] At the Latin American Congress on Evangelism (Bogotá, November 21-30, 1969),[15] Samuel Escobar read a paper on 'The Social Responsibility of the Church'[16] in which, 'In words that echoed the anguished cry of the disinherited, he charted the direction of evangelicals toward a sorely needed involvement in the social order'.[17] The *Evangelical Declaration of Bogota* underlined the need for the example of Jesus Christ to be incarnate 'in the critical Latin American reality of underdevelopment, injustice, hunger, violence and hopelessness'.

The note of social responsibility was echoed at the European Congress on Evangelism (Amsterdam, August 28-September 4, 1971),[18] especially by Paavo Kortekangas in his paper on 'Social Implications of Evangelism'.

A milestone in the awakening of the social conscience of evangelicalism in the United States was the Thanksgiving Workshop on Evangelicals and Social Concern held in Chicago, November 23-25, 1973. The *Chicago Declaration of Evangelical Social Concern* that came out of it was enthusiastically received by many people who saw in it clear evidence that evangelicals were transcending the traditional dichotomy between evangelism and social responsibility. The 473-word statement was essentially an affirmation of God's total claim on the lives of his people, a confession of failure in demonstrating God's justice in society, and a call for evangelicals 'to demonstrate repentance in a Christian discipleship that confronts the social and political injustice of our nation'. It eventually became the basis for *Evangelicals for Social Action* in the United States of America.[19]

With all these antecedents, no one should have been surprised that the International Congress on World Evangelization (Lausanne, July 16-25, 1974)[20] turned out to be a definitive step in affirming that both evangelism and social responsibility are essential to the mission of the Church. The fact, however, is that the Congress was expected to concentrate on the *how* of world evangelization. 'As Berlin was the theological launching pad for Lausanne,' said *Christianity Today* 'now Lausanne must be the launching pad from which the people of God go on to finish the work of proclaiming the Gospel to every creature.'[21] The implication was clear: no time would be wasted in theological discussions at Lausanne since the theological foundation had already been laid in Berlin; the point was now to consider the strategy and methods to evangelize the world. A symbol of this emphasis was a digital population clock activated at the beginning of the Congress, according to which the world population had grown by 530,193,076 since Berlin (1966) and had an increase of 1,852,837 during Lausanne.

For those coming to Lausanne with this type of expectation the Congress was obviously a disappointment. To begin with, one of the topics attracting the greatest attention during the conference was the social responsibility of the Church.[22] More important still is that this topic was openly discussed in plenary sessions and found its way into *The Lausanne Covenant*, where it was given a place of prominence together with other subjects as dear to evangelicals as the authority of Scripture, the uniqueness of Jesus Christ, and evangelism. There was recognition that Christians should share God's concern 'for justice and reconciliation throughout human society and for the liberation of men from every kind of oppression' and that 'evangelism and socio-political involvement are both parts of our Christian duty'. It was stated that 'The message of salvation also implies a message of judgment upon every form of alienation, oppression and discrimination, and we should not be afraid to denounce evil and injustice wherever they exist' (section 5).

The Lausanne Covenant was a death blow to every attempt to reduce the mission of the Church to the multiplication of Christians and churches through evangelism.[23]

The plea to keep evangelism and social responsibility together was further strengthened at Lausanne by *A Response to Lausanne* presented by the *(ad hoc)* Radical Discipleship Group at the end of the Congress.[24] Almost five hundred participants signed it just before leaving, and it was welcomed by the chairman of the drafting committee, John Stott, as an addendum to the Covenant. Its definition of the Gospel of Jesus Christ as the 'Good News of liberation, of restoration, of wholeness, and of salvation that is personal, social, global, and cosmic' provided the strongest statement on the basis for wholistic mission ever formulated by an evangelical conference up to that date. Social involvement had finally been granted full citizenship in evangelical missiology, mainly under the influence of people from the Two-Thirds World.

From Lausanne '74 to Pattaya '80

The Lausanne Covenant was received all over the world with great interest and even exhilaration by Christians of different theological persuasions. Granted its limitations, many regarded it as a very commendable evangelical statement and sought to delve deeply into its implications for the life and mission of the Church.

By contrast, others interpreted Lausanne as a dangerous departure from biblical truth and a tragic compromise with 'ecumenical theology'. One of its most articulate critics claimed that the 'large evangelism' of the International Missionary Council (1921-1961), influenced by the 'social gospel', had been replaced by 'wholistic evangelism' at Lausanne. 'The Evangelical must recognize,' he warned, 'that the theological foundations of wholistic evangelism, as noble as it sounds, is built not only upon the theology of an errant Bible but also the universalism of New Delhi that justifies a horizontal salvation as equal to, or superior to, the evangelical concern for the personal or individual salvation.'[25] John Stott in particular came under fire for defining social action as 'partner of evangelism', thus dethroning evangelism as '*the* only historic aim of mission'.[26]

In his response to such criticisms published in *Christianity Today*, John Stott[27] reasserted the importance of 'a primary commitment to world evangelization'. He then went on to say, however, that the distinction between evangelism and social action 'is often artificial' and that the relation between the two was 'the theological question that Lausanne left unresolved and that still needs to be pursued'. If social action is a *consequence* of evangelism, he argued, then we should expect that those who are the consequence of our evangelism should become involved in social action, and we ourselves

The Best in Theology

should do likewise, since we also are the consequence of other people's evangelism.

In spite of its opponents, most of them identified with the North American missionary establishment, the wholistic approach to mission continued to find support among evangelicals, especially in the Two-Thirds World. This is reflected in the statements emerging from the various conferences held in this period. Thus, the *Madras Declaration on Evangelical Social Action*,[28] produced at the All India Conference on Evangelical Social Action (October 2-5, 1979), laid down the basis for responsible Christian action in the face of 'the increasing oppression of the underprivileged classes, the continuing entrenchment of casteism and the rising rate of communal violence'. The *Pastoral Letter* issued by the Second Latin American Congress on Evangelism (Lima, October 31-November 7, 1979)[29] echoed a deep concern for 'those who are hungry and thirsty for justice, those who are deprived of what they need in order to survive, marginalized ethnic groups, destroyed families, women who have no rights, young people dedicated to vice or pushed to violence, children suffering because of hunger, abandonment, ignorance, or exploitation'.

Finally, *An Evangelical Commitment to Simple Lifestyle*,[30] which came out of the Consultation on Simple Lifestyle (Hoddesdon, March 1980) sponsored by the Theology and Education Group of the Lausanne Committee and the Unit on Ethics and Society of the World Evangelical Fellowship Theological Commission, expressed the growing consensus among evangelicals around the world on the intimate connection between the personal and social dimensions of the Gospel. The 2,450-word statement was primarily meant to expound the implications of the 'duty to develop a simple lifestyle in order to contribute more generously to both relief and evangelism', acknowledged by *The Lausanne Covenant* (section 9). Taking that 'duty' as its starting point, however, the *Commitment* denounced 'environmental destruction, wastefulness and hoarding' and deplored 'the misery of the poor who suffer as a result of these evils'. It condemned involuntary poverty as 'an offense against the goodness of God' and claimed that 'the church must stand with God and the poor against injustice, suffer with them and call on rulers to fulfil their God-appointed role'. It recognized that 'the call for a New International Economic Order expresses the justified frustration of the Third-World' and 'in many cases multi-national corporations reduce local initiative in the countries where they work, and tend to oppose any fundamental change in government'. It also stated that 'all Christians must participate in the active struggle to create a just and responsible society'. It thus established the link between a responsible lifestyle and evangelism.

Quite clearly, evangelicals had turned a corner at Lausanne with regard to their understanding of the social implications of the Gospel. It would not be difficult to prove, however, that the organizers of the next major international event sponsored by the Lausanne Committee for World Evangelization

(LCWE), the Consultation on World Evangelization (Pattaya, Thailand, June 17-27, 1980),[31] made a special effort to ensure that the task of world evangelism was dealt with in isolation from social responsibility. Under the motto 'How Shall They Hear', Pattaya was to be 'a working consultation with the main objective of developing realistic, evangelistic strategies to reach for Christ hitherto unreached peoples of the world', as the programme of the Consultation stated.

That the organizers were almost exclusively concerned with the 'how' of the (verbal) communication of the Gospel to 'people-groups' around the world was made evident by many of the materials that were circulated in advance.[32] This preoccupation also undoubtedly explains the tight control that was exercised by the leadership during the conference—there was the fear that the discussion of the social aspect of the Christian mission would again divert attention from evangelism, as had (supposedly) happened at Lausanne! In words of a participant, 'Pattaya was somehow prepackaged'.[33]

Much creative thinking, however, was done in the seventeen mini-consultations that had been planned in advance to consider the strategy to reach non-Christians in an equal number of people-groups. As a result, the attempt to keep the conference within the straitjacket of a narrow definition of mission was counterbalanced at the grassroots level. An editorial in *Christianity Today* later reported that 'Some tried to transform COWE into a conference on social concern, but the leadership managed for the most part to keep the group on track'.[34] Some of the Lausanne Occasional Papers published after the Thailand Consultation[35] ratify that the mini-consultations left aside the 'official' concern for strategy and 'went ahead on the gains of Lausanne'.[36]

Some of the issues discussed in these mini-consultations became the basis for a 1,000-word *Statement of Concerns on the Future of the Lausanne Committee for World Evangelization* which without the help of official publicity was signed by 185 people within twenty-four hours.[37] The Statement chided the Lausanne Committee for not being 'seriously concerned with the social, political and economic issues in many parts of the world that are a stumbling block to the proclamation of the gospel'. Evidence of this is shown by the fact that at Pattaya there was a working group on 'Reaching Refugees' but 'none of those who are largely responsible for the refugee situation around the world: politicians, armed forces, freedom fighters, national oligarchies and the controllers of international economic power'. It called the Lausanne Movement to help Christians 'to identify not only people-groups but also the social, economic and political institutions that determine their lives and the structures behind them that hinder evangelism' and to give guidance on how evangelicals lending support to repressive regimes or to unjust economic policies 'can be reached with the whole biblical gospel and be challenged to repent and work for justice'.

This Statement was presented to the LCWE as a 'genuine attempt to build bridges between evangelical Christians who at present are not yet agreed about the relationship between evangelization and socio-political involvement'. The conference leadership ignored it; no plenary discussion of it was allowed. Because of it *The Thailand Statement*—the official document issued by the conference—was, however, substantially revised so as to stress incarnational, rather than exclusively verbal, evangelization.[38] Thus despite all the problems, the Pattaya Consultation proved once again that the wholistic approach to mission is here to stay.

From Pattaya '80 to Wheaton '83

The Lausanne Covenant had stated that 'evangelism and socio-political involvement are both part of our Christian duty' (section 5). It also stated that 'in the church's mission of sacrificial service evangelism is primary' (section 6). As time went on the need to clarify the relationship between evangelism and social responsibility, and to understand in what sense evangelism is primary, became increasingly pressing. The Consultation on the Relationship between Evangelism and Social Responsibility (CRESR) meeting in (Grand Rapids, Michigan, June 19-25, 1982), under the sponsorship of the Theology and Education Group of LCWE and the Unit on Ethics and Society of the World Evangelical Fellowship Theological Commission, was held in order to deal with these questions.

The CRESR Report, *Evangelism and Social Responsibility*,[39] represents a milestone in the evangelical understanding of the Christian mission in the modern world. CRESR was an attempt to settle a question that had become divisive among evangelicals. The Report represents a further step in the process of renewal of evangelical missiology. Almost as if by a miracle, it includes many of the concerns which the Lausanne Congress had summed up in its affirmation that 'evangelism and socio-political involvement are both part of our Christian duty'. The writer can himself vouch to the long and painful course that the group and plenary discussion followed in order to produce this statement. Only the Spirit of God could have enabled the participants to overcome their fear and to allow space for a position in which evangelism and social responsibility are no longer conceived of as in opposition to one another but as united in a partnership which is 'in reality, a marriage'. As the Report puts it, 'evangelism and social responsibility, while distinct from one another, are integrally related in our proclamation of and obedience to the Gospel'.

If the relationship between evangelism and social responsibility is defined in these terms, it is obvious that the primacy of evangelism mentioned in the Lausanne Covenant (section 6) could not mean that evangelism is to be regarded as more important than its partner *every time* and *everywhere*. If that were the case, something would be wrong with the marriage! One of the values of the Grand Rapids Report is that, in contrast with all the previous documents produced by evangelicals in the last few years, it clarified that the primacy of evangelism can be stated only in a relative, not in an absolute, sense. It is, in the first place, a logical priority, since 'The very fact of Christian social responsibility presupposes socially responsible Christians, and it can only be by evangelism and discipleship that they have become such'. It is, in the second place, a priority derived from the fact that 'evangelism relates to people's eternal destiny and in bringing them Good News of salvation, Christians are doing what nobody else can do'. This way of understanding the primacy of evangelism simply reflects the Christian conviction that the widest and deepest human need is wholeness of life through the power of the Gospel. However, no room is left for the notion that social responsibility may be dispensed with. In fact, the Report admits that the choice between evangelism and social responsibility is 'largely conceptual'.

The 'marriage' between evangelism and social responsibility as a wholistic approach to mission was confirmed by the Consultation on the Church in Response to Human Need sponsored by the World Evangelical Fellowship, (Wheaton, June 20-July 1, 1983).[40] The document that emerged from it viewed *the whole of human life* as subject to the transforming power of God. In unequivocal terms it affirmed the inevitability of political involvement: 'either we challenge the evil structures of society or we support them'. It challenged individualism, 'the unspoken assumption that societies operate best when individuals are most free to pursue their own self-interests'. It questioned private property as an absolute right: 'When either individuals or states claim an absolute right to ownership, that is rebellion against God'. It also condemned the arms race, 'While millions starve to death, resources are wasted on the research and production of increasingly sophisticated nuclear weapon systems'. It pointed to the problem of international injustice. 'Injustice in the modern world has reached global proportions' and recognized the prophetic ministry of the Church: 'Our churches must also address issues of evil and of social injustice in the local community and the wider society'. By emphasizing that the Kingdom of God is 'both present and future, both societal and individual, both physical and spiritual', it laid a sound theological basis for the mission of the Church, with no dichotomy between evangelism and social responsibility.

Wheaton '83 completed the process of shaping an evangelical social conscience, a process in which people from the Two-Thirds World played a decisive role.[41] It made it evident to evangelicals that evangelism cannot be divorced from meaningful involvement with people with all their needs.[42]

Notes

[1] There were 938 participants, of whom eight came from Africa, nineteen from Asia and twenty-eight from Latin America. According to Eugene L. Smith, the 'Delegates brought from other countries were of notable ability and training' (*Christianity Today* 10 (May 27, 1966): 867).

There were one hundred and fifty missionary societies represented, two-thirds of them affiliated to IFMA or EFMA, plus thirty-eight special mission interest groups, fourteen non-North American agencies, and fifty-three schools. The Congress was regarded by *Christianity Today* as 'the biggest and most representative meeting of evangelical missionary leaders ever held' (*CT* 10 (April 15, 1966): 743).

  [2] Donald H. Gill, 'They Played It Safe in Wheaton', *World Vision Magazine* 10 (June 1966): 31.

  [3] 'The Wheaton Declaration', *Evangelical Missions Quarterly* 2 (Summer 1966): 231-44. According to *Christianity Today* 10 (May 13, 1966): 852, this Declaration 'represents a broad consensus on evangelical strategy for the years immediately ahead'. The stand on racial equality, human freedom, and social justice was not in the original draft of the Declaration but was added as a result of the debate at plenary sessions.

  [4] Harold Lindsell, *Christianity Today* 10 (April 29, 1966): 795. It must be said, however, that the person in charge of presenting the paper on 'Mission and Social Concern' was a North American, namely, Horace L. Fenton, Jr., General Director of the Latin America Mission. Of this paper Ruben Lores wrote, shortly after the Congress, that 'it should help dispel the false fears and correct the wrong perspective that makes many evangelicals equate social action with liberal theology' (*Evangelical Missions Quarterly* 3 (1966-67): 13-14). At the same time, however, Fenton regarded it as necessary to reaffirm his conviction that 'whatever the social implications of the Gospel, our primary task is to take this redeeming message of personal salvation to every creature, and to use every legitimate means for the evangelization of the world in our generation' ('Debits and Credits—the Wheaton Congress', *The International Review of Missions* 55 (1966): 479).

  [5] Cf. Robert Booth Fowler, *A New Engagement: Evangelical Political Thought, 1966-1976* (Grand Rapids: Wm. B. Eerdmans, 1982). According to Fowler, the emphasis on evangelicalism in the middle sixties in the United States 'was on individual conversion and individual action and witness in daily life' and the result was that 'evangelicalism was leery of major social and political changes' (p. 5). By contrast, evangelicals in the Two-Thirds World were becoming increasingly concerned about the social implications of the Gospel. Writing shortly before the Wheaton Congress, C. Peter Wagner said: 'On mission fields such as Latin America, where people are deeply involved in one of the most explosive and widespread social revolutions in history, the relation of the Church to society is a top-priority issue. There is no pulling back. Christians, like everyone else in Latin America, are caught in a whirlpool of rapid social change, and they demand to know what the Bible has to say to them in this situation' (*Christianity Today* 10 (January 7, 1966): 338).

  [6] Eugene L. Smith, *Christianity Today* 10 (May 27, 1966): 867.

  [7] There were 1,111 participants from one hundred countries at the Berlin Congress. Despite this world-wide representation, the Congress was 'predominantly Western in organization and expression', as is acknowledged by Arthur P. Johnston (*The Battle for World Evangelism* (Wheaton, Illinois: Tyndale House Publishers, Inc., 1978), p. 158). The proceedings were published in *One Race, One Gospel, One Task*, edited by C. F. H. Henry and W. S. Mooneyham (Minneapolis: World Wide Publications, 1967), in two volumes.

  [8] 'Why the Berlin Congress', *Christianity Today* 11 (November 11, 1966): 133. According to Billy Graham, social needs are one of the motivations for evangelism, for 'The preaching of the Cross could do more to bring about social revolution than any other method' (135). Cf. *World Aflame* (Minneapolis: Billy Graham Evangelistic Association, 1965), pp. 168-69. In response to those who have criticized the so-called 'social gospel', however, he argues that 'Jesus taught that we are to take regeneration in one hand and a cup of cold water in the other. Christians, above all others, should be concerned with social problems and social injustices . . . The Christian is to take his place in society with moral courage to stand up for that which is right, just, and honorable' (*ibid.*, pp. 176-77).

  [9] *Christianity Today* 11 (November 25, 1966): p. 226. According to the same report, 'Congress highlights included strong demands voiced for racial equality, for identification with the world, and for much wider demonstration of Christian compassion'. The heated debate on social responsibility in the small groups is illustrated by the discussion between Maxey Jarman,

chairman of GENESCO Corporation, and Louis Johnson, a black Detroit Baptist. In answer to Jarman's claim that 'Because individual Christians feel their own individual weakness, they are greatly tempted by the seeming strength of political power to force reforms and improvements among people', Johnson said that the 'law did for me and my people in America what empty and high-powered evangelical preaching never did for one-hundred years'.

[10] Arthur P. Johnston, *The Battle* . . . , p. 221. In all fairness it must be said that several Congress speakers reflected a more integrated view of evangelism and social responsibility than the one Johnston would apparently allow for. Paul Rees, for instance, was reported as affirming that 'It is a terrifying thought that in a presumably free society, abject poverty, family disorder and disintegration, work insecurity and joblessness, can erect psychological barriers to the reception of the Gospel that are as real as the suppression of free speech' (*Christianity Today* 11 (November 25, 1966): p. 227). A similar chord was struck by Samuel H. Moffett, Harold Kuhn, and Michael Cassidy in their respective papers.

[11] There were 1,100 Asian participants from twenty-four different countries. According to Sherwood E. Wirt, 'The first Asia-South Pacific Congress on Evangelism was called into being by Mr. Graham to bring into focus, on the world's largest and most populous continent, the challenge of Berlin 1966. The Singapore meeting was directed by Dr. W. Stanley Mooneyham of the Graham Team, assisted by a staff of Asian and Australian workers' (*Decision* Magazine 10 (February 1969): 9).

[12] *Christ Seeks Asia*, ed. W. S. Mooneyham (Hong Kong: Rock House Publishers, 1969), pp. 120, 122. Kyung Chik Han, chairman of the executive committee of the Congress, also said that 'The church which is alert in helping the poor, the sick, the needy, orphans, widows, and all people—in other words, the church which has most earnest social concern—is always the most thronged with people. When a church becomes the centre of all kinds of services in the community, it is bound to grow. This does not mean that we should help people with a selfishly evangelistic purpose, i.e., merely for the sake of our church's growth, but it does mean that when we are concerned about people's bodily needs and meet their physical needs, we are usually also on the way to saving their souls' (*ibid.*, p. 208).

[13] There were 4,700 delegates from ninety-three denominational traditions, including Southern Baptists and Missouri Synod Lutherans. The proceedings of the Congress were published in *Evangelism Now* (Minneapolis: World Wide Publications, 1970).

[14] Carey Moore, 'Moving!', *Decision* Magazine 10 (December 1969): 6. Moore reports that at Minneapolis evangelicals were also affirming what the Rev. Nelson Trout of the American Lutheran Church evangelism staff put in more colourful terms: 'Evangelism and social action have been like the old steamship trying to cross the English Channel. When it whistled it couldn't move, and when it moved it couldn't whistle'. According to David E. Kucharsky, 'Secular newsmen were surprised to learn the degree of social concern on the part of evangelicals' ('U.S. Congress on Evangelism: "Much Given . . . Much Required",' *Christianity Today* 13 (September 26, 1969): 1148). Kucharsky also reports that 'For many delegates, the high point of the congress was an eloquent, fifty-minute address by Tom Skinner, a 27-year-old black evangelist from New York . . . For many, he related more articulately and meaningfully than anyone else biblical truth to the black revolution. Delegates repeatedly interrupted his speech with applause and at the close gave him a standing ovation' (1149). In his paper on 'Evangelism in a Day of Revolution' (*Christianity Today* 14 (October 1969): 62-68), Leighton Ford argued that 'Love goes beyond justice, and only the saving power of Jesus Christ can produce real love. But love is not a substitute for justice, and since not all men are or will be converted to Christ, and since we Christians have imperfect lives, we have a responsibility to seek justice in society' (67). According to Arthur P. Johnston (*The Battle* . . ., p. 252), 'Ford's call for the Church to become involved in social action as well as evangelism was not supported biblically or theologically'. A conservative critic of the U.S. Congress referred to it later as '90 percent social gospel' (*Christianity Today* 14 (April 10, 1970): 648). Obviously, there were people who expected the U.S. Congress to major on the 'how' of evangelism. Cf. *Christianity Today* 13 (October 25, 1968): 73.

[15] There were 920 delegates from twenty-five countries. The proceedings of the Congress were published in Spanish in *Acción en Cristo para un continente en crisis* (San Jose, Costa Rica:

Editorial Caribe, 1970). For a report on this gathering, see C. Peter Wagner, 'The Latin American Congress of Evangelism', *Pulse* 5 (February 1970): 3-6.

[16] The English translation of this paper was published in *Is Revolution Change?*, ed. Brian Griffiths (London: Inter-Varsity Press, 1972).

[17] Sherwood E. Wirt, '!Vivan los Evangélicos!', *Decision* Magazine 11 (March 1970): 6. Escobar's paper was received with a standing ovation. Cf. 'CLADE Surpasses Expectation' *Pulse* 4 (December 1969): 1-2. Quite evidently, not only Escobar (as Johnston suggests), but the whole Congress 'seemed unwilling to admit the danger of blunting the evangelistic edge which enables the continued growth and influence of Latin American evangelicalism' (Arthur P. Johnston, *The Battle . . .*, p. 256).

[18] There were 1,064 participants from thirty-six countries. The proceedings were published in *Evangelism Alert*, ed. G. W. Kirby (London: World Wide Publications, 1971). According to Bill Yoder, 'Those who expected the European Congress on Evangelism to produce a significant, definite strategy for evangelism on the Continent were certainly disappointed. An attempt was made on the final afternoon to divide the delegates into national groups, but it was too much to expect that within two hours a group of heterogenous delegates, even from one country, could agree on a strategy to reach their country for Christ in the seventies' ('European Congress on Evangelism', *Evangelical Missions Quarterly* 7 (Winter 1972): 113).

[19] Cf. *The Chicago Declaration*, ed. Ronald J. Sider (Carol Stream, Illinois: Creation House, 1974). About fifty people attended the conference. The Declaration was drafted by John Alexander, William Bentley, Frank Gaebelein, Paul Henry, Stephen Mott, William Pannell, Bernard Ramm, Lewis Smedes, and Jim Wallis. In an interview with *Christianity Today* shortly after the Chicago meeting, Billy Graham stated: 'We have a social responsibility and I could identify with most of the recent Chicago Declaration of Evangelical Concern. I think we have to identify with the changing of structures in society and try to do our part' ('Watergate,' *Christianity Today* 18 (January 4, 1974): 394). Evangelicals for Social Action is based at PO Box 76560, Washington, DC 20013, USA.

[20] This Congress, described by *Time* Magazine as 'a formidable forum, possibly the widest-ranging meeting of Christians ever held', had 2,473 participants and about 1,000 observers from 150 nations and 135 Protestant denominations. The proceedings were published in *Let the Earth Hear His Voice*, ed. J. D. Douglas (Minneapolis: World Wide Publications, 1975).

[21] 'From Berlin to Lausanne,' *Christianity Today* 18 (July 5, 1974): 1154. Cf. Paul E. Little, 'Looking Ahead to Lausanne,' *Christianity Today* 18 (November 23, 1973): 208-10. In his keynote address at the beginning of the Congress, however, Billy Graham expressed the hope that Lausanne issue a statement on the relationship between evangelism and social responsibility. Cf. Billy Graham, 'Why Lausanne,' *Christianity Today* 18 (September 13, 1974): 1320.

[22] There were two major papers dealing with this subject, namely, 'Evangelism and the World,' by C. René Padilla, and 'Evangelism and Man's Search for Freedom, Justice and Fulfilment', by Samuel Escobar. Carl F. H. Henry also read an important paper on 'Christian Personal and Social Ethics in Relation to Racism, Poverty, War, and Other Problems' in a commission that drew more than a hundred participants from more than twenty countries. At Lausanne and later, John Stott admitted that his understanding of social responsibility had changed since the Berlin Congress. 'I now see more clearly,' he said, 'that not only the consequences of the commission [in Matthew 28:20] but the actual commission itself must be understood to include social as well as evangelistic responsibility, unless we are to be guilty of distorting the words of Jesus' (*Christian Mission in the Modern World* (London: Falcon, 1975 and Kingsway, 1984), p. 23).

[23] Section 5 of the Covenant, dealing with 'Christian Social Responsibility', was considerably strengthened for the final draft. In it social responsibility was subordinated yet intimately related to evangelism. According to Carl F. H. Henry, this statement is still 'too imprecise to foster significant dialogue and too bland to be biblically adequate' ('The Gospel and Society', *Christianity Today* 18 (September 13, 1974): 1365). For a careful discussion of this whole section of *The Lausanne Covenant*, see Klaus Bockmuehl, *Evangelicals and Social Ethics* (Downers Grove: Inter-Varsity Press, 1979).

[24] This document was published in *International Review of Mission* 63 (October 1974): 574-76; J. D. Douglas (ed.), *Let the Earth Hear His Voice* (World Wide Publications, 1975), p. 1294-1296; Christopher Sugden *Radical Discipleship* (Marshall Morgan and Scott, 1981), p. 172-176; and René Padilla and Christopher Sugden (eds.) *Evangelical Texts on Social Ethics 1973-1984 I* Grove Books (Bramcote, Nottingham, 1983).

[25] Arthur P. Johnston, *The Battle . . .*, p. 147.

[26] *Ibid.*, p. 292.

[27] *Christianity Today* 23 (January 5, 1979): 418-19.

[28] This document is included by Christopher Sugden in *Radical Discipleship* (London: Marshall Morgan & Scott, 1981), pp. 184-89.

[29] This letter was published in *America Latina y la evangelización en los años 80* (Mexico: Fraternidad Teológica Latinoamericana, 1980), pp. xix-xx. For a report on this conference, see Dayton D. Roberts, 'Latin America News Front,' *Latin America Evangelist* 60 (January-February 1980): 18.

[30] This document was published with all the papers in *Lifestyle in the Eighties: An Evangelical Commitment to Simple Lifestyle*, ed. Ronald J. Sider (Philadelphia: The Westminster Press, 1982). For a commentary on it, see Alan Nichols, *An Evangelical Commitment to Simple Lifestyle: Exposition and Commentary*, Lausanne Occasional Papers No. 20 (Wheaton, Illinois: LCWE, 1980).

[31] There were 650 participants, plus 225 observers or staff, from eighty-seven countries. The reports of the 'mini-consultations' have been published in the collection of Lausanne Occasional Papers.

[32] In preparation for the Consultation, a great deal of material was circulated on the strategy concept known as the 'people-groups' or 'homogeneous unit principle' approach to world evangelization. On the very first morning of the conference this approach was outlined by C. Peter Wagner. Wade T. Coggins reports that 'Critics perceived the concept to be heavily based in the social sciences and in western technology. Others perceived it as encouraging segregation and bias, thus contradicting the unity of the body of Christ' (*Evangelical Missions Quarterly* 16 (October 1980): 228).

[33] David J. Bosch, 'In Search of Mission: Reflections on "Melbourne" and "Pattaya" ', *Missionalia* 9 (April 1981): 17. Shortly before the Consultation, Peter Williams, editor of *Churchman*, wrote: 'The reassertion of the conviction that the gospel has a social dimension has been one of the most interesting developments within evangelicalism during the last fifteen years. There is some evidence of a backlash against this understanding, of an attempt to argue that social and political radicalism is incompatible with evangelical belief. It is surely important that Pattaya resist any proposal to go back on the advances made at Lausanne in understanding the relevance of the gospel to the whole man' ('Melbourne and Pattaya, *Churchman* 94 (April-June 1980): 101).

[34] *Christianity Today* 24 (August 8, 1980): 880.

[35] Cf. especially 'Christian Witness to Marxists', 'Christian Witness to Large Cities' and 'Christian Witness to the Urban Poor', Lausanne Occasional Papers (Wheaton, Illinois: LCWE, 1980).

[36] Vinay Samuel and Chris Sugden, 'Let the Word Become Flesh', (A Personal Report on the Consultation on World Evangelisation held at Pattaya, Thailand, June 17-27), *Third Way* September 1980, pp. 5-8 (37 Elm Road, New Malden, Surrey).

[37] This document was included by Andrew Kirk in *A New World Coming: A Fresh Look at the Gospel for Today* (Basingstoke, Hants: Marshall, Morgan & Scott, 1983), pp. 148-51. Out of 185 who signed it in Pattaya, 75 came from the Two-Thirds World. Six of the international co-ordinators of the mini-consultations also signed it.

[38] Those attending the Consultation pledged themselves 'to live under the lordship of Christ', 'to work for the evangelization of the world and to bear witness by word and deed to Christ and his salvation', 'to serve the needy and the oppressed, and in the name of Christ to seek for them relief and justice', 'to love . . . and to identify with them in their needs', 'to study God's Word . . . and to relate it to ourselves and our contemporaries', 'to go wherever Christ may send us', 'to

The Best in Theology

labour to mobilize Christ's people, so that the whole church may take the whole gospel to the whole world', 'to cooperate with all who share with us the true Gospel of Christ', 'to seek the power of the Spirit of Christ', and 'to wait with eagerness for Christ's return, and to be busy in his service until he comes'.

[39] (Exeter: The Paternoster Press, 1982). Fifty participants from twenty-seven countries were present. The papers presented at the Consultation are published in *'In Word and Deed'*, Bruce Nicholls (ed.), (Paternoster Press, 1985).

[40] Wheaton '83 was an international conference on the life and mission of the Church, and it had 300 participants from about sixty countries. The Consultation on the Church in Response to Human Need was one of three 'tracks' and it had about 100 participants. The final document was published in *Transformation* 1 (January-March 1984): 23-28. A study guide by Vinay Samuel and Rob Bellingham was published by Tear Fund Australia as a supplement to *On Being* June 1984 (2 Denham Street, Hawthorn, Victoria 3122 Australia).

[41] For further material the following documents referred to in this process are published in *Evangelical Texts on Social Ethics 1973-1983 I* edited by René Padilla and Christopher Sugden (Grove Books, Bramcote, Nottingham), 1985: The Chicago Declaration, The Statement on Radical Discipleship, The Madras Declaration on Evangelical Social Action, The Pastoral Letter from Lima, The Evangelical Commitment to Simple Lifestyle, The Statement of Concerns from Pattaya. Important companion reading is provided in 'Proclaiming Christ in the Two Thirds World' by Orlando Costas in *Sharing Jesus in the Two Thirds World* edited by Vinay Samuel and Christopher Sugden (Eerdmans, 1984).

[42] John Stott surveys the progress of the consultation towards agreement in 'Seeking Theological Agreement' *Transformation* 1, Jan-March 1984: 21-22.

A PREMILLENNIAL VIEW OF LAW AND GOVERNMENT

NORMAN L. GEISLER
Professor of Systematic Theology
Dallas Theological Seminary

Article from *Bibliotheca Sacra*

This approach to the topic of the Christian and civil law is doctrinal rather than historical or ecclesiastical. The issues that differentiate one evangelical view from another are more clearly focused this way. The crucial difference of viewpoints regarding Christian involvement in the political arena is more closely associated with one's view of how the present kingdom of God relates to the future kingdom than with what one's ecclesiastical tradition is. And the clearest line of demarcation on the relationship of the present and future kingdoms is between the premillennial and postmillennial views.

Postmillenarians believe that the church is obligated to usher in the kingdom. They believe that the future kingdom (millennium) "is to be brought about by forces now active in the world."[1] Hence it is understandable that their view manifests the closest relationship between church and state, between God and government. On the other hand premillenarians hold to a discontinuity between the present kingdom and the future kingdom (which only Christ will personally inaugurate). Hence they manifest less identity between the kingdom of God and civil politics. Amillenarians fall somewhere in between. But on the crucial point of whether there is continuity between the present and the future kingdom, amillenarians most often side with the premillenarians in answering no.

N.B. DEFINED NOT BY CHRONOLOGY, BUT BY REL. of PRES. TO FUTURE.

History of the Premillennial View

The extrabiblical roots of premillennialism go back to the first century. "Among earlier writers the belief was held by the authors of the Epistle of Barnabas [4, 15], the Shepherd, the Second Epistle of Clement, by Papias, Justin, and by some of the Ebionites, and Cerinthus."[2] There are no references to the millennial belief in the writings of Clement of Rome, Ignatius, Polycarp, Tatian, Athenagoras, or Theophilus. But even Bethune-Baker admits that "we are not justified in arguing from their silence that they did not hold it."[3]

The premillennial view was also shared by Irenaeus, Melito, Hippolytus, Tertullian, and Lactantius.[4] In fact the Gnostics were the first to reject the premillennial view. They were followed by Caius, Origen, and Dionysius, all of whom engaged in allegorical interpretation of the Bible.

Eusebius recorded the millennial beliefs of Cerinthus, saying that he believed that "after the resurrection there would be an earthly kingdom of Christ."[5] Of Papias, Eusebius wrote, "He says there would be a certain millennium after the resurrection and that there would be a corporeal reign of Christ on this very earth."[6]

Justin Martyr declared, "I and others, who are right-minded Christians on all points, are assured that there will be a resurrection of the dead, and a thousand years in Jerusalem, which will then be built, adorned, and enlarged, [as] the prophets Ezekiel and Isaiah and others declare."[7]

Tertullian wrote, "We confess that a kingdom is promised to us upon earth, only in another state of existence; inasmuch as it will be after the resurrection for a thousand years in the divinely built city of Jerusalem."[8]

The premillennial view continued strong until the fourth century when it was at first embraced by Augustine. However, he later gave it up in an apparent overreaction to some extreme form of chiliasm. But Augustine never undertook to refute the premillennial view. He even conceded that it would not be objectionable as long as the premillenarians did not "assert that those who then rise again shall enjoy the leisure of immoderate carnal banquets."[9]

Augustine's reaction to premillennialism prevailed in medieval Roman Catholicism up to the Reformation, in which the primary concern was with soteriology, not eschatology. During the Reformation the premillennial view was strongly represented by the Swiss brethren such as Conrad Grebel, Felix Manz, and George Blaurock. The Dutch Anabaptist, Meno Simons (d. 1561), was also premillennial. The German Calvinist, Johann Heinrich Alsted (1588-1638), returned to the premillennial view of the early church fathers in his book *The Beloved City* (1627), which caused the learned Anglican scholar, Joseph Mede (1586-1638), to become a premillenarian. In America the millennial position was forwarded by Cotton Mather (1691) who held that "there will be a Time, when Jerusalem shall be Literally Rebuilt, and People all over the world shall be under the Influence of that Holy City."[10] John Edwards (1637-1716) believed in six dispensations and a thousand-year reign of Christ, albeit a spiritual one. But crucial for this study is Isaac Watts (1674-1748), who was not only premillennial but also a forerunner of dispensationalism. He outlined six dispensations plus a millennium which correspond exactly to those of the Scofield Bible.[11] He also referred to his view of civil government.

Johann H. Bengel, Isaac Newton, and Joseph Priestly carried on the premillennial view in the 18th century. In the 19th century Edward Irving of the Church of Scotland fostered a widespread interest in premillennialism. The latter part of the 19th century witnessed a full-blown form of dispensational premillennialism in the writings of John Nelson Darby (1800-1882).[12]

At the turn of the century C. I. Scofield, through his enormously popular reference Bible, had a wide influence on American premillennialism. And through Lewis Sperry Chafer and Dallas Theological Seminary (established in 1924), dispensational premillennialism has spread throughout the world.

Premillennialism dominates a broad section of American theological schools (many of which are dispensational as well). These include Bethel Theological Seminary, Covenant Theological Seminary, Dallas Theological Seminary, Denver Conservative Baptist Seminary, Liberty Baptist Seminary, Talbot Theological Seminary, Temple Baptist Seminary, Western Conservative Baptist Seminary, Wheaton Graduate School of Theology, and most Bible colleges. To say the least, the premillennial view has an early and venerable history and is perhaps the dominant evangelical view in the United States today. It is important then to look at how premillenarianism, in contrast to postmillennialism, affects one's view toward law and government.

The Postmillennial Position

Although the early American tradition was largely dominated by postmillenarians, few evangelicals today hold that view. Hence it is a misdirection for contemporary premillenarians (and amillenarians) to call America back to its so-called Christian foundations. For whatever Christian influence there was in early America was largely postmillennial, not premillennial (or amillennial). But the unfounded optimism of the postmillennial view has been severely undermined by the reality of centuries of history since then.

In fact today not a single evangelical seminary is committed to postmillennialism. The strongest postmillennial influence in America today comes from the tiny Chalcedon group who are disciples of Rousas J. Rushdoony. These reconstructionists and theonomists, such as Greg Bahnsen, Gary North, and others, believe that Christians are obligated to set up a Christian government in America. As Rushdoony put it, "the saints must prepare to take over the world's government and its courts."[13]

Rushdoony opposes democracy, saying, "democracy requires identification with the continuum, and such identification necessitates a surrender of all exclusive and aristocratic concepts."[14] He believes that democracy is opposed to Christianity, insisting that "the choice, ultimately, is the basic one between democracy and traditional Christian theology."[15] More than this, "supernatural Christianity is basically and radically antidemocratic."[16] Indeed, Rushdoony believes, "democracy is the great love of the failures and cowards of life, and involves a hatred of differences."[17]

Rushdoony is equally opposed to equality, saying, "The only conclusion of such a course of action is bankruptcy, both moral and financial bankruptcy, because the very idea of law is against equality."[18] In fact "equality is a highsounding but impossible dream."[19] Rushdoony actually favors a kind of caste system, contending that "no society has ever existed without class and caste lines."[20]

Bahnsen carries through consistently Rushdoony's idea of theonomy and concludes that Christians should still practice the Old Testament law today, including capital punishment for homosexuals and rebellious children. He concludes "that there is a continuity between the law of God in the Older Testament and New Testament morality: Christ has confirmed every jot and tittle of the law."[21] This means that the state must be based on the Bible. For "the doctrine of the state presented by Paul in Romans 13 is a *reaffirmation of the essential Older Testament conception of the civil magistrate."*[22]

While most amillenarians disavow the extremes of postmillennialism, some have come perilously close to setting up their own kingdom. Calvin's Geneva is a case in point. The Roman Catholic Church, holding an amillennial Augustinian view, has also manifested this propensity from Constantine to this century. However, unlike the postmillennial view, nothing inherent in amillennialism demands that Christians politically prepare for the setting up of Christ's kingdom. On the contrary, most amillenarians look to the future return of Christ and to His eternal reign as discontinuous with the present.[23] Hence they do not view their present social involvement as directly related to the emergence of the future kingdom of God. In this respect amillenarians are more like premillenarians and have thereby often escaped some of the extremes of postmillennialism.

The Premillennial Contribution

Although premillennialism does not have the inherent extreme which postmillennialism has, some premillenarians have gone to an opposite extreme on social and political issues. Some have urged believers not to polish the brass rails on the sinking social ship. Rather, they urge Christians to be engaged in "saving souls." A famous contemporary premillennial evangelist quips that he has no time to clean up the cesspool because he is too busy fishing (for souls) in it. Early this century I. M. Haldeman insisted that "trying to save the world by socialism was like cleaning and decorating the staterooms of a sinking ship."[24]

Most premillenarians, however, have been deeply involved in social matters. In spite of his unfounded earlier conclusion to the contrary, Timothy Smith has subsequently recognized the important role of premillennial thought in social renewal.[25] This was true of earlier fundamentalists and evangelicals, as well as contemporary ones. A. C. Dixon, editor of *The Fundamentals* (1910-1915), even went so far as to encourage Christians to organize political parties "for the carrying forward of any great reform."[26] James Gray, president of Moody Bible Institute, and William Riley, an influential Baptist pastor from Minneapolis, both had strong social emphases in the early 20th century, as did A. J. Gordon of Boston. Wheaton College has also had a strong premillennial influence in social and cultural areas.

Much of the strongest influence for premillennial social involvement in contemporary America has been and is being generated by leaders such as Francis Schaeffer, Jerry Falwell, Timothy LaHaye, and Pat Robertson.

What is of interest here is to explore the genius of premillennialism, especially as it relates to law and government. In order to do this, attention is drawn to the early roots of the modern premillennial movement, especially to some of the dispensationalists. Several characteristic features of premillennial dispensationalism enabled it to avoid the extremes into which the postmillenarians and even some amillenarians have fallen. Three features combine to form this moderating view between noninvolvement on the one hand and setting up a kind of theocracy or theonomy on the other.

The belief that only Christ's return will bring in the Kingdom

Premillennialists believe that there will be no true theocracy or theonomy until Christ returns to earth. Hence they are relieved of the unnecessary and heavy burden postmillenarians have placed on themselves to bring in the kingdom. Actually this postmillennial idea is humanistic at root. Indeed it can be argued that early American postmillennial optimism paved the way for Darwinism[27] and Unitarianism, from which modern American secular humanism emerged. Postmillennial optimism overlooks the depravity of man and attempts by human resources to bring in the millennium without divine intervention. Indeed Marxism is an atheistic form of postmillennialism, as are other humanistic utopias.

To bring in the kingdom of God, postmillennialists realize that they must Christianize the world. Hence they are infected with the unfounded optimism that eventually "evil in all its many forms will be reduced to negligible proportions" and "the race, as a race, will be saved."[28] Even Warfield expressed this same incurable optimism characteristic of postmillennialism when he wrote, "It is solely by reasoning that it [Christianity] has come thus far on its way to its kingship. And it is solely by reasoning that it will put all its enemies under its feet."[29]

The early 20th-century Scottish theologian, James Orr, also believed in the evolutionary development of the race to the point of millennial perfection.[30] This is why, contrary to what one might expect, the early fundamentalists were favorable to Darwinism, while the liberals opposed it.[31] They saw natural selection as a divinely appointed natural means for the biological and social evolution of the race. American political aspirations for the "New Deal," the "Great Society," and the like are secular hangovers of the Puritan postmillennial hopes for a New Jerusalem.

Premillenarians, on the other hand, do not believe the millennium will come about by any political process continuous with the present. They insist rather on a divine, cataclysmic, and supernatural inauguration of the reign of Christ on earth. This relieves premillennialists of any divine duty to Christianize the world. Their duty is to be salt, light, and to do good to all men. But they do not need to set up a theonomy. They can be content with a democracy or any government that allows freedom to preach the gospel. For, unlike postmillennialists, premillenarians do not need to Christianize all nations, they need to evangelize all people (Matt. 28:18-20). Their obligation is not to bring all men to Christ, but to bring Christ to all men. And their obligation to government is to promote a good and just government (1 Tim. 2:1-4), not necessarily a uniquely Christian one.

The premillennial position bears no obligation to make distinctly Christian laws. It works rather to assure that the laws are not anti-Christian. Along with this it recognizes that the unregenerate cannot live out the demands of God's laws. It believes that society must be changed from the inside out, not from the outside in. Premillennialists believe that transformation must come by evangelization, not by legislation. This leads to a second characteristic of premillennialism.

The belief in religious pluralism

Premillennialists, unlike postmillennialists, do not attempt to set up a distinctly Christian government; they work rather for good government. Premillenarians need not work for Christian civil laws but only for fair ones. Their effort is not to achieve religious superiority for Christianity, but religious equality before the law for all religions. In short, the premillennial position is compatible with a true pluralism. It fits well with the First Amendment of the United States Constitution which is against the state's establishing (or preferring) one religion over another.

Postmillenarians, on the other hand, are uncomfortable with religious pluralism. They sometimes concede religious liberty to others under their Christian-dominated state, but even this has its limits. In early America there was discrimination against those who chose not to be religious. The Puritans persecuted those who would not conform. Many states required belief in God (theism) as a prerequisite for public office, something that lingered on the law books into the 1940s. This is consistent with the postmillennial need to establish God's rule on earth. Premillenarians, however, can await that day and meanwhile can be content with true religious (and irreligious) pluralism.

The Ten Commandments are a case in point. Postmillennial theonomy, and its stepchild biblionomy, demands that the Ten Commandments are the basis for civil law. This, however, is impossible if true freedom of religion is to be allowed. For the first commandment(s) demands allegiance to a monotheistic God as opposed to all false gods or idols. If the civil law of the United States followed the Ten Commandments, then there would be no freedom of religion for polytheists, Taoists, Hindus, Buddhists, secular humanists, or atheists. So making the Bible the basis for civil law is a contradiction to freedom of religion such as exists in the United States today. But if the Bible is not the basis for civil law, then what is? This leads to the next characteristic of the premillennial contribution.

God's revelation in nature is the basis for civil government

While premillennialists, especially dispensationalists, do not believe that Christians are living under the Old Testament Law today, this in no way means they are antinomian. To be sure, dispensational premillenarians insist that the Old Testament Law was given only to the Jews and not to Gentiles.[32] And they argue that the Old Testament Law has been done away by Christ (2 Cor. 3:7-13; Gal 3:24-25). However, most premillenarians recognize that God has not left Himself without a witness in that He has revealed a moral law in the hearts and consciences of all men (Rom. 2:14-15).

Isaac Watts, an early dispensationalist, is exemplary of this position. Building on the natural law ethic of Richard Hooker, an Anglican, who followed Thomas Aquinas, Watts argued that "the design of civil government is to secure the persons, the properties, the just liberty and peace of mankind from the invasions and injuries of their neighbours."[33] Further, neither "the things of religion, nor the affairs of a future state come within its cognizance."[34] Nevertheless, "civil government is an ordinance of God, and appointed by him according to the light of reason. Thus government itself is a necessary thing in this world, and a natural moral institution of God among persons of all sorts of religion, whether heathen, turks, or Christians to preserve them in perfect peace."[35] According to Watts, government should not alter any of these religions, "nor do any of these religions alter the nature of civil government."[36]

Government is not based on special revelation, such as the Bible. It is based on God's general revelation to all men. Thus Watts avoided the extremes of theonomy and antinomianism by an appeal to natural law. He followed John Locke in "showing that the Jewish government was a theocracy wherein God, even *Jehovah, the one true God*, was their political king, and therefore the acknowledgement of any other God was treason against the state; but it was never so in any other nation upon earth."[37] Since civil law is not based on God's special revelation, it is tolerant even of idolatry.

Thus civil law, based as it is in natural moral law, lays no specifically religious obligation on man. For "everyman, both governor and governed, ought to have full liberty to worship God in that special way and manner which his own conscience believes to be of divine appointment."[38] But "this is a personal obligation which natural conscience, or the light of reason, which *is the candle of the Lord* within us, lays on every individual person among mankind" and "peculiar religion does not break in upon the just rights or the peace of our neighbors."[39]

So "the supreme power of any state, has no right to impose the profession or practice of any one peculiar religion upon the people."[40] In short, "the power of civil government reaches no further than the preservation of the natural and civil welfare, rights and properties of mankind with regard to this world, and has nothing to do with religion further than this requires."[41] Watts is emphatic in his conclusion that "the gospel of Christ does not pretend to erect a *kingdom of this world*, and therefore it alters nothing in the nature of civil government; but leaves *to* Caesar the things that are Caesar's; Matt. 22:21."[42]

Based on this general revelation, man enters into social contracts in which "he engages himself with his powers and capacities to defend and preserve the peace, order, and government of the society." Indeed "the very reason of man and the nature of things shew us the necessity of such agreements."[43]

The civil law, however, does have a moral basis in what Watts called variously, "nature," "laws of nature," "natural rights," "natural conscience," "reason," "principles of reason," "light of reason," "divine revelation," "candle of the Lord," and "ordinance of God."[44] For Watts the natural moral law includes such things as honesty, justice, truth, gratitude, goodness, honor, and faithfulness to superiors. The laws of nature also include personal duties such as sobriety, temperance, frugality, and industry.[45] In brief they include the kinds of things addressed in the second table of the Mosaic Law (attitudes and actions toward men) but not the first table of the Law (those toward God). These are the same kinds of things C. S. Lewis listed as part of the natural law which he found in all major cultures.[46]

While dispensationalists' views are not monolithic on this point, major contemporary proponents are in general agreement on the nature of general revelation. This provides a true pluralism in the present form of the kingdom before Christ returns to earth. Chafer quoted with approval *The Scofield Reference Bible* (p. 16) when he wrote, "the Christian is called upon, then, to recognize [existing] human government as of God (Rom. 13:1-7; 1 Pet. 2:13-17; cf. Matt. 22:21)."[47] Chafer balanced this by the recognition that "in Luke 4:5-6 it is clearly indicated that the governments of this world system (cf. Matt. 4:8-9) are under Satan's authority."[48] So the present form of the kingdom is "a mixed bag." There are good fish and bad fish, wheat and tares.

For these premillenarians the present (mystery) form of the kingdom (Matt. 13) is different from the future (messianic) form of the kingdom. Both Scofield[49] and Chafer[50] recognize that a real pluralism will exist in the present kingdom until Christ comes. Scofield wrote, "the parable of the wheat and tares is not a description of the world, but of that which professes to be the kingdom."[51] Chafer is more precise when he noted that "the kingdom of heaven is the rule of God in the earth, [and] it is now present to the extent to which He is exercising authority over the affairs of the *cosmos*."[52] But he adds, "certainly this does not depict a regenerated world. It clearly pictures an outcalled people [the church] together with the full ripening of iniquity in the unregenerate portion of humanity."[53]

According to dispensationalists <u>the wheat and the tares must be allowed</u> <u>to grow together in this present age</u>. Religious pluralism must prevail. Only when Christ comes will He (not Christians) pluck out the wheat. Meanwhile believers must be content to plant and cultivate wheat, not to cut down tares. This does not mean that there is no common moral basis for society. Most dispensationalists recognize a general revelation for all men (Rom. 1:18-20; 2:14-15). Chafer even goes so far as to claim that this general revelation or "natural theology" is part of the data (along with the Bible) of systematic theology.[54] As Witmer noted "the Law is not to be found only on tablets of stone and included in the writings of Moses; it is also inscribed in their [moral Gentiles'] hearts and is reflected in their actions, consciences, and thoughts."[55]

Postmillennialists reject this conclusion, insisting that Christians must begin to establish Christ's kingdom now before He returns. Hence postmillenarians must work to eliminate true politically-encouraged religious pluralism. Herein lies the difference between premillennialists and postmillennialists in their views on government. And it has great relevance to the kind of involvement called for in the present social and political arena. Postmillenarians work to make a Christian America. <u>Premillenarians work</u> <u>for a truly free America.</u>

Combining these two features of non-theocracy (or non-theonomy) and natural law, premillennial dispensationalism makes a unique contribution to the relationship of Christians to civil government. For it avoids on the one hand the need to establish a kingdom, and on the other hand it avoids an antinomian basis for civil government. By denying the postmillennial theocratic basis for civil government the premillennial position avoids destroying religious freedom, and by basing civil government in the general moral law of God, it avoids destroying any moral basis for society.

A word of warning is called for here for premillennialists. It is disastrous for them to deny any general moral-law basis for civil government, as some have done.[56] For then society would be left without an ultimate moral ground and would be subject to political tyranny and social pragmatism. This is contrary to the general revelation of Romans 2:14-15 and to the command in 1 Timothy 2:2 to pray (and work) for a godly, tranquil life.

A Case in Point: Civil Disobedience

The premillennial view of government may now be applied to the question of civil disobedience. This will serve to clarify a consistent premillennial view from a consistent postmillennial view on a hotly debated contemporary issue. Many evangelicals are calling for civil disobedience, even revolution, against a government. Francis Schaeffer, for example, insisted that Christians should disobey government when "any office commands that which is contrary to the word of God."[57] He even urges a blood revolution, if necessary, against any government that makes such laws. He explains that "in a fallen world, force in some form will always be necessary."[58]

Schaeffer's personal beliefs were premillennial. Nonetheless it appears that in actual practice at that point his views were postmillennial. It is interesting to note that Schaeffer's son, Franky, who is leading social activism based on his father's principles, has given up his father's premillennial view. This is consistent. For if one takes Francis Schaeffer's suggestions seriously, then *all* civil laws must be based on the Bible—at least none contrary to it are allowed. This would be a biblionomy, that is, a Bible-based civil government. But nowhere in the Bible is God's judgment of the nations based on His special written revelation (the Bible). Rather, it is always based on general principles of goodness and justice known to all men by general revelation (cf. Amos 1; Obad. 1; Jonah 3:8-10; Nahum 2). Furthermore there was God-ordained civil government (cf. Gen. 9:6) long before there was a Bible.

What then is the essential difference between the premillennial and the postmillennial views regarding Christian obedience to government? The former can be summarized as follows:

Civil government is ordained by God for all men
According to Scripture civil law is not based in the *Christian* mandate to preach the gospel to all nations (Matt. 28:18-20) but in the *cultural* mandate to subdue all things in creation (Gen. 1:28). This was reinforced by God by ordaining the sword for capital punishment of capital crimes (Gen. 9:6).

The God-ordained nature of human government is clearly spelled out in Romans 13:1-7 (and in 1 Pet. 2:13-14). Several facts stand out in the Romans passage.

First, even oppressive governments have God-ordained authority, such as Nero's Rome, which is referred to in this passage. Indeed, Nero was called a "minister of God" (Rom. 13:4).

Second, the reference in Romans 13 is to de facto governments (ἐξου-σίαις) not de jure ones. That is, the legitimate government is the one in power. According to Romans 13:1 the "existing (οὖσαι) governments are ordained of God." Thus Christians (and all men) are to "submit" to them (Rom. 13:1) and to "obey" them (Titus 3:1).

Third, there is no conditional clause in Romans 13 such as "obey governments *only if they are just.*" Likewise the command to pay taxes (Rom. 13:7) is not accompanied by any condition such as "pay taxes only *if the government is using one's money for moral causes.*" Even as the Princeton theologian Charles Hodge's comment on this passage indicates, "we are to obey all that is in actual authority over us, whether their authority be legitimate or usurped, whether they are just or unjust."[59]

Disobedience is allowed only when government usurps God's authority
Since Romans 13:1 notes that all authority comes from God, it is assumed

here (and made clear elsewhere) that human authority cannot usurp God's authority over the individual. Hence disobedience to government becomes necessary when the government usurps the authority of God. Indeed, there are numerous examples in Scripture of divinely approved disobedience to human government. The following is a complete list of circumstances when God clearly approved of believers' disobedience to civil law:

1. When it does not allow worship of God (Exod. 5:1).
2. When it commands believers to kill innocent lives (Exod. 1:15-21).
3. When it commands that God's servants be killed (1 Kings 18:1-4).
4. When it commands believers to worship idols (Dan. 3).
5. When it commands believers to pray only to a man (Dan. 6).
6. When it forbids believers to propagate the gospel (Acts 4:17-19).
7. When it commands believers to worship a man (Rev. 13).

All these cases have this in common: whereas believers are always to obey government when it takes its place *under* God, they should never obey it when it takes the place *of* God. In short, governments and laws can *permit* evil but they cannot *command* it. For example, they can *allow* citizens to worship idols but they cannot *insist* that all do so. The authority of government ends where the conscience of the believer begins.

The Bible places limits on how one can disobey government
There are biblical limits on how and when believers can disobey government. First, disobedience is not allowed simply because the government *limits* religious freedom. Rather, government must *negate* freedom. All laws limit freedom. It is the nature of law to draw lines so that one may know where his freedom ends and another person's begins. Thus government regulations regarding zoning, parking, and safety are not in themselves oppressive and should be obeyed, even though they limit the freedom a church has. But if the government mandates teachings or practices contrary to Scripture, the Christian should refuse to comply. That is, the government must eliminate religious freedom, not simply regulate it, before a believer should disobey the government.

Second, Christian noncompliance to oppressive laws should be a *refusal*, but not a *revolt*. That is, their disobedience should be *passive*, not *active*. They can be insubmissive, but they must not be insubordinate. Even when a believer cannot submit to the law, he must be willing to submit to the consequence of that law. Peter refused to stop preaching Jesus, but he did not refuse to go to prison (Acts 5). Daniel refused to pray to the king, but he did not refuse to go to the lion's den (Dan. 6). And the three Hebrew young men would not bow, but they were willing to burn (Dan. 3). A good example of this attitude comes from the Hessian Anabaptists (c. 1538 A.D.). Having been accused of sedition, their response was: "These who are not obedient to the authorities . . . should be punished with the sword by the imperial edict. We do not want to be disobedient to worldly authorities. If we have done evil, then we accept the adequate judgment."[60] This same attitude was true of many Anabaptists in the 16th and 17th centuries in Switzerland, Germany, Austria, Moravia, and the Netherlands.

?!
A NON-ISSUE

To contemporize the principle, Christians should refuse to kill a human life by abortion, even if the government commands it. But they should not revolt against a government (or withhold taxes) from a government which allows abortion. Of course they may work legally to change the abortion law. But commanding Christians to have an abortion, and simply permitting non-Christians to do so, are two different things. Or to change the illustration, commanding a Christian to worship an idol is oppressive, but laws merely permitting others to worship idols are not oppressive and should not be overthrown.

The Israelites *refused* to obey Pharaoh's command but they did not *revolt* against him. They followed a "love it or leave it" policy with Egypt, but they did not attack it. Nowhere in Scripture is the sword given to the citizens against the state. Rather, the sword is given to the government to use on the governed (Gen. 9:6; Rom. 13:4). The only legitimate use of the sword for citizens is to protect themselves against other citizens (Exod. 22:4). Jesus said, "those who take up the sword will perish by the sword" (Matt. 26:52). Revolutions in Scripture are not condoned, including Korah's, Absalom's, and Rehoboam's. The revolution of those who killed wicked Queen Athaliah and installed Joash was a special divinely approved event in order to preserve the blood line of the Messiah (2 Chron. 22:10; 23:3). Therefore it cannot serve as a basis for other revolutions any more than the theocratic command for Israel to slaughter the Canaanites can be used to promote the genocide of

JESUS & the ZEALOTS ?

a country today. In fact the Bible forbids even associating with revolutionaries, saying, "My son, fear the Lord and the king: Do not associate with those who are given to change" (Prov. 24:21). Keil and Delitzsch describe those named here as "dissidents, oppositionists, or revolutionaries."[61]

By contrast to this premillennial perspective, it is consistent with postmillennialism to use arms to overthrow one's government if it falls short of God's demands. As a theocracy Israel fought for God, and if the church assumes Israel's role, as postmillenarians claim it does, then it is consistent to claim that the church also assumes the use of Israel's sword. And if the sword can be used to promote the kingdom of God on earth, why should a postmillenarian, who believes he is commissioned to promote God's kingdom rule in present civil government, refuse to use the sword?

Herein lies the crucial difference between the premillennial and postmillennial perspectives on the Christian's relationship to civil government. Premillenarians can promote true religious pluralism; postmillenarians cannot. Premillenarians can await Christ's coming with His armies to set up His kingdom (Rev. 19:11; 2 Thess. 1:7-9); postmillenarians cannot. For the latter view themselves as the army of God to usher in Christ's kingdom here and now. This principal difference has a wide range of ramifications for contemporary conflicts between church and state.

The genius of the premillennial view is that while it avoids a repressive theonomist perspective, it nonetheless provides a common moral basis for civil law in God's general revelation to all men. In this way Christian social and political action (e.g. to change abortion laws), can be performed without hesitation because such is based on a common moral law revealed to all men. On the other hand, Christians should be careful to resist any attempt of government to provide a religious advantage to any one religion over another, even if it is theirs.

But in the postmillennial view the church assumes the role of Old Testament Israel, not of a distinctly new group called out of the world. Hence there is no sufficient reason why it should not set up a society like Israel's which is based on biblical principles (that is, a biblionomy). This same danger is inherent in the amillennial view too, since it believes that the New Testament church carries on the mission of Old Testament Israel. There is, however, one difference that saves amillennialism from the extremes of postmillennialism. Amillenarians believe that there is a future kingdom (the eternal state) which does not grow naturally out of the present one, but which will be inaugurated only by Christ. It is this similarity with the premillennial view which saves them in part from the need to set up a kingdom here and now, though not all amillenarians have made this connection. But premillennialism, in contrast to the liabilities of both postmillennialism and amillennialism, can avoid the extremes of social neglect on the one hand and of theonomy on the other hand. Thus premillennialism is uniquely capable of providing a moral basis for society (in general revelation) without denying religious freedom to any by setting up a monotheistic theonomy or biblionomy.

Notes

[1] Loraine Boettner, "Postmillennialism," in *The Meaning of the Millennium: Four Views,* ed. Robert G. Clouse (Downers Grove, IL: InterVarsity Press, 1977), p. 117.

[2] J. F. Bethune-Baker, *An Introduction to the Early History of Christian Doctrine* (London: Methuen & Co., 1942), p. 69.

[3] Ibid.

[4] Ibid., p. 70.

[5] Eusebius Pamphilus, *The Ecclesiastical History of Eusebius Pamphilus* (Grand Rapids: Baker Book House, 1955), p. 113.

[6] Ibid., p. 126

[7] Justin Martyr, *Dialogue with Trypho* (*The Ante-Nicene Fathers*, ed. Alexander Roberts and James Donaldson, 9 vols. [Grand Rapids: Wm. B. Eerdmans Publishing Co., 1977] 1:239).

[8] Tertullian, *Against Marcion* (*The Ante-Nicene Fathers*, 3:342).

[9] Augustine, *City of God* (*The Nicene and Post-Nicene Fathers*, ed. Philip Schaff, 14 vols. [Grand Rapids: Wm. B. Eerdmans Publishing Co., 1956], 2:426).

[10] Cotton Mather, *Things to Be Look'd For* (New England: N. p., 1691), 1.4.

[11] Isaac Watts, *The Works of the Rev. Isaac Watts, D.D.,* 7 vols. (Leeds: Edward Baines, n.d.)2:625.

[12] John Darby, *The Collected Writings of J. N. Darby*, ed. William Kelly, 34 vols. (reprint, Sunbury, PA: Believers Bookshelf, 1971) 2:568-73.

[13] Rousas J. Rushdoony, "Government and the Christian," *The Rutherford Institute* 1 (July-August 1984):7.

[14] Rousas J. Rushdoony, *The Messianic Character of American Education* (Phillipsburg, NJ: Presbyterian and Reformed Publishing Co., 1963), p. 149.

[15] Ibid., p. 198.

[16] Ibid., p. 157.

[17] Rousas J. Rushdoony, *Thy Kingdom Come* (Phillipsburg, NJ: Presbyterian and Reformed Publishing Co., 1971), p. 39.

[18] Rousas J. Rushdoony, *Bread upon the Waters* (Nutley, NJ: Craig Press, 1969), p. 87.

[19] Ibid.

[20] Rousas J. Rushdoony, *The Foundations of Social Order* (Phillipsburg, NJ: Presbyterian and Reformed Publishing Co., 1968), p. 193.

[21] Greg L. Bahnsen, *Theonomy in Christian Ethics* (Nutley, NJ: Craig Press, 1979), p. 398.

[22] Ibid.

[23] Anthony A. Hoekema, "Amillennialism," in *The Meaning of the Millennium: Four Views,* p. 150.

[24] I. M. Haldeman, *The Mission of the Church in the World* (New York: Book Stall, 1917), pp. 280-87.

[25] Timothy L. Smith, *Revivalism and Social Reform* (Baltimore: Johns Hopkins University Press, 1980), pp. 257-58.

[26] See George M. Marsden, *Fundamentalism and American Culture: The Shaping of Twentieth-Century Evangelicalism: 1870-1925* (Oxford: Oxford University Press, 1980), pp. 88-89.

[27] James R. Moore, *The Post-Darwinian Controversies* (Cambridge: Cambridge University Press, 1979).

[28] Boettner, "Postmillennialism," pp. 118, 123.

[29] Benjamin B. Warfield, "Introduction," in Francis R. Beattie, *Apologetics* (Richmond, VA: Presbyterian Committee of Publication, n.d.), 1:26.

[30] James Orr, *The Christian View of God and the World* (Grand Rapids: Wm. B. Eerdmans Publishing Co., 1948), chap. 9.

[31] Moore, *The Post-Darwinian Controversies*.

[32] Lewis Sperry Chafer, *Systematic Theology,* 8 vols. (Dallas, TX: Dallas Seminary Press, 1947), 4:234-43.

[33] Isaac Watts, *The Works of the Rev. Isaac Watts, D.D.,* 3:328.

[34] Ibid., 3:330.

[35] Ibid.

[36] Ibid.

[37] Ibid., 3:336.

[38] Ibid., 3:343.

[39] Ibid.

[40] Ibid., 3:356.

[41] Ibid., 3:361.

[42] Ibid.

[43] Ibid., 3:329-30.

[44] Ibid., 3:328-30, 334, 341, 343.

[45] Ibid., 3:334-35.

[46] C. S. Lewis, *The Abolition of Man* (New York: Macmillan Co., 1947), pp. 95-121.

[47] Chafer, *Systematic Theology*, 7:177.

[48] Ibid.

[49] C. I. Scofield, *The Scofield Reference Bible* (New York: Oxford University Press, 1967), pp. 1014-15.

[50] Chafer, *Systematic Theology,* 7:177.

[51] Scofield, *The Scofield Reference Bible*, p. 1015.

[52] Chafer, *Systematic Theology*, 5:352.

[53] Ibid.

[54] Ibid., 1:4-5.

[55] John A. Witmer, "Romans," in *The Bible Knowledge Commentary, New Testament Edition*, ed. John F. Walvoord and Roy B. Zuck (Wheaton, IL: SP Publications, Victor Books, 1983), p. 446.

[56] J. N. Darby, *Exposition of the Epistle to the Romans* (London: G. Morrish, n.d.), p. 25.

[57] Francis A. Schaeffer, *A Christian Manifesto* (Westchester, IL: Crossway Books, 1981), p. 90.

[58] Ibid., p. 107

[59] Charles Hodge, *Commentary on the Epistle to the Romans* (1886: reprint, Grand Rapids: Wm. B. Eerdmans Publishing Co., 1947), p. 406.

[60] G. Franz, ed., *Urkundliche Quellen zur hessischen Reformationsgeschichte* 4: Wiedertäuferakten 1527-1626, trans. Timothy Dalzell (Marburg: Waldeck, 1951), p. 179.

[61] C. F. Keil and F. Delitzsch, "Proverbs," in *Commentary on the Old Testament in Ten Volumes* (reprint, [25 vols. in 10]; Grand Rapids: Wm. B. Eerdmans Publishing Co., 1975), 6:138.

CLEAR, UNDERSTANDABLE, BUT —

BEGS MANY QUESTIONS RE: GOV'T PROBS.
FEW ARE PURE POSTMILLENIALISTS
FEW ARE ENTIRELY CONSISTENT PREMILLENIALISTS.

BETTER: DROP the TERMS, DISCUSS QUES. of
RELA. TO THIS WORLD
  — i) N.T.
  — ii) THEO.
  — iii) CONTEMP. IMPLICAS.

A GUIDE TO DEVOTIONAL READING

JAMES M. HOUSTON
Professor of Spiritual Theology
Regent College

From the series *Classics of Faith and Devotion*
Multnomah Press

"Wilt thou love God, as He thee! then digest,
My soul, this wholesome meditation,
How God the Spirit by angels waited on
In heaven, doth make His Temple in thy heart."
John Donne, *Holy Sonnet* 15

If someone asked you if you were a "devotionalist" today, you would be excused for not knowing what he meant. If someone talked about being devotionally-minded, you might raise an eyebrow in wonder.

This century is possibly the first one in which action has been emphasized and valued more than contemplation. Today we *do* things. We think contemplation wastes time, produces nothing, and bumps awkwardly into our schedules. Devotional reading is a questionable priority for most successful people today.

But are we "successful" Christians if we are so busy organizing and propagating the Christian faith that we really do not know God personally—or intimately? Christian devotional reading helps us find intimate union with God. What is its motivation? To love God with all our heart, mind, and will.

Devotional Reading—A Great Awakening

The writer of Ecclesiastes realized that God set eternity within our hearts.[1] Augustine saw that God made man for Himself, and our hearts are restless till they find their rest in Him. This eternal yearning forms the basis of devotion.

We are created with infinite longings. We may try to conceal them and hide behind lesser values such as the recognition of beauty, or the desire for truth and authenticity. On the other hand, we may apologize for the adolescent ideals, incurable optimism, or indulgent romanticism connected with our longings. But once we have been awakened to heaven as a possibility, nothing else will do but to learn more about it. Then we are like pilgrims who have finally discovered where the Holy Grail is located. Or maybe we are like schoolboys. The mystery of mathematics is before us as we struggle to grasp

269

the essentials of algebra and geometry, and we have to believe the teacher's enthusiasm that they do have intrinsic beauty.

We further discover that God's desires for us are not dissimilar from our truest, innermost desires for ourselves. Yet the connection between them at times seems terribly warped by selfishness and self-will. We reflect and we begin to see that the deepest form of nostalgia—to be loved, or to be understood, or to be reunited with the Infinite beyond all the universe—is "no neurotic fancy," according to C. S. Lewis. Rather it is "the truest index of our real situation."[2]

In Christ we also discover that it is not God's personhood that is vague and intangible. It is our own personalities which are incoherent, bitty, and inadequate. So the reality of prayer in the name of Jesus is the search for a fuller, richer personality, the personality we most deeply long to have.

In this light we see devotional reading not just as a pious option to reading a good thriller or even a serious work. It is more in the nature of an awakening, as the prodigal son had at the swine trough. Our animal existence is simply not good enough when we discover inwardly that we have a royal Father and that we are made in the image and likeness of God.

The reading habits of the swine trough cannot ever satisfy a son and a swine at the same time. The reading habits of the "hired servants," guided by the mesmerization with "how-to" books that define life by action and buy acceptance by self-achievement, will not do either. For a beloved son or daughter, though a prodigal, responds to his or her acceptance in Christ. It is all we ever can "do." And it is more like lovers holding hands than corporate businessmen making decisions in the board room.

Indeed we find that life consists of a number of progressive awakenings. When we first study seriously, we are excited by the awakening of our mind's activity to reasoning and understanding in our world. We awaken again in the experience of taking responsibility for our lives when we have to be decisive about major acts or decisions. We awaken also when we are acted upon in suffering. For pain is a great awakener to realities that had previously slumbered in our lives. But it is the awakening to the love of God which transcends all other forms of human consciousness.

Today we are in grave danger of politicalizing our faith, organizing it to death, and making it a cold ideology. We need once more to stand still and to see God. Then we shall begin to live again more like a child of God than like an entrepreneur before men. Deep emotions will be reopened. Memories will begin to be healed. The imagination will be redirected. And whole new possibilities will open out of dead-end streets to show us vistas of love and joy we never knew we could experience. Hope will succeed despair. Friendship will replace alienation. For we wake up one morning and discover we really are free to fall in love with God.

Then we can begin to understand what John Calvin meant when he called faith a firm knowledge of God's benevolence which is sealed in the heart. Calvin's affirmation recalled the burning heart in many a man before him: Jeremiah, the disciples on the Emmaus road, Augustine, Jonathan Edwards. This is how God instills the awareness that we are in the communion of saints, and that we are simply sharing what many others before us have already joyously experienced. We too, like them, now realize that heaven is our horizon after all.

Devotional Reading Changes History

Nothing can exceed the practice of prayer or the devotional reading of Scripture in one's daily devotions. Yet both of these practices need reinforcement and orientation from the example of others, from the sharing of their experiences. Perhaps the devotional use of Scripture is disappearing so fast that it can be rediscovered and made common practice today only with the help of other books. The results of such readings are often far-reaching. In fact, the accidental encounters with great classics of faith and devotion have triggered a whole series of unforeseen reactions.

This was so with C. S. Lewis. He came across such classics as the writings of Richard Hooker, George Herbert, Thomas Traherne, Jeremy Taylor, and John Bunyan as a result of his English studies.[3]

As a student, Alexander Whyte—the Scottish preacher of the late nineteenth century—undertook to index Thomas Goodwin's works of the seventeenth century. But he became so absorbed by them that, later in life, he wrote his *Spiritual Life* based on Goodwin's teachings. He confessed, "I carried his volumes about with me till they fell out of their original cloth binding, and till I got my bookbinder to put them into his best morocco. I have read no other author so much or so often."[4]

When John Bunyan married, his father-in-law gave him a dowry consisting of Arthur Dent's *The Plaine Man's Path-Way to Heaven* (1601) and Lewis Bayly's *The Practice of Pietie* (1613). Bunyan later acknowledged that these two works "beget within me some desires to Religion."[5] Their popularity clearly showed with many of his contemporaries.

One is also reminded of Ignatius of Loyola who, as a frivolous young knight, was wounded at the siege of Pamplona in 1521. There he was forced to spend his convalescence with only two books in his hands, *Life of Jesus Christ* by Ludolph the Carthusian and *Flower of the Saints* by Jacopo de Voragine. These works left a deep impression upon him which led to a radical change of his life.

Christian friends deliberately introduced Augustine to the *Life of Antony* which was written by Athanasius. This did not immediately impress Augustine, although his friend went on to tell him how at Trèves in Gaul a state official "read it, marveled at it, and was inflamed by it." While this official read, he began to think how he might embrace such a life of monasticism in the Egyptian desert. He thought about giving up his worldly employment to serve "You [God] alone; . . . and the world dropped away from his mind . . . while he was reading, and in his heart tossing thus on its own flood, at last he broke out in heavy weeping, saw the better way, and chose it for his own."[6]

Augustine adds a note about the result of reading such an example as Antony. This man and his companion were led to build "a spiritual tower at the only cost that is adequate, the cost of leaving all things and following You."[7]

The influence of mystical writers upon Martin Luther has been well documented. He read deeply the sermons of Johannes Tauler (1515-1516), and edited the anonymous mystical treatise which he entitled *German Theology* (1516, 1518). When he defended the ninety-five theses in 1518, he confessed that there was more good theology in Johannes Tauler's *Sermons*, more "pure and solid theology" than in all the works of scholasticism. Of *German Theology* he declared that "only the Bible and Augustine had taught him more about 'God, Christ, man, and all things.' "[8]

Sometimes the writings of mystics can prolong the struggles to know God personally. The readers are then caught up in their exercises and spiritual insights instead of in encountering God Himself. This was the case with John Wesley. From his mother he learned about many devotional works, especially when he first went up to Oxford as an undergraduate. He found the studies there, "an idle, useless interruption of useful studies, horribly and shockingly superficial."[9]

But Wesley was enchanted by Cardinal Fenélon's *Discourse on Simplicity*; it gave him the realization that simplicity is "that grace which forces the soul from all unnecessary reflections upon itself."[10] On vacation, his friend and spiritual guide Sally gave him a copy of Jeremy Taylor's *Rule and Exercise of Holy Living and Dying.* He admits that this volume "so sealed my daily practice of recording my actions (which I have continued faithfully until this moment) that I later prefaced that first *Diary* with Taylor's Rules and Resolutions. This helped me to develop a style of introspection that would keep me in constant touch with most of my feelings."[11] One wonders how far Fenélon and Jeremy Taylor contradicted the convictions of a confused young man.

About this time, Sally also encouraged John Wesley to read Thomas à Kempis's *Imitation of Christ.* This, too, made its mark upon him, and he determined either to belong to God or to perish. Yet these works in a sense only prolonged for some thirteen years the need for John Wesley to recognize that he must be "born again," and accept God as his own Savior. At the same time they left their mark indelibly upon his character and ministry.

Finally, we think of C. H. Spurgeon and of the profound influence the Puritan writers had upon his whole life and preaching. He had a collection of some twelve thousand books, about seven thousand of them being Puritan writings. Over and over again, Spurgeon read *Apples of Gold* by Thomas Brooks. He also devoted much time to Brooks's *Precious Remedies Against*

Satan's Devices. He delighted in all of Brooks's sweet devotional works.

But books by Thomas Goodwin, John Owen, Richard Charnock, William Gurnall, Richard Baxter, John Flavell, Thomas Watson, and of course John Bunyan, were also Spurgeon's companions.[12] Then in his own *Chat About Commentaries*, he confesses that Matthew Henry's *Commentary* on the Scriptures is his first selection as the Christian's constant companion. He recommended that all his students read it in the first twelve months after they had finished college.[13]

The influence of books upon Christian leaders and their impact in turn upon the renewal movements of the church is clear. As Richard Baxter pointed out in his *Christian Directory* in the seventeenth century, "many a one may have a good book, even any day or hour of the week, that cannot at all have a good preacher."[14]

Sometimes the book and the author are now totally unknown, yet their consequences have been conspicuous and permanent. Who reads today Arthur Dent's *Plaine Man's Path-Way to Heaven;* yet John Bunyan's *Pilgrim's Progress* has been translated into over 198 languages. Few know today of Florentinus of Deventer; yet the book of his pupil, Thomas à Kempis, *Imitation of Christ* has been issued in over 2000 editions. Francisco de Osuna's *The Third Spiritual Alphabet* means nothing to most Christians now; yet it inspired Teresa of Avila's writings on prayer, writings which still influence us strongly. Nicholas Scupoli's *Spiritual Combat* (1589) was Francis de Sales's bedside reading along with the Bible for over sixteen years. Yet it is de Sales's own *Introduction to the Devout Life* that has had such profound impact on so many.

So the message is clear to us all. Open the windows of your soul in meditative reading, and the potentials of God's presence in your life can be, as Paul prays, "exceeding abundantly, above all that we can ask or think."[15]

There Are No Innocent Readers

There is no such thing as "just reading." Reading is an instrument also of our emotions and our spirit, our motives and our objectives. The monastic art of *lectio divina,* the practice of reading meditatively and prayerfully for spiritual nourishment and growth, is little known outside the Catholic traditions of spirituality today. The loss of such devotional assimilation of the Scriptures reflects upon the impatience many have with the spiritual readings of the great masters of Christian faith. Or it possibly shows the sheer neglect or ignorance of such works.

C. S. Lewis speaks of "the strange idea abroad that in every subject, the ancient books should be read only by the professionals, and that the amateur should content himself with the modern books . . . a shyness," he adds, "nowhere more rampant than in theology."[16] But it would make a topsy-turvy confusion in Christianity if we were always contented with a shallow draught of what is said about its origins and never motivated to drink personally from the fountain source.

We are also guilty when we do not distinguish fundamental reading from accidental reading, or edifying reading from recreative reading. For they are all distinct.[17] Accidental reading is what catches our attention for the tactics of life so that we absorb a wide range of know-how, trivial and significant. All that is required of this kind of reading is mental mastery. Fundamental reading, that which we do strategically for training in a profession or discipline, demands docility and perseverance. The shift from the first to the second type of reading is from information to formation, and so the attitude of mind also changes.

Reading which relaxes is also tactical, yet it can catch us off guard sometimes. To absorb trivia which we label as "recreational" can be time wasted. Worse, it can take and divert our minds and spirits from the paths of righteousness and purity.

Such reading may really test our spirits and be evidence of the lack of a Christian imagination in our lives. Stimulating reading is dependent on more deliberate choices that we make. If we wish to be more sensual, then we will indulge in more of the pictorial pornography with which our society is so awash today. Or if we want to breathe the cleaner air of personal authenticity, we will enjoy good biography, be moved by the prayers or journals of great warriors of the faith, or even dwell in the parables of our Lord. It becomes an intense resource in times of depression to keep at hand favorite authors, inspiring pages, and familiar themes, to reinvigorate the flagging spirit.

We are not innocent readers, even when we choose not to read at all! We become guilty of blending our thoughts with the culture that we so readily accept. The TV set, for example, tempts us with deep, manipulative tendencies. For we can at the press of a button translate ourselves into a dozen different artificial environments. We can literally choose the environment we want to live in and live by. Are we not then also going to be tempted to manipulate our spiritual longings and needs also? Submission to the will of God seems to recede more than ever. This attitudinal revolution so deepens our egocentricity that listening to spiritual writers becomes hard indeed. Yet it is docility, not mastery, that is the essence of spiritual reading and the meditative life.

We also have a very short span of attention. Our style is disjointed: Our sentences break off readily, our messages are not always meaningful. We live to be entertained as a spectator rather than to be involved as a participant in life. Our books reflect the staccato of modernity. Messages are given in precise form and in shallow dosages. Likewise, our lifestyles change because procrustean man changes to each new fad and enthusiasm of the moment. It is a divorcing society, where one changes one's partner as one's mood also changes. The solid meat of the Word that the apostle speaks of is rejected not just for milk but for Coca-cola. Classics of faith and devotion are not attrac-tive to a generation that lives on a diet of popcorn and chewing gum.

We tend to live also on the externals of life. It is all show-biz and how we can impress other people. As Christians we are more concerned about the promotion of our faith than its private practice. Busyness is more significant than godliness. We are afraid to listen to God because we are more con-cerned about what other people think. The herd mentality and the tyranny of consensus—what Aldous Huxley once called "herd intoxication"—makes us afraid of solitude, of facing God alone, or indeed of our facing the inner feelings of guilt and self-betrayal.

Yet devotional reading is such a private, interior affair. It does require the moral courage of humility, of openness to life-changing perspectives, and of respect for my own inner being. It does mean shifting gears so that we operate with the fear of the Lord rather than be concerned about the fear of man.

We also play the numbers game. Everybody is doing it! we exclaim. How then can I, or should I, be odd man out?

In reply Kierkegaard would ask us to deliberate: "Do you now live so that you are conscious of yourself as an individual?"[18] Above all, do you realize the most intimate of relationships, "namely that in which you, as an individ-ual, are related to yourself before God?"

In nature there does seem to be a prolific waste of sunlight, of plants, of lesser and greater animals in the great food-chains of our ecosystems. In the callousness of man's violence against his fellows, numbers still do not seem to matter. In our disobedience to the voice of conscience, our personal reading habits, prayer life, and lack of spiritual progress also do not seem to matter if we see Christianity as the crowd.

But God does not judge as the crowd. Rather, as a Father He knows the fall of every sparrow; every hair of our head is counted by Him. "In eternity you will look in vain for the crowd . . . in eternity you, too, will be forsaken by the crowd."[19] This is terrifying unless we prepare for eternity by meeting with God now, constantly and longingly.

Devotional reading helps us, then, to have an eternal consciousness, not a herd consciousness; it is the primary consciousness of man before his Maker, and of me before my Savior. "In eternity," adds Kierkegaard, "there are chambers enough so that each may be placed alone in one . . . a lonely prison, or the blessed chamber of salvation."[20] Is then my spiritual reading and its reflection helping me to see myself "in place," in the will and love of God? True individualism is not following the fashion, but following God.

The Place of Intimacy with God

It is no coincidence that the theme of "following God" for the Israelites in the Exodus was a desert experience. Our desert is not normally the Sahara or the

Gobi, or even the great Australian outback. Our desert is the space to reflect on our shattered dreams, the alienation no touch can connect between even loved ones, the trackless uncertainty of tomorrow, and the experience of inner darkness. There God calls us to Himself, not from our usefulness but for ourselves.

When we say yes to God, He then takes us into the desert. There are no clear directions, nothing systematic, no concrete proposals, no exciting blueprints, no promising opportunities; there is just the promise to be unafraid to be. It is surrender, utterly so. It is docility, whatever the cost. It is divine companionship, regardless of the consequences.

Carlos Carretto acknowledged that the great gift the desert gives us is prayer.[21] The desert is the place of silence before God where the quietness makes the heart's awareness of His presence come closer than our own breathing. In this silence of attentiveness, we listen to God speaking through His Word. Silence becomes stale without the Word, but the Word loses its recreative power without the silence of the desert.

The desert experience is not just an environment for stoicism. It is the place of intimacy with God. It needs the quiet withdrawal—at least temporarily—from the world of men, to be alone with God. It is a reflective dwelling place where one sees things in the light of eternity and therefore in true proportions. It is the removal from agitation, bustle, and speed to see things in stillness. It is where we silence our passions and recede from our tensions. Like a desert wanderer, we learn to discover the oasis where searching is no longer necessary. There we rest, refreshed and renewed.

The desert life has a way of reducing needs to the bare essentials of water, food, and shelter. In the desert alone with God we discover He is enough to satisfy every need. Our only remaining need is simply to need Him more. Of all the lessons the desert teaches, none is greater than finding the intimacy of God.

No wonder, then, that some of the most vital literature of spiritual renewal has come from the Desert Fathers—Antony, Athanasius, Origen, Pachomias, Evagrius, Basil, Gregory of Nyssa, and many unknown men whose sayings we still treasure. What later became institutionalized as "monasticism" is none other than the reflection on the desert life alone with God. We are reminded that without the desert experience of self-emptying, of detachment from idolatry, of surrender in commitment to God, and of our spiritual awakening to God, devotional reading has no significant part to play in our lives. For these are the basic motives and desires needed for devotional reading.

Space and time are required to actualize the desires for the desert. "The quiet time" is either a pious blank in the morning, or it is the most important space in our daily lives. Our bedtime reading is another time for our devotions. Fixed moments during the day give devotion spiritual reality.

Emotionally, too, our desert experiences are not just the spaces God should be invited to fill; they are reminders of what He really wants to occupy in our lives. Indeed, our solitude is the space in which we are conscious of needing Him. Devotional literature will help us to see what an expanding universe His presence should fill. This is the measure to which we see spiritual progress—our increasing neediness for God. This is not weakness but the secret of our greatest strength.

However, a journey into the desert requires a guide, in case we get lost. We need guidance lest we succumb to its dryness of discouragement and defeat. In the same way, our spiritual journey requires a guide.

Supremely we have the Holy Spirit as our Guide. But His presence depends also upon the condition that we do not grieve Him or quench Him. We therefore have the counsels, inspiring examples, and the spiritual experiences of God's people to help guide us. For church history is properly the actualization of the communion of saints whose faith we are exhorted to follow.

The shallowness of much contemporary Christian life is its modernity. We need all twenty centuries of the life of devotion to help us become devotees of Christ at the end of the twentieth century.

So let us learn to enjoy the communion of saints, reliving their lives, rethinking their thoughts, and re-expressing the ardor and fervor of their desires for God. When we get discouraged, these examples of the past show us that when Christian ideals are really tried, they will bear rich fruit. Their devotional writings can revitalize the lifelessness of our formalities like the dry bones in desert wastes that became revitalized in Ezekiel's vision. In another metaphor, Paul speaks of the cloud of witnesses that cheer on the athlete in the race. Devotional works do just that; they encourage us on to the finishing post.

Reading Guidelines that Are Life-Changing

In spite of the spate of new books and of reprints of spiritual literature, there is little guidance offered as to how the art of spiritual reading can and should be cultivated. We have hinted already that the art of devotional reading is not exegetical, not informational, and not literary in its emphasis. Spiritual reading is essentially formative of the soul before God. We need, then, to read it in such a way that it helps us to be inspired and in tune with God in the "inner man." For it is writing which turns us heavenward, and it is formative of our character in Christ.

1. Spiritual reading requires a primary emphasis on the devotional use of Scripture.

"LISTEN."

Do not allow the first excitement of tasting devotional literature to detract you from the priority that you should still give to Bible study and meditation.

Remember, the Scriptures are the canon of the devotion of God's people. They saw the Scriptures uniquely as the final revelation of God's purposes for man. They saw the Scriptures guided by the Holy Spirit.

However, what needs recovery or significant revision in the spiritual exercises of many Christians is how to use and meditate upon the Bible devotionally. For we have tended since the Reformation to flatten the interpretation of Scripture into the one process of historical criticism; we want to see it as we believe the text to have been originally written by the author. The medieval scholar-monk saw it, however, much more richly, as the following hermeneutical rhyme summarizes its fourfold meaning:

> The letter shows us what God and our fathers did;
> The allegory shows us where faith is hid;
> moral meaning gives us rules of daily life;
> The anagogy shows us where we end our strife.

While we do not systematically look for such fourfold levels in every verse of Scripture, nevertheless the literal or plain meaning of the text, as we believe it to be, requires also the use of symbolism to remind us of its mysteries. The use of moral application for the individual believer is also required, as well as the awareness of the transcendent realities of eschatology hidden in the text. This treatment is best seen in the Psalter, which has always been the most popular book of the Bible in the liturgical readings of the Church.

2. The art of devotional reading is less a matter of techniques than it is a matter of attitudes of the heart.

Taking note of the pressures and obstacles of our culture that would negate and sterilize the values of devotional reading is like developing a "sixth sense." It is a process akin to developing spiritual discernment and desire. It is clearly different from the curiosity for more information or the intellectual challenge to master rational understanding. The attitude is changed from a longing for information to a willingness to be reformed and a desire to be transformed. The creation mandate to have dominion over the earth by the *imago dei* is surpassed when we move to the redemptive mandate to be conformed to the image of Christ.

This involves a new way of knowing with a different mindset. Informational reading is more a search for questions and answers. Devotional reading dwells more on the basic issues of living before God. The former looks for transparency in understanding, the latter is living contentedly with mysteries in appreciation and adoration. Again, informational reading is more dialectical and comparative; logic is important. But devotional reading is more docile and receptive rather than critical and comparative.

Informational reading tends toward being dissective. Data are taken to pieces by analysis in order to increase the range of one's ability to learn new things in new arrangements. But devotional reading is the readiness to leave all initiative in God's hands, to recollect and wonder at what God has already done, and to be united with God in living and dynamic ways. It is like the captain of the ship inviting the pilot to take the bridge. For this reason, devotional reading is much more personal and involves self-surrender, docility, and a willingness to change course in deep resolutions and by inner disciplines. The keeping of a spiritual journal may now begin to mark the changes of attitudes and of the desires before God.

Such devotional reading which encourages changes of character may therefore encounter severe spiritual battles and deep emotional struggles. It will require gentleness of spirit to avoid guilt trips, to sustain enjoyment of spirit, and to avoid being unrealistically harsh with one's self. It will require patience and the long view of Christ's control of our lives.

3. Devotional reading has more of the character of a spiritual awakening out of cultural sleep than it has the idea of improving existing attitudes.

We readily "sleep" within our culture until we travel abroad and are surprised by how differently other societies live and behave. The apostle implies we need to spiritually awaken out of our cultural conformities, mindset, and attitudes that we share with the world around us; we need to live to God freshly and honestly (1 Thessalonians 5:6). Often this requires a renewed brokenness of spirit, a new or deepened sense of sin, or a profound reevaluation of our priorities. Then we begin to discover two Christians can share the same orthodoxy of doctrine and yet have profoundly differing attitudes of spirit.

Much distress and confusion in the church today demands all the more discernment of attitudes among Christians to avoid what Bonhoeffer called "cheap grace" and to exercise true devotion before God. We may need then to "travel abroad" as the Desert Fathers did when they left the cities of men. We may need to explore as the medieval mystics explored, or suffer as the Puritans suffered, in order to learn how secular their contemporary species of Christianity really was, and ours is today.

Confession and repentance must therefore be the consequences of devotional reading. It stirs the heart too uncomfortably to be ever confused with entertaining reading. It is too radical to leave us safe within the sphere of our own mastery and control of new information. For the pathology of the heart is revealed in its deceptions, its hiddenness of sin, and in sin's inability to be controlled.[22]

Confession, then, implies both the need to acknowledge (*confiteri*) the holiness of God and to make confession (*confessio*) of guilt and sin.[23] Only sacrifice can unite the sinner with God, and the only sacrifice that unites man with God is that of Jesus Christ. The value of all other sacrifices derives from this. Then confession becomes praise, a thanks-offering. So Bernard of Clairvaux exhorts us, "By the confession of sins and by the confession of praise, let your whole life confess Him!"[24] With praise as a garment, confession becomes the act of one who has recovered an inner beauty, the budding of glory to come.

If we think of some spiritual writers such as Thomas à Kempis in his *Imitation of Christ* as too astringent and severe, could it be that our own lives are not confessional enough? Could it be that they are therefore lacking adequate praise? For praise flows out of gratitude, and gratitude springs out of confession of sin in the realization of who God is. Contemporary theological expression of faith as a belief system has come a long way from twelfth century men such as John of Fecamp, who regarded theology as primarily a task of praise, adoration, and prayer, touched off by the contemplation of God.[25]

It is in the confession of sin that we discover new dimensions of self and of self-love that need to be dealt with. An awakening to the consciousness of indwelling sin in the believer such as that so vividly exposed by John Owen gives a new sensitivity to the reality of Satan that drives us to our knees. Temptation becomes a deeper reality that requires more moral wakefulness in more devotional reading.[26] Repentance becomes a lived reality that needs the support and comfort of the communion of saints.

So a desire to reset our course of life after failure and dishonesty with our own soul will intensify our search to learn from others how they dealt with these issues. Seeing life now with deeper meaning calls forth greater spiritual resources than we previously ever imagined we would need. Once in pilgrimage and away from the *status quo*, we are on a long journey. We have awakened out of a long, dull sleep. Like John Bunyan's Christian, we shall need many spiritual companions.

4. Devotional reading has its own pace, a slower pace.

Once we have begun to see discipleship as a long obedience, then we have to resist the impatience of our "Instant Society." If our devotional reading is to be life-changing and life-forming, we cannot look for instant results. It is, therefore, futile to rush through a devotional work in a hurry. Unlike an Agatha Christie novel, we cannot get through it in an evening.

Much inauthenticity arises in our lives because we do not differentiate speeds; we do things too fast. As it is, I think faster than I can talk, I talk faster than I can act, and I act faster than I have character for so many actions. So I tend always toward the inauthentic.

Spiritually, we need to slow down and spend more time in reflection and silence. We need the slowly measured pace of regular fixed times of reading, even if this is only fifteen or thirty minutes a day. To absorb a few lines of a writer in one's heart and through the bloodstream of one's attitudes is far more effective than to anxiously speed-read merely for the sake of curiosity. If the problem of many churches is how the speed of boardroom decisions can be communicated in a community spirit, then the problem of devotional reading is how the impatience of the mind can be restrained from its lust for more information.

Space, as well as time, is required for devotional reading. Literally this may lead to the habit of developing a particular environment, an area in one's room that locates an "altar" of devotion. Physically it may require a comfortable posture, perhaps a particular chair, where one can most readily relax and where an atmosphere is created specifically for such exercises of devotion as prayer and contemplation. It may be that we should first take spiritual reading seriously when we are on holiday or vacation; there we sense the relaxing, recreational atmosphere of spaciousness we need for such spiritual exercises and disciplines. A facetious advertisement reads on a Los Angeles freeway, "With ice cream every day can be a sundae." The truth is that, with every day nurtured by spiritual reading, all days are Sundays.

5. Choose classics of faith and devotion from a broad spectrum of God's people.

We have noted that the poverty of Christendom today requires the resources of all twenty centuries of spiritual traditions, be they Orthodox, Catholic, or Protestant. Need we hesitate, then, to receive the diverse and catholic range of experiences that other saints of God have experienced throughout the ages and across the cultures of mankind? Indeed, those who most experience the riches of God's grace can most afford to be eclectic in their spiritual reading. This they can do without losing in any way their firmness of faith and doctrine, nor be in any way careless with the essential truth of the gospel.

How such wide reading can enrich a Christian is exemplified in the life and ministry of Dr. Alexander Whyte, an influential member of the Free Church of Scotland, a church not known for its catholic interests. When he was fifty-six years old (1892), Alexander Whyte began to read the collected works of William Law. He wrote an anthology of Law's works in his book *The Characters and Characteristics of William Law*. In the preface he said of this Anglican, "The study of this quite incomparable writer has been nothing else than an epoch in my life."[27]

Then Whyte was led to study Teresa of Avila of whom he also wrote. He wrote other tributes of Lancelot Andrewes, Sir Thomas Browne, Samuel Rutherford, and the Russian Father John of Cronstadt. In a period of seven

years, Alexander Whyte came to see a vast new vista of spirituality in writers
whom he had never known before. So he began to realize that the admiration
and love of the great saints of God is indeed a study of great worth.

"Exercise the charity," Whyte used to exhort, "that rejoices in the truth,"
wherever it is found, and however unfamiliar may be its garb. "The true
Catholic, as his name implies, is the well-read, the open-minded, the hospi-
table-hearted, the spiritually-exercised Evangelical; for he belongs to all
sects, and all sects belong to him."[28]

6. Enjoy spiritual friendships with soul-friends so that you can mutu-
ally benefit in a group-study or in a shared reading program.

Such a group can meet every two or four weeks to hear and discuss books
reviewed in turn by members of the group. At first, such reading may intensify deep spiritual challenges and generate a whole new sense of awareness
to realities. It is a common reaction to question one's self whether one is
becoming unbalanced or even crazy to have such convictions and longings.
For just as the recovery from a severe illness, the threat of death, or an
experience of deep brokenness may open up new doors of perception, so the
fresh challenge of reading Christian mystics may do the same. It is then very
important to be encouraged and led on wisely by those more experienced.
Moreover, differing reactions give one a sense of proportion or correct one-
sided impressions. The common goal of growing up into Christ, argues the
Apostle Paul, is a corporate maturity (see Ephesians 4:13-14).

A spiritual friend, says the twelfth century writer Aelred of Rievaulx in
Spiritual Friendship, is one who is loyal and has right motives, discretion, and
patience in order to help his friend know God better.[29] Since there is no end
to the extent to which I can and do deceive myself, I need a spiritual guide to
keep me honest. Moreover, the love of God is only effectively developed
when my friend helps to draw me out of myself and to show me how I can
enter into a wider circle of insights where I can be more honest with myself.

Thus revelation and honesty can give shape to spiritual companionship.
Spiritual life rests upon revelation: the revelation of Christ who continually
calls us in the power of the Holy Spirit into a relationship with Him. It rests on
honesty: honesty with regard to what is there to be seen and to be reckoned
with. So spiritual companionship is a process of both nurture and of confrontation, both of which are helped by reading and the discovery of devotional
literature together.

A true friend in Christ will wake me up, help me to grow, and deepen my
awareness of God. For God's love is mediated through human relationships,
by those who care for me, encourage me, and desire my affections to become
God-centered. Indeed, says Aelred, God is friendship, and so friendship with
the spiritually-minded will lead me toward godliness. Perhaps few of us
today take spiritual friendship quite so seriously.

7. Recognize that spiritual reading meets with obstacles that discourage, distract, or dissuade you from persistence in your reading.

the INFLU.
OF SATAN
IN YOUR
LIFE (EPH 6)

Often we are not discerning enough to see or to question why a book may not grip our immediate attention, or why it seems so irrelevant to us. It may be caused by our own despondency or spiritual state as referred to earlier. Discouragement may rear its ugly head even when there are clear signs that we are being blessed. What the Desert Fathers called *acedia*, boredom, flatness, or depression, may also be our affliction when we are tempted to believe we are making no spiritual progress at all.

We may also be distracted from reading the Fathers because we have never learned to live by a book; the book has meant only entertainment. After a casual flicking through TV programs, concentrated reading is perhaps a new discipline. Or perhaps we have never known the experience of awe and wonder in the presence of God, such as some spiritual reading will incite. This attitude may therefore need development before we enjoy some of the spiritual masters.

We may also be dissuaded from going far into the spiritual classics because of their timebound cultural and theological frame. For instance, the fourfold levels of exegesis of medieval use of Scripture needs some understanding and sympathy before the sermons of Bernard of Clairvaux may mean very much to us today. Middle English mystics such as the unknown author of *The Cloud of Unknowing*, Richard Rolle, Margery Kempe, Walter of Hilton, or others make it difficult for us when they insist we put away all human thought in our contemplation of God. They argue it is love rather than reason itself which gives such true understanding. They speak of "discretion," a spiritual sensing of grace, humility, contrition, and deep contemplation of God that is truly required.

Even later literature such as that of the Puritans may put us off because of their Latinized style or their "precision" in tabulating major and minor headings and subheadings.[30] One can understand their nickname of the "Precisians" in the ways they often categorized point after point. It is for this reason of changed vocabulary, loquaciousness, changes in style, etc., that we have undertaken to rewrite in more contemporary fashion some of these classics, a task many other publishers and editors are also now undertaking. So there is little excuse today for the modern reader to say such material is unintelligible or unascertainable.

It is, of course, true that the literary imagery of such works is often that of a bygone culture. Bernard's *In Praise of New Knighthood,* or Teresa of Avila's *Interior Castle*, or Bunyan's *Holy War* may seem like out-of-date symbols. Yet they also contain principles for spiritual warfare, for the surrender of self to the communion with God, or for watchfulness in temptation; they remain as timeless principles. For mortification always remains a vital exercise, or series of exercises, in the Christian's life.

8. Seek a balance in your reading between modern and ancient writings.

Remember that modern writing is untried, lacks vintage, and often reflects the fads of the marketplace. As C. S. Lewis has said:

> A new book is still on trial, and the amateur is not in a position to judge it. . . . The only safety is to have a standard of plain, central Christianity ("mere Christianity" as Baxter called it), which puts the controversies of the moment in their proper perspective. Such a standard can only be acquired from old books. It is a good rule, after reading a new book, never to allow yourself another new one till you have read an old one in between. If that is too much for you, you should read an old one to every three new ones.[31]

In spite of such a precaution, when *Christianity Today* did a popular survey of "100 Select Devotional Books," (September 25, 1961), less than one-third were over a hundred years old. Most that were chosen were contemporary works. Rightly excluded were works of general religiosity such as the popular books of K. Gibran, works of speculative mysticism such as those of Meister Eckhart or Jakob Boehme, works reflecting contemporary positive thinking, or works of sweetness and light, all of which types have an unrealistic view of sin in human life.

At the same time, many of us may find the need for some entry point into a deeper spiritual experience by the use of modern writers who clear the trail to follow beyond the secular, modern mind and back to the ageless truths of Christianity. C. S. Lewis himself needed the sanity and humor of G. K. Chesterton, as well as the Christian imagination of George MacDonald, to feed him symbolically. Then he could go back to Boethius's *On the Consolations of Philosophy* which gave Lewis a firm awareness of the solidity of eternity that was more than measureless time. But it is typical of life-shaping literature that very few authors really can do this for us. So Lewis would assure us, as so many have experienced this, that reading too widely may leave very little profound effect, however broadly we may become informed.

Michel Quoist's book *Prayers of Life* has revolutionized the prayer life of many today, and brought life and humanity into their devotions. I was stirred first of all in the challenge of Søren Kierkegaard's *Purity of Heart Is to Will One Thing*. It shakes one to the roots to mean business with the Almighty. P. T. Forsythe in *The Soul in Prayer* reminds us that "the worst sin is prayerlessness." Oswald Chambers in *My Utmost for His Highest* has lifted many on to the spiritual quest. At the same time, no devotional book, past or present, can do anything decisive if we are not already longing for a deeper spiritual life and prepared to receive it.

Just as there are Psalms for all the moods and needs of life, so there should be a balance in our reading. Sometimes we may need the solid theological reading of Calvin's *Institutes*. At other times the joyous celebration of Thomas Traherne's *Centuries*, or the poems of George Herbert's *Temple*, are more suitable. John of the Cross combines some of the finest lyrics in Spanish literature with expressions of the most intense suffering and fervor for God in the *Dark Night of the Soul*. The hymns of John and Charles Wesley, or the *Journal* of George Whitefield, or the *Letters* of Fénélon, or the *Pensées* of Pascal, cover rightly varied expressions of the soul before God. The diversity aids balance in our spiritual diet.

9. Accompany your spiritual reading with the keeping of a journal or some reflective notebook.

The Puritans used to argue that as the captain of a ship kept his log, or as the doctor recorded his case studies, or as a businessman audited his accounts, so the Christian should keep accounts with God; indeed daily, short accounts.

Indeed, from this tradition of keeping a journal we have some of the great treasures of spiritual literature. We think of John Bunyan's *Grace Abounding to the Chief of Sinners*, the *Memoirs* of David Brainerd, the Quaker journals of men such as George Fox and John Woolman, the journals of John Wesley and George Whitefield. Their examples still encourage us not just to record spiritual successes, but note also the goodness of God in our failures, depressions, and recoveries. They also point us to the consideration of small matters that may seem trivial and unimportant, yet are also maintained within the provident care of God. Likewise, there will be times when our aridity of spirit may appear to make our devotional study and meditation pointless and useless. Then it is that the faithful and sustained recording is kept up as a labor of love, and we honor Him in all circumstances.

Writing things down is also a helpful, reflective exercise. It often helps to clarify thoughts when our emotions are confused or lazy; it helps to keep things memorable and edifying. The fruits of our meditations are also preserved when "wonderful thoughts" could so easily evaporate again.

For some, keeping a journal seems too grand an exercise for their diary jottings. Others may never get into the habit of having one. Nevertheless, their spiritual autobiography is still vital to them, for they have been taught to see every significant event as happening since their conversion. In some circles this can lead to an unhealthy emphasis on a once-for-all experience that settles past, present, and future in such a way that no spiritual progress is ever made subsequently. It all happened once and for all. No, if we are pilgrims, then life still lies open before us, and so our spiritual autobiography is still in the making. Premature attempts to finish the "story" either at conversion, at a "second blessing," or at the reception of a specific gift or insight should be resisted.

Perhaps, then, we need to exercise more sense of a spiritual autobiography in our lives, either by journal keeping, diary jottings, memoirs, or just an ongoing list of gratitude for the many events God has transformed in our

286   The Best in Theology

experiences. But we do need to be guarded by too frequent expression of public testimonies which can be exaggerated or spiritually wasted by over-exposure. Dostoevsky's hero in *Notes from Underground* argues that "con-sciousness is a disease."[32] The self-fulfillment cult of this "Me-Generation" certainly is a deadly plague among us today. Perhaps the recovery of spiritual autobiography will help us. For all autobiography is a search for a meaningful pattern to life, and all such quests are doomed to futility without reference to our Creator and Redeemer. For the absence of God from our thoughts and decisions, desires and delights, is that which makes self-con-sciousness so often demonic.

The keeping of a journal around our devotional reading will thus help to maintain our reading as a steady diet. It may also be a form of self-direction in the cultivation of conscience, a knowledge with God rather than knowl-edge on my own. It is a way of living that prepares us for heaven. Bishop Joseph Hall, who recorded many of his meditations, reminds us that such reflections so recorded are "the Christian's heavenly business, for it is no more possible to live without a heart than it is to be devout without medita-tion."[33] Such meditative recording will remind us constantly of the long journey of the soul before God.

10. Choose carefully the devotional work that you desire to read for life-changing benefits to your soul. Pray seriously and seek someone to help you in the quest.

There is such a range of books available of a spiritual character that you may be discouraged at the beginning by the very variety. So first of all, distinguish between the "primary" classics that are basic reading, and the supportive "secondary" sources that are only minor classics. We may then call "tertiary reading" the background histories of spirituality, biographies, and other material that help to fill out the context of the primary classics. The "fourth" kind of reading is the vast range of contemporary devotional litera-ture which has not yet been sorted out as having permanent or passing interest and value.

Do not imitate someone else's choice of a classic, because your needs may be very distinct. So the advice of a spiritual friend may be needed to help you discover the right book that may remain as your friend for life. If you are still without such a spiritual guide, the following suggestions may help.

If you feel that your worst enemies are still inside you—guilt, lust, a constantly defeated Christian life—then Augustine's *Confessions* may just be the book for you. Many of us will identify with Augustine's recognition that he postponed exploring and submitting to Christianity because he really wanted his lust for sex, beauty, and success to be satisfied rather than cured. "Lord, make me chaste, but not yet." Augustine's honesty and openness before God refresh and relieve us if we have spent a lifetime bottling things up and postponing a much-needed catharsis of soul.

If you mean business with God, and have felt the absence of a real discipleship before God, then Thomas à Kempis's *Imitation of Christ* may be the astringent call you are looking for. The tradition out of which this small work arose was the notes (*ripiaria*) or collection of sentences from the Scriptures and the Fathers that became a focus for meditation, not only for Thomas à Kempis but for countless generations of "the committed ones." Why not join the august band of devotees?

If you see life as a constant struggle, and feel tempted to give up in discouragement and weakness, then perhaps Lorenzo Scupoli's *Spiritual Combat* is your need. Second only to *Imitation of Christ*, it has had the most profound influence, especially in eastern Europe, since it was published in 1589. Francis de Sales kept it by his bedside for sixteen years, "the golden, dear book" that he read every day. For those needing to be gentle with themselves in self-rejection, Francis de Sales's own meditations, *Introduction to the Devout Life,* is a sweet bouquet of daily refreshment for many sensitive spirits.

Falling in love with God seems a fearful thing for many Christians. Perhaps one begins this experience by reading the classic of Jean Pierre de Caussade, *Abandonment to Divine Providence*. It was recently retranslated by Kitty Muggeridge as *The Sacrament of Every Moment* and has the same theme as this work. Brother Lawrence's *The Practice of the Presence of God* is in the same tradition of seventeenth century French devotion.

All this may encourage you to return to the twelfth century, which like our own today was much preoccupied with the discovery of the individual through romantic love. The response of Bernard of Clairvaux and his friends was to see the love of God as the source of true personhood. Man's being calls out for love, and love's source is God Himself. Our integrity and deepest understanding of ourselves deepen when we fall in love with God as a permanent reality. So short works such as *On Loving God, Spiritual Friendship*, and meditations on the *Song of Songs* help us to enter into this reality.[34]

If you feel the need to nurture your devotional life with solid theological study also, then it is often overlooked that Calvin's *Institutes*, part three, is written precisely for that purpose. Before you get there, you may find it helpful to read William Wilberforce's *Real Christianity*, a spirited attack on civil religion by the abolitionist leader against slavery.[35] If your theology may be clear, but your feelings are still confused and weak toward God, then Jonathan Edwards's *Treatise on the Religious Affections* remains unique in this need of disciplined desire for God.[36] This is a book that requires much recovery for post-modern man.

Perhaps we also need to return to books of childhood, such as Bunyan's *Pilgrim's Progress*, to see at deeper levels what is timeless for all generations. Recovering our childhood for God may help us redeem the past for future enrichment as C. S. Lewis did with the tales of George MacDonald. Prejudices of childhood sometimes need to be unfrozen by rereading sources that previously blocked our progress.

In his *Maxims*, John of the Cross sums up what we have attempted to say. "Seek by reading, and you will find meditating; cry in prayer, and the door will be opened in contemplation."[37] But he admits, they who are "pilgrims for recreation rather than for devotion are many." So he warns us, "Never admit into your soul that which is not substantially spiritual, for if you do so, you will lose the sweetness of devotion and recollection." He adds, "Live in the world as if God and your soul only were in it; that your heart may be captive to no earthly thing."

Notes

[1] Ecclesiastes 3:11.

[2] C. S. Lewis, *The Weight of Glory* (Greensboro, N.C.: Unicorn Press, 1977), p. 10.

[3] C. S. Lewis, *God in the Dock*, Walter Hooper, ed. (Grand Rapids, Mich.: Wm. B. Eerdmans, 1970), pp. 200-207.

[4] Quoted in G. F. Barbour, *The Life of Alexander Whyte* (New York: George H. Doran Co., 1925), pp. 117-18.

[5] Quoted in Richard L. Greeves, *John Bunyan* (Grand Rapids, Mich.: Wm. B. Eerdmans, 1969), p. 16.

[6] F. J. Sheed, ed., *The Confessions of St. Augustine* (New York: Sheed & Ward, 1949), p. 164.

[7] Ibid.

[8] Steven Ozment, *The Age of Reform, 1250-1550* (New Haven, Conn.: Yale University Press, 1980), p. 239.

[9] Robert G. Tuttle, *John Wesley: His Life and Theology* (Grand Rapids, Mich.: Zondervan, 1978), p. 58.

[10] Ibid, p. 100.

[11] Ibid, p. 65.

[12] Earnest W. Bacon, *Spurgeon: Heir of the Puritans* (Grand Rapids, Mich.: Wm. B. Eerdmans, 1968), p. 108.

[13] C. H. Spurgeon, *Commenting and Commentaries* (London: Banner of Truth, 1969), pp. 2-4.

[14] Richard Baxter, *Practical Works*, William Orme, ed. (London: James Duncan, 1830), 4:266.

[15] Ephesians 3:20.

[16] C. S. Lewis, *God in the Dock*, pp. 200, 201.

[17] A. G. Sertillanges, *The Intellectual Life,* (Westminster, Md.: Christian Classics, 1980), pp. 152-54.

[18] Søren Kierkegaard, *Purity of Heart Is to Will One Thing* (New York: Harper & Row, 1954), p. 184.

[19] Ibid, p. 193.

[20] Ibid.

[21] Carlos Carretto, *Letters from the Desert,* (London: Darton, Longman, Todd, 1972), p. 32.

[22] See John Owen, *Sin and Temptation,* James M. Houston, ed. and J. I. Packer, cont. ed. (Portland, Ore.: Multnomah Press, 1982).

[23] Jean Leclerc, *Contemplative Life* (Kalamazoo, Mich.: Cistercian Publications, 1978), p. 109.

[24] Quoted by Leclerc, *Contemplative Life,* p. 117.

[25] Ibid, p. 116.

[26] John Owen, *Sin and Temptation.*

[27] G. F. Barbour, *Life of Alexander Whyte,* p. 378.

[28] Ibid, p. 389.

[29] Bernard of Clairvaux and his friends, *The Love of God*, James M. Houston, ed. (Portland, Ore.: Multnomah Press, 1983), pp. 233-51.

[30] See for example Richard Baxter, *The Reformed Pastor,* James M. Houston, ed., and Richard D. Halverson, cont. ed. (Portland, Ore.: Multnomah Press, 1982).

[31] C. S. Lewis, *God in the Dock,* pp. 201-202.

[32] Quoted by Roger Pooley, *Spiritual Autobiography* (Grove Books, Bramcote, Notts., 1983), p. 6.

[33] Joseph Hall, *The Works* (London: M. Flesher, 1647), p. 114.

[34] Bernard of Clairvaux, *The Love of God.*

[35] William Wilberforce, *Real Christianity*, James M. Houston, ed., and Sen. Mark O. Hatfield, cont. ed. (Portland, Ore.: Multnomah Press, 1982).

[36] Jonathan Edwards, *Religious Affections*, James M. Houston, ed., and Charles W. Colson, cont. ed. (Portland, Ore.: Multnomah Press, 1984).

[37] David Lewis, ed., *The Works of St. John of the Cross* (London: Thomas Baker, 1891), pp. 586, 603.

THE "FINGER OF GOD" IN EVANGELISM

LEIGHTON FORD
Chairman, Lausanne Committee for World Evangelization

Article from *World Evangelization*

Evangelism includes the offer of God's presence to fill our spiritual emptiness, and the promise of God's power to overcome our spiritual tyrannies. In this, the Holy Spirit is God in action.

When Jesus was asked by his disciples to teach them to pray, he gave them a model prayer—the "Our Father" accompanied by a story and a demonstration. The story was of the friend who comes to a neighbour by midnight, saying that an unexpected and hungry visitor has arrived and that he has nothing to set before him. He overcomes his sleepy neighbour's reluctance by begging until he gets what he wants. Jesus concludes, "How much more will your Father in Heaven give the Holy Spirit to those who ask him!" (cf. Lk. 11:9,13).

Then follows a demonstration of the power of the Kingdom as Jesus drives out a demon that had caused muteness. His critics accuse him of driving out demons by Beelzebub, the prince of demons, but Jesus gives his classic counter, "If I drive out demons by *the finger* of God, then the kingdom of God has come to you" (Lk. 11:20). In the parallel passage in Matthew 12, Jesus says, "If I drive out demons by *the Spirit* of God then the kingdom of God has come upon you" (Mt. 12:28). In one sense, the Spirit of God is the finger of God.

What do we do with our fingers? We may write, beckon, grip, point, work. So in the gospel ministry of Jesus and the apostles, we see the Holy Spirit acting as God's finger, pointing and guiding to areas of evangelistic opportunity, beckoning as he convicts men of sin and shows them Christ, gripping new believers as he assures and seals them, writing God's Word upon their hearts, and working to destroy the tyranny of the devil and to build up the Kingdom of God.

The promise of the Spirit as God's presence and power is a key theme in Luke and Acts, and a key element in all evangelistic ministry.

The Promise to Believers

Jesus promised that the Father will "give the Holy Spirit to those who ask Him." This is more than an isolated text; it is a central reality in Luke and Acts. The structure of both books is waiting—receiving—ministering. In the early chapters of Luke we see God-fearing people like Zechariah (1:12-17), Simeon (2:25,26), and Anna (2:36-38) *waiting* in Jerusalem in the temple for the promised Messiah. When Jesus appears he *receives* the Holy Spirit at his baptism (3:21-22) and is marked out as the beloved Son. Then, after being led into the desert and tempted, he begins to *minister*, proclaiming, teaching, healing, and casting out demons, and having his authority recognised by evil spirits. Acts follows a similar pattern. It begins with the disciples *waiting* (again, in Jerusalem and near the temple) for the promised Spirit (Lk. 24:49; Acts 1:4,5), and then *receiving* the Spirit at Pentecost, which is the baptism of the church, and marks the disciples as witnesses to the beloved Son. Then they begin *ministering* in the name of Jesus, preaching, teaching, and seeing signs and wonders done in the authority of his name. The waiting for Jesus' birth and the coming of the Spirit at Jesus' baptism is strikingly similar to the waiting of the church at Jerusalem and the coming and the descending of the Spirit at Pentecost.

In England today, as in some other areas, there is a noticeable emergence of what is often called "Celebration Evangelism," defined as the combination of praise, testimony, drama, music, and preaching in an atmosphere of worship. Often lengthy periods of time are given to worship, more than is common in most evangelistic meetings. The belief is that "God inhabits the praises of his people," and that when non-Christians come into the atmosphere of worship, they will be convicted by the reality of God's presence and the joy of the assembled worshippers and will thereby be more prepared to receive the Word. Not all agree with this approach, and currently there is considerable debate as to the forms of "Celebration Evangelism."

Yet however much worship is incorporated into evangelistic meetings, there is growing recognition of the importance of worship, praise, and prayer, at least in the preparation for evangelism, if not in the actual presentation. Much of the effectiveness of Mission England with the Billy Graham team came from the spirit of expectancy created through the 50,000 or more persons taking part in the "Prayer Triplets" scheme—in which three believers met regularly to pray for their unconverted friends.

The Promise to Unbelievers

As the Spirit is promised to empower the waiting and worshipping believers, so he is also offered to nonbelievers. At Pentecost, Peter answered the question, "What shall we do?" of his convicted hearers with, "Repent and be baptized, every one of you, in the name of Jesus Christ so that your sins may be forgiven. And you will receive the gift of the Holy Spirit. The promise is for you and your children and for all who are far off—for all whom the Lord our God will call" (Acts 2:38,39). The Spirit is as much a gift as is forgiveness. As with forgiveness, the life-giving Spirit is a gift of grace, not of works. Peter's premise is that Jesus "has received from the Father the promised Holy Spirit and has poured out what you now see and hear" (Acts 2:33).

The typical preaching in Acts offers both forgiveness and the Spirit. Of the evangelistic sermons and messages recorded by Acts, the coming of the Spirit is either promised or accompanies the preaching in seven of them. In four instances (Peter to the rulers 4:8; Paul at Lystra 14:8-9f; Paul to the jailer 16:31; and Paul to the philosophers of Athens 17:22 ff) salvation is offered without specifying either forgiveness or the gift of the Spirit. Only in one instance, in Paul's preaching at Antioch, is forgiveness offered without the promise of the Spirit (13:38,39). Richard Lovelace has suggested in *Dynamics of Spiritual Life* that an in-depth presentation of the gospel should include not only justification, *"you are accepted in Christ,"* but also the promise of sanctification *"you are free* from the bondage of sin in Christ" (p. 75). Such a pattern indicates that our evangelistic presentations should emphasise not only the pardon that is available in Christ, but also the power.

In Luke 11, Jesus makes an apt comparison to the human personality. An evil spirit is purged, leaving a house swept clean and in order, but when left empty it is reinvaded by seven more wicked spirits. A true and complete conversion must involve both the sweeping clean that takes place in forgiveness and the occupying of the cleansed spirit when the Holy Spirit takes up residence. Certainly for the first Christians it was clear that a complete conversion included accepting the Word of God, being baptised in the name of Jesus, and receiving the Holy Spirit. The coming of the Spirit upon the Samaritans (chapter 8) and upon Cornelius (Acts 10) was evidence that God accepts Samaritans and Gentiles, and completed the missionary triad— Judea, Samaria, and the uttermost parts—showing that Jesus is Lord of all.

The Holy Spirit Gives Authority in Evangelistic Ministry

After the Holy Spirit descended upon Jesus, he was led into the desert and later returned to Galilee in the "power of the Spirit" (Lk. 4:14). This power was seen in three specific ways. His teaching was with authority (Lk. 4:33-37); and he laid hands on people and healed them (Lk. 4:40). This power of the Spirit continued to be present with Jesus as his authority was seen in the calling of disciples, the healing of a leper, the forgiving of sins, and his teaching about fasting and about the Sabbath. When he passed on some of this authority to the seventy-two, their new authority brought joy to Jesus because it confirmed that "all things have been committed to me by my Father" (Lk. 10:22).

When the apostles in Acts taught and healed, the same authority and power of the Spirit was with them. It was an authority and power that pointed to Jesus. Peter preaching at Pentecost said, "Men of Israel, listen to this: Jesus of Nazareth was a man accredited by God to you by miracles, wonders and signs" (Acts 2:22). And when the crippled beggar at the temple was healed, Peter asked, "Why do you stare at us as if by our own power of godliness we [have] made this man walk? . . . [B]y faith in the name of Jesus, this man whom you see and know was made strong" (Acts 3:12,16). Similarly, when they were all filled with the Holy Spirit and "spoke the word of God boldly" it was with great power that "the apostles continued to testify to the resurrection of the Lord Jesus" (Acts 4:31,33). Whether the Spirit worked in teaching, healing, or releasing from demonic power, his characteristic work was to manifest the authority of Jesus and to see that he was recognised as Lord (1 Cor. 12:3). The spiritual authority which the Scriptures describe is never just an unusual attribute of gifted people. It is always for the recognition of Jesus.

I was with a Church in England clergyman at the end of a Billy Graham meeting in Liverpool where nearly 4,000 people had walked down to stand for Christ and be counseled. "I thought to myself," the clergyman said, "that I could have preached a better sermon. But, oh how I wish that the power of God was upon my ministry as it is upon his." It was not great preaching but great power in Christ that he sensed.

Somewhere it is said of John Wesley that before his conversion his preaching was like that of a man shooting an arrow. Its strength and effectiveness depended upon his ability to draw the bow. But after his experience of God's power in his own life, his preaching became like a rifle, impelled by the authority and power of God.

The "Unpredictable" Spirit

The study of the coming of the Spirit upon people in Acts is interesting for the very reason that the pattern seems somewhat unpredictable. I quickly went through the following instances: the coming of the Spirit at Pentecost upon the disciples, upon others, upon the Samaritans, upon Paul, upon Cornelius, upon the Ethiopian eunuch, and upon the twelve at Ephesus. In three instances there was speaking in tongues; in four, there was not. In four instances they were hearing and believing the gospel for the first time, and in three they were not. In five instances they were baptised at that time, in one they were baptised earlier, and in one there was no baptism recorded. In five instances they were not prayed for, in one they were. In two instances hands were laid on them, and in five they were not. In six instances confession or praising of God was present, and in one it was not. None were alone when they received the Spirit. The only common factors that stand out were the hearing and believing of the gospel (in four instances), baptism, and confession or praise of God. Even a quick study should warn us against seeking to impose phenomena and patterns upon God the Spirit and the way he converts people.

The Holy Spirit in Conversion

According to Acts 11, those who had been scattered by the persecution in connection with Stephen travelled to various places and then to Antioch. When they told the good news about the Lord Jesus "The Lord's hand was with them, and a great number of people believed and turned to the Lord" (Acts 11:21). On the analogy of the Holy Spirit being God's finger, the "hand of the Lord" likely refers to the Spirit. So the Holy Spirit as the hand of God reaches out and turns people from darkness to light and from their sins to the Lord. When the Jerusalem church heard about this, they sent Barnabas to check it out. He not only saw the evidence of the grace of God, but himself began to evangelise. "He was a good man, full of the Holy Spirit and faith, and a great number of people were brought to the Lord" (Acts 11:24).

Aristotle in his *Rhetoric* spoke of persuasion as involving the *logos*, that is, the relevance and clarity of the message; *pathos*, the appeal to the underlying life motives and emotions of the hearers; and *ethos*, which is the perceived credibility of the communicator. Based on his model, we might speculate that in the conversion process the Holy Spirit illuminates the truth and relevance of the message, pierces the conscience, opens the minds and stirs the hearts of the hearers to grasp its urgency, and bestows the gifts and graces that incarnate the message in the messengers.

The Holy Spirit Guides the Evangelist to Those He Wishes to Reach

As God's pointing finger, the Spirit guides the church into evangelistic situations. Again and again, the evangelistic initiatives in Acts come from the Spirit's movement. It was the Spirit who directed Philip in the desert to go near the chariot of the Ethiopian eunuch so that he could explain to him the Scripture, and the Spirit who took Philip away after the conversion was complete (Acts 8:29-39). It was the Spirit who overcame Peter's reluctance to enter a "nonkosher" situation, going with Cornelius's messengers in order to preach the gospel to a Gentile household (Acts 10:19). It was the Spirit who directed the church at Antioch to set apart Barnabas and Saul as a cross-cultural missionary team to the Gentiles (Acts 13:2,4). Again, the same Spirit restrained the evangelists from going into Asia or Bithynia, and instead directed them to Macedonia. There the businesswoman Lydia had her heart opened to respond to the message, and later the jailer was literally shaken on the way to salvation (Acts 16:6,7). The Holy Spirit was working at both ends of the evangelistic encounter. He prepared and directed the evangelists, and he also prepared and opened the evangelised, causing them to seek. Through prayer and intuition, through the study of situations, societies, and peoples, through inner and outer promptings, the Spirit is the master strategist, and the church must seek to be sensitive to him and his promptings.

If we are listening he will direct us to particular people. I was with Billy Graham at Mission England in Birmingham. A large overflow crowd had gathered outside the stadium to watch on closed-circuit television, and I went out to speak a word of welcome and encouragement. On my way back into the stadium a middle-aged man stopped me. "Does Billy Graham have any literature for bereaved parents?" he wanted to know. "Why do you ask?" I replied. "I've been here several nights and I know some people who lost children," he said, "and I'd like something to help them." "Have you been through that experience?" I asked. He told me that 18 months before he had lost a 20-year-old daughter in a very tragic situation.

I told him that two-and-a-half years before we had lost a 21-year-old son during heart surgery. For the next few minutes we talked as one bereaved and grieving father to another, empathizing at the human level but also meeting at a deeper level of the Spirit. Gerald, who was a dentist, told me that he had an intellectual faith but not much more, and that he was "a rotten soul." We prayed and I told him I would write him.

I went on into the stadium, but something prompted me to go back out again. I asked the Lord to help me find him, if he was working in that man's life—and out of all that crowd I spotted him. When I asked him if he wanted to go forward he said he wasn't worthy, and he didn't want to take my time. When I told him it wasn't a question of worthiness but of grace, he said, "I'll go." And that night I stood in the midst of several thousand inquirers next to one man to whom God had led me. Why, at that very moment, had he been on the street? Why, out of all the people who were there had he come up to me, whom he did not know, the one person perhaps in that area who had an experience and could identify with him? Why, if not by the guidance of the Spirit?

The Holy Spirit Gives Wisdom in Communicating

The folk in Jesus' hometown were amazed at the gracious words that came from his lips, as the teachers in the temple had been amazed before at his understanding and his answers to their questions (Lk. 4:22; 2:47). Through the Spirit, the risen Christ gives the gift of wisdom to his communicators. Stephen is a great example. He was one of those selected to oversee the daily distribution of food because he was known "to be full of the Spirit and wisdom" (Acts 6:3). In addition, he was a man "full of God's grace and power" who did great wonders and miraculous signs (Acts 6:8). And when certain members of the synagogue began to argue with Stephen "they could not stand up against his wisdom or the Spirit by which he spoke" (Acts 6:30). Wisdom in gospel preaching is that combination of insight into God's truth and intuition into men's hearts and minds which enables the evangelist to probe, to anticipate objections, to answer questions, to locate that crack in the conscience, or the flaw in the reasoning that makes the Word come home with telling power.

It seems to me there is no one way in which the Holy Spirit gives this power. Sometimes it comes by careful research into, and preparation for, the situation to which the evangelist is going. Again it may come in a moment when an immediate response is needed to a situation. Jesus promised that when his followers were brought before kings and governors they were not to worry about how to defend themselves, for "I will give you words and wisdom that none of your adversaries will be able to resist or contradict" (Lk. 21:15).

Once in Australia when a crowd had come forward at an invitation, I felt led to say something I have never said before or since. "It may be," I said, "someone who is here tonight has had an abortion and you feel that is a sin that can never be forgiven, and you feel terribly guilty. But God will forgive and cleanse and give you a new beginning." Afterwards I found that a university girl had come forward that night who indeed had had an abortion and was feeling tremendously guilty. Her counselor that night was a senior nursing supervisor who was able, when the girl told her of her situation, to counsel her with great wisdom. In days to come, that young lady herself was able to minister to other young women facing a similar dilemma.

The Spirit Gives Cross-Cultural Wisdom

Often evangelists will be going into new territory, geographically or socially, where they must learn to distinguish between what is essential to the gospel and what is merely cultural. Often this requires of the evangelist particular sensitivity in language, or customs, or in matters concerning life-styles and standards. Here too, the Holy Spirit can be depended upon to bring fresh light from the Word of God and to shine it on that situation. Acts 15 tells of the council called at Jerusalem to consider reports that had come of Gentiles converted through the ministry of Paul and Barnabas. Two questions were raised: 1) Were the conversions geniune? and 2) If so, should the Gentiles now be required to be circumcised according to the law of Moses? After much discussion, Peter spoke. His key point was that when Gentiles earlier had heard from his lips the message of the gospel and believed: "God, who knows the heart, showed that he accepted them by giving the Holy Spirit to them, just as he did to us" (Acts 15:8). This was evidence that God purified their hearts by faith (15:9) and that it is only through the grace of the Lord Jesus that Jews are saved, as are Gentiles (15:11). When the council wrote an official letter to affirm the faith of the Gentiles, and to recommend that they abstain from certain practises (such as eating food sacrificed to idols or from sexual immorality), they stated their position this way: "It seemed good to the Holy Spirit and to us" (Acts 15:28).

cf J.W.

Captivity to tradition and culture has often bound the expression of God's Word and hindered evangelism. A bishop once said that the church in Europe was like an old man hobbling up a mountain with a great burden on his back, and that burden was tradition. This is not to say that tradition and culture are to be despised or rejected out of hand. It is to recognise that the confusion of the gospel with any particular culture or tradition may either blunt the cutting edge of the gospel or hide its glory.

The culture trap is always with us. In the council at Jerusalem the question was whether Gentiles could become followers of Jesus without becoming orthodox Jews. Today a similar question is whether Jews can become followers of Jesus without adopting Gentile life-styles and forms! The emergence of Jewish evangelistic movements and so-called "messianic synagogues" has been one attempt at genuine cross-cultural evangelism. So have the efforts of certain missionaries in the Muslim world to express the gospel in forms and ways that are at home and not alien to the ways of Muslim peoples. The Holy Spirit becomes our faithful guide in the cross-cultural translation of the gospel. "He has made us competent as ministers of a new covenant—not of the letter but of the Spirit; for the letter kills but the Spirit gives life," and "where the Spirit of the Lord is, there is freedom" (2 Cor. 3:6,17). Yet it must be noted that the freedom the Spirit gives is not *apart from* the gospel but *rooted in* it.

The Spirit Appoints Evangelists

All believers are called to be filled with the Spirit, to demonstrate the fruit of the Spirit, and to be witnesses. Some are especially appointed and anointed as evangelists. Again, just as the gift of the Spirit is received and poured out by the risen Christ, so the gifts of ministry, including that of evangelist, are received and bestowed by the ascended Lord (Eph. 4:11). He is the Evangelist *par excellence* and he is the one who makes evangelists. Through the Holy Spirit, he sets apart some for special missionary and evangelistic tasks, as he called Barnabas and Saul to missionary work from Antioch (Acts 13:2). In the setting apart of evangelists, the gift is *initiated* by the Spirit (the Holy Spirit said, "Set apart for me Barnabas and Saul for the work to which I have called them"), *mediated* and recognised by the church ("they placed their hands on them and sent them off," Acts 13:3), and *activated* by the obedience of the evangelists ("the two of them, sent on their way by the Holy Spirit, . . . when they arrived . . . proclaimed the word of God," Acts 13:4,5).

The gift of evangelism isn't one for us to choose for ourselves apart from the gift of God. Rather, all gifts are "the work of one and the same Spirit and he gives them to each man, just as he determines" (1 Cor. 12:11). But there is a responsibility that the church has to look for the gift of the evangelist, to note when someone seems to have received it, and to call on him or her and support that person in using it. The would-be evangelist will need to discover whether he or she has that burning desire to share with others the precious gift God has given, the mind on fire, the will aflame, the life ready to be poured out for God's glory and the salvation of the lost. And the gift is realised in using it.

PRACTICAL THEOLOGY: PASTORAL PSYCHOLOGY AND COUNSELING

David G. Benner, area editor

PASTORAL PSYCHOLOGY
AND COUNSELING

DAVID G. BENNER
Professor of Psychology
Wheaton College

Introduction

In the journal by the same name, pastoral psychology is described as the application of psychology to issues encountered in the ministry. Thus its focus is ministry and its method is psychological, that is, bringing psychological theory, research, and practice to bear on the understanding and practice of Christian ministry.

Perhaps the best known area of pastoral psychology is pastoral counseling. Here the theory and practice of counseling within the pastoral context is examined in light of what is known of counseling from its study in psychology and related mental health fields. The goals, techniques, dynamics, results, and problems encountered in pastoral counseling all are illuminated by the much broader and more thoroughly studied field of psychological counseling.

This is not to assume that pastoral counseling is the same as psychological counseling or psychotherapy. It is not. And in fact, the differences are increasingly obvious as pastoral counseling is studied in relation to psychological counseling. But related they are. And that relationship, as well as the cross-fertilization that can occur, is the focus in the study of counseling within the field of pastoral psychology.

However, pastoral psychology is much broader than pastoral counseling. It includes all aspects of the pastoral functions of ministry. Thus, journals that carry articles relevant to the field of pastoral psychology might examine such topics as the dynamics of forgiveness, guilt, anger, conversion, family life, or helping relationships—all of these viewed from a Christian perspective. These, and many many similar topics are vital for the pastor or person in Christian ministry.

A number of journals carry articles related to pastoral psychology. Some of the most available and possibly most relevant to *The Best in Theology* readers include *Journal of Pastoral Care, Pastoral Psychology, Journal of Pastoral Counseling, Journal of Psychology and Christianity*, and *Journal of*

Psychology and Theology. In this present volume we draw articles from two of these.

Stanley Hagemeyer's article "Making Sense of Divorce Grief" presents a theoretical and yet very practical assessment of the grief associated with divorce. Understanding the stages of such grief and the dynamics of a person's adjustment to the experience of divorce should be helpful to anyone involved in formal or informal helping relationships with divorced or divorcing persons.

The next article, "Healing in the Koinonia" by Leigh Bishop, presents an examination and case study of what it means for the church to function as a therapeutic community. This article should be of particular interest to those in churches who have made significant efforts to develop a body-life ministry.

Bruce Narramore's examination of the concept of responsibility in psychopathology and psychotherapy addresses a crucial issue for anyone involved in helping relationships. Here he examines seven alternate ways of understanding responsibility, and evaluates these in light of what he considers a biblical perspective.

For further reading I recommend John McDargh's article entitled _God, Mother and Me: An Object Relational Perspective on Religious Material_ (_Pastoral Psychology_ 34 [Summer 1986], 251-63). It presents an insightful consideration of how to listen to and understand religious material presented in the counseling context. This article utilizes the framework of a contemporary movement within psychoanalysis called object relations theory, a movement that many Christians are finding more useful than some of the more reductionistic earlier psychoanalytic traditions. McDargh's article will challenge and inform one's thinking and listening, and will repay the careful thought it might require.

A number of journals carried special issues this past year in tribute to Seward Hiltner, whose death in 1984 terminated almost four decades of leadership in American pastoral care. "Pastoral Care and the Gospel: A Theoretical Foundation for Hiltner's Pastoral Care" appears in such a tribute issue (_Journal of Psychology and Christianity_, 4 No.4 [1985] 79-85). In this article, LeRoy Aden examines the theological foundation for pastoral care, using Hiltner's vision of pastoral care as a framework. He argues that pastoral care is an indispensable aspect of the proclamation of the gospel. He then suggests ways this understanding can inform all pastoral activities.

This issue of _The Best in Theology_ presents three striking samples of what the past year has produced in pastoral psychology. They provide the pastor or person in Christian ministry with help through understanding. There is nothing here of a cook-book approach to pastoral care. Those days are, and should be, past. Contemporary pastoral psychology is a rich and developing field which in years to come will increasingly not only take the insights of psychology and apply them to pastoral practice, but will reverse this direction and demonstrate the wisdom of good pastoral practice.

About the Area Editor

David G. Benner (M.A., York University; Ph.D., York University) is a Canadian citizen, and currently professor of psychology at Wheaton College (Ill.). He is editor of *Baker Encyclopedia of Psychology* (1985).

MAKING SENSE OF DIVORCE GRIEF

STANLEY HAGEMEYER
Pastor, Saranac Community Church (Mich.)

Article from *Pastoral Psychology*

As more and more pastors, counselors, and lay leaders are confronted with the need to respond to divorce, it becomes more important to understand the process of recovery from divorce. Not all experiences of divorce are alike. Although many are increasingly recognizing common patterns, they continue to be confused because emotional stages seem to repeat in cyclical fashion. A person may appear to be falling into repetitious cycles rather than making progress.

These patterns do make sense, however, when seen as an interaction between distinct losses on one hand, and the emotional stages of grief that respond to the losses on the other hand. Recognizing the interlocking dynamic between the losses that occur and the stages of grief that follow them, can help a person make sense out of the cyclical nature of the experience of grief. This framework may assist in bringing some perspective and stability into what most often is a confusing and painful journey. Some tools will be suggested that can help identify those losses that cause the greatest distress and present the most challenging tasks for people being treated.

It is my purpose to provide a sort of road map showing the basic outlines of the route traveled by many divorced persons. Knowledge of the pitfalls, detours, and hidden dangers will help disarm those demons of despair, confusion, and fear that so often raise their heads. Some who might otherwise settle down in one of the stations along the way, may find that this information can help them move on through this experience to a new life with wholeness and purpose.

Sequence, Order, and Disorder in the Stages

Researchers have offered numerous theoretical models to describe the process of recovery from divorce. Salts[1] divided such models into two general classifications: those that focus on the emotional or affective dimensions of the process (denial, etc.), and those that describe the process with a focus on the dimension of behavior and event (that is, such matters as the court ceremony of legal divorce, etc.). In the first category, Herrman[2] applied

Kubler-Ross's[3] five stages of grief to the process of recovering from divorce. Wiseman[4] and Kraus[5] put forth similar descriptions with slight variations. These five steps may be described as, first, shock and denial; second, anger or guilt, a time of fixing blame; third, anxious bargaining to salvage some of what is being lost; fourth, depression and resignation; and finally, acceptance and renewal. The intense emotions and confusion that accompany these stages are often very troublesome to the individual and the care giver. They do not always appear in the same order and often repeat in various combinations. The experience of actually "going around in circles" adds an extra dimension of frustration and pain. Confusion and self-doubt often arise because of the instability perceived by both the subject and the care giver.

What has been said to this point will hardly be news to experienced pastors, counselors, or researchers. The stages of grief have often been identified, although it appears to date that little empirical research verifies the process. I propose that these familiar emotional stages appear repeatedly in response to a predictable series of identifiable losses. These losses have been identified, for the most part, by a group of researchers in Salts's second category.

This category includes the approaches that analyze the process from an event/behavior perspective. Bohannan's six stations of divorce (the emotional, legal, economic, co-parental, community, and psychic "divorces") constitute one of the best known of these models.[6] Another in this category is Kessler's[7] seven stages of divorce. She approaches the process more as a series of tasks to perform. Other models of this kind are presented by Waller,[8] and by Kressel and Deutsch.[9] There are serious problems with these and other models. Definitions vary among different writers. People do not experience the stages or events in the same order. There is sequence, but it is not fixed. Patterns appear and recur in a wide array of varieties. Some researchers refer to them as cyclical, although the stages do not repeat neatly. Salts's attempt to integrate the various theories has helped by clarifying the different subject matter that each contributor has been using.

These two types of categories of models serve as a background for a more recent integration of both types by Crosby, Gage, and Raymond.[10] They attempted to test the hypothesis that the widely recognized stages of grief actually do occur in sequence during divorce. They did not find that to be the case. They emphasize that the experience is characterized by *circular* rather than *linear* progression. They develop the conception that people experience both downward and upward spirals wherein the emotional grief, the thinking process, and personal behavior patterns often repeat. A person may repeat stages, skip some, or have stages occur simultaneously. They affirm that order, intensity, and duration vary from one person to another.

It seems to me that there is a simpler interlocking dynamic between the two types of models, one that can help us understand the cyclical nature of these experiences. The reason the emotional stages have often confused observers is that we are observing at the same time a series of specific losses identifiable on quite a different plane. These are losses that represent the important psycho/social components of a marriage that occur one or more at a time. The losses may occur either prior to the separation, during separation, or after the actual divorce decree. We can see the emotional stages, therefore, as responses to the actual or threatened losses that are occurring.

Each loss brings an emotional response. The emotional response will be determined in part by the lost item's value in one's psychic makeup, or by the value placed upon it by a cognitive belief system. As each new loss is perceived, singly or in groups, it may again set in motion a whole series of emotional stages, reverberating one after the other, deepening or moderating one another like waves upon water. Some stages seen before, like shock or denial, may not appear at all, while others, such as anger, may rise briefly to new heights of intensity and then pass on quickly to acceptance. Before describing the interaction in more detail we will first look at the losses we have identified.

A Succession of Losses

Divorce brings the loss of the psycho/social components that together have made up the meaning and content of a marriage. We can also view each loss as a crisis the person has to resolve in order to go on to new health and wholeness. Bohannan's six stations of divorce, the emotional, legal, economic, co-parental, community, and psychic, may be expressed as losses. To these I would add the loss of the dream and the loss of physical accessibility. They are described in the order that often occurs, although it must be emphasized that the pattern will vary from case to case.

The Loss of the Dream
Marriage most often includes some idealization of the spouse and unrealistic expectations about the happiness and fulfillment marriage will bring. It is the experience of losing this fancied ideal that Barnett[11] refers to as the "Fall." The person married was expected to bring happiness, sexual fulfillment, security, personal growth, or any number of other things. These expectations are eventually disappointed, to some degree. With the disappointment of this dream—the loss of the ideal partner or relationship that was hoped for—depression frequently occurs in one of the partners. This loss will likely occur in all marriages at some time, and the partners may go on to develop a more mature relationship built upon more realistic expectations, goals, and negotiated commitments. However, if not resolved, the loss frequently brings on other manifestations of marriage difficulties.

The Loss of Intimacy

The loss of complete openness and trust, Bohannan's "Emotional Divorce," develops when one or both partners begin to make commitments that take precedence over the marriage partner. This experience is the opposite of the courting process, where in preparation for marriage one was lifted out of the rest of humanity and selected for extra attention, appreciation, and given the highest value. Now a marriage partner experiences being "deselected." Emotional distance develops as partners find other interests and commitments. Children, jobs, friends, or even sexual affairs focus the emotional energies away from the unfulfilling relationship. An attitude of trust and commitment to one another is replaced by mistrust and a concern for self-protection. Constant criticism, even in the presence of friends, may occur in place of appreciation and compliments. Intimacy, vulnerability, honesty, and trust shrink to specific, recognized areas. The two partners know what they share and what they do not. In a marriage that appears to be well on the surface, devastating grief and loneliness may be carefully hidden from the outside observer. Reflecting on the tension of sharing his partner's home and bed but having no physical contact, one man stated sadly, "I feel such a terrible loneliness when I am in her presence." The loss of emotional intimacy is often signalled by loss of sexual satisfaction, and by decreased involvement or the complete absence of sexual activity.

The Loss of Physical Accessibility

Gradually, partners spend less time together in day-to-day activities. Separate lives are lived through jobs, friends, clubs, and children. Interests developed during the loss of intimacy take up more and more of their time. Fewer meals are shared together. During this period, there is often a seething anger in at least one of the pair at the deep disappointment in the marriage. This may be demonstrated by a harping criticism, which is met by defensiveness and criticism in return. As the rift widens, both partners find more appreciation and satisfaction away from each other and go on to develop those relationships. As an alternate pattern, however, the couple might be together regularly at social events, while at home, separate bedrooms signal a loss of accessibility. A couple may persist in living together when all hope for a relationship appears to be gone. Nevertheless, the physical accessibility that remains can still seem comforting to some. In this case, ambivalent love/hate feelings are often close to the surface. A way of life may develop and last for years with no real marriage beneath the surface. The couple may have accepted their identity in that marriage with its clear limitations, comforts, and benefits. Finally, they may crystallize the loss by obtaining separate living quarters; a publicly recognizable separation emerges. The real loss of accessibility may have been developing for years.

For most people separation is a time marked by severe loneliness, unless a new partner has been waiting in the wings for immediate companionship.

The emotional isolation experienced before, within the home, is now confirmed by the physical isolation from one another. Thereby, the loss of accessibility is nearly complete. The world seems desolate of potential attachment, barren, silent, dead.[12]

The Loss of Parenting Role

Separate living quarters open up the question of custody and parenting roles for those children still at home. For a few, relief from the burden of parenting is welcomed. Most, however, experience a deep sense of loss. Visitation times may be strictly limited. After each visit, a sense of loss and grief can well up again and again as the reality of being only a part-time parent settles in. Knowing that one's children are not within one's daily control hurts. One misses out on the numerous and varied experiences at school or play. The little things that make up the interchange of parent and child are now compacted into visits.

The same feeling of loss is often experienced by the parent *with* custody, who must release the children to the other for weekends or other brief visits. Relinquishing young children even for those visits can be very difficult, for example, when young children are handed over to the former spouse who is perceived as immoral, devious, or irresponsible. The emotional turmoil of one weekend of waiting for their return can be an intense drama, with all of the stages of denial, anger, guilt, and depression rising up to high tide.

The Loss of Legal Standing

The legal divorce, when initiated, or finalized, may become a ceremonial turning point in recognizing the dissolution of the marriage. The symbolic potential of this experience is great. It may be the occasion that signals loss of some social standing among friends or business associates. For some this carries little weight, but again, for others it is a day of intense grief, even though it has been long sought. The event may set off a celebration, with the euphoria of release from a prison. But when the day of court action comes, for very few does it pass without a deep sense of this being an important turning point in one's life.

The Loss of Money and Property

For the majority, divorce brings a drop in income. Two households cannot live as cheaply as one.[13] Temporary arrangements for the partner leaving the family domicile are often at a lower standard of living, and for the person staying in the family home, the income level drops. The severe losses in the area of family savings, property, and accompanying lowered status can bring a sense of bitterness. It seems there is no justice. Often, both parties feel wronged and cheated by the legal system. Even when attempts at a fair division are carried out, the loss of furnishings and items of sentimental value leaves a sense of diminished identity. One man in his fifties reported,

"Our divorce is almost over, but I moved back in to take care of the house for a while. She had let so many things go to pot, I just couldn't stand it. The place was becoming a wreck." The last part of a marriage, in his case, was the joint property.

The Loss of Community
Friends usually take on a changed view of the individual experiencing divorce. Some social circles, especially couples, may exclude one altogether, in part because of their own uncomfortable feelings rather than outright disapproval. Likewise, a change in attitude by the faith community is often unintentional, but nevertheless experienced as ostracism and disapproval. For many, the divorce from community may make it seem that nothing in the world is stable.[14] In addition, the time between separation and the eventual legal divorce is a limbo that for most people is a singular period of highest stress.[15]

If during this time one's normal social supports are found lacking, the stress of alienation is compounded by those friends or associates who have withdrawn. Some of them may feel they need to be neutral, but their actions are perceived as negative and critical. Anger may focus on those who have turned their backs, as loneliness and alienation are magnified. On the other hand, the more contacts that can be maintained—continuing relationships with people on the job or in other routines—the easier it is to hold on to some sense of stability.

The Loss of Attachment
The last loss to be described is perhaps the most mysterious, one Bohannan referred to as the "psychic divorce." As Weiss[16] most clearly describes, the attachment bond can persist long after all other aspects of the marriage have disappeared. A feeling of "belonging" to one another can persist in the absence of love over a long period of time. The most difficult work of the divorce appears to revolve around the rebuilding of a separate identity, without the former spouse as a key reference point. Often a person, in a marriage believed hopeless, will recognize the attachment and curse himself or herself for weakness and dependence.[17]

Attachment in a negative form can become a way of life as the lost partner becomes the focus of repeated confrontations, harassment, or games played to settle old scores, or to express the anger, loss, and perceived injustice of the divorce. As the attachment ebbs away, the former spouse is no longer seen as a reference point to relate one's daily experiences to. For some, that reference point may never disappear completely.

Losses and Grief before Divorce
In early research, Goode[18] reported that only two-thirds of the sample studied experienced significant separation distress. Similarly, Spanier and Casto[19]

found that for a substantial minority of people, the loss of attachment does not present significant difficulty post-divorce. These reports raise the question as to whether this distress is really such a universal phenomenon as Weiss indicated. Using our framework, however, we see that for some people the grief process may have been in motion long before a word about divorce was uttered. Therefore, it is not surprising that for a large minority of people, the time for grieving is nearly over when the divorce arrives. We might compare it to the death of a loved one following a lengthy illness during which the life has ebbed away. Grief in response to losses that occurred months or years before has already been accomplished in some cases.

Interaction of Losses with Emotional Stages

The loss of each component of the marriage has the potential for setting in motion the emotional stages described earlier. Thus, during the marriage, the early perception that the intimacy and trust of the marriage have disappeared can set off the succession of stages: shock/denial, anger/guilt, and bargaining ("What do I have to do to get you to love me the way I love you?"). After despair/depression, resignation and acceptance may finally arrive. At a later time, when separation and single parenting roles occur, each event can deliver an impact that may re-start the process, or at least distort or enhance parts of the recognizable pattern of grief. Thus, each wave of emotions set off may reinforce waves already in motion, enhancing their depth, or adding new ripples to an already confusing pattern of "disturbance" just as when one pebble after another is dropped into a pool, creating new circles of reverberating waves.

As we have indicated, the losses may not all occur separately and not necessarily in the order described. Losses can occur more or less simultaneously, with a shocking element of surprise, thus enhancing the sense of trauma and the depth of emotional spiral experienced. One woman reported that her husband brought her to a hospital for surgery, and as he left, explained that the marriage was over. He would move out of the home that week, was planning to marry a different woman, and would not be coming to visit her at the hospital. She had had no previous intimation that the marriage was in trouble.

Some may face one or two such intense experiences. However, others may, instead, experience a slow recognition of the numerous losses over a period of years, with emotional reverberations going on almost endlessly. Little wonder, then, that therapists report a bewildering array of stages, emotional journeys, or steps toward healing. Most likely the time of the emotional response will be determined by the time the loss is perceived as threatening or actually occurring, regardless of how it is seen by others.

Illustration 1

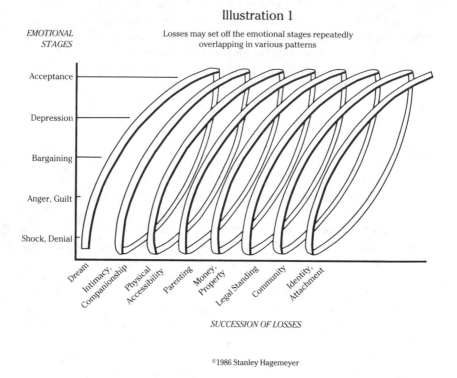

EMOTIONAL
STAGES

Losses may set off the emotional stages repeatedly
overlapping in various patterns

Acceptance

Depression

Bargaining

Anger, Guilt

Shock, Denial

Dream
Intimacy, Companionship
Physical Accessibility
Parenting
Money, Property
Legal Standing
Community
Identity, Attachment

SUCCESSION OF LOSSES

©1986 Stanley Hagemeyer

Illustration #1 portrays the way a sense of spiralling motion within the stages could occur. At any one time a person could have reason to be experiencing a number of different feelings, each adding to or being confused with the others.

It is worth mentioning that the losses need not be irreversible. Early recognition of problems, the loss of the dream, the loss of intimacy and trust, can lead to healthy and productive bargaining to create a new and realistic contract for the marriage. Destructive patterns can be reworked if the losses energize a couple into creative negotiation and love building.

Assessing the Meaning and Intensity of Emotional Stages

For most people, becoming married is the major attempt at gaining a certain part of one's identity. Becoming separated is a process of losing that part of the identity. Many liken it to losing a limb. Each specific loss is like the loss of another part of their identity. Letting go of parenting, driving the favorite car, gardening in the familiar back yard, eating with the family, enjoying the home and property, being seen by others together with the spouse and family, each slice diminishes the person and brings on a form of crisis in identity.

The loss becomes even more profoundly disturbing when one's identity is unknown outside the marriage. This is most often seen in the woman who has been married for many years and has invested everything in the husband's career and the family needs, and has not pursued her own autonomous identity. To the extent that an individual's sense of the meaning of the marriage may be concentrated on the particular component being lost, the impact of that loss will be more intense at that time. Property, children, or even one's church may be bartered away with a sense of bitter loss.

Erikson's thematic theory of development is a helpful framework for understanding the likely impact of the losses of divorce. Within this system the basic psycho/social crises of a person's life may be reopened by a marriage breakdown. Each needs to be resolved anew. The adequacy of previous resolution of crises will be tested, and unresolved parts reactivated.[20] Divorced or separated people often experience a sense of return to adolescence. At the same time, themes typically met with in later stages of life come rushing forward early, demanding attention. The crisis of generativity vs. stagnation, for instance, presents itself early to the father without custody who questions whether he will have any further opportunity to give of himself to his children or have any lasting influence on them.

Instead of progress as expected through the course of life, the divorced person is busied with a dialectical pattern in which he or she must find new forms of clarity and meaning.[21] A great deal of work must be done within. Therefore, it is not surprising that people often report the value of intensive journaling or other methods of carrying on an active internal dialogue. Small groups of supportive people in seminars or intentional programs provide another similar opportunity.

This theory suggests that people usually have one major theme in their life, such as trust vs. mistrust, or industry vs. inferiority. The discovery of that theme can be a helpful guide to predict which losses will likely produce the most profound disturbance in the individual. Recognition of a loss is very likely met with attempts to replace what is lost. The struggle to hold on to or to replace will likely bring up the same themes. For instance, the loss of community, and attempts to find new friends or circles of companionship, will bring up the theme of intimacy vs. isolation. Smart has applied Erikson's theory to divorce recovery with some success.[22] To her connections we have added our own to create a suggested list of the Erikson themes corresponding to losses, shown in Illustration #2.

Without getting into further detail about the theory, we offer it as a starting point for those familiar with the theory, and as a stimulant to further research.

Illustration 2

LOSSES IDENTIFIED	RELATED TO ERIKSON THEMES
The dream; ideal	Trust/mistrust Integrity/despair
Intimacy	Trust/mistrust Intimacy/isolation
Physical Accessibility	Autonomy/shame, doubt
Money and Property	Autonomy/shame, doubt Industry, inferiority
Parental Role	Generativity/stagnation
Community; Legal Standing	Initiative/guilt Intimacy/isolation Identity/diffusion
Attachment	Identity/diffusion Integrity/despair

Crosby *et al.* recognize that a major delimitation of their study is the inability to take into account the correlates of recovery such as economic stability, physical and emotional health, previous crisis experience, familial pressure, scripts, definitions of marriage, belief systems, and values.[23] We offer the Erikson thematic approach as one avenue of elucidating these and other correlates that will have a major influence on the way any one person responds to the losses encountered in divorce.

Conclusion

We have presented a theoretical framework that identifies eight major areas of potential loss in the divorce experience. We propose that each of them has the potential for setting off a wave of emotional distress with many of the familiar components of grief. With this expectation, it is hoped that the care giver and the one experiencing divorce can gain perspective on this confusing array of interacting emotional waves. By seeing the losses in this fashion, it may be possible to pass through them with more confidence, and carry on a more thoughtful approach to the corresponding needs that will arise. Further research is in order to clarify the usefulness of instruments for measuring the correlates, component stressors, and various interactions that can occur. The effectiveness of programs or counseling strategies for the separated or divorced may thus be evaluated and enhanced as well.

Notes

[1] C. J. Salts, "Divorce process: Integration of theory," *Journal of Divorce* 2 (Spring 1979): 233-240.

[2] S. J. Herrman, "Divorce: A grief process," *Perspectives in Psychiatric Care* 12 (Spring 1974): 108-112.

[3] E. Kubler-Ross, *On Death and Dying*, (New York: Macmillan, 1969).

[4] R. S. Wiseman, "Crisis Theory and the Process of Divorce," *Social Casework* 56 (4) (1975): 205-212.

[5] S. Kraus, "The Crisis of Divorce: Growth Promoting or Pathogenic?" *Journal of Divorce* 3 (2) (Winter 1979): 107-119.

[6] Paul Bohannan, "The Six Stations of Divorce," in *Divorce and After*, ed. Paul Bohannan (Garden City, NY: Doubleday, 1970), 29-55.

[7] Sheila Kessler, *The American Way of Divorce: Prescriptions for Change*, (Chicago: Nelson-Hall, 1975).

[8] W. Waller, *The Family: A Dynamic Interpretation*, (New York: Holt, Rinehart & Winston, 1951).

[9] K. Kressel, and M. Deutsch, "Divorce Therapy: An In-depth Survey of Therapists' Views," *Family Process* 16 (4) (1977): 413-443.

[10] J. F. Crosby, B. Gage, and M. Raymond, "The Grief Resolution Process in Divorce," *Journal of Divorce* 7 (1) (Fall 1983): 3-18.

[11] John E. Barnett, Jr., "The Natural History of a Marriage," *Pilgrimage* 9 (Spring 1981): 5-19.

[12] Robert S. Weiss, *Marital Separation* (New York: Basic Books, 1975), p. 32.

[13] Aric Press, et al, "Divorce American Style," *Newsweek* (January 10, 1983): 42-48.

[14] Bohannan, p. 31.

[15] Sharon P. Bonham and Jack O. Balswick, "The Non-institutions: Divorce, Desertion, and Remarriage," *Journal of Marriage & Family* 42 (November 1980): 962. The authors refer to numerous research efforts by others, in this broad survey of divorce literature of the 1970s.

[16] Weiss, p. 45.

[17] Op cit.

[18] W. Goode, *Women in Divorce* (New York: Free Press, 1956).

[19] G. B. Spanier and R. F. Casto, "Adjustment to Separation and Divorce: An Analysis of 50 Case Studies," *Journal of Divorce* 2 (3) (Spring 1979): 241-53.

[20] Laura S. Smart, "An Application of Erikson's Theory to the Recovery-from-divorce Process," *Journal of Divorce* 1 (Fall 1977): 71.

[21] Donald Capps, *Pastoral Care: A Thematic Approach* (Philadelphia: Westminster, 1979), p. 139.

[22] Smart, "An application of Erikson's theory," pp. 67-79.

[23] Crosby, "Grief resolution," p. 17.

HEALING IN THE KOINONIA:
THERAPEUTIC DYNAMICS OF CHURCH COMMUNITY

LEIGH C. BISHOP
Assistant Professor,
Chief, Adult Psychiatry Outpatient Clinic
Medical College of Georgia

Article from *Journal of Psychology and Theology*

The concept of healing community has been an integral one in social psychiatry over the past three decades. Since the years following World War II, when Maxwell Jones (1953, 1968) and others gave the idea a definitive form in experiments with "therapeutic community," the concept has expanded to include various forms of communities that have as a primary purpose the healing of their members. As Richard Almond (1974) demonstrates, the essential dynamics of healing communities appear to cut across cultural lines, and such communities can be found within many widely varying cultural groups.

In the past two decades, healing communities that identify themselves as Christian in belief and practice have become increasingly common. Indeed, there are many historical precedents for Christian healing communities, among them the Geel boarding system in Belgium, in which an entire town has become the healing community; the Modum Bads Nervesanatorium at Vikersund, Norway, where whole families were included in the healing community; and the York Retreat under the English Quaker William Tuke (Ravensborg, 1982; Roosens, 1979; Rosenblatt, 1984). In recent years, Christian healing communities have appeared both within and without established church bodies (Harper, 1973; Tidings, 1977; Vanier, 1979).

This article will review the social and psychological dynamics of healing communities in general and then examine a particular church community as an example of how the dynamics of healing community may be operative in an established church congregation. For purposes of this article, the terms healing community and church healing community will presuppose communalism as an element of community, though this may not always be true of healing communities (Almond, 1974). In the church, this recalls the concept of the *koinonia*, the sharing communion. Though this particular understanding of community may seem somewhat narrow, it is not intended to be exclusive but rather to emphasize the degree of interdependence and sharing that seems to provide the most suitable condition for healing community to function.

An adequate exploration of healing community in more traditional church settings would lengthen this study considerably and will be deferred for a future article. In reviewing the dynamics of healing community, I will draw heavily from the work of Richard Almond (1974).

Dynamics of Secular Healing Community

Typically, those who suffer mental illness in our culture undergo a labeling process that both labels them as sick or deviant and begins to isolate them, oftentimes long before they receive professional attention. In many other cultures, and in special cases within our own, there exist groups of people identified as communities, fraternities, or special societies for whom the deviant behavior is requisite for membership. Healing community acts to redefine the meaning of the deviant behavior as well as to include the individual in a group of fellow sufferers, with whom identification occurs.

Two qualities of the healing community are integral to this process. The first is the sense the community imparts to its members of being part of a special group in which each member is unique, yet important to the group as a whole and fully a participant. Almond (1974) labels this quality *communitas*. Communitas implies membership as having a central importance in the individual's life. It also implies shared norms and a shared belief system within the community. The second quality is the sense of specialness the community imparts to the individual members, one that encourages them to go beyond their accustomed roles and to become what they would like to become. Almond (1974) calls this quality *healing charisma*. Healing charisma also implies the member's belief in the healing power residing in other members of the community. It is reflected in the sufferer's belief that it is possible to become, and then his or her actually becoming, a member of the group, relieved of sickness and able to help others become relieved of their own sickness. Specifically, in psychiatric therapeutic communities, it is manifested by the concept of the patient as therapist for self and for others. Through these two dimensions and by other active processes, the healing community redefines the patient's behavior, previously defined as sick, in terms of its own norms and belief systems. While the community recognizes the deviant behavior as a reason for a given individual membership, it also communicates to patients that their individual specialness no longer derives from their sickness, but from that part of them that is healthier, and from their ability to move beyond accustomed roles.

The New Member in Healing Community

As the newcomer enters the community, a process of transactions around community norms and individual roles begins that will be one of the most powerful forces for change and healing that the community exerts. Ideally, this process will eventually culminate with the internalization of the community norms, although in some communities where a greater degree of commitment to the community is possible, the member ultimately may undergo integration into the community and not merely identification with it. Initially however, the group norms are chosen by the member as a more or less conscious adaptive maneuver. That is, it is the negative alternatives of failure to adopt the normative system, rather than the positive alternatives that the normative system offers, that most influence the new member. He or she is an insider who would yet live by the law of the outside if only it were possible.

Once received into the community, the member becomes aware of the healing charisma of the various roles of each member of the community. Typically in healing community, this charisma is reinforced by the norms of the community that allow members at all social levels to function beyond their usual roles. Healing charisma is not confined to those in traditional leadership roles. In a process not greatly unlike transference, the member imbues both leaders and other members with the power to heal. Just as important, the community imparts a healing charisma to the member. As a new member, one begins to sense that here one will not be simply acted upon, the object of healing, but that one will oneself be a means of healing. The power of the community to draw the new members into itself also begins to draw them to take responsibility for their individual healing and to some degree for the healing of others.

Interaction and Joining the Community

Other processes are active also. Early on, the members are exposed to a flood of new experiences that saturate their abilities to attend and focus. Indeed, part of the power of the healing community is that it is an experience unlike any the new members have had before, rendering many of their pathological adaptations ineffective. They find themselves in a social environment different from any they have known, and become the object of inquiry, confrontation, and expectation. This saturation of attention draws each individual out of isolation and focuses his or her attention on the processes of the community. It may serve to confuse the member, but the confusion itself is useful in moving the member toward a release of defenses and a heightened state of awareness. Even before the member's attention becomes focused, however, he or she is moved toward taking an active role in the community, even if ignorant of how to do so. This may at first mean nothing more than stating one's name and one's reasons for joining the community in a community meeting. Thus the member moves not only from isolation to involvement, but from passivity to activity. The new member may attempt to escape this wave of events, but the power of communalism prevents avoidant behavior. Privacy is rarely available, and withdrawal becomes a bid for inquiry.

Almond (1974) has noted that in most healing communities, the movement toward activity is expedited by two powerful events: confession and catharsis. By some means, the new member is induced to acknowledge his or her own contribution to the problem. This serves several purposes: It acts as a way of resolving guilt that has accrued because of the effect of the member's behavior on others. It also signals the possibility of accepting new ways of being and behaving, specifically those of the group, and it represents a move toward actually joining the community. It is a kind of rite of passage. In Alcoholics Anonymous, for example, the member's verbal identification before the group of himself or herself as an alcoholic represents the group norm of confession. Catharsis is the affective fulfillment of the essentially cognitive act of confession. It serves an abreactive function, heightening the member's sense of identification with the group and the group's identification with the member. Functionally, the primary importance of confession and catharsis is the general arousal of the member and a refocusing of the member's attention on the activities and norms of the community. Dynamically, a type of conversion occurs, similar to a religious conversion, with the possibilities of a new identity for the convert.

Roles and Behavior Change

Throughout this process, and probably throughout the duration of membership in the community, behavior modification is at work in complex patterns as the member is rewarded socially for accepting the community norms and demonstrating them by his or her own behavior. Advancement in social standing in the group as evidenced by changes in privileges, open recognition of leadership status, or more subtle operations, is a reward for perceived intrapsychic change.

The member also learns a new role by imitating the behavior of other community members. This represents the initial stage in a process of role paralleling, which results in the new member becoming an agent of healing like others in the group. The healing charisma that is identified with the leaders and other members draws the newcomer to behave in the way that they do.

A more advanced stage of role paralleling than imitation is identification. Identification as an intrapsychic process is more affectively charged than imitation. The member is no longer simply accommodating the norms of the community, but is actively looking to other group members for evidence of the possibility of real and internalized change. Identification implies an incorporation of the qualities of more experienced community members as well as a greater flexibility of role for the identifying member. As it involves internalization of norms and role expectations, it prepares the individual to deal effectively with situations for which mere imitation would be inadequate.

In groups that allow or require long term commitment, the member may progress beyond identification to integration. While identification has primarily to do with the member embracing the norms and values of the community, integration suggests the incorporation of the community into the member's anticipated life trajectory as an ongoing and central social context in which the member lives. Integration suggests a long-term or indefinite commitment by the member to be a part of the community as well as a reciprocal sense by most other members that this particular member provides an integral part of the community's identity.

As mentioned before, members of the healing community are expected and encouraged to live in a way that transcends their previous life roles. The processes of community life can be understood to identify and draw out of the members certain personality capacities. Among these, Almond (1974) notes the capacities for membership, faith, conformity, immersion or letting-go, altruism, and malleability. To this list might be added empathy and, pertaining to Christian healing communities, two other capacities that in our secularized culture receive relatively little attention, namely the capacities for awe and reverence.

A Church Healing Community Examined

At least within the mainline denominations of Christianity, healing community as a social phenomenon represents the intersection of two converging movements: a movement toward deeper experiences of community life, and a movement toward translation of religious values into corporate social action. The Christian healing community may be organized around a particular church congregation, several congregations, or it may be a community in itself without either congregational or denominational affiliations. It may have an ecumenical composition, its members representing different theological and sacramental backgrounds. Generally, however, the community has a theology that is largely shared by its members.

In 1975-76, I was privileged to be directly involved with such a community and to observe firsthand the processes of community life and the healing experiences of several people within the community. The Church of the Redeemer, a member congregation of the Episcopal Diocese of Texas, is located on the lower east side of Houston in an economically declining neighborhood that at that time, in terms of racial profile, was primarily Mexican-American and black. Under ordinary circumstances, I would disguise the identity of the church for purposes of an article such as this; but Redeemer is not an ordinary church, and there have been books and articles published about it already.

The history of the development of the community at Redeemer has some bearing on any consideration of it as a healing community, but it is too lengthy to detail in this article, and is available from other sources, notably Michael Harper's book (Harper, 1973). Redeemer, in some sense, was a healing community by secondary intention. As a church congregation, it developed a communal lifestyle in the 1960s in an attempt to deal practically with the difficulties inherent in fulfilling a corporate vision of ministry to an impoverished and decaying neighborhood. However, from the early days of its life as a community, it provided a place of refuge and healing for many with varying degrees of psychological and social impairment. It was probably as well equipped as any church congregation to do so. Graham Pulkingham, rector and parish priest, had served for some time prior to coming to Redeemer as chaplain to the University of Texas Medical Branch in Galveston, and had been a treatment team member for the Multiple Impact Family Therapy program at the Medical Branch. In addition, other professionals with knowledge of mental health issues, including two family physicians and a psychiatrist, were members of the community. However, to a great degree, the parishioners of Redeemer had to learn together, often painfully, how to address the needs of the psychological casualties which sought refuge there.

By 1974 the community (that is, those who chose to live together in households in the immediate neighborhood) numbered between 300 and 400 with a considerably larger full church membership. There were altogether twelve households with as many as eighteen people or as few as four people per household. Households were often organized around a nuclear family, but at least three households were composed of single unrelated adults. Each household was under the leadership of two or three household heads, appointed by the body of church elders.

Though survey data is not available to confirm it, the degree of communitas could be considered to be quite high in the community. Members generally considered the community to be a very special place where healing might be found for those who unsuccessfully had been seeking it elsewhere. The community's evangelical Christian belief system and its corporate sense of mission to the Eastwood neighborhood contributed to the conviction of the church community as being of central importance in the lives of the members. There was a strong emphasis on openness in relationships, free expression of feeling, and freedom to confront one another. This emphasis was largely fostered in response to the demands of a communal lifestyle, and was often summed up in the scriptural phrase "speaking the truth in love." Open expressions of caring and affection, usually in the form of hugs, were so frequent as to become almost a trademark of the community's lifestyle.

Included in the community were those with alcohol and drug abuse histories, personality disorders, marital problems, histories of criminal behavior, and thought disorders. The community was not equipped to deal with active psychotics and generally referred them elsewhere for professional care.

The primary social units of healing interaction in the community were the households and the relationships within them. The community's belief that any member could potentially manifest charismatic gifts (in the religious sense) heightened the degree of healing charisma (in the psychological sense) present in those relationships.

Household meetings led by the household heads occurred on a regular basis and as needed, and often were characterized by an intensity of interpersonal interaction typical of group psychotherapy. Also, through these experiences healing charisma was reinforced, and household relationships often took on the depth and character of familial relationships. Prayer was frequently utilized as a mode of healing in the households and in the larger community meetings.

Other healing activities in the church included pastoral counseling, which was provided quite frequently if necessary, special "sharing groups" that approximated group therapy, and daily work activities. Those who came to the community for healing very often did not have a job, had recently lost it, or were asked by the pastoral staff to leave their job in order to give themselves more fully to the life of the community. Several work and activity crews met daily under the leadership of more experienced community members and specialized in certain types of work, such as remodeling of households, construction of church furniture, janitorial care of church buildings, secretarial work, day care for children of working mothers in the neighborhood, or volunteer work in the local public elementary school. For members, this work was in addition to regularly assigned household tasks. Often, a newcomer was given work of a type that corresponded to the community's needs rather than his or her own experience or training, if any. In this way, new members were put in the position of having to try out new roles and to adapt to the needs of the larger group.

Not infrequently, married couples or whole families joined the community in need of help with problems in the family relational system. The flexibility afforded by the community's lifestyle allowed couples or families to live together in a single household, or to separate for a time and live in separate households while still being mutually supported by the one community. This provided a means by which stress in the family system could be temporarily relieved and individual problems addressed, while the preservation of the system as a whole could be maintained.

Authority resided primarily in the elders of the church, elected according to church law by the congregation. Most were in the 25-40 year age range. As a community norm, major life decisions were submitted to the elders for consultation and advice. However, members were discouraged from looking to the elders for guidance without having also considered carefully the problem on their own and with members of their household. As normative groups, pastors, elders, and parishioners were well integrated. While authoritative, pastors and elders expressed discomfort with an authoritarian stance, and often shared quite openly about their own personal struggles.

History of a Member

An understanding of the healing process in the Redeemer community is probably best obtained by following the history of one member, whom I will call Kay (names of the household and its members are pseudonyms). Kay was a divorced 44-year-old white female who was referred to the community by a friend. Kay had a long psychiatric history which included abuse of alcohol, prescription medications, and street drugs, multiple suicide attempts, a history of auditory and visual hallucinations, delusions, depression, and estranged family relationships. Prior to joining the community she had been living in the downtown Houston Y.M.C.A. and receiving episodic psychiatric care from overworked residents in Houston's Ben Taub Hospital emergency room. At the time of joining the community, she was taking amitriptyline and chlorpromazine, which she had received in the emergency room, and was continuing to experience hallucinations, although delusional thought content was absent or well-masked. Her thought processes were somewhat loose with an inappropriate and bland affect. Her mood was depressed. Her appearance was that of an overweight woman younger than her stated age, appropriately and neatly dressed, with a notable stare. She probably would be diagnosed as having a borderline or schizotypal personality disorder by DSM-III criteria.

As was usual after referral to the community, Kay met with members of the pastoral staff who obtained a history and, after determination that placement in a household was appropriate, she was assigned to one of the singles households, Dallas Street House. The household was composed of five men and three women, all single except for one of the women who had been abandoned by her husband, plus that woman's three-year-old daughter. Except for complaints of chronic depression in one of the men and reactional symptoms of anxiety and depression in the abandoned mother, no other members of the household had notable psychological impairment. As was usual, the two heads of the household had no professional training, but received support and supervision from the pastoral staff.

Kay moved into Dallas Street House with her few possessions and immediately began to be integrated into the life of the household. At the first meal, she was met with questions about her background and her reasons for coming to the community. Although some newcomers to the community might find such direct questioning at first meeting intrusive, Kay gave little indication of reluctance to talk about her difficulties. Neither did she protest the next day when assigned a light schedule of household duties. Newcomers to the community learned early that they were not guests. In her first week in the household, Kay was evaluated by one of the family physicians in the church and it was elected to discontinue all medications, with a two-week tapering of amitriptyline.

Household members' responses to Kay could be described as caring, but her past difficulties were regarded somewhat casually and it was clear that whatever special role she might fill in the life of the household, it would not reflect an identity as a "sick" person. Her occasional comments about past hallucinations or drug experiences were met with near-indifference. Her somewhat gratuitous personal style was challenged in particular by Daniel, one of the household heads, who was quick to express disbelief at Kay's frequent denials of feelings such as anger and sadness, that in her experience had been unacceptable. Yet while certain aspects of her behavior were challenged, it was clear that other household members were sincerely making an effort to care for Kay, if not to take care of her. Accepting Kay unconditionally was another powerful way of drawing her out of the sick role. As she experienced an unconditional acceptance, being in the sick role was less useful for her. Not all of the household members were equally able to do this. During discussion at the supper meal one evening, one of the men, Bill, became aware that he had felt anger toward Kay for some time. As other members of the household gently helped him explore the feelings, he discovered that he had resented being asked by Kay to assist in household tasks because he had felt socially superior to her. Once he had confessed this to the household, and had experienced not being rejected by the household or Kay, he was able to relate to her with greater ease and warmth. In this way and others, Kay became herself a means of healing for other people, thereby demonstrating and reinforcing her own healing charisma, and her move toward wholeness.

As the effect of medications began to recede, it seemed that much of Kay's bland affect began to diminish also. Although she expressed fearfulness of her hallucinations returning, none did and she began to interact with increasing spontaneity and a wider affective range. She began to express her feelings more frequently in household meetings and other settings. During her first month, Kay reported that she had new understanding of Christian salvation through faith, and that she had made a confession of faith in Christ and received a salvation experience.

In her second month in community, Kay was assigned to work half days with the clean-up crew at the church building. The crew met daily before work for a time of Scripture study and personal sharing. Outside of the household, Kay developed her closest and most supportive relationships on this crew. She expressed an increasing concern for the quality of work that she did on the clean-up crew. This work represented for her something more of herself that she could bring to the community, and signified an increasing identification with it.

After four months in the community, Kay had changed in appearance. She had lost much of her excess weight and appeared relaxed and calm. She no longer stared, though her affect remained somewhat bland. After eight months in community, Kay began expressing an interest in finding a job outside of the community and getting her own apartment. After ten months, and with the support of the pastoral staff and her housemates, Kay began training as a beautician and acquired her own place. At six months after moving out of the household, she was continuing to do well and maintained her job.

Anecdotal though it is, perhaps Kay's history at Redeemer demonstrates some of the rehabilitative processes of the church healing community.

The Koinonia as Healing Community

The life of the community at Redeemer demonstrates how the essential elements of healing community may be found within an established church body, albeit in this case a somewhat unusual church body. As Almond (1974) has suggested, the church may provide an almost ideal setting for the formation of healing community, with its "shared beliefs, involvement with and caring about fellow members, [and] charisma, the sense of something out of the ordinary" (p. 365). In theory, the unique qualities of the *koinonia* may modify the usually observed dynamics of healing community in such a way as to make the experiences of both healing and community more intense than might otherwise be the case.

The church community differs from most other kinds of healing communities in that it is a community that is not defined by sickness, at least not by sickness in the psychological sense. Its membership includes both those who are well and those who are ill. Consequently, though it may truly be "set apart from the world" in other ways, it provides a microcosm that is more like the real world than is the healing community that is defined by the common sickness of its members. Presumably, this adds to the power of the community to help the impaired member move beyond the sick role.

However, the church is also a community defined in some degree by its members' recognition of their individual and collective "spiritual sickness"; that is, all members are recognized as sinners in need of healing of their breach in fellowship with God. Therefore, to that degree the members, sick and well alike, share a common and radical need, and a common identity. The *koinonia* thus provides for a wider variety of role models while preserving and even intensifying communitas.

Regarding healing community in general, healing charisma implies the member's belief in the healing power residing in other members of the community. Specifically in many Christian communities, the same dynamic is suggested by the practice of having newer members of the community guided, nurtured, or "discipled" by members of greater experience and maturity in the faith and life of the community. Thus a kind of healing charisma may be imparted to those more experienced members. Yet the newer member partakes of this charisma also as he or she is invited from the first into full fellowship with the communion of believers and learns the doctrine of the interrelatedness and essentialness of the body's members (1 Corinthians 12). The relatedness of the individual member to the church community, and of the local church itself to the church universal, with its wealth of shared faith and spiritual heritage, provides for an experience of identification with group norms and values that extends beyond that of most other types of healing communities. In theory, this suggests the possibility of a more intense and pervasive experience of realignment of the individual's values.

Conclusion

In this article I have not discussed the intrapsychic aspects of the individual's religious experience or intellectual worldview in the healing process. This is not to suggest that such experience is either irrelevant or immaterial, but an adequate review is beyond the scope of this article. Suffice it to say that the social and psychological dynamics of healing communities in general may be seen to be present in specialized ways within the church healing community. In addition, the special qualities of the *koinonia* provide for an intensity of healing experience that may extend beyond that of the secular healing community.

Works Cited

Almond, R. (1974). *The Healing Community: Dynamics of the Therapeutic Milieu.* New York: Aronson.

Harper, M. (1973). *A New Way of Living.* Plainfield: Logos International.

Jones, M. (1953). *The Therapeutic Community.* New York: Basic.

Jones, M. (1968). *Beyond the Therapeutic Community.* New Haven: Yale.

Ravnsborg, I. (1982). "The Inpatient Care of Families at Vikersund." In F. Kaslow (Ed.). *The International Book of Family Therapy.* New York: Brunner/Mazel.

Roosens, E. (1979). *Mental Patients in Town Life.* Beverly Hills: Sage.

Rosenblatt, A. (1984). "Concepts of the Asylum in the Care of the Mentally Ill. *Hospital and Community Psychiatry, 35,* 244-250.

Tidings, J. (1977). *Gathering a People.* Plainfield: Logos International.

Vanier, J. (1979). *Community and Growth.* New York: Paulist Press.

THE CONCEPT OF RESPONSIBILITY
IN PSYCHOPATHOLOGY AND PSYCHOTHERAPY

BRUCE NARRAMORE
Professor of Psychology
Rosemead School of Psychology
Biola University

Article from *Journal of Psychology and Theology*

The concept of responsibility is a central issue in all forms of psychotherapy. Even when not addressed explicitly, the therapist's assumptions about the role of personal and societal responsibility in the development and resolution of adjustment problems has an impact on the entire treatment process. A large number of therapeutic interventions either teach or imply who we think is "at fault" for our patient's problems and who we believe is "responsible" for their resolution. Since an understanding of responsibility is intricately bound up with one's views of human nature, sin, psychopathology, and sanctification, a clearly thought-out understanding of responsibility should be foundational for Christian therapists. We cannot hope to have a biblically consistent approach to counseling until we come to grips with the concept of responsibility.

The purpose of this article is three-fold. It is designed (a) to survey alternative ways of looking at the concept of responsibility, (b) to evaluate briefly those viewpoints to see which are most consistent biblically and most helpful therapeutically and (c) to offer a corrective to a superficial view of responsibility frequently held by Christians. In regard to this latter objective, it seems to me that many Christians (including some Christian counselors) have erred by conceiving responsibility primarily as right actions or right thinking and by failing to stress responsibility for one's hidden inner wishes and feelings, and sinful nature.

This limited view of responsibility is reflected in the superficial criticisms some Christian authors have made of various psychological theorists. Jay Adams (1970), for example, claims that "All that can be said of Freud is that his views have encouraged irresponsible people to persist in and expand their irresponsibility" (p. 17). Yet Freud (1923/1961) himself wrote:

> To believe that psycho-analysis seeks a cure for neurotic disorders by giving a free rein to sexuality is a serious misunderstanding which can only be excused by ignorance. The making conscious of repressed sexual desires in analysis makes it possible, on the contrary, to obtain a mastery over them which the previous repression has been unable to achieve (p. 252).

Freud's position on responsibility is in stark contrast to Adams's caricature. In fact, in another place Freud (1914/1961) writes that the therapist sets about

> a perpetual struggle with his patient to keep in the psychical sphere all the impulses which the patient would like to direct into the motor sphere; and he celebrates it as a triumph for the treatment if he can bring it about that something that the patient wishes to discharge in action is disposed of through the work of remembering (p. 153).

While Freud clearly stated that patients must become responsible for their previously repressed wishes and feelings, many Christians persist in believing that depth therapies promote irresponsible acting out. In the following pages I will attempt to reconcile these apparently conflicting understandings of responsibility, in order to present a comprehensive understanding of responsibility that is biblically consistent.

The Meaning of Responsibility

Before entering into a discussion of alternative ways of viewing responsibility we need first to agree on the meaning of the word. *Webster's New Collegiate Dictionary* (Woolf, 1979) defines responsibility as "liable to be called to account as the primary cause, motive, or agent" (p. 979). Two aspects of this definition are relevant to the concept of responsibility in psychopathology and psychotherapy. The first is that responsibility involves locating the primary *cause* or source. The second is that responsibility involves *accountability*.

Since for some people, accountability or liability stirs visions of guilt feelings and condemnation, I would like to say at the outset that as I understand Scripture, the problem of the Christian's condemnation has already been solved (Romans 8:1) at the moment he placed his faith in Christ and His atonement. Consequently to locate in an individual the cause or cure of his or her own problems, or those of others, should *not* create feelings of neurotic guilt or condemnation. It may (and frequently should) create the "godly sorrow" Paul talks about in 2 Corinthians 7:7, and it may lead to genuine repentance. But it should not create punitive feelings of psychological guilt. Because of prior conditioning and their own self-atoning (punitive) dynamics people may well respond with guilt feelings when they see their responsibility, but these feelings do not come from God. They were most likely already in existence, although unconsciously, and they can be resolved with proper understanding. When I am speaking of responsibility, therefore, I speak of where we locate the source or solution to a problem, not about who should be blamed in a guilt-inducing way.

Responsibility in Psychopathology

Simplistic attempts to dichotomize theories of psychopathology and therapy into those who "blame" the parents and other socializing agents on the one hand, and those who promote personal responsibility on the other, do not do justice to the complexity of the problem. In fact, we can identify at least seven different ways of looking at responsibility both for the development of problems of adjustment and for their resolution.

In answer to the question "What is the *source* of problems of adjustment?" (or "Upon whom do we place responsibility?") we could answer any of the following: (a) the conscious, specific willful sins of the individual; (b) the (at least partially) unconscious sinful nature of the individual; (c) a combination of specific willful sins and the sin nature of the individual; (d) the conscious willful sins of the parents or significant others in the client's life; (e) the (at least partially) unconscious sinful nature of parents or significant others; (f) a combination of the willful sins and the sinful nature of others; (g) a combination of the willful sins and the sin nature of both the individual and his or her significant others.

Table 1 illustrates the several possible options. Although secular authors would not use the label "sin" and while probably no theorist fits totally in any one category, I have included one theorist in each cell who seems to come closest to representing that viewpoint.[1] Although it is a logical possibility, I am not aware of any theorist who places the responsibility almost entirely on the human sinful condition of others.

Table 1
Responsibility for Pathology

	SELF	OTHERS
SINS (Specific Conscious Sins)	J. Adams	B. F. Skinner & C. Rogers
SIN (Sin Nature)		M. Klein

If we locate responsibility for the cause of personal maladjustments in the conscious personal sins (actions or choices) of the individual we may, for example, see a woman as responsible for her marriage problems because she refuses to be submissive. Or a man's depression may be attributed to his failure to carry out his responsibilities at work or to confess his sins. This view of responsibility focuses largely on behavior and conscious actions and thoughts. Its concept of responsibility is that we have chosen to do the wrong thing and that is why we have problems. This seems to be the most superficial view of responsibility. While it certainly contains an important truth (our choices do strongly influence our adjustment), it is limited because it focuses too exclusively on conscious behavior, it minimizes or denies the responsibility of others, and it neglects the impact of our fallen sinful natures which cannot easily be reduced to consciously willed thoughts or actions.

The second alternative is to locate responsibility for the development of pathology in the inner sinful nature of the individual. This view has a great deal to commend it, and is consistent with the Bible's stress that overt actions grow out of attitudes of the heart (Matt. 12:34). It is a deeper concept of responsibility than one that locates the problem in specific acts or sins. The psychoanalytic perspective of Melanie Klein's et al. (1973) probably comes closest to fitting these categories. Her view of the innate destructive-ness of libido which is projected out into the world and is the source of most of our pathology, is reputed to have been labelled by Ernst Jones a mater-nalized version of original sin. Klein believes that while good parenting is vital to sound psychological development, the ultimate source of pathology lies in the child's inherent destructive impulses.

Views such as those of Klein's et al. (1973) that stress the importance of the total sinful nature and of hidden wishes, thoughts, and feelings, have caused concern among some Christians, perhaps because they fear that if we look beyond overt behavior to these deeper, sinful feelings, our clients might act upon them. They fail to see that only when we *face* the shadowy side of our lives can we really begin to make fully responsible choices. Responsible behavior in the context of repressed sinful wishes is a limited and shallow form of responsibility even though it may initially seem safer than struggling with sinful wishes and feelings.

The fourth and fifth possibilities are to locate the responsibility in the parents or other agents of socialization. In this view the child is seen as essentially good (or at least morally neutral), and problems are believed to be caused by the negative or sinful impact of others (either "willful" or "natural." The behaviorism of B. F. Skinner (1971), of course, suggests that all behaviors are controlled by the environment and that the belief that the individual initiates his own actions (and is consequently responsible) is an illusion.

From a totally different perspective Carl Rogers also places most of the responsibility on the environment. In *Becoming a Person*, Rogers (1961) writes of the enjoyment young children have in making a bowel movement any time or place they wish, and in hitting or trying to do away with their baby brother. According to Rogers, these feelings "are not necessarily incon-sistent with the concept of self as a lovable person." Then he writes:

But then to our schematic child comes a serious threat to self. He experiences words and actions of his parents in regard to these satisfying behaviors, and the words and actions add up to the feeling "You are bad, the behavior is bad, and you are not loved or lovable when you behave in this way." This constitutes a deep threat to the nascent structure of self. The child's dilemma might be schematized in these terms: *"If I admit to awareness the satisfactions of these behaviors and the values I apprehend in these experiences, then this is inconsistent with my self as being loved or lovable"* (pp. 499-500).

For Rogers, environmental conditions of worth that cause the child to repress the true self or shape himself or herself to others' expectations lie at the source of psychopathology. Views such as those of Skinner and Rogers, while contributing to our understanding of the role others play in the development of psychopathology, suffer from an essential denial of personal sin and of any personal responsibility for the etiology of pathology.

The final three options for looking at responsibility in psychopathology (c, f, and g) are simply variant combinations of personal versus societal and specific sins versus sin.

Responsibility in Therapy

Just as responsibility for the *source* of pathology can be looked at from the perspective of the relative weight attributed to personal or societal factors and from the perspective of specific conscious actions or humanity's basic sinful nature, so can the responsibility for resolution of problems.[2]

We can summarize our options for conceptualizing responsibility for solving problems or maladjustment much as we did their etiology.

1. The individual is immediately responsible for altering the problem behavior (regardless of who was responsible for its origin).

2. The individual is responsible for maturing in a way that alters his or her inner sinful patterns (nature) that led to the problem.

3. The individual is responsible for altering both the sins and the sinful nature.

4. Parents, spouses, therapists, or others are responsible for evoking specific behavioral changes.

5. Parents, spouses, therapists, and others are responsible for evoking changes in the sinful disposition (nature).

6. Parents, spouses, therapists, and others are responsible for effecting changes in both specific behavior and the inner nature.

7. Both patients and others have a responsibility for changing both specific sins and the sin nature.

If we locate the *source* of adjustment problems in specific sins of the individual we are likely to conceptualize responsibility as involving changing one's overt behavior in a relatively short period of time. If, in contrast, we emphasize the role of one's inborn sinful nature in the development of pathology, we are more likely to stress growth as a process involving insight into previously hidden sinful desires and hurts. Adams presents one of the clearest expressions of the belief that the fundamental element in the therapy process is changed behavior. He writes:

> When a client feels depressed or high, or anxious, or hostile, there really is no problem with his emotions. . . . It is true that his emotions are not pleasant, but the real problem is not emotional, it is behavioral. . . . People feel bad because of bad behavior (Adams, 1970, p. 93).

Although this is certainly one aspect of responsibility, it does not appear to encompass the full range of options. While Adams believes changed behavior will change inner feelings and attitudes, the problem as he defines it and consequently the locus of responsibility is at the behavior level. Christ accused the Pharisees of being "whited sepulchres" (Matt. 23:27) even though their external behavior was impeccable in nearly every detail. And the apostle Paul acknowledged that growth was an ongoing process involving the continual renewing of the mind (Phil. 3:12-14, Rom. 12:1-2). Just as placing all of the responsibility for the development of pathology on the individual's specific sins overlooks the deeper, inner aspects of personality and the responsibility of others, so does limiting responsibility for change to immediate or short term behavior change.

The treatment of homosexuality is a case in point. An extreme emphasis on the environmental or biological causes could lead to the conclusion that the homosexual has no responsibility for the development of his or her pathology, that he or she is a victim, and consequently cannot be held responsible for change. At the other extreme, the person may be told that whether he or she was responsible for the development of the pathology, he or she is responsible for changing the behavior *now*. The latter view certainly has something to commend it. But a third option seems to be both more biblically and psychologically consistent. That view would acknowledge that homosexuality is the result of (a) being a sinner, (b) being sinned against, and (c) sinning. It would also say that at this point the homosexual has a responsibility both to behave biblically and to set out on a path to alter the underlying attitudes that lie at the root of his sinful actions. This view does not excuse or condone the acting out of sinful wishes, but it does stress that overt actions are a result of inner sinful patterns, and as such are symptoms, not the actual problem.

Comprehensive Responsibility

It seems that any view of responsibility that does justice to all the facts must give attention to both one's personal responsibility and the responsibility of others, and to both one's specific sinful acts (sins) and his or her sinful nature. It must also include responsibility for both immediate and long term changes. If we underemphasize the impact of others on our clients' adjustment, we deny the fundamental social nature of humanity and excuse the sins of others. But if we fail to acknowledge that even with perfect parenting children would commit sins and develop problems, we distort the reality of humanity's fallen nature. If, in therapy, we focus too largely on immediate, conscious, willful changes we are in danger of reinforcing our clients' repressions and helping them avoid the depth of their hurts (from being sinned against) and sin. Yet if we focus on long-term hidden feelings, needs, and wishes in a way that suggests behavior is unimportant, we can promote the acting out of our clients' sinful wishes.

I have observed this latter phenomenon in some psychologically sophisticated clients who, in rebelling against legalistic or rigid Christian upbringing, use the fact that they are "in process" or "getting in touch with their real selves" as an excuse for irresponsible (sinful) behavior. Honesty about their feelings (including their resentment toward those who have sinned against them) and the need to overcome past repressions and restraints is seen as warrant to engage in sinful behavior as long as they are "growing"!

A comprehensive view of responsibility avoids both this irresponsible acting out, and unhealthy repression. It acknowledges both that we have been sinned against and that we are sinners. It acknowledges that both our specific sinful choices and the sinfulness inherent in our fallen natures contribute to our problems. And it acknowledges that we are responsible even for our unconscious sins—not because we purposefully choose them but because they grow out of our own fallen natures. They originate in ourselves, not simply in our environment.

This comprehensive view of responsibility also affirms that while we may have been deeply sinned against, at the present time we have a major responsibility for taking steps to initiate change. We do not, however, have to undertake that responsibility in isolation, since other members of the body of Christ have a responsibility to help us grow (James 5:16, Gal. 6:1,2). The process is also likely to take a significant period of time, since the resocialization occurring in counseling will often have to assist the one counseled in overcoming the long term effects of being sinned against by parents and others. Van Kaam (1968) demonstrates several aspects of this comprehensive view of responsibility when he writes:

> I-as-willing must take into account all the aspects which are involved in the change which I work to make in my life. I-as-willing should not set myself apart from I-as-feeling, I-as-thinking, I-as-imagining, I-as-remembering, I-as-participant-in-my-social-milieu, I-as-passionate, I-as-weak-and-sinful, and I-as-looking-toward-the-future (p. 113).

Here Van Kaam mentions our own willing, our thinking, our feelings, our environment, our fallen nature and the interaction of all these processes.

Summary

Attempts to dichotomize therapists into those who promote irresponsibility by blaming others for one's problems, and those who hold the client totally responsible, do not do justice to the complexity of the problem of responsibility. A comprehensive view of responsibility must incorporate both the impact of the individual and his or her socializing agents, the individual's specific sins and sinful nature and the role of the individual and others (therapists, members of the body of Christ, and so forth) in both altering sinful actions and in growing toward greater maturity in one's total personality. Consequently Christian counselors should help those counseled to become fully aware of the effects of both their own sinfulness and of being sinned against, and to accept willingly the importance of the therapeutic relationship in altering problems stemming from each of these sources.

Notes

[1] Adams, for example, writes of both the sin nature and of being sinned against. When it actually comes down to his theory of pathology, however, he lays most of the responsibility at the feet of the individual. He writes: "That others have done much to shape our lives, no one can deny. However, each individual must bear personal responsibility for how *he has allowed others to influence his conduct*" (Adams, 1970, p. 214). Note his emphasis on *conduct* and on *allowing* others to influence.

[2] The position one takes on responsibility for the development of pathology, however, does not have to determine fully our view of responsibility in therapy. Even though one may trace the *causes* of a counselee's problems totally to their socializing agents, he or she need not place the responsibility for *change* totally (or even partially) on those or other societal agents. Rogers (1961), for example, in discussing his process conception of psychotherapy, speaks of increased "feelings of self-responsibility in problems" (p. 138).

Works Cited

Adams, J. (1970). *Competent to Counsel*. Grand Rapids: Baker.

Freud, S. (1961). "Remembering, Repeating and Working Through." In J. Strachey (Ed. and Trans.), *The Standard Edition of the Complete Psychological Works of Sigmund Freud* (Vol. 12, pp. 145-156). London: Hogarth Press. (Original work published 1914)

Freud, S. (1961). "Psycho-analysis." In J. Strachey (Ed. and Trans.), *The Standard Edition of the Complete Psychological Works of Sigmund Freud* (Vol. 18, pp. 235-254). London: Hogarth Press. (Original work published 1923)

Klein, M., Heimann, P., Isaacs, S., & Riviere, J. (1973). *Developments in Psycho-analysis*. London: Hogarth Press.

Rogers, C. (1961). *On Becoming a Person*. Boston: Houghton Mifflin.

Skinner, B. F. (1971). *Beyond Freedom and Dignity*. New York: Knopf.

Van Kaam, A. (1968). *Religion and Personality*. New York: Doubleday.

Woolf, H. B. (Ed.). (1979). *Webster's New Collegiate Dictionary*. Springfield, MA: G. & C. Merriam Company.

PRACTICAL THEOLOGY: MISSIONS

Miriam Adeney, area editor

MISSIONS

MIRIAM ADENEY
Lecturer, School of Religion, Seattle Pacific University,

Introduction

Why bother with missions? Because the love of Christ constrains us to be ambassadors of reconciliation. Because the Word is fire in our bones. God is creator of the peoples of the earth. He is their redeemer. He is their lawgiver. He is their reconciler, their peacemaker. He is conqueror of the powers of darkness, both within individuals and within multinational structures. We do mission so that His name may be praised explicitly and with understanding among every people. We do mission out of love for our neighbors, in this interdependent world. If we sell wheat to people overseas, if we buy electronic components from them, can we keep silent? Is Christ less than wheat?

How we do it is another matter.

Straightforward, pragmatic, and conversionist, C. Peter Wagner's article in this volume is a good baseline as we begin to explore American mission strategy in 1985-86. Others, however, have raised questions about this "church growth" emphasis, with its measurable components. Is quantification—social science—a way to gain significant truth about what God is doing? Does a conversionist preoccupation faithfully express God's full-orbed love? Are ethnic churches racist? Et cetera.[1]

The power of the Holy Spirit surely must rank high in mission strategy. Many articles this year focus on the Holy Spirit. I recommend, but could not include for reasons of space, "After Twenty Years Research on Pentecostalism," by Walter Hollenweger. He distinguishes between classical Pentecostals; charismatics, who function in non-Pentecostal denominations; and "indigenous nonwhite churches." "The total membership of all three streams was over 100 million in 1980 and is expected to grow to 250 million by the year 2000."[2]

Regarding the third stream, Dean Gilleland asks: "How 'Christian' Are African Independent Churches?" He offers four useful categories:[3]

1. Primary Evangelical-Pentecostal Type: Originating in a historical American or European church.

2. Secondary Evangelical-Pentecostal: "Almost totally unrelated to any movement outside Africa."

3. Revelational-Indigenous Type: "The direct word that comes to the leaders carries more authority than reference to the Bible."

343

4. Indigenous-Eclectic: These "have retained so many features of the traditional religion that their claim to be Christian is in doubt."

In choosing whether to aim to fellowship with a group or to evangelize it, Gilleland has found these criteria helpful: the place of Christ, the role of the Bible, sacraments, discipline, and the direction in which the church is moving over a period of time.

Other articles, such as Warner's (which is included in this volume of *The Best in Theology*), challenge the missionary to take hold of God's power for healing, exorcism, and defense.

Close on the heels of the power of the Holy Spirit comes the power of money, a very mixed blessing. Not printed in this volume but recommended reading, is "The Curses of Money on Missions in India"; here three Christian leaders document abuses.[4] This may complement the inclusion this year of "ecclesiastical embezzlement" as a significant and measurable category in the annual roundup of statistics tabulated by David Barrett, editor of the *World Christian Encyclopedia.*[5]

Yet money *is* a blessing. Faced with its abuse, our giving should not decrease, but should be armored with questions concerning accountability. Of these, financial accountability should be only one part. One journal helping church mission committees to give more wisely, especially for physical needs, is published for development practitioners by World Vision: *Together.*[6]

After money, politics is often mission strategy.[7] Other significant focuses this year include: the Vatican twenty years after Vatican II[8]; Urban mission[9]; Blacks in mission[10]; and women in mission.[11] Looking to the future, "new demands, new items, and new questions" in mission are explored in Harvie M. Conn's "Missions and Our Present Moment in History," printed in this volume.

Notes

[1] For 140 comments on this approach, drawn from around the world in the past year, see: "Comments on Donald McGavran's 'A Giant Step in Christian Mission'," *A Monthly Letter on Evangelism* (Committee on Evangelism, World Council of Churches, Geneva, Switzerland), August 1985-April/May 1986.

For further contrasts of opinion on strategy see:

Sharon Mumper, "Where in the World Is the Church Growing?" *Christianity Today*, July 11, 1986.

David Stoll, "What Should Wycliffe Do?" and R. Daniel Shaw, "Ethnohistory, Strategy, and Bible Translation: The Case of Wycliffe and the Cause of World Mission," *Missiology*, Vol. XIV, No. 1, January 1986.

[2] Walter Hollenweger, "After Twenty Years' Research on Pentecostalism," *International Review of Mission*, Vol. 75, No. 297, Jan. 1986, pp. 3-12.

See also Grant McClung, "Explosion, Motivation, and Consolidation: The Historical Anatomy of the Pentecostal Missionary Movement," *Missiology*, Vol. XIV, No. 2, April 1986.

[3] Dean Gilliland, "How 'Christian' Are African Independent Churches?" *Missiology*, Vol. XIV, No. 3, July 1986, pp. 259-272.

[4] Rajmani Stanley, Roger Hedlund, and J. P. Marsh, "The Curses of Money on Missions to India," *Evangelical Missions Quarterly*, Vol. 22, No. 3, July 1986.

[5] David Barrett, "Annual Statistical Table on Global Mission: 1986," *International Bulletin of Missionary Research*, Vol. 10, No. 1, Jan. 1986, pp. 22-23.

[6] For example of such helpful guidance, see Tom Houston, "A Biblical Context for Relief Ministries," *Together*, No. 11, April-June 1986, pp. 24-27.

[7] J. Dudley Woodberry, "The Bombing of Libya and Christian Witness," *The Zwemer Institute Newsletter*, Summer 1986, p. 3.

James Dekker, "Searching for Ways of Mission in Revolution," and William Taylor, "Provocative Analysis Needs Alternatives," *Evangelical Missions Quarterly*, Vol. 22, No. 2, April 1986, pp. 142-59.

Sidney Rooy, "Social Revolution and the Future of the Church," *Occasional Essays of CELEP*, Vol. 13, Nos. 1 and 2, June-Dec. 1986, pp. 60-89.

David Bosch, "Afrikaner Civil Religion and the Current South African Crisis," *Princeton Seminary Bulletin*, Vol. VII, No. 1 (New Series 1986), pp. 1-14. This article appears in the current volume of *The Best in Theology*.

[8] See especially two articles and two documents in the *International Bulletin of Missionary Research*, Vol. 9, No. 4, Oct. 1985:

W. Richey Hogg, "Vatican II's *Ad Gentes*: A 20 Year Retrospective."

Paul Pierson, "Roman Catholic Missions Since Vatican II: An Evangelical Assessment."

"*Nostra Aetate*: The Declaration on the Relation of the Church to Religions," Pope Paul, 1965.

"The Attitude of the Church Toward the Followers of Other Religions," Vatican Secretariat for Non-Christians, 1984.

[9] See especially *Urban Mission*, published by Westminster Theological Seminary.

[10] Gayraud S. Wilmore, "Black Americans in Mission: Setting the Record Straight," *International Bulletin of Missionary Research*, Vol. 10, No. 3, July 1986, pp. 98-103.

[11] Ruth Tucker, "African Women's Movement Finds Massive Response," *Evangelical Missions Quarterly*, Vol. 22, No. 2, July 1986, pp. 282-93.

About the Area Editor

Miriam Adeney (M.A. in Journalism, Syracuse; Ph.D. in Anthropology, Washington State University) is adjunct professor of missions and cross-cultural communications at Regent College, and lecturer in missions at Seattle Pacific University. She is also concerned with evangelization of Muslims, church outreach to international students in Canada and the U.S., and fostering literature and media programs relevant to developing countries. She is the author of *God's Foreign Policy* (1984) and numerous articles.

A VISION FOR EVANGELIZING THE REAL AMERICA

C. PETER WAGNER
Professor of Church Growth
Fuller Theological Seminary

Article from *International Bulletin of Missionary Research*

Residents of the state of Oregon are required to pay an annual fee of $42.50 for rights to hunt and fish during a specific season designated by the Department of Fish and Wildlife. That is, all residents except Klamath Indians. After some hard-fought legal battles during the 1970s in which the state of Oregon bent all efforts to bring the Klamath Indians into line and make them obey state hunting and fishing laws, the U.S. 9th Circuit Court of Appeals ruled in favor of the Indians in the early 1980s. The Klamath Indians now may hunt and fish without being bound by state regulations because the U.S. Congress did not declare otherwise when the treaty was signed over eighty years ago.

In San Gabriel, California, a Chinese businessman retained a real estate agent to help buy a home, but none of the houses listed appealed to him. As they were driving back to the office, the Chinese spotted a house and said that it was the one he wanted. The agent tried to explain that it wasn't for sale, but his client insisted. The woman of the house came to the door and the Chinese challenged her to put a price on the house. Just playing games, she said, "One million dollars." "Sold!" said the Chinese. She immediately called her husband home from work because the house would not have listed for a quarter of that price. When they agreed on the sale, the Chinese opened a briefcase and turned over one million dollars in currency.

In the St. John Valley of Maine, nuns teach religion in public schools. The Supreme Court might as well be light years away from Maine's 400,000 Franco-Americans who now comprise a full one-third of the state's population. In fact the 30,000 people who live in small towns on the American side of the St. John River consider themselves primarily citizens of La République de Madawaska (the land of the porcupines), even though they dutifully submit their 1040 forms to the Internal Revenue Service on an annual basis. New England has over two million people whose mother tongue is French, not English. Their ancestors first began to arrive in 1755, and in the beginning years of our own century trainloads of French Canadians poured in to work in Maine's textile mills and shoe factories. They now call themselves Franco-Americans and they are here to stay.

The Real America

Whether in Oregon, California, or Maine, this is the real America. Today's America is a multi-ethnic society on a scale that boggles the imagination. The teeming multitudes of all colors, languages, smells, and cultures are not just a quaint sideline in our nation; they are America. And it is this America that God has called us to evangelize.

Jesus said, "Go, therefore, and make disciples of all nations" (Mt. 28:19). The Greek from which "all nations" is translated is πάντα τὰ ἔθνη. Ἔθνη, of course, is the word from which our English word "ethnic" is derived. Because our Lord has commanded us to evangelize πάντα τὰ ἔθνη, many American Christian leaders have been developing a new awareness of ethnic America. Many are saying to the ethnics around us, "We care." We care about the millions upon millions of Asians and Hispanics and Middle Easterners and Europeans and American Indians and Caribbeans who have come to a land of freedom and opportunity. We care about the Mexican working in the restaurant in Minneapolis. We care about the Greek in the butcher shop in New York. We care about the Romanian sewing dresses in Chicago. We care about the Japanese wholesaling stereo equipment in Los Angeles. We care about the Arab pumping gasoline in Detroit. Why do we care? Because God cares.

God cares for their bodies, their souls, their minds, their spirits, and their social relationships. And he call us as Christians, no matter what our racial or national background, to be his instruments for reaching them with the message of the kingdom of God. God claims them as his own. He sent his Son to die for them. He wants them to be born again and thereby to see and enter into the kingdom of God.

What an enormous vision. The Bible says that where there is no vision the people perish (Prov. 29:18). It also says that God is not willing that any should perish (2 Pet. 3:9). This vision undoubtedly has many, many parts. I would like to begin to bring three of them into focus in this essay, namely, the social vision, the spiritual vision, and the strategic vision.

I. The Social Vision

I should think that when historians of the twenty-first century look back on the United States of the twentieth century, they will judge that the most significant decade was that of the 1960s. The two world wars, the Great Depression, the advent of space travel, and the cybernetic revolution will certainly be important. But I believe that even more important has been the civil rights movement of the '60s.

This movement, stimulated largely by black Christian leaders, has permanently changed America's self-image from that of an assimilationist to a pluralistic society. Most of us learned in school that America was a melting pot. We were led to believe that when people came across our borders from other nations, they would quickly forget about their past and become so-called Americans. The American way was to abandon all claims to Frenchness or Polishness or Irishness or Chineseness or Mexicanness and to adopt the so-called more civilized Anglo-American cultural values. This attitude also applied to the peoples who were here before the Anglos such as the Mohawks or the Sioux or the Comanche or any of hundreds of other Indian tribes. It was fully expected that they would inevitably recognize the superiority of Anglo culture and melt into the melting pot.

Up to the decade of the 1960s, most Americans actually thought the melting pot had worked. With only a few exceptions, ethnics were socially and legally invisible. Sociologists studied Americans only as individuals, and did little work on analyzing their group loyalties, which were not even supposed to exist. Mild doses of non-American behavior were tolerated and even regarded as somewhat colorful. St. Patrick's Day, French restaurants, and Polish jokes were a part of American life. But at levels that might affect government, law, or economics, ethnic behavior was frowned upon. At worst ethnicity was a serious threat to society, and at best it was a nuisance it was hoped would disappear in a generation or two.

America's Stewpot
Ethnicity did not disappear in a generation or two, nor will it. The real America is not a melting pot; it never was. The real America is a stewpot. While some prefer using analogies of salad bowl, mosaic, tapestry, or rainbow, I prefer the stewpot. Here each ingredient is changed and flavored by the others. The changes are for the better. The carrots, potatoes, meat and the onions all taste better after they come in contact with each other in the stewpot. While they enrich each other, each ingredient nevertheless maintains its own identity and integrity. If the stew is overcooked, the ingredients lose their identity and the contents become unpalatable mush.

In the new American society that emerged from the civil rights movement of the 1960s, each ethnic ingredient now has the potential to be enriched through intercultural contact with the others. But ideally they are no longer under social pressure to become culturally Anglo-American in order to "make it" in our country. It is true that we have not always lived up to the ideal, but the sweep of social history over the last two decades is encouraging. American blacks in particular have taken giant steps toward the ideal, with mayors in four of the six largest cities in the nation, two black Miss Americas, a black Tournament of Roses queen, and a presidential candidate who accentuated his blackness instead of pretending to ignore it. Other ethnic minorities are advancing as well. We need to recognize that this could not be happening under the melting-pot ideal.

What does this stewpot look like?

Time magazine called the Los Angeles area, where I live, "The New Ellis Island." Waves of immigrants flood in. Parts of the city change almost overnight from one ethnic group to another. Blacks in south-central Los Angeles are complaining that Mexicans are "spoiling the neighborhood." In Hollywood a fast-food stand, operated by Koreans, sells "Kosher tacos." Students in the Los Angeles Unified School District speak 104 languages, with over 1,000 students speaking each of these languages: Spanish, Korean, Vietnamese, Cantonese, and Armenian.

The Los Angeles metropolitan area has the greatest population of Koreans outside the Orient, with estimates as high as 270,000. Despite the fact that Korean immigration started only in the '70s, there are now four daily Korean language newspapers, a Korean telephone directory, three banks, one savings and loan, 130 Korean schools, five art galleries, two symphony orchestras, 300 voluntary associations, and 430 churches.

For the past eight years I have been collecting and updating facts concerning the ethnic makeup of the Los Angeles area. Here are the known groups with the best estimate of population: Hispanics (4 million), blacks (972,000), Germans (450,000), Italians (350,000), Koreans (270,000), Armenians (225,000), Iranians (200,000), Japanese (175,000), Arabs (160,000), Yugoslavs (150,000 divided sharply between Serbians and Croatians), Chinese (150,000), Filipinos (150,000), Vietnamese (100,000), American Indians (95,000), Russians (90,000), Israelis (90,000), Dutch (75,000), Hungarians (60,000), Samoans (60,000), French (55,000), Thai (50,000), Greeks (50,000), British (50,000), Asian Indians (30,000), Dutch Indonesians (30,000), Egyptian Copts (10,000), Romanians (10,000), Turks (5,000), and Gypsies (5,000). I expect information on other groups to surface as time goes by. One television station, KSCI, has programs in English, Spanish, Arabic, Farsi, Armenian, Vietnamese, Korean, Japanese, Cantonese, and Mandarin.

What is said about Los Angeles could be said about cities across the land. Minorities now make up a majority in at least twenty-five major United States cities, including Miami, Newark, Washington, Atlanta, Detroit, El Paso, New Orleans, Chicago, Hartford, and Jersey City, as well as many more. Miami is the second largest Cuban city. Downtown stores carry window signs "English spoken here." There are more Jews in New York City than in Tel Aviv. Chicago is the world's second largest Polish city, and Los Angeles the second largest Mexican city. There are more Hispanics in Los Angeles than in seven of the Latin American countries. The United States is the fifth largest Spanish-speaking country in the world. New York is the second largest Puerto Rican city. The projection is that by the year 2,000, more than fifty major United States cities will be composed predominantly of ethnic minorities.

Census figures are the chief source of information on United States population, but they frequently need refining for a more accurate broadscale picture. For example, they do not include undocumented aliens and many discrete ethnic groups are not enumerated as groups at all. With an evangelistic purpose in mind I have used the 1980 census, with interpolations done by the Southern Baptist Home Mission Board and myself. The following breakdown of United States population emerges.

Notice that the deaf are listed separately. Although they are not an ethnic group as such, they do need a specialized kind of evangelism, since they have their own language, a highly endogamous marriage pattern, and behavior patterns distinct from the dominant culture.

America's "Melting Pot"

	Millions	Percent
Europeans	94.0	41.0
Anglos	67.0	29.0
Blacks	26.5	11.0
Hispanics	23.0	10.0
Deaf	14.0	6.0
Asians	3.5	1.5
American Indians	3.5	1.5
Totals	231.5	100.0

The Europeans include those who claim a self-identity as German or Irish or Italian or Polish or Norwegian or Dutch or Greek or some other. Many with European ancestry, even some first-generation Americans, have assimilated into the Anglo culture and regard themselves as Anglos rather than Swedes or French or Russians or what have you. They are not counted as Europeans above. The most surprising statistic is that, according to this breakdown, Anglos now comprise only about 30 percent of America's population, though most of the national cultural structures and forms remain Anglo.

Ethnics on the Increase
It is one thing to know the numbers of the colorful ethnic mosaic that is the real America, but it is another to know the trends. Non-Anglo minorities are likely to increase disproportionately as the years go by. For one thing, generally speaking, they have a significantly higher birth rate than Anglos. For another, the immigration patterns have been on the increase. Notice how the numbers of immigrants have been increasing as the decades have gone by:

U.S. Immigration Patterns	
	Numbers per Year
1930s	53,000
1940s	104,000
1950s	252,000
1960s	332,000
1970s	429,000
1980s	over 600,000

These figures do not include the undocumented immigrants. No one knows exactly how many illegal aliens enter the United States each year, but it is known that the Immigration and Naturalization Service in 1976 apprehended and deported an average of 2,400 per day, and that by 1983 that daily average was up to 5,500 or over two million per year. Some estimates say that conservatively we can believe that 600,000 undocumented persons enter the United States per year for permanent residence. While most of these are Mexicans, large numbers come from a variety of other countries as well.

The Hispanic population of California is increasing so rapidly that, at the present rate, sometime before the turn of the century California will once again be a Spanish-speaking state. California legislators spend a good bit of time debating the issues that this raises. All voting material in the state is now bilingual, but a bill has been introduced to remove the Spanish from the voting materials. This is obviously a feeble effort to force Hispanics to forget their language and learn English. But, on the other side, another bill has been introduced that would require fluency in Spanish if one is to graduate from high school in the state. Neither bill has passed as of this writing.

The increase of American Indians, or Native Americans, through the years has been dramatic, particularly in view of the persistent effort of the whites to eliminate not only tribalism but the entire race through forced assimilation. The first census of Indians was made in 1890, when 248,000 were counted. By 1970 there were 1.5 million and in 1980 the figure was up to 3.5 million. The 95,000 Indians in the Los Angeles area represent more than 100 of the 493 federally recognized tribes. Over the last ten years the number of Indian-owned businesses in California has risen from fifty to 600.

It is obvious even to a casual observer that the vast majority of America's ethnics live in the cities. Seventy-five percent of America's blacks live in cities. Eighty-four percent of Hispanics live in cities. East Los Angeles, California, is 96 percent Hispanic. When immigrants come from abroad they settle in the cities. Internal migration has been from the rural to the metropolitan areas throughout American history, with a brief reversal in the mid-seventies. It is appropriate, then, that the city become a focal point for ethnic evangelization. We are learning a great deal about the city through the Lausanne Strategy Working Group under the leadership of Ray Bakke of Northern Baptist Seminary. Westminster Seminary has developed a high-level urban program with Professors Harvie Conn and Roger Greenway. Larry Rose and Kirk Hadaway have established an influential Center for Urban Church Studies in Nashville, Tennessee. Others are emerging.

This, then, is the social vision. It is a vision of a nation of ethnics blended into an urban stewpot. The Statue of Liberty has long expressed America's invitation to the world: "Give me your tired, your poor, your huddled masses, yearning to breathe free." The current extensive renovation of the statue itself is indication enough that America intends to keep the doors open. I like the way a brochure from the Southern Baptist Language Missions Department expresses this sentiment:

> It is unlikely any other nation in the world is so *intentionally* pluralistic: the people of the United States have chosen to come to these shores: men, women and children giving up home and family, status and stability, human beings drawn by things more powerful than might or wealth; for here triumphs the concept of freedom and hope, here promises a fresh start, an equal chance: the opportunity to be *somebody*.

II. The Spiritual Vision

If the real America is a multitude of multicolored, multilingual, multicultural human beings, the spiritual vision for the real America is summed up in an extraordinarily challenging evangelistic task. America is a multitude to be won to Jesus Christ.

What the exact parameters of this evangelistic challenge are, I do not know. Information on the status of evangelization in each of the distinct ethnic groups is spotty and largely private. Many individuals have up-to-date information, but such information does not readily enter the public domain. Obviously more research is needed.

We do know that American ethnics are under-evangelized, compared especially to Anglos and blacks. About 74 percent of America's 26.5 million blacks are affiliated with churches, and about 68 percent of whites are church members. Church membership, of course, is never the whole story when planning evangelism, for many church members are nothing more than nominal Christians and are not born again. They, too, need to be evangelized by what is known as E-0 evangelism (bringing nominal Christians into personal commitment to Christ, with "zero" cultural distance between evangelists and hearers). Nevertheless the number of active Christians in the black and Anglo communities of the United States is fairly high.

This is not true about most of the ethnic groups. I do not have hard data for Hispanics in Los Angeles, but some guesstimates have been floating around. Most Hispanics are nominal Catholics, but the number of active Catholics may be only around 10 percent, not unusual when compared to many Latin American countries. However, the number of Protestants, called *evangelicos*, is probably less than 4 percent, lower than most Latin American nations. By contrast, Protestants in Guatemala are now pushing toward 30 percent of the population.

My hunch is that similar low figures will apply to most ethnic groups across the nation. We know for sure that three million Muslims and 2.4 million Hindus are almost totally unevangelized. Earl Parvin, in his recently published book *Mission U.S.A.* (1985) estimates that 95 percent of Native Americans, Franco-Americans, and recent immigrants are unevangelized. The Samuel Zwemer Institute of Pasadena, California, reports that there are now over 300 mosques or teaching centers of Islam in the United States, and that Muslim Student Association chapters are now on the campuses of 150 universities. Their goal is a chapter on every university campus.

The Pattern of Acts

All this adds up, as I have said, to an enormous evangelistic challenge. The spiritual vision for the real America needs to be a vision firmly rooted in the Word of God. The book of Acts is significant for understanding this because it is a book on the cross-cultural communication of the gospel. Up to the time of Pentecost the spread of the gospel had been confined largely to a relatively small ethnic group, namely Aramaic-speaking Galilean Jews. This, not coincidentally, was the people group in which Jesus and the apostles were born and raised. While Jesus did have touch with some Hellenistic Jews and some Samaritans and some Gentiles, they were marginal. He sent his disciples to "the lost sheep of the house of Israel" (Mt. 10:6) and declared that he himself had been sent to the people of Israel (Mt. 15:24). After Jesus' ascension, the people who went out to proclaim the gospel on the day of Pentecost were noteworthy in Jerusalem because they were all Galileans, according to Acts 2:7.

But while the gospel first took root in a rather tight ethnic group of Galilean Jews (who, incidentally, would be almost directly analagous to Appalachians in the United States today), it was by no means Jesus' intention that the gospel stay there. This is why the Great Commission was such an incredible challenge to the apostles. Jesus specifically commanded them to carry the good news of the kingdom to πάντα τὰ ἔθνη, all the peoples. As a starter it was to include Jerusalem, Judea, and Samaria; then it was to go to the uttermost parts of the earth. These details, given in Acts 1:8, establish the outline for the book of Acts, and the story unfolds in twenty-eight exciting chapters.

The first step was crossing the cultural barrier to the Hellenists on the day of Pentecost. Thousands and thousands of very sophisticated Hellenistic

Jews had come to Jerusalem for the feast from every part of the Roman empire. For a motley group of Galileans to preach to them would be like an evangelistic team from a Kentucky coal-mining village to speak on the commons at Harvard. It could be done only with the supernatural power of God, and, at Pentecost, this power came in the form of the miracle of tongues. Three thousand were converted, and the gospel spread through Jerusalem and Judea.

Still, almost all believers were Jews. Then Stephen, one of the Hellenists and Christianity's first missiologist, preached his watershed sermon, which gave a theological legitimation for carrying God's message to non-Jews. Stephen lost his life for it, but his friend Philip, another Hellenist, implemented the theory by taking the gospel to the Samaritans. Peter and John, both Hebrews, visited Philip, confirmed his work, and themselves began preaching to some Samaritans.

The final challenge was the uttermost part of the earth, namely, the Gentiles. Peter, somewhat reluctantly, broke the ice in the house of Cornelius, but he never turned out to be much of a cross-cultural worker. God raised up the apostle Paul, a self-declared Hebrew, but with Hellenistic roots, to be the great apostle to the Gentiles. Through him and his missionary bands, this, the most formidable cultural hurdle, was crossed and the gospel was rapidly moving out to πάντα τὰ ἔθνη.

This pattern in the book of Acts is God's pattern for today also. The gospel is designed not to be captive to a particular ethnic or people group, but to jump cultural barrier after cultural barrier.

Some Excellent Progress
Fortunately we are not starting from scratch. While the task is formidable, excellent starts have been made by many churches and denominations.

At the top of the list in ethnic ministries in the United States are the Southern Baptists. Their Language Missions Division under the leadership of Oscar Romo has set the pace over the last ten or fifteen years. Southern Baptists are the most ethnically diverse denomination, worshiping in 87 languages in more than 4,600 language-culture congregations every Sunday. This is an aggregate of 250,000 ethnic believers praising God in their own churches. Over 20,000 new ethnics are professing faith in Jesus Christ each year through their ministry. To illustrate the scope of Southern Baptist ethnic ministries, permit me to list the languages, other than English, in which Southern Baptists in the state of California alone will be worshiping on a Sunday: American Indian, Cambodian, Laotian, Thai, Chinese (several dialects), Estonian, Filipino, Hebrew, Hungarian, Indonesian, Italian, Japanese, Korean, Arabic, Egyptian, Afghan, Pakistani, Yemeni, Iraqi, Chaldean, Sudanese, Armenian, Assyrian, Portuguese, Romanian, Russian, Slavic, Ukranian, Spanish (representing sixteen different cultural groups), and Vietnamese.

Other denominations significantly crossing ethnic barriers in the United

States include the Church of the Nazarene under the leadership of Raymond Hurn, and the Assemblies of God under Robert Pirtle. In fact, 35 to 40 percent of new Assemblies of God churches each year are ethnic. In the last couple of years new churches have started among Asian, black, deaf, Filipino, German, Guyanese, Haitian, Hmong, American Indian, Japanese, Korean, Portuguese, Romanian, Samoan, Spanish, and Tongan peoples.

The textbook for the Houston '85 National Convocation for Evangelizing Ethnic America, *Heirs of the Same Promise*, mentions denominations such as the United Methodist Church, which has adopted "developing and strengthening the ethnic minority local church" as its missional priority for 1985-88. In the California-Nevada Conference there are already Chinese, Filipino, Japanese, Korean, Taiwanese, Black, Hispanic, and Native American Methodist churches. Their goal is to have 25 percent of their conference made up of ethnic minority churches. The Lutheran Church of America is seeing considerable growth in black, Hispanic, Asian, and American Indian churches. The Presbyterian Church (U.S.A.) has 100 Native American congregations. It has recently established an innovative Korean-American presbytery in Southern California.

I think of Enrique Torres, a Chilean-American Christian leader who came to study with me at Fuller a few years ago. He was earning his way through school by planting Hispanic churches for the American Baptists around Los Angeles. Enrique's Doctor of Missiology studies required eighteen months. During that period of time he planted nineteen new churches!

I think of Pastor Kwang Shin (David) Kim, a successful Korean landscape architect who was also an atheist. He was saved in 1978 and decided to leave his business to study at Talbot Seminary and then to plant a Christian and Missionary Alliance church in Norwalk, California, near Los Angeles. The church grew rapidly, and leased an entire unused high school campus. They are already nearly filling the 2,000-seat auditorium on Sunday, and Kim's goal is to have 7,000 members by 1988. But this is also a church with a vision for cross-cultural ministry. Their missions budget is now approaching a half-million dollars annually, and they hope to raise $2.5 million per year for missions by 1988. They have already established Filipino and Cambodian congregations as well as an Anglo congregation. The Korean church pays the Anglo pastor's salary!

This reminds me of an Assemblies of God Korean church in Manhattan pastored by Nam Soo Kim. The church is investing in a thirty-three story building on West 33rd Street, just one block from Madison Square Garden. They are building a sanctuary to seat 3,000. The total budget for it was $5 million, and in one day the congregation came up with pledges of $2 million.

Multiply these examples by hundreds and you will have a glimpse of the exciting things God is already doing among the ethnics of our nation. Our spiritual vision is to accelerate these efforts until the πάντα τὰ ἔθνη of America have become disciples of Jesus Christ.

FINANCES, OLG'S BY PROSPEROUS MINORITIES THEMSELVES!

III. The Strategic Vision

A vision for the real America sees a multitude of ethnics in an urban stew-pot, a multitude that needs to be won to Christ. But how is this to be accomplished? The final part of the vision is a strategic one—the vision of a harvest field ready to be reaped. How to do the reaping in the most efficient manner is the question at hand.

I see four major aspects of this strategic task: motivation, mobilization, contextualization, and kingdom ministry. Each deserves an essay, but I shall outline briefly what I feel needs to be done.

Motivation

The first step in reaching ethnic America for Christ is to want to do it. Motivation is key.

For one thing, ethnics need to be motivated to reach ethnics. This is monocultural, or E-1, evangelism in the categories used by the Lausanne Committee for World Evangelization.[1] The old saying that "nationals can evangelize better than missionaries" has always been true. Since 1970, 430 Korean churches have been planted in the Los Angeles area. Virtually all of them were planted by Koreans using E-1 evangelism. One of my Taiwanese students, Felix Liu, has planted seven Taiwanese churches in the past five or six years. Such activity needs to be multiplied. Ethnic churches that are not actively involved in evangelism and church planting need to be motivated to do it. Happily, most of them already are.

For another thing, Anglo churches and denominations need to be motivated for cross-cultural evangelism and church planting. This is E-2 and E-3 evangelism. A great amount of responsibility lies on the Anglo churches because, even though Anglos are a numerical minority, they still control the key structures of American society. They can make things happen in this country that many ethnic groups simply cannot make happen. Anglo Christians must not say, "Let the ethnics take care of their own evangelism." Under God, they need to say, "Let us use our resources of people, money, and influence to make sure ethnic evangelism gets done, and that ethnics have what they need to do the best job possible." I am not advocating Anglo paternalism at this point, but neither am I advocating Anglo detachment. A wise balance of partnership must be found.

I have already mentioned many Anglo denominations that are doing this well. More need to join forces with them. I was pleased just the other day to hear that the Christian Reformed Church is beginning to take cross-cultural evangelism seriously. Here is a traditionally Dutch denomination that now has churches worshiping in eleven different languages. If present trends continue, by the year 2000 there will be more Asians than Dutch in Christian Reformed Churches across the United States.

As all United States churches, denominations, and other Christian organizations are sensitized to the possibilities, challenge, and feasibility of greatly increasing the evangelistic ministries to unreached individuals and people groups in the United States, Christian leaders across America will catch fire, and great advances will be made toward finishing our evangelistic task.

Mobilization

Motivated people are ready to take action. But the energy that is released must be channeled productively. I see three key areas for which God's people should be mobilized.

First, they should be mobilized for prayer. Prayer is supreme, for we do not wrestle against flesh and blood but against principalities and powers. I must confess that for a large part of my own Christian ministry I thought that the inclusion of prayer under suggestions for strategy was simply a mandatory Christian platitude. Now I understand how wrong I was and how vital prayer really is for accomplishing God's purpose.

Second, God's people should be motivated to plant churches. New church planting is the single most effective evangelistic methodology known under heaven. Denominations that are successfully winning ethnics are doing so because they are multiplying new churches and church-type missions. Some of these ethnic churches are started by existing ethnic or Anglo churches. For example, my own church, Lake Avenue Congregational Church of Pasadena, California, now has Chinese, Indonesian, Hispanic, Filipino, and Korean congregations right on the same campus. This needs to increase, but also we need separate agencies dedicated to starting churches. In *Mission U.S.A.*, Earl Parvin states that 12,000 home missionaries are currently serving in the United States. I don't know how many of them are planting churches, but the majority should be. Some foreign mission agencies such as CAM International and the Latin America Mission have taken the bold step of declaring the United States a mission field, and are now using their overseas church-planting experience to help win American ethnics.

Third, workers should use their energies well by concentrating on the responsive segments of society. God wants laborers in the harvest fields, but not all fields ripen at the same time. Years of research in the resistance-receptivity theory has shown that new arrivals are frequently much more ready to accept the gospel than long-term residents. It is strategically important to discover where ethnics are moving in, whether as foreign immigrants or from other parts of the United States, and concentrate church-planting teams there. While we must not neglect anyone, nor should we bypass the resistant, we nevertheless should give a high priority to the receptive, the ripe harvest fields.

Contextualization

The Lausanne Committee for World Evangelization has popularized the "people approach to world evangelization" in recent years. Its basic thrust is to identify the people groups that are as yet unreached and move in with an objective of planting churches to fit the culture of the group. We Anglo-Americans have been particularly guilty of believing that everyone should do it just the way we do. We would rather persuade the ethnics to join our churches than plant new ethnic churches. We continually attempt to force new wine into our old wineskins, and wonder why it does not stay. I like the way Oscar Romo puts it: "We are seeking to evangelize, not to Americanize." He contends that "we must allow culture to set the agenda for our sharing the love of Jesus Christ for all people."

We need to realize that not all ethnics are the same. Some are nuclear ethnics and they require language churches. Some are fellow-traveler or marginal ethnics and they need bilingual or English-speaking churches. A few are alienated ethnics, and they will be very happy in Anglo churches. If we are evangelizing ethnics, we must not major in telling them what we think they need, but rather we must minister to them on their own terms.

Leadership selection and training is a crucial area that has hindered many denominations from undertaking successful ethnic evangelism. Denominations that require college and seminary for ordination will not be able to move ahead rapidly in planting churches in most ethnic groups. Ordination requirements, like all other aspects of church life, should be contextualized to fit the culture; they should not be superimposed by the Anglo churches.

Kingdom Ministry

Finally, our strategy for reaching the real America must be biblical. It must be a strategy of the kingdom of God. It must be wholistic and deal with all aspects of need that ethnic people have. We must be sure that the evangelistic mandate and the cultural mandate are in biblical balance.

The Lausanne Covenant rightly recognizes that the evangelistic mandate is primary because evangelism brings eternal life. Successful social ministry is good, but at best it brings peace and prosperity only for life here on earth. This of course must not be neglected and we must love and care for the poor just as Jesus did. Many ethnic groups are poor, but not all. Asian Americans, for example, showed the highest per-capita group income in the United States in the 1980 census—higher even than Anglos.

One of the social conditions that we must be acutely aware of is racial prejudice and discrimination. The ethnics we are attempting to evangelize are often victims of injustices, and these must not be tolerated. Prejudice is rarely removed by legislation; it is most often removed by love. Love is a fruit of the Holy Spirit, so as both ethnics and others receive Christ, love will be more prevalent, and barriers of discrimination will be broken down. We may not assume, however, that racism will disappear by itself. We must work at it, recognizing that it can occur between Vietnamese and Italians or between Armenians and Mexicans just as readily as between whites and blacks.

There is one area in which kingdom ministry relates directly to contextualization, and I think it is more important for ethnic evangelism than many of us might realize. That is the relationship of supernatural signs and wonders to ethnic evangelism. When Jesus sent out his disciples, he said, "Preach, saying the kingdom of heaven is at hand. Heal the sick, cleanse the lepers, raise the dead, cast out demons" (Mt. 10:7-8). When he gave the Great Commission he told his apostles to wait in Jerusalem until they were endued with power from on high (Lk. 24:49). Power to heal the sick and cast out demons is a formidable asset in communicating the gospel cross-culturally.

I am not suggesting that we all become Pentecostal or charismatic. I am neither myself. Yet for four years we have been teaching courses on this at Fuller Theological Seminary and have discovered that God is more than willing to give the rest of us the same power of the Holy Spirit that the Pentecostals and the charismatics have enjoyed for years. Many of us have not been open to it, however, largely because of the pervasive influence of secular humanism on Anglo-American culture. This same secular humanism has not influenced many ethnics nearly as much. The world of the supernatural with demons and angels, visions and dreams, is much more real to them than to many of us. Part of our kingdom ministry to them, as I see it, is to allow the power of God to be demonstrated among them in supernatural ways, not for the sake of being spectacular, but because it is a New Testament way of encouraging the message of the gospel to be heard and accepted.

Conclusion

This, then, is my vision for reaching the real America. I hope you share it with me. It is a vision of a few sparks now, which will soon be fanned into flames by the power of God. John said that Jesus would baptize with the Holy Spirit and fire. The disciples on the Emmaus road said, "Did not our hearts burn within us, while he talked with us by the way, and while he opened to us the scriptures?" (Lk. 24:32). It is this kind of fire for which I pray. The fire of the Holy Spirit must begin in the hearts of those of us who have ears to hear. This is the fire that will produce a burning desire to see ethnic America won to Jesus Christ.

Notes

[1] These categories are described in Ralph Winter, "The Highest Priority: Cross-Cultural Evangelism," in Gerald H. Anderson and Thomas F. Stransky, eds., *Mission Trends* No. 2 (Grand Rapids, Mich.: Eerdmans, 1975), pp. 109-22.

MISSIONS AND OUR PRESENT MOMENT IN HISTORY

HARVIE M. CONN
Professor of Missions and Director of the Urban Missions Program
Westminster Theological Seminary

Article from *Missionary Monthly*

Forecasting the future of world missions is hazardous; even while talking about the present we may court disaster. The prophet is likely to be more rash than right. And like other prophets before, we can sound pessimistic. Like Nehemiah's builders, we are tempted to say, "There is much rubbish" (Neh. 4:10).

I present this message in hope. I cry, "Let us arise and build!" (Neh. 2:18). But I remind you that missions is always "missions under the cross." Where else can it begin? "The cross is the place of humiliation and of judgment; but it is also the place of refreshment, of enlightenment and of power."

The rendering of Psalm 96:10 given in some manuscripts of the Septuagint is not original but it is true: "Tell it out among the heathen that the Lord hath reigned from the tree."

Our "Now" in History: Polarizations and Pressures

What is the setting in which we are called to mission? It is a dizzying world of rapid social change, of pressures and polarizations. We face what Alvin Toffler a decade ago called "the premature arrival of the future."

In 1947 [the founding year of the Association of American Bible Colleges, to which this article was originally addressed], we were more assured about mission. We agreed on our definitions more easily. The world was vast but, it seemed to us, more reachable. Our paternal perceptions of other cultures were stronger, the cultures themselves seen by us as less dynamic. Colonial expansion was assumed, entrepreneurial wealth was more accessible. The flow of mission was one-way, from the West to the Third World. Our assumptions made the task easier. We needed only to ask, How can the churches grow?

J. H. Bavinck began to question our optimism in his 1954 classic, *An Introduction to the Science of Missions*. His picture for the future was "in general not particularly encouraging." He saw ecclesiastical self-preoccupation and growing religious hostility to the church. He saw shortages of Christian leadership and literature. Asia and Africa were said to be "busy detaching themselves in an over-hasty tempo from their old cultural and social ties." The rush to westernization was increasing its pace.

Thirty years after Bavinck made his predictions, many of us can call him generally a true prophet. But to his list we can add other frustrations and realities he saw only dimly.

(1.) *We face the growing world gap between affluence and poverty*. The rich, indeed, are getting richer and the poor are having children. More than a decade ago the crisis was described in these words:

> It is generally accepted that up to two billion people—one half of the world's population of four billion—are now poor. The World Bank describes one billion of these people as "individuals who subsist on incomes of less than $75 a year in an environment of squalor, hunger and hopelessness. They are the absolute poor, living in situations so deprived as to be below any rational definition of human decency. . . . It is a life at the margin of existence." For the other billion who are living slightly above this absolute poverty level, life is nearly as joyless and has improved little, if at all, through decades of "development" efforts.

Two-thirds of the human family go to bed hungry every night. Fifteen thousand people starve to death every day. In Third World countries, reports the United Nations Children's Fund, 90 million children—runaways, school dropouts, or abandoned—live on the world's streets.

What hurts especially is the alignment of this gulf with the old categories of "sending churches" and "receiving churches." The world's wealth still is largely located in the Anglo-Saxon community. In 1976, North America represented only 6.1 percent of the world's population, but its gross national product represented 30 percent of the world's wealth. Behind it comes Western Europe, with 13 percent of the world's people and 31.8 percent of the world's wealth. From these two centers still comes over 85 percent of the world's mission force, missions proceeding out of affluence.

Part of Ezekiel's mission was to sit where the people sat (Ezek. 3:15). How can mission out of such affluence sit with the poor?

(2.) *This gap grows as urbanization grows*. "Nowhere else is the economic, political, and social distance between the few rich and the masses of the poor greater than in the towns of the Third World" (Peter Gutkind, *Urban Anthropology*). In so-called developing areas, the rate of urbanization is occurring three or four times as fast as the rate in industrialized countries.

In 1950, Mexico City's population was 2.2 million. It is expected to become 30 million by the end of this century. In 1950, the urban population of Third World countries was less than 16 percent. By the end of this century, if the Lord tarries, it will be close to 41 percent.

The urban way of life is viewed as the model of the good life, the new life. The city draws the migrant to what is perceived as economic opportunity, diversity, self-expression.

Yet here festers the future arena of major confrontations. For here the invisible poor become visible. In Rio de Janeiro, the *favela* (shantytown) population grew from 400,000 in 1947 to over a million in the early sixties. Between 1947 and 1967, Caracas and Bogota grew at the incredible rate of just under seven percent per year. Most of it was in shantytown areas.

The great Peasant Trek to the city has produced the urban poor, the largest percentage of urban population. Rising expectations have produced rising frustrations. Facing status-loss, marginalization, hunger, and rootlessness, the poor are formed into what Oscar Lewis calls a new culture. And all this in the cities, where so few of us venture in missions.

3. *The luxury of a society-dominating church died in the 1940s and '50s.* It died with the end of Western colonialism and the end of the "Vasco da Gama era" of mission. And now the church finds itself struggling with the political absolutes of society-dominating ideological structures.

Nationalism no longer is the problem. The problem is larger and more awesome. It is that of territorial and extra-territorial ideologies, blueprints of the future made by a certain ideologue or group of elite within the community, to move the masses. Human beings are steered, exploited, conditioned, and manipulated by these comprehensive strategies.

Ideologies form governments of the left and of the right. A political scientist has observed that nearly every Third World nation today is under an authoritarian government. He predicts that within twenty years nearly every country in the world will have an authoritarian form of government. The only difference among them will be those who benefit from the structures—the elite few in the society, or the masses. Marxist and Muslim, capitalist and socialist, they all move back and forth between parliament and prison, calling for regulation or revolution.

What is the mission of the church in such situations? In the People's Republic of China and in South Africa, in North Korea and the Philippines? How do we live and witness to our faith under conditions of oppression and authoritarianism? How should kingdom discipleship face suppression of human rights, hindrances to evangelism, the torture of dissidents, the strictures against baptism and church building?

Recently, some evangelicals defined mission in terms of worship, service, proclamation, and fellowship. What is the place of justice in our definitions of mission?

The oppressed of the world listen for compassion, not sympathy. And the difference between sympathy and compassion is our willingness to see people not merely as sinners but also as the sinned against. Racism remains the white leftover of colonialism that obliterates that difference.

(4.) *Against this social, economic, and political backdrop, we remind our-selves of the awesome size of the world's non-Christian population.* In Jesus' time, it numbered about 250 million people. When world population was over 4 billion around 1970, an estimated 2.8 billion were non-Christian—eleven times as many non-Christians as when Jesus preached the Sermon on the Mount. By A.D. 2000, world population will have increased fifty percent. Christians, according to some, will constitute only 15 percent of that vast multitude.

Breaking down this figure into task-oriented information has been diffi-cult in the past. But in the last decade, the concept of "unreached peoples" has arisen to offer some help.

What is an unreached people group? The most recent consensus seems to be this: a people group within which there is no indigenous community of believing Christians able to evangelize this people group without outside (cross-cultural) assistance.

"Reaching" such a people group means incorporating this group into Christ's fellowship, into His church. It calls for culturally-appropriate com-munities. It calls for border-crossing servants of our King to leave their cultures and societies and move into settings foreign to them to finish the job. There are at least 16,000 such networks to which we must journey.

Complications in Meeting These Challenges

How will the evangelical church and centers of education rise to meet these challenges? Several factors complicate our task. Notice, I did not say "prob-lems"; I said "challenges." And I did not say "hindrances"; I said "com-plications."

(1.) *There is a new shift of global ecclesiastical gravity.* Our gravity center moves from Pasadena and Wheaton and Grand Rapids to Mexico City, to Seoul, to Madras and Nairobi. By the end of the 20th century, the population strength of the world church will have moved from the northern to the southern regions of the world.

The old centers of theological influence in Europe and North America are becoming new peripheries. Meanwhile, the new centers of vitality and importance in church growth and theological construction are in Asia, Africa, and Latin America—where the majority of Christians will be living in A.D. 2000.

This exciting shift already is appearing in the area of world missions. A 1972 study uncovered at least 210 missionary societies sending out a mini-mum of 3,404 missionaries from Africa, Asia, and Latin America.

Studies in 1983 have updated this information to 368 sending agencies. And they are sending not 3,404 workers but an estimated 13,000 foreign missionaries. David Barrett suggests that the figure is closer to 32,500.

Why is this a complication? We must ask new questions. How will our schools help prepare northern hemisphere missionaries to work in fraternity with southern hemisphere missionaries to finish the task? Do we have a role to play in helping this new task force avoid the mistakes about church-mission relations that we have made in the past?

In world missions today, we are called on to be brothers and sisters, not mothers and fathers—partners, not foremen. Will our thinking about the global task become *global thinking* about the global task?

(2.) *There is a growing gap between evangelicals in the two hemispheres over the shape and agenda of the theology*. Christian missions in its earliest days was "the mother of theology," not its grandchild. Under the direction of the Holy Spirit, Paul shaped his theology out of his mission and for his mission. He did his theologizing with an eye always on "those who are without" (Col. 4:5, 1 Thess. 3:12).

The spiritual "outsiders" were before Paul as he uttered his theological malediction of "shame" on Christians who instituted lawsuits against other Christians (1 Cor. 6:1-5). His theological deliberations on spiritual gifts were prompted by his pastoral sensitivity to the church and to how all this would be perceived by the unbeliever (1 Cor. 14:23-24).

The renewal of theologizing in the 16th century repeated the same pattern. The renewed mission of the church brought forth a renewal of theological activity. Creeds and catechisms were produced as genuine evangelistic "confessions of faith." The communication of the gospel required more than little booklets or 7-color wall charts.

In its times of greatest glory, northern hemisphere theology was nothing more than reflection *in* mission and *in* pilgrimage on the road calling cultures to Christ. It also was reflection *on* mission, *on* Jesus Christ as the good news, and *on* the church as salt and light and leaven, the bearer and model of the good news. The creeds were simply reflections of this missionary task of theology.

Through the years, that missionary dimension often has been lost in the theologies we teach in our schools. David Bosch, an evangelical author, has suggested that theology increasingly has defined itself "as a metaphysical science of speculation," with philosophy as its only "outside partner." In the process, it often has forfeited the missionary thrust that gave it birth. Some of our brothers in the Third World (or the Two-Thirds World), say that theology has become a luxury dispensed to so-called "younger churches" through the banking method of the "mother churches." The art of doing theology as a missionary conversation between the Scriptures and the world too often has been reduced to theology as the mission-less result of that conversation.

As a result, a different kind of evangelical theology seems to be developing in the Two-Thirds World. It addresses questions not usually dealt with by evangelical mainstream theologians in the northern hemisphere.

This different theology retains a clearcut commitment to Scripture as the source and norm of theology. The Bible still sets the theological agenda. Salvation by grace through faith still rings as an evangelical affirmation. The evangelical still speaks of conversion as a distinct experience of faith. The call to a new life still is regarded as a demonstration of that work of the Spirit in the believer.

What then is different? Says Orlando Costas, "Evangelical theologians in these parts of the world are appropriating the best of their spiritual tradition and are putting it to use in a constructive critical dialogue with their interlocutors, in and outside of their historical space. For them, the evangelical tradition is not locked into the socio-cultural experience of the West. They insist that they have the right to articulate theologically the evangelical tradition in their own terms and in light of their own issues." They are rediscovering the evangelistic, missionary dimension of theology.

Why is this a complication? It can be frightening for white folks in the north. If we do not understand their unique contexts, Southern hemisphere theologies can sound to us like a compromised form of Marxist capitulation, or a syncretistic alliance with Muslim concerns. Without a renewed reminder of the missionary task of theology, we may regard them as too localized to be permanent, too particularized to be universal. And without any serious interaction on our part, these theologies sound even more frightening to us.

Contextualization of theology, then, sounds to us whites like syncretism climbing in the back door, like relativism tearing away at the gospel once for all delivered to the saints.

3. *I mention one other complication*, although there are many more. It could be called the complication relating to priorities. Which is louder: the cry of the poor, or the cry of the lost? Which comes first: evangelism or social involvement?

Which role should the church play in an ideological state: that of a priest for a bruised people who need healing, or that of a prophet in the house of Herod?

Which sins demand our attention: those of heterodoxy, or those of heteropraxy? Should Christian missions focus the major part of available resources on frontier mission to unreached people, or should our resources be devoted to interchurch aid?

Should we picket only abortion clinics, or should we also participate in anti-apartheid demonstrations?

My own hope is that we will reaffirm the need for balance, not *either-or*, but *both-and*—soul and body, word and deed, individual and society, doing justice and preaching grace. I think that this is the direction the Lausanne Committee for World Evangelization urges us to take.

We will warn against those who narrow the scope of God's kingdom activity only to making individuals new creatures and alleviating minor social distress, backache, and upset stomachs. And we will fear those who allow the boundary line between the church and the world to be blurred.

We do not want the church to become just another agency for the betterment of society. Nor do we want the church to be simply a guerrilla band carrying out Rambo-like evangelistic commando raids into enemy territory to find isolated prisoners or those missing in action.

Why is this a complication? David Bosch suggests some reasons. "Each of us is inclined to incarcerate the gospel within the narrow confines of his or her predilections. We find it extremely difficult to live permanently in tension. We find it difficult to have clear-cut answers. We are irresistibly pulled towards one-sidedness and reductionism. We all tend to delineate the gospel too sharply and handle the biblical material too self-confidently."

Our own history sometimes does not help us in avoiding one-sidedness. We remember the failure of the social gospel, and some of our noses become fine-tuned to smell it when it may or may not be there.

Others of us fear the bad side of pietism which sometimes has locked world missions into what has been called "a quest for souls with ears." We become theological bloodhounds sniffing out pietism gone bad in every trail that speaks too loudly of the individual.

Our latest debates over the "primacy" of evangelism in world missions display to me traces of both mistakes. Lots of heat . . . and not much light.

Our Renewed Calling as Mission Training Schools

Where do we go in the future? The role of our training schools for northern hemisphere missionaries will continue, I hope. In fact, I pray it will be stepped up and accelerated. As it is reinvigorated, some old emphases will be reemphasized and some new demands will be made on us.

1. *Evangelism and church planting must remain high on our training agenda.* Our quest for balance never must make our missiological agenda so crowded that the evangelistic dimension will be pushed to the periphery. Our legitimate concerns over racism and injustice, our calling to combat world hunger, and our duty to resist ideological de-humanization can become cups of cold water given without the name of Jesus. And naming that name is what distinguishes the wholistic mission of the church from amateurish efforts in social reclamation beyond our depth.

Our agenda of concerns must not overwhelm us again with what Peter Wagner has called a new "Babylonian captivity of the Christian mission." We must not go on writing our books about the relation of evangelism to social action, or "search evangelism" versus "harvest evangelism"—while over three billion people in the world do not know Christ and continue to die, pressing their faces against the outside of our study windows in Des Moines or Kalamazoo.

2. *At the same time, our research and our teaching of missions will have to become wider.* Or is "deeper" a better image? An evangelism without discipleship produces nominalism, a major problem in the world church. And discipleship is more now than simply lessons about how to study the Bible, how to pray, church life, or leadership development.

Preparation for world missions must add *new items* to a growing agenda: how to carry on spiritual warfare in animistic cultures where Satan still bares his teeth; how to function as Christians in ideological and totalitarian states; how to reach out to the poor with integrity and a hope that is more than words; how to evaluate Marxism and Islam (and even capitalism) as ideologies; how to function as a Christian minority in a Hindu social culture.

We have *new questions* to add to the missions agenda of our schools. Where are the unreached peoples of Nigeria and Bangkok and Sao Paulo? What is the role of signs and wonders in church growth? What is the role of the Christian in nation-building, including nations which are Muslim or even tilt to Marxism? What legitimate, biblical role is there for the church in a religiously plural society?

Can Westerners serve as idea brokers in the formation of new evangelical, global theologies? If we can, how? What can we learn from these emerging theologies about our own theologizing? "Third world theologies" no longer can be an elective in our curricula. Our theology teachers must stop teaching as if the theological world was still flat and not round.

3. *A new location for reaching unreached peoples must be placed on our study curriculum—the city.* In most Middle Eastern countries, more than one-third of the population now live in cities. The city is not on the fringe of the Islamic system. "It is the system."

Super cities continue to appear. In 1950, only two cities, London and New York, had over 10 million people. As of 1980, 10 cities had reached that size. By the end of this century, if the Lord tarries, 25 cities will be like that. And there will be five cities with over 20 million people.

Men and women need to know "how to read cities." Till now we have focused on rural and tribal situations. That must change. We need training schools located in inner-city America to effect that change.

Some of our educational institutions now begin to call, "Reach the city!" However, almost all of them issue that call from a situation of suburban safety. That must change.

Our teaching staffs, by and large, are monocultural, made up of white folks trained in our suburban colleges and our suburban seminaries. That must change. We need a teaching staff that *lives in* and understands the city.

We must encourage the diligent recruiting of students and faculty among American blacks and ethnic minorities, the people who know North America's cities best. And we need a support basis for our institutions from urban center city churches, who have promised God they will not leave the city until He gives a blessing.

In all this we do not desert our past. We build on it again. The missionary images stir us again—the shepherd searching, the father awaiting the prodigal son with outstretched arms, the host welcoming the beggar to the dinner table. The church can do no less and still be church.

TEACHING POWER ENCOUNTER

TIMOTHY WARNER
Director, School of World Mission and Evangelism
Trinity Evangelical Divinity School

Article from *Evangelical Missions Quarterly*

"His eyes were glassy, his clothes ragged, his hair matted, and he was desperate. 'I'm going to kill this animal,' he repeated three times." A demon in a man trapped in spiritism was challenging the crowd of people around him, including an evangelical missionary.

> I remembered the words of Jesus, "Behold, I give you power over all the power of the enemy, and nothing by any means shall hurt you." I felt I should rebuke the demon in the name of Jesus, but what if nothing happened? All the people gathered would ridicule me. I slipped behind another man and watched as the man finally got up and started down the street being held by two men. Abruptly he threw them off and started running. . . .
>
> There I was—a defeated missionary in the interior of Brazil, ready to pack up and go home. When face to face with the enemy I was afraid. Who had told me how to deal with demons?[1]

Unfortunately, this story could be repeated over and over from various parts of the world because missionaries have been sent to the field with no preparation for power encounter with the demonic forces at work in the world.

One of the most glaring gaps in our missionary curriculums is in our failure to help missionaries understand the reality of demons in the world today and to equip them to deal with the demons from a position of spiritual authority. An increasing number of writers are indicating an awareness of this problem, however. Alan Tippett has pointed it out frequently in his writings. He says:

> A missionary geared to a metaphysical level of evangelism in his generator cannot drive a motor of shamanistic voltage. It is a tragic experience to find oneself with the right kind of power but the wrong kind of voltage.
>
> There may be theological or missionary training institutions which provide for this but they are few and far between.[2]

In the same article Tippett points out that if this subject were to be offered, the professor would be hard pressed to find good textbooks or other resource material. Most of what has been written on the subject of demons and spiritual power encounter has not been in a missionary context.

The fact is, however, that most of the people in the unreached areas of the world practice a religion at the folk level that is dominated by concepts of spirit power. Donald Jacobs, the Mennonite anthropologist, contends that "most people in the non-Western world convert to another faith because of seeking more power."[3]

Alan Tippett reinforces this when he says, "Western missions might do well to face up to the statistical evidence that animists are being won today by a Bible of power encounter, not a demythologized edition."[4]

Tippett supports this by citing the contention of the secular anthropologist Melville Herskovitz that "it is no accident that the type of Protestantism most successful in Haiti is the form most hostile to *voodoo*, because it comes into *encounter* with it on a meaningful level. . . ."[5]

I look back on my own missionary experience in a tribal village in West Africa with a combination of regret and incredulity that I attempted ministry there with almost no understanding of either the biblical teaching on demons or of the reality of the demonic world to the people with whom I lived and worked.

While I have spoken on the issue in the years since my days in Africa and have continued to study the subject, it was only this year that I ventured to teach a whole course on the subject. The response from the missionaries in the classes has been overwhelmingly positive. Many have expressed thoughts like, "If only I had had this course before I went to the field!"

I should perhaps add that a stimulus to venture into teaching has come in the form of personal experience in dealing with demonized people in the area in which we live. Being able to use illustrations from personal experience rather than just from the experience of others makes the instruction more credible.

I always begin the course with a brief discussion of my philosophy of balance as expressed in the statement, "The Christian life is the exciting process of trying to keep your balance." This stems from the more basic consideration that evil is always the perversion of a good that God has written into his order for man. Satan is on all sides of an issue and doesn't care whether we are on one side or the other—just so we are not at the balance point where God intends us to be. This subject is no exception. There are those who find demons everywhere, and there are those who find them nowhere. Both extremes are unbiblical, but most of us have sought a place of safety in simply avoiding the subject. Unfortunately, there is no place of safety in this conflict—only places of ineffectiveness.

In connection with the idea of balance, it is important to make clear at the beginning that this is not a panacea for missionary ills or a strategy or methodology that can or should dominate missionary ministry. It is simply one approach that is essential in many areas of the world to effective communication and effective ministry, because without the confidence to confront demonic powers, we will forfeit the opportunity to minister to many people.

To deal with the subject of power encounter, it is essential to deal with the concept of worldview, especially the difference between the animist view, the Western view, and the biblical view. We often encounter syncretism in the Third World churches, but we fail to understand that we as missionaries are also syncretistic, but from the opposite end of the continuum. Our worldview has been influenced by the secularism and materialism around us more than we want to recognize, and we end up as victims of Hiebert's "flaw of the excluded middle."[6]

The aim is to develop a biblical worldview that includes angels and demons as functioning elements in everyday life, not just for animists or people in other cultures, but for everyone. Without such a worldview, the subject will never have the reality it must have if it is to become a vital factor in our ministries.

This discussion leads very naturally into an examination of the biblical teaching on Satan and demons. It is important, I believe, to see the big picture, that is, to understand the key issue in the conflict between God and Satan. That issue will be clearly demonstrated in the antichrist as the personification of Satan who "even sets himself up in God's temple, proclaiming himself to be God" (2 Thess. 2:4). The issue is the glory of God. Satan is gripped with envy, desiring to have the glory God has. He realizes that he will never have it; so he is now out to gain all the satisfaction he can by depriving God of all the glory he can. From an eternal perspective that is impossible, but in the present order of things, he can achieve his objective partially and gain some satisfaction by causing men to live at a level below their privileges as God's children—children by creation or children by redemption.

This article is not the place to develop that concept; but it is very helpful, if not imperative, to see this perspective on the conflict in which we are all engaged whether we want to be or not. It is important that the role of angels be clarified in the treatment of this topic so that we do not get an unbalanced view of the spirit world.

As part of this section I also review and clarify the position of victory and authority of the Christian based on being "in Christ." The fear of the demonic world evident in so many Christians is essentially an expression of unbelief. Early in the course the absolute victory of Christ over Satan and all of his hosts and our participation in that victory must be made crystal clear. Without it there will be no victory in spiritual power encounter on the mission field.

So it is always wise to deal with the positive side of the question early in the course, but just as we need to know the authority on the basis of which we wage spiritual warfare, and the resources available to us in that warfare, we also need to know our enemy. Paul said that he was not "unaware of [Satan's] schemes" (2 Cor. 2:11). Those "schemes" are studied as a basis for our resisting him "standing firm in the faith" (1 Pet. 5:9).

I prefer the term "demonization" to "demon possession" for the generic term denoting the various relationships between men and demons. I see these relationships falling along a continuum of influence ranging from temptation and harassment to actual control in the more classical concept of demon possession. A study of the Greek words used in passages dealing with demonized people is helpful.

Having laid the biblical foundation, I next move to the application of this specifically to the missionary. This is done first in terms of possible areas of attack on the missionary. One of the primary aims of Satan for Christians is to render them ineffective in Christian life and ministry. This can be accomplished in many ways; and when the source is not recognized as being demonic, it is very effective. It is always important, however, to make clear that the normal old nature-new nature conflicts cannot be avoided or solved by casting out demons. We can, however, prevent demons from taking advantage of such conflicts to bring us into deeper bondage.

The second area of missionary application is ways in which *missionaries take the initiative in claiming territory held by Satan.* This begins with *evangelism* (bringing people "from the power of Satan to God"), but it also includes the *destruction of occult objects* or paraphernalia, *healing, confrontation of practitioners* of the black arts, and the *casting out of demons.* I do not suggest that missionaries go on a "lion" hunt, trying to set up a series of dramatic power encounters. But neither do I suggest that we back off in fear when the power and glory of God are being challenged by men under the power of demons.

The course is concluded with a presentation of the practical methodology used in confronting demons. It is essential that we do not see our effectiveness in such a ministry as residing in saying the right words or phrases. This becomes magic. It is the flow of Christ's power and authority through us that produces the desired results. But it is helpful to be able to learn from the experience of others.

Audio tapes of actual confrontations are helpful in bringing an air of reality to what is too often just more theory. Nothing can substitute for experience in learning about this subject, but it is seldom possible to bring such experience into the classroom. Tapes for this purpose are available from Faith and Life Publications, 632 N. Prosperity Lane, Andover, KS 67002.

Some will question the absence of any historical perspectives on this subject. They have been omitted in the course I teach only because of time constraints. I think it is more important to deal with the current situation than to trace the historical positions on the subject.

There are other related areas which could also be included in such a course, but the important thing is to equip missionaries to engage in power encounter when that is required.

Notes

[1] Paul Lewis, *Attack from the Spirit World* (Wheaton: Tyndale Press, 1973): 203-4.

[2] Alan R. Tippett, "Probing Missionary Inadequacies at the Popular Level," *International Review of Missions* 49 (1960): 413.

[3] John P. Newport, "Satan and Demons: A Theological Perspective." In John W. Montgomery, *Demon Possession* (Minneapolis: Bethany House, 1976): 334.

[4] Alan R. Tippett, *Solomon Islands Christianity* (Pasadena: William Carey Library, 1967): 1000.

[5] Alan R. Tippett, "Spirit Possession as It Relates to Culture and Religion." In John W. Montgomery, *Demon Possession* (Minneapolis: Bethany House Publishers, 1976): 156.

[6] Paul Hiebert, "The Flaw of the Excluded Middle," *Missiology* 10 (1982): 35-47.

PRACTICAL THEOLOGY: HOMILETICS

Haddon W. Robinson, area editor

HOMILETICS

HADDON W. ROBINSON
President, Denver Conservative Baptist Seminary

Introduction

Worthwhile literature about preaching that offers assistance to a thoughtful minister seems as rare as a relevant biblical sermon on a Sunday morning.

Articles passed off as scholarship sometimes suffer from being so specific that they appeal only to the most esoteric homiletician. On the other hand, titles holding a more universal appeal usually have a Doctor of Ministry project attached to them. Relatively few of these well-intentioned exercises measure up to the promise of their title.

Two new journals have appeared in the past two years, however, that propose to get down where the preacher meets his people. *Preaching*, while tilting a bit toward Southern Baptists, brings in an assortment of authors who write on subjects ranging from "The Personal Computer and Preaching" (July/August 1986) to a five-part series by Wayne Oates on "Preaching and Pastoral Care" (starting November/December 1985). In addition to feature articles, each issue offers several sermons, mostly topical, a biographical sketch of a noted preacher, and a page or two of illustrative material.

A second offering is *The Journal of the Academy for Evangelism in Theological Education*. Each annual issue will explore the teaching of evangelism in theological education, and, in addition, provide serious reflection on evangelism for pastors and denominational executives. In the first volume, Richard Peace writes on what we must do to communicate effectively in a visually oriented society. What he describes applies to any minister confronted by the fact that his people think of Sunday as a day set aside to watch the National Football League on television.

While biblical scholars and preachers should make a good marriage, in practice they have had a hard time getting together. The historical critical investigation of the Scriptures has, for the most part, moved away from the pulpit. And many pastors, finding little help from the scholars, have actually given up trying to preach the Bible to modern congregations. If topics point to trends, however, then it appears that biblical scholars and preachers may be trying to make a go of it. Four articles serve as examples. D. A. Hagner, in *Expository Times* (February 1985), argues that a call to preaching that is truly biblical is committed to what the text meant, as well as to a vital, fresh, and creative expression of what the text means today.

Fred Craddock, in an article on "The Sermon and the Uses of Scripture" in *Theology Today* (April 1985), maintains that the biblical preacher must not only derive his content and authorization from the Scripture, but he will also employ allusions from the Bible to enrich and drive home his message.

Thomas A. Jackson wrote "From Text to Sermon: The Proper Use of the Bible in Preaching," in *Faith and Mission* (Fall 1985). He analyzes the process and problems a minister faces when, in his study, he considers how to preach the text relevantly on Sunday morning.

Richard C. White adds his insights to the discussion in "Building Biblical Sermons" in *The Lexington Theological Quarterly* (April 1983). He takes a detailed look at some of the barriers and benefits in building "biblical sermons." The primary emphasis in the article deals with what stands in the way of letting the text speak to the people.

About the Area Editor

Haddon W. Robinson (Th.M., Dallas Theological Seminary; M.A., Southern Methodist University; Ph.D., University of Illinois) has been president of Denver Conservative Baptist Seminary since 1979. He was ordained in 1955 by the Conservative Baptist Association. He was professor of homiletics at Dallas Theological Seminary from 1970-79). He is co-editor (with Duane Litfin) of *Recent Homiletical Thought* (1983), and author of *Biblical Preaching* (1980).

THE NEW MEDIA ENVIRONMENT:
EVANGELISM IN A VISUALLY-ORIENTED SOCIETY

RICHARD V. PEACE
Associate Professor of Missions and Evangelism
Gordon-Conwell Theological Seminary

Article from *Journal of the Academy for Evangelism
in Theological Education*

"Do the mass media impact our lives substantially?" Most of us would answer with little hesitation, "Yes, of course." We all have an intuitive sense of the power of media. We know that we are daily bombarded by messages shouted out by radio, magazines, films, newspapers, billboards and signs, records, and television—especially television. And we know that all this affects us. Yet if we were asked to describe the nature of the impact the mass media have upon us—our value system, our aspirations, our very perceptions of reality—most of us would find it difficult to be specific. When it comes to media we have become, to borrow an illustration from Ben Logan of the Media Action Research Center, like the goldfish in a bowl, for whom water is so familiar that it forgets about its existence. We know that we exist in a media-oriented society, but our environment has become so familiar and so pervasive that we forget it is even there, much less notice its impact on us.

And yet I believe the emergence of our present media environment, even though it is relatively new, has had marked consequences for us as individuals and as a nation. It is as if our goldfish gradually learned to breathe air. At the end of that metamorphosis, it would become a different creature, and probably as oblivious to the air in its environment as it previously was to the water. In the same way, we are different creatures now from what we were 30 years ago, before TV.

All this has serious consequences for Christians, individually as we strive to grow up into the fullness of Jesus Christ, and as a community that seeks to be faithful to the Great Commission. Let's explore this further.

T.V. and Our Time

It is obvious that Americans spend a great deal of time with the media. It is not uncommon for a person to spend thirty minutes each morning reading the newspaper over breakfast. Then he or she listens to the radio while driving to work. Coffee breaks and lunch might be spent with a book or magazine. In the evenings and on weekends there is, of course, television.

Television consumes more of our time than any other medium of communication. In the average American home, the TV set is on for 6 1/4 hours a day. Each person in that home will watch it nearly 4 hours a day for 7 days a week—that is over 1,400 hours a year of TV viewing. (The average person spends 2,000 hours a year at work.) In addition, it has been calculated that the average adult spends an additional 200 hours a year reading newspapers, and another 200 hours reading magazines. That same average American, however, reads books only *10 hours* a year.

With children, it is worse. Over half our nation's 12-year-olds watch TV 6 or more hours each day. One quarter of each 24-hour day is spent passively in front of a TV set at an age when a child has a desperate need to learn relational skills. By the time the average student has graduated from high school, he or she will have spent 50 percent more time with TV than in the classroom. In the course of this TV watching, this student has witnessed 18,000 murders and seen 350,000 commercials. TV is no longer an alternative educational system. In terms of hours of input, it has become our *prime* educational vehicle.

Needless to say, sheerly by virtue of all the hours they consume, mass media, and especially TV, have become dominant forces in our lives. The length of a day is still pinned at 24 hours. Let's subtract 8 hours for sleep, 8 hours for work, and 2 hours for travel, eating and chores. If 4 of the remaining 6 hours are then spent with TV, and an additional hour with newspapers and magazines, little time is left for involvement in church activities, much less evangelism and spiritual growth. The media consume inordinate amounts of time in the life of the average American.

And this affects the choices we make in our involvement in church. I can remember the conflict I felt as a teenager between knowing I should go to the Sunday evening service, and wanting to watch "The Wonderful World of Disney." I am sure it is not the only factor, but I wonder how much the high quality of Sunday evening TV programming—it is the best of the week—has contributed to the demise of the Sunday evening service. Not only has all this TV-watching reduced the number of people participating in activities other than the Sunday morning service, but it has limited what the church can do in outreach. Heaven help the visitation team that stops by when the "CBS Evening News" is being aired! And even on Sunday morning, we must now contend with the competition offered by the so-called Electronic Church.

Media and Reality

This immersion in media has had an even more serious impact on our culture. The mass media do not simply and innocently consume our time; they change the way we perceive reality. We can see this, for example, in the urban riots in 1966-67. Researchers have suggested that one factor contributing to the rioting was the constant, unrelated display on TV of the "good life" money could buy. The people in the ghettoes compared what they possessed to what they saw on TV, and they demanded a better break. But TV did not simply raise the level of expectation and hence the level of frustration; it also showed people how to get what they felt was their due. As Albert Bandura, professor of psychology at Stanford University, has said

> It has been shown that if people are exposed to television aggression, they not only learn aggressive patterns of behavior, but they also retain them over a long period of time. There is no longer any need to equivocate about whether televised stimulation produces learning effects. It can serve as an effective tutor.

TV enters at a third point in any analysis of the 1966-67 riots. In its report on civil disorder in America, the Kerner Commission devoted an entire chapter to mass media. It found that the very act of televising riots tended to generate similar upheavals elsewhere. TV modeled how to conduct a riot! Not only that, the Kerner report also pointed out the impact of denying blacks access to mass media. As Dr. Martin Luther King put it: "Lacking sufficient access to television, publications, and broad forums, Negroes have had to write their most persuasive essays with the blunt pen of marching ranks."

It is naive to think that any of us is unchanged as a result of living in this new media environment. Our values, our expectations, our understanding of people, all have been influenced by the media. Take, for example, our values. By merely thumbing through a magazine and glancing at the advertisements, one can get a sense of what is considered desirable in our culture. Advertising executives know how to sell. They know what appeals to us, and so there it is, in crisp, living color—alluring cars, cigarettes, fur coats, gadgets, dream vacations, beautiful people, etc. The American dream, so it seems, is to *acquire*—things, power, popularity, and a "zest for living." Because after all, "We're only passing this way once."

This has implications for our evangelism. As we call men and women to repentance and faith, the media are calling them to self-assertion and materialism. Furthermore, since we the evangelists are not immune to this same allure (have you visited the opulent headquarters of some evangelistic organizations?), we often sound an unsure and indistinct note in our proclamation. We even come to wonder if we should be proclaiming at all; or, even worse, our proclamation of the gospel gets mixed up with the proclamation of materialism.

Not only do the mass media teach us to value the wrong sorts of things; they also mislead us as to the worthwhile goals in life. As Christ calls us to a life of sacrifice, giving, and caring, TV proclaims as ideal the young, single, self-centered, affluent, responsibility-free life. For example, only 15 percent

of the females on television are more than 40 years old. Only one third of TV
males are married men. TV's stereotypes of the "good life" are all wrong. We
learn to value the wrong things, to strive in the wrong direction. While TV is
not the sole culprit in this shift of values and aspirations, it is unquestionably
the single most pervasive and influential purveyor of these new perceptions.

Coping Strategies

What can we do about all this? Mass media are not going away. If anything,
with the advent of inexpensive devices that will enable home TV sets to
receive satellite transmissions directly, the impact of the media will expand.
We cannot insulate ourselves from their direct, much less indirect, influence. Even if we could persuade all Christians to turn off their radios and TV
sets, and put away their magazines, newspapers and records—a course I
would never advocate—still the rest of America would go on tuning in and
turning on to the media way of life. Our general culture is going to continue to
bear the marks of the media. And this is important to realize because it is all
those people out there in media-land whom we are trying to reach with the
gospel. We must first accept the reality and ubiquitous nature of the media;
second, we must learn how to blunt its more deleterious impact; and third,
we must be willing to learn from it how to present our own message better.
How are we to achieve these three aims?

1. Educate our congregations in the art of TV viewing
Like the goldfish who has forgotten what water is like because it is so much a
given in its life, so we have grown too accustomed to the media world we live
in. The first step in any coping strategy is to become sensitized to our media
environment. Until we are conscious of the impact of TV in particular, and
how this impact is made, we cannot initiate any kind of change.

Various consciousness-raising programs are available. One designed for
church use that I personally know works, is called *Television Awareness
Training (TAT)*. It was developed by MARC, The Media Action Research Center
in New York City, a project of the United Methodist Church, the Church of the
Brethren, and the American Lutheran Church. This program can be run in an
abbreviated form as a single session, or fully in eight modules. It discusses
topics such as stereotyping, violence, TV and children, and sexuality.
Recently, MARC added Sunday School materials for use with various age
groups. The program has a very pragmatic end in view. Not only does one
begin to *understand* the issues involved, but one learns how to defuse the
power of television. As we begin to distance ourselves from the impact of
TV, we begin to develop the kind of perspective that allows us to use media
rather than be used by them. As we begin to understand our environment and
cope on a personal level with the impact of the media, so we also develop the
kind of insights that help us in reaching out to the people around us.

2. Develop sensitivities to the real needs of people

As we start to get free from the grip of media sensitivities, we likewise begin to develop new perspectives on the real needs of the non-Christian population. We see how agonizing the struggle is for a lot of people to acquire all the possessions peddled in TV land. We see how warped our perspectives about sex and violence have become. We see how lonely it is when the only conversation in our family occurs during commercial breaks. We discover how dulling all that input becomes when a person has no way to *respond* to it. And especially we discover that, deep down below that seeming commitment to materialism, a spark continues to burn in most people, by which they know that there is more to living than they have yet experienced. In the average person, submerged though it may be, still lies a yearning for something more—something that looks suspiciously like a craving for spiritual reality.

In other words, we need to develop a new sensitivity to the real needs of real people. We must get beyond what our culture tells us about people's needs; and when we are in touch with such needs, we must let the gospel speak to them. Then, and only then, have we identified a *point of contact* between a person and our message. This is foundational to any effective evangelism.

3. Develop authentic fellowship units

The thing TV lacks and culture craves is the warmth of human contact. TV is but a flickering cold fire around which a group of isolated individuals huddle. Moreover, since over half the homes in America have two TV sets, and probably a quarter of the homes have as many as three, more and more TV viewing is done all alone. One of the needs that has emerged with new urgency in our media age is the longing for authentic fellowship. *If a church is fostering deep and meaningful fellowship, in which people can share burdens with honesty and caring love, then it can compete with any TV show for the time and attention of people.*

This is another key to evangelism. It is not enough simply to reach people for Jesus Christ, and then bid them "good luck." We have an obligation to nurture them. And this means introducing them to a congenial environment of caring Christian people. In fact, an introduction into that environment alone is often the most powerful means of evangelism. Where non-Christians experience for any length of time true Christian fellowship, they will almost always seek out the Source of that fellowship.

4. Revise our modes of communication

The mass media have irrevocably altered the way we receive information, and the church must pay attention to these changed modes of communication if it is to be heard.

Notice how TV operates. For one thing, it tells a lot of stories. TV programming is filled with situation comedies, dramas of various sorts, soap-operas, and feature films. And there is a reason for this. People like stories. They always have and they always will. Jesus knew this, so he told a lot of stories during his ministry. We, however, seem to have written off Jesus' style of teaching as mere husk, in our eagerness to get at the kernel of truth contained in the story which we then present as didactic rhetoric. Therefore people tune us out, and will do so increasingly, as the pre-electronic-media generation passes away. If our message is to be heard, we must learn once more how to tell stories.

Notice, too, how the stories are told on TV and in films—with humor, with lots of action, and with surprises. These characteristics have, of course, been the cause of a great deal of *bad* television and film. As each producer tries to outdo the other, the stories become more violent and more sensational. The settings move from the exotic to the bizarre, and the dialogue becomes more and more risqué and titillating. We can, of course, resist these extremes and still learn the lesson—that the best stories are action-filled, full of suspense, and have a touch of good fun about them.

Notice, further, how on television the input is broken up into small palatable sections. TV news is a prime example. Ten news stories per half hour used to be the norm. Now the tendency is to discuss up to twenty stories each half hour, which means that we get our information in smaller discrete units. The same tendency is seen in sports coverage. While baseball games are still broadcast *in toto*, many sports events are shown in small segments intercut with other events. We see a little gymnastics, then a few rounds of a fight, and we end with a look at the World Mud Racing Championship. Variety shows continue to be popular, and they follow the same format—short, discrete units of entertainment. In fact, even the editing of TV shows bears this characteristic. The picture cuts to a new frame every 7 to 10 seconds.

All this stands in sharp contrast to the heavy, fairly didactic sermon delivered in so many of our churches for 20 to 30 minutes. I am convinced that our congregations are becoming less and less able to "hear" us anymore in this format. It is hard enough for those raised in a church to sit through most sermons (notice how attention picks up when a story is told). For a non-Christian who wanders into a church on Sunday, the sermon must be akin to culture shock, given present-day media conditioning. We must start experimenting with different time formats for our preaching and teaching. There is nothing sacred about a half-hour, continuous monologue, placed at the end of the service. If people are better able to absorb three connected, well-constructed ten-minute statements interspersed throughout the service, then perhaps it is time to alter our order of worship.

Another area in which TV has had an impact on churches is technical preparation. While not all TV is first-rate, much of it is beautifully and skillfully constructed. Even the "bad" shows are technically brilliant by comparison to TV even 15 years ago. As a result, people have a high level of expectation when it comes to our teaching and preaching. They want it well done. They are used to solid content, carefully crafted phrases, and well-timed delivery. Now of course TV looks and sounds good because numerous hours of highly paid talent have been directed toward making it that way. While we need not try to compete directly, still the burden is upon us to use words skillfully and colorfully, and to keep our insights in touch with the real needs of real people. The mass media have raised the level of expectation in churches.

TV has also made us more entertainment-oriented. I react against the kind of worship service that rings of "show-biz," even though it invariably seem to draw large congregations. Still, without succumbing to the glibness, flash, and superficiality of the media, we ought to think long and hard about how we construct our worship experiences and teaching sessions. Are the hymns carefully planned, and not randomly chosen at the last moment? Do they serve to move the service forward thematically, and on a feeling level? Is all the music characterized by careful presentation, variety, and thoughtful choice? Is there a flow and rhythm to the service itself? Is there a pageantry to our worship? Most of the time, it seems, an "order of worship" is inherited and little attention is paid to it.

Our teaching ministries suffer even more. The easiest thing to do is to lecture people. They sit passively for forty-five minutes while we talk. It is also the least effective way of making an impact. Reflect on how information is communicated on TV. Sit for a few hours with the children's shows that have an ostensible teaching purpose, and notice *how they do it*—the variety (cartoons, puppets, skits, music, characters), the repetition (but not in a boring way), the noncondemnatory attitudes of the characters (the "teachers" smile and exude a sense of "learning is fun"), the short, discrete but interconnected segments, the way the teaching issues are discussed in the context of the needs and interests of the target audience, the rhythm and flow to the whole show. Then go to your study and try to design a series of seminars on "Sharing Your Faith," using these principles.

Finally, in discussing what we can learn from TV about how to communicate in this new environment, it must be noted that the new electronic media have shifted our orientation from the verbal to the visual. We have become a visually-oriented society. If you doubt this, you do not even have to turn on your TV. Just pick up a wide-circulation magazine. Notice the layout. Even in heavy-print magazine makes a serious attempt to appeal to the eye. There are ample spaces and margins, excellent photographs and line-drawings, and in general a pleasing "look" to the magazine. Examine the advertisements: beautiful color photographs, eye-catching captions, a minimum of words. When a manufacturer gives technical details, it is relegated to very small type, tucked away down at the bottom of the advertisement. A magazine, after all, appeals basically to the eye, not the ear. Yet we in the church, and especially in the nonliturgical tradition, still rely heavily on words. The focal point of our experience together is a verbally delivered sermon. To be sure, we use print. Our commitment to the Bible has made us a print-oriented people. Yet how often do we design our books and tracts to appeal to the eye? To communicate effectively, both to our people and to those outside the church, we must become more visually oriented.

Final Notes

Having said this much about the relationship between media and our evangelistic responsibility, we must deal with one more matter. We have said nothing about how the church can use mass media directly for evangelistic purposes. This omission has been intentional. I have become increasingly wary as to our ability to use media skillfully. Indeed, my impression is that most of the direct use of media by Christians is evangelistically counterproductive. I suppose a case could be made that Christians have used media skillfully in nurturing their own community. Christian radio and TV provide church folk with useful spiritual insights. Yet my point remains. My feeling is that even these shows, *from an evangelistic point of view*, are counterproductive. Imagine the average non-Christian tuning across a Christian radio program. What would he or she hear? For one thing, the format would be totally foreign. Christian radio programs do not sound like any other programs. When music is played, it often has an antique ring to it. And then there are all those words, all those monologues. And what words they are—"washed in the blood," "sanctification," "sold out to God," etc. It is like a new language to the non-Christian listener—which, of course, it is.

And this is the problem. Our media efforts make public our Christian subculture, with its unique concerns, ways of doing things, and vocabulary. That subculture is not wrong. But people outside the church simply do not understand it. And the aim of all good evangelism is to foster understanding—to help a person grasp in a clear, unequivocal way the incredible message of Jesus Christ. And to do so not simply with their minds, but with their whole beings. The best response we can hope for from most non-Christians exposed to a Christian media production is that they will be mildly curious and ask questions. How often, however, are they bored, cynically amused, or even annoyed by what to them sounds and looks like condemnatory gobbledygook?

Why don't Christians do a better job with media? That is a big question, and outside the scope of this paper. But briefly it has to do with at least four factors. First, money. Good media productions are *very* expensive. All too often there has been unwillingness to provide the resources necessary to do an adequate job. Second, talent. Too often Christians have tried to produce films or do TV with only prayer and a vision, without having spent the ten or fifteen years necessary to master a complex craft. Third, there is often a refusal to take seriously the unique parameters of the chosen medium. It seems as if we are always trying to make our media products look and sound like a church meeting. And so we misuse the medium. Last, we seem to have a curious inability to see ourselves as others see us. Our evangelistic programs seem to be produced to ensure an enthusiastic response from our brothers and sisters in the faith, rather than to provide interest and insight for the non-Christian. And, needless to say, while there have been some very good Christian films, radio shows, records, and TV programs, as well as some fine Christian books and magazines, these, alas, have been the exception, not the rule.

It must be said in conclusion that the media are not inherently evil. Nor are all, or even most media products suspect in themselves. I love films. I watch a lot of them, and I even assist in making some. I have worked in TV and radio. The problem is that, taken together, the mass media do propagate a secular vision of reality in a most powerful and persuasive way. Not only that, the unique aspect of electronic media is not their values and vision, for the secular vision has long been with us. It is that they have totally altered our modes of learning and communicating. We are deluged with instant information, skillfully presented in discrete, entertaining packages, largely visual in orientation. This has made us very impatient with the turgid, the dull, the over-long, the didactic.

Whether this is good or bad must be decided on other grounds. All that matters now is that this is the way things are in America today. It is not going to do any good to launch an anti-media campaign. The mass media are here to stay—with their good and bad elements. It is up to us to learn to work in this new environment if we are going to reach people with the gospel.

It amounts to a question of communication, which is of course what evangelism is all about—the communication of a very special, uniquely life-changing message. We must learn to communicate this message with power and clarity to our media generation.

PRACTICAL THEOLOGY: CHRISTIAN EDUCATION

Kenneth O. Gangel, area editor

CHRISTIAN EDUCATION

KENNETH O. GANGEL
Professor and Chairman of the Christian Education Department
Dallas Theological Seminary

Introduction

Marching along at mid-decade, Christian education as an academic and theological discipline has never been in greater health. Record departmental enrollments (particularly at the graduate level), newly-initiated doctoral programs, and a generally higher level of scholarship among evangelicals has made it a good year for journal articles in the field.

Furthermore, it is precisely these promising conditions that offer bright hope for the rest of the century. The newly reorganized National Association of Professors of Christian Education will attract over 100 professionals to its annual convention in October 1986, and the membership is far larger. The names and articles of evangelicals have been appearing in non-evangelical publications with increasing frequency, a phenomenon unknown twenty years ago.

No longer the simplistic scissors-and-chalk activity of the era prior to World War II, Christian education today occupies a rightful, if hard-earned place among other essential disciplines in both graduate and undergraduate education. Its faculty are often among the most highly-trained and field-experienced in the modern seminary movement, and their productivity in scholarly and practical arenas increases annually in both quantity and quality.

Professional Christian educators must be somewhat schizophrenic by demand. Whereas an archaeologist or Semitic scholar may give his or her total attention to academic and scholarly pursuits, those serving the "practical disciplines" dare never lose sight of the "So what?" questions. Pragmatism is hardly the base of our authority, but inerrant truth must translate into real life for pastors, teachers, lay leaders, parachurch directors, and students, or Christian education has no reason for existence. It is imperative to talk to God on the mountain, but meanwhile the real world awaits down in the valley.

All of which affects the choice of articles for this publication. Criteria sought to identify articles of a conceptual nature for educated but nontechnical readers. Table talk between disciplinary specialists is not included. The ultimate restriction, however, was space, and my selection process identified the "top 20" articles in the field, narrowed to 10 and grudgingly chipped away to five, allowing the editorial committee to determine what follows. Painfully laid aside were excellent articles dealing with such crucial disciplinary topics as women's roles in church leadership, studies of public versus private schooling for Christians, the status and future of Christian higher education, andragogy and gerogogy, family life education, and lay leadership development. Even this modest topic sampling demonstrates the breadth of what we have come to call "Christian Education." But a word is in order about the five articles I consider the best sampling. I received valuable assistance from these colleagues: Timothy Hui, of the Dallas Theological Seminary Library; Fred Wilson, of Talbot Theological Seminary; and D. Campbell Wyckoff, retired from Princeton Theological Seminary.

D. Bruce Lockerbie, a Gaebelinian disciple and protégé was invited to deliver the 1985 W. H. Griffith Thomas lectures at Dallas Seminary. The field was Christian education, and the general topic, "Thinking Like a Christian." Part three of that series issues a call for a distinctively Christian humanism set against the obtuse and often bizarre attacks by some who have confused secular, religious, and Christian humanism into a hopeless generalization obfuscated by the absence of adjectives.

Lockerbie not only corrects the error, but shows in unmistakably biblical, theological, and philosophical patterns how true humanism centers in an evangelical epistemology. This work speaks to the *why* questions of Christian education, which serve, of course, as foundational to the what and how questions. *The Best in Theology* readers are urged to follow through with the other three articles in his series.

Rarely are scholarly articles so accurately titled and easily read as the informative piece by Bruce Shelley, professor of church history at Denver Seminary. Exploring the roots and fruits of Youth for Christ, Young Life and InterVarsity Christian Fellowship, Shelley lays out no fewer than ninety documented references and offers readers insights few have been privileged to glimpse. At first glance this appears to be just another historical survey, the stuff of which history of education classes consist. But it is much more. Since World War II these three parachurch organizations "informally allied with the Graham organization" have accounted for thousands of conversions and countless young men and women entering some form of ministry. Their story is one Christian leaders ought to hear.

Klaus Issler, a seminary professor, applies the magic word "excellence" to the process of teaching, and uncovers five categories housing eleven "elements" or "variables." Some will fault his denial of the crucial process-product dyad, but the article has humble goals and open ends, a primer raising solid questions for those who would go further and deeper. We could have wished for more significant theological insights which this author is qualified to provide, but perhaps these fall into the "further and deeper" study mentioned above. According to Issler, "Excellent teaching is not an

activity solely confined to the classroom, but it is rather a habit, a way of life."
Selah.

Warren Bryan Martin is a Senior Fellow at the Carnegie Foundation for the Advancement of Teaching. His essay, not printed here, deals with the authority for education, and again pushes Christian educators to ask the *why* questions. The small Christian college, in Martin's view, offers a prototype for society, a pocket of resistance in a culture that has abandoned character. Although biblical support is not the intent of the author, evangelical readers will want to strain Martin's concepts of "virtue," "morality," and "ethics" through a theological sieve before dumping them into the educational soup. What appears is not in error; what is lacking must be made up. (Refer to "Education for Character," *Faculty Dialogue* [Winter 1985-86]: 7-17.)

Also recommended but not printed here is Edward Farley's, "Can Church Education Be Theological Education?" His presuppositions and handling of authority are vastly different from Lockerbie's. Many will not agree with his treatment of the status of Scripture (this editor could wish for much clearer commitment to biblical authority) but we can doubt neither the relevance nor the wisdom of his conclusions. Farley defends the premise that the church takes seriously education for its clergy but not its laity. Contrary to James Michael Lee and others who posit a social science base for Christian education, Farley places strong emphasis on the theological nature of the discipline, a thesis which evangelicals can and should affirm. This delicate balance of faith and knowledge is threatened by the "darkened posture" (sin) and the biblical functioning of the church is plagued by elitism. Here is a short preview: "Once this narrowing [of theology to systematics] takes place, theology is expelled even from the clergy, the ordained leaders, and is restricted to teacher-scholars who preside over clergy education or over one of its fields." (Refer to *Theology Today*, Vol. XL11, No. 2 [July, 1985]: 158-171.)

About the Area Editor

Kenneth O. Gangel (M.Div., Grace Theological Seminary; M.A., Fuller Theological Seminary; S.T.M., Concordia Theological Seminary; Ph.D., University of Missouri at Kansas City) is professor and chairman of the Department of Christian Education at Dallas Theological Seminary. He is an ordained minister in the Christian and Missionary Alliance. He edited *Toward a Harmony of Faith and Learning* (1983), and has recently written *Unwrap Your Spiritual Gifts* (1983); and *Christian Education: Its History and Philosophy*, co-authored with Warren Benson (1982).

A CALL FOR CHRISTIAN HUMANISM

D. BRUCE LOCKERBIE
Staley Foundation Scholar-in-Residence
The Stony Brook School

Article from *Bibliotheca Sacra*

The novel *The Great Gatsby* ends with Nick Carraway, the narrator, musing on what he calls "the last and greatest of all human dreams."[1] It is that, certainly: the *last* and *greatest*, as F. Scott Fitzgerald writes; but it is also the *first* and *foremost*, the primary dream. Anthropologists and students of myth recognize it as such; even casual readers of the Bible find this same dream tracing its way from Eden to Mount Ararat and beyond to a midnight conversation between a Pharisee named Nicodemus and an itinerant Teacher from Nazareth. This "last and greatest of all human dreams," this first and foremost aspiration, is the dream of starting all over again.

Other similar expressions are in use, such as "turning over a new leaf," "making a fresh start," "creating a new identity," "achieving a new consciousness." The hope contained in these terms is that, somehow—by an act of the will, by a physical uprooting from one location to another, by a deliberate change in behavior—new conditions can be formed that will lead to a happier life.

In specifically Christian terms, this experience is provided for by the new birth—being born again. The gospel offers this hope in spiritual rebirth by faith, regeneration, and renewal. Indeed Christians look back to their time of rebirth; but they can also look forward to a time when God the Creator will fulfill His promise to make everything new, the ἀποκατάσασις ("restoration") of prophecy and apostolic preaching.

Defining Humanism

This is God's plan, to be performed in God's time. But to the God-denying secularist, for whom there is no supernatural dimension, no ultimate power outside this natural sphere, "God's plan" and "God's time" are nonsense. If anything new is to come about, says secular man, it will happen only because human beings themselves achieve it. This certainty, this self-assurance, stems from the belief, declared by Protagoras in the fifth century B.C., that "man is the measure of all things."[2] This is the philosophy of the egocentric self, the vanity that exalts the individual over any other authority.

Even his Greek contemporaries—the playwright Sophocles, for instance—
recognized the heresy of Protagoras, who also wrote, "About the gods I have
no means of knowing whether they exist or do not exist or what their form
may be."[3]

If, then, the concept of God is at best irrelevant, if human ingenuity is all
there is to rely on, there is no course open but to establish the supremacy of
human values and the legitimacy of human claims to control human destiny.
This is the attitude popularly known as humanism; but because that word
has been so loosely used and abused in many quarters, the term "secular
humanism" may be used. This is the dogma that exalts the human being as
the god of this age. For secular humanism is the religion of the contemporary
culture. It has its own shrines and cathedrals, its idols and icons, its scriptures and creed, its hymns and bumper stickers. All these proclaim belief in a
naturalistic universe defined by time and space, denial of any supernatural
or eternal reality, denial of human accountability to a personal and transcendent God. The magazine *Free Inquiry* condenses the creed to a sentence:
"Secular humanism places trust in human intelligence rather than in divine
guidance."[4]

A serious blunder is being made by well-meaning Christians in the pulpit
and the classroom, before television cameras, and in widely read books. This
is the common practice of assuming that all humanism is the same as secular humanism, that the historic tradition known as "Christian humanism" is
an oxymoron, a contradiction as puzzling as "liberal Republican." To give
the proper setting for this point, some broad strokes of historical survey
need to be made.

The Roots of Biblical Humanism

Christians trace the revelation of truth about God to the historical Chaldean
whose willingness to trust the God of the covenant resulted in the righteousness of faith. All believers are the "sons and daughters" of Abraham, his
spiritual descendants (Rom. 4:12; Gal. 3:29). But Christians are therefore also
heirs of culture as well as heirs of faith. Yahweh's covenant with Abraham did
not invalidate the patriarch's need to eat and sleep. His tents prospered, his
flocks increased, his wealth and power expanded. Abraham became the
associate of kings, as well as being priest of Mamre and Beersheba, the stout-
hearted father on Mount Moriah. Furthermore those covenant promises of
God were to be fulfilled through an ever-enlarging penetration by Abraham's
children. "Your descendants will take possession of the cities of their enemies," said the Lord, "and through your offspring all nations on earth will be
blessed, because you have obeyed me" (Gen. 2:17-18, NIV).

Clearly the call of Abraham to leave the culture of Ur and trek the Fertile
Crescent to Canaan was not a call to cultural isolation. It was a call to

reestablish an order of living in which God's authority was supreme, a call to thinking and acting on godly principles, a call to living in full obedience and full delight. The same must be true for Abraham's spiritual descendants today. Christians are called not only to the test of faith but also to the blessings concomitant with faith. Believers have inherited the rich legacy that begins with recognition of God and continues through mankind's unique relationship with God as Creator and Lord. From this same legacy springs the revelation in the written Word and the incarnate Word, the doctrine that "God was in Christ reconciling the world to Himself" (2 Cor. 5:19). From this legacy of faith, new hope brings dignity to all of life, dissolving the old fear of death; a new regard for all persons—men and women, husbands and wives, parents and children, masters and servants—eliminating the old bondage to pride and caste. From this legacy a new social order evolves, in which Jesus Christ is Lord. Wherever this recognition obtains, that domain becomes known as Christendom; the cultures that come under the saving knowledge of the gospel combine to form a way of life that may be called a Christian civilization, marked by a consciousness of the Cross and the empty tomb.

From the beginning of Christianity's influence on the Mediterranean world, some 250 years before the Emperor Constantine proclaimed the church as his own, its role as conservator of social and domestic values has been clear. In a culture where the home and hearth were, first, honored in the worship of patron goddesses, then debauched in fornication at temples, Christian apostles and teachers called for faithfulness in marriage. At the same time, when Gnostic heresy began to infect Christian doctrine with denial of material worth, the writers of the New Testament letters affirmed the goodness of God in nature and the sanctity of all that God had created, including the human body, confirmed by the incarnation, resurrection, and exaltation of God-in-flesh in the person of Jesus of Nazareth. By extension, therefore, Christian doctrine calls for a recognition of the sacramental possibilities in every human act and artifact. For if "culture" may be defined as "the work of men's minds and hands,"[5] then within every culture lies the potential for believers to praise God.

The Breadth of Truth

So for all its emphasis on conserving the truths of Jewish and early Christian teachings, Christian doctrine never excluded truth from other sources as well. Paul occasionally made reference to pagan literature (e.g., Acts 17:28; Titus 1:12) in teaching his new message to Greeks familiar with the old ways. Of course Paul was not thereby acknowledging the validity of all pagan writings. He was simply recognizing an element of truth in some of that literature. While God's ultimate revelation of truth is embodied in Jesus Christ, truth is not limited to Christ's few years of earthly life.

Justin Martyr, the second-century apologist, spoke of this truth. Prior to his conversion he had been a teacher, entitled to wear the blue robe marking his profession. After he became a Christian, he continued to wear the robe, having determined that the Logos for which he had been seeking in philosophy was now made known to him in Jesus Christ.

More than 250 years after Justin, at the beginning of the fifth century, Augustine of Hippo, in his treatise *On Christian Doctrine,* argued against those who would restrict Christians from studying and learning to appreciate the work of nonbelievers. In a passage of sublime insight Augustine wrote, "Every good and true Christian should understand that wherever he may find truth, it is his Lord's."[6]

By so recognizing the universality of truth and its divine origin, and by following the examples of both Justin Martyr and the apostles, Augustine established a model for thinking Christians to emulate. But today many Christians seem to have lost much of this breadth of truth. They have become victims of their own narrowness and defensive views. Now as never before they need to liberate their minds and hearts—their intellects and emotions—from all that would enshackle them; they need to become open and free to all that is reasonable and lovely, orderly and inspiring, stimulating to further knowledge and at the same time overwhelming in its awesome beauty. They need to reclaim for God what He has given and they have squandered, offering back to Him what their mind and hands find to do. If thinking Christians were to live each day in full realization that every area of life belongs to God, they would see again the kind of art, literature, education, government, and social order that marked much of Christendom in earlier centuries. The church would experience again culture captured for Christ, culture embraced by Christians throughout every aspect of living, as was the case during the 15th and 16th centuries in Europe.

In the Middle Ages, when infant mortality was high and life expectancy short, when the serf system bore down heavily on most people, when education was limited to a few, the church had little to offer by way of comfort for this life. Its eye was fixed on the prospects of life-to-come, "the life everlasting" of the creed. Human life and human endeavor seemed to count little when weighed against eternal values. Against this bleakness arose the reaction known as the Renaissance, stirred by a revival of interest in ancient Greek and Latin writers whose work had offered a brighter view of human worth.

It is hard for people today to imagine that there was ever a time when books had the same power as the television screen to rule lives and set forth values. But so it was, just as there had also been a time in Athenian society when public discourse determined the highest ethic. The revival in Europe of classical literature asserted human and humane values idealized in love sonnets and sculpture, in painting and fine speech. This preoccupation with the present life became known as humanism, but it was not necessarily

Protagoras's kind of rebellion against God's standard of measurement; rather, it was a reaffirmation of the biblical appreciation for human experience lived in a mutually caring and responsible relationship with God the majestic yet loving Father. Certainly it is true that, under the guise of reasserting human worth and individual importance to God, humanism in some of its forms exalted the creature of the Creator; some men renewed Protagoras's agnosticism, raising a battle cry against divine authority. But if some aspects of humanism led to a perverse sense of human autonomy, humanism also led to a breaking of the medieval church's stranglehold on the free expression of faith, for humanism led to the Reformation.

In the nominally Christian states of Europe the church passed its laws compelling baptism and uniform church attendance, but nothing could compel the spirit to believe or the mind to accept as necessary a God propped up by a human prince. Medieval scholars plodded through their constructs of questions and answers, but could their cold, formalistic reasoning warm men's hearts with the love of God? Could men and women learn to see the goodness and grandeur of God in His works of common grace? What of man's attempts to glorify God in return? Can art and architecture, poetry and song reflect anything heavenly by means of earthly expression? Or, to put the question plainly, can a person be both a Christian and a scholar, a Christian and an artist?[7]

Christian Humanists   ← RENAISSANCE

An affirmative reply may seem straightforward and obvious today, but it was a radical response when, after A.D. 1300, Dante began writing his epic *The Divine Comedy* in vernacular Italian rather than ecclesiastical Latin; or after A.D. 1400, when Flemish and Italian painters began depicting religious themes by means of realistic figures of common people in familiar settings. Little by little, artists and then scholars began to make the worship and love of God less ethereal, less other-worldly, less spiritual, less remote, less divine—more human! Was this not in keeping with the gospel itself and its doctrine of the Incarnation? Had not God chosen to become human, thereby sanctifying by His very bodily form and substance the life known by human beings?

Little of this humanizing reality, this mystery of God-in-flesh, came through the categorical theology of that time. The gospel was being suffocated by too great a reliance on systematics and dialectics. There were no translations of the Bible in the common European languages. Furthermore, until the advent of Johann Gutenberg's printing press around 1456, access to manuscripts was limited, and learning necessarily depended a great deal on rote acceptance rather than inquiry and discovery for oneself.

But by the middle of the 15th century, aided by Gutenberg's invention, ancient texts and scholars who could read them began finding their way into Italy, Germany, and France. Here were men who knew not only the classical poets but also the language of the New Testament and the Eastern Church Fathers. Subsequently a new interest in learning Greek and Hebrew sprang up, and with this interest in the Bible's original languages came the translation of the Scriptures into common tongues.

Three names from this era are important to remember. Lorenzo Valla (1405-1457), a linguist, goaded theologians into understanding that their hermeneutics must be based not on their knowledge of theology but their knowledge of the Bible itself. Next John Colet (1466-1519), an English priest, founder of St. Paul's School and dean of St. Paul's Cathedral, gave his Oxford lectures in 1496, on Romans and 1 Corinthians. These were unlike anything before their time. Instead of turning every line of text into allegory, Colet actually treated the text as if a man named Paul had written an important letter to other men and women in a real city called Rome or Corinth. He brought Paul to life; he brought Paul's readers and their problems to life; he made the Bible breathe with vitality.

Colet's friend Desiderius Erasmus (1466-1536) is the third name. Erasmus may have been the greatest scholar in history. His accomplishments were numerous, but among his most important were these: his translation of the New Testament from the Greek text; his call for Bible study by everyone, including women; and his paraphrases of the Gospels and the Epistles, eventually translated into German, French, and English. Erasmus is responsible for some of the most profoundly striking statements, as these instances show:

> People say to me, How can scholarly knowledge facilitate the understanding of Holy Scripture? My answer is, How does ignorance contribute to it?
>
> Only a few can be scholars, but there is no one who cannot be a Christian.
>
> To be a schoolmaster is next to being a king. Do you count it a mean employment to imbue the minds of your fellow-citizens in their earliest years with the best literature and with the love of Christ, and to return them to their country honest and virtuous men? In the opinion of fools it is a humble task, but in fact it is the noblest of occupations.
>
> All studies, philosophy, rhetoric are followed for this one object, that we may know Christ and honor Him. This is the end of all learning and eloquence.[8]

Thinking in Christian Categories

The commitment of Erasmus and others like him to a program of studies so singlemindedly Christ-centered sets him and other Christian humanists of his time among the forerunners in the search for an authentic integration of faith and learning. Their sense of wholeness in studies and teaching, in art and science, in politics and government, puts to shame many of today's so-called "Christian schools" and "Christian colleges," whose index of forbidden pleasures may be their highest measure of orthodoxy; whose curriculum and instruction resemble not at all T. S. Elliot's understanding that "the purpose of a Christian education would not be merely to make men and women pious Christians. . . . A Christian education would primarily train people to be able to think in Christian categories."[9]

The Christian humanists of long ago knew how to think in Christian categories. They devoted their lives to serving Jesus Christ by making His Word more accessible. By their example they encouraged artists and musicians to follow their vocations in representing the truth of Scripture in human terms. Of course these men were flawed. Erasmus, for instance, chose to remain a Roman Catholic and debated bitterly with Luther. No doubt many believers today would disagree with Erasmus (and Luther too) on some points, but is their work to be ignored and their integrity transgressed by today's ignorance?

Peculiarly, television preachers and film lecturers and writers of predigested history books often fail to deal with Erasmus and other Christian humanists. But history is not to be bent to suit one's prejudice; nor does a word like "humanism" lose its primary meaning just because it is adopted by atheistic naturalists. The Ethical Culture Society, The British Humanist Association, and the publishers of *Free Inquiry* have corrupted the word "humanism," and the nature of "language laziness" is such that, once a word has been commandeered and its usage made familiar, it is all but impossible to redeem that word from corruption and restore its historic meaning. Such corruption is witnessed in the now-standard use of "gay" to mean "homosexual." "Humanism" is another word worthy of redemption.

In a 1972 book, *The Way They Should Go,* this writer offered the phrase "Christian artists and scholars" as a palliative to anyone who might gag over "Christian humanists." He was too timid to call for a revival of the spirit of Christian humanism by name—Christian humanism as exemplified by saints and singers, artists, and poets since the day of Pentecost. Today this writer hopes to atone for that blunder by issuing for a call for Christian humanists, a challenge to thinking Christians everywhere to reclaim for God the life of the mind, the world of imagination, the things of the spirit. This is a call for Christians to begin enjoying the abundant life promised them—their utterly human and dependent walk with Jesus Christ. To heed this call, Christian educators are needed at every level and in every sphere who understand the legacy of Christian humanism and are not ashamed of their inheritance as modern Christian humanists. Such leaders are needed to point the way to a *BUT the PRIORITY ?* Christian renaissance.

But while many Christian educators know their purpose, many in the church have grown suspicious of their supposed erudition. What will win them to an enlightened understanding of God's benediction on learning? Only an unremitting allegiance to Jesus Christ revealed in the Word of God. Erasmus—towering thinker that he was—could nonetheless write the following:

> I utterly disagree with those who do not want the Holy Scriptures to be read by the uneducated in their own language, as though Christ's teaching was so obscure that it could hardly be understood even by a handful of theologians, or as though the strength of Christian religion consisted in men's ignorance of it. . . . I hope the farmer may sing snatches of Scripture at his plough, that the weaver may hum bits of Scriptures to the tune of his shuttle, that the traveler may lighten the weariness of his journey with stories from the Scripture.[10]

This is the vision of the true Christian humanist.[11] At Dallas Theological Seminary, at The Stony Brook School, throughout formal Christian education—wherever Jesus Christ is professed—teachers and students alike should labor to regain that vision of their predecessors. Christians today are challenged to join with Paul and Timothy, with Justin Martyr and Jerome, with Augustine and Alcuin, with Calvin and Knox, with Luther and Erasmus, with Comenius and Milton, with T. S. Eliot and C. S. Lewis, with Gresham Machen and Griffith Thomas and Frank Gaebelein—Christian humanists all. May Christians join together in renewed commitment to their treasured task as conservators and proclaimers of the good news.

Editor's Note: This is the third in a series of four articles delivered by the author as the W. H. Griffith Thomas Lectures at Dallas Theological Seminary, November 5-8, 1985.

Notes

[1] F. Scott Fitzgerald, *The Great Gatsby* (New York: Charles Scribner's Sons, 1925), p. 182.

[2] Bernard M. W. Knox, *Oedipus at Thebes* (New Haven, CT: Yale University Press, 1957), p. 45.

[3] Ibid., p. 161.

[4] *Free Inquiry* 1 (Winter 1980/81), cover page.

[5] H. Richard Niebuhr, *Christ and Culture* (New York: Harper and Row, 1956), p. 33.

[6] Augustine, *On Christian Doctrine*, trans. D. W. Robertson, Jr. (Indianapolis: Bobbs-Merrill Co., 1958), p. 54.

[7] For an expanded treatment of this problem, see E. Harris Harbison, *The Christian Scholar in the Age of the Reformation* (New York: Charles Scribner's Sons, 1956). This writer is happy to acknowledge his debt to Harbison's scholarship. The opening paragraph of his book reads: "The Christian scholar—like the Christian poet, the Christian musician, or the Christian scientist—has always run the risk of being dismissed as an anomaly. What has learning to do with salvation of the soul, or satisfaction of the mind with peace of the spirit? . . . Yet the fact is that almost from the beginning of Christianity there have been those who pursued learning as a Christian calling, in the belief that they were following God's will" (p. 1).

[8] See ibid., chap. 3, "Erasmus," pp. 69-102; and H. C. Porter, "Introduction," *Erasmus and Cambridge* (Toronto: University of Toronto Press, 1963).

[9] "The Idea of a Christian Society," in *Christianity and Culture* (New York: Harcourt, Brace, and World, 1949), p. 22.

[10] Harbison, *The Christian Scholar in the Age of the Reformation*, pp. 100-101.

[11] For further reading on this topic, see "A Christian Humanist Manifesto," ed. James I. Packer et al., *Eternity*, January 1982, pp. 15-22. See also James I. Packer and Thomas Howard, *Christianity: The True Humanism* (Waco, TX: Word Books, 1985).

THE RISE OF EVANGELICAL YOUTH MOVEMENTS

BRUCE SHELLEY
Professor of Church History
Denver Conservative Baptist Seminary

Article from *Fides Et Historia*

During the Great Depression a small storefront mission on the near-north side of Chicago provided bread and soup for long lines of people. As part of the ministry to the community, leaders of the mission surveyed 2,000 homes in the immediate area and discovered that 50 percent of the children never attended church services or Sunday School.[1]

As a result, the founders of the mission, Herbert J. Taylor (1893-1978) and his wife Gloria, reached a conclusion: they had to provide organizations and people who could reach unchurched children and, eventually, direct them toward the church. Soon Taylor, president of the Club Aluminum Products Company, was ready to put his convictions into action.

First, he created a nonprofit foundation: The Christian Workers Foundation. The original trustees, in addition to himself, were his wife, Gloria, and his attorney, Lysle Smith. Taylor gave twenty-five percent of the Club Aluminum Company's stock to the foundation.[2]

With this financial base Taylor was ready to create or to help finance organizations capable of reaching the unchurched young people of America. He had in mind an extensive plan that included Christian evangelistic works starting with collegians and moving on down through high school teens, junior high school students, and elementary school children. As Taylor later expressed it, "With God's help, . . . we intended to help pioneer and finance the nondenominational organizations we felt would do the best job of reaching these young people with the Lord's word."[3]

These "nondenominational organizations" turned out to be the Inter-Varsity Christian Fellowship, Young Life Campaign, Youth for Christ, Christian Service Brigade, Pioneer Girls, and Child Evangelism Fellowship— parachurch evangelistic organizations that can be considered the evangelical heirs of revivalism. Taylor's line of thinking is significant. Though a Methodist layman, he did not turn to his church. He looked instead to new interdenominational agencies.[4]

Today parachurch organizations have changed the face of American Protestantism. Many recent observers have noted a shift in religious loyalties from the traditional denominations to the parachurch movements.[5] Youth for Christ points to 1065 Campus Life clubs in the United States and work in 56 foreign countries. Young Life has over 500 full-time staff members contacting nearly 200,000 teenagers annually. Inter-Varsity has work on 850 college and university campuses and draws 17,000 collegians to its massive Urbana Missionary Conferences every three years.[6]

A studied look at the beginnings of these movements calls for some terminal point.[7] One possibility is 1957. In that year, when Billy Graham considered an invitation to hold a crusade in New York City, the heirs of fundamentalism were divided over who should sponsor the meetings: the Protestant Council of New York City or a group of fundamentalists led by evangelist Jack Wyrtzen. Graham accepted the invitation of the Protestant Council and the separatistic fundamentalists never let him forget it. As a result, after 1957 the distinction between "evangelical" and "fundamentalist" gained acceptance in wider and wider circles.[8] So 1957 is a convenient terminal point for a study of evangelistic organizations during the 1940s and '50s.

The best known of these movements is the Billy Graham Evangelistic Association. Informally allied with the Graham organization were three youth ministries: Youth for Christ, Young Life, and Inter-Varsity. How did these three agencies arise in the forties and how do we explain their significant growth on the evangelical horizon?

Youth for Christ

The origins of Youth for Christ are almost impossible to trace. The movement had no founder; it had an explosion.[9] Probably the first youth rally director in America was fiery Lloyd Bryant, who organized weekly rallies for youth in the early 1930s. For seven years he ministered to teenagers in Manhattan at the Christian and Missionary Alliance Tabernacle at 44th Street and Eighth Avenue. During these same years Percy Crawford launched his Young People's Church of the Air and set a pattern for future rapid-fire Youth for Christ preachers.

The youth style rally became nationally known, however, when Jack Wyrtzen, at the urging of Percy Crawford, launched a youth broadcast in Manhattan. Wyrtzen, a converted insurance salesman and dance band trombonist, called his radio broadcast "Word of Life Hour" and linked it with rallies held at Bryant's old meeting place, the Christian and Missionary Alliance Tabernacle. The first rally came on October 25, 1941. Later, Word of Life moved to Carnegie Hall, but soon outgrew it. Several rallies, beginning in 1944, drew more than 20,000 to Madison Square Garden.[10] This combination—radio and rally—became common in Youth for Christ circles.

After Oscar Gillan in Detroit, Roger Malsbary in Indianapolis, Dick Harvey in St. Louis, Glen Wagner in Washington, D.C., and George Wilson in Minneapolis initiated youth rallies in their cities, a group of young men in

Chicago decided it was time their city had such a ministry.[11] Beverly Shea, then on the staff of Moody Bible Institute, had worked with Wyrtzen in his Word of Life Hour in New York. He urged Torrey Johnson, pastor of the Midwest Bible Church, to take the leadership of the Chicago rally.

After some hesitation, Johnson agreed to organize a rally, and secured prestigious Orchestra Hall for 21 Saturday nights in 1944. Also, with the help of Herbert Taylor, he booked a half-hour on radio station WCFL. He enlisted his brother-in-law, Bob Cook, to lead the singing for the first rally. And for the first night's preacher he turned to a young, neighboring pastor at Western Springs, Billy Graham. Then he prayed, "Lord, put this meeting on a miracle basis." He was not disappointed.[12]

On Saturday, May 27, 1944, over 2,000 people crowded into Orchestra Hall and so it went for the next 20 weeks. On October 21, a "Victory Rally" at Chicago Stadium drew 28,000 to hear, among others, Gil Dodds, national champion miler, and Herbert J. Taylor give their testimonies, and evangelist Merv Rosell make the evangelistic appeal.[13] Taylor helped the movement financially too, with checks from time to time in the range of $500 to $1000. The Chicagoland YFC quickly became the focal point of Saturday night rallies across North America and the organizing center for Youth for Christ International.[14]

Rally after rally followed a similar pattern: Saturday night in a big auditorium, lively gospel music, personal testimonies from athletes, civic leaders, or military heroes, and a brief sermon, climaxing with a gospel invitation to receive Jesus Christ as personal Savior. This was revivalism tailored to youth.

In a passion for novelty and entertainment, many rallies got caught in a "one-upsmanship" trap: magicians, gospel whistling, musical saws, single-string oil cans. The most outlandish attraction was a "gospel horse" called MacArthur. He moved his jaws to show "how the girls in the choir chew gum" and demonstrated his knowledge of the Bible by tapping his hoof three times when asked "how many Persons are in the Trinity?"[15]

Appeal to the patriotic spirit of the country was open and direct.[16] For Memorial Day 1945, Torrey Johnson planned a mammoth rally at Soldier Field. Chicago had never seen anything like it. In the stands sat 70,000 people. Five hundred uniformed nurses formed a living white cross before the platform. The assembled crowd honored war dead in a solemn ceremony. Navy Chaplain and war hero Bob Evans, in full uniform, gave his testimony. Percy Crawford preached to the throng and appealed for those "moved by the Holy Spirit" to hand decision cards to the ushers. Hundreds did.[17]

One month later the Hearst newspaper chain carried a full page story on the new movement reaching half a million youth every Saturday night. When right wing preacher Gerald L. K. Smith came out in support of Youth for Christ, charges of fascism surfaced. The *Christian Century* put no stock in the fascist charges but roundly criticized "this streamlined evangelism" for its "milky abstractions" and its lack of concern for social and ethical problems.[18]

That summer, on July 22, 1945, forty-two delegates met at Winona Lake, Indiana, for the founding of Youth for Christ International. Torrey Johnson, the keynote speaker, interpreted the significance of the gathering. "The youth movement has grown and spread so rapidly," he said, "that it is no longer possible for cities to isolate themselves from one another." The delegates adopted a constitution that included the doctrinal statement of the one-year-old National Association of Evangelicals, and elected Johnson as president.[19]

Johnson recruited Billy Graham as the first full-time evangelist for the movement. In 1945 the young itinerant traveled 135,000 miles, and United Airlines cited him as their leading civilian passenger. In two years' time Graham preached in forty-seven of the forty-eight states and throughout Canada. He also developed friendships with a team of young men who would in time emerge as the nucleus of the Billy Graham Evangelistic Association.[20]

By the fall of 1945, the war was over but Youth for Christ had hardly begun. Chaplains, G.I.'s, and missionaries provided a bridge for overseas expansion. "Who knows," said Torrey Johnson, "but what we've got an army of occupation for the purpose of establishing Youth for Christ." Rallies appeared in Paris, Manila, Frankfurt, London, Okinawa, Guam, Seoul, Lisbon, Stockholm, Belfast, Oslo, Brussels, and Johannesburg.[21]

The Palermo brothers, Louie and Phil, went to Italy, and held rallies throughout the land of their parents.[22] Spencer DeJong and Don De Vos, both of Dutch descent, flew to Holland and were welcomed as American heroes.[23] Watson Argue and Frank Phillips headed south for rallies in Jamaica, Cuba, Venezuela, Brazil, and Argentina. Bob Pierce, Hubert Mitchell, and David Morken went to India and then to China before the country fell to the Communists.[24] When the YFCI Convention met at Winona Lake in 1947, Johnson, re-elected president for a third term, reported that the international office was "in touch" with 800 rallies in North America, and Billy Graham announced that YFC teams had gone to forty-six countries the previous year.[25]

All, however, was not sparkle and sound. Early in the summer of 1948 Torrey Johnson shocked the fourth YFCI Convention at Winona by asking that he not be renominated for president. His reason, he said, was a desire to "travel more in evangelism."[26] He recommended Bob Cook to succeed him and, in spite of some objections, the convention elected Cook. He seemed to be the man to guide YFCI toward greater maturity.

The direction of that maturity soon appeared. Under Bob Cook's leadership YFC continued its vigorous evangelistic efforts, including scores of teams sent overseas, but the new president sensed that the movement could not keep running on enthusiasm and promotion alone.[27] He deplored the "talented opportunist who was in YFC for self-interest." As a result, he drew guidelines for rally directors and stressed financial accountability.[28]

By 1951 Cook was convinced the one-shot rally approach was in serious trouble in many cities. "The rally idea," he said, "is sound but in most places the . . . rally is just the show window. Let's get something on the counters the rest of the week."[29]

What went "on the counter" was Bible clubs. The Kansas City YFC already had a successful club program going under the leadership of Jack Hamilton and his wife Mary Jeanne.[30] In twelve high school clubs they led students through the New Testament by a series of quizzes, then staged competition between clubs at the Saturday night rallies. The idea spread across the country when Jack left Kansas City to travel with Don Lonie to promote the program in other cities.[31]

In the early fifties many conservative parents and pastors were frustrated by the Supreme Court decision in the *McCollum* v. *Board of Education* case (1948), which apparently removed the Bible from the public schools.[32] They were eager to counteract the ruling. At almost every stop, Hamilton said, "The Court is taking the Bible out of the high schools. With Bible clubs we can put it back in through the lives of the young people on fire for God."[33]

By March 1952, when *Time's* Henry Luce discovered "a more serious interest in religion in America than in thirty years," YFC clubs passed the 1,000 mark. By 1955 Jack Hamilton, in the national office, reported 1956 clubs in forty-one states and seven foreign countries.[34] Clearly, Bible clubs in YFC had become for the fifties what Saturday night rallies were in the forties. *post WWII*

Another significant YFC ministry, developed during the years of Bob Cook's leadership, was the Youth Guidance Program. Cook noticed in the early fifties that YFC was reaching "comparatively few from the so-called 'seamy side of town'." "One reason," he said, "is that so much of our advertising and programs are slanted to happy Christian youngsters. Let's do something to reach the teens outside."

Like the Bible club idea, the work with delinquents started in local ministries. Oakland, California; Victoria, British Columbia; and Los Angeles were the pioneers. As a consequence, the national office recruited Gordon McLean in 1952 as the first Youth Guidance Director. Later, Wendy Collins, a Chicagoan who had developed a successful youth work in Wyoming, succeeded McLean and made Youth Guidance a major facet of YFC's ministry. By 1963 the Youth Guidance program was operating 110 summer camps for delinquent youngsters.[35]

Ten years after the organization of YFC many of the early leaders had moved on to other evangelical endeavors. Of these Billy Graham is the most famous. Graham built his evangelistic team of former YFC leaders. His business manager, George Wilson, was from the Minneapolis YFC. His crusade organizer, Walter Smyth, came from Philadelphia. His song leader, Cliff Barrows, had served on the YFC field staff. Associate evangelist Leighton Ford and pianist Tedd Smith came from YFC in Canada. In a sense, Billy Graham never left YFC; he took it with him.[36]

The same, however, was true of others. As a result of evangelistic junkets in the Far East, Bob Pierce created World Vision. After years of overseeing YFC rallies in Europe, Bob Evans resigned and founded the Greater Europe Mission. Paul Freed, while traveling for YFC in North Africa, determined to build Trans World Radio. In 1950, after a YFC tour of Taiwan, Dick Hillis decided to form Overseas Crusades. And Bob Finley, YFCI's second staff evangelist, while traveling in China, projected a ministry with international students, diplomats, and businessmen visiting the United States; the result was International Students, Inc.

By 1955 so many of his former colleagues had left YFC that Bob Cook lamented "everybody's bailing out except me." Two years later, on Valentine's Day, 1957, Cook himself resigned as president to accept a position with Scripture Press, a publishing house in Wheaton, Illinois. He left behind a stronger, if less sensational YFC than he had inherited.[37]

Young Life

Unlike Youth for Chirst, which seemed to explode like a fireworks display, Young Life was the result of a fuse burning in one young man. To this day the organization reflects the outlook, the principles, and the experiences of Jim Rayburn.

Rayburn was raised in a Presbyterian home during the Great Depression. The son of an evangelist, Jim graduated from Kansas State College and pursued graduate study in mineralogy at the University of Colorado. In 1933, unable to find a job in engineering, Jim and his young bride Maxine accepted an invitation to a remote region of southern Arizona and New Mexico as Presbyterian home missionaries. During these three years Jim found his greatest satisfaction from his work with young people and his greatest disillusionment with traditional church life.[38]

One day, however, while living in Clifton, Arizona, Rayburn came across a dirty, coverless copy of Lewis Sperry Chafer's book, *He That Is Spiritual*. It turned his life in a new direction. "True spirituality," it said, "does not consist in what one does not do; it is rather what one does. It is not suppression: it is expression. It is not holding in self; it is living out Christ."[39] The book set Rayburn thinking about better preparation for ministry. In 1936 he and Maxine packed all their possessions into their old Chevy and headed east to Dallas Theological Seminary, where Louis Sperry Chafer was president.[40]

At Dallas Seminary, Rayburn wasted little time exploring ways to reach teenagers. He spent his first two years working in two churches in Dallas, but no one seemed to know how to reach unreached teenagers. Along with two seminary friends, Addison Sewell and Walden Howard, Jim put up a tent with a "God Bless America" banner. They invited high school students to the meeting where Rayburn brought a Bible story to life with his humor. Slowly he developed his own style of youth evangelism.

During the summer of 1938 Rayburn tested his methods in Gainesville, Texas, a town eighty miles north of Dallas. He discovered that he was not the only one interested in this mission to teens. Clyde Kennedy, pastor of the Gainesville Presbyterian Church, asked Rayburn to join him on weekends as a youth minister but with a specific assignment to reach the 600 young people in town outside the church. Rayburn accepted the challenge.[41]

In the fall of 1938, Rayburn started driving to Gainesville on weekends. He formed a Miracle Book Club that met once a week after school in a classroom, but the results were disappointing. The next year he decided to change his tactics. He continued to spend his Friday nights and Saturdays watching ball games and hanging around with the high school students. But he moved his club to an evening hour and invited his young friends to a home instead of a classrom. The club exploded. Rayburn had stumbled onto some basic principles of Young Life:

1) Hold meetings with teenagers away from school. They are more comfortable in homes than they are in school or in church. Teenagers will go where their friends are.

2) Aim for leaders in the school; others will follow.

3) Make the meetings enjoyable: skits, jokes, singing.[42]

Through the Gainesville experience, Rayburn moved step by step from the traditional revival tent to the suburban living room, the new platform for his youth evangelism.

To this day Young Life evangelism reduces to a network of personal contacts. A leader forms a friendship with a teenager, on campus, at a ball game, at the local MacDonald's, or wherever youth hang out. Friendship gives the leader the right to be heard. It leads naturally to a club, meeting throughout the school year. There, usually once a week, the leader has the opportunity to share his deepest beliefs about personal trust in Jesus Christ.[43]

By April, 1940, the Gainesville club was cramming 125 young people into the living room where they met, and the seminarians had spun off new clubs in other towns: Dallas, Weatherford, and Tyler.[44] With the approach of summer and new tent campaigns, the seminarians felt they needed a distinct name. At seminary in 1937 Rayburn had heard about a youth organization in England led by the Reverend and Mrs. Frederick Wood. It was called the National Young Life Campaign. Rayburn liked the campaign idea.[45] After contacting the Woods, who saw no problem with the use of the name in Dallas, the sign for the tent meetings appeared: "Young Life Campaign—Hear Jim Rayburn." The next concern was financial backing.

Down the hall from the Rayburn's seminary apartment lived Ted and Mary Lou Benson. Ted was from Chicago and worked with Herbert J. Taylor's Christian Workers Foundation. Knowing of Taylor's plan to assist an effective youth organization, Benson wrote to him about Jim Rayburn. Taylor liked what he read and in May agreed to cover the expenses of Rayburn's campaigns up to $100 a month. So with Taylor's financial backing and Add Sewell and Tim Hatch at his side, Rayburn swept through a score of towns throughout Texas. His first report to Taylor covered thirty-three meetings in eleven towns. Some of them started with a dozen youngsters and ended with 500 or more in attendance.[46]

In September Taylor paid Rayburn's way to Chicago and together they explored ways to appeal to teenagers across denominational lines and outside the institutional church. Taylor agreed to continue his financial backing, so Rayburn threw himself into the club work during the fall months.[47] On December 24, 1940, he brought together three men to form a board of directors: John E. Mitchell, a business man, Ted Benson, and Louis Sperry Chafer.[48] It was Herbert Taylor, however, who kept urging Rayburn to think big: "You'll have to go national, Rayburn," he told his young friend, "or I'll not give you another dime."[49] The first moves in that direction came in 1941 when Young Life Campaign was incorporated, and four Dallas Seminary men joined the staff: Wally Howard, George Cowan, Gordon Whitelock, and Addison Sewell. They scattered west, south, and east of Dallas organizing clubs. Early in 1941, sixty clubs were meeting throughout Texas.[50]

During the next three years the movement spread from Texas to Oklahoma, Arkansas, Tennessee, Missouri, and Washington.[51] This growth usually came on the heels of Rayburn's travel, sometimes with a quartet, for meetings on weekends.[52]

During these early days, Rayburn also tried a series of high school assemblies. Some staff member would contact the principal and arrange a date. Then Rayburn would speak before the student body. In his shy, quiet way he knew how to get next to young people. They would cheer him and howl at his jokes, such as the one about the cross-eyed teacher the principal had to fire because she couldn't see eye to eye with her pupils.[53] Assemblies and one night rallies with Gil Dodds in 1945 reached almost 40,000 young people.

Gradually, however, the growing Young Life staff began to feel uneasy about the big rallies, the tents and assemblies—just as Youth for Christ came to question their Saturday night extravaganzas. From June 24 to July 8, 1945, thirty staff members met for their first staff conference at Manitou Springs, Colorado. They prayed and planned and shared ideas. They were trying to discover what made teenagers tick.[54] Young Life, it seemed, was most effective when leaders contacted teenagers one on one. That is one reason camping proved so effective.

At first the leaders tried renting campgrounds, but in 1946 Young Life's realtor, Guss Hill, found a site for sale near Pike's Peak in Colorado, and Rayburn and Taylor agreed to meet in Colorado Springs to see the property.[55] Taylor arrived from Chicago but Rayburn failed to keep the appointment. Taylor, acting alone, was so persuasive in his dickering that he got the $100,000 marked price reduced to $50,000 and put $1,000 down to secure the deal. When Rayburn's delayed plane finally arrived, Taylor announced, "We just bought Star Ranch."

That proved to be true, literally. When Taylor called the board meeting to approve the deal, not one member would vote to support Taylor. They could not understand why Young Life needed a camp when they scarcely had enough money to pay staff salaries. Taylor, however, refused to surrender his $1,000. He sold some preferred stock in Club Aluminum, and bought Star Ranch himself, then leased it to Young Life for $1 a year.[56]

The ranch soon became the nerve center of Young Life. During the following winter, leaders moved the headquarters of the campaign from Dallas to the ranch, where they remained until 1961, when leaders moved their offices to Colorado Springs.[57] Other ranches soon followed. In September, 1949, the Campaign purchased Chalk Cliff Lodge near Buena Vista, Colorado, for $56,000 and held the first camp during Christmas vacation that year. Young Life later renamed the lodge Silver Cliff Ranch.[58]

A year later an announcement in *The New Yorker* led Rayburn to Round-Up Lodge, next to Silver Cliff Ranch. It was for sale for $250,000. He went to the board meeting in January 1951, and secured permission to raise the money. Thirty days later he had eleven donors who had agreed to cover the cost of the property. Young Life called the property Frontier Ranch.[59]

The next year, 1952, a Seattle businessman flew Rayburn into British Columbia to show him yet another piece of property, an amazing site a hundred miles by water from Vancouver. The Malibu Club, as it was called, had been an exclusive yacht resort, but its owner, Tom Hamilton of Los Angeles, had closed it because it failed to meet his financial expectations. In December, 1953, Hamilton set a price of $300,000, provided the deal could be settled at once. Rayburn contacted the board's executive committee by phone and the biggest deal in Young Life's history was soon closed.[60]

Star Ranch, Silver Cliff, Frontier, Malibu. That is how Young Life became so deeply involved in camping as a method of evangelism. Over 4,000 campers attended a camp in 1952. Unlike most other camping programs at the time, Young Life ranches stressed personal relationships between leaders and campers: laughing, singing, hiking, eating, praying. And just as the clubs were designed to attract non-Christian young people, so the camping experience was tailored for teenagers from unchurched families. One girl while hiking through a breathtaking Alpine meadow exclaimed. "We don't have the teensiest chance against God out here! You guys have got it rigged."[61]

Rigged or not, Rayburn seemed to have found the answer to his question, how do we reach unreached kids? By 1977, when the staff reached 600, over 70,000 teenagers were attending Young Life Clubs.[62]

The third evangelistic organization that became a prominent part of the conservative evangelical scene in the 1940s was the Inter-Varsity Christian Fellowship. And again Herbert J. Taylor played a major part in the story.

Before it came to the United States in 1940, Inter-Varsity had a long history in Great Britain, going back to Cambridge University in 1877. It opened work in Canada as early as 1928, and in 1934 C. Stacey Woods, an Australian, assumed leadership of the Canadian ministry.[63] From time to time Woods would encourage student groups in the United States. In 1939 he helped organize the Michigan Christian Fellowship at the University of Michigan.[64] At the same time the Canadian Inter-Varsity Board appointed two Americans to serve in the United States: Grace Koch to work in Pennsylvania and Herbert Butt for ministry in the Pacific Northwest. Another U.S. staff member, Charles Troutman, moved from Canada to Michigan.[65]

In October 1939, Ted Benson brought Stacey Woods and Herbert Taylor together[66] and the two of them began to explore the possibility of Inter-Varsity establishing an office in the United States.[67]

On April 6, 1940, Taylor went to Toronto to meet with the Executive Committee of the IVCF Board. The committee agreed that a board of directors should be formed in the United States and that an office should be opened in Chicago. The members accepted Taylor's offer to begin work in the offices of the Christian Workers Foundation, and his pledge of $10,000 to launch the ministry.[68]

The move became official on May 31, 1941, when the Canadian board, meeting at the University of Toronto, appointed eight staff workers for the United States and Stacey Woods as the general secretary. The U.S. board, meeting at the same time, adopted a constitution for the new work. By September 1941, at the inception of the U.S. ministry, forty-one chapters were linked to IVCF.[69]

The purpose of each chapter was twofold: to witness of the Lord Jesus Christ so that fellow students could be led to personal faith in him as Savior and Lord, and to strengthen the spiritual life of the members of the chapter through Bible study and prayer. Chapters maintained ties with IVCF by subscribing to the basis of faith and the general policy of the Fellowship.

Unlike Young Life Campaign, which depended heavily upon the personality and skills of the staff leader, Inter-Varsity chapter meetings were planned and conducted by the students themselves. Staff members served primarily as a link between the scattered chapters.[70] Meetings were usually held on campus and consisted of hymn singing, praying, and studying the Bible, often under the leadership of a guest speaker.[71] These early IVCF meetings showed no signs of traditional American revivalism. Evangelism was based on personal friendships and the reinforcement of a Christian fellowship. In his history of these early years Stacey Woods confessed that IVCF was "a British export." The British "ethos was carried *in toto* to the United States" and part of the difficulty the movement had in the 1950s and early 1960s was its "struggle to establish its identity as a completely American movement."[72]

Inter-Varsity had scarcely launched work in the United States when the country was caught up in World War II. In spite of the war's dislocations, however, at the end of hostilities Inter-Varsity had grown to almost 200 chapters in the States. By 1950 the figure had reached 561.[73] And decisions for Christ were a big part of the picture: in 1950 alone, 2,000 students professed faith in Christ.[74]

This growth in only ten years was aided by the addition of the Christian Nurses Fellowship. As early as 1936 three nurses at the Children's Hospital in Chicago began meeting for prayer. This modest beginning led to other groups in the greater Chicago area and under Alvera Anderson's leadership a fellowship was forged. The Nurses Christian Fellowship was formed in 1941. From the beginning chapters received help from IVCF field staff. In 1948 NCF became a department of IVCF and leaders appointed Tressie Myers the first full-time secretary. Within a year forty-two NCF chapters were active participants in IVCF.[75]

During this important decade Herbert Taylor served as chairman of the Board of Directors in the United States. Stacey Woods' association with Taylor was so close during these years that he later confessed that people felt that "H. J. Taylor and Stacey Woods rigged everything to suit themselves." Woods preferred to call this "influence" rather than control.[76]

In any case, in July 1945, under Woods's influence, IVCF initiated a summer training program for students and chapter leaders at their Campus in the Woods, located 140 miles north of Toronto. The facility on Fairview Island on the Lake of Bays was made available by Cameron Peck, then treasurer of Inter-Varsity. While conditions were rustic at best, about 100 adverturesome students made the trek each July to study the Bible, theology, apologetics, and evangelism under evangelical guest teachers.[77]

In 1948 a second summer program opened at The Firs Conference Center near Bellingham, Washington. In 1951 this West Coast venture moved to an abondoned camp on Catalina Island. Two years later Gene Thomas, staffman in the Rocky Mountain region, discovered a small but well equipped camp not far from Colorado Springs. Since the buildings were on national forest land, IVCF could not secure the land outright, but for $50,000 they purchased the property; that year, 1953, Bear Trap Ranch opened its doors to a year-round ministry to students, internationals, and chapter leaders.[78]

Through these early years, however, Herbert Taylor was laying plans for Inter-Varsity's own facility, a resort center like Young Life's Star Ranch. He owned some property on the north shore of Prentiss Bay in the upper Michigan Peninsula. In the early fifties he began buying property around the bay with a view to obtaining an old logging camp and village that seemed like an ideal site for IVCF. After contacting the nine heirs who held title to the property, he succeeded in buying the property for Inter-Varsity and building a beautiful lodge seating 200 people for dining and 200 more in the meeting room. In 1958 he donated the entire property, called Cedar Campus, to IVCF.[79]

Inter-Varsity's place in the evangelical sun, however, was soon to be associated with the huge Urbana Missionary Conferences. This leadership came as a result of a merger with another evangelical student organization, the Student Foreign Missions Fellowship.

The Student Foreign Missions Fellowship was sparked by Robert C. McQuilkin, president of Columbia Bible College and leader in the American Keswick Conferences. In June 1936, fifty-three students were attending a conference at the Ben Lippen Conference Center outside Asheville, North Carolina. During the week of June 15-22, students from Columbia Bible College and Wheaton College set up, with McQuilkin's assistance, a tentative organization for student involvement in the foreign missionary cause.[80]

The first national convention, meeting at Keswick, New Jersey, ratified the constitution of the Student Foreign Missions Fellowship in December, 1938. Summer deputation teams of students helped to extend the impact of the movement. By October 1941 there were thirty-six chapters of SFMF with 2,628 members scattered about the country.[81]

Similar aims brought IVCF and SFMF together.[82] In May 1945 the IVCF executive committee discussed the possibility of a merger. In December it became a reality: SFMF became the missionary arm of IVCF. The merger set the stage for the first student missionary convention, held in 1946 at the University of Toronto during the Christmas vacation. Approximately 580 students from 151 campuses in the United States and Canada attended the six-day event. On New Year's Eve, the delegates crowded into the Ontario College of Education auditorium to hear Robert C. McQuilkin challenge them to complete Christ's commission as soon as possible. Nearly 250 volunteered for missionary service.[83]

The last student had hardly left Toronto before talk began about the next convention. Herbert Taylor proposed that the next convention be in the Chicago area. It was. In 1948 the convention moved to the University of Illinois at Urbana and attracted 1,200 students.[84] The new location gave the convention its popular tag "the Urbana Convention." By 1979 attendance had reached 17,000.

How do we explain this surprising surge of evangelism among young people? William G. McLoughlin argues that the evangelical resurgence led by Billy Graham was the "nativist phase" of the "Fourth Great Awakening" in America. He contends that from time to time the United States experiences culture-wide phenomena called "revitalization movements." These "awakenings" bring the nation back to a common core of beliefs that shape American history and culture. This individualistic, pietistic, perfectionist, millenarian ideology is in its fourth period of testing and anxious search for renewal. One option for a recovery of faith in the post-war era is the traditional gospel of the three groups we have studied, "the nativist phase" of the fourth awakening.[85]

In one important sense, however, these groups were not traditional: they were a reflection of the emerging youth culture in America. As Dwight

MacDonald pointed out in an article in *The New Yorker* in 1957, the United States was the first country in the world to develop the concept of "teen-ager." The youth culture suggested by that term is more than an apprentice-ship for adulthood. It is more than a transitional period combining the values of both childhood and adulthood. It has roles and values and ways of behaving all its own. It emphasizes sexual attractiveness, immediate pleasure, and comradeship in a way that is belligerently non-adult. After World War II, catering to this teenage market emerged as the nation's commercial passion.[86]

Evangelism in this environment was both a reflection of the youth culture and a rejection of it. In a letter to his fellow students at Dallas Seminary in the summer of 1940 Wally Howard said, "This is a *young people's* day."[87] Most of these evangelists felt that deeply. Torrey Johnson and his YFC colleagues designed their rallies to appeal to youth: the music, the personalities, the pace of the Saturday night meetings were all tailored to youth tastes. No one, however, made a more persistent attempt to understand the teenager than Jim Rayburn. "Every young person" he said, "has the right to hear the Christian message in terms that make sense to him." He adopted the youth dialect of the time. For example, "gang" and "swell" are sprinkled throughout the early issues of *Young Life.* But more important, he pursued the basic principles of communication in another culture like a foreign missionary.

At the same time youth evangelism was, in one important sense, a rejection of youth culture. Kenneth Keniston has argued that juvenile delin-quency was a primary expression of youth culture.[88] If so, these youth ministries were only a limited part of the culture. Leaders of these ministries constantly stressed during the forties and fifties that the country needed evangelism among teenagers in order to counteract juvenile delinquency. This widely recognized crisis gave youth evangelism the appearance of a national cause.

In a *Christian Life* interview in 1954, Jim Rayburn acknowledged that teenagers in America were "on a rampage." He blamed parental neglect and John Dewey's philosophy of self expression in the schools for contributing to this "rowdyism and crime." He proposed a remedy, however, in "the knowl-edge of God." This meant evangelism. And that is where the churches came in for their share of blame.[89]

The most glaring failure of the traditional denominations was in their youth ministries. For example, the once vital Student Volunteer Movement was no longer a powerful voice for evangelism. By the 1940s it was a whisper of its former self. As a result the Student Foreign Missions Fellowship and Inter-Varsity broke the silence. In the same way denominational youth min-istries were often Sunday night exercises in futility. Church seemed to have no connection with the high school or university campus. In 1948 the *Watch-man-Examiner* applauded Youth for Christ's Saturday night rallies for addressing a need the churches had totally neglected: "In the midst of community revelry and promiscuity and irresponsibility the churches were utterly indifferent and incompetent to meet the situation."[90] As a result, parachurch youth ministries arose and spread. As with Herbert and Gloria Taylor's survey in the 1930s, the need constituted the call.

Notes

[1] Herbert J. Taylor, *God Has a Plan For You* (Carol Stream, Ill.: Creation House, 1972), p. 47.
[2] Ibid., p. 58.
[3] Ibid., p. 50.
[4] For an early discussion of this trend see *Moody Monthly*, Feb. 1946, p. 345.
[5] See Richard G. Hutcheson, Jr., *Mainline Churches and the Evangelicals* (Atlanta: John Knox, 1981), pp. 49-61.
[6] See *Moody Monthly*, Oct. 1980, pp. 40-42.
[7] See Willard L. Sperry, *Religion in America* (Boston: Beacon Press, 1946, 1963), pp. 160-62, and W. W. Sweet, *Revivalism in America* (Nashville: Abingdon, 1944), for attitudes toward revivalism in 1940.
[8] Jerry Falwell (ed.), *The Fundamentalist Phenomenon* (Garden City, N.Y.: 1981), pp. 128-31.
[9] The early 1940s saw the rise of the Miracle Book Club (later named the Hi-C Club) in Chicago, the Hi-BA (Born Againers) in the New York City area and the Dunamis clubs on the West Coast. Leslie B. Flynn, "These Teenagers are not Delinquents," *Christian Life*, Nov. 1951, pp. 72 ff.; *United Evangelical Action*, Sept. 15, 1949, p. 13; and Betty Lee Skinner, *Daws* (Grand Rapids: Zondervan, 1947), pp. 140-41 and 178-79.
[10] Forrest Forbes, *God Hath Chosen* (Grand Rapids: Zondervan, 1948), p. 54. Marvin Goldberg, "Youth Alone and Liked," *Sunday*, April 1946, pp. 19 ff.
[11] James Hefley, *God Goes to High School* (Waco, Texas: Word, 1970), pp. 19-22.
[12] Torrey Johnson and Robert Cook, *Reaching Youth for Christ* (Chicago: Moody Press, 1944), pp. 15-19; H. J. Taylor, *God Has a Plan*, p. 64.
[13] *Watchman-Examiner*, Nov. 30, 1944, p. 1176; *Sunday School Times*, Nov. 25, 1944, pp. 859, 891; *King's Business*, Dec. 1944, pp. 400 ff.
[14] Johnson and Cook, *Reaching Youth*, pp. 23-24. Mel Larson, *Young Man on Fire* (Chicago: Youth Publications, 1945), pp. 81-86; "History of Youth for Christ," *Christian Life*, July 1946, pp. 61 ff. The *Chicago Daily News* soon took note of the movement in an article (Feb. 3, 1945) titled "Bobby Sox Hit Sawdust Trail."
[15] Hefley, *High School*, p. 17.
[16] Torrey Johnson, on occasion, linked Youth for Christ with saving America from Nazi Germany. *King's Business*, Sept. 1945, pp. 329 ff.
[17] Clyde H. Dennis, "Great Soldier Field Rally," *Youth for Christ Magazine*, June 1945, pp. 1-2.
[18] *Time*, Feb. 4, 1946, pp. 46-47. Harold E. Fey "What About 'Youth for Christ?' " *Christian Century*, June 20, 1945, p. 729; Nov. 14, 1945, pp. 1243-44.
[19] Hefley, *High School*, pp. 26-27; Mel Larson, *Twentieth Century Crusade* (Grand Rapids: Zondervan, 1953), pp. 24-25.
[20] Hefley, *High School*, p. 32.
[21] Hefley, *High School*, p. 29.
[22] *Watchman-Examiner*, Aug. 28, 1947, p. 879.
[23] *United Evangelical Action*, Aug. 15, 1946, pp. 12-13; Dec. 1, 1946, p. 8.
[24] *Watchman-Examiner*, Nov. 20, 1947, p. 1158.
[25] Hefley, *High School*, pp. 37-39; Larson, *Twentieth Century*, pp. 26-27.
[26] *United Evangelical Action*, Aug. 5, 1948, pp. 14-15. The following February Johnson had a throat operation which was also a factor in his resignation. *Watchman-Examiner*, March 24, 1949, p. 270.

[27] *United Evangelical Action*, March 1, 1949, p. 26.

[28] Hefley, *High School*, pp. 45-46.

[29] Hefley, *High School*, p. 47.

[30] *United Evangelical Action*, Sept. 1, 1949, p. 12.

[31] *United Evangelical Action*, Jan. 15, 1950, p. 16.

[32] Louis Casper, *Fundamentalist Movement* (Paris: Mouton, 1963), p. 90. Hefley, *High School*, p. 49.

[33] Hefley, *High School*, p. 49.

[34] *Watchman-Examiner*, Sept. 8, 1955, p. 792; *United Evangelical Action*, Jan. 15, 1956, p. 13.

[35] *Watchman-Examiner*, June, 26, 1952, p. 642. *United Evangelical Action*, Mar. 15, 1956, p. 26. See also H. J. Taylor, *God Has a Plan*, p. 83; and Hefley, *High School*, p. 72.

[36] Hefley, *High School*, pp. 65-66 and Larson, *Twentieth Century*, p. 28.

[37] Hefley, *High School*, p. 69 and *Watchman-Examiner*, Feb. 28, 1957, p. 190.

[38] Arline Pritchard Harrison, "Winning the High School Heathen," *Christian Life*, May 1950, pp. 23 ff. *His*, May 1944, pp. 22-23.

[39] Lewis Sperry Chafer, *He That Is Spiritual* (Union City, PA: Bible Truth Depot, 1918).

[40] Char Meredith, *It's a Sin to Bore a Kid* (Waco, Texas, 1978), p. 16.

[41] Ibid., pp. 18-19.

[42] Ibid., pp. 20-21.

[43] Harrison, "High School Heathen," pp. 45-56; "Young Life," *King's Business*, July 1953, pp. 11-12.

[44] *Young Life*, April 1944, p. 7; May 1944, p. 7.

[45] *Young Life*, Nov. 1944, p. 20.

[46] Jim Rayburn letter to Ted Benson June 20, 1940 and Ted Benson letter to Jim Rayburn July 16, 1940, from the Archives of the Billy Graham Center at Wheaton College, collection 20, box 12, folder 8.

[47] Jim Rayburn letter to Ted Benson Aug. 29, 1940. Archives of the Billy Graham Center, collection 20, box 12, folder 8.

[48] Young Life Campaign letter sent by Jim Rayburn, Jan. 30, 1941. Archives of the Billy Graham Center, collection 20, box 69, folder 26.

[49] Meredith, *Sin to Bore*, pp. 29-30.

[50] Brochure program for Young Life Rally at the Baker Hotel, Dallas, Texas, Feb. 24, 1941. Archives of the Billy Graham Center, collection 20, box 69, folder 26. By March 1941, Rayburn dropped all ties with the Miracle Book Club, Jim Rayburn letter to Ted Benson Mar. 2, 1941. Archives of the Billy Graham Center, collection 20, box 11, folder 7.

[51] Rayburn bulletin to the board of directors, Dec. 16, 1944. Archives of the Billy Graham Center, collection 20, box 69, folder 29.

[52] In the summer, 1944, Rayburn spoke at YFC rallies in Chicago and St. Louis. Jim Rayburn letter, Aug. 1, 1944. Archives of the Billy Graham Center, collection 20, box 69, folder 29.

[53] Meredith, *Sin to Bore*, p. 36. During 1943-1944 Christian Workers Foundation was supporting Young Life with $100 a month. In addition, four staff workers received $25 support per month and an occasional $1000 gift arrived for the work. Archives of the Billy Graham Center, collection 20, box 69, folder 29.

[54] *Young Life*, May 1944, pp. 2-3; Sept. 1945, pp. 4-7.

[55] These early camps are listed in a Rayburn letter to friends of Young Life, May 5, 1944. Archives of the Billy Graham Center, collection 20, box 69, folder 29.

[56] Meredith, *Sin to Bore*, pp. 41-43; H. J. Taylor, *God Has a Plan*, p. 76; Emile Cailliet, *Young Life* (New York: Harper & Row, 1963), pp. 24-25.

[57] *Young Life*, Aug. 1945, pp. 8 ff.; Cailliet, *Young Life*, p. 25.

[58] Cailliet, *Young Life*, p. 26.

[59] Cailliet, *Young Life*, pp. 26-27; Meredith, *Sin to Bore*, pp. 56-57; H. J. Taylor, *God Has a Plan*, p. 77.

[60] Cailliet, *Young Life*, pp. 31-32; Meredith, *Sin to Bore*, p. 66.

[61] Meredith, *Sin to Bore*, p. 70.

[62] Cailliet, *Young Life*, p. 29; Meredith, *Sin to Bore*, pp. 11-12.

[63] Douglas Johnson (ed.), *A Brief History of the International Fellowship of Evangelical Students* (Lausanne: IFES, 1964), pp. 44-45; *His*, Oct. 1945, pp. 17-20; *United Evangelical Action*, July 1, 1946, p. 7.

[64] A forerunner of Inter-Varsity on American campuses was the League of Evangelical Students, which arose at Princeton Seminary. By 1936 the League had 60 chapters with about 1,500 students. Two thirds of these chapters were in colleges and universities. Stacey Woods and some students in the Chicago area, however, felt that the League was ill-equipped to meet the needs of undergraduates. See Charles Troutman's manuscript "Backgrounds of Evangelical University Witness in the United States" in Archives of the Billy Graham Center, collection 111, box 20, folder 1.

[65] C. Stacey Woods, *The Growth of a Work of God* (Downers Grove, Ill.: Inter-Varsity Press, 1978), pp. 18-19.

[66] Personal letter from Ted Benson to H. J. Taylor, Oct., 6, 1939, in Archives of Billy Graham Center, collection 20, box 11, folder 11.

[67] C. Stacey Woods's letter to H. J. Taylor, Jan. 18, 1940, in Archives of Billy Graham Center, collection 20, box 60, folder 2. See also Woods, *Work of God*, p. 20.

[68] C. Stacey Woods' letter to H. J. Taylor, April 24, 1940, in Archives of Billy Graham Center, collection 20, box 60, folder 2. See also Woods, *Work of God*, pp. 163-64.

[69] Woods, *Work of God*, pp. 23-24; 30.

[70] For an early explanation of the ministry see Robert Walker, "Winning College Students for Christ," *Revelation*, Sept. 1942, pp. 393 ff.

[71] *His*, Oct. 1945, pp. 17-20; *King's Business*, March 1949, p. 9.

[72] Woods, *Work of God*, p. 30.

[73] Woods, *Work of God*, p. 27; *His*, Oct. 1945, p. 17; *United Evangelical Action*, July 1, 1946, p. 7. In 1945 the Christian Workers Foundation (CWF) was contributing $1200 a year to the regular ministry of IVCF and $200 a month to the missionary work, letter from Judith Carlson (CWF), Nov. 28, 1945 in Archives of Billy Graham Center, collection 20, box 62, folder 2.

[74] Woods, *Work of God*, p. 28.

[75] Charles E. Hummel, *Campus Christian Witness* (Chicago: Inter-Varsity Press, 1958), p. 186; Woods, *Work of God*, p. 136. In 1952 the original name, Christian Nurses Fellowship, was changed to Nurses Christian Fellowship.

[76] Woods, *Work of God*, p. 75.

[77] *His*, Oct. 1945, pp. 7-9; April 1946, pp. 29-31; April 1947, p. 9; Woods, *Work of God*, p. 83.

[78] Woods, *Work of God*, pp. 83-84; *His*, Feb. 1954, p. 3.

[79] H. J. Taylor, *God Has a Plan*, pp. 78-80; Woods, *Work of God*, pp. 84-85.

[80] David M. Howard, *Student Power in World Evangelism* (Downers Grove, Ill.: Inter-Varsity Press, 1970), pp. 98-99; Woods, Work of God, p. 130.

[81] Howard, *Student Power*, pp. 100-101.

[82] See letter from Neill Hawkins to IVCF Board of Directors, April 11, 1942, in Archives of Billy Graham Center, collection 20, box 60, folder 24; *His*, January 1946, pp. 3-5.

[83] *His*, March 1947, pp. 10-12; *Watchman-Examiner*, Jan. 30, 1947, p. 98.

[84] Howard, *Student Power*, pp. 102-103; *His*, Jan. 1946, pp. 3-5; Feb. 1949, pp. 17-20; *Sunday School Times*, Nov. 6, 1948, p. 990.

[85] William G. McLoughlin, *Revivals, Awakenings and Reforms* (Chicago: Univ. of Chicago Press, 1978), pp. 1-12, 212-216.

[86] Erik H. Erikson (ed.), *Youth: Change and Challenge* (New York: Basic Books, 1963), p. 131.

[87] Wally Howard's letter, dated Aug. 26, 1940, is in the archives of the Billy Graham Center, collection 20, box 12, folder 8.

[88] Kenneth Keniston, "Social Change and Youth in American," in Erikson, *Youth*, pp. 176-80.

[89] Jim Rayburn, "Teenagers on the Rampage" *Christian Life*, Feb. 1954, pp. 28-30.

[90] *Watchman-Examiner*, March 18, 1948, pp. 274-75.

A CONCEPTION OF EXCELLENCE IN TEACHING

KLAUS ISSLER
Assistant Professor of Educational Ministry
Western Conservative Baptist Seminary

Article from *Education*

A great portion of our human and financial resources has been invested in the mission of teaching the children and youth of America. Despite this effort, many still lack understanding about the fundamental nature of excellence in teaching. A perusal of the literature will convince one that very little theory undergirds research on teaching. In one review of research on behavior in teaching, Brophy admits that "most of this research is heavily empirical, guided by no systematic theory and, in fact, very little theory at all."[1] This lack of theoretical knowledge affects our attempts to improve instruction. As indicated by Travers, "There is no single concept of what the teacher should be undertaking in the classroom."[2] Consequently, each teacher has his or her own conception of teaching, however inconsistent and implicit it might be.

Green explains that a conception is a rule: "When someone learns a concept, without exception, what he has learned is a rule, a rule of language, or more generally, a rule of behavior."[3] Hyman notes the implications of this for teaching when he states that "a person setting out to teach needs to clarify his concept of teaching because the concept he holds directly influences the activities he will engage in."[4]

Clarifying a conception of teaching (and excellence in teaching) is not necessary only for each teacher, but it is also critical for those who evaluate and do research on teaching. How can teaching be evaluated or studied unless specific factors are identified for investigation? A conception of teaching, and more important, a conception of excellence in teaching, should elucidate these essential elements. This article will attempt to shed light on both of these concepts.

What Is Teaching?

The word *teach* is used in a variety of contexts. In the broadest sense it may refer to an occupation with its attendant institutional activities (e.g., attending meetings, taking roll, patrolling hallways, etc.). Our concern will be the use of this word in a more narrow sense as it pertains to the act of teaching (e.g., questioning, motivating, testing, explaining, etc.). Some teaching activities and concerns are "context-specific," that is, they are more relevant for specific age groups, specific ability levels, or specific subject matter.[5] The focus of this study will be on those teaching activities and concerns that constitute teaching in general, regardless of such contextual factors.

A dominant model for research on teaching continues to be the process-product approach in which a specific set of teacher competencies can be dependably linked to student achievement.[6] The weakness of this model is that it assumes a simple, linear, cause-effect relationship between teaching and learning. Dunkin and Biddle, in their approach to studying classroom teaching, have identified at least eight classes of variables, besides that of the teacher's behavior, that should be studied for influence on student learning.[7] Of these variables, three deal solely with the student, involving the student's characteristics and classroom behavior. Thus, it becomes evident that a number of factors influence student learning, and only one of these factors is teaching.

Little attention has been directed to the notion of student responsibility for learning. It has been largely assumed in our tendency toward an efficient, mechanistic approach to education that "since behavior is controlled by the environment, the pupils cannot be held responsible for whether they do or do not learn. If the classroom manager provides favorable conditions for learning, then the pupil will learn. If the pupil does not learn, then the conditions provided by the teacher must be blamed."[8] However, one important student characteristic that must be considered is the disposition of the student, especially the student's receptivity to teaching. Even the great teachers, Socrates and Jesus, experienced strong opposition from some of those they taught. Can we expect complete responsiveness from our students?

At this point it will prove helpful to make a decision between teaching as intention and teaching as achievement.[9] In teaching as achievement, a direct, causal relationship exists between teaching and learning. Yet this disregards what is commonly experienced, that teaching may occur without learning. Although, in many cases, teaching may be considered a necessary condition for learning, it is not a sufficient condition. For this reason, Magee suggests that we view the word *teaching* as a task word and not an achievement word. Of course, there must be some relationship to achievement since words develop a "task" sense only when they often result in achievement. In sum, it can be said that teaching *intends* to bring about learning in students, but sometimes it may not be successful.

Current emphasis on the information-processing model of cognitive learning has brought to light the importance of an active and meaningful involvement on the part of the student during the learning process. Psychologists such as Ausubel and Anderson, as well as Piaget and Inhelder, have suggested that a student's cognitive structures play an important role as ideational anchors.[10] By interacting with the environment, students build and adjust their schemata, and thus personally construct their own knowledge and experience. If students have not formed relevant schema, they may be incapable of learning, or they may be impaired in fully comprehending specific information.

The creation of the taxonomies for the cognitive and affective domains has clarified a variety of levels of learning. It is conceivable that a higher level of learning may not be realistic for some students whose learning abilities have been arrested at lower levels through a conditioning process of only experiencing lower level teaching, or possibly because of a lack of initiative, or for other reasons. Thus, in assessing the effectiveness of teaching, we should also consider the factor of the level of content that is taught and learned. At what level of learning is the teaching aimed? At what level is the student learning?

Students not only learn through what the teacher says, but also through what the teacher does. Another emphasis in learning theory relates to observational-social learning.[11] As McLuhan has popularly stated, the medium is the message. Both the modeling the teacher does, and the environment of schooling, may either complement the intended message, or contradict it and hinder learning. Although the teacher is partly responsible here, a host of variables influence student learning—variables that are institutional and societal—beyond any teacher's direct control.

What has been described, then, is that many more factors affect student learning than just teaching. They include: (a) the entry characteristics of students, especially receptivity to teaching, (b) the meaningfulness and level of learning, and (c) the harmony or consistency between the teaching and the social context of the educational setting. Thus, teaching should not be viewed in a purely cause-effect association with learning. Then how should teaching be viewed in relationship to the teacher, the student, and student learning? It is suggested that teaching is an intentional activity in which a teacher, by word and deed, and in conjunction with (and sometimes in spite of) the circumstances of the educational setting, directs the opportunity for students to involve themselves actively and meaningfully in personally constructing their own knowledge and experience of a particular subject.

Toward Excellence in Teaching

With this conception of teaching as a general framework, a discussion of excellence in teaching can proceed. To provide a framework for this inquiry, the following commonplaces of teaching will be utilized: (a) the teacher, (b) the student, (c) the aims of teaching, (d) the activities of teaching, and (e) the outcomes of teaching. Within these broad categories, eleven variables are identified as elements that constitute excellence in teaching. Each of the eleven elements is presented and briefly discussed in the following section.

The teacher

Lifestyle of the teacher. Because of the implications of observational-social learning, an assessment of excellent teaching must consider the teacher's lifestyle. Are the aims taught exemplified by the teacher? The popular concept of "master teachers" bears out this emphasis on his personal life. Those who have given testimony to their great teachers have recalled how these master teachers[12] were consumed by their particular subject, as well as by their desire to teach students how to think. These teachers were great thinkers themselves who strongly urged students to think critically. Socrates exemplified a life devoted to seeking truth, to living virtuously, and to producing a state of discomfiture for those who claimed to know truth. Jesus manifested the holiest life of all, preaching and living the truth. Jersild indicates that only teachers who are themselves moving toward self-actualization are in a position to guide this process in others.[13] Thus, excellent teaching is not solely confined to the classroom, but is rather a habit, a way of life.

Mastery of the subject matter. This achievement by the teacher will affect his ability to teach excellently. Subject matter may be conceived either as isolated, or in relationship to other disciplines. It may be viewed as a group of facts (content), or as both content and process (the skills requisite for gathering and interpreting the facts of the subject). Subject matter may also be mastered at a variety of levels (whether it be a part of the cognitive or affective taxonomies).

The student

Student responsibility for learning. In the past, this may have been considered a given, but today the obligation of the student to put forth his best effort can no longer be assumed. With what disposition does he enter the teaching-learning milieu? What degree of receptivity to teaching is there? Are the student's psychological and emotional needs so great as to incapacitate any learning, no matter who the teacher is? Has the student made a decision to commit himself or herself to participate in learning the subject matter? This aspect of cooperation between teacher and student may be similar to that of a marriage where both partners bring a determined resolve to invest themselves in the marriage relationship. Such a high degree of partnership may be possible with only a few students.

The aims of teaching

Worthiness of the teaching aims. Of the utmost importance in education is the selection of constructive and worthy aims. Effectively teaching someone how to steal or kill may receive high marks on a process-product evaluation form, but it will promote neither social progress and the advancement of civilization, nor the good for the individual and for society. Socrates confronted his listeners with questions pertaining to fundamental reality. Jesus directed His audience to decide about their participation and commitment to the kingdom of God. Jersild and Rogers both suggest that teaching should be aimed at aiding the student in attaining self-actualization.[14]

The criteria one selects to judge the worthiness of aims will reflect a view of life, education, and mankind. Worthy aims promote emotional, moral, and social, as well as cognitive growth. Teaching should aim at encouraging students to perceive and live out the implications of their own knowledge and convictions. Worthy aims allow students the opportunity to wrestle with issues at higher levels of learning, both in the cognitive and affective realms.

The activities of teaching

Teaching preparation. Jackson has made a useful distinction when he identifies "preactive" teaching as those activities the teacher usually does alone (for example, lesson planning, reading, creative thinking, arranging classroom furniture), and "interactive" teaching as the aspect of teaching involving both student and teacher.[15] Many qualitative efforts of thinking, studying, planning, and organizing are invested in excellent teaching.

Use of students' intelligence. To what degree does the teacher allow an open and rational discussion of the matter at hand? Green designed a continuum in which teaching activities were related to their use of students' intelligence.[16] Activities such as conditioning and indoctrinating that do not encourage the students to use their intelligence were not considered true teaching. True teaching should reflect a view of the student as capable of critical thinking and self-direction, and not as an animal to be manipulated or as a dupe to be brainwashed.

Classroom working relationships. Thelen entitled this factor "productivity."[17] It relates to the supportive, social cooperation that is fostered—the kind of working relationships promoted by the teacher. Student activities may be cooperative, parallel, or competitive. What does the teacher do to encourage a mutual cooperative effort by the students, all the while incorporating their diverse abilities and interests? How does the teacher station himself or herself: on a pedestal, behind a barrier, or as a friend and partner in the quest of learning? Is there a continuity between the teacher's relationship with students in and out of class? By means of the relationship a teacher establishes with students, the teacher reflects his or her views of the learner and the learning process.

Opportunity for meaningful learning. To what degree does the teacher provide the opportunity for the student to be actively involved in the learning process? This need not necessarily be physical activity. A teacher may be able to stimulate student mental activity that can be very important.[18] Regardless of whether it is mainly mental activity of a student listening to a lecture, or more active participation in a group discussion, are students challenged to construct personally their own knowledge and experience, or are they directed only to regurgitate the teacher's or textbook's knowledge?

Does the teacher foster the development and refinement of cognitive structures through activities such as advanced organizers, puzzling dilemmas, or perceptive questions? The teacher should encourage the student to learn at higher levels of conceptual and experiential learning.

Knowledge of student needs. How well does the teacher heed student feedback (both verbal and nonverbal) during the interactive aspect of teaching? Is the teacher capable of making adjustments in the lesson plan when student needs would suggest a different teaching approach? Does each student have a clear understanding of his or her specific responsibilities for participation? Because of the differences in the ability and disposition of students, there may be a need to have differing aims for differing groups of students. An excellent teacher is sensitive to and takes into consideration the needs of the students.

Commitment to pursuing excellence in teaching. With regard to the teacher's lifestyle, preparation, and interaction with students, is the teacher committed to the pursuit of excellence? Would the teacher rate his or her own efforts of teaching at the 100 percent level? 75 percent? 50 percent? Does the teacher pursue excellence consistently, or only infrequently?

The outcomes of teaching

Effect of student learning. Though teaching does not guarantee learning, a close relationship exists between the two. As mentioned earlier, a number of factors may influence learning in students, and one of these factors is teaching. A variety of unobtrusive measures may be used in tandem with, or instead of, obtrusive measures for gauging student learning. Consideration should be given for both short- and long-term effects, and learning in the affective realm as well as the cognitive and psychomotor realms. Since teaching intends to bring about learning, we should expect learning—but learning of what quality and duration, and in how many students?

Conclusion

summ.

How one views teaching significantly affects how one practices teaching. The process-product orientation to teaching presumes too much of a causal relation between teaching and learning, and therefore requires a greater degree of accountability from the teacher than is realistic and necessary. A more circumscribed conception of teaching is offered as the basis for an inquiry into excellence in teaching. The eleven factors identified as essential may prove useful as a suggestive guide for the evaluation and improvement of instruction.

Different questions still remain. To what degree need each of these variables be in evidence to fully constitute excellence in teaching? And in what proportion should each of these variables be manifested? Further study will be required to deal with these issues.

Notes

[1] J. E. Brophy, "Teacher Behavior and Its Effects," *Journal of Educational Psychology* 71 (1979): 738.

[2] R. W. Travers, "Criteria of Good Teaching," *Handbook of Teacher Evaluation* (Beverly Hills, CA: Sage Publications, Inc., 1981): 22.

[3] T. F. Green, "A Topology of the Teaching Concept," *Contemporary Thought on Teaching* (Englewood Cliffs, NJ: Prentice-Hall, 1971): 71.

[4] R. T. Hyman, *Ways of Teaching* (Philadelphia: J. P. Lippincott, 1974): 35.

[5] N. L. Gage, "The Generality of Dimensions of Teaching," *Research on Teaching: Concepts, Findings, and Implications* (Berkeley, CA: McCutchan Publishing Corp., 1979).

[6] D. M. Medley, "The Effectiveness of Teachers," *Research on Teaching: Concepts, Findings, and Implications* (Berkeley, CA: McCutchan Publishing Corp., 1979). Also see W. Doyle, "Paradigms for Research on Teacher Effectiveness," *Review of Research in Education* 5 (1977): 163-79.

[7] M. J. Dunkin and B. J. Biddle, *The Study of Teaching* (New York: Holt, Rinehart and Winston, 1974).

[8] Travers, *op. cit.,* 17.

[9] J. B. Magee, *Philosophical Analysis in Education* (New York: Harper and Row, 1971).

[10] D. Ausubel, *The Psychology of Meaningful Verbal Learning* (New York: Grune & Stratten, 1963). Also see R. C. Anderson, R. J. Spiro, amd M. C. Anderson, "Schemata as Scaffolding for the Representation of Information in Connected Discourse," *American Educational Research Journal* 15 (1978): 433-39; and J. Piaget and B. Inhelder, *The Psychology of the Child* (New York: Basic Books, 1969).

[11] A. Bandura, *Social Learning Theory* (Englewood Cliffs, NJ: Prentice-Hall, 1977).

[12] J. Epstein, ed., *Masters: Portraits of Great Teachers* (New York: Basic Books, 1981).

[13] A. T. Jersild, *When Teachers Face Themselves* (New York: Teachers College, 1955).

[14] *Ibid.* Also see C. R. Rogers, *Freedom to Learn for the '80s* (Columbus, OH: Charles E. Merrill, 1983).

[15] P. W. Jackson, "The Way Teaching Is," *Contemporary Thought on Teaching* (Englewood Cliffs, NJ: Prentice-Hall, 1971).

[16] Green, *op. cit.*

[17] H. A. Thelen, "Authenticity, Legitimacy, and Productivity: A Study of the Tensions among Values Underlying Educational Activity," *Journal of Curriculum Studies* 14 (1982): 29-41.

[18] Ausubel, *op. cit.*

ABOUT THE AUTHORS

LEIGH C. BISHOP (B.A., Houston Baptist University; M.D., University of Texas Medical Branch [Galveston]) is at Medical College of Georgia (Augusta), where he is assistant professor of psychiatry, and chief of Psychiatry Outpatient Services. He is a Diplomate, American Board of Psychiatry and Neurology, and attends First Presbyterian Church, Augusta, Ga.

KLAUS BOCKMUEHL (Th.D., University of Basle) is professor of theology and ethics at Regent College (Vancouver, B.C.). A citizen of the Federal Republic of Germany, he is an ordained minister in the Evangelical Church of the Rhineland. His most recent books are *The Challenge of Marxism: A Christian Response* (IVP, 1980; Helmers and Howard, 1986), and *Evangelicals and Social Ethics* (1979).

DAVID J. BOSCH (B.A., B.D., M.A., University of Pretoria; Th.D., University of Basel, Switzerland), is professor of missiology, and dean, Faculty of Theology, University of South Africa. He is ordained, and affiliated with the Dutch Reformed Church, South Africa. He has been a missionary in Transkei, Southern Africa. His most recent books include *The Lord's Prayer: Paradigm for a Christian Lifestyle* (Pretoria: Christian Medical Fellowship, 1985); *Witness to the World: The Christian Mission in Theological Perspective* (London: Marshall, Morgan & Scott; Atlanta: John Knox Press; 1980).

HARVIE M. CONN (A.B., Calvin College; B.D. and Th.M., Westminster Theological Seminary) is professor of missions and director of the Urban Missions Program, Westminster Theological Seminary (Philadelphia). He was ordained by the Orthodox Presbyterian Church and served as a missionary in Korea (1960-72). Recent books include *Eternal Word and Changing Worlds* (1984); and *Evangelism: Doing Justice and Preaching Grace* (1982). He is editor of *Reaching the Unreached* (1984) and *Missions and Theological Education in World Perspective* (1984).

JAMES L. CRENSHAW (B.A., Furman University; B.D., Southern Baptist Theological Seminary; Ph.D., Vanderbilt University) is professor of Old Testament, Vanderbilt University Divinity School. He is an ordained Baptist minister. Former editor of the Society of Biblical Literature's Monograph Series, books he has recently written include *Story and Faith* (1986) and *A Whirlpool of Torment* (1984).

LEIGHTON FORD (B.A., Wheaton College; M.Div., Columbia Theological Seminary, Decatur, Ga.) is president of Leighton Ford Ministries and chairman of the Lausanne Committee for World Evangelization. He was program chairman in 1983 and 1986 for the International Conference for Itinerant Evangelists (Amsterdam). He is an ordained Presbyterian minister. His most recent book is *Sandy: A Heart for God* (1985). His biography, by Norman Rohrer, is titled *Leighton Ford: A Life Surprised* (1981).

R. T. FRANCE (B.A., M.A., Oxford University; B.D., London University; Ph.D., Bristol University) is vice-principal, London Bible College. He was ordained by the Church of England. He has been lecturer at University of Ife, Nigeria, and at Ahmadu Bello University, Zaria, Nigeria. He has also been librarian and warden at Tyndale House Library for Biblical Research (Cambridge, England). Recent books include *The Evidence for Jesus* (1986); and *Matthew* in the Tyndale New Testament Commentary series (1985). With D. Wenham he edited *Gospel Perspectives* I-III (1980-83).

NORMAN L. GEISLER (B.A., M.A., Wheaton College; Ph.D., Loyola University) is professor of systematic theology, Dallas Theological Seminary. He was ordained in the Evangelical Free Church and currently attends Scofield Memorial Church, Dallas, Tex. Recent books includes *Decide for Yourself: How History Views the Bible* (1982); *Miracles and Modern Thought* (1981); *Biblical Errancy: Its Philosophical Roots* (1981).

NORMAN K. GOTTWALD (A.B., Th.B., Eastern Baptist Theological Seminary; M. Div., Union Theological Seminary [New York]; Ph.D., Columbia University) is professor of biblical studies, New York Theological Seminary. He was ordained by the American Baptist Convention. His most recent book is *The Hebrew Bible—A Socio-Literary Introduction* (1985). He edited *The Bible and Liberation: Political and Social Hermeneutics* (1983).

ROBERT H. GUNDRY (B.A., B.D., Los Angeles Baptist College and Seminary; Ph.D., Manchester University) is professor of New Testament and Greek, Westmont College. His most recent book is *Matthew: A Commentary of His Literary and Theological Art* (1982).

STANLEY HAGEMEYER (B.A., Hope College, Holland, Mich.; M.Div., Western Theological Seminary) is pastor of Saranac Community Church (United Church of Christ) in Saranac, Michigan. He was ordained by the Reformed Church in America, and is pursuing a D.Min. degree at Western Theological Seminary. He is co-author, with Sue Richards, of *Ministry to the Divorced* (1986).

JAMES M. HOUSTON (M.A., Edinburgh University; D. Phil., Oxford University) is professor of spiritual theology, Regent College. He has been bursar and lecturer at Hertford College, and lecturer at Oxford University. He is editor of the series *Classics of Faith and Devotion.* He is author of *The Benefit of Christ: Living Justified Because of Christ's Death* (1984).

KLAUS ISSLER (B.A., California State University, Long Beach; Th.M., Dallas Theological Seminary; M.A., University of California, Riverside; Ph.D., Michigan State University) is assistant professor of educational ministry, Western Conservative Baptist Seminary (Portland, Oreg.). Born in Stuttgart, Germany, he is a United States citizen, and was ordained by the North American Baptist Conference. He is currently affiliated with a Conservative Baptist church.

DAVID C. LINDBERG (B.S., Wheaton College; M.S., Northwestern University; Ph.D., Indiana University) is Evjue-Bascom Professor of the History of Science at the University of Wisconsin, Madison. With Ronald Numbers he edited *God and Nature: Historical Essays on the Encounter Between Christianity and Science* (1986). Recent books include *Roger Bacon's Philosophy of Nature* (1983).

ROBERT D. LINDER (B.S., Emporia State University; M.R.E., M.Div., Central Baptist Theological Seminary; M.A., Ph.D., University of Iowa, post-doctoral study, Oxford University, Cambridge University) is professor of history, Kansas State University. He was city councilman, Manhattan, Kans., 1969-79, and mayor, Manhattan, Kans., 1971-72 and 1978-79. He was also editor of *Fides et Historia*, 1968-78. He is co-author of *Twilight of the Saints: Biblical Christianity and Civil Religion in America* (1978), and American editor of *Eerdmans' Handbook to the History of Christianity* (1977).

D. BRUCE LOCKERBIE (A.B., M.A., New York University) is Staley Foundation Scholar-in-Residence, The Stony Brook School (New York), and president of Fatherlove, Inc., and Stewardship Consulting Services. He is affiliated with an Episcopal church. Recent books include *The Cosmic Center* (1986); *The Christian, the Arts, and Truth* (1985); and *In Peril on the Sea* (1984).

PATRICK D. MILLER, JR. (A.B., Davidson College; B.D., Union Theological Seminary [Virginia]; Ph.D., Harvard University) is professor of Old Testament theology, Princeton Theological Seminary. He was ordained by the Presbyterian Church U.S. and is affiliated with the Presbyterian Church (U.S.A.). His recent books include *Interpreting the Psalms* (1986); and *Sin and Judgment in the Prophets* (1982).

DOUGLAS MOO (B.A., De Pauw University; M.Div., Trinity Evangelical Divinity School; Ph.D., University of St. Andrews) is associate professor of New Testament, Trinity Evangelical Divinity School. He is affiliated with The Missionary Church. Recent books include *The Letter of James* (1986); *The*

Rapture: Pre-, Mid- or Post-Tribulational? (1984, co-author); and *The Old Testament in the Gospel Passion Narratives* (1983).

BRUCE NARRAMORE (B.A., Westmont College; M.A., Pepperdine University; M.A., Fuller Theological Seminary; Ph.D., University of Kentucky) is dean and professor of psychology, Rosemead School of Psychology, Biola University. He is a Licensed Psychologist, State of California, and a Licensed Marriage, Family, and Child Counselor, State of California. He has been involved in periodic consultation and in-service training seminars for educational, psychological, and religious organizations (Australia, Brazil, Ecuador, Mexico, Micronesia, The Netherlands, Puerto Rico, and the United States). He is affiliated with Whittier Area Baptist Fellowship (Whittier, Calif.) Recent books include *No Condemnation* (1984); *Adolescence Is Not an Illness* (1980); *Why Children Misbehave* (1980). He is Series Editor for the Rosemead Psychological series, and in this series, co-author with J. Carter of *The Integration of Psychology and Theology: An Introduction* (1979).

RONALD L. NUMBERS (B.A., Southern Missionary College, now called Southern College [Tennessee]; M.A., Florida State University; Ph.D., University of California, Berkeley. He is professor of the history of medicine and the history of science at the University of Wisconsin, Madison. With David Lindberg he edited *God and Nature: Historical Essays on the Encounter Between Christianity and Science* (1986). With Darrell W. Amundsen he also edited *Caring and Curing: Health and Medicine in the Western Religious Traditions* (1986).

C. RENÉ PADILLA (B.A., M.A., Wheaton College; Ph.D., University of Manchester [England]) is general secretary, Latin American Theological Fraternity (Buenos Aires), and editor of *Misión.* He has been general secretary for Latin America for the International Fellowship of Evangelical Students, and director of Ediciones Certeza Publishing House. He is affiliated with a Baptist church in Buenos Aires. His most recent book is *Mission Between the Times* (1985).

RICHARD PEACE (B.E., Yale University; M.Div., Fuller Theological Seminary; Ph.D. candidate, University of Natal [South Africa]), is associate professor of evangelism and media, and director of media education, Gordon-Conwell Theological Seminary. He was a founding member of African Enterprise, and of Clear Light Productions. He was ordained by the United Church of Christ. Some of his recent publications include *A Church's Guide to Evangelism* (1982), and he has written or edited *Serendipity New Testament for Groups* (1986); *Study Guide for the Book of Ephesians*, Mastering the Basics series (co-authored with Lyman Coleman, 1986); and *Pilgrimage: A Handbook on Christian Growth* (1984).

BRUCE SHELLEY (B.A., Columbia Bible College; M.Div., Fuller Theological Seminary; Ph.D., University of Iowa) is professor of church history at Denver Conservative Baptist Seminary. He is ordained in the Conservative Baptist Church. Recent books include *Christian Theology in Plain Language* (1985); and *Church History in Plain Language* (1983).

GRANT WACKER (B.A., Stanford University; Ph.D., Harvard University) is associate professor of religious studies, University of North Carolina at Chapel Hill. He has written *Augustus H. Strong and the Dilemma of Historical Consciousness* (1985).

C. PETER WAGNER (B.S., Rutgers University; M.Div., Fuller Theological Seminary; Th.M., Princeton Theological Seminary; M.A., Fuller Theological Seminary School of World Mission; Ph.D., University of Southern California) is professor of church growth, Fuller Theological Seminary. For sixteen years he was a missionary to Bolivia. Ordained by the Conservative Congregational Christian Conference, he is a member of Lake Avenue Congregational Church (Pasadena). He is a charter member, Lausanne Committee for World Evangelization, and founding president, North American Society for Church Growth. He edited *Church Growth: State of the Art* (forthcoming). He is author of *Strategies of Church Growth* (forthcoming); *Spiritual Power and Church Growth* (1986); and *Leading Your Church to Growth: The Secret of Pastor/People Partnership in Dynamic Church Growth* (1984).

TIMOTHY M. WARNER (A.B., Taylor University; M.Div., New York Theological Seminary; M.A., New York University; Ed.D., Indiana University) is associate professor of mission, and director, Professional Doctoral Programs, Trinity Evangelical Divinity School. He has been a missionary to Sierra Leone, West Africa (1956-59), professor of missions, Fort Wayne Bible College (1959-70), and president, Fort Wayne Bible College. He was ordained by The Missionary Church, and attends North Suburban Evangelical Free Church (Deerfield, Ill.). Recent publications include contributions to *Evangelism on the Cutting Edge* (1986); and *Toward a Harmony of Faith and Learning* (1983).

ACKNOWLEDGMENTS

Leigh C. Bishop. "Healing in the Koinonia: Therapeutic Dynamics of Church Community." *Journal of Psychology and Theology* 13 (1985): 12-20. Reprinted by permission.

Klaus Bockmuehl. "Secularisation and Secularism: Some Christian Considerations." Reprinted by permission from *Evangelical Review of Theology* 10 (Jan. 1986): 50-73; published by The Paternoster Press, Exeter, England, for the World Evangelical Fellowship Theological Commission. Condensed by the author for *The Best in Theology*.

David J. Bosch. "Afrikaner Civil Religion and the Current South African Crisis." Reprinted by permission from *The Princeton Seminary Bulletin* 7 (New Series 1986): 1-14.

Harvie M. Conn. "Missions and Our Present Moment in History." Reprinted by permission from *Missionary Monthly*, Feb. 1986: 3-5, 23-25. The address of *Missionary Monthly* is Box 6181, Grand Rapids, Michigan 49516-6181.

James L. Crenshaw. "Education In Ancient Israel." Reprinted by permission from Scholars Press and *Journal of Biblical Literature* 104 (1985): 601-15.

Leighton Ford. "The 'Finger of God' In Evangelism." *World Evangelization* March 1986: 5-8. Published by the Lausanne Committee for World Evangelization. Reprinted by permission.

R. T. France. "Liberation In the New Testament." *The Evangelical Quarterly* 48 (1986): 3-23. Published by The Paternoster Press, Exeter, England. Reprinted by permission.

Norman L. Geisler. "A Premillennial View of Law and Government." *Bibliotheca Sacra* 142 (1985): 250-66. Reprinted by permission.

Norman K. Gottwald. "Social Matrix and Canonical Shape." *Theology Today* 42 (1985): 307-21. Reprinted by permission.

R. H. Gundry. "Grace, Works, and Staying Saved in Paul." *Biblica* 66 (1985): 1-39. Used by permission. Slightly condensed by the author for *The Best in Theology*.

437

Stanley Hagemeyer. "Making Sense of Divorce Grief." *Pastoral Psychology* (1986): 237-50. Reprinted by permission of the publisher, Human Sciences Press.

James M. Houston. "A Guide to Devotional Reading." Taken from the series of books *Classics of Faith and Devotion*, of which Dr. Houston is General Editor. The series, published by Multnomah Press, Portland, Oregon, presently has nine volumes. "A Guide to Devotional Reading" by Dr. Houston appears in each volume. The series includes *Religious Affections* (Jonathan Edwards), *Sin and Temptation* (John Owen), *Toward a Perfect Love* (Walter Hilton), *The Benefit of Christ* (Juan de Valdés and Don Benedetto), *Evangelical Preaching* (sermons by Charles Simeon), *A Life of Prayer* (St. Teresa of Avila), *The Love of God* (Bernard of Clairvaux), *Real Christianity* (William Wilberforce), and *The Reformed Pastor* (Richard Baxter). Dr. Houston's article also appeared in *Crux* 22 (1986): 22ff. *Crux* is published by Regent College.

Klaus Issler. "A Conception of Excellence in Teaching." This article first came to the attention of *The Best in Theology* in a publication of Scripture Press, *Christian Education Journal* September 1985: 19-23. It originally appeared and was copyrighted in *Education* 3 (1983): 338-43. Used by permission of *Education* and the author.

David C. Lindberg and Ronald L. Numbers. "Beyond War and Peace: A Reappraisal of the Encounter between Christianity and Science." *Church History* 55 (1986): 338-54. Reprinted by permission. A similar article appeared as the Introduction to *God and Nature: Historical Essays on the Encounter Between Christianity and Science* published by University of California Press, 1986.

Robert D. Linder. "Religion and the American Dream: A Study in Confusion and Tension." This article first came to the attention of *The Best in Theology* in *TSF Bulletin* Jan.-Feb. 1985: 13-17. It originally appeared and was copyrighted by *Mennonite Life* Dec. 1983. Reprinted by permission.

D. Bruce Lockerbie. "A Call for Christian Humanism." *Bibliotheca Sacra* 143 (1986): 195-204. Reprinted by permission.

Patrick D. Miller, Jr. "Current Issues in Psalms Studies." *Word and World* 5 (1985): 132-43. Copyright by Luther Northwestern Theological Seminary, St. Paul, Minnesota. Reprinted with permission. A form of this article appeared in *Interpreting the Psalms*, published by Fortress Press (1986).

Douglas J. Moo. "Jesus and the Authority of the Mosaic Law." *Journal for the Study of the New Testament* 20 (1984) 3-49. Reprinted by permission. Slightly condensed for *The Best in Theology* by the author.

Bruce Narramore. "The Concept of Responsibility in Psychopathology and Psychotherapy." *Journal of Psychology and Theology* 13 (1985): 91-96. Reprinted with permission of the author and the publisher, Rosemead School of Psychology, Biola University, La Mirada, California.

C. René Padilla. "Evangelism and Social Responsibility: From Wheaton '66 to Wheaton' 83." *Transformation: An International Dialogue on Evangelical Social Ethics* July-Sept. 1985: 27-32, inside back cover. Reprinted by permission.

Richard V. Peace. "The New Media Environment: Evangelism in a Visually-Oriented Society." *Journal of the Academy for Evangelism in Theological Education* 1 (1985-86): 36-45. Reproduced here by permission.

Bruce Shelley. "The Rise of Evangelical Youth Movements." *Fides et Historia* 18 (1986): 47-63. Reprinted by permission.

Grant Wacker. "The Functions of Faith in Primitive Pentecostalism." *Harvard Theological Review* 77:3-4 (July/October 1984): 353-75. Reproduced in *The Best in Theology* by permission.

C. Peter Wagner. "A Vision for Evangelizing the Real America." *International Bulletin of Missionary Research* April 1986: 59-64. Reprinted by permission of publisher and of the author, who holds the copyright.

Timothy Warner. "Teaching Power Encounter." *Evangelical Missions Quarterly* 22 (1986): 66-71. Reprinted with permission of the Evangelical Missions Information Service, Box 794, Wheaton, IL 60187.